God's Doctrine
for
DUMMIES

A Study of Basic Doctrine Taught in God's Word

B. N. Lightsey

ISBN 978-1-64515-627-7 (paperback)
ISBN 978-1-64515-375-7 (hardcover)
ISBN 978-1-64515-376-4 (digital)

Christian Faith Publishing, Inc.
832 Park Avenue
Meadville, PA 16335
www.christianfaithpublishing.com

Printed in the United States of America

It has been my privilege to be Pat and Bill Lightsey's pastor and friend for years. During these years I have found them to be faithful to the Lord Jesus and His Church. Bill is committed to the Word of God and inerrancy of scripture and the truth of basic Biblical doctrine. He is a gifted speaker and teacher and I trusted Him to teach a series on the material in this book to our church. He and his material was a blessing to our membership.

God's Doctrine for Dummies is written, not for theological scholars but for the faithful Christian that wants to grow in their knowledge of solid Biblical doctrine. Bill has taken complicated material and made it understandable and useable in living the Christian life.

I recommend God's Doctrine for Dummies without reservation and with the promise it will be a blessing to all who read it.

Dr. Hal Kinkeade
Pastor of First Baptist Church
Springtown Texas

Psalms 19:7-8

"The law of the Lord is perfect, reviving the soul, the testimony of the Lord is sure, making wise the simple, the precepts of the Lord are right, rejoicing the heart, the commandment of the Lord is pure, enlightening the eyes."

Prologue

As a member of the laity, I am part of a vast ocean of Christians that view the work of God through a different set of eyes than those of many ordained pastors and professors. I have interest in the deep theology of scripture and recognize the need to always be immersed in God's Word, as do my "called" brethren. I am not, however, burdened with the personal responsibility of growing a Church. And it is not my responsibility to meet the social, spiritual, emotional, and physical needs of a vast congregation. As a member of the laity, I have a more narrow focus on God's Word. I primarily want to know what God wants me to become and how I am to live this life. Second, I want to know how I should witness to my family and always present God in my teaching and my personal behavior. I also want to know what God's Word teaches about Himself. My approach to Bible study is, perhaps, selfish. I understand that my view of spiritual responsibility may be narrower than that of most pastors. Nevertheless certain truths prevail.

In the earlier days of our country, school systems concentrated on giving students "reading, writing, and 'rithmatic." They made those basics the core of school curriculum. As a Church member hungry for the basics of God's Word, I encourage a return of our Churches to the "reading, writing, and 'rithmatic" of our spiritual curriculum. I seek to hear from the pulpit and from bible study groups not what makes me feel good, but what convicts me to be righteous. I seek what God's Word tells me I need to change in my life. I need to be pleasing unto God. I seek to hear not what my teacher, preacher, or professor thinks but what God knows and wants to convey to me.

We hear a lot about the love of God, and well we should because God is a loving God who cares for his children. But we also need to hear about the wrath of God. God's Word is full of warnings of God's wrath. God warns us because He loves us. Romans 1:18 tell us, *"For the wrath of God is revealed from heaven against all ungodliness and unrighteousness of men, who suppress the truth in unrighteousness."*

We hear a lot about the glory and splendor of heaven. We rejoice to hear of this home where we will live with God, without pain, without worry, without stress, and without sin. This truth in God's Word is the light of our path and puts joy in our heart. However, God also warned us of the pit of Hell created for the devil and his angels. And God, in His love, warned us over and over again that the abyss of Hell will be populated with all nonbelievers in Jesus Christ. Jesus Himself told us in Matthew 25:41, *"Then He will also say to those on the left hand, 'Depart from me, you cursed, into the everlasting fire prepared for the devil and his angels.'"*

I gave my heart to Jesus Christ at the young age of nine, when the Holy Spirit pounded on my heart's door and said open up your heart and let me come in. I did not give my heart to Christ that day because of a magnificent sermon. I was, however, ready to respond to God's calling because of a Church environment that preached the Word of God and taught salvation by faith through the grace of God. For me the steady feeding of foundational truth from the pulpit in that West Texas Church helped me be ready when the Holy Spirit said, "Bill it is time." Untold thousands are saved under the influence of magnificent Bible based preaching. That is the primary medium the Holy Spirit uses to touch hearts and invite eternal acceptance. But whether it is under the influence of magnificent preaching, steady Church urging, the guidance of a Godly mother or father, or some cataclysmic event God sends into our lives, we all come under conviction and faith the same way. We find salvation by believing Jesus Christ chose to die on Calvary for our sins and that He rose from death on the third day so that we might be saved. Our faith in what Jesus did and does combines with God's almighty grace, to bring about a Holy Spirit induced change in our heart, making us a new spiritual creature. We call that being "born again." As a member of the Kingdom of God I need to hear a steady reminder of God's gift of life. It is not only necessary for new converts but it is necessary for those on the way to spiritual maturity. I need to hear the foundations of our faith preached, taught, lived, and prayed every day of my life.

A social gospel that teaches joy, happiness, fulfillment and success in this life give us a spiritual buzz that makes us forget the realities of sin for a short time. However, God does not want us to forget the realities of sin. He wants us to be imbedded with the reality of sin and He wants us to seek His love of redemption. We need to understand that God did not promise the path of Christianity would be smooth and comfortable. He warned us of the opposite. He told us that if we want to be followers of Christ we must pick up our cross daily and deny ourselves and follow him.

Jesus was not trying to gain members in a political or social crusade. Christ died on the Cross of Calvary with us on His mind. He was so concerned about our sin infestation before God He was willing to give His life for our sin. Christ warns us about the coming day of sin's accountability. We have a need to understand the basic doctrines of our faith so eloquently presented in God's Word. We need to hide those truths in our heart that we might not sin against God.

Unfortunately, America is turning away from its spiritual heritage. Most of America and the world as well, go through each week barely brushing their mental understanding that mankind is predominately a spiritual being and secondarily a physical being. They neither seek, nor receive, spiritual insight and, while most Americans are good moral people, they do not understand the sin-based definition of whom and what they are. As a layperson, I also sense many professed Christians, receive only a light portion of basic doctrine on a regular basis. Perhaps this is because a steady teaching of the full gospel of God makes people uncomfortable and is harmful to Church attendance.

I understand the complex problem of pastors and elders who say, "If we drive them away they will not hear any of God's Word and how can the masses profit from that approach?" Jesus Christ faced the same problem. He gave us the example of seeking the uncommitted and striving for their commitment. His top priority was not a huge congregation. Christ challenged us that our responsibility is to inform people not to enroll them. That is God's work. Witnessing and telling the full truth about God's Word is the primary mission we have been challenged by God to accept.

God's Doctrine for Dummies addresses the need we have in America, and in the world, to teach basic doctrine as presented directly from God's Holy Word. Our need for the Word of God to be part of our everyday life is no different than it has ever been in the history of mankind. In Matthew 4:4 Jesus said, *"But He answered and said, "It is written, 'Man shall not live by bread alone, but by every word that proceeds from the mouth of God.'"* Note this truth from our Lord tells us the whole Bible must be studied and taught. We must teach and preach more than just a feel good scripture. Logic would tell us that people would learn from the Hebrew children. God led them in the wilderness for forty years because they would not listen and obey Him. The Hebrew children had multiple periods of bondage captivity because of their unfaithfulness to God. Yet in America our people are turning away from Him in greater numbers every day. We need to study the basic doctrines as outlined by God in His Scripture. *God's Doctrine for Dummies* is a review of God's outline of truth as revealed in the Bible. In Acts 17:11, we are commanded by God to study His Word for doctrinal truth when he wrote*: "These were more fair-minded than those in Thessalonica, in that they received the word with all readiness, and searched the Scriptures daily to find out whether these things were so."*

I greatly desire that you will read this book along with an in-depth study of Scripture noted and recommended. I have primarily used the Eastern Standard Version (ESV) translation of Scripture, with a desire to meet the interest and understanding of most age groups and different lifestyles. Occasionally, you will note the use of mankind being referred to in the masculine terminology of "man." The intent of such terminology is always to use "mankind" or "man" as a call to everyone not a separation of gender. Jesus Christ was and is the greatest liberator of women and minorities the world has ever known. Men and women who come to know Jesus Christ as savior began a road of freedom of discrimination taught by Christ and commanded by Christ. The Scriptures we quote may use the term "man" to mean "mankind." Such wording is always inclusive of both male and female gender.

You will also note I do not identify specific sources of inspiration I received to help write this book. Certainly many great articles, great sermons, great advisors, and great books have channeled me to patterns of thought and to Scripture that should be studied. But the source of inspiration is, and has consistently been, the Word of God. It is from the Holy Spirit interpreting to me God's Word and no other power that has enabled me to identify these truths. As you read this book I urge you to also use the Word of God to determine authenticity of this book's content. Content based on my knowledge is shallow and highly debatable. But content based on the Holy Word of God is deep, eternal, unshakable, omniscient, omnipotent, and beyond human challenge.

I trust you will find God's will for your life as you read and study.

B. V. Lightsey

Contents

CHAPTER ONE

God's Holy Word
God's Revelation of Himself to Mankind

The Bible, God's Holy Word, is God's communication with us. God desires that we understand and know Him, yet because of our sinful nature, we have created a sin barrier between God and ourselves. Man created this barrier, not God. Because of that barrier of sin we cannot, on our own, communicate with or be in the presence of God. We are not capable of looking upon, or grasping, the holiness of God. In order to better reveal Himself to mankind, God, in the early history of man, used prophets to record what He told them to write. These prophets were men inspired by God to record the thoughts of God. Through this medium God elected to reveal Himself to mankind through the written word. These selected men were inspired by God to write what He told them to write. The word testament is a derivative of the Latin word *testamentum*. It means a covenant with God. We call these writings the Old Testament.

After the birth of Jesus, after His sinless life on earth, after His death on the Cross of Calvary, and after His triumphal resurrection from the dead; God inspired His apostles, and other selected disciples, to record His continuing revelation of Himself to mankind. We call that collection of writings, inspired by God, the New Testament. With the death and resurrection of Jesus a new covenant was created between God and man.

A popular position of many that attempt to explain the presence of error in God's Word is that the Bible was written for a specific time and culture and does not fit our culture today. In other words many people try to tell us the Bible is out of date. God, however, tells us in His Word that He is timeless. He is eternally righteous, just, holy, and full of grace and truth. God is always the same, yesterday, today and tomorrow and His truth is just as true today as it ever has been. His Word, therefore, is also unchanging, timeless, and never goes out of date.

Why does God reveal Himself to Mankind?

God wants His creation to know who He is and to understand His values and character. God wants us to adore and appreciate Him.

God wants to fellowship with us. God wants us to love Him. To accomplish this God very definitely reveals His identity to man and His expectations of man as well. One of the principle ways God chose to reveal Himself was in His written Word. God used select men to record His revelations to us, but He is the author. The thoughts in the Bible are God's thoughts. The Bible is the record of God's revelation of Himself to man. His Word is perfect, without blemish, without error, and it is sufficient to meet all the needs of mankind throughout the generations. God reveals the foundational truths by which He judges us. These truths are the supreme standard by which all human conduct, thoughts, opinions, and values must be formed. Nothing else is acceptable to God.

God does not just tell us His word is holy, supreme, and divine. He gives us compelling evidence that support His statement. The design of the Bible itself is compelling evidence of its having been created by a divine authority that is beyond the scope and concept of man. It was written over a period of 1,500 years by vastly different writers. Yet every book is consistent in its message. The Bible contains sixty-six books covering the subjects of history, prophecy, poetry, and theology. The Bible encompasses vast differences in writing styles and cultures. The books of the Bible were written by hand, without the technology of the printing press. Yet the constant, consistent harmony of the sixty-six books, present a continuous testimony of a divine, common author; directing, guiding and inspiring the writers. Only through the divine inspiration of a divine being that is beyond time and physical limitations; could sixty-six authors over a period of thousands of years of people and their lifestyles, create a document that unfalteringly stays on the same theme, the same purpose, and the same message.

Ancient writings were on fragile materials like papyrus and parchment. This material has vanished over the course of time however many copies of the Old Testament scriptures survived. The Dead Sea Scrolls were discovered between 1947 and 1956 in eleven caves on the northeast shore of the Dead Sea, a salt lake in Jordan. These Scrolls consist of nine hundred documents. From them, texts from the Hebrew Bible, known as the Old Testament, were written. They include documents written 150 years before Jesus Christ was born. They were written mostly in Hebrew, with some in Aramaic. They give testimony of God's authorship of His Word.

However, the authority of God's Word does not come through the evidence of history. It comes from God's personal testimony to us that we can believe God. In the book of Timothy Paul clearly informs us that every word of the Bible came from God and is valuable in directing, controlling and inspiring mankind.

2 Timothy 3:16
"All Scripture is breathed out by God and profitable for teaching, reproof, for correction, and for training in righteousness."

God inspired Paul to record for our use, the words "All Scripture is God-Breathed." This means every word in the original manuscripts used to record what God revealed to us, was directly from God. "God-Breathed" means God put the thought into the heart and mind of the scribe who recorded it and then put into the heart of the scribe an overpowering urge to record it. In 2 Timothy 3:16 that scribe was "The Apostle Paul." God directs us to read and study His Word and decide for our spiritual health if it is true or false. The decision to believe is called faith and not to believe is unbelief.

God tells us His Word came from God and God alone. God knew man would try to twist, modify, and change the Bible to say what man wants it to say. God therefore warns us mankind does not have the ability or authority to create or change scripture. **"God-Breathed"** inspired the Apostle Peter to record the following words as evidence of the intent of God.

2 Peter 1:20–21
"Knowing this first of all, that no prophecy of Scripture comes from someone's own interpretation."

In the second book of the Apostle Peter, God informed us that no thought, word, or record of God's Word came because of the intellect of man. Man's thoughts are too fallible, too changeable, too imperfect, and too corruptible to be suitable as part of God's Word. Therefore, over a period of hundreds of years, God placed in the heart of His select writers, through the Holy Spirit, what to record. The words the scribes recorded reflect their own personalities and experiences, but the thoughts conveyed are directly from God.

God emphasized this point through many writings by various authors. In 1 Corinthians, the Apostle Paul tells us the total Bible, through the inspiration of the Holy Spirit, is directly from God. Paul felt impelled to inform us what he recorded in his letters to the Christian Churches, was not his thoughts and not his ideas but were the thoughts and ideas of God. We often refer to Paul as the author of Corinthians, Galatians and other books. We refer to David as the author of Psalms and so on. In absolute correct dialog we should refer to these great men of God as scribes who recorded the words of God. God is the author of the entire Bible with many scribes chosen by Him to record His word.

1 Corinthians 2:13
"And we impart this in words not taught by human wisdom but taught by the Spirit, interpreting spiritual truths to those who are spiritual."

The Bible informs us that these spiritual truths never become out of date. God is timeless and does not change. His spiritual truths are also timeless and do not change. The Apostle Matthew was told by God to document that His Word, the Bible, would never go out of date, would never cease to be practical and applicable to the world we live in. Until God Himself comes to reign with us in the millennium and thereafter, the Word of God is unchangeable, unshakable, unmovable, and eternally true.

Matthew 5:18
"For truly I say unto you, until heaven and earth pass away, not an iota, not a dot, will pass from the law until all is accomplished.

In today's world, the terminology "jot" and "tittle" are not used. We often pass by these words in reading scripture. However, Matthew 5:18 tells us much about God's Word. "Jot" is the Hebrew word "YODH." It is the tenth letter of the Hebrew alphabet and also the smallest letter. "Tittle" is not a word but is the small decorative spur placed at the end of "YODH." The "tittle" gives emphasis and passion to the word "YODH." Therefore, we find that in Matthew God is telling us that not one of the smallest letters in the original text, and not even one instance of emphasis and passion of His Word will ever be lost to mankind. This will be true until Christ comes back in His second coming to live with His believers in the millennial reign. This verse, straight from God, tells us His Word will never be obsolete, will never be out of date and will always be as applicable to human needs as when it was written.

Is the Bible Always Accurate?

Inerrancy of scripture is the belief that the Bible, in its original revelation to man by God, is entirely true and without error whether it relates to doctrine, ethics, or as a record of events. God confirms the complete and total accuracy of His Word in His revelation to man. Therefore, if God is truth and God is holy, then His word is without error. Biblical inerrancy is rather different than what many non-scholars think. Skeptics can show variances from the different translations. Biblical inerrancy does not mean the translators were without error. It means the words of God, as given to those originally inspired to record it, was without error. Many original Greek, Aramaic or Hebrew words can be translated into several similar but slightly different English meanings. This can lead to slightly different emphasis in various translations. And the translations were not always made from divine inspiration. Some translations from the original scrolls were made for very human motivations such as financial profit. And yes, some translations are closer to the original text meanings than others. Yet even the different translations, when translated from the original manuscripts, to the extent we have them, are amazingly close to the original manuscripts. This is true because over the centuries, God has protected His Word and its accuracy.

Throughout the ages, ever since the first century Church, some have challenged the view of inerrancy of scripture. This challenge, based by many who call themselves theologians, is based on three principles. The principles are true but the resulting conclusion of challenged inerrancy is flawed. The principles are:

1. Humans are limited in knowledge and have a selfish and sinful nature. We tend to interpret information regarding God's Word, from the viewpoint of what we wish it to say, rather than what the context of Scripture tells us.
2. We do not possess for interpretation all the documents that bear on Bible inerrancy, and we do not have all of the original texts of scripture, many of which are probably lost forever.
3. The ancient scrolls containing the Word of God are difficult to read and interpret. When they were recorded by God's inspired writers no formatting existed. Until 900 AD no punctuation marks were included in the scripture texts. No verse or chapter numbers existed until centuries later. Prior to 900 AD the texts were written in Scriptua continua. This means there were no spaces between words or sentences. There was no capitalization and no punctuation.

The issue of inerrancy of scripture comes down to belief in God's truthfulness or belief in man's logic. God tells us that His Word is true and we ultimately believe God or we do not. To doubt the accuracy of the Bible is to doubt the truthfulness of God. If we accept the statements of God that His Word is totally accurate and without error; we answer the critics as follows:

1. Humans are weak and have limited knowledge. We are selfish and want the work we do to turn out the way we want it to turn out. Yet God tells us His Word is inspired. It is "God-Breathed." This means the Holy Spirit, or God

in spirit imputed into the authors the words God wanted printed. The authors often were recording things they did not understand. Their knowledge was weak and limited but God's knowledge knows no boundaries. They were often self-centered people, just as we are.

However, Old Testament believers believed in Yahweh, in God Jehovah, and they believed in God's promise of the coming Messiah. They believed their only hope for salvation was the promised Messiah. The entire Old Testament is focused on that future event. Yet their understanding of this promise of God only gave them a limited grasp of the future event of Christ's birth, life, and crucifixion. The authors wrote the books of the Bible because they recognized God was telling them what to write and they were in awe of God.

2.   It is true we probably do not possess all of the scriptures recorded by man about God. Yet God has insured we have what Scripture we need for full revelation to man. We know we have what God wanted us to have. The Scripture we possess was saved by God. They were revealed by God in the Dead Sea Scrolls. If there are scriptures we have not yet discovered they will only add to the amazement of God's truth being revealed. What we have is the fulfillment of prophecy contained in the Word. What we have is the total accuracy of the scripture after having been written over 1,500 years. What we have speaks of the determination of God to preserve His Word for us so we might have proof of His truth.

3.   And the third basis on which men deny the inerrancy of Scripture is that the original documents are so hard to understand. Yes, we agree, but mankind has continued to have the amazing inspiration of God the Father to help us understand. The significant point here is that we do not understand God's Word based on our intelligence. We understand it based on the interpretation of the Bible as the Holy Spirit reveals to us. This means His Word was imputed or imbedded into the hearts of His chosen scribes.

We believe in the inerrancy of Scripture not because of the proof given by scientists and prophets. We believe in the inerrancy of Scripture not because of theologians who proclaim doctrine and theories supporting inerrancy. We believe in the inerrancy of Scripture because in His Word God told us He does not lie. And we believe in the inerrancy of the Scripture because God Himself told us His Word is totally accurate, true, and sufficient to meet all our needs.

Numbers 23:19
"God is not man, that He should lie, Nor a son of man, that He should change His mind. Has He said, and will He not do it? Or has He spoken, and will He not make it fulfill it?"

Hebrews 6:18
"That by two unchangeable things, in which it was impossible for God to lie, we who have fled for refuge might have strong encouragement to hold fast to the hope set before us."

Many places in His Word, God tells us He does not lie. This is undoubtedly because God knew mankind would challenge His truthfulness. We also have the comfort of knowing that inerrancy was part of the early Church's base doctrine from its inception. It was taught as an accepted unchallenged fact by those who believed by faith and studied the scriptures for knowledge and authority. In the early Church, St. Augustine, who lived from 354 AD to 430 AD stated,

"I have learned to yield this respect and honor only to the canonical books of scripture: Of these alone do I most firmly believe that the authors were completely free from error."

The two great reformers, Luther and Calvin bear testimony to biblical infallibility. Luther said,

"But everyone, indeed, knows that at times they (the fathers) have erred, as men will, therefore, I

am ready to trust them only when they prove their opinions from scripture, which has never erred."

Mankind often chooses to question the total truthfulness and accuracy of the scripture because mankind often finds instruction in God's Word is in conflict with what our mind's logic says. Is it logical to believe that Jonah was swallowed by a whale and after three days was coughed up and continued his mission for God? No, but God said it and that settles it. God cannot lie. Is it logical to believe that Jesus walked upon the water or fed the five thousand from three fish? No, but God said it and that settles it. Is it logical to believe that Jesus Christ died on the cross of Calvary and after three days rose again with victory over death? No, but God said it and that settles it. Many of the miracles of Jesus cannot be explained by logic of man. Those who do not have faith to believe are left to explain the inexplicable by logic. These miracles cannot be explained by man so mankind seeks ways to compromise the scripture. It is not logical to explain the creation of the earth and sky and seas and especially the creation of humans. Yet reality is that we exist and the earth is real. God's Word tells us He created all that is and that ever will be. God cannot lie. He said it and that settles it.

Mankind, desiring to rely upon his logic rather than faith in God, tends to explain the revelation of scripture by saying the Bible contains error. When nonbelievers find instruction that conflict with the type of life they want to lead, they find ways to say the scripture really means something else. The world says whip your fellow man because you are in conflict with him. God's Word says love your fellow man because you are your brother's keeper. The world says gather material things, because that is how we measure success and happiness. God's Word says do not worry about where you will sleep or what you will eat because God will take care of His children. The reason so many of us explain scripture away is we are uncomfortable with it. This means we have to come up with a justification of why God's Word is in conflict with what we want it to say.

However, if we accept that the Bible was God-Breathed, or inspired by God, if we accept the thoughts and concepts recorded are directly from God, and if we accept that God is without error, the only coherent conclusion is that the Bible, as originally God-Breathed to man, is, was, and will always be, without error.

Jesus taught the Bible is absolutely true and without error. In the Old Testament, He established the authenticity of His New Testament text. For example, Jesus used the Old Testament law to create the foundation for His teachings to love your enemies. It is conflicting to our human spirit to love or even to try to love our enemies. Our desire is to crush our enemies. But Jesus told us that, if we love God, we will love all of His children. To understand that we have to consider what true love means. It means to be willing to sacrifice our needs, or comfort and even our safety for their needs, comfort and safety.

Matthew 5:43–47
"You have heard that it was said, 'You shall love your neighbor and hate your enemy.' But I say to you, love your enemies, bless those who curse you, do good to those who hate you, and pray for those who spitefully use you and persecute you, so you may be sons of your Father in heaven; for He makes His sun rise on the evil and on the good, and sends rain on the just and on the unjust. For if you love those who love you, what reward do you have? Do not even the tax collectors do the same? And if you greet only your brethren what more are you doing than others? Do not even the tax collectors do the same?"

Jesus also taught the accuracy of the commandments given to the people by God, through Moses, when he told them the most important commandment was, and had always been to love the Lord your God with all your heart.

Matthew 22:36–40
"Teacher, which is the great commandment in the law?" and He said to him, "'You shall love the Lord your God with all

your heart, with all your soul, and with all your mind. This is the great and first commandment. And the second is like it: You shall love your neighbor as yourself.' On these two commandments, depend all the Law and the Prophets. "

The accuracy of the scripture is established by the testimony of God the Father who gave us His word through the prophets and apostles. It is established by God the Holy Spirit who breathed the word of God into the hearts of God's scribes to record it, and it is established by Jesus Christ the Son of God who relied on the inerrant word of God to be the foundation of His teachings to man.

Is the Word of God Sufficient to Meet Man's Needs?

God's Word is inerrant, meaning it is always true and is without error. However, is God's Word sufficient to meet the needs of man or does it require support? Many take the position that God's Word alone, without the interpretation of and guidance of something else, is not sufficient to meet man's needs.

Perhaps a prime example of mankind feeling something more is needed than God's Word alone is the way we worship in Church. Can Churches continue to exist and accomplish Gods will by simply preaching and teaching the word of God? In the modern world where every aspect of our society appeals to the entertainment of man, do Churches also need entertainment to thrive and succeed? If Churches must appeal to the material and entertainment needs of people, they are saying that simply preaching and teaching the contents of God's Word is not sufficient to support the work of the Church. A similar question is whether Churches need something more than proclamation of the word of God to grow and thrive. This question implies that a thriving, successful Church must include growth. What does God ask of His Church?

First of all, God wants His Church to praise, honor, and glorify Him. The purpose of the Church is to exalt the Savior, to evangelize the lost, to encourage the believer, to equip the saints and to empower His workers. However, we do not accomplish this by empty words of praise. We accomplish this by dedication of our heart, our mind, our strength, our soul and our spirit to Jesus Christ God's Son. As we reach a state of mind that yields dedication to Christ, we will strengthen the Christian, encourage the believer, enlist the uncommitted, evangelize the lost, lift up the downtrodden, minister to the needy, and witness to the lost. We must not, however, lose sight of the reality that the primary purpose of God's Church is to exalt the Savior. To exalt the savior we must teach truth. Every effort must have as its focus the intent of exalting our Savior. We are not supposed to go to Church to get a blessing. We go to Church to worship our Savior and in return we often receive the blessings of God. To achieve these important goals we must understand and believe that the study of, commitment to, and belief in the sufficiency of God's Word is critical. Otherwise we will invariable begin to yield to man's intellect, man's creativeness, and man's passion to achieve the goals of the Church. In so doing we will not be pleasing God and we will fail in our goal of exalting the Savior, even if we achieve huge congregations.

If we use psychology and modern methods of counseling, at the exclusion of God's Word in trying to reach out and meet the needs of a needy people, we are saying God's Word is insufficient to meet the needs of a modern society. Why does the modern Church reach this conclusion? Could it be that Satan is trying to persuade us to rely on something other than the Bible? Would Satan tell us modern techniques are more productive than simple reliance on the word of God? Satan is sly and devious. He does not tell us God's Word is inadequate, he simply tells us that the addition of man's logic and intellect is better in the modern world. God knew Satan would temp man to do this. Satan tells us that we cannot reach the world in today's environment, without an increased intellect of man. Thus we seek signs and wonders. Satan will assist us with amazing results if it leads people to this false teaching.

2 Corinthians 3:5
"Not that we are sufficient in ourselves to claim anything as coming from us, but our sufficiency is from God."

27

Paul teaches us the temptation to rely on our entertainment ability, or to rely on our interpretive ability, or to rely on our own intellect rather than the Word of God is not a new concept. It has always been in existence and has always been false. Paul told the Christians at Corinth and he tells us today, **"Our sufficiency is of God."** What did Paul mean by this statement? He meant our ability to please God and meet the needs of man, comes from God. The intellect of man is not sufficient to accomplish this. Too often man gets this statement out of context and says our sufficiency to please man and meet the needs of God comes from our dedication and application of our minds to the task. When Paul wrote this passage he was writing to those whom the Holy Spirit had come to dwell within their hearts. They, therefore, had the in-dwelling assistance of God on a second by second basis. The assistance of God to live a spirit filled life is not available to those who do not believe on Jesus Christ. Paul is even more specific in writing to us as recorded in his correspondence to the Christians at Corinth.

2 Corinthians 9:8
"And God is able to make all grace abound to you; that you, having all sufficiency in all things at all times, you may abound in every good work."

Paul tells us that God is sufficiently able to make available to us, as believers, His total inventory of grace. His grace is without limit therefore we may successfully achieve a life of good work in the sight of God. Paul does not say that God is able, with the assistance of psychologists and social workers, to give man the spirit filled life we seek. God does not need man's help. In fact, as we add these false sources of help we cut out God and hinder His willingness to help us. This is not to say there is no value in professional psychologists and social workers. It is to say we must rely first on God and interpret every other vehicle of help from the venue of God's Word.

In his first letter to the Christians at Corinth, Paul addressed this subject quite clearly. They were having the same problem hundreds of thousands of Christian experience today. They were trying to explain the Holy Spirit and the Word of God based on man's logic and intellect. Sermons preached and lessons taught based on the speaker's intellect and study, are insufficient to convey the power of God. We will only be taught the wisdom of God as we listen to God and as we allow the Holy Spirit to speak quietly to our heart. God's Word is sufficient to teach God's truth. God's Word is sufficient to give us answers to our problems and our needs. Relying on anything else is asking for disappointment and failure.

1 Corinthians 2:13
"And we impart this in words not taught by human wisdom but taught by the Spirit, interpreting spiritual truths to those who are spiritual."

Jesus Christ taught us the sufficiency of God's Word. As He walked and taught on earth, Jesus did not answer the problems He faced by His own power but by the power of God the Father. When Jesus faced Satan in the wilderness, as He prepared for His ministry on earth, Satan came to temp Him. Jesus answered Satan by saying over and over again, *"It is written."* It is written in the Word of God. If the Word of God was sufficient for Jesus in that horrific hour it is certainly sufficient for us regardless of whatever problems we might face. The writer of Hebrews speaks to the issue of the sufficiency of God's Word as well.

Hebrews 4:12
"For the word of God is living and active, sharper than any two-edged sword, piercing even to the division of soul and spirit, of joints and marrow, and discerning the thoughts and intentions of the heart."

God told us His Word is living and active and is the most powerful weapon existence in penetrating our soul to compare our desires with God's desires. This verse tells us that to rely on any substitute other than the word of God is to teach the way of the Lord is foolish.

God's Word does tell us that we should do good works. God's Word tells us that if we are "born again" Christians we will have a nature that wants to feed the hungry, clothe the needy, and minister to the sick and downtrodden. We will want to counsel the distressed and depressed among us. But the Word of God also tells us that the Scripture is the strength and guidance to empower and enable us to accomplish these tasks. Anything we use to help us must be used with the clear intent of reliance upon God's Word as the all-powerful source of strength. And we must remember that our mission is primarily to make disciples of men, to teach the way of salvation, and to grow in the way of the Lord. God has vested His power in His word. We can do no less than rely on it.

God's Word tells us exactly why it is sufficient to meet our needs and ultimately our desires. Psalms 19:7–9 speaks clearly to what man needs and what God provides.

Psalms 19:7–9
"The law of the LORD *is perfect, reviving the soul; The testimony of the* LORD *is sure, making wise the simple; The precepts of the* LORD *are right, rejoicing the heart; The commandment of the* LORD *is pure, enlightening the eyes; The fear of the* LORD *is clean, enduring forever; The rules of the* LORD *are true and righteous altogether."*

The Psalmist recorded what God told him to write when he gave these incredible promises. God reveals six timeless, unchangeable, precious facts.

1. First: The law of the Lord is perfect. Law means the guidelines or the commandments of God are always correct and without error. They are complete and need nothing added. They are everlasting and timeless and they are true and all encompassing. They meet every problem, every need, and every weakness of mankind. They are so vast and rich that when we accept God with a heart to glorify and please him, God converts our soul from its carnal physical being, to

a spiritual being that is clean of all sin. This is because of God's Gift of His Son.

2. Second: The testimony of God is sure. This means that what God tells us in His Word is truth. This teaching from God reassures us that there is such a thing as absolute truth and God is absolute truth. His Word often does not make sense to nonbelievers, but when we rely on His Word the Holy Spirit gives us understanding. We then become wise rather than foolish, we rely on God rather than ourselves, and His wisdom seems right and true and obvious to us through the Holy Spirit.

3. Third: The precepts or statues of the Lord are right. This means His commandments to us, His believers, are just and right. We need to do what God commands. We should follow His commandments not only because to do so is pleasing to God but also because to do so is positive and fulfilling for us. To do other that what God commands brings sorrow, confusion, regret, guilt and eternal damnation. To do what God commands brings joy, peace, fulfillment and satisfaction. And it brings this inner joy and peace not only in eternity with Him but also on this earth. in this lifetime.

4. Fourth: The emphasis of God is that His commandments are pure and enlighten the eyes. In this powerful scripture, God uses the law of the Lord, the statues of the Lord and the commandments of the Lord separately, to give us powerful insight into the identity of God. Likewise it gives us insight into what we must become to please Him and to earn His blessings.

5. Fifth: The point made is that fear of God is natural. It is a good thing. It is common sense. It will last forever. This does mean we are to be awed by God. It means we are to recognize our inadequacy with relation to God. It means we are to recognize His awesome characteristics. It means that in comparison we are so inadequate we stand in awe of God. We are amazed at who and what God is. That com-

parison will last forever even throughout eternity. It is a fear that brings amazing love and adoration. It is not a fear that brings terror and destruction. It is a fear that gives glory to God and in return He gives love to us.

6. Sixth: The point of Psalms 19:7–9 is that His judgments are true, and they are righteous. No falseness can survive, we cannot fool God. He knows our inner heart. He sees beyond what we do and knows why we do it. He knows our thoughts. Yet God loves us. This verse is as much a condemnation of those who are not believers and who do not trust Him as it is a reassurance of those who trust and believe in Him.

Psalms 19 is God speaking to us and telling us His Word is sufficient to save us from our sins and revive our soul. His Word is sufficient to provide us truth. His Word is sufficient to make us wise not because of our intellect but because of God's grace. His Word is always right, never wrong, never misleads or leads us astray. His Word is without end, unchanging, unshakable, immutable, instilling in our hearts a fear of disobedience that is needed for our good. And His Word is sufficient to provide us the reminders needed to stay on the path of righteousness if we stay true to him.

God's Word is not only sufficient for our needs. To rely on anything other than God's Word is to begin to walk the path of destruction. Any urging we have to rely on man's intellect, man's programs, man's technology, or man's teachings is to reject God.

Who did God intend to receive and understand His Word?

Mankind has trouble grasping a foundational truth that has massive application to our understanding of Scripture. The entire Word of God is inerrant, is sovereign, is unchangeable, is sufficient for my needs and applies to all mankind. But the Word of God was written to three groups of people. Although the entire Word applies to all, it's focus and therefore it's message is directional. This means God's revelation for each of these groups varies. It also says that to gain clear understanding of Scripture we need to know to whom each passage of Scripture was written.

The Bible is addressed to three categories of people. These three are Jews, Gentiles, and the Body of Christ also known as "The Church." Jews are the lineage of Israel, also the chosen people of God. The Jews are people who have a special, preordained mission and purpose, as anointed by God. The world thinks of Gentiles as meaning people who are not Jews. In the Bible, the word Gentile refers to people who have not accepted Jesus Christ as their Savior and are therefore foreigners to the select of God. That can be of Jewish descent or any other group of people as long as they are not believers in Jesus. The "Body of Christ" or "The Church" includes both Jews and Gentiles who, after the death, burial and resurrection of Christ (known as His glorification) place their faith in Christ for future deliverance from their sins. God gave "The Church" too Jesus Christ and He, along with the Holy Spirit, empowered "The Church" to become part of the family of God with eternal salvation.

Ephesians 1:22
"And he put all things under his feet and gave him as head over all things to the church."

At times in the Scripture, God speaks primarily to the Jews, at times to the Gentiles, and at times to His Church. If we do not understand this the message delivered can seem contradictory and confusing. If we understand this and grasp what God's plan and intended revelation of scripture is for each group, the message is clear and makes perfect sense.

Faith in Christ and His resurrection from the dead has always been the door of salvation. However, in the Old Testament people did not have full revelation of the death, burial and resurrection of Jesus Christ. Therefore their faith did not include the name of Jesus but did include belief in the promised coming of "The Messiah." Because they did not have Jesus in front of them as the model of what they should be and do they needed something that would help them know when they were pleasing God and when they were not. Therefore, God gave them "The Law" a specific set of instructions of how they were to live, think, and react toward God. Their salvation required faith in the coming Messiah. Their salvation also required faith in God the Father to care for His people and obedience of God's commandment to keep the Law. Obedience to keep God's commandments did not require those in faith to be perfect in keeping the law. No one could do this. However, it did require them to maintain a constant desire to keep the law. It also required a constant desire to repent when they failed, and a willingness to offer burnt sacrifices to God in their petitions of forgiveness for their failures. In truth and spirit this is not different than our path to salvation today. Much of the Old Testament and some of the New Testament is a record of God working with these people.

Galatians 3:23 tells us that keeping the law did not save those people in the Old Testament. Old Testament people were saved because of their faith in God to deliver His promises and their belief in the Grace of God to forgive their sins. They did not know Jesus would be the Messiah. But they trusted God to deliver a Messiah. Their salvation was based on their faith in God and His announced plan to send a Messiah. It was not completed until the death, burial and resurrection of Jesus Christ.

Therefore Scripture written for the Old Testament people or pre-Church people, addresses people with a different revelation from God than given to "The Church." In the Old Testament the Law was a measuring guide to alert people when they sinned. However, after the death, burial and resurrection of Jesus Christ, people no longer needed the law as a measuring board. The life of Jesus Christ became their measuring board. He sent the Holy Spirit to live in our hearts as our mentor. In the Old Testament people were not saved based on how well they kept the law. They were saved on whether they believed in God the Father and trusted Him to save them from their sins. Salvation during any Dispensation has never depended on obedience for salvation. To those in "The Church" obedience to God shapes us as we grow in spirit and builds faith in our Savior. Scripture written to "The Church" will focus on the life of Christ to be our measuring board. Scripture written to Old Testament people did focus on the Law because it was their measuring board. Look at how Paul specifically identifies the group of people he is writing to as "The Church." This scripture would have not meant anything to Old Testament saints.

Galatians 3:26–27
"For in Christ Jesus you are all sons of God, through faith. For as many of you who were baptized into Christ have put on Christ."

In the above verses God is talking to "The Church." He is talking to people who have believed on Jesus Christ as the risen Savior and thus His message is not to Old Testament Saints. Paul addresses this change when He says you are sons of God through faith in Christ Jesus, as opposed to Old Testament Saints who become part of the family of God (not the Body of Christ). He goes on to say that "as many of you as were baptized into Christ have put on Christ." This type message would make no sense to Old Testament Saints just as Gods message to the Old Testament Saints does not totally apply to "The Church." Paul further states that when you accept Jesus Christ you cease to become Greek (Gentile) or Jew. You cease to be slave or free person. You cease to be male or female. We are all one in Christ.

The Bible has sections specifically addressed to these different groups. How are we to react to sections not addressed to "The Church"? Romans chapter 15 specifically addresses this question.

Romans 15:4
For whatever was written in former days was written for our instruction that we through endurance and encouragement of the Scriptures we might have hope.

Therefore we are to study all Scripture, but be aware of who the Scripture was intended. But all Scripture teaches us how God works with His people and has value for us.

How did God put together His Word?

The Pentateuch

The first writings of God's Word include five books that are collectively called the Pentateuch. They are the foundation upon which all of the Old Testament rests and upon which the New Testament rests. These five books are God's revelation to man about the creation of humanity, the fall of man, and the establishing God's law. These five books were written by Moses approximately 1,445 years before the birth of Jesus Christ. God's Word itself provides the authenticity of Moses as the writer and God as the author of these books.

Deuteronomy 31:24–26
"When Moses had completed writing the words of this law in a book to the very end, Moses commanded the Levites, who carried the ark of the covenant of the LORD, saying: "Take this Book of the Law, and put it beside the ark of the covenant of the LORD your God, that it may be there as a witness against you."

The five books of the Pentateuch are Genesis, Exodus, Leviticus, Numbers, and Deuteronomy. God gave us these books to accomplish the following:

1   **Genesis** is a book of beginnings in which God gives man limited insight into our origination. Genesis tells us everything that exists, is of God. God is the author and creator of this universe and nothing exists outside of his authorship and creator role. God gave us Genesis to counter an array of false philosophies that every culture has advanced through every century of man's existence. God, however, wants mankind to know and acknowledge that He and He alone is the creator of all that exists.

2   **Exodus** describes the departure of God's people from slavery to freedom. It gives us insight into the trials and struggles they suffered because of their lack of faith in God.

Moses was chosen by God to lead God's chosen people, the Israelites, from bondage to freedom. God then instructed Moses to teach them what responsible freedom means with relation to being pleasing in God's sight. Major themes include the name and glory of God and the agreements (covenants) between God and Israel.

3   **Leviticus** reveals to us our sin nature. Leviticus tells us man can never be Holy unless God makes us Holy. We see ourselves in the Israelites as they try to circumvent the will of God. This book presents to us a broken relationship with God restored because of His love and man's repentance. Leviticus is a book of holiness.

4   **Numbers** is a book of the history of God's people. It reveals to us lessons we need to learn. Numbers tells us disobedience to God has consequences.

It begins with the exodus generation and takes us through the thirty-nine years of wandering in the wilderness. It shows the faithfulness of God and the infidelity of God's people.

5   **Deuteronomy** is the "Second giving of the law." The Ten Commandments were given on Mt. Sinai forty years earlier and Moses now repeats the Ten Commandments stressing that the law and nature of God is unchanging.

Jesus recognized and accepted the division of the Old Testament. God told Matthew to record that His arrival on the scene of mankind was not to destroy the Law but to fulfill the law.

Matthew 5:17–18
"Do not think that I came to abolish the Law or the Prophets. I have not come to abolish them but to fulfill them. For truly, I say to you, until heaven and earth pass away, not one iota not one jot will pass from the law till all is accomplished."

Today we are not bound by the law because the Holy Spirit lives in our hearts and is our mentor to righteous living. But the law is not abolished by the coming of Jesus Christ. Matthews 5:17–18 tells us the law still gives us today a good picture of what we must do to be within the will of God. Therefore it is of value to understand the Ten Commandants. They were given to Moses about 1,300 BC. They are:

1. "You shall have no other Gods before me." (Exodus 20:3)
2. "You shall not make for yourself a carved image…" (Exodus 20:4)
3. "You shall take the name of the Lord in vain…" (Exodus 20:7)
4. "You shall remember the Sabbath day and keep it Holy…" (Exodus 20:8)
5. "You shall honor your father and your Mother…" (Exodus 20:12)
6. "You shall not murder…" (Exodus 20:13)
7. "You shall not commit adultery…" (Exodus 20:14)
8. "You shall not steal…" (Exodus 20:15)
9. "You shall not bear false witness…" (Exodus 20:16)
10. "You shall not covet anything that is your neighbor's…" (Exodus 20:17)

These ten commands of God to all mankind are quite sufficient to meet His goal of righteousness. His commandments are complete and applicable to all generations. In this scripture, Jesus himself validates the complete Old Testament and declares the Old Testament to be adequate for study, for instruction, for guidance and for knowledge throughout all time. The later inclusion of the New Testament did not invalidate the Old Testament. The New Testament validates the Old Testament. Both the New and Old Testaments are validated by Jesus himself. The coming of Jesus was to fulfill the promises of the coming Messiah and to fulfill the events that must happen for the conclusion of time with relation to God and His people.

The Historical Books

The second section of the Old Testament, described as "The Prophets," can be broken down into sections. These sections are the former prophets, sometimes called History, the Major Prophets, and the Minor Prophets. Many Christians today misunderstand the role of prophets in the Old Testament. Their role was not to foretell the future but to understand the world they lived in and determine the will of God for the people of their time based on:

1. History of the Hebrew people
2. The prophets understanding of God, and
3. God's revelation to the prophets.

The classification of "Major" or "Minor Prophets" refers to the length of the book by that prophet's name. Major or minor refers to the book and not the person and does not indicate varying degrees of importance of the book in God's Word. This classification is used with prophetic books in the Old Testament. There are twelve shorter books collectively referred to as the "Minor Prophets." The remaining prophetic books in the Old Testament are considerably longer in length and referred to as "Major Prophets."

The "Minor Prophets" record the history of Israel from the initial conquest and settlement of Canaan or the land promised by God to Israel. They continued to record the history of Israel through the almost one thousand years of the judges and kings. The following books make up the "Minor Prophets":

1. **Joshua** is a history of the Israelites entering the promised-land; their conquering the people there, and the dividing into twelve tribes.
2. **Judges** is an early history of the Israelites in Canaan. They became loosely organized into a loose federation of tribes who were led by various judges. These judges were to be faithful to God and where to lead their federation to be faithful to God.

3. **Ruth** is an account of a young woman who would become an ancestor of King David and ultimately of Jesus Christ

4. **1 Samuel** is the history of God establishing King Saul as the first king of Israel. It covers Saul's lack of faithfulness to God, and God's raising-up David as Saul's successor.

5. **2 Samuel** is the history of how David ascends to the kingship of Israel and his love of God even as he evidences weaknesses as a man.

6. **1 Kings** is the history of kings following David in Israel, including Solomon and the civil war that divided Israel into two nations.

7. **2 Kings** is a continuation of the history of the kings that followed Solomon and their unfaithfulness to God. This history reveals Israel being destroyed by the Assyrians and Judah later being destroyed by the Babylonians because of the nation's unfaithfulness to God.

8. **1 Chronicles** is a history of the kings of Judah that parallels 1 Kings.

9. **2 Chronicles** is a history of the kings of Judah that parallels 2 Kings.

10. **Ezra** a history of how Ezra led a group of Jews back to Jerusalem from exile in Babylon and rebuilt the temple.

11. **Nehemiah** is a history of how Nehemiah led a group of Jews back to Jerusalem from exile in Babylon and rebuilt the wall of Jerusalem

12. **Esther** is history of a Jewish woman who became Queen to one of the Persian kings and helped the Jews avoid persecution.

The Major Prophets are called "major" only because the books they wrote are longer than the "Minor Prophets." These books are the following:

1. **Isaiah** is the record of a prophet to the northern kingdom of Israel who warned Israel of their coming destruction by the Assyrians if God's people did not repent. God also

revealed to Isaiah many great revelations regarding the coming Messiah. Isaiah is believed to have prophesied from about 740 BC to 698 BC.

2. **Jeremiah** is the record of a prophet to the southern kingdom of Judah who warned of the destruction of Judah by the Babylonians that would result in exile if the people did not repent. He was often called the "weeping prophet" because of his sorrow about the fate of the Jewish people and he prophesied from about 626 BC to about 580 BC.

3. **Lamentations** is a record of the deep sorrow and depression of Jeremiah as he could see the forthcoming destruction of both Israel and Judah. It is widely accepted the author of Lamentations was Jeremiah.

4. **Ezekiel** is a record of a prophet who lived in Jerusalem and was deported by Nebuchadnezzar to Babylon in the exile. Ezekiel includes many visions of God speaking to His people. Ezekiel began prophesying at the age of thirty in the year 592 BC until about 570 BC. He was a contemporary of Jeremiah.

5. **Daniel** is a record of the prophet to whom God revealed prophetic visions of the future. Daniel was carried off to Babylon during the exile of the Jewish people about 606 BC. His prophesy or revelation of God's prophetic visions came late in his life.

The minor prophets lived and served as God's spokesmen to the people between 850 BC and 440 BC. The prophets who worked with the Northern Kingdom of Israel were as follows:

Hosea** Joel**** Amos ****Obadiah****
Jonah, and,**** Micah**

The prophets who worked with the Southern Kingdom of Judah were as follows:

Nahum** Habakkuk**** Zephaniah***
Haggai*** Zechariah*** Malachi**

The Books of Wisdom

The third and final section of the Old Testament is often called "The Books of Wisdom." They include the following:

1. **Job** is the account of a man who was faithful to God even though many hardships were placed upon him. It features the question of why the righteous must suffer.
2. **Psalms** is a record of praise and requests of God by various authors. Most songs are recognized as having been written by King David. The collections of songs and poems cover a wide span of years and exact time of authorship is not known.
3. **Proverbs** is a collection of short statements of wisdom. King Solomon is recognized as the principle writer of Proverbs.
4. **Ecclesiastes** is a reminder to us that God is bigger and our life is more out of our control than we imagine or think. Most scholars recognize Solomon as the author of this book of Wisdom.
5. **Song of Solomon** is a play that illustrates the love between God and man by outlining the union between man and woman bathed in love.

How did we get the Old Testament?

Canonization is a term that defines the process that resulted in the selection of books to be accepted into the Bible. It took several centuries. It included different practical stages over a vast number of years. These stages were not always chronological but sometimes overlapped. They include.

1 Many manuscripts were written as recording of oral stories of first hand witnesses.
2 Manuscripts were circulated through communities of believers and became validated and accepted.
3 The manuscripts were gathered together in single scrolls and later into books.

This process was guided by God to protect and sustain His Word. Through His divine guidance the manuscripts were collected and emerged as His divine truth.

The canonization of the Old Testament rests upon God's deliverance of the Law and Prophets. Moses is widely believed to have written the books of the law when he wrote the books of Genesis, Exodus, Leviticus, Numbers, and Deuteronomy. Moses used scrolls that described ancient historical events to frame his writings and was guided by the Holy Spirit who is the true author of the law. In addition, he lived through the forty years of the Exodus so he had ample authentication for his writings. Jesus Christ accepted the books of the law, sometimes referred to as "The Law and The Prophets" as truth. He accepted them to be God's choice for divine direction, instruction, guidance, and devotion for God's people.

Deuteronomy 31:9
*"Then Moses wrote this law and gave it to the priests,
the sons of Levi, who carried the ark of the covenant
of the LORD, and to all the elders of Israel."*

The word canon comes from the Greek word *kanon*, which means a measuring. Canonization basically means writings that measure up to sacred standards. Therefore the Old Testament canon refers to all writings that measured up the very strict standards of authenticity. What were these standards? First and foremost writing had to be seen, over a number of years as being inspired by God and not having been born out of the motives of man. Over a period of time from the early fifth century through approximately 400 BC writings were scrutinized and evaluated and tested to determine if they met the standards as outlined below.

1   **Authenticity:** The writings had to be viewed as having come from God. This meant that the writings had to be accepted as not coming from the mind of man and this view had to be tested over time by different cultures and generations.

2   **Prophetic:** The author of the book had to be viewed as God Himself, who inspired one of His selected servants to record His words. This selected servant was called a prophet. So if the writing did not come from a Prophet of God it did not pass the standard of canonization.

3   **Dynamic:** The content of the Book was required to include evidence of life-changing power of God Himself. The writing had to give evidence of God's self-proclaimed power and message to man.

4   **Acceptability:** The writing had to have been accepted by people of God as meeting the above three standards.

5   **Continuity:** The writings had to teach doctrine and values consistent with the Law and the Prophets as outlined to Moses and presented to the people of God.

We look at four widely used and generally accepted collections of ancient manuscripts which comprise the Canon as accepted down through the centuries and are accepted today. These are as follows:

1   **The Hebrew Bible:** This canon (compilation of man-uscripts) is what the Hebrew people through the centuries accept as the Bible. It remains today, unchanged and accepted by the Hebrew people as God's Word. The Hebrew religion does not accept the New Testament and does not accept Jesus Christ as the Messiah. The Hebrew Bible, in substance, agrees with the compilation of man-

uscripts Baptists and most Protestants accept as the Old Testament.

2   **The Greek Septuagint:** This is the Greek translation of the Hebrew Bible which included "The Apocrypha."

3   "The Apocrypha" is a compilation of manuscripts that were not regarded by the Hebrews as inspired Scripture and are not viewed by Baptists and most Protestants as inspired Scripture.

4   **The Latin Vulgate:** This is the translation of the ancient manuscripts that were written after the birth of Jesus Christ into Greek from Hebrew and Aramaic. Saint Jerome (c. 347, September 30, 420) worked from the well-known Greek manuscripts and made the first effort to define the New Testament. He later learned Hebrew and translated the Hebrew Bible into Latin. This body of work is called the Vulgate. The Vulgate is the standard version of the Bible observed by the Catholic Church for well over a thousand years.

5   **Modern Translations:** A flurry of translations in European languages and English followed. Of these the King James Version, authorized by King James of England in 1604 was the most influential and continues today to be one of the most relied on versions of the Bible. Currently the top ten translations used today are as follows: (1) New International Version, (2) King James Version, (3) New Living Translation, (4) English Standard Version, (5) New King James, (6) Reina Valera, (7) New International Reader's Version, (8) Christian Standard Bible, (9) Common English Bible, and (10) The Message.

What is the Value of the Old Testament today?

The New Testament Scriptures are the body of sacred writings that outline the guidelines by which God judges mankind. In the minds of many that raises the question about why the Old Testament has any value to us in our daily living. While the question is valid, the answer to the question is absolute and complete. The Old Testament gives us the foundation of faith upon which mankind could and would accept the death, burial, and resurrection of Jesus Christ. The fulfillment of prophecy could not have been accomplished without the prophecy of the coming Messiah. The fulfillment of this prophecy establishes that the death, burial, and resurrection of Jesus Christ were ordained by God from before the creation of mankind. We learn of this prophecy and God's provision of grace in the Old Testament. The Old Testament provides us glimpses of the glory of God and of His abounding love for man.

The initial chapters of Genesis provide a history of the origin of the Universe and the beginning of mankind. It is through Genesis that we learn that God is the creator and that the entire creation of everything we know and experience today was created over a period of six twenty-four-hour days.

Genesis 1:1
"In the beginning God created the heavens and the earth."

Genesis 1:31
"Then God saw everything that he had made and behold it was very good. And there was evening, and there was morning, the sixth day."

In Genesis, we learn God created man in God's own image. God wanted to have fellowship with man. God wanted to love man and be loved by man. In Genesis God tells us He created man without sin. Man was without blemish and God was pleased with His creation. Man was created to reflect back to God the same love and adoration that God demonstrated to man. Man was created in the image of God and was intended by God to exhibit the characteristics of God.

Genesis 1:27
"So God created man in his own image, in the image of God He created him, male and female He created them."

Genesis teaches us about Adam's decision to disobey God. The book of Romans tells us that when Adam sinned he separated all of mankind from God because God will not take on the cloak of sin in either Himself or His family.

Romans 5:12
"Therefore, just as sin came into the world through one man, and death through sin, and so death spread to all men because all sinned."

We learn about our sin nature for the first time and we learn of our inherited sin.

Genesis 3:8–13
And they heard the sound of the LORD *God walking in the garden in the cool of the day, and the man and his wife hid themselves from the presence of the* LORD *God among the trees of the garden. But the* LORD *God called to the man and said to him, "Where are you? And he said, "I heard Your voice in the garden, and I was afraid because I was naked; and I hid myself." He said, "Who told you that you were naked? Have you eaten from the tree of which I commanded you not to eat?" Then the man said, "The woman whom You gave to be with me, she gave me of the tree, and I ate." And the* LORD **God said to the woman, "What *is* this you have done?"**

The Old Testament tells the history of God's revealing Himself to man. God's working with mankind is an evolving story. It includes the failure of mankind to listen to God and man's history of infidelity with God. The Old Testament reveals how God has interacted with man and gives us an insight into what God wants from man. From the books of Genesis through Malachi we see God is a loving, merciful, and compassionate God. But we also see God is just, holy, and is capable of wrath and anger against the sin of man. The purpose of the Bible is for God to reveal Himself to man. In the Bible God reveals to us the standards and expectations He has for us and the penalty that awaits us if we fail to meet those standards. The Old Testament reveals to man God's hatred of unrighteousness. It reveals man's desire to be independent and to be selfish in his actions and thoughts.

The Old Testament reveals the wrath of God. God cannot be a God of justice, of holiness, of truth and take on any part of sin and unrighteousness. The Old Testament reveals that His wrath against our sin reveals who God is and His expectation of what we are to and will eventually become. For example the Old Testament reveals God's destruction of the Egyptian army at the crossing of the Red Sea. It reveals God's wrath when He allowed only two of the Israelites to enter the Promised Land because of the Israelites infidelity to Him. The utter destruction of the people who occupied the Promised Land was ordered by God. God declares Himself to be a God of violence and wrath against those who oppose Him. God reveals to us His wrath in the Old Testament not to make us fear him but to direct our paths to righteousness. God wants us to know the truth so that we might not have to suffer His wrath.

Psalms 76:10
"Surely the wrath of man shall praise You; the remainder of wrath You shall put on like a belt."

Psalm 21:9
"You shall make them as a blazing oven when You appear; The Lord shall swallow them up in His wrath, And the fire shall consume them."

The Old Testament reveals to us the promises and prophecies of God. The greatest revelation is the coming Messiah. It is in the Old Testament that the foundation for the plan of salvation of man is revealed. If we only had the New Testament we would not understand why the Jews were looking for the Messiah. We would not understand the full miracle of the virgin birth of Jesus Christ or the mass of prophecies that had to be fulfilled to pave the way for the coming of Jesus. Without the Old Testament the validity of the sermons of John the Baptist, the forerunner of Christ, would have been empty preaching. The significance of the birth place, the lineage of Jesus, the virgin birth itself, would have been passed over without our knowledge of their preordained preparation from before the beginning of time.

Isaiah 7:14
"Therefore the Lord will give you a sign: Behold, the virgin shall conceive and bear a Son, and shall call His name Immanuel."

Genesis 3:15
"And I will put enmity between you and the woman, and between your offspring and her offspring: he bruise Your head, and You shalt bruise his heel."

The Old Testament gave us the Law which established the parameters of the expectations of God for man. We would be unable to grasp the miracle of grace if we did not have the law to help us measure how far short of God's expectations we fall. God's gift to us of the Law helps us understand, in more depth, the impossibility of our living without sin.

Romans 5:20
"Now the law came in to increase the trespass, but where sin increased, grace increased all the more."

The Old Testament is a wealth of knowledge of how man is supposed to interface with God. The books of Psalms and Proverbs are vast reservoirs of instruction and advice. They show that God's Word gives us answers to every problem we will face if we will seek it. Romans chapter 5 tells us that the input of the law made man much more aware of the sin they committed but everywhere sin existed the grace of God matched and exceeded the price of that sin. And the price paid was Jesus dying on the Cross of Calvary.

Psalm 1:1–2
"Blessed is the man who walks not in the counsel of the wicked or stands in the way of sinners or sits in the seat of scoffers. But his delight is in the law of the LORD, and on His law he meditates day and night."

Between the Old and New Testaments

The last book in the Old Testament is Malachi. After God inspired Malachi to write his book historians tell us four hundred years passed between the Old and New Testament in which God was silent. Imagine, the United States has been in existence for slightly over two hundred years. Twice that time God was silent and did not speak to the Israelites. In this time period we do not have a record of God's working with man. But this does not mean God was inactive. God was preparing for the giving of His Son, Jesus Christ to come to earth and pay the price of mankind's sin. At the close of the Old Testament period the nation of Israel existed in the land of Palestine after Babylonian captivity. They were under the domination of the Persian and Medio-Persian Empire. The temple was restored at far lesser glory than that built by Solomon. The lineage of King David was in difficult and evil days.

At the height of Persian power and influence, Phillip of Macedon emerged as the leader of Macedonia. Macedonia would become known as Greece. Phillip of Macedon would be followed by his son, Alexander the Great. In 330 BC, Alexander the Great, only twenty years old, defeated the Persian Empire in one of the great battles of history. Greece became the next world power. Grecian influence became a strong force in Palestine. A movement of people called the Hellenists emerged who were dedicated to bring Grecian culture into the Israelites. They also wanted to liberalize many of the Jewish laws. The Hellenists eventually emerged as the strong political party known in the Bible as the Sadducees or the liberals. They were opposed by the traditionalists known as the Pharisees.

In 284 BC the Hebrew Scriptures were translated into the Greek language. This translation was called the Septuagint. For the first time most of the known, literate population could read the Bible.

In 203 BC, Antiochus the Great became the ruler of Syria and captured Jerusalem from the Egyptians. He became one of the most vicious and violent persecutors of the Jews in their history. This is a significant fact because Jerusalem is the most captured city in all of history. Palestine is the battle ground of the most wars of any country in the world. In about 170 BC Antiochus became so enraged at Palestine he engaged the temple of God in a battle in which forty-thousand people were killed. He destroyed the scrolls of the law and butchered a sow and offered it upon the sacred alter. He then made a broth of the sow and sprinkled the entire temple, intentionally defiling its sanctuary.

The people of Israel were so despondent at their eternal bondage and the violent abuse they suffered, they became more and more convinced that their only hope was the coming of the Messiah as predicted in Isaiah. However they believed the Messiah would give them release from oppression. They were looking for a physical King not a spiritual one. They wanted a king who would impose fierce military rule against the Romans. Therefore when Pompey captured Jerusalem for the Roman Empire in 63 BC, and Palestine was placed under the domination of Rome, the scene was set for the fullness of time as predicted in the scripture.

Galatians 4:4–6

"But when the fullness of the time had come, God sent forth His Son, born of woman, born under the law, to redeem those who were under the law, so that we might receive the adoption as sons. And because you are sons, God has sent forth the Spirit of His Son into your hearts, crying out, "Abba, Father!"

How does the New Testament relate to the Old Testament?

The New Testament consists of twenty-seven books. The word "Testament" means "covenant or agreement" just as it does in the Old Testament. However, the word "new" is used in contrast to the word "Old" to reflect the way God relates to mankind after the coming of Christ. The New Testament is not a replacement of the Old

Testament but a continuation of God's revelation to mankind His will and our obligations. It is, however, a new agreement between God and man, based on the following teachings of God.

- The birth, life, death, and resurrection of Jesus Christ fulfilled all Old Testament Prophecy concerning the Messiah. It completed the purpose of the Old Testament which was for believers to worship looking forward to the coming of the Messiah.

- The Old Testament was a life under the Law as given by God through Moses. The law was to be a measuring device to help people understand how much they failed to meet God's Holiness. The New Testament is a covenant for life under the Holy Spirit. In this new covenant the Holy Spirit becomes the measuring device to help people know when they fail to meet God's Holiness.

- The basic standard of God's Holiness in both the Old Testament and New Testament is the requirement to trust God and rely upon Him and Him alone for salvation. With the advent of Jesus Christ the understanding of God is exemplified in His son Jesus Christ.

- In the New Testament era those who believe on Jesus Christ have been given the Holy Spirit as a daily companion to give interpretation and guidance in the new age of grace.

- The Old Testament basically focused on the Children of Israel and God's working with them in their failures. It also features God's patience being stretched to the breaking point. In the New Testament the focus is on the entire world, first with the Jew and then the Gentile. In the Old Testament God's focus was on the Hebrew nation.

The New Testament is the fulfillment of prophecy in the Old Testament. Understanding the Old Testament is essential to understanding the New Testament. Both the Old Testament and New Testament are inspired by God. The New testament contains several thousand references and quotes from the Old Testament in relation to the (1) fulfillment of prophecy concerning the promised Messiah, (2) the completion of the Law and institution of the age of Grace and the Church, and (3) the replacement, by God, of the nation of Israel with the Christian Church as God's instrument to evangelize the world.

What is "The Apocrypha"?

As the Greek language and culture spread due to the conquests of Alexander the Great, the need arose for a Greek translation of the Hebrew Scriptures. So the Hebrew Bible was translated into an authoritative Greek version of the Old Testament. This Greek version of the Old Testament is commonly called the Septuagint. The Septuagint contained some writings which were not found in the Hebrew Bible. These writings were interspersed among the Old Testament Books and have commonly been called "The Apocrypha." The Apocrypha comes from the Greek language and means "things that are hidden." Various views exist concerning these writings so far as their application as inspired scripture.

Some view "The Apocrypha" as Holy Scripture. The Roman Catholic Church in the Council of Trent April 8, 1546, officially declared the Apocrypha to be inspired, authoritative, and equal with the books of the Old Testament. Others including Baptists and most Protestant denominations believe these Scriptures contain content that is other than from the original manuscripts. This view believes these writings contain questionable or heretical content. This foreign content is believed to have occurred when the Catholic Church "doctored" such scriptures to correspond with views of the Catholic Church.

During the days of the Reformation, Martin Luther's translation of the Scriptures contained The Apocrypha in the appendix of the Bible and he wrote these are "books which are not held equal to the Holy Scriptures but yet are profitable and good to read."

The Apocrypha includes the following writings: Tobit, Judith, Esther (The Greek Version), Wisdom, Sirach, Baruch, the Letter of Jeremiah, The Prayer of Azariah, and the Song of the Three Young

Men, Susanna, Bel and the Snake, and First Maccabees, and Second Maccabees. Most non Catholic denominations do not recognize "The Apocrypha" as part of the Bible because it cannot be authenticated as inspired. It does have some historical value and gives some authentication of events but it is not recognized as inspired and therefore is not included as part of our base of worship.

What is the composition of the New Testament?

Any consideration of how the New Testament canon was established must start with the understanding that the Church, established by Jesus Christ and empowered through his apostles, was never without a canon to establish doctrine. From the beginning of the Church the Old Testament existed and was a source of authority. With the advent of the Holy Spirit the new covenant arrived as a completion of the old.

The Church existed for about twenty years with no New Testament writings. They only had the oral teachings of the Apostles and the Old Testament. Even after manuscripts were written, they were mostly available to small, local congregations. Local congregations began to accept documents and manuscripts that were written, based on their best understanding of the works of Jesus Christ and the Holy Spirit. Most Bible scholars believe the 27 books of the New Testament were written in the first century although definitive proof of dates they were written does not exist.

In the first century New Testament Church, the Apostles represented Jesus Christ. They were the ultimate authority because they walked and talked with Jesus. He authorized them to do exactly what they did and that is to build, structure, support, and strengthen the New Testament Church. They did not immediately recognize the need for documentation. They did not immediately record their teachings of the good news because they did not view their teachings to be applicable for generations to come. They felt Christ would come back within their lifetime. The spread of the "Good News" was done verbally. Paul, however, realized he could not get to all places he was needed. Therefore, he began to write letters supporting the faith.

These letters become the unchallenged core of the New Testament canon because they represent the documentation of the Apostle's faith. The New Testament Church widely accepted the authenticated thirteen letters written by Paul as divinely inspired. They became part of the New Testament canon. These letters include nine letters written to Christian communities or congregations which are:

1. **Romans:** Paul wrote this letter to the Christians in Rome. Paul's purpose in the letter was to explain the doctrines of judgment and righteousness, law and grace, free will and predestination. Paul presents the plan of Salvation outlined by God to Jew and Gentile.

2. **1 Corinthians**: Paul wrote this letter to the Christians in the Greek city of Corinth. He wrote it in response to conflicts arising within the membership of that body of Christ. Paul explains God's expectations of believers in practical issues such as law suits, communion, spiritual gifts, women in the Church, matters of conscience, and the resurrection of Christ. The theme of the letter is how Christians are to relate to one another in love and grace.

3. **2 Corinthians:** This is a second letter written by Paul to certain leaders in the Church at Corinth who had questioned Paul's authority. Paul defends his calling and his right to apostolic authority and in so doing establishes for Christians throughout the ages the foundation of his teachings.

4. **Galatians:** Paul wrote this letter to the Christians in the Roman province of Galatia. We call that area of the world Turkey. Paul explains that Christians are released from the ceremonial laws of the Old Testament. The theme of Galatians is that salvation is belief on Christ Jesus, or Salvation by grace through faith and nothing else.

5. **Philippians:** Paul wrote this letter from prison to the Christians in the Greek city of Philippi. It is about the joy of salvation and is an encouraging supporting letter regarding the Christian faith.

6   **Colossians:** Paul wrote this letter to the Christians in the Greek city of Colosse. It centers on the magnificence of Jesus Christ and His being worthy of trust adoration and faith

7   **Ephesians:** Paul wrote this letter to the Christians in the Greek city of Ephesus. The purpose of this letter is to clarify what the Church is and how God wants to use it.

8   **1 Thessalonians:** Paul wrote this letter to the Christians in the Church in Thessalonica. The members of this Church were primarily Gentiles. Paul writes to encourage them and ask them to continue the work of righteousness and being faithful to God while they await the return of Christ.

9   **2 Thessalonians:** Thessalonica was the second city in which Paul established a Church. This letter is in response to some Christians in the Church who became concerned about what happened to those who died prior to the second coming of the Lord. They were being subjected to false teachings being done in the Church body and Paul wrote them to encourage them to remain faithful to the teachings of faith that Paul instructed them when he was with them.

    Paul also addressed letters to four individual Christian leaders. These are personal instructional letters to understudies of Paul for their development and encouragement:

10   **1 Timothy:** Paul received an inquiry from Timothy who was considering joining Paul on missionary efforts. Paul answered Timothy's inquiry and encouraged him to stay on the field in Ephesus. In this letter, Paul gives specific instruction regarding qualifications of deacons and pastors as well as other instructions of Church ministry. Paul also warns us about false teachers that will try to lead Christians astray.

11   **2 Timothy:** This is one of the last letters Paul wrote. He believed he would die sometime in the near future and makes a heartfelt plea for Timothy to join him. Paul also asks Timothy to bring Mark and certain items such as a cloak and his parchments.

12 **Titus:** Titus was a companion of Paul on a missionary journey and was serving as leader of a Church on Crete. Paul
wrote this letter to encourage Titus. Paul asks Titus to complete the missionary work needed on Crete and in so doing
encourages Christians to persevere in the faith.

13 **Philemon:** This is a short personal letter to Philemon. Paul
met Philemon's runaway slave and sent this letter implor-
ing Philemon to accept the return of his former slave and
brother in Christ.

The four Gospels are four views of Christ's ministry to different
groups. Each presentation is given from an individual perspective
reflecting that persons interests, observations, and values. Each presentation presents the Gospel, or the Good news, of the coming of
the Messiah and the fulfillment of scripture.

1 **Matthew:** Matthew was a tax collector. He wrote to convince a Jewish audience that Jesus was the Messiah promised in the Old Testament. He understood his audience
valued the Old Testament and therefore emphasized how
Jesus fulfilled Old Testament prophecy. The message of
Matthew, while directed to Jewish people is fully applicable
to all believers. This evangelistic message of Matthew gives
us the Great Commission (28:18–20). In it he challenges
all believers to spread the Gospel to every land and to all
people.

2 **Mark:** Mark was the first Gospel to be written. Matthew
and Luke used it as foundation for some of their teachings.
Mark gives us a vivid composition of the ministry of Jesus.
He does so through relaying the activities of Christ as He
traveled throughout the land. Mark portrays Jesus as the
Son of God sent to rescue humanity by serving and by sacrificing his life.

3 **Luke:** Luke was a physician and was the only non-Jew-
ish author in the Bible. He also wrote Acts and was not
one of the original apostles. He was a traveling companion

of Paul. Luke's Gospel is the most organized of the four Gospels and gives us more detail than the other Gospels. Luke gives us limited understanding of the youth of Jesus. It is the Gospel of Luke that lets us know Jesus was thirty years old when He was baptized. Luke was not a Jew and his Gospel was written primarily for Gentiles although it is applicable to all mankind.

4   **John:** John is the theological book of the four Gospels. John's focus was to

Teach that Jesus was, is and always will be the incarnate Word of God. John tells us God the Father is revealed to us through His Son Jesus. John clearly presents Jesus as the long awaited Messiah and teaches the only way to salvation is through Jesus Christ.

5   **Acts:** Luke, the physician, wrote Acts. In this book Luke reveals the power of the Church. The book is titled "The Acts of the Apostles" but it more accurately depicts the "Acts of the Holy Spirit." Luke gives us understanding of the way the Holy Spirit works through the Church and the individual believer.

6   **Hebrews:** We do not know who God told to record the book of Hebrews. It emphasized the doctrine of Jesus Christ, using the Old Testament as a foundation. Hebrews clarifies that Jesus Christ is the fulfillment of the Old Testament.

7   **James:** James is a short but powerful letter about the importance of faith. It is a kind of New Testament book of proverbs.

8   **1, 2 Peter:** Peter, among other things, has a focus on how the Christian is supposed to respond in adversity. It covers the subjects of sanctification, suffering and obedience.

9   **1, 2, and 3 John:** These are three letters by the same John who wrote the Gospel of John.

10   **Jude:** Jude is a short letter featuring serving God with purity and integrity.

11 **Revelation:** Revelation is the book of prophecy. It is understood as the most difficult to understand of all books in the Bible. Revelation contains an account of visions in symbolic and allegorical language borrowed extensively from Old Testament books like Ezekiel, Zechariah, and Daniel. The book is a both an encouragement and command to Christians to stand firm in the faith despite the threat of adversity and martyrdom. Revelation tells of God's promises of eventual victory over evil and commands Christians to wait patiently for the fulfillment of God's mighty promises. The triumph of God is to be accepted in faith and longed for in hope. Revelation instructs Christians to persevere in the faith even if it results in a martyr's death.

Why have various translations?

For over three hundred years, the King James Version was the prominent translation used in most Protestant Churches. However, as the English language continued to change and as people became more demanding of a translation they perceived to be "easier to read," scholars sought to update the scriptures into more contemporary language. Word meanings change with the passage of time. To some degree the need for new translations is justified because of changes in meaning of words in our language. Primarily, however, the new translations have been efforts to gain a more applicable translation from the original manuscripts to common language used by people of today.

New translations have generally been welcome contributions to the comprehension of scripture, but they have also been sources of division and controversy. Many well intentioned Christians feel the King James Version is the only version without error. The original manuscripts given to us by God are the only ones without error. The King James Version is a translation of the original manuscripts. However, to the extent the new translation, including King James, portray the thought and concepts of God, it is of great value. Today there are about twenty-four thousand translations of part or whole sections of the original manuscripts. In choosing a translation we need to make sure our main and over-riding consideration is how close the translation portrays the original text. If we could, the Dead Sea Scrolls would be our best translation. However, most of us would not understand what it says and would not study it. It was written without punctuations and without identification of chapters. Thus translations that assist our effort to interpret the original manuscripts of God's Word are critical to our worship.

What different translations are available?

- **King James Version** is the first version of Scripture authorized by the Protestant Church and was commissioned by King James. It was first published in 1611 and has since withstood many revisions.
- **American Standard Version:** A revised version of the King James Version. It was completed in 1885 and edited and reissued in 1901.
- **Revised Standard Version:** A revision of the American Standard Version and was published in 1952.
- **English Standard Version:** A literal, word for word translation from original transcripts with the goal to be an exact translation of the original texts.
- **The New Revised Standard Version**: Is an edited and published version of the Revised Standard Version. It was published in 1990.
- **The New English Bible** was translated from the original manuscripts in 1970. It adds clarification to original text of the manuscripts thus stands criticized as straying from the original texts.
- **New International Version** is a result of a desire to create an international translation that was not focused on American or English thought patterns. It has, however, received much criticism for choices made in the translation for having added to the original translations. The critics claim that in trying to clarify the original manuscripts, the

NIV changes thought of the original manuscripts. The NIV is widely used and accepted but it brings substantial doubt as to being the most accurate of the translations available.

- **The Living Bible** is the work of Kenneth N. Taylor who paraphrased the scripture for the purpose of not being a research Bible but being a family study Bible for family devotions. It has the author's interpretation and viewpoint built into the text and therefore varies widely from the original text. Many do not recognize it is not an original translation but is a commentary on the Bible.

- **New American Standard:** It is highly respected as the most literal English Translation of the Bible. It is considered very accurate but is sometimes difficult to read. It was revised to improve readability in 1995.

- **New King James Version** is not related to the King James Version other than in name. It is considered an accurate translation and is easier to read than the King James Version.

- **The New American Bible** is a translation focused for the Catholic layman. It is a very good Bible for Catholics but it definitely has built into it the Catholic doctrine and thought process.

- **The New Jerusalem Bible** is a product of the best Bible scholars in the Roman Catholic Church.

- **The New Living Translation** is an effort to change the Living Bible from being a paraphrase Bible into a true Translation. In the end, however, it is a revision of the Living Bible and still a paraphrase.

Apart from these versions and countless others not mentioned here, many publications exist that feature study helps, commentaries or references added as a supplement to a particular translation. Among these include:

- **The Scofield Reference bible**
- **The Open Bible**

- **The Thompson Chain Reference Bible**

Opinions regarding which translation is the best vary greatly from Church to Church and even more so from individual member to individual member. We rely on the Holy Spirit to convict people hearts regarding their interpretation of God's Word. Reading of the Scripture should not be dictated by man but by the Holy Spirit and that the Holy Spirit can and will convict us of our interpretation of God's Word. That said: one should beware of paraphrased editions of God's Word. They are, by definition, someone else's interpretation of a translation.

CHAPTER TWO

The Doctrine of Creation
God's Presents Himself as the Creator of everything

All cultures, nationalities, and religions have, throughout the ages, asked; "Where did we come from?" Most creation myths speak of gods and goddesses who came from a place above the earth and seeded a race called humanity. All such myths strive to answer the question without success. Today in America, the prevailing question regarding our origination centers on the theory of evolution and the concept of creation. One tries to find proof in science while the other relies on faith in God.

Changing Cultures

Only a few generations ago laws prevented teaching the theory of evolution in many communities of the United States. The Bible was generally accepted as the true and reliable account of our origin. But now the opposite seems to have happened. The Bible is banned from classrooms in American schools. Any serious discussion of creation is forbidden and is deemed as violation of the law. Any criticism of the theory of evolution is ruthlessly suppressed. Why is this true? The reason such a fierce attack on the truth of creation is being staged in our world today is that Satan wants to poison the minds of people and deny the reality of God. Satan has employed this tactic though out the ages. Satan will use any false belief to hinder mankind from recognizing God as the creator of everything.

In America today, we do not find much pressure to believe in gods and goddesses of fertility; as people in other cultures have for the ages. In fact, in our culture, we find very few images set as Gods that man is tempted to worship. Instead Satan has focused on tempting man to believe all of creation came about by chance. We call this myth the "Big Bang Theory" otherwise called the theory of evolution. Both the theory of evolution and the myth of gods and goddesses of fertility are in conflict with God's Word. To believe either in effect says God is lying when He tells us He is the only God and that He is the beginning and the end of all things created.

What does God tell us?

Christians are people of the book (Bible) and believe God's Word is without error true and accurate. Therefore, the answer must be found in God's Word. God knew man would seek to know more about his origin. Therefore God answers that question in the very first book of the Bible. In fact in the very first words of Genesis God tells us He created the heavens and the earth. "Where did I come from?" The answer is God created everything and everybody.

Genesis tells us God created the skies and the earth. Then, because His creation was dark and God is a God of light, He created light and divided the light and darkness. He called the light day and the darkness night. The scripture says "God said." He did not use evolution to create the world. God spoke it into existence. We even know how much time God took to create all creation. The Bible tells us very clearly and specifically that God created all that exists in six twenty-four hour days. To believe in anything other than God the creator, means we either refute the entire Bible or we have decided some of the bible is in error and man has the freedom to pick and choose that part he wants to believe.

God's Word tells us God not only spoke the world into existence, He did it from nothing. Before God's creation, only God the Father, God the Son and God the Holy Spirit existed. God does not reveal to us when He created the angels. God tells us that He created the world as we know it today in six twenty-four-hour days. To believe anything else adds to God's Word and in effect says that "God did not explain clearly His creation so I will do it for Him." God outlined for us His creation sequence in the form of six days.

Day One: Creation of Matter and Light

Genesis 1:1–5
"In the beginning God created the heavens and the earth.
The earth was without form, and void; and darkness was
on the face of the deep. And the Spirit of God was hovering
over the face of the waters. Then God said, "Let there be

light"; and there was light. And God saw the light; that it was good; and God separated the light from the darkness. God called the light Day, and the darkness He called Night. And there was evening and the morning, the first day."

God's Word is precise in its definition of creation. It declares first the creation of matter. When God tells us the earth was without form and was void He tells us it did not exist. Light did not exist. Time did not exist. God's creation of matter took the form of gaseous liquid that God's Word calls water. No light existed and creation existed in total darkness. Therefore during the first twenty-four-hour day God created matter, created light to illuminate his creation, and then separated the light from darkness. In so doing, he created day-time and nighttime.

This is a noteworthy when we understand God created the stars and the sun and the moon on the fourth day. If God is not speaking of the creation of the sun, moon and stars then what is the light of which God speaks of when He said' "And let there be light"? Please note that verse 2 of Genesis chapter 1 says the earth was without form, was empty (void) and dark. And God said let there be light and let the light be distinct from darkness. So in day one God created night and day. This is significant because God declared day would have twelve hours and night twelve hours. The first amazing creation of God on day one was matter. His second amazing creation was time. Time had never existed before. His third creation was light. In the New Testament, Jesus Himself verifies the time creation of twelve hours in the day and twelve hours in the night.

John 11:9
"Jesus answered, "Are there not twelve hours in the day? If anyone walks in the day, he does not stumble, because he sees the light of this world."

The Bible does not specifically state that on day one God created time. But it tells us God created light to divide time into day and night. In Genesis we see God named the light day and the dark night and then Jesus Christ himself tells us the day has twelve hours. We know God created time after matter and after light. This was not the light that would come from the sun and moon and stars. The light created on the fourth day was light that set in motion the universe as it rotates on its axis. This is something much different than the light created on day one. Time began with the creation of day and night.

The creation of matter, light, and time was done by God speaking it into existence. This speaks of the power and intellect of God which is vastly superior to that of man. People have difficult grasping such power and intellect so they try to explain it away with an explanation that more nearly meets the logic of man. In today's world we call this the theory of evolution which is nothing more than man's effort to reject God as the creator.

However, we have not yet answered the question of what did God mean when He created light and divided it from darkness on day one of creation? First John 1:5 gives us this answer.

1 John 1:5
"This is the message we have heard from Him and proclaim to you, that God is light, and in Him is no darkness at all."

However, we have not yet answered the question of what did God mean when on day one He separated light from dark? Prior to creation, God was light therefore had no need to create light. Used in this context light means two things. One is light is substance and darkness is nothing. The second is that light is truth and darkness is evil. Yes, the Bible tells us that God created the deep and darkness was on the face of the deep. The Bible does not say God created the deep and darkness. God's Word says He created the deep or substance and size to His creation. Then it says darkness was on the face of the deep. That means that other than the substance God created there was nothing. God was, before the creation of the world substance and truth. God is still substance and truth. God created the world to be substance and truth.

Day Two: Creation of Our Atmosphere

Genesis 1:6–8
"And God said, "Let there be an expanse in the midst of the waters, and let it divide the waters from the waters." And God made the expanse, and separated the waters which were under the expanse from the waters which were above the expanse; and it was so. And God called the expanse heaven and there was evening and there was morning, the second day."

On the second twenty-four-hour day God took the gaseous liquid created on the first day (substance also called matter), and formed it into what we understand as the atmosphere. It is easy to read this revelation of God and miss its magnificent revelation. It also stands alone as a powerful, accurate revelation of God the creator that dismisses any legitimacy of the Theory of Evolution.

On this incredible twenty-four-hour day, God looked upon the matter, referred to in Genesis 1:6 as "the waters," and said, **"Let there be an expanse in the midst of the waters and let it separate the waters from the waters."** The word expanse in Hebrew is firmament and both words mean a vastness. In Psalm the writer refers to the same concept when he tells us God stretches out the heavens like a curtain.

Psalm 104:2
"Covering Yourself with light as with a garment, stretching out the heavens like a tent."

Genesis 1:8 tells us God called the expanse or firmament heaven. We will see there are three levels of heaven and the firmament (vastness or our atmosphere) is level one. God tells us that in the bottom Heaven He divided the waters which were under the firmament from the waters that were above the firmament. Most surface readers of this verse interpret the dividing of waters as the separation of sea and land. No, that happens the third day on the lower level of the firmament. God is telling us there is water above the atmosphere we call space. Scientists have established that our atmosphere is very complex and extends approximately four thousand miles above sea level. That vastness, which is above our atmosphere, constitutes our middle level Heaven. However the part of our atmosphere we concern ourselves with is only five to ten miles above sea level and is called troposphere. Far above the troposphere lies Heaven level two, another level of water created when God placed the firmament between the bodies of water. From this level of water our rain comes down. Scientists know an unbelievable, unmeasurable amount of water exists far above the troposphere. This was part of God's original creation of the firmament. This part of the firmament was not used to water the earth through rain until the flooding of the world in Noah's age. God brought up dew from the land itself to water the land.

Genesis 2:6
"But a mist was going up from the land and watered the whole face of the ground."

In later Scripture, we will see that God used the lower and middle heavens when He saw the sinfulness of man in the days of Noah. God, in His decision to flood the world and eliminate all of His human creation except Noah and His family, also opened the windows of heaven and flooded the earth with rain. The flooding of the world was accomplished by bringing waters up from the earth and down from the heavens. Note in this verse God calls the firmament level of water above the atmosphere to be heaven. Let's revisit the truth that God called the firmament that divided the waters, our atmosphere or troposphere, heaven in Genesis 1:8. Scripture also refers to the ultimate place the saved will go to live with God in eternity as heaven. This is the top level of the Heavens. So we see that God created at least three levels of heaven. In review, they are our atmosphere or space as we understand it and this is the lower level Heaven. Then the waters beyond our atmosphere which are involved in the watering of the earth and the weather patterns of earth constitute the middle level Heaven. And the eternal home of God and His believers constitute the Upper level Heaven. In addition to the three layers of firmament called "heaven" God also created a layer of firmament He called earth. God had a busy second twenty-four-hour day.

Genesis 7:11
"In the six hundredth year of Noah's life, in the second month, the seventeenth day of the month, on that day all the fountains of the great deep were burst forth, and the windows of heaven were opened."

Day Three: Formation of Land and Seas with Vegetation and Trees Growing on the Land

Genesis 1:9–13
Then God said, "Let the waters under the heavens be gathered together into one place, and let the dry land appear"; and it was so. And God called the dry land earth, and the waters that He gathered together He called Seas. And God saw that it was good. And God said, "Let the earth sprout vegetation, plants yielding seed, and fruit trees bearing fruit in which is their seed, each according to its kind on the earth"; and it was so. And the earth brought forth vegetation, plants yielding seed according to their own kinds, and trees bearing fruit in which is their seed, each according to its kind, and God saw that it was good. And there was evening and there was morning the third day."

In review, God had created matter, light, and time on day one. On day two God created the lower and middle heavens. This means on day two he created water below our atmosphere and water above our atmosphere and our atmosphere that we know as space. God is now ready to focus on the earth as we know it. At the beginning of the third day the earth was made up of a gaseous liquid named water. But God's creations at this point were not something that would support life. God was not yet ready to create man.

Can we see how our loving God so thoughtfully prepared His creation for mankind? God created the world for man and for man's enjoyment. How God loves us and how we disappoint Him. On the third twenty-four-hour day God again spoke into existence the dry ground that he called land. He also gathered the waters under the atmosphere together and called them seas.

Think of the magnitude of this act. God took a creation of matter and raised land among the waters on the lower level of His firmament. God then created an ocean floor that we know to be at times thirty-seven thousand feet deep and separated water from land. He did it all for mankind.

He then made the land grow vegetation and trees that were designed to perpetually reproduce their own kind. Earth was getting closer to being ready for mankind but not yet.

God tells us another noteworthy fact in these verses. He says, "And the earth brought forth grass, the herb that yields seed according to its kind, and the tree that yields fruit, whose seed provides life of that fruit, according to its kind. God is telling us distinctly that evolution is not the way creation happened. God created vegetation according to His divine intent and purpose, not left to chance regarding into what it might evolve. We will later see that God creates animals according to their own kind and mankind according to His divine purpose. Evolution is not part of how God created.

Day Four: Creation of the Sun and Moon and the Universe

Genesis 1:14–19
"Then God said, "Let there be lights in the expanse of the heavens to separate the day from the night; and let them be for signs and seasons, and for days and years; and let them be for lights in the expanse of the heavens to give light on the earth"; and it was so. Then God made two great lights: the greater light to rule the day, and the lesser light to rule the night. He made the stars. God set them in the expanse of the heavens to give light on the earth, and to rule over the day and over the night, and to separate the light from the darkness. And God saw that it was good. And there was evening and thee was morning the fourth day."

On the fourth day of creation, God had now created a place to put the sun, the moon, and the stars and that was and is the middle level heavens. God was ready to execute His plan of maintaining His creations. God created time on day one and He was now ready to create the system in which earth would fit time. He also created the system in which earth would be the home of mankind for whom time was created.

Yet many struggle over the question of how God could have created light the first day when the sun, moon and stars were not created and still needed to create the sun, moon, and stars on the fourth day. Let's look in depth at what God said. God told us he made two great lights with the greater light to rule the day and the lesser light to rule the night. And then Genesis 1:14–19 tells us God also made the stars. God then makes an interesting but often misunderstood statement. "God set them in the firmament of the heavens (note plural heavens) to give light and to rule over the day and over the night and to divide the light from the darkness."

The primary job of the sun, moon and stars is to rule over the day and night. This means the primary job of the universe as we understand it is to put in place the rotation system God implemented to maintain perfect timekeeping of the world He created. Only secondary was the need for light on an ongoing basis.

Where did the light come from on day one through three before God created the sun, moon, and stars? God was the light. God provided the light the plants created needed to survive. God was the light that separated night from day. But God knew He would not continue to live among man because He knew man would sin. Therefore God created the sun, moon and stars to continue as a source of light after He withdrew His presence from His creation. One day, in eternity after the end of time, God will again live among men and will be the light for man. But He will only be the light for men who believe on Jesus Christ as the almighty Messiah and Savior of the world. And because God will be with the redeemed it fits Gods statement that in Hell there will be total darkness.

It is a shame that man was going to sin and separate himself from God and God in His all-knowing nature had to prepare for man's survival even through man was going to betray God's love.

Day Five: Creation of the Fish and Fowl

Genesis 1:20–23
Then God said, "Let the waters swarm with swarms of living creatures, and let birds fly above the earth across the expanse of the heavens." So God created great sea creatures and every living creature that moves, with which the waters swarm, according to their kind, and every winged bird according to its kind. And God saw that it was good. And God blessed them, saying, "Be fruitful and multiply, and fill the waters in the seas, and let birds multiply on the earth" and there was evening and there was morning the fifth day.

On the fifth twenty-four-hour day God looked upon the vastness of space in the first atmosphere (lower heaven) and upon the vastness of the oceans created for mankind. He spoke and created the teeming swarms of every kind of fish and sea creature ever to exist. God created or spoke into existence these creatures. This is another example of the awesome nature of our God the creator.

God then created every kind of winged creature we have ever known and placed them in the air or in the atmosphere. God ordained that the sea would be the home of the fish and sea creatures while the air would be the home of the winged creatures. Both were created for mankind. Then God created all of the great creatures of the sea. As we will see this creation was done for the pleasure and sustenance of man. Man was created on the sixth day to have dominion over all of God's creation.

We must also note that God created each creature according to their own kind. God is emphasizing the truth that He did not use evolution in any form, to implement creation. According to the word of God every one of His creations were created complete and did not evolve by chance into what it became.

The nature and purpose of God's creations are to give a magnificent environment to bring mankind into to live. How the Bible speaks of God's love for us. How much God wanted us to adore Him for what He had done and for who He is. How we disappointed and disappoint God today.

Day Six: Creation of the Animal Kingdom and Human Beings

Genesis 1:24–26

Then God said, "Let the earth bring forth the living creature according to its kind: livestock and creeping things and beasts of the earth, each according to their kinds"; and it was so. And God made The Beasts of the earth according to their kinds, and the livestock according to their kind, and everything that creeps on the earth according to its kind. And God saw that it was good. Then God said, "Let Us make man in Our image, according to Our likeness; let them have dominion over the fish of the sea, over the birds of the heavens, and over the livestock, over all the earth and over every creeping thing that creeps on the earth."

By the end of the fifth day everything was in order for the most magnificent of all of God's creations. The greatest creation was yet to come. God was about to create living beings on the sixth day. God wanted animals that could think, could react, could hurt, could live and could die. God created the animals, like the birds and sea creatures for the enjoyment and enrichment of man.

The spectacular nature of all of God's creation is that it was done for the enjoyment and comfort of mankind. God glorified in His creation of mankind because mankind was intended to love God, communicate with God, and be a companion in deep love with God. God wanted that relationship with mankind. And God wanted man to be happy and live in great luxury and in great adoration of God and God's provision.

Therefore on the sixth twenty-four-hour day God created all of the animal kingdom. This included domesticated animals and wild animals. It included serpents and all of the reptile family. God also emphasized that each of His creations were of their own kind. In so stating God eliminates any possibility of evolution. God created species of animals, birds, fish, reptiles and man the way they were going to exist through the ages. They would reproduce in their own species but without evolution into other species. God then looked on all His creation but it was not yet complete. He wanted to create a creature that would be made in His own image.

The Godhead's Involvement in Creation

It is also interesting to note the wording of God as He records His creation. God uses the word "us" to declare the identity of the creator. The word "us" cannot refer to man because man had not yet been created. God specifically says "Let us make man in our own image." God the Father, the ultimate creator, is speaking to God the Son and God the Holy Spirit who are also involved in creation. The book of Colossians tells us that it was through God the Son, Jesus Christ, that all things were created. This confirms the roles of the Godhead. God the Father conceives, plans, and sets in motion creation. God the Son does the will of His father and actually creates all of creation. The Holy Spirit assists God the Son in creation and maintains all that is created.

Colossians 1:16
"For by Him all things were created in heaven, visible or invisible, whether thrones or dominions or rulers or authorities. All things were created through him and for him."

We previously studied scripture saying God the Holy Spirit was involved in creation. These scriptures reaffirm the doctrine of the Trinity in which God is one God and yet also exists in the form of Father, Son, and Holy Spirit. It is of interest the way mankind jumps to conclusions about Scripture that says things like; God made. When the Bible says God created it means the Godhead created in the three roles of the Godhead.

Genesis 1:1
"In the beginning God created the heavens and the
earth. The earth was without form and void, and
darkness was upon the face of the deep, and the Spirit
of God was hovering over the face of the waters."

Creation versus Evolution

In reality, the Bible itself stands or falls with the historical accuracy of Genesis 1. If we cannot trust the creation account, then why should we trust anything else on the pages of scripture?

There is not one word of support in God's Word for the evolution of man from the lower creatures. The Bible teaches the opposite in both the Old and in the New Testament. How then, can we say we believe God's Word and also endorse the theory of evolution? Evolution is denial of God's Word? If we believe in evolution we say God lied in His scripture. God did not use evolution as a tool to create. God simply spoke the world into existence. The Bible presents man as the crowning masterpiece of creation. When God created each of His masterpieces on the first five days He ended the day by saying it was "good." But when He concluded the creation of man he said it was "very good." This is also implied in the statement that God created him in His image, for the scriptures declare, "All His work is perfect."

Genesis 1:27–31
"So God created man in His own image; in the image of God He
created him; male and female He created them. And God blessed
them, and God said to them, "Be fruitful and multiply; fill the
earth and subdue it; have dominion over the fish of the sea, over
the birds of the heavens, and over every living thing that moves
on the earth." And God said, "Behold, I have given you every
plant yielding seed that is on the face of all the earth, and every
tree with seed in its fruit; you shall have for food. And, to every
beast of the earth, to every bird of the heavens, and to everything
that creeps on the earth, everything that has the breath of life, I

have given every green plant for food"; and it was so. Then God saw everything that He had made, and indeed it was very good. And there was evening and there was morning the sixth day."

We accept that we were created in God's image because God tells us so in the above verses. But what does that mean? We know that man was created in the image of God meaning man was created without sin and without a nature of sin. Man was created with a nature that caused him to want to please God. God created man with the capacity to rule over all of creation. The nature of man included the ability to think independent of God which gave man the capacity to disobey God but not a nature to do so. And of course, we know that man eventually elected to disobey God and came into disfavor of God because he took on the nature of sin. Several important images of God imputed to man, need to be reviewed to understand how God created man with the ability to sin yet created him without sin.

God created man with freedom of will. God has the ability to do whatever He wishes. He has total and complete freedom of will. God wanted mankind to relate to Him. God wanted mankind to converse with Him to love Him. For love to be true it has to emerge out of ones choice to love. God decided to create man because of what man could be but he had to be given freedom of choice to become what God wanted. Mankind was given the choice to return love to God or to not return love to God.

Galatians 5:16–17
"But I say, walk by the Spirit, and you will not gratify the desires of the flesh. For the desires of the flesh are against the Spirit, and the desires of the Spirit are against the flesh, for these are opposed to each other, to keep you from doing the things you want to do."

To not give man that choice made it impossible for man to fill the intent of God's creation. Every man and woman is given the ability to choose for his or her self a course of action. All of God's human creation is born morally aware. Yes, we have to reach a certain age before we are mentally aware of that nature God has given us.

However, once we reach that age of mental awareness, man forever understands that some choices are good and moral and some are evil and in opposition to God. Before man made the horrible world changing decision to disobey God in the Garden of Eden, Adam and Eve had no knowledge of good and evil. They had been fully instructed by God about what they should not do and had been advised of the consequences of disobeying God.

The question of all mankind is; why did God give man the freedom to choose righteousness or sin? The answer is that we cannot gain the freedom to truly love unless we have the freedom to reject. The necessity of God's creative intent, to make man in the image of God with freedom to choose, became the downfall of man who was weak and fell into Satan's lure. We should also recognize that God created man with the ability to reason. None other of God's creation has this ability. God is a rational being and operates by values and upon the basis of these values He determines right from wrong. To God right and wrong are expressed in terms of righteousness and unrighteousness. Man does not make the decision of what is right or wrong. Man does, however, choose what is righteous and what is unrighteous based on God's Values. Man is made in the image of God in that he is given the ability to review situations, assess what is righteous and unrighteous and elect which path he will take. This image of God takes freedom of choice another step. Man is the only creation of God given the true capacity for rational thinking. Man is intelligent, aware of his surroundings, aware of situations and choices to be made. Man was created to act not on instinct but to act according to value choices made with the intent of pleasing God.

Isaiah 1:18
"Come now, let us reason together, says the LORD: though your sins are like scarlet, they shall be as white as snow; though they are red like crimson, they shall become like wool."

We should also recognize that only man was made with the capacity to be aware of God and to fellowship with God. This part of man was exercised freely before the fall or before man decided to disobey God. As people we are able to comprehend God's existence, recognize the choices God has laid out for us, and decide what our choice will be. But unless we have given our heart to Christ and trusted in His death on Calvary and His resurrection from the dead, we cannot have fellowship with God. This is because of the sin barrier covered in chapter 1.

We also need to accept that man was made in the image of God in that man was created sinless. Man was made without sin, without any desire to do or be anything that was not just, or holy, or loving, or true, or righteous. Mankind gave up that image of God when He chose to follow Satan's temptation. The scripture tells us that from the day Adam and Eve violated the desire and order of God, all people born after Adam's fall were born with the imputed nature of sin. This is because when God made Adam He made more than a man. God made mankind. All of mankind was represented by Adam. When Adam sinned we lost our nature of innocence. Better said, we gave away our nature of innocence and we pay the highest sacrifice possible for that decision. However, we can praise God because Jesus paid for our sins on Calvary. We don't have to pay for our disobedience of God.

We have lost some of our image of God because of the decision of Adam and Eve. Yet we remain created in His image. And as Christians we have assurance that we will, at the second coming of Christ, be given back the very nature of God in every aspect. In Corinthians we are told that we still have the nature of God even after the fall.

1 Corinthians 11:7
"For a man ought not to cover his head, since he is the image and glory of God; but woman is the glory of man."

God is spirit and does not have a physical body. That does not keep Jesus, the second member of the Godhead from taking on a physical body. God told us in John 4 that God is spirit and does not reside in a physical body. Yet because man is created both as a physical creature and a spiritual creature we cannot separate the two in this physical life. The Spirit is intended to control the physical, yet the physical body houses the spirit and deeply influences the spiritual side of man. Both the physical side of man and the spiritual side of man must unite in harmony to fully grasp and utilize the image of God imputed to man. God wanted mankind to understand what He referred to when He stated He made man, "In His Image." To be "in the image of God" we must join together the spiritual and physical side of our being to grow and implement the following images of God imbedded within us:

- We are capable of fellowship with God.
- We are an intelligent creature who can communicate with God.
- We are a creature who can feel love and emotion and praise for God.
- We are a creature who has a will of our own and the capability to disobey or obey the desires of God.
- We are a creature who has the ability to rationalize and make decisions based on good and evil and based on the desire of God our creator.

We live in a world in which the masses fight the truth of creation in every advent of life. We see this in our schools, the media, and our education systems. Christians have become increasingly confused about what to believe. We have compromised God's Word and we try to rationalize what the Bible says with what the world says. We are trying to come up with explanations that find universal acceptance.

Creation versus evolution should not be a litmus test to one's salvation. It is, however, important for us to examine false teachings about creation and examine why such teachings are false. The evidence of creation is all around us.

How do we know God created in six twenty-four-hour days?

Certainly the scientific community desires to destroy the possibility of God having created the world. They want to find their own explanation for creation. Their theory of evolution is far more unbelievable than creation. In addition, they want to poison our minds to say that if God did create, He did it through evolution. The liberal forces of our world totally denounce the idea of God creating the world in six twenty-four-hour days. They say such thinking is irresponsible.

People who wish to rewrite the Bible to fit their predetermined conclusions often compromise by trying to make the six days that God used to create longer than twenty-four hours. They also like to create a "gap" between Genesis 1:1 and 1:2 thereby creating the possibility of evolution. The problem is they are adding to the text as presented by God and changing His revelation to mankind. The literal interpretation of Genesis, without added words from man, is supported by much scientific evidence regarding the age of the earth although the science community actively tries to deny and suppress this evidence. Regardless of what nonbelieving scientists proclaim, the message God conveyed to us is clear. He created the world as we know it in six twenty-four-hour days. To add anything to this is in violation of God's command to not add or change any "jot" or "tittle" of His Word until the end of time.

God's Word gives us substantial "faith-evidence" that the Genesis 1 twenty-four-hour days are twenty-four hours as we know them today. First the normal meaning of the word "yom," which is Hebrew for day, is twenty-four hours. The text of Genesis gives no indication that the word "yom" refers to anything but a twenty-four-hour day. In addition, the number of the days, in the creation of everything, is in series. God speaks of the first day, then the second, third, fourth, fifth, sixth days of creation and then seventh day of rest. There is no exception to this anywhere in the Old Testament.

Then we see God uses the terminology "Evening and Morning" in referring to His days. *"And there was evening and there was morning."* The Jewish calendar day was twenty-four hours and began at sunset and ended before sunset the next day. The Jewish calendar was based on the teaching of God to Jewish forefathers.

The Jewish work week, according to the law given to Moses, began at sunset on Sunday and went through six days with rest on

Saturday. No, God did not create according to the Jewish work week. The Jewish work week was established according to the guidance given by God and it coincided with the days of creation. Therefore the Jewish work week was patterned after the days of creation.

God told us to accept His Word at face value. He told us to not add to it, to not modify it to fit our logic, and to not take from its content. Without doubt, God clearly communicates God created all of creation within six ordinary twenty-four-hour days.

God's Word provides us with confirmation that God created in six, twenty-four-hour days. Consider these scriptures:

- **Genesis 1:5:** *God called the light Day, and the darkness He called Night. And there was evening and the morning, the first day.* **God Himself named the light to be daytime and the night to be nighttime. These were set into a twenty-four-hour solar day. The Hebrew word** *"Yom,"* **means "day." God refers to "Yom" in Genesis 1:5. The same Hebrew word is used 410 times in the Bible. In every incident of usage it refers to a twenty-four-hour solar day.**

- **Genesis 1:5, 8, 13, 19, 23, 31: In these verses God completes a day of creation. After each day God clearly declares His work has been completed in one day. God knew mankind would try and twist His creative act. God wanted to be crystal clear of how and when His creation took place.**

- **Exodus 31:17:** *It is a sign forever between Me and the people of Israel, that in six days the LORD made heaven and earth, and on the seventh day He rested and was refreshed."* **God established the day seven to be the Sabbath day, or Saturday as we know it. He established it to be a remembrance forever. This means the Sabbath day was to be a sign between Him and Israel forever.**

- **John 11:9:** *Jesus answered, "Are there not twelve hours in the day? If anyone walks in the day, he does not stumble, because he sees the light of this world.* **In His ministry on** earth, Jesus Himself reminded us that there are twelve hours in the day. He reminded us that we work in the day (light) because we can see by the light God created. Jesus is telling us clearly that the light God created was for man so man could work and get things done and it was a twenty-four-hour solar creation.

- 1 Corinthians 15:21: *For as by a man came death, by a Man has come also the resurrection of the dead.* Several places in the Scripture God tells us that death came because of the decision of Man to defy God and rebel against God. This means that death did not have exist prior to man's creation. But if the world had been in existence millions of years prior to the evolution of man from an ape then death would have been in existence prior to man. This would mean the Word of God was not accurate.
- *Luke 3:23: Jesus when He began His ministry at about thirty years of age, being the son (as was supposed) of Joseph, the son of Heli,* the genealogy of Jesus, as traced in Scripture indicates the world was about six thousand years old.

What method did God use to create?

God is the creator of all things. God's Word tells us so in unmistakably clear language. The only question is what method He used to create. God's Word tells us He spoke all things into creation. It is important we grasp this truth. For in His clear precise language, God eliminates any possibility of evolution. He tells us He simply spoke His creation into existence. And His Word tells us that when He created man, He created man in His image. If man was created as a lower species of monkey to eventually evolve then man was not created in the image of God.

If creation occurred over billions of years then God needed billions of years to speak. God's Word tells us that He spoke and it happened within a twenty-four-hour day. That eliminates any possibility of evolution.

God's purpose in creation would not have been fulfilled in evolution. God is love. Love, by its nature must be shared and needs an object that can receive and give love. God created a magnificent world for man to live in. God created it with ultimate beauty because He wanted man to be pleased. God's creation of the universe, the earth, the atmosphere, animals and birds and all of creation was for the pleasure of God and man. God wanted man to return love and adoration and to do it immediately, not through an evolution process of billions of years.

God desired a creation that He could love and who could love Him back. God's creation was centered on the creation of man. God's creation of man "in His own image" tells us of His intent of creation. The purpose of human life is to return love to God. This is why God created man with a human spirit. The spirit that God gave man is the greatest example of God having made man "in His own image." God is Spirit and He created man with a human spirit so that man could receive His spirit. However, for man to return a true love it had to be a love of free will. So man was given a choice, and from the actions of Adam and Eve, we know man made the wrong choice.

Creation Accepted by Faith

We can prove creation but to do so violates the will of God. We do not try to prove creation. We accept it by faith. Like so many things, concerning our relationship with God, we are instructed to accept God's Word by faith and not try to prove it. In fact, the presence of proof weakens the substance of faith. We are specifically instructed in Hebrews to accept creation by faith. God tells us that He created our world from nothing and we are to accept His word.

Hebrews 11:3
"By faith we understand that the universe was created by the word of God so that what is seen was not made out of things that are visible."

So although it is interesting to examine the reasons that creation is feasible according to scientific fact, such research, if relied upon, is meaningless. God told us to accept His Word as it was written.

Creation Challenged

The acceptance of Creation as the beginning of man has been challenged throughout time. Sinful man has an inborn need to explain away God. Yet great men of faith in our history, arrived at the truth. Martin Luther believed the world was relatively young, and he believed in creation for the same reason you and I should; because that is what the Scripture says. Luther stated:

"We know from Moses that the world was not in existence before six thousand years ago" He said, "God employees the term "day" and evening" without subjective meaning, just as we do. Moses spoke in literal sense for God spoke the world into existence in six days. If we do not comprehend the reason of this let us remain pupils and leave the job of teacher to the Holy Spirit."

Jesus taught us that Adam and Eve were created in the beginning of creation, not billions of years after the beginning. In the book of John, Jesus made it clear that all of mankind was to believe the writings of Moses.

John 5:45–47
"Do not think that I will accuse you to the Father. There is one who accuses you: Moses, on whom you have set your hope. For if you believed Moses, you would believe Me; for he wrote of Me. But if you do not believe his writings, how will you believe My words?"

Jesus establishes the groundwork to tell mankind Moses was correct when he stated that the world was created in a literal six, twenty-four-hour days.

Exodus 20:11
"For in six days the LORD made heaven and earth, the sea, and
all that is in them, and rested on the seventh day. Therefore
the LORD blessed the Sabbath day and made it holy."

The testimony of Jesus verifying the accuracy of Moses's declaration that creation happened immediately rules out any form of evolution.

Essential Truths Regarding the Doctrine of Creation

The following essential truths regarding creation are eternal:

God is the creator of everything.

Psalms 104:24
O LORD, how manifold are Your works! In
wisdom have You made them all.
The earth is full of Your creatures.

This scripture and many others that state the same truth, eliminate the possibility that creation involved evolution. The theory of evolution is not a theory it is a false doctrine. One either believes the Word of God or denies the Word of God. God's Word says all of creation was created and did not evolve.

God has always existed.

Genesis 1:1
"In the beginning God created the heavens and the earth."

Perhaps this is the most amazing truth to grasp in all of creation. God is, God was, and God always will be. God was not created. He is the creator. God, in the form of God the Father, God the Son, and God the Holy Spirit all existed before time began. God created time for the benefit of man. God does not need time because God is eternal. Man needs time because he is mortal.

The sequence of creation has value for us to consider. We know that for an infinite period of time before the creation of the Universe God existed.

God existed in His three roles we come to know Him and those are God the Father, God the Son, and God the Holy Ghost. What about the angels? When were they created? The Scripture is not definitive on this question but the context of Scripture leads us to believe the angels were created during the six day period of creation of our Universe. In Ezekiel 28:13b God tells us that Lucifer was created during the first six days of creation when God created the beautiful stones of sardius, topaz, diamond, beryl, onyx, jasper, sapphire, emerald, carbuncle, and gold.

Ezekiel 28:13b
"On the day that you (Satan) was created they (precious stones) were prepared."

We also know from Scripture that Lucifer was created to be the guardian of the angels and was created as the most beautiful of all angels. We can therefore believe both Lucifer and the angels were created during the six day of creation. The Bible is clear nothing was created before the creation of the heavens and earth because we find God telling us that "In the beginning God created the Heavens and Earth" (Genesis 1:1). This verse firmly established nothing was created before God began His creation of the heavens and earth.

The beauty of God's creation surpasses our ability to describe it. The magnificence of God who created such intricate detail in the atom, yet created the vastness of space, is beyond our capacity to understand. Because of His love for man and His desire to please His creation, God packaged His works in such a way that man could live in incredible comfort. We ask the question of God, "How could You love me so?" God created so we would return His love. Yet we are creatures who give little pleasure to God and are disobedient, arrogant children. We are full of pride and we try to exclude God from our lives. Yet God loves us. We do this intentionally because we do not want to face the reality that we are subject to the almighty God.

We twist God's Word to mean something that it clearly does not mean, not because His Word is difficult to understand, but because His Word convicts us of our dependence upon Him. We feel the presence of Satan in our lives telling us to rebel and we decide to yield to that presence rather than the presence of the Holy Spirit.

The majesty and power of God is quite well described by Stuart K. Hine in 1899 when he put words to the timeless hymn "How Great Thou Art."

CHAPTER THREE

The Doctrine of Sin
Man's Decision To Turn from God

All sin originates with Lucifer. Lucifer is a created being, unlike God. God always has been, and is not a created being. God created Lucifer as an angel. In Ezekiel 28:12–17, the Bible gives us information concerning Lucifer who is also known as Satan. The passage below refers to Satan as the one in the Garden of Eden. Satan was created beautiful. His beauty is compared to that of precious stones. He was the highest of all the angels God created. He had a special place of prominence. Many are surprised to learn that Satan was created perfect without sin.

Ezekiel 28:12b–17

"You were the signet of perfection, full of
wisdom and perfect in beauty.
You were in Eden, the garden of God; every precious stone
was your covering: sardius, topaz, and diamond, beryl,
onyx, and jasper, sapphire, emerald, and carbuncle, and
crafter in gold were your settings and engravings.
On the day you were created they were prepared."
"You were an anointed guardian cherub; I placed you;
You were on the holy mountain of God; In the midst
of the stones of fire you walked. You were blameless
in your ways from the day you were created,
'till iniquity was found in you."
"In the abundance of your trade you were
filled with violence in your midst,
And you sinned; so I cast you as a profane thing
from the mountain of God; and I destroyed
you, O guardian cherub,
From the midst of the stones of fire."
"Your heart was proud because of your beauty;
You corrupted your wisdom for the sake of your splendor;
I cast you to the ground, I exposed you before kings,
to feast their eyes on you."

When was Lucifer created? Many state Lucifer was created before the creation of the world but God's Word says that is not true. In Ezekiel 28:13 God tells us that Lucifer was created during the first six days of creation. God created the angels and Lucifer as He created the most beautiful parts of His creation. Unfortunately Lucifer's pride and obsession with his own beauty made him want to be equal, even superior, to God. God cast him out of his privileged position (Isa. 14:12–14), God calls Satan "Lucifer" meaning the bright one, *"the son of the morning. And the Shining Star."* But Lucifer became enraptured by his own beauty to the point he elected to challenge God for supremacy. He determined to set up his own throne that men might worship him. God, however, is holy, just, and righteous. The definition of sin is anything that displeases God. Rebelling against God is sin. Lucifer sinned and became the horrible creature named Satan.

When was Satan cast out of Heaven?

God's Word does not give us a clear, definite time when Satan was cast out of Heaven. But the Bible does give us some insight and we must assume it is all God intended for us to consider. The conduct and punishment of Satan is identified as being in stages.

God's Word is clear that Satan let his arrogance and pride overcome being God created. His vanity and pride made him decide to defy God. We know this did not happen until after the creation of man. In Genesis 2:1 God told us *"the heavens and the earth…and all the host of them were very good."* We do not know how many years passed from when God created Adam and Adam disobeyed God and was cast out of the Garden of Eden. Sometime during these years, Satan grew disobedient to God and his disobedience was climaxed when he used Adam and Eve to be his weapons to defeat God. The context of Scripture implies that at this time God eliminated Satan's right to be part of the Heavenly Host and imposed certain penalties on him. These penalties are as follows:

1. Satan lost the privilege to be God's lead angel and to be revered by the angels in heaven. Evidently Satan has rallied

quite a following of the angels in heaven because one third of all angels elected to defy God and follow Satan.

2.   Satan lost the incredible beauty that he was created to be. We know that in Revelation he was described as a "Dragon." He is pictured as being capable of appearing in the form of guile but He was made the picture of evil in his natural state.

3.   Satan and the angels that followed him were cast out of Heaven. This apparently means Satan was no longer recognized as welcome in Heaven but he was not imprisoned and could still travel from earth to heaven as he wished. We see Scripture evidence of this.

Job 1:7
"Now there was a day when the sons of God came to present themselves before the LORD, and Satan also came among them."

4.   We also note in Revelation 12:13 that Satan will not be allowed in Heaven during the Seven-Year Tribulation. He will be confined to earth although will have freedom to reign on earth as he wills. This means that when all of the saints of the Old Testament, "The Church," and the Tribulation Saints gather around the throne of God Satan will not be there.

5.   During the Seven-Year Tribulation Satan will be confined to earth and will endure the pain and despair as he sees God prevail and sees his fate emerging.

6.   Satan will be imprisoned in a place that he cannot escape from during the one thousand year Millennial Kingdom presided over by Jesus Christ.

7.   Satan will be released from prison to rally forces on earth to war against God at the very end of the one-thousand-year Millennial Kingdom.

8.   Satan will then be defeated by Jesus handily and will be permanently cast into the Lake of Fire.

The Fall of Man

Sometime after Satan rebelled against God and came into conflict with God, he looked upon the creation of God, and elected to use man in his war against God. The third chapter of Genesis tells us of the act of Satan who was in rebellion against God.

Genesis 3:1–5

Now the serpent was more crafty than any beast of the field that the LORD God had made. He said to the woman, "Did God actually say, 'You shall not eat of any tree in the garden'? And the woman said to the serpent, "We may eat of the fruit of the trees of the garden; but God said, "You shall not eat of the fruit of the tree that is in the midst of the garden, neither shall you touch it, lest you die.'"
But the serpent said to the woman, "You will not surely die, for God knows that when you eat of it your eyes will be opened, and you will be like God, knowing good and evil."

Genesis chapter 3 teaches us many things. First, it confirms that prior to eating of the tree of knowledge Adam and Eve had no knowledge of, or understanding of evil. They knew no sin. Satan knew God told Adam and Eve to not eat of the tree in the middle of the Garden of Eden. Satan desired to defeat God and be greater than God. He chose man as the focal point of his rebellion against God. Note that God allowed Satan to temp mankind even knowing man would fall to Satan. This was because man had to have the right to choose to be able to return a free love back to God. Because of the omniscience (all knowing) nature of God He knew what Satan would choose and what man would choose. Satan plotted to recruit mankind to his side of the conflict. Satan approached Eve when she was alone and told her that God lied to her and Adam when He told them they would die if they ate of the fruit of the tree in the middle of the Garden. Eve's curiosity and desire made her vulnerable to disobey God. So she followed the temptation of Satan. She then convinced Adam to do the same.

God told Adam that he was not to eat of the tree of knowledge of good and evil (Gen. 2:17). When God warned Adam to not eat fruit of the tree in the middle of the garden, God gave Adam the choice of serving God in holiness and truth because of Adam's faith in God, or rebelling against God in evil and wickedness. In this truth we see that as far back as Adam, God's plan of salvation was faith in God through the Grace of God. Adam was given a free choice. That free choice was intended to return a free love back to God.

Genesis 2:17
"But of the tree of the knowledge of good and evil you shall not eat, for in the day that you eat of it you shall surely die."

Adam had always sought to please God in his thinking and actions. The idea or temptation to displease God had not occurred to Adam. Adam loved God and had daily communications with God in a love relationship. For an unknown period of time Adam chose to follow God and to love God. God gave Adam the freedom to choose to obey God or not obey God. Adam had to have that freedom to fulfill the purpose of man's creation. This answers the basic question of, "why did God create man?" The answer was God wanted a free love returned to Him from His creation. For God to give Adam the ability to return a free love, Adam had to have a will that gave him the potential to sin. At first, Adam and Eve exercised their will in favor of God and had fellowship with Him.

The Original Sin

The Bible tells us in Genesis that Adam and Eve were placed in the Garden of Eden, a magnificent creation that contained an abundance of food and beauty, beyond their ability to comprehend. Genesis tells us the Garden of Eden had no weeds or thorns but had every kind of fruit tree and bush needed to provide food and beauty for Adam and Eve. Sin had not come into the world, therefore death had not come into the world and meat was not used as a food. All animals were not afraid of Adam or Eve and were not afraid of other animals.

Adam and Eve were given work to do. They were to cultivate the land, grow the fruit God had provided and maintain the Garden. They had work to do, but their work was not hard. It was a pleasure. They were also charged with naming all the animals God had created. A fear relationship did not exist between Adam and the animals God created. Adam often walked and talked with God. Adam was able to communicate directly with God because he had not sinned. God cherished the relationship even while knowing it was not going to last. Because God is timeless, He is already at the end of time, as man understands time. God, therefore, knew from the creation of man that man would eventually disobey Him. God knew man would sin, be separated from Him and therefore God put together the plan of man's salvation even before man sinned.

To put this plan in place, God created the choice for man to decide to be obedient to God or to disobey. That choice was a tree in the middle of the Garden that God called the tree of knowledge of good and evil. The popular opinion voiced is that the tree was an apple tree. However there is no scriptural basis that informs us what kind of fruit the tree bore, if any. And as God knew would eventually happen, man finally did disobey God. Lucifer, who became known as Satan came to earth in the form of a serpent, temped Eve, who temped Adam to disobey God.

Genesis 3:1–6
*Now the serpent was more crafty than any other
beast of the field that the L*ORD *God had made. And
he said to the woman, "Has God indeed said,
"You shall not eat of any tree of the garden"?" And the woman
said to the serpent, "We may eat of the fruit of the trees of the
garden, but of the fruit of the tree which is in the midst of the
garden, God said, "You shall not eat it neither shall you touch it,
lest you die."" But the serpent said to the woman, "You will not
surely die, for God knows that when you eat of it, your eyes will
be opened and you will be like God, knowing good and evil."*

So when the woman saw that the tree was good for food, and
that it was a delight to the eyes, and a tree was to be desired
to make one wise, she took of its fruit and ate. She also gave
some to her husband who was with her, and he ate."

None of these life-changing events happened as a surprise to God. God had a plan for the redemption of man before Adam took of the offering of Eve. God was not surprised at the betrayal of Satan and He had, and has, a plan for the eventual containment and punishment of Satan and his followers. However, with the decision Adam and Eve made, sin entered the world.

The Bible does not tell us what food the tree of knowledge of good and evil contained. Milton in *Paradise Lost*, written in 1667, took liberties with scripture and speculated it was an apple. Thus through the ages, most people have come to believe the Bible tells us Adam ate of the apple. Whatever it was, it constituted the original sin of man and ushered in a new covenant with God. That covenant was one of separation because God could no longer coexist with sinful and defiled man.

Genesis 3:17
"And to Adam he said, "Because you have listened to the voice
of your wife and have eaten of the tree of which I commanded
you, 'You shall not eat of it,' The LORD God took the man
and put him in the garden of Eden to work it and keep it."

There is a fallacy in our society by some that physical labor is the curse laid on Adam when he sinned against God. Technically this is wrong. Work is the privilege given to mankind so man can be creative, so man can be busy, and so man can utilize the amazing talents God gave him.

Genesis 2:15
"The LORD God took the man and put him in
the Garden of Eden to work it and keep it."

Because Adam disobeyed God, God took one of the great enjoyments of Adam, toiling the soil, and made it hard, made it physically almost impossible and cursed the ground. ***"The LORD God took the man and put him in the garden of Eden to work it and keep it."*** Man would now have to work in tilling the soil to reap food so he could live. Before Adam and Eve sinned, the ground was watered by dew every morning. There were no weeds. The ground must have been soft, very fertile. There were no rocks and no barriers that hinder us today. The weather in the Garden of Eden was mild. How that changed because of Adam's sin. Now Adam had to clean the ground, plant seed, cultivate it, protect it from hail and storms, water it, and harvest it. And it changed for all time not just the period of Adam's life. Just as the curse of sin was passed to all men because of Adam's sin so were the punishments of Adam's sin.

Eve also sinned. Her sin was no greater or lesser than Adam's but both were in disobedience to God and had sinned. Eve's punishment was similar to Adam's in that man and woman, after the fall of Adam and Eve, were burdened with having to make a living for themselves. But Eve's was twofold in addition to Adam's. First she would suffer pain in childbirth. And second, she would be obedient to Adam in life decisions.

Genesis 3:16
"To the woman he said, "I will surely multiply your pain in childbearing; in pain you shall bring forth children. Your desire shall be contrary to your husband, but he shall rule over you."

Throughout our society we still have issues of what is the proper relationship between husband and wife. God's Word spells it out for us although women often do not like it. First, other Scripture tells us a marriage is to be a relationship of love. That means no mistreatments by either man or woman. It means that in most instances there should be discussion of life's issues and agreement reached. But the Bible clearly states that because of Eve's sin of disobedience to God and because she misled Adam into disobedience she would often view life differently than her husband and in such instances he would have authority over her. The question of "Who's in charge?" has existed since Adam and Eve and is part of God's punishment to Eve. The second part is that of childbirth. In today's medicine giving birth is painful but not like it was many years ago. God said in Genesis that the pain of childbirth would be multiplied several times over that prior to Adam and Eve's fall. Of course, Eve had had no children before she disobeyed God so we have no knowledge of what God's plan for childbirth then would have been. Eve's desire implanted into almost all women is the desire for children. But the price they pay because of their sin is the pain of childbirth.

Prior to the disobedience of Adam and Eve, God created in such a way that Adam and Eve and all of the birds or the air, animals on earth and fish in the sea lived on plant food. Probably plant food was different then. Certainly animals were different then. There was no desire or temptation for animals to kill each other for food or defense. There was no hatred from one creature to another.

Genesis 1:29–30
And God said, "Behold, I have given you every plant yielding seed that is on the face of all the earth, and every tree with seed in its fruit. You shall have them for food. And to every beast of the earth and to every bird of the heavens and to everything that creeps on..."

Yet the most serious of all results of man's original sin was separation from God. The separation consisted of two forms of separation. One was immediate and physical because Adam and Eve were cast out of the Garden of Eden. Adam and Eve now were creatures of sin and God will not coexist with sin. So Adam no longer would walk and talk with Adam. God no longer communicated with Adam on a daily basis. While in the Garden of Eden, Adam and Eve were created with a desire in their heart to please and satisfy God. They were placed with love for God. But a love that God place there and man had no choice but to obey was not true love as God wanted. God wanted Adam and Eve to love Him because they wanted to love Him. So God not only gave mankind the capacity to love God but also the capacity to disobey God. When Adam and Eve disobeyed God they sinned against God. They sinned not only for themselves but for all mankind that would follow. The primary punishment that came to Adam and Eve in their disobedience was the truth they would immediately be cast out of the Garden of Eden and out of the confidence and trust of God. They were separated spiritually from God for the length of their physical life and were limited in years that the physical life could exist. They were penalized with physical death. They were also penalized with permanent spiritual death (separation from God) if they did not meet God's plan of salvation He drew up before their creation.

Adam and Eve were born with a nature to worship God. They knew no sin at Adam's creation and Eve's birth. God created Adam as His test model to represent all mankind that was to come. Therefore when Adam sinned against God all Adam and Eve's offspring, forever, were henceforth "imputed" or born with a nature to sin. The "nature to sin" is identified by our desire to do what we want to do rather than what God wants us to do. Satan constantly tempts us to disobey the will of God.

Why did God create Satan?

The opening statements of this chapter quoted God in outlining the beauty and perfection of Lucifer when God created him. God's purpose in creating Lucifer was to receive a free and perfect love from him. But Lucifer had to be given a free choice of loving God or rebelling against God in order for that love to be free. In His omniscience, God knew Lucifer would rebel against Him. Therefore God planned to create mankind from the beginning of time to be the vessel that would defeat Lucifer. Yes, most of mankind will fail and eventually suffer death and Hell. But God's plan will be fulfilled in the end and Lucifer will be defeated by God through mankind. That is because an incredible host of mankind will accept God's plan of salvation. They will elect to trust that Jesus Christ, the Son of God, who paid the price of their salvation, and therefore by their trusting

Jesus, God defeats Satan; through man's decision, which is made possible through Jesus Christ.

Lucifer, or Satan, was created to become the temptation man would face that ushered in the fall of man. It was God's plan that man would refuse Satan's temptation and remain faithful to God. Through Lucifer, or Satan, man was given free choice. Satan continues to tempt mankind today and still man has a free choice of following Christ or following the lust of Satan. Mankind was not created with a sin nature. Adam and Eve did not have a sin nature. But as punishment of their rebellion of God all following mankind was given, or "imputed" a sin nature. The decision to follow God and reject the sin nature or temptation of Satan is a choice we make every minute of our lives.

1 John 3:8b
"Whoever makes a practice of sinning is of the devil, for the devil has been sinning from the beginning. The reason the Son of God appeared was to destroy the works of the devil."

What is sin?

What is sin? This is a question man has tried to answer for generations and too often tries to answer based on his own opinion. Sin is any thought, deed, intent, or state of mind that would not be pleasing to God. Sin is disappointing God. If righteousness describes God, then unrighteousness is just the opposite. Sin is doing or thinking the opposite of what God desires. In Romans 6:13, Paul encouraged the brethren not to be instruments of unrighteousness, but rather instruments of righteousness.

Romans 6:12–14
"Let not sin, therefore, reign in your mortal body, to make you obey its passions. Do not present your members to sin as instruments for unrighteousness, but present yourselves to God as those who have been brought from death to life, and your members to God as instruments

for righteousness. For sin shall have no dominion over you, since you are not under law but under grace."

The words God give us in Romans 6 are amazing. *"For sin shall have no dominion over you, since you are not under law but under grace."* This brings to our understanding that Old Testament people who believed in God and wanted to please him were still held accountable to every little thing they did that was not in total obedience to the law as outlined to them by God. Their condemnation for their acts, were not because of what they did but because of the reason they did it. Likewise, New Testament people, or "The Church," are held accountable for every deed we do and thought we have. We are held accountable according to whether we please God. Anytime we sin against God it is because we decide to follow our own desires rather than God's desires. In Romans 6, we are told God no longer holds us responsible for violations against Him if we believe in Jesus Christ and trust His blood to cover our sins. This is because of the grace and love of God. Our sin takes the form of two categories both displeasing to God.

Sin Involves Acts of Commission (Transgression)

In the Old Testament, three Hebrew words are used in the understanding of the English word sin. Avon is an Old Testament word that defines the overall state of sin as being iniquity. It means being depraved or guilty of perversity. Pesha is an Old Testament word that means transgression. The meaning of this involves rebellion or revolt. And the third word in Hebrew is Chattah. This word is translated in the King James Version as sin meaning to miss the mark.

In the New Testament, the word in Greek related to sin is *hamartano*. It means to miss the mark. Therefore the Bible teaches us that sin is a state of depravity in which we are guilty of perversity. We reach this state because of one of two conditions of mind. One is transgression and the other is missing the mark. But the question is transgression against what, and missing what mark? The mark the Old Testament is speaking of is the Mosaic Law. The Mosaic Law gave the Hebrew people a measuring stick to determine when they were displeasing God or missing the mark set by God for their conduct. God did not intend for Hebrew people to be focused on keeping the law. God intended the Hebrew people to be focused on pleasing God. The Mosaic Law simply was given to them to help them understand when they were displeasing God and therefore sinning. In the New Testament also called the "Church Age," the mark was and is the life of Jesus. If we do anything or think any thought that Jesus would not have done or thought we are missing the mark. Therefore we understand the Apostle John when he explains that anyone who "misses the mark of the law in the Old Testament" or "misses the mark of the life of Jesus in the New Testament, commits sin because they are displeasing to God."

1 John 3:4
"Everyone who makes a practice of sinning also practices lawlessness; sin is lawlessness."

When John states sin is lawlessness he refers to a state of mind that willingly and intentionally elects to impose our own will instead of keeping the will of God. So when a person intentionally displeases God they are guilty of sin and the sin is the result of the attitude toward God more so than the specific act itself. Yet the act is also sin because it displeases God also. Transgression against God involves our acts that result in displeasure to God.

How then can we avoid sin? John answered that question when he said we can purify ourselves through Jesus Christ because Jesus Christ is pure and He has paid the price of the sins of believers.

1 John 3:3
"And everyone who thus hopes in Him purifies himself, as He is pure."

We all have heard the term "I'm only human, nobody's perfect." The Bible says the same thing. Romans 3:23 says we are all sinners and we all do things that displease God. That is why we often feel estranged from God, because God is Holy and good and we are not. What action, attitude, state of mind is required to purify ourselves through Christ? The answer found in Mark 7 tells us we must take on the nature of Christ and stop doing and thinking the way Satan influences us to do.

Mark 7:21
"For from within, out of the heart of men, come evil thoughts, sexual immorality, theft, murder, adultery, coveting, wickedness, deceit, sensuality, envy, slander, pride, foolishness."

Sin Involves Acts of Omission (Missing the Mark)

"Sin is lawlessness" is correct and eternally true. But lawlessness does not define the complete scope of sin. If sin is doing things that involve violation of the Mosaic Law or the life of Christ, it is also not doing things that are the will of God for us to do.

James 4:17
"So whoever knows the right thing to do and fails to do it, for him it is sin."

Sin is not only "not doing evil"; it is not doing the good that we know we should do. The more we know, the more accountable we are to God. The more we know the more God expects of us, and the more God expects us to come closer to the mark or goal that He has set for us to attain. God expects us to meet His standard of righteousness. That means we are to always present a pure heart that coveys love for God, love for our fellow man, compassion towards others, and patience with those who disagree with us. We are to be righteous, not just "not do evil." God tells us He wants us to be in a state of love and obedience to Him always. When we stop being what He wants us to be in our attitude and thoughts we are in violation of sins of omission, or our failure to please God. To review, acts that displease

God are sins of transmission and failure to be the person God wants us to be are sins of omission. Both are sin.

Lack of faith in God is a state of sin.

The nature of man is to be independent. We take pride in our ability to get things done, to solve mysteries ourselves, and to be self-sufficient. That is not what God wants. God wants us to be in constant partnership with Him. He wants us to lean on Him, to trust Him, to confide in Him, and to include Him in every part of our life. God wants us to have faith in Him to be there for us, to heal our wounds, to solve our problems, to give us strength to go through the day, and to give us joy and fulfillment regardless of the world's troubles.

For us to do anything less is sin because it misses the mark God has for us. Whatever is not of faith, whatever action, conduct, or thought that is not done in faith is Sin, and is "missing the mark."

"Missing the mark" is the same as displeasing God.

Hebrews 11:6
"And without faith it is impossible to please Him, for whoever would draw near to God must believe that He exists, and that He rewards those who seek Him."

Sin is the state of mind of people. Sin is our attitude that brings forth action. For example, the act of murder is sin. However the intent to murder is sin also whether or not we convert the intent into an act. The foundation of sin is the state of mind that caused that action. God wants our hearts to be pure. God wants our motives to be pure. God does not want us to be in rebellion (transgression against God) against God. God wants us to be in harmony with Him. This is the positive. In other words He wants us to be righteous. We struggle with that because our minds are not the same as God's. We do not think the same way.

Isaiah 55:8–9
"For My thoughts are not your thoughts, neither are your ways My ways," declares the LORD. "For as the heavens are higher than the earth, so are My ways higher than your ways and My thoughts than your thoughts."

The Unpardonable Sin

Many Christians are greatly troubled by fear they have committed "The unpardonable sin" as outlined in Mark 3:28–30. In this passage Jesus Christ makes an overall evaluation of the sin question in response to the accusations made against Him by the Scribes in Jerusalem.

Mark 3:28–30
"Truly, I say to you, all sins will be forgiven the children of man, and whatever blasphemies they utter; but whoever blasphemes against the Holy Spirit never has forgiveness, but is guilty of an eternal sin"—for they were saying, "He (Jesus) has an unclean spirit."

What is God telling us, in the third chapter of Mark, when He refers to a statement man might make, *"He (Jesus) has an unclean Spirit."* Jesus is telling us that whoever has the imbedded attitude that Jesus has an unclean Spirit, cannot be forgiven of that sin. God sees this person who places the unholy spirit of Satan on Jesus as one who has an unchangeable attitude of rebellion against the act of God in sending Jesus Christ to die for our sins. In this verse, the Scribes of this time period hated Jesus and rationalized He was evil. Take into context the statements of Christ when He said "I and my Father are one." He has told everyone who would listen that God the Son, God the Father and the Holy Spirit are one and the same. To accuse Jesus as being like Satan is to accuse the Holy Spirit and God the Father of being like Satan.

How, then, can we measure our self and determine if we have committed the "Unpardonable Sin"? The answer is to ask ourselves if, deep into our mindset, we believe Jesus Christ is the same as Satan. Do we believe Jesus is evil and do we therefore refuse to follow him? If the answer is yes we are guilty of the "Unpardonable Sin." However if your answer to this question is no, you can still be restored into the Kingdom of God.

Those thousands of people, who fear they have committed the unpardonable sin, have not done so. The mere fact they are worried and feel they should repent of whatever it is they have done, and the mere fact they do not want to be separated from God insures that they have not committed the unpardonable sin. Christ is quiet clear all acts against God will be forgiven if the guilty party comes to Christ in truth seeking forgiveness with a repentant heart. But the one who has the mindful, willful, unchangeable attitude of antagonism toward God has committed the unpardonable sin because they have refused to ask God for forgiveness.

Man's Sin Nature

If Adam had not chosen to sin would the world be sinful? The correct answer to this is no human being knows. And the answer is this question is meaningless because God in His omniscience or all-knowing nature knew Adam would sin. Remember God is timeless. God, at the creation of the universe and mankind was also at the timeslot that is after the one-thousand-year millennial reign. God knew what man would do and knew what Adam and Eve would do. The better question is this. "Knowing man would sin, why did God consider it worth-while to create mankind?" The answer to that question is that God, in His omniscience considered the love of those who would love Him was worth it all.

Yes, I know I have not answered the question quoted above. Our best answer, perhaps guess, to this question is yes the world would be sinful. This is because every human being ever created was born with the choice of obeying or disobeying God. If not Adam and Eve someone else would have chosen to rebel against God. As a penalty for the sin of Adam, we are born with a basic nature to please ourselves over and above anything else. At birth we do not understand our nature and have no understanding of God. We do not sin until we make a conscious decision to put self above God. Sin is a decision to disobey, or displease God, followed by the action of sin. Infants who have no knowledge of righteousness or unrighteousness are born with a nature to sin but they have not made the decision to follow nature. Unfortunately each person soon reaches a point of knowing and understanding that God wants us to be one kind of person and we choose to be something else. This nature of sinning against God was imputed into us when Adam chose to disobey God. We are born with the desire to advance self over all other. If Adam had not made that decision, Cain or Abel or someone else would have made it. You and I have that natural desire inbred into our nature. We want to please ourselves rather than God.

The Apostle Paul, writing under the inspiration of God told us in Romans that every human ever born of man comes short of the holiness of God and is a sinner. This does not include Jesus Christ. Jesus did not have an earthly father. He was not born of man and was therefore not imputed with a sin nature. Christ had to choose to serve God or self, as we do, but He was not born with the inherent nature to sin. In Romans 3:23 Paul speaks of mortal man when he says,

Romans 3:23
"For all have sinned and fall short of the glory of God."

The apostle John told us that if we say we have not sinned, we are saying Jesus Christ is a liar and the spirit of God is not in us. That means we are not of Jesus Christ. God wants us to see the seriousness of sin and how everyone is affected by this problem.

1 John 1:10
"If we say that we have not sinned, we make
Him a liar, and His word is not in us."

We have a war going on inside of us from birth that struggles with doing what is righteous. Doing what is righteous means making the focus of our life pleasing God. Doing what is sinful is doing what we want, not what God wants. Even after we accept Jesus Christ as our savior we still battle with the desire to satisfy lust of the flesh, as opposed to the urgings of the Holy Spirit. And we still fail from time to time and act to serve self rather than God but our overall desire is to always please God. Saved people do sin but they never lose the desire in their heart to please their Lord and Savior.

Christians sin because we have a nature of sin. Every time we feel a desire to do something displeasing toward God, that desire is of Satan. God does not temp people to sin. God abhors sin. Some people take this fact and say they should not be held accountable for sin because they have no choice but to sin. This is not true. Having a sin nature does not mean we cannot tell the difference between right and wrong. It does not mean we cannot tell the difference between righteousness and disobedience of God.

What is "imputed" sin?

Vast numbers of people have no concept of imputed sin. The Bible tells us that at the age of one hundred and thirty years old, Adam became the father of a son "In his own likeness." All of mankind are born "in the likeness" of Adam, and Adam was punished for his disobedience of God by receiving a nature to disobey God. Adam and all of Adam's offspring had built into them the desire to please God. However they lost that desire to please God when Adam disobeyed God. This is imputed sin. They were left with a basic nature to serve self rather than God.

Romans 5:12
"Therefore, just as sin came into the world through one man, and death through sin, and so death spread to all men because all sinned."

Psalm 51:5
"Behold, I was brought forth in iniquity, and in sin did my mother conceive me."

In this verse, David verifies that he was born with a nature to sin. His statement that in sin my mother conceived me does not refer to his birth being outside of marriage, it refers to the fact that his father and his mother had a sin nature and when he was born he inherited that nature. David makes this fact clearer in Psalm 58.

Psalm 58:3
"The wicked are estranged from the womb;
They go astray from birth, speaking lies."

We are divinely informed therefore that all people have an inherited nature to sin that was imputed into them because of the disobedience of Adam. Yet we bear full responsibility for our sin. We cannot blame Adam and Eve we have to blame ourselves. In the days of Adam and Eve, God used the conscience of man to reveal the reality of their sin or disobedience of God. This was the Dispensation of Conscience. With the giving of "The Law" to Moses, God's method of governing mankind changed and God initiated into the world a new method of revealing to man when he was falling short of the righteousness required of God. This was the Dispensation of Law. From the day of Moses, mankind was expected to be aware of their sin through the measuring stick of the law. When they realized they fell short of the righteousness of God, God provided a process of burnt offerings to allow mankind to ask God for forgiveness of that sin. But whether before the day of Moses, or after "The Law" was given to Moses, or even unto the day of the Prophets, God held mankind accountable for their sins.

When Do We sin?

When do we actually sin? God gives us this answer in many places in His Word. Let's review what God tells us in the book of James.

James 1:13–14
Let no man say when he is tempted, "I am being tempted
of God"; for God cannot be tempted with evil, and He

himself temps no man:, but each person is tempted,
when he is lured and enticed by his own desire.

God tells us that we all feel the desire in our heart to do what we want to do regardless of what anyone else or God thinks. God told us in James that desire is temptation. God does not temp us. Temptation is always of Satan. Therefore, when we feel an urge to do something that we know is against what is holy and righteous it comes from Satan. Often we do not recognize that temptation as being from Satan. We think someone else is tempting us. That someone else may very well be a vessel of Satan but it is Satan who is the source of temptation to displease God. Often that temptation is, within itself, not grossly bad in the eyes of man. But if it is not pleasing to God it is temptation and can result in sin if we yield to it. For instance, if we decide to not go to Church, or to not pray, or to treat someone else badly because we want to, that is sin.

James 1:15
"Then desire when it is conceived, gives birth to sin;
and sin, when it is fully grown, brings forth death."

When we recognize that our desire to satisfy our own cravings are not acceptable in the sight of God, and we still elect to disobey God, we fall victim of Satan's temptation and we commit sin. This means we are guilty of sin the second we decide to engage in the sin. We are not sinning by just considering sin. Temptation alone does not constitute sin. It is when that desire is conceived or we decide to act upon it, we sin.

Can any of us say truthfully we have not done things or entertained desires that are displeasing to God? Hatred, lust, selfishness, greed, envy, taking God's name in vain, profanity, harmful acts to others, all these are acts of sin. All have sinned and come short of the glory of God. We can sin by having certain types of thoughts. Thoughts that are not pleasing to God, and we know they are not pleasing to God, become sin when we allow those thoughts to linger in our mind and enjoy thinking about them. For example, lusting is a sin. God addresses this in Matthew.

Matthew 5:28
"But I say to you that everyone who looks at a woman to lustful intent has already committed adultery with her in his heart."

Sin is the result of wrong desire in which the person mulls that desire around, enjoys thinking about it and then perhaps acts because of it. Acting on temptation can simply be the decision to continue to harbor, in our mind, the thought that we know to be displeasing to God. Temptation does not have to result in a physical act to become sin. However temptation, of itself, when we have not yielded to it, is not sin. The Holy Spirit unites with our spirit to identify when we are about to displease God. We know when we are not being righteous. When we are tempted, we are face to face with the question of standing up to the mark of righteousness that God defines so clearly to us. We sin when we "miss His mark of righteousness." If we demonstrate desire to do what we are tempted to do we are missing the mark. And earlier in this chapter we learned that missing the mark of Christ was sin.

Yet we have not transgressed against God until we make an active decision to do what we want to do even though it is displeasing to God.

The Price of Sin!

Adam and Eve paid a stiff penalty for their sin. That penalty was an abundance of things dealing with pattern of life but the ultimate penalty of sin as outlined many places in God's Word is death.

Romans 6:23
"For the wages of sin is death, but the free gift of God is eternal life in Christ Jesus our Lord."

The Bible clearly teaches that sin brings about death. We all understand physical death. And yes, physical death is a result of man's sin. However death also means a spiritual separation from God and eternal punishment. The death referred to in scripture is beyond our physical death.

God's Word tells us that those who do not know Jesus Christ will experience a second death. The second death refers to spiritual death. All of mankind, except Jesus Christ, Elijah, and those believers in Jesus who will be alive at the rapture of the Church, will experience physical death. Nonbelievers will experience a second death which is separation from God.

Why does God hate sin?

Many might ask why God is so intolerant of sin. If God imputed into us a sin nature is it our fault that we just follow our nature? And if God put into us a sin nature why does God hate sin? God hates sin because He is righteous. We understand that oil and water do not mix. They are opposites. We understand that heat and ice do not coexist. We must understand that God and sin do not coexist when we begin to understand God. God has certain characteristics that make Him God. He is truth. He is just. He is love. His love demands a free and unforced return of His love from man. But God is also holy. This means God is different from man, separated from man by nature, and uncompromising with regard to His nature.

Psalm 5:4
"For You are not a God who delights in wickedness,
evil may not dwell with You."

God is righteous. God is Holy. God is love. God is Just. He is who He is and will ever be who He is. God cannot tolerate any evil. He hates sin because it appalls Him. God hates sin because He is Holy. Holiness is perhaps the forefront characteristic of God.

Isaiah 6:3
And one cried to another and said: "Holy,
holy, holy is the LORD of hosts;
The whole earth is full of His glory!"

God also hates sin because it separates Him from His creation of man. Isaiah pointed out to all people that the sin of mankind is what separates us from God. We are corrupt with sin. God is righteous. The two cannot co-exist.

Isaiah 59:2
"But your iniquities have made a separation
between you and your God;
And your sins have hidden His face from you,
So that He does not hear."

Sin or disobedience of God caused Adam and Eve to run away from God in the Garden of Eden after they had eaten of the tree of knowledge of good and evil. They were aware of their guilt and they could not stand in the presence of God. God would not appear any longer in their presence because of their sin.

God also hates sin because it tempts us to partake of the worldly opportunities of pleasure, fame, wealth, materialism, and self-gratification. To sin against God is to disobey. Most of these opportunities are not wrong within themselves but when they possess us and become the direction of our life they close God off from us and then they become sin.

God also hates sin because it blinds us to truth. Just as light is opposite from darkness God is opposite from sin. As we begin to pursue the things we desire we become blinded to the desires of God.

1 John 2:11
"But he who hates his brother is in darkness and
walks in the darkness, and does not know where he is
going, because the darkness has blinded his eyes."

Transgressions and omissions against God have a result. God has declared that the price of sin is death. That means the price man must pay for sin is physical death in this life and eternal spiritual separation from God. But God wants a healthy relationship with mankind. God desires a relationship of righteousness but not at the price of becoming unholy.

Romans 6:16
"Do you not know that if you present yourselves to anyone as obedient slaves, you are slaves of the one whom you obey, either in sin, which to death, or of obedience which leads to righteousness?"

Human beings never operate on earth without guidance from one of two sources. Those two sources are Satan or God. God hates sin because it weakens our love for Him. We struggle trying to love God and serve Satan. The Hebrew Children would love God for a time and then rebel and hate God blaming Him for all their ailments. We also tend to love God and then regress to a desire of self-satisfaction. To the degree we are consumed with self we are neglectful and disobedient of God.

CHAPTER FOUR

The Doctrine of God the Father
God the Father Reveals Himself to Man

There is only one living and true God. He is an intelligent, spiritual, and personal being. He is the creator, redeemer, preserver, and ruler of the universe. God is infinite in holiness and all other perfections. To Him we owe the highest love, reverence, and obedience. The eternal God reveals Himself to us as Father, Son and Holy Spirit with distinct personal attributes.

The Trinity

The concept of the Trinity, also known as the Godhead, or the three personifications of God, is presented to us as early as the first chapter of Genesis. God described Himself with the word Elohim which translates into plural personifications of one divine being. This same word is used over 2,500 times in the Old Testament. God speaks in the plural of His own person. This is a fascinating scripture because it captures God speaking to Himself or to His other personifications as He says *"Let Us"...in our image: "after our likeness."* God inspires Moses, in writing Genesis, to say God created man in His own image. In the Old Testament, God, speaking of Himself, often makes reference to Himself and "My Spirit."

Genesis 1:26, 27
"Then God said, "Let Us make man in Our image, after Our likeness; let them have dominion over the fish of the sea, over the birds of the heavens, and over the livestock, over all the earth and over every creeping thing that creeps on the earth." So God created man in his own image; in the image of God he created him; male and female he created them."

The Bible speaks of God the Father as God in Philippians 1:2. God's Word also refers to Jesus as God in Titus 2:13. And God refers to the Holy Spirit as God in Acts 5:3–4. When we speak of the three personifications of God are we talking about three different ways of looking at God, or simply ways of referring to three different roles that God plays? The answer must be no, because the Bible also indicates that the Father, Son, and Holy Spirit are distinct Persons.

Proverbs 30:4
"Who has ascended to heaven and come down? Who has gathered the wind in His fists? Who has wrapped up the waters in a garment? Who has established all the ends of the earth? What is His name, and what is His Son's name, Surely you know?"

God's Word gives us an account of God the Father (the one who sends the Son (see John 3:16), God the Son (the one who is sent from the Father (John 16:28), and the Holy Spirit (the one who is sent by the Son from the Father—John 14:26; John 15:26). The Holy Trinity is revealed in the earliest Scripture of the Old Testament, although the word trinity is not used. A partial list of Scripture that record the presence of all three God the Father, God the Son, and God the Holy Spirit includes the following:

Matthew 1:20, 21
Matthew 3:16, 17
Mark 1:9–11
Mark 12:35
Luke 1:35
Luke 12:9
John 3:5
John 15:26
Acts 2:32, 33
Acts 5:31, 32
Romans 8:2, 3
Acts 20:21–22

The Doctrine That God Is One

Deuteronomy 6:4
"Hear, O Israel: The LORD our God, the LORD is one."

The Trinity or the Godhead is too deep and too complicated for man to fully grasp it. But as believers in His complete Word, we accept His Word knowing that someday we will understand. However, God tells us He is three personifications, God the father, God the Son, and God the Holy Spirit. This is evidenced by a host of scripture. Yet God also says He is one. Although full explanation of this is not provided in scripture, we do understand each of the personifications of God, interlinks with the other to the extent they think as one with the same characteristics and same values. Jesus said **"to be with me is to be with the Father."** They are one and yet each personification of God has a distinct and specific role in the Godhead.

2 Corinthians 13:14
"The grace of the Lord Jesus Christ, and the love of God, and the fellowship of the Holy Spirit, be with you all."

In Corinthians Paul expresses to us the blessings of all three parts of the Trinity. To the Church at Ephesus Paul further clarifies the Trinity when he says that the Church is to be one just as God the Father, God the Son, and God the Holy Spirit are one.

Ephesians 4:4–6
"There is one body and one Spirit, just as you were called to the one hope that belongs to your call; one Lord, one faith, one baptism; one God and Father of all, who is over all, and through all, and in all."

God states many times in His Word that God the Father, God the Son, and God the Holy Spirit are one. That means more than to say they think alike. They do not just act as one; they are one. God wants man to be united with Him in motivation, value, thought, desire, mission, purpose and deed. The Godhead exists as one in all things while being separate and God wants us to exist in all ways as one with Him while being separate

The Creation of Man gives insight of God

God the Father God the Son and the Holy Spirit have existed forever. They are separate beings yet one in mind, in mission, in character, and in purpose forever. It is difficult to explain how God can be one and yet three. However, we can visualize God as three entities each with a role in the Trinity. Yet each is exactly the same in Spirit, in Character, in purpose, and in action.

A simple explanation of how God made man somewhat explains the Trinity of God being three yet one. Man has three parts. We have a physical body. We have a Spiritual body. And separate from those two exists the soul of man. The physical body we understand, to the extent we can understand this amazing creation. The Spirit of man is more difficult for us to understand because we cannot see it or touch it. Most of us do not have a very deep understanding about our soul. God distinctly tells us however He created man "in His own image" with the three component of body, spirit and soul.

1 Thessalonians 5:23
"Now may the God of peace, Himself sanctify you completely, and may your whole spirit, and soul and body be kept blameless at the coming of our Lord Jesus Christ."

The Body of man is the physical housing of the spirit and soul of man. The spirit of man is the spirit of life God breathed into man making him a living being. In creation of man God gave us a piece of His Spirit so we could communicate with Him as long as we remained sin free. The spirit is that element of our being that gives us the ability to have a close spiritual relationship with God. It is our Spirit that "connects" with God because God is spirit. Our spirit is intended to have a love relationship with God. Yet in order to allow man to return a free love back to God, God had to create man with the capacity to make a choice of having our Spirit commune with God or reject God. That decision is made by the Soul of man.

The Soul of man is where our Spirit joins with our physical body. So our Soul is both physical and spiritual. As human beings we have a spirit but we are not spirits. We also have a soul but we are souls. As we understand our body the soul is the composite of our mind, our emotions, and our intellect. Our soul is influenced by our Spirit but our body is controlled by our soul. If the soul of man believes and loves God then his spirit will never be separated from God. But if our soul chooses to worship something other than God our Spirit will be separated from God for eternity. The soul is removed from the body at the time of physical death. If the spirit of man believed in Jesus the soul of man joins Christ in eternity. If the spirit of man chooses to follow our own selfish desires, then our soul is separated from our body and joins Satan in eternity. To the one who is lost eternity involves the following: (1) our separation from God, (2) our existence in Hell, a place of torment throughout eternity, and (3) our eternal knowledge of the glory of heaven and vision of those who have gone on to heaven.

The body of man as we know it is temporary, yet God speaks of those who are redeemed in His blood, as having a glorified body. The two bodies are not the same. The physical body we currently have ceases to exist at our death. But those who die believing in Jesus Christ, will be given a glorified body separate and distinct from our physical body here on earth. That glorified body will be immortal and cannot die. Our physical bodies here on earth are physical in structure but our spiritual bodies will be spiritual in structure. Our physical bodies here on earth are adapted to earth but our resurrected bodies will be perfectly adapted to heaven. We will have form and can be touched physically.

Luke 24:39
"See my hands and my feet, that it is I myself. Touch me, and see. For a spirit does not have flesh and bones as you see that I have."

Our resurrected bodies will have no limitations on travel.

John 20:19
On the evening of that day, the first day of the week, the doors being locked where the disciples were

*for fear of the Jews, Jesus came and stood among
them and said to them, "Peace be with you."*

We will be able to enjoy food, but will not be driven to it by
necessity for nourishment nor fleshly desire.

Luke 24:40–43
*"And when he had said this, he showed them his hands and his
feet. And while they still disbelieved for joy and were marveling,
he said to them, "Have you anything here to eat?" They gave
him a piece of broiled fish, and he took it and ate before them."*

The reality of God being three in one should not be foreign to
man because we are three in one. We have the three components yet
they operate in harmony.

Attributes of God the Father

God the Father is one of the three personifications of the Trinity.
Mankind simply does not understand God the Father. Because of the
holiness of God and the sinfulness of man, mankind cannot even
look upon God. The Bible gives us insight into who God is and what
roles God uses in interfacing with man. To understand God with
the limitations our human capacity allows it is helpful to study the
attributes of God that are outlined in Scripture.

God Is Eternal

We have often heard it said that God is the past, present and future.
In terms of what man understands that is correct. Yet it understates what
God is in terms of time. To God there is no past and no future. There is
only present because to God time does not exist. God created time for
the benefit of man. God has no beginning or end as man understands
time. God exists. God describes it by saying He is, "I Am."

God understands that man cannot cope with timelessness.
Man is subject to time because he is mortal. Man will physically die.

Because the days God granted for man to live make time essential to the being of man while on this earth. God created time for man but lives outside the parameters of time. Therefore God can see the beginning of our lives and the end of our lives, as we understand them to be. Our entire lives are happening in the present for God. When God tells us what events will precede us and will come to pass after our existence on earth we can be confident of His accuracy and truth. We can live in peace knowing that His promise of taking the believers home with Him to eternity will come to pass. God is already there at the end of time as we understand it.

Psalm 90:4
"For a thousand years in your sight are but as yesterday when it is past, or as a watch in the night."

God lives or exists in the present. However all time, from before creation through eternity God controls, understands, and monitors. God is never surprised and in never confused. Mankind cannot grasp such understanding.

God Is Holy

God is holy. He is perfect in every way. No imperfection is found in Him. He is far above all His creation in His holiness. The term holy means to be set apart, to be a plateau above. We immortals recognize to be holy means to be without sin. Yet to be holy means so much more. It means to be beyond comprehension of sin.

Exodus 15:11
"Who is like you, O Lord, among the gods? Who is like You, majestic in holiness, awesome in glorious deeds, doing wonders?"

1 Samuel 2:2
"There is none holy like the LORD, for there is none besides You, There is no rock like our God."

Isaiah tells us that God is not only holy; but is Holy, Holy, and Holy. Isaiah could not find words to express how far God's righteousness and purpose exceeds ours. Holy, Holy, Holy, gives reference to the Trinity of God. He is Holy as God the Father, God the Son, and God the Holy Spirit. The Holiness of God excludes our sinful state and casts us out of His presence unless the blood of Jesus cleanses us of our sin. Included in the definition of Holy is to be set apart. God is not like man. God is different than man yet man is made in the likeness of God. Much of our nature is similar to but vastly different than God. God is truth, God is just, God is love. God is righteous. God has to change the very heart of man after salvation for man to be even acceptable in the sight of God.

We, as humans, understand the word "holy" or "holiness" to carry a strong connotation of moral purity. And we are correct, but moral purity is not the foremost characteristic Scripture is talking about in the use of holiness. Instead, the most basic meaning of the word is to be "set apart" or "dedicated."

"I will be your God, and you will be my people," God tells us in Leviticus 26:12 and again in Hebrews 8:10. Therefore, far more important than morality, biblical holiness is focused on a unique *relationship* that God has established and desires with his people. When the Bible says "God is Holy" it means God is "set aside" from man in that while man can sin, God cannot sin. While man can be weak and listen to Satan, God will not coexist with Satan. Satan is weak compared to God. God is strength and has no weakness. To be Holy, is to be set aside as a unique, one of a kind creature.

God Is truth

God is truth. His life is truth. His actions are truth. His words are truth. God is the source of all truth. There is a vast difference in saying someone told the truth and saying someone is truth. God's Word describes Him as being truth. Truth can be painful yet God never compromises it. People often hide from the truth and do not want to confront exactly who and what they are in the sight of God.

Paul points out the problem we have with God's truth in his letter to the Roman Christians:

Romans 1:18, 25
"For the wrath of God is revealed from heaven against all
ungodliness and unrighteousness of men; who, by their
unrighteousness, suppress the truth." Because, they exchanged
the truth about God for the lie, and worshiped and served the
creature rather than the Creator, who is blessed forever. Amen."

People do not accidentally sin. They choose to take a path away from what God desires. In so doing they choose to disobey God. God is holy. We are unholy. God is truth. We choose to accept the untruth. This carries a severe penalty. Wrath and anger are all actions of a gracious and loving God who is Holy, Just, and full of Righteousness and cannot abide with evil.

Romans 2:8–9
"But to those who are self-seeking and do not obey the truth
but obey unrighteousness there will be wrath and fury.
There will be tribulation and distress, for every human
being who does evil, the Jew first and also the Greek..."

Because God is truth we can be confident that everything He has promised will come to pass. He does not lie. That means He keeps His promises. What He has said in the Bible about Himself is true. This is extremely important to believers in Christ because we have placed our hope of eternal life squarely on His promises.

God Is Righteous (Just)

The word *righteous* in the Hebrew language is "tsaddiy." It means to be just, lawful, and accountable. That is more than how you act. That means what you are. To be righteous means one's value system is just lawful and correct. The word righteous in the New Testament comes from the Greek word *"dikaios."*

"Dikaios" means to be faultless, innocent, accountable, and without guilt. It also speaks beyond what one does and addresses what their inner being is. We can be unrighteousness and still not be a wicked person. The bad news is that true and perfect righteousness is not possible for man to attain without the help of Christ. We can refrain from being wicked based on the values our parents teach us a children. We can achieve a level of not being wicked based on man's teachings but we cannot achieve the level of being righteous without God's intervention. The good news is that true righteousness is possible for mankind, but only through the cleansing of sin by Jesus Christ and the indwelling of the Holy Spirit. We have no ability to achieve righteousness in and of ourselves. But Christians possess the righteousness of Christ. Our measuring rod of righteousness is the life of Jesus.

Acts 17:31
"Because He has fixed a day on which He will judge the world in righteousness by a man whom He has appointed and of this He has given assurance to all by raising Him from the dead."

To be righteous means to have all the good qualities in perfect balance and to always make the right decision in all instances using those qualities. God is right in everything He does. He never makes a decision that could have been a little bit more correct. To be righteous means to never displease God. God has all wisdom and all power and His Word is true and His decisions are right. God is the source of righteousness. To say God is righteous is also to say God is Just. Both terms means His actions are always consistent with His nature and values. God does not sometimes act or think one way and other times act or think another way. Man acts and thinks inconsistently but God does not.

God is also holy, meaning He is set apart from man to be without sin. His righteousness is the natural product of His being Holy. God is not like human beings so far as characteristics are concerned. He is pure and always moral. God is, therefore, always against sin and will not tolerate sin. This is the reason God separates Himself from man and is the reason man cannot communicate directly with God. We know God through Jesus. Jesus told us God rules judgment of righteousness not by what man sees on the outside but by what is in man's heart. Therefore true righteousness is not only what we do and say, but is why we do it and say it. We, as believers can be viewed by God the Father as sinless because the blood of Jesus Christ who died on Calvary covers our sin with His ultimate payment for our sin.

God Is Love

Love is of the highest priority to God. The Bible tells us *"All the law and the prophets hang on the two love commandments."*

Matthew 22:37–40
"And He said to him, '"You shall love the LORD your God with all your heart, with all your soul, and with all your mind.' This is the great and first commandment. And a second is like it: 'You shall love your neighbor as yourself.' On these two commandments depend all the Law and the Prophets."

Love is that characteristic that allows us to care for another to the extent of sacrificing self for that person's good. God instructs us to love the Lord, your God with all your heart, and with all your soul, and with your mind. That means every fiber of our being is to be focused for the good and well-being of God. God also tells us that He loves us the same way He wants us to love Him. God loves us so much He gave His only begotten Son to die on Calvary for our sins. We do not deserve His love but He loves us anyway.

Human love is conditional while God's love is unconditional. We love others as long as certain conditional things are true. God loves us regardless of situational conditions. Our love is based to a huge extent on what we see in others and what we desire for our own good. God's love is based on His nature, not what we can become. We love others largely because we are attracted to them. God loves us even though we are totally unattractive.

The closest love man can grasp, that parallels God's love for us, is the love of a parent for children. In most cases parents love their children almost unconditionally. Regardless of what the child does, becomes, or thinks, the parent continues to love. That is not to say there cannot be a time the child forces a separation between the parent and child. In such cases parents tend to be truly sacrificial trying to restore the relationship of parent child in love. God's love is similar in that He loves us unconditionally. He knows that we will cause Him pain and that we will disobey Him, yet He cherishes the love we can return. This is not just because God loves. It is because God is love. God loves us so much He sent His only begotten Son, Jesus Christ, to die on Calvary to restore a relationship with His children.

Yet we must understand that God is also just and righteous. His nature of being just and being always right, commands that His love must be consistent with justice. His just or righteous nature commands that penalty must be paid for sin. Without such there is no righteousness. Yet God's love demands that there be love for even the sinful and fallen. Without it there would be no salvation and no restitution to God.

1 John 4:9–10
"In this the love of God was made manifest among us, that God sent His only Son into the world, that we might live through Him. In this is love, not that we have loved God, but that He loved us and sent His Son to be the propitiation for our sins."

God Is Omnipotent
(All-Powerful)

The world will tell us that this earth is a contest between God and Satan. However, the contest is only in the mind of Satan. God's Word tells us that God is omnipotent. Omni means all and potent means powerful. So God is all-powerful and can do anything He desires. Often God's character of Holiness, Love, and Righteous require action that is painful to God. God is limited only to the characteristics He possesses that are unchangeable. While dealing with the Children of Israel in the Old Testament God's love existed even through His wrath. The prophet Isaiah gives us a broad view of God's omnipotent power.

Isaiah 55:11
"So shall my word be that goes out from my mouth; it shall not return to me empty, but it shall accomplish that which I purpose, and shall succeed in the thing for which I sent it."

God's power can be defined as absolute without beginning or end. Absolute power means God has the power to do anything He wishes. God could destroy Satan and end the conflict, but His divine wisdom elects to not do so at this time. We have the promise of God that Satan will, at the end of time, receive eternal punishment of fire and sulfur. We do not understand all of God's decisions. For instance, God has promised He will come again and establish His kingdom. He has not done it yet. But through faith, we know he will do so. We know this because He has to power to do so and has promised He will do so.

The most prominent evidence of God's all powerful nature is in creation. God created from nothing. God did not use evolution. God did not use tools. God the Father through God the Son, with the assistance of the Holy Spirit, created. God simply said "Let it be so" and it happened. God's power is also seen in his preservation of His creation. All life on earth, both human, animal, foul, and vegetation would cease to exist if God did not continue to provide everything needed for order and preservation. God defines limits for the seas to operate. God defines limits for space to hang and maintains distances necessary for the solar systems to not collide. God also defines limits for Satan to operate and for evil to prevail.

God also provides limits for current governments and leaders to operate. God brings nations down and creates nations. All that exists is subject to God's omnipotent power.

God Is Omniscient
(All-Knowing)

Romans 11:33
"Oh, the depth of the riches and wisdom and knowledge of God! How unsearchable are His judgments and how inscrutable His ways!"

Mankind is jealous of God and wants to be on an equal level with God even though we know that is impossible. In that consideration are we unlike Satan? We try to pull God down to the level of man because we do not want to have to submit to a God that is all powerful and all knowing. God has knowledge without limitations. Mankind cannot identify with the wisdom of God. God's Word proclaims God the Father, God the Holy Spirit and God the Son to understand everything. That means there no knowledge mankind can discover that God does not already grasp and master. After all God planned, created, and maintains everything. There is no financial merger ever created God does not understand. There is no technical invention God is not the master of and there is no persuasion of others God does not master. This does not mean man is destined to do certain things and has no choice. It means God created us and understands us completely. If a mother lets her young child who has just learned to crawl go without guidance that child will eventually crawl into a place of harm and danger. The mother knows it will happen because she knows the nature of the child. Yet the child has full freedom to make the decision as he or she wishes. God knows us so much better than the mother knows the child. Why are we surprised? God is never surprised. God knows everything.

The significance to man regarding the omniscient God is that God always knows everything about us. God knows our every thought. He knows our every temptation. He knows our temptation before we face it and knows our decision before we make it. God knows our heart and therefore knows what we will decide. This is the omniscient nature of God. God is not limited by time as is man. God already exists at any point in the future man has reason to consider. God knows everything about nature because He created it. God never forgets as man does.

God is omniscient not only about us, mankind, but He is omniscient regarding the universe into which He placed us. God knows every detail about His creation. He knows the vastness of space yet fully knows every atom ever created. David was amazed at the omniscient of God when He views the stars.

Psalm 147:4
"He determines the number of the stars;
He gives to all of them their names."

Because God is all-powerful (omnipotent) and all-knowing (omniscient) it should be clear to man that God is able to fulfill every promise He ever made. Nothing, no promise ever made, no plans ever created is impossible for Him. And God has promised to never fail us if we will trust in Him. God has known us from before creation of Adam, before creation of matter. He knew where we would appear in time and whom we would interact with. He promised us eternal security and glory with Him in heaven after the close of time, if we put our faith in His Son. God in His omniscience foresaw the sinfulness, ugliness, and depravity of man. God saw and understood how man would deny Him, how man would be selfish, and yet God loved His greatest creation enough to still create us. And praise the Lord He loved us enough to provide a path of Salvation through Jesus Christ His Son.

God Is Immutable
(Unchanging)

It is impossible for God to change. Influences that cause change in our lives do not change God. God does not compromise and His values are always constant. God's plan is unchangeable. That gives us confidence in predicting our destiny. His plan for man has existed from before creation of man and still exists unchanged today. We are part of God's plan. God's unchanging character and unchanging word equips us with truth.

It is not necessary for God to change because He is perfect. Change implies an effort to improve something in some way. God is the creator of all and God is perfect. To know God is immutable or to know God cannot and will not change is so reassuring to us. It means God will not change His mind regarding Heaven and eternity. To us, mankind, our eyes are set on the Son of God, Jesus Christ.

Hebrews 13:8
"Jesus Christ is the same yesterday, today, and forever."

Change also has to happen within the boundaries of time. God is eternal and is not limited to time. Change implies something is getting better or worse. God is perfect and will not coexist with anything that is not perfect meaning both complete and without blemish. And finally change often means new technology or new data has been developed. God is all wisdom and all knowing. No technology is ever discovered that surprises God.

God Is Omnipresence
(Always Present)

This theological term means, "always present." Since God is infinite, His being knows no boundaries. So clearly He is everywhere. David voiced this truth for all mankind in Psalm when he articulately stated, "Where can I go from Your Spirit?"

Psalm 139:7–12
Where can I go from Your Spirit? Or where shall I flee from Your presence? If I ascend to heaven, You are there; If I make my bed in Sheol, You are there, If I take the wings of the morning, and dwell in the uttermost parts of the sea, even there Your hand shall lead me, and Your right hand shall hold me. If I say,

"Surely the darkness shall cover me, and the light about me be night; even the darkness is not dark to you, the night is bright as the day for darkness is as light are with You."

The omnipresence of God is a burden to nonbelievers who seek to separate from God. However, it is a blessing to the believer who seeks to follow God and rests in the comfort of His love. We are never alone. God is aware of every situation we get into and is never out of touch when we call upon His name. It also tells us there is never a situation that is beyond the ability of our omnipotent God to handle. That means we do not have to be filled with fear at every turn of life. God's omnipresence is not just an attribute but is a promise. And God keeps His promises. In a unique and special act of love, God promises to be especially available to those who trust in His Son Jesus Christ. God outlines His expectations for us to be righteous in thought and deed, to be caring to those we meet, to spread His Gospel to all lands and all people we see. He has promised that when we call upon His name He will hear us and will answer our prayer. The availability of God to His children is promised and described in Psalm 23:1–3.

Psalm 23:1–3
*"The L*ORD* is my shepherd; I shall not want.*
He makes me lie down in green pastures;
He leads me beside the still waters. He restores my soul;
He leads me in the paths of righteousness
For His name's sake."

God Is Timeless

We have previously discussed this characteristic of God. God exists outside of the boundaries of time, as man understands time. God tells us He is the beginning and the end. Time, as we understand it, was created by God and the ending, as we understand it, is created by God. God is beyond the boundaries of time, beginnings, and endings. To God, everything that is happening, that has happened, and will happen, occurs in the present.

John 8:58
"Jesus said to them, "Truly, Truly, I say to
you, before Abraham was, I AM."

Psalm 90:2
"Before the mountains were brought forth,
Or ever You had formed the earth and the world,
from everlasting to everlasting, You are God."

These verses, along with many others God gave us, clearly establish that God existed way before the creation of matter. And they tell us God will exist forever, all powerful, all knowing, all present, unchanging and timeless. Perhaps the most significant feature of understanding the timelessness of God is that of the doctrine of atonement.

If God is timeless and exists in a continuous state of the present, then He was present the day Christ died for my sins. He was present the day I gave my heart to Jesus Christ. It means that when I gave my heart to Christ, God was there to forgive me through the blood shed for me by Christ on Calvary two-thousand-plus years ago.

God Is Sovereign

Most people, even most Christians do not know what the sovereignty of God means. The sovereignty of God is the climax of all other attributes and defines our relationship with Him. The sovereignty of God simply means God is in control of everything. Yet even in the context of that control, God delegates to man certain privileges and responsibilities. However, God is in control of every person ever born, every person now living, and every person who will ever be born. Nothing happens in the universe that is outside of God's influence and authority. Yet the responsibility of much that happens in the Universe, so far as people are concerned, is a shared responsibility between God and man. This is because God delegates to people the responsibility of making a free choice regarding righteousness and regarding eternity. God has decreed He will not make that choice for us. He influences us. He urges us. He directs us but He gives man the free choice to decide to follow Satan or Jesus Christ. The responsibility of that choice is man's not God's. God has given mankind full warning of the consequences of sin just as He gave Adam and Eve a warning of what would happen if they disobeyed Him.

The fact, however, that man chooses to disobey God; as the Hebrew children did, and as we are doing; does not change the fact that God is in full control. He will, in His chosen time, proclaim rewards and punishments as so earned by mankind for man's actions. God is not limited in any way and Satan has no power or control over God. God's Word tells us in Revelation 21:6 that He is "above all things and before all things. He is timeless and immortal. He is omnipresent, capable of relating to everyone in the Universe on a personal basis.

Revelation 21:6
"And He said to me, "It is done! I am the Alpha and the Omega, the beginning and the end. To the thirsty I will give from the spring of the water of life without payment."

God further tells us that He is the creator of everything. It is important to God that we know and believe He is the creator. We know that because He so clearly tells us it is true.

Colossians 1:16
"For by Him all things were created in heaven and on earth, visible and invisible, whether thrones or dominions or rulers or authorities—all things were created through Him and for Him."

God can do anything. As creator he proved this. God is the Lord of the minutiae and of the huge. His knowledge understands the slightest parts of the atom; yet understands the vastness of space. Nothing is too difficult for God. Nothing happens that God does not make or allow too happen. This means God is in control of everything that has and will happen in our lives. We can trust God to care for us. Yes, hardships and tragedies come into our lives, and we do not know why, but God knows and God is in control of our lives. Often we do not know why God does certain things or allows certain things to happen but God has a reason and that reason is for our good. Anything God wants to happen in the universe will happen. Now, we must realize that God wants man to have freedom of choice. This means the results of God's decision to give man free choice is that often we make decisions God does not agree with and things happen He does not approve. But God also has foreordained that man must pay the penalty of his disobedience.

God has power and authority over everything. This means God is in control of governments. God is in control of the future and the past. God is in control of all angels and every created being including demons and Satan. God controls our weather and our storms and our rain. God is in control of our technology. Mankind never "invents" anything we just occasionally discover more of God's creation. Satan himself has to ask God's permission before he can make things happen. God sometimes grants Satan's wish for whatever end result God deems worthy and sometimes God's rejects Satan's request. What is so significant about God's sovereignty? The answer is found in Romans 8:28.

Romans 8:28
"And we know that for those who love God all things work together for good, for those who are called according to His purpose."

This promise of God tells us that God is totally, without reservation, in control of everything. And God has promised that everything that happens is for the good of those people who are totally dedicated to the love and adoration Him. Yes things will happen that in the short term we do not understand. God tells us to trust Him and not to worry unduly about such things. He will, in His own time, turn what we see as bad into good. We can trust this promise because our God is an all-knowing, all-powerful, all-loving, just, holy and truthful God. This means that we, as people who have put our trust in Christ and who believe His Word, need not fear because nothing will ever come into our life that God does not understand. Nothing will come into our life that God cannot control. We can take comfort in the promise God is sovereign, in control over everything, whether it be our health, our parents, our kids, our marriage, our finances, our social world, our emotional world, or our spiritual world. God is sovereign. He is in control and that allows us to live a life of freedom from undue anxiety and fear.

God's Grace

The very definition of God's Grace is unmerited favor. His goodness is toward those who have no claim to express, no reason to expect, no right to receive, gifts from God that we so deeply do not deserve. The principal manifestation of God's grace has been in the form of a gift. The very word grace is music to a believer's ears. But not just grace but the grace of God. It is music because it is our salvation. It is our life. It is our hope and future. The wonderful, amazing grace of God! God is our source of grace. Jesus entered His earthly ministry filled with God's grace. God's grace flowed through Christ to all of us. The entire human race benefits from God's grace.

John 1:14
"And the Word became flesh and dwelt among us,
and we have seen His glory, glory as of the only son
from the Father, full of grace and truth."

God's grace allows people to be born, grow up, live their lives and make a choice. The very fact that people are allowed to live is based on the grace of God. Everything we have is because of God's grace. The Apostle Peter said it well in his first letter to the church at Ephesus.

Ephesians 2:8
"For by grace you have been saved through faith; and this is not your own doing: it is the gift of God."

Man's only contribution to salvation is faith in Jesus Christ as the Son of God who died on Calvary for our sins. The actual changing of us from a lost and condemned soul to a saved soul is by the unmerited favor God chose to pour out on us. However that grace is conditional. It depends on our believing that Jesus Christ, the Son of God died on the Cross of Calvary to save us from our sins. Such belief is called faith. But God even clarifies this to mankind lest we become proud of our part of salvation. God tells us that our faith is not something we earned but is the gift of God who gives us the capacity to believe so that we might be acceptable to God.

The Wrath of God

It is not complete to discuss the Grace of God and not recognize the wrath of God. When we list all the great characteristics of God it is easy for us to view God as being a sweet, love everybody God that is never hard on anyone. That is not true. As we consider the wrath of God it is of value to review one of the greatest sermons of all time and certainly a sermon that is applicable in the troubled world in which we live. July 8, 1741, the great Jonathan Edwards preached his most famous sermon entitled "Sinners in the Hands of an Angry God." We like to preach and teach that God is a God of love ready to forgive if we will just wrinkle our brow in forgiveness. God is a God of love, God is also a patient God and a God of compassion. But God will not forever hold back His wrath against man. God does want us to be happy. But that is not God's primary goal. First He wants us to be righteous. He wants us to conduct our lives according to the pattern Jesus provided for us. We react to the demands of God not God reacting to the demands of mankind. Our sin blocks the righteous word of God and for that God's wrath spews forth.

Romans 1:1
"For the wrath of God is revealed from Heaven against
all ungodliness. And unrighteousness of men, who
by their unrighteousness suppress the truth."

How can God be a God of love and still a God of wrath? The answer is that the opposite of love is hate not wrath. We love our children but when they disobey we still get mad with them and justly so. Anger and love can go hand in hand in our physical life and in God's view of mankind. Let's also recognize that love binds wrath to a point of self-control not lack of self-control. God does not lose His temper even in the last Seven Years of Tribulation. He reacts to man according to a plan drawn up before the creation of man. People who only see the love of God and do not want to accept the wrath of God do not have a full view of God's Word.

Today people have it backwards. We tend to judge God. How could Hell be justified? We ask. Why did God take that loved one from me because of illness? We ask. Why did God allow me to get in the financial shape I am in? We ask. No, God is the judge of us. He does not have to ask questions to which He has no answers because He knows all the answers. So God says, because they disobeyed me I shall. God understands us and wants to forgive us. But forgiveness has to fit into a master plan for our lives. Forgiveness comes after our repenting of our sin and asking God to forgive. People also have little concept of imputed sin. We have little understanding of the fact that because Adam sinned we entered the world deserving to die for our sin. Therefore as soon as we have enough mental capacity to willfully disobey God, we fall under the righteousness of God, the wrath of God and praise the Lord we also fall under the Grace of God. It is therefore of great value to understand certain principles of God's wrath toward us.

1. God's wrath is always deserved: We never experience God's wrath that we do not deserve it and more. **Romans 2:5: "But because of your hard and impenitent heart you are storing up wrath for yourself on the day of wrath**

when God's righteous judgment will be revealed. "Why do we ever experience God's wrath? The answer is because we have a hard and impenitent heart. When will we, for certain, know what God's punishment will be? Sometimes very quickly and sometimes not until the "Day of The Lord" judgment day. That day is not known to mankind.

2. God's wrath is awesome. **Matthew 25:46: *"And these will go away into eternal punishment, but the righteous into eternal life."*** It is impossible for mortal man to understand the horror of eternal punishment. And yes, Hell is the ultimate punishment for unforgiven sinners. God is a loving God but God will not forgive those who do not claim the price Jesus paid for their sins on Calvary.

3. God's wrath is consistent and parallel with His love. **Hebrews 10:31: *"It is a fearful thing to fall into the hands of the living God."***

4. God's wrath is paid in full by the blood of Jesus Christ. **Romans 3:26: *"It was to show His righteousness at the present time, so that He might be just and the justifier of the one who has faith in Jesus."***

The Names of God

To us as people, our names are important. We try to live a life that does not tarnish our name. As Christians we carry the name of Christ in our title of Christians and we desire to not tarnish or bring disgrace to the name of Christ. The Hebrew culture also valued names greatly. People knew who and what a person was by their name. Their name was a tangible vision of their autobiography and character.

God also gave Himself many names. He gave names to reveal His character and autobiography. It is good for us to learn the names God gave Himself and in doing so better understand God. The Old Testament was written largely in Hebrew as opposed to the New Testament being written in Greek. Therefore the following is a listing of the names God gave Himself in the Old Testament and recorded in Hebrew.

Psalm 8:1
"O LORD, our Lord, How magestic is Your name in all the earth,
You have set Your glory above the heavens!"

- Yahweh is the personal name God gave Himself. It is Hebrew. Because Hebrew was originally written without vowels it is truly "YHWY" a name that means "The Lord" and referring to God's salvation power.
- Elohim means simply "God" and is a reference to God's power and might. *See Genesis 1:1 or Psalm 19:1.*
- Adonai means "Lord" and is a reference to the sovereignty of God. *See Malachi 1:6.*
- Jehovah-Yahweh is a reference to God's divine salvation. *See Genesis 2:4.*
- Jehovah-Maccaddeshem means "The Lord the sanctifier." *See Exodus 31:13.*
- Jehovah-Shammah means The Lord who is present." *See Ezekiel 48:35.*
- Jehovah-Rapha means "The Lord our healer." *See Exodus 15:26.*
- Jehovah-Tsidekenu means "The Lord our righteousness." *See Jeremiah 23:6.*
- Jehovah-Jireh means "The Lord will Provide." *See Genesis 22:13–14.*
- Jehovah-Nissi means "The Lord our banner." *See Exodus 17:15.*
- Jehovah-Shalom means "The Lord is peace." *See Judges 6:24.*
- Jehovah-Sabbaoth means "The Lord of Hosts" *See Isaiah 6:1–3.*
- Jehovah-Gmolah means The God of Recompense. *See Jeremiah 51:6.*
- El-Elyon means "The most high God." *See Genesis 14:17 and Isaiah 14:13–14.*
- El-Roi means "The strong one who sees." *See Genesis 16:13.*

- El-Shaddai means "The God of the mountains or God Almighty." *See Genesis 17:1 or Psalm 91:1.*
- El-Olam means "The everlasting God." *See Isaiah 40:28–31.*
- Pater means "Father of His people" in Greek. *See Deuteronomy 32:6, Isaiah 63:16 and Isaiah 64:8.*

Abba is Aramaic for Pater. It is the term Jesus used in the New Testament when speaking of His Father in Aramaic. *See Mark 14:36, Romans 8:15, Galatians 4:6.*

God's Word gives God the title and attributions of Father. In the old and modern Judaism, *YHWH* is called Father because he is the creator, law-giver, and protector. Likewise, in Christianity, God is called father for the same reasons, but especially because of the Father-Son relationship revealed by Jesus Christ. In general, the name of *Father,* applied to deity, signifies that he is the origin of whoever and whatever is subject to him. God is a supreme and powerful authority, a patriarch, and protector. Yet we make a mistake if we assume that God the Father created God the Son and the Holy Spirit. That thought meets man's logic but is not scriptural. The Bible teaches that God the Father is not the origin of God the Son or the Holy Spirit. Each of the three of the Godhead had no creation and no end. God describes himself using the special name *Elohim* (God) and *Yahweh Elohim* (Lord God). He is called God in relation to Jesus Christ, who is the *'Christ of God'*, and who addressed Him as *'My God'*. He is likewise called God in relation to the Holy Spirit, who is referred to repeatedly as the Spirit of God.

Father of Israel

The Old Testament refers to the fatherhood of God as He relates to His covenant relationship to Israel. God the Father declares Himself to be the father to the house of Israel. Moses refers to God as the Father of the Israelites.

Jeremiah 31:9
"With weeping they shall come, and with
pleas for mercy I will lead them back.
I will make them walk by the brooks of water in a
straight way in which they shall not stumble; for I am
a Father to Israel, and Ephraim is My firstborn."

The New Testament was written in Greek and the names for God are recorded in Greek. The New Testament records the following names given by God to us so we might know Him better.

- **"God"**: God uses the Greek word "theos." which is equivalent to the Hebrew word Elohim, one thousand times in the New Testament to describe Himself. It is used in reference to God's power and might.
- **"Lord"**: God uses the Greek work "Kurios" six hundred times in the New Testament. In these instances the word "Kurios" refers to "Jehovah" in Hebrew.
- **"Godhead":** God refers to Himself as part of the trinity or Godhead in 2 Corinthians 13:14.

2 Corinthians 13:14
"The grace of the Lord Jesus Christ and the love of God
and the fellowship of the Holy Spirit be with you all."

- **"Savior":** God refers to Himself as the Savior of the World in

Luke 1:47
"And my spirit rejoices in God my Savior."

- **"Highest"**: God refers to Himself as the highest.
- **"Word"**: God refers to Himself as the Word.
- **"Jesus"**: derived from the word "Joshua" or "Y'Shua" or "Je-Hoshua."

Christian Relationships with God the Father

Christ used the term Father, as His most common designation for God. However, He used it to designate a relationship that was uniquely His. The name 'Father' very particularly defines His relationship to God the Son and the Holy Spirit. It is an eternal relationship that always has been and always will be. God the Father does not mean God the creator of Jesus or the Holy Spirit. So in this usage God the Father does not mean creator but defines a relationship with God the Son. We can imagine a father and son both in existence forever and identical in every way but with different roles. Christ claimed this relationship for Himself in a sense that could not be shared even with His disciples. It is a relationship that cannot be understood by the human mind. God did not try to explain the Trinity as the words of Christ seems to suggest:

Matthew 11:27
"All things have been handed over to Me by My
Father, and no one knows the Son except the Father.
And no one knows the Father except the Son, and
anyone to whom the Son chooses to reveal Him."

Jesus told us that no man can know the Father, except through the Son. This is because man has the sin curse and is not presentable to God except when seen through the blood of Jesus. The Jews sought the destruction of Christ because He said God was His Father, making Himself equal with God (John 5:18). To Jesus the term Father signified a unique relationship of equality, love, respect, and responsibilities between Him and God the Father. Believers understand God the Father is distinctive in His role as our creator, protector, and originator. He is distinctively unique in that we do not have direct access to God the Father but do have access through the Son. That does not separate God the Father from the God the Son or the Holy Spirit. And it does not separate us from The Son and the Holy Spirit. God gives us access to God the Father through the Son and access to the Son through the Holy Spirit.

Only those who have given their heart to Jesus Christ and have the Holy Spirit as an interpreter of the Word can understand, to a limited degree, the significance of this relationship. God the Father is hallowed ground to His believers. When God refers to us as His children He certifies our relationship. Yet we have that relationship not by natural birth but because of the price Jesus paid for our sins which made it possible for us to be adopted unto the family of God. God's Fatherhood to His true believers is based on the closer eternal relationship to the Only Begotten Son. Paul indicates that it is this relationship to Christ that gives us our relationship to God:

Galatians 3:26
"For in Jesus Christ you are all sons of God through faith."

Galatians 4:4–5
"But when the fullness of the time had come, God sent forth His Son, born of woman, born under the law, to redeem those who were under the law, so that we might receive adoption as sons."

The Holy Spirit communicates this experience of "Sonship" to believers. Paul instructed us it is the Holy Spirit who maintains the consciousness of this relationship in the Christian heart.

CHAPTER FIVE

The Doctrine of Jesus the Messiah
God's Fulfillment of Messianic Prophecy

Prophecy of the Coming Messiah

A divine prophecy is a prediction of something that, made under the divine revelation of God, will happen in the future. Of the hundreds of prophecies made in the Old Testament regarding the coming of the Messiah, every one of them came true prior to the birth of Jesus Christ. All of the Old Testament was written between 1450 BC and 430 BC. Therefore the prophecies were made as far back as one thousand years before the birth of Jesus Christ. Yet every single prophecy was fulfilled according to the timetable of God and was fulfilled before the birth of Jesus.

The Messianic prophecy is the prediction of the future related to God's promise that He would send someone to save the Jewish people from their sins. Messianic prophecies provide for Israel's eternal destiny with God. Although the focus of the Messianic prophecy was the Hebrew nation it also would be the prophecy for Gentiles as they would be adopted into the Family of God. God gave the Jewish people the Messianic prophecies so:

They might be comforted to know their future with God was secure, in spite of the necessity of their punishment for being disobedient to God.

1. The Jewish people would be able to predict the coming of the Messiah and would be ready to recognize and would receive Him when He came.
2. God wanted the Jews to understand the Messiah's coming was the highlight of their lives and He wanted them to look forward to His coming. The Children of Israel did get the message of the coming Messiah but they misunderstood why He would come.

But first let us consider a basic question that is often misunderstood. What information did God reveal to Old Testament believers concerning the Messiah? The reality is that as the Old Testament was revealed to the Hebrew nation, from Genesis to Malachi the picture of who the Messiah would be gradually, over centuries, became clearer to the Hebrew people.

And we must base all such discussion on the truth that is taught from Genesis to Revelation regarding Salvation. That truth is that there is no salvation without the shedding of blood of Jesus Christ, the Son of God. There is only one plan of salvation for Old Testament believers, New Testament believers, Tribulation believers or even one-thousand-year Millennial Kingdom believers. When God gave us the following revelation He meant it to apply to all mankind throughout all ages.

John 14:6
"Jesus said to him, "I am the way, and the truth, and the life. No one comes to the Father except through me."

Jesus was discussing this with the New Testament people but His truth does not say *"No one comes to the Father except through me"* and mean, except of course, those people in the Old Testament. God confirms this truth in a verse well known to all New Testament Christians (John 3:16).

John 3:16
"For God so loved the world, that he gave his only Son, that whoever believes in him should not perish but have eternal life."

God is quite clear in this verse in which He reveals more than we sometimes see in it. *"God loved the world, not just the Jews, or Gentiles, or Old Testament or New Testament, but the whole world that He gave His only Son, Jesus Christ, that all who believe in Him will have eternal life."*

The fact, however, that the only way to salvation is through Jesus Christ the Son of God does not mean that throughout the Old Testament, people of that day and time, had a full understanding of who the Messiah would be. The earliest revelation to Old Testament people in the Bible was in the book of Genesis and must have been confusing to them.

Genesis 3:15
"And I will put hostility between you and the woman and between your offspring and her offspring; her offspring will attack your head, and you will attack her offspring's heel."

This verse is given to mankind in the context of God giving punishment to Satan for having deceived mankind and for all eternity given mankind a basic nature of sin. God loved Lucifer and was undoubtedly broken hearted at Him for choosing to rebel against God. God was undoubtedly also quite angry at Lucifer for what he had done. Just consider how God in His omniscience looked over the forthcoming thousands of years and saw the pain, defeat, punishment, and horror man would endure because of what Lucifer, now called Satan, had caused. Yes, the fault was also man's fault but in this verse God is talking to Satan. He announces that there would be for all eternity hostility between Satan's offspring (all people in the future who would choose to not trust in the coming Messiah to save them) and the woman's offspring (because Mary would someday bear forth a son and His name would be Jesus the Son of God, God speaks of Jesus as the offspring of The Woman). However, the offspring of "The Woman" is more inclusive than just Jesus. Because Jesus would pay the price of salvation for all mankind, male, female, Old Testament or New Testament, who would believe on Him they would be adopted as children of God and they too become the offspring of the woman and the receiver of the evil of Satan.

Then God announces that as punishment to Satan, the offspring (now talking about Jesus Christ) would bruise the head of Satan. This took place on Calvary when Jesus conquered the precious tool of Satan called death. God told Satan that the offspring of Mary would crush and eventually destroy Satan. Satan understood exactly what God was telling him, but of course, mankind would not really understand this when revealed some hundreds of years after Satan deceived man.

Then God announces to Satan that the creation of God, mankind, would also suffer because this deceit had occurred. God announces that the Serpent (the form of Satan now because of his deceit) would crawl on the ground and would only be able to harm mankind by striking his heal. That meant that is so doing Satan would put sin into the life of all mankind and that sin would result in eternal death unless mankind believed in the Son of God.

Now we see in Genesis 3:15 that God announces at the beginning of mankind's life that the way to salvation was through Jesus Christ. But God, in His Omniscience elected to not reveal to the Old Testament people that Jesus of Nazareth would be the Messiah. God wanted faith of man to be turned to Him with the slightest possible amount of revelation. So at the beginning of creation man had revealed to him that salvation came only through the coming Messiah. That Messiah would be Jesus Christ the Son of God but man was not told this until the time was right.

Let's move forward now to the book of Deuteronomy where we find God taking another step in revealing to His chosen people who the Messiah would be. God does not tell them the Messiah would be Jesus Christ the Son of God but instead tells them He would be a great prophet.

Deuteronomy 18:15
"The LORD your God will raise up for you a prophet like me from among you, from your brothers—it is to him you shall listen."

God now takes another step of revelation to the Old Testament people who wish to believe Him but do not understand because they have limited revelation from God of God's plan. God tells them, therefore tells us, that God would raise-up a prophet. What does a prophet do? A prophet is one who speaks for another and in so doing reveals truth he is sent to reveal. Jesus would be the prophet for God the Father. Jesus came to earth not in His own power but in the power of God the Father. The Old Testament people of Abraham and forthcoming prophets were now holders of information that told them the forth coming Messiah would be one who would reveal truth to them. God expected the Old Testament believers to have enough faith in Him to wait for clarification of the message. What we see is a gradual revelation from God the Father first of all that Satan would be defeated and it would be at the hand of the Son of God. Second we see God telling the people He would send a powerful prophet to reveal His truth. Now we see in Proverbs that God reveals to the Old Testament people that prophet would be the Son of God. But the name Jesus was not revealed to be the coming Son of God.

Proverbs 30:4
"Who has ascended into heaven and descended? Who has gathered the wind in His fists? Who has wrapped the waters in His garment? Who has established all the ends of the earth? What is His name or His son's name?"

God reveals through Daniel's vision that after sixty two weeks of the seventy weeks (remember God is using the Hebrew Idiom of one week equals seven years) future of Israel, an anointed one who is appointed to be the sacrifice for man's sin (meaning Jesus but not naming Him) would be sacrificed. This is another step in which God reveals to Old Testament people more about the Messiah but not the name Jesus Christ. At this point in history believers knew the Messiah would be the Son of God but He did not reveal the name of the Messiah. God did reveal to the people the fact that the anointed one would be sacrificed for the sins of believers.

Daniel 9:26
And after the sixty-two weeks, an anointed one shall be cut off and shall have nothing. And the people of the prince who is to come shall destroy the city and the sanctuary. Its end shall come with a flood, and to the end there shall be war. Desolations are decreed.

The revelation of God to the Hebrew people was always focused on the people having faith in God for salvation regardless of the amount of revelation He elected to yield. As the people did not respond God, in His love for them, continued to slowly increase the amount of knowledge they had about the promised Messiah. What they came to know was that God would send an anointed one who would be sacrificed for their sins. To be saved people had to believe in that truth from God. If they believed their actions would demonstrate their belief. God who is omniscient would know if they believe or not. But if they believed in God to the point of letting God direct how they lived then they were saved subject to the ultimate sacrifice of the Son of God in the future.

Why did the Children of Israel reject the Messiah?

The Hebrew people understood the prophecies very well. The children were taught the prophecies of ancient prophets and the Hebrew people were religious people. Hebrew prophets warned the Hebrew people over and over again of the forth coming of the Messiah. They were given in the book of Daniel, as well as other scripture, reasonable precise time guidelines regarding His birth. They were provided an amazing number of evidence events that should have made them ready to accept and worship the newborn Christ child. Yet they did not. The Jewish nation in Israel today does not accept Jesus Christ as the Messiah. They still have all the prophecies. They still have all the fulfillment of the prophecies and yet they do not believe. To Christians it seems amazing that the Children of Israel reject the Messiah when they were taught for hundreds and hundreds of years how to recognize and accept Jesus Christ as the Messiah.

Acts 7:51–53
"You stiff-necked people uncircumcised in heart and ears! You always resist the Holy Spirit; as your fathers did, so do you. Which of the prophets did your fathers not persecute? And they killed those who announced beforehand the coming of the righteous One, whom you have now betrayed and murdered? You who received the law as delivered by angels and did not keep it."

A committed follower of Christ, Stephen, gave us an insight into the nature of the Jewish people and why they refused to accept Jesus Christ as the Messiah. He said they knew what the teachings of the ancient Prophets were but they did not like those teachings and they refused to believe those teachings should direct their lives. Stephen said they did not want to yield to the teachings of the Prophets so they persecuted and in some cases murdered those God sent to be His messengers. Stephen's words were applicable to the Jews who did not believe in the time period of Christ's walking on the earth. They are applicable today. They are applicable to more than Jews. They are applicable to America and the rest of the world. Many of the peoples of the world, in fact the vast majority, are stiff-necked and uncon-verted in their heart and ears. They do not want to hear the Word. They do not want to follow the Word. They want to do their own thing in a way that gives them joy and perceived happiness. They do not want to submit to the power and righteousness of God. We are so much like the Jews of the day of Stephen that we cannot criticize them without criticizing ourselves.

The five hundred years between the Old Testament and New Testament

The Old Testament closes with the death of Malachi about 450 BC. We know God did not appoint a prophet to speak to the Children of Israel during this time. Many Bible scholars label this almost five hundred years as the intertestamental period or the gap between dispensations in the Old and New Testaments. Without a prophet, people began to divide into what we would call today polit-ical parties although to the Hebrew people they were a combination of political/religious parties. The two were yoked together. The lead-ers of these groups focused more on personal power and economic gain than seeking an understanding of what God wanted His people to do. Had they sought after God's will could they have found it? We do not know because God decided to be silent and not communicate with His people during this time. Why did God keep silent during this time? One reasonable answer is to help fulfill the prophecy outlined to the Israelites in Daniel. Another is to punish His people for their lack of faith. But the best answer is to help prepare the people of Israel for the coming Messiah. The Israelites suffered greatly in these years. They were the subject of war after war. They were in and out of slavery and toward the end of that time period they had little hope except for the promise of God that He would send the Messiah to save the Israelite people.

The promise of the coming Messiah should have made people ready to receive Jesus Christ as the coming Messiah. But the people chose to believe God would send a military ruler that would lead the Hebrew nation in victory over the hated Romans, who were in power at the end of this period. So the scene was set for the prophet, promised by God, to address the people. John the Baptist, was to be that prophet but his message was not one of military victory over the Romans but was one of a coming Messiah who would advance love, peace, and worship of Jehovah. The message of John the Baptist, and then the message of Jesus Christ, was unable to overcome the traditions and beliefs that had developed during the intertestamental period. As we understand these approximate five hundred years and the confusion that accompanied them, we can understand more about the Savior's ministry and renew our commitment to follow Him.

The Promised Messiah

Malachi 3:1
"Behold, I send my messenger, and he will prepare the way before me. And the Lord whom you seek will suddenly come to his temple; and the messenger of the covenant in whom you delight, behold, he is coming, says the LORD of hosts."

In Malachi 4:5, the promise of a prophet to succeed Malachi was given by Malachi to the Hebrew nation. Malachi predicted the coming of the Messiah as promised by God and as hoped for so fervently by the Israelites. He did not yet understand the mission of that Messiah. He only knew God would send the Messiah to save the Hebrew people. He had not placed the Messiah as being the Son of God and he certainly did not see the coming Messiah come in a "suffering servant" role. And Malachi added another promise the people did not understand perhaps because it had no timeline. He promised "Elijah the Prophet" would return as a forerunner of the coming Messiah. For the next five hundred years the Hebrew people looked forward to the coming Messiah, but still expected Him to be a mighty military ruler who would devastate all nations ruling over them.

It is important to understand that the fulfillment of the promise of the advent of "Elijah the Prophet" was not in error but was fulfilled through the coming of John the Baptist.

Matthew 11:13, 14
"For all the Prophets and the Law prophesied until John and if you are willing to accept it, he is Elijah who is come."

John the Baptist was not the same man as Elijah was but was the same promise of God. Elijah, Malachi, and John the Baptist all preached of the coming Messiah. The main difference is that John the Baptist understood that the coming Messiah was the Son of God, Jesus Christ. Old Testament prophets did not know this and were not ready to accept it. Malachi 3:1 is very importance because it helps us understand the nature of the Son of God.

Malachi 3:1
"Behold, I send my messenger, and he will prepare the way before me. And the Lord whom you seek will suddenly come to his temple; and the messenger of the covenant in whom you delight, behold, he is coming, says the LORD of hosts."

In the verse, Yahweh God is speaking, and He says that a prophet, "Elijah the Prophet" would prepare the way *"before me."* This means the LORD God Himself is coming. Then, God describes Himself *"the Lord"* as being *"the messenger of the covenant."* We also see that God outlines that *"the messenger of the covenant"* was fulfilled by Jesus. Therefore, *"Yahweh"* and *"the Lord"* are personified in Jesus.

We know the Hebrew people were not ready to accept Christ as the promised Messiah. Praise God, however, many Jews did accept Jesus Christ as their Savior. If that were not so we would not have the account of Matthew, Mark, Luke, John, Peter, Paul, and others who believed and repented of their unbelief. After salvation they dedicated their lives to the glory of Christ. Under the preaching of Peter three thousand people, we assume most were Jews, became believers on the Day of Pentecost. In the first seven chapters of the book of Acts the Jewish believers remained in Jerusalem. However, after the stoning of Stephen, it became apparent the torture, murder, and extinction of Christians, led by Saul of Tarsus, scattered these believers into Judea and Samaria. Fortunately they continued to witness their belief that Jesus Christ was the long-awaited Messiah.

Acts 8:1
"And Saul approved of His (Christs) execution and there arose on that day a great persecution against the Church in Jerusalem. And they were all scattered throughout the regions of Judea and Samaria, except the apostles."

In part because of the persecution and murder of Christians after the death, burial and resurrection of Christ, Christianity spread rapidly. It spread because of the commitment of Jewish and Gentile believers who put the cause of Christ above their own lives. It spread to the point that the Roman government became concerned Christians might revolt and overtake parts of the Roman Empire. Christianity spread to the point that somewhere between two hundred and three hundred years after the resurrection of Jesus, the influence of Christianity was a common and dominant power in shaping the thoughts of people.

However, that growth of Christianity did not continue because believers did not continue to keep the faith. They acted much like the Hebrew children. They were hot for Christ for a time after His resurrection. Then they grew cold and Christianity faded. Are we, today, any different? We have the prophecies of old. We have the spoken word of Christ. We have the Old and New Testaments yet our faith is hot for a spell and then we turn cold. The pattern of faithlessness in the Hebrew people is found in today's gentile population. It is eating into the moral fiber of America as it has in years past for countless groups of people

The Fulfillment of Prophecy

We learn in the Gospel of Luke that Gabriel, God's messenger, acting on the directions of God, delivered a message to a young Jewish girl named Mary. God had promised a Savior; the Messiah who would save The Jews and all of mankind, from their sin. God's promise was that Messiah would be delivered to earth through a young virgin of God's choosing.

This is the sensational and mysterious background truth of the events surrounding the birth of the Savior of Man. One of the Godhead of God the Father, God the Son and God the Holy Ghost, yes none other than Jesus Christ the Son of God stepped forward to become human in order to deliver humanity from the depravity of man's own sin and rebellion against God. Over two thousand years ago God determined it was time for the Savior to come to earth. God the Son elected to accept this challenge. God, as recorded in Genesis, before the creation of man, foretold that the birth of Jesus Christ, the Messiah would stop the revolt of Satan and implement his final destruction.

Genesis 3:15
"I will put enmity between you and the woman, and between your offspring and her offspring: he shall bruise your head, and you shalt bruise his heel."

Old Testament prophets, or spokesmen for God, had for hundreds of years prior to the birth of Christ, foretold of the virgin birth of the forthcoming Messiah. The Hebrew prophet, Isaiah, foretold of the virgin birth of the coming Messiah more than six hundred years before its advent.

Isaiah 7:14
"Therefore the Lord Himself will give you a sign:
Behold, the virgin shall conceive and bear a Son,
and shall call His name Immanuel."

The doctrine of the virgin birth is not a new teaching. The apostles and the first generation of Church fathers recognized the need to document, record and forward to successive generations the truth that was revealed to them. The advent of the Messiah formed a new relationship of God to man and gave man hope for eternity. The first century Church did not have the New Testament as foundation of its faith but did have the Old Testament and its record of God's promises. And they had the testimony of the Apostles who personally walked and worshipped with Jesus. The first century Church universally affirmed the supernatural origin of Jesus of Nazareth, as the revealed Messiah.

Isaiah 9:6
"For to us a child is born, to us a son is given, and
the government will be on His shoulders. And His
name will be called Wonderful Counselor, Mighty
God, Everlasting Father, prince of Peace."

Unfortunately, the Jewish world was not ready to accept the coming of Jesus Christ as the Messiah. Old Testament scripture is precise in its declaration that the coming Messiah would have the objective of establishing a spiritual kingdom for the purpose of defeating Satan and releasing man from the penalty of his sins. The prophecies proclaimed the coming New Testament, or new contract between God and man, would be one of grace and faith through Christ Jesus. The Old Testament gave sign after sign that should have been more than sufficient to justify the Israelites faith in Jesus Christ as the coming Messiah. The Messiah was said to descend from Abraham, from the tribe of Judah, and from the lineage of King David. Jesus Christ met that prophecy. The Old Testament said the Messiah would be born to a virgin in the city of Bethlehem. Jesus met that prophecy.

The Old Testament also prophesied the Messiah would preach, would be meek and compassionate and would be betrayed. It prophesied He would suffer and die of crucifixion and would rise again the third day. The children of Israel did not want to hear this truth. They did not want a Messiah that would be meek but wanted a King that would be a great warrior and gain independence and revenge against the Romans. They did not want a Messiah that would die and rise again the third day they wanted a Messiah that would be immortal and be above death because they were consumed with their oppression of Rome.

They should have known. They had the Old Testament which was written over a period of more than one thousand years. The Old Testament was specifically intended to announce the coming birth of the Messiah. It gave hundreds of prophecies of the coming Messiah. Every one of these prophecies was completely fulfilled prior to the birth of Jesus Christ. Each pointed to Jesus as the coming Messiah. They had proof that should not be challenged that these prophecies were made and fulfilled. The Greek translation of the Old Testament was written two hundred years before Christ's birth and was found in its original form in the Dead Sea Scrolls.

The Old Testament laid the foundation for the first advent of Jesus Christ but the world did not want to listen because they had conceptualized what the Messiah would be and would do. The first advent simply means the first coming of Christ. The world was not ready for the virgin birth of our Savior.

The Virgin Birth of Jesus

The New Testament Gospels of Matthew and Luke record the story of the birth of Jesus. God's Word, as recorded by Luke, reveals to us Jesus's birth was the result of the Holy Spirit working within Mary's body. The spiritual (Holy Spirit) and the physical (Mary's womb) were both involved. Only God could perform the miracle of the Incarnation. God, in His wisdom, ordained that Jesus Christ would come to earth as both God and man. The physical conception of Mary by God for the birth of Jesus is the means God elected to establish the existence of Jesus taking on the form of man while still being God. Scripture teaches that Jesus was fully human, with a physical body like ours. This He received from Mary. At the same time, Jesus was fully God, with an eternal, sinless nature. Jesus had the capacity to sin when He came down from heaven, because He had freedom of choice even as we have freedom of choice. However, because Christ was not born of man but born of God He was not imputed with sin as man is. Christ was not born with a sinful nature. He had to live a life here on earth and be faithful unto God the Father without sin.

Luke 1:27–28
To a virgin betrothed to a man whose name was Joseph, of the house of David. And the virgin's name was Mary. And he came to her and said, "Greetings, O favored one, the Lord is with you!"

Luke 1:31
And behold, you will conceive in your womb and bear a Son, and you shall call His name JESUS.

Luke 1:34–35
And Mary said to the angel, "How can this be, since I am a virgin?"
"And the angel answered her, "The Holy Spirit will come upon you, and the power of the Most High will overshadow you; therefore, the child who is to be born will be called Holy—The Son of God.

Luke 1:37–38
For nothing will be impossible with God."
Then Mary said, "Behold I am the servant of the Lord! Let it be to me according to your word."
And the angel departed from her."

We have stated previously that God created mankind perfect, without sin, but with the capacity to sin. God wanted man to return a free heartfelt love to God. The only way man can give a free heart felt love back to God was for him to have free choice of electing to trust and follow God with all his heart and mind or to disobey God and follow Satan.

God viewed Adam not just as a single man but as mankind. Adam was the creation of God and all of mankind would be burdened with Adam's choice to disobey God. Adam chose to disobey God. Man's penalty was physical and spiritual death. Spiritual death is total and eternal separation from God. When man made that choice he created a barrier between himself and God that man could not cure. God had to cure it and God never stopped loving mankind. Even before we were created, God knew mankind would eventually be imputed with a sin nature because of Adam's sin. Yet God created a plan prior to the beginning of time to bring man back into God's grace.

We have a tendency to believe the decision of God to create the plan of salvation for man was of God the Father. We have a tendency to think God sent Jesus Christ, His Son, to earth to provide a plan of salvation for mankind. We, in so thinking, fail to recognize the Jesus Christ is also part of the Godhead or Trinity. God the Father did conceive the plan of salvation that required a perfect, sinless being come to earth, be tempted to sin in every way mankind is tempted, and yet never sin. God the Father conceived of a plan whereby the Son of God would be that sacrifice for mankind and God would rise Jesus the third day with victory over death.

We must also recognize that Jesus Christ, part of the Godhead, equal with God the Father, had such great love for mankind that He volunteered to be the one who would sacrifice His throne in heaven. He volunteered to face the temptation of the world, and to live a perfect, sinless life for about thirty-three years. And He volunteered to die on Calvary for our sins. Jesus was not sent, He volunteered.

Jesus came to earth because He loves us. He came to earth because man was doomed to eternity in Hell separated from God. He came to earth because the Godhead, God the Father, God the Son and God the Holy Spirit all loved man enough to sacrifice for us. Jesus came to earth because someone, who was perfect and sinless had to die for the sins of man.

The Gospel of Luke gives us a detailed account of the interface between God and Mary thus the humanity of Christ. The book of John is more direct in proclaiming the humanity of Jesus Christ while retaining the deity of God.

John 1:14
"And the Word became flesh and dwelt among us.
And we have seen His glory, glory as of the only
Son from the Father, full of grace and truth."

Adam sinned against God. With Adam's sin, man took on the nature of sin, and from that time forth all of mankind passed on the sin nature through the lineage of Adam. Jesus, however, did not have the lineage of Adam because He was not born of an earthly father. Jesus was not created with His birth but was transformed from heaven's portals to earth. It is important for us to understand the significance of Jesus having the earthly mother Mary. God placed on Christ the capacity to be human through Mary. Yet Christ retained the deity of God. Jesus was not born in sin; that is, He had no sin nature. Man has a sin nature. We are born with that sin nature and it is passed down from generation to generation. The virgin birth circumvented the transmission of the sin nature and allowed the eternal God to become a perfect man. The fact Jesus did not have a sin nature at birth does not mean he did not feel and face temptation. Jesus had the capacity to sin. He felt temptation from Satan to sin but never did yield to temptation.

Romans 5:12
"Therefore, just as sin came into the world through
one man, and death through sin, and so death
spread to all men because all sinned."

Romans 5:17
"For if, because of one man's trespass, death reigned
through that one man, much more will those who receive

abundant of grace and the free gift of righteousness
reign in life through the one man, Jesus Christ."

Romans 5:19
"For as by the one man's disobedience the many
were made sinners, so by the one man's obedience
the many will be made righteous."

The Doctrine of Incarnation

The doctrine of **incarnation** is that Jesus Christ, the second of the Triade of God the Father, God the Son and the Holy Spirit, voluntarily came down from Heaven to earth, became flesh, assumed a human nature, and became a man in the form of Jesus. Jesus is outlined in Scripture as the second person of the Trinity. One of the mysteries of God's Word is the clear definite statements of God that Jesus Christ, the Son of God is both human and God. The virgin birth facilitated this change that was planned before the beginning of time. Jesus Christ volunteered to come down from His throne on high with God the Father and the Holy Spirit and to enter earth becoming both God and man. This was accomplished in that the virgin birth gave Jesus an earthly mother but a heavenly father. Joseph was not the father of Jesus. Perhaps we should recognize that there is no mystery about the reality of Jesus being both God and man. The mystery is how God could accomplish this miracle.

A term theologians sometimes use to describe how God the Son took on human nature and yet remained fully God is the hypostatic union. The English adjective is a derivative of the Greek word hypostasis. The Greed word is found in the New Testament four times. It defines Jesus to be "the radiance of the Glory of God and the exact imprint of His nature." The discussion of the incarnate being of Christ leads us into the discussion of the Trinity or Godhead. We know God is one yet has three distinct natures. Each nature is separate and distinct from the other. And yet all three are made in the same imprint or nature as each other. In English hypostatic means personal and union means to join so what we find hypostatic union to refer to is the personal union of Jesus Christ's two natures, those of God and Human.

John 1:14
"And the Word became flesh and dwelt among us, and we have seen His glory, glory as of the only Son from the Father, full of grace and truth."

The virgin birth of Jesus was the way God introduced into the world the two natures of the Messiah. With His virgin birth, Jesus took on the nature of man. They are united. While on earth, Jesus functioned within human limitations. This is seen in His weariness in the story of the woman by the well.

John 4:6
"Jacob's well was there. So Jesus, wearied as He was from His journey, was sitting by the well. It was about the sixth hour."

Often, however, we see Jesus operating in the power of His deity.

John 11:43
"When He had said these things, He cried with a loud voice, "Lazarus, come forth!"

The hypostatic union is more easily understood as the Doctrine of Incarnation. The Doctrine of incarnation is the teaching that Christ was both God and Human. The Doctrine of Incarnation includes the complex concept of how Jesus could have always existed and was not a created being, yet was conceived by Mary for the purpose of an earthly physical birth. The two concepts reflect the two natures of Christ.

The concept of Jesus being both God and human is mind-stretching and hard to grasp. However it gives us reassurance that Jesus can and will save us from our sins. Jesus did not have to become man to understand our sinful state and the depth of Satan's temptation. Jesus is God and knows all. He already knew about our sinful state, about our weakness for following Satan, and the power of our temptation. However, Jesus had to come to earth and become man so He could be tempted just as we are and could reject Satan's temptation. Only in that manner could His death on the cross justify our sins and not be needed for his own.

Jesus Christ, the human paid the price for our sins by His death on the cross. Jesus Christ, part of the Godhead, saved us from our sins by His resurrection from the grave and His victory over death for all time to come. No being can satisfy the longing of the human heart like Jesus Christ. That is because we have the Holy Spirit ever reaching out for us and influencing us to trust God and to honor Him. Yes, we also, because of man's failure to continually honor God, have imputed in us the nature of sin, but praise God we also have in us the Holy Spirit to guide us.

The Sinless Life

In chapter 3, The Doctrine of Sin," we outlined that *"sin is transgression of the law."* Paul tells us that **"all have sinned and fall short of the glory of God"** (Romans 3:23). Paul later tells us **"The wages of sin is death"** (Romans 6:23). God will not compromise with His holy and righteous law. Jesus said that *"one jot or tittle will by no means pass from the law till all is fulfilled"* (Matthew 5:18). The penalty for breaking that law will be paid.

Since we have all sinned, we have all earned spiritual death. Spiritual death is eternal separation from God. That is the fate of all human beings—unless in some way the price of our sins could be paid by another. Jesus did this. Chapter 4, "The Doctrine of God the Father," outlines the fact that God created a plan for the redemption of man. No life of an ordinary human being could be sufficient to satisfy the law's demand for all of humanity. A life that could satisfy the penalty for the sins would have to be a life that had no sin. So to satisfy the demands of God, the person who would pay the price of our sins would have to have a sinless life or His death would only pay for His own sins. If Jesus was to be the redeemer of mankind, he had to live a sinless life.

2 Corinthians 5:21
"For our sake He made Him to be sin who knew no sin, so that in Him we might become the righteousness of God."

Jesus Christ did not have to be told by God the Father why He was sent to earth to redeem man from his sin. Jesus is God. Jesus is part of the Godhead that made the decision prior to the beginning of time that this would be the redemption of man. Jesus knew His purpose of coming to earth and becoming man in addition to God, was to take on the sin of man and give His life in payment for that sin. In the book of John, as well as other places in Scripture, Jesus predicts His forthcoming crucifixion.

John 12:27
"Now is my soul troubled, and what shall I say? 'Father, save me from this hour'? But for this purpose I have come to this hour."

At His trials the accusers of Jesus had to resort to false witnesses because no one could testify to any wrong He had ever committed. Even those who were not His disciples agreed that the character of Jesus of Nazareth was without blame. Pilate's verdict was, *"I find no fault in Him."*

John 19:6
When the chief priests and officers saw Him, they cried out, saying, "Crucify Him, crucify Him!" Pilate said to them, "Take Him yourselves and crucify Him, for I find no guilt in Him."

The centurion, who oversaw Jesus's execution, having experienced time with Christ stated, *"Certainly this was a righteous Man!"* Jesus lived a sinless and virtuous life as confirmed by those who knew and observed Him in everyday life, as well as difficult circumstances.

The essence of authentication of the perfect life of Jesus came, however, from none other than God Himself. As Jesus was entering His ministry period God looked down at the moment of baptizing

Christ by John the Baptist and said, *"This is my Son, whom I love with Him I am well pleased."*

Matthew 3:16–17
And when Jesus was baptized, immediately He went up from the water; and behold, the heavens were opened to Him, and He saw the Spirit of God descending like a dove and coming to rest on Him. And behold, a voice came from heaven said, "This is my beloved Son, with whom I am well pleased."

God will not coexist with sin. Yet He looked upon Jesus who had left His thrown in Glory to become equal with man, and God said He was pleased. That meant Jesus had fulfilled every desire of God and was without sin. His state of being sinless enabled Christ to take on our sin and be our Savior.

The Miracles of Jesus

Jesus's life was marked by miracles from the beginning. He was born of a virgin, He turned water into wine, He walked on water, and He quieted the storm. He multiplied bread to feed the multitude, He opened the eyes of the blind, and He healed the lame and made lepers whole again. He healed all manner of sicknesses among all kinds of people, cast out demons and even raised the dead to life again. Jesus pointed to the miracles as proof of who He was. Jesus used the miracles as credentials to us that He was, and is, the Son of God.

John 10:25
"Jesus answered them, "I told you and you do not believe. The works that I do in My Father's name bear witness about me,"

John 10:37–38
"If I am not doing the works of My Father then do not believe me; but if I do them, even though you do not believe me, believe the works, that you may know and understand that the Father is in me, and I am in the Father."

The messengers from John the Baptist, the forerunner of Christ, ask Christ if He was the one who had come to fulfill all the messianic prophecies. The answer Jesus gave them is also His answer to us:

Matthew 11:4–5
Jesus answered them, "Go and tell John what you hear and see: The blind receive their sight and the lame walk; lepers are cleansed and the deaf hear; the dead are raised up and the poor have the good news preached to them."

Many well intentioned Christians believe the motivation of Jesus to heal the sick and perform miracles was done because of His compassion for the needy. Jesus did, and does, love mankind and has great compassion for those in need. However, He understood that our spiritual needs are much greater than our physical needs. Therefore, His ultimate motivation for everything He did was to provide redemption for the sins of mankind. The miracles Christ performed met those criteria. Jesus fully expected John the Baptist to understand that the miracles He performed would be all the evidence John needed to believe He was the Messiah. The miracles demonstrated clearly who Jesus was, just as He intended. He healed one paralyzed man with the accompanying words, *"Son, your sins are forgiven you"* (Mark 2:5). He explained to those gathered around Him that He had healed the man so they could know He was the Messiah for whom they had searched throughout the centuries. Christ performed His miracles to establish in the minds of mankind that He was the long awaited Messiah.

Mark 2:3–5
"Then they came, bringing a paralytic carried by four men. And when they could not come near Him because of the crowd, they removed the roof above him. And when they had made an opening, they let down the bed on which the paralytic lay. When Jesus saw their faith, He said to the paralytic, "Son, your sins are forgiven."

The miracles of Jesus are listed here in our best understanding of their identification of chronicle order.

1. Born of a Virgin
2. Changing water into wine
3. Healing of the officer's son
4. Healing of the demoniac
5. Healing of Peter's mother-in-law
6. Healing of the sick in general
7. Catching a host of fish
8. Healing a leper
9. Healing a Centurion's Servant
10. Healing a paralyzed man
11. Healing a withered hand
12. Raising a widow's son
13. Calming the Storm
14. Healing a man possessed by demons
15. Healing a woman with internal bleeding
16. Raising Jairus's daughter
17. Healing two blind men
18. Healing a mute man possessed with demons
19. Healing a thirty-eight-year invalid
20. Feeding five thousand men and their families
21. Walking on water
22. Healing a deaf man
23. Feeding four thousand men and their families
24. Healing two blind men
25. Catching a fish with a coin in its mouth
26. Healing a blind and mute man
27. Healing a woman with an eighteen-year-old infirmity
28. Healing a man with dropsy
29. Healing ten lepers
30. Raising of Lazarus
31. Healing of blind Bartimaeus
32. Curses the fig tree so it gave no fruit
33. Restored a severed ear

34. Resurrected from the dead
35. Catching 153 fish
36. The Ascension of Jesus

In the physical miracles, such as healing ten lepers, Christ, took the laws of nature set by God and set them aside to perform something that was obvious to even the strongest disbeliever. They could not be denied as supernatural. Spiritual and moral miracles such as cleansing people of demons broke Satan's grasp on these people leading them to the point of salvation through their faith.

The greatest miracle was the resurrection of Christ followed by the miracle of His ascension back to glory. These miracles convince us of Christ's willingness to go all the way to provide a way for His people to be redeemed.

Prophecy of His Death and Resurrection

Prophecies of Christ's Death, Burial, and Resurrection		
Prophecy Scripture	*Prophecy Meaning*	*Fulfillment Scripture*
Hosea 6:1–2 *Come, and let us return to the Lord; For He has torn us that He might heal us; He has struck us down and He will bind us up. After two days He will revive us; On the third day He will raise us up, That we may live before Him.*	*Hundreds of years before Christ, Old Testament prophecy foretold of His death his burial and His resurrection the third day. In Luke the fulfillment of that prophecy is concluded.*	Luke 24:5–7 *And, as they were frightened and bowed their faces to the ground, the men said to them, "Why do you seek the living among the dead? He is not here, but has risen! Remember how He told you while He was still in Galilee, 'That the Son of Man must be delivered into the hands of sinful men, and be crucified, and the third day rise."*

Jonah 1:17	Christ Himself refers to	Matthew 12:40
and the Lord appointed a great fish to swallow up Jonah. And Jonah was in the belly of the fish three days and three nights.	the Old Testament record of Jonah in the great fish and Himself in the grave and connects the resurrection of both	For just as Jonah was three days and three nights in the belly of the great fish, so will the Son of Man be three days and three nights in the heart of the earth.
Isaiah 53:3 He was despised and rejected by men, A Man of sorrows and acquainted with grief. And as one from whom men hide their faces He was despised and we esteemed Him not.	Old Testament foretells of His rejection by Jew and Gentile while New Testament tells of the fulfillment of that prophecy	John 1:10–11 He was in the world and the world was made through Him, yet the world did not know Him. He came to His own, and His own people did not receive Him.
Isaiah 53:5 But He pierced for our transgressions, He was crushed for our iniquities; Upon Him was the chastisement that bought us peace and with His wounds we are healed.	Old Testament foretells of His rejection by Jew and Gentile while New Testament tells of the fulfillment of that prophecy	John 19:28–30 After this, Jesus, knowing that all was now finished, said (to fulfill the Scripture), "I thirst." A jar full of sour wine stood there and they put a sponge full of the sour wine on a hyssop branch and held it in His mouth. When Jesus had received the sour wine, He said "It is finished," and He bowed His head and gave up His spirit.
Psalm 16:10 For You will not abandon my soul to Sheol, or let Your Holy One see corruption.	Old Testament foretells of His rejection by Jew and Gentile while New Testament tells of the fulfillment of that prophecy	Acts 2:31 He foresaw and spoke about the resurrection of the Christ, that He was not abandoned to Hades, nor did His flesh see corruption.

The sacrificial death of Jesus was prophesied in the Old Testament long before He came to earth to walk among men. The New Testament records over sixty prophecies which were directly fulfilled at the birth of Jesus. Throughout history, those who received Jesus as their personal Savior proclaimed His name and the forgiveness of sins which is found in Him alone. The Apostle Paul preached to Jews and Gentiles that the saving power of Jesus Christ was the same saving power that had been prophesied through the ages in the Old Testament.

1 Corinthians 15:1–4

"Now I would remind you brothers, of the gospel I preached to you, which you received, in which you stand. And by which you are saved, if you hold fast that word which I preached to you—unless you believed in vain. For I delivered to you as of first importance what I also received: that Christ died for our sins according to the Scriptures, that He was buried, that He was raised on the third day in accordance with the Scriptures."

The scripture Paul refers to, as he writes to the Church in Corinth, is the Old Testament Prophecies of the death burial and resurrection of Jesus. Our belief in Jesus Christ as the one who paid for our sins on Calvary needs to be accepted in the light of truth. That is in the light of the fulfillment of Old Testament Prophecy because within that light we begin to understand just who Christ is and what He accomplished for us. We need to understand why His death on the Cross and His total complete fulfillment of scripture prophecy is vital to our salvation. If Jesus Christ is not the Son of God incarnate in the flesh, meaning He took on the nature of both God and human, then His death is not sufficient to save us. If Jesus Christ is not the one sent by God the Father; if He is not the one of the Godhead who volunteered to come to earth and become man so He could die for our sins, then His death was in vain. The Jews had trouble accepting Jesus as the Messiah primarily because He died a physical death. They did not believe in His physical resurrection. This is understandable in terms of logic because resurrection from the dead was considered to be physically impossible. Jews who would not believe in the physical resurrection of Christ would not believe in His power over death demonstrated during His life on earth. To help us understand what the Jewish people failed to understand we need to look at the Old Testament prophecy of the resurrection.

CHAPTER SIX

The Doctrine of Jesus the Redeemer

Jesus Pays for Man's Sin

Why the Cross?

Mel Gibson's film *The Passion of the Christ* brought to the attention of tens of thousands and perhaps millions of people the reality that Jesus Christ voluntarily gave up His life to pay the price of our sins. At no time have most of us every seen a more vivid picture of the suffering Jesus endured to pay the price of our sins. But God is all powerful, He is omniscience and being all powerful why could He not have discovered a more gentle way of paying for our sins? Have you ever wondered this? Most people have that thought go through their mind. Two renowned doctors of religion in the thirteenth century also asked these questions. St. Augustine of Hippo and St. Thomas Aquinas, biblical scholars of their time and throughout history came up with two questions. They are the following:

1. Is there another way that Jesus could have paid the price of our sins, other than death, and yet met the expectations of His Father? And if death, indeed, was required to pay for our sins does that mean God is limited in His ability to find solutions to problems?

2. If the price of our sins had to be death and the blood had to flow why could He not have been the subject of much less suffering and death? And if God could not find a solution to the problem of man's sins other than crucifixion on the cross what does that say about God being a kind and gentle God?

   We know in Scripture that God is all powerful and nothing is impossible for God. Therefore the answer is Yes, God could have selected another plan for our salvation.

Luke 1:37
"For nothing will be impossible with God."

It is true that nothing is impossible for God. But it is also true that God is a just God and that means God will do what is right and there is a difference between right and wrong. There is a difference between righteousness and sin. God knows the difference. Often, man knows the difference also, although in a much lesser way than God. Yes, man knows the price of sin is death because it is imputed into us yet we often vary from that standard. God abides by a strict standard of righteousness and demands that man also abide by the same standard. Look at what Jesus told Peter in Matthew the sixteenth chapter. This came after Peter was told Christ had to go to Calvary and be killed and would raise up the third day. Peter told Christ "Far be it from you, Lord! This shall never happen to you." Jesus replied:

Matthew 16:23
"But He turned and said to Peter, 'Get behind me, Satan! You are a hindrance to me; for you are not setting your mind on the things of God, but on the things of man."

God further explains the price for sin. There is a price for sin that is just and God determines what is just. In Romans 6:23 He told us the price of sin is death.

Romans 6:23
"For the wages of sin is death, but the free gift of God is eternal life in Christ Jesus our Lord."

So God reveals to us the answer to the questions listed above. God is a just God which means God is a Holy God. The combination means God's standard for one who sins is that the just penalty for that is death. Therefore if Jesus is to pay the price of our sins He had to pay that price in death. And because mankind is so very sinful, so distant from God by nature, the price had to be severe. The Cross of Calvary met that price.

The Crucifixion of Christ

When Christ walked on earth the Sanhedrin served Israel as the equivalent of America's Congress, Supreme Court and the national religion; if we had a national religion. The Sanhedrin felt threatened by the growing followers of Jesus Christ. They hated Jesus because He openly condemned them for their selfish sins. They were people of great pride and Christ challenged their pride. They were people of great power and Christ questioned the reality of such power. Most members of the Sanhedrin were solid Israel citizens with the love of their country. However, most had, over time, learned to enjoy the power and glory of being on the Sanhedrin. They adopted the Hebrew practices and adopted them to build up the Sanhedrin. Jesus told them openly they were misguided in their purpose for the state and not worthy of their goals.

They hated Jesus because He forced them to look at themselves. They saw but did not want to believe the teachings of Christ. They became jealous of the massive crowds that followed Jesus and of His miracles. They could not explain His source of power and resented it. Everywhere they went people asked them to explain what this man named Jesus had done. They could not. They finally decided they had to find a way to kill Him. However, the Sanhedrin did not have the right to kill a man without the approval of the Roman governor. So they took Jesus to Pilate the Roman Governor and charged Him with trying to start an uprising against Rome.

Although no evidence was presented against Jesus at His mock trial, the Jewish people, as a whole and especially the Jewish leaders, demanded that He be crucified. In an attempt to satisfy the desires of the Jewish leaders Pilate, the Roman governor, had Jesus scourged or flogged. Pilate hoped this would satisfy the Jewish leaders and it would not be necessary to crucify Jesus. Scourging was done with a whip made of strips of leather. Each strip had two balls of lead at the end. Jesus's clothes were removed and His hands were tied to a pole above His head. As He was whipped the balls of lead would at first bruise and then sink into His back as the tissues broke down under the repeated beating. Blood flowed first from the broken skin and then from the muscles and veins as they were lacerated. Jewish law limited the number of scourges to forty, and the Pharisees limited it to thirty-nine in case they miscounted. The road to Calvary, called Via Delarosa, was an excruciating journey. The patibulum of the cross was tied across His shoulders. The procession of the condemned Christ, two thieves, and the execution detail of Roman soldiers headed by a centurion, began the 650 Yard journey to Golgotha. The rough beam dug into the lacerated shoulders of Christ. The weakened and bleeding Christ became unable to carry the beam, so a visitor from Cyrene who happened to be looking on was forced to carry it the rest of the way.

At the scene of the execution Jesus was again stripped of His clothing except for a loin cloth. Jesus was thrown to the ground on top of the patibulum and a large square nail was driven though the small depression in the front of each wrist. Jesus was then lifted to the top of the stipes. A sign reading "Jesus of Nazareth, King of the Jews" was nailed in place.

At the trial Pilate found no evidence of violation of Roman law but yielded to the pressure of Jewish leaders to have Jesus killed. They decided to use the common method of killing criminals which was crucifixion. Crucifixion involved placing a cross of heavy wooden timbers on the ground, and having the victim lay down on the cross. Roman soldiers would then nail his hands and his feet to the cross with huge spikes. The Roman cross consisted of an upright pole and a cross arm. The upright pole was called the stipes. The cross arm was called the patibulum. The patibulum could be attached either toward the top of the stipes to form a "T" or lower down to form what was typically call the "Latin cross." Most historical evidence suggests that it was the "T" shaped cross used to crucify Christ.

The cross was then lifted and dropped into a hole that had been dug into the ground and the total weight of the victim's body tore the hands and feet and caused ripping and tearing of flesh. The pain was almost beyond human endurance. Blood began streaming out of the wounds and rushing through the body as shock set in.

The intent was to make the crucifixion as painful as possible so it would serve as a deterrent to other criminals. As the victim laid on the "T" cross, they would have to put pressure on their spiked feet to lift the body so they could get a breath. This activity went on and on as the bodily pain increased with the passage of time. As the cells of the body began to break down the victims of crucifixion would die. Death could be from a few hours to a few days depending on the health and strength of the victim.

Jesus in His flesh feared the cross. But Jesus in His Spirit welcomed the cross. This is because He came for the very purpose of dying on the Cross of Calvary for our sins. Even with all the pain, Jesus's focus was on the millions of people who depended on Him paying the price for our salvation. A wonderful spiritual song recites the words "When He was on the Cross, I was on His mind" That song captures the spirit of Christ at Calvary. He said *"Father, forgive them for they know not what they do."*

On either side of Him there was a thief crucified with Him. When one of them expressed faith in Jesus, the Savior answered, *"Today shalt thou be with me in paradise."* As His body weakened and His pain increased He finally moaned, *"I thirst,"* and was offered vinegar, which He would not drink. God blotted out the sun as if to let us know how black the deed being done was. Then, out of the blackness Jesus cried, *"My God, My God, why hast Thou forsaken me?"* His final words expressed his complete surrender to the will of God as He said, *"It is finished; Father into Thy hands I commend my spirit."* In truth, the Romans and Jews at Calvary did not take His life. He gave it up voluntarily and suffered the pain of the cross for you and me.

Mark 15:22, 25–27, 33–34, 37; John 19:19–20
And they brought Him to the place called Golgotha (which means "Place of a Skull)…and It was the third hour when they crucified Him. And the inscription of the charge against Him read: "The King of the Jews." And with Him they crucified two robbers, one on His right and one on His left… and when the sixth hour had come there was darkness over the whole land until the ninth hour, and at the ninth hour Jesus cried with a loud voice, "Eloi, Eloi, lerna sabachthani?" which means "My God, My God why have You forsaken me?"

Sequence of Events at Calvary

Jesus was on the Cross at Calvary for six hours, and, with His life and words, He left us a most beautiful testimony of God's love, sin, redemption, the cross, forgiveness, heaven, Hell, the Church, and prophecies fulfilled. The sequence of events was as follows:

1. His arrival at Golgotha (Golgotha =Skull, Calvary) (Mark 15:22)
2. He was offered a benumbing drink (wine mixed with gall, myrrh) which He declined (Mark 15:23; Matthew 27:34)
3. The Romans stripped His clothes off of Him (Mark 15:24, John 19:23–24)
4. The Crucifixion (Mark 15:24–25, at 9:00 AM)
5. The Title "Jesus of Nazareth, King of the Jews" (Mark 15:26)
6. First Words: *"Father, forgive them, for they do not know what they are doing"* (Lk. 23:34).
7. The parting of Jesus's garments (Mt. 27:25, Jn. 19:23–24)
8. Jesus mocked (Mt. 27:39–44, Mk. 15:27–32)
9. The thieves rail on Him, but one believes (Lk. 23:39–43)
10. Second Words: *"Truly, I say to you, today you will be with me in Paradise"* (Lk. 23:43)
11. Third Words: *"Jesus said to His mother: "Woman, this is your son." Then to the disciple He said: "this is your mother"* (Jn. 19:26–27).
12. The darkness fell on the earth (Mt. 27:45, Mk. 15:33).
13. Fourth Words: *"And about three o'clock Jesus cried out with a loud voice: "Eloi, Eloi, lema sabackthani?" which means "My God, my God, why have you forsaken me?"* (Mt. 27:46, Mk. 15:34).
14. Fifth Words: *"I thirst"* (Jn. 19:28).
15. Jesus is given a sponge with vinegar, sour wine (Jn. 19:29).
16. Sixth Words: *"It is finished," "it is accomplished"* (Jn. 19:30).

17. Seventh Words: ***Jesus cried out in a loud voice, "Father, into your hands I commend my Spirit"*** (Lk. 23:46).
18. Breaking of the bones of the two thieves (Jn. 19:32–33).
19. The side of Jesus pierced, with blood and water coming out (Jn. 19:34).
20. The curtain of the Temple was torn in two, and the earthquake (Mt. 27:51–54, Mk. 15:38).
21. Jesus is taken down from the Cross (Mk. 15:46, Lk. 23:53).
22. The burial of Jesus (Mt. 27:5, Mk. 15:46, Lk. 23:53, Jn. 19).

Between the Cross and the Resurrection

Scripture tells us Jesus was in the "heart of the earth" for three days and three nights. He uses the three days and nights Jonah was in the great fish to relate the reality of Christ being in the heart of the earth three days and three nights.

Matthew 12:40
"For just as Jonah was three days and three nights in the belly of the great fish, so will the Son of Man be three days and three nights in the heart of the earth."

Yet scripture also clearly tells us Jesus was not in the tomb for three twenty-four-hour days as we consider a solar day. How is this difference explained? First let's acknowledge that Scripture tells us, without controversy, that Christ was crucified on Friday. In several of the Gospels we are told Jesus was taken to the Chief Priests, scribes and elders of the Sanhedrin early in the morning of Friday or the day before the Sabbath. In Jewish understanding of a twenty-four-hour solar day Christ does not have to be in the tomb for a full twenty-four hours on Friday for Friday to count as a day. To the Jew the day Friday began with sundown on Thursday and ended with sundown on Friday. Anything that happened in that time span would be considered Friday and they made no separation of a partial day of Friday. The Scripture does not tell us Jesus was in the tomb a full seventy-two hours. It says three days and three nights. Scripture tells us when Jesus was crucified.

When was Jesus Crucified?	
Mark 15:25 *"Now it was the third hour, when they crucified Him."*	John 19:14 *"Now it was the day of Preparation of the Passover, It was about the sixth hour. He said to the Jews, behold your King!"*

This is a scripture that provides ammunition for those who try to show the Bible contains error. Mark and John appear to site a difference of opinion as to when Jesus was crucified. However, more study of the scriptures shows they say the same thing. Mark is speaking in Hebrew thought pattern while John is talking to the Jews and speaking in the language of Romans. The Jewish Friday began at sundown or about 6 PM of the previous Thursday night and ended with sundown Friday. The Roman time is the same as English and American time. Roman time would be that 12:00 AM would be the same of our 12:00 AM. Roman time was, therefore ahead of Jewish time.

All scripture records Jesus as being crucified approximately 9:00 AM and enduring the torture of crucifixion for about six hours. He was removed from the cross at about 3:00 PM. Scripture also shows that the morning of the first day of the week (Sunday) the women found the tomb to be empty and the stone rolled away. We can therefore recognize that Jesus's body was in the tomb as follows according to the Jewish time system:

- From about 3:00 PM Friday to Sundown Friday—the first day. This is because although it was not a twenty-four-hour day the Jews counted it as a full day. This is recorded as the day of Sabbath preparation.
- From Sundown Friday through Sundown Saturday—the second day. This was a full twenty-four-hour day and rec-

ognized by Jews as a full day. This was also the Sabbath Day.

- From Sundown Saturday to Sundown Sunday. However Jesus was discovered by the women at dawn Sunday to be risen from the grave. This was therefore a partial day of Sunday but recognized by the Jews as a full day since a partial day is counted as a full day.
- The three nights prophesied as clearly Friday night, Saturday night, and Sunday night.

During the period of time Christ was in the tomb what did He do and where did He go? We have limited scripture on this but those who say Christ did not want us to understand the answer to this question overlook certain specific scriptures.

1 Peter 3:18–19
"For Christ also suffered once for sins, the righteous for the unrighteous, that He might bring us to God, being put to death in the flesh but made alive by the Spirit, in which He went and proclaimed to the spirits in prison."

So many people have huge trouble reconciling the fact that sinless Jesus Christ descended into the "middle of the earth" for an unknown period of time. We know it occurred after His death but before His resurrection. To understand this we have to grasp these questions and answers:

- "Where is the middle of the earth, Hades, Hell, or the tomb"?
- "Did Jesus's spiritual and earthly body descend or just the spirit"
- "Why did He descend into the middle of the earth?"

In Hebrew the word to describe the realm of the dead is Sheol. This means the place of the dead. Because the Old Testament was basically written in Hebrew the word for the realm of the dead in the Old Testament is Sheol. It means where the dead or those who have died a physical death go who have physically died. There are no bodies there so Sheol is the place of souls and spirits. Early recordings of the Old Testament show God's revelation of Sheol as very limited. But early recordings of the Old Testament reflect Sheol as the lowest parts of the earth and a place no one could avoid or escape. Toward the end of the Old Testament, God revealed He would provide a resurrection of the dead (*Isaiah 26:19*). God tells us Sheol will not contain the dead forever. Instead, God tells us the coming and promised Messiah, will conquer death. When that happens, God said faith will be rewarded as righteousness and righteousness with everlasting life. Those without faith in God and God's promise of the coming Messiah will be denied victory over death. They will experience eternal death and separation from God.

Sheol is divided into two divisions and those who had faith is God are counted as righteous and resided in a part of Sheol called Abraham's Bosom. The place for those without faith is just described as Sheol.

With the death, burial and resurrection of Jesus the promise of the coming Messiah was fulfilled. With the death, burial, and resurrection of Jesus the revelation that the coming Messiah was the Son of God, Jesus Christ, was completed. God's Word records in the New Testament that after the resurrection of Christ believers in Sheol will go immediately to be with the Lord, where He abides around His throne.

2 Corinthians 5:8
"Yes we are of good courage, and we would rather be away from the body and at home with the Lord."

Sheol in the Old Testament and Hades in the New Testament is a place where those who were not found faithful in the Old Testament reside. They are in torment although not as great as it will be later when they go to the Lake of Fire. The Lake of Fire is known as Hell.

Luke 16:23
"And in Hades, being in great torment he lifted up his eyes and saw Abraham far off and Lazarus at his side."

In the New Testament the word "Hades" is used to describe the place in New Testament time where nonbelievers wait, in torment, for the second coming of our Savior. Those who believed in the coming Messiah as God promised and who were found faithful to God, after Jesus went down to the depth of Hades and resurrected them spiritually, went to the Throne of God in Heaven to await the End Times.

Hades today refers to a place for the spiritually dead. The rich man said he lifted up his eyes in Hades (not Hell) and was in torment. This tells us that although Hades is a temporary place for souls to wait, it has torments. Note this does not yet mean the "Lake of Fire" (Hell). This scripture also tells us a man lifted up his eyes and saw Abraham and Lazarus in Abraham's bosom (also referred to as Abraham's side) afar off.

Note: This event took place in the Old Testament when Hades had a realm that contained nonbelievers and a realm that separately contained believers. Both groups were in Hades but in very different sections of Hades. Therefore the great chasm described in Luke 16:26 is an event that happened in the Old Testament and is being described in the New Testament period.

Luke 16:26
"And besides all this, between us and you there is a great chasm has been fixed, in order that those who would want too pass from here to you may not be able, and none may cross from there to us."

When Jesus died on the cross because of the Crucifixion, His soul went immediately to "Paradise" or "Abraham's bosom." His fleshly body stayed in the tomb. However the Spirit of Christ went to "Abraham's bosom" not to reside there but to deliver all believers who had believed in the promises of God, including the promise of the coming Messiah. Christ claimed them and took them to Heaven to be with Him

Resurrection from the Dead

The resurrection of Jesus Christ is the very heart of Christianity. The apostle Paul, writing to the church at Corinth and ultimately to all mankind outlines the importance of the resurrection of Christ on 1 Corinthians.

1 Corinthians 15:12–14
"Now if Christ is proclaimed as raised from the dead, how do some of you say that there is no resurrection of the dead? But if there is no resurrection of the dead, then not even Christ has been raised. And if Christ has not been raised, then our preaching is in vain and your faith is in vain."

If Jesus Christ was not raised from the dead there is no victory over death. The price of dying for our sins that Jesus paid on Calvary was insufficient to satisfy the debt of our sins unless He would then be raised from the dead. Paul goes on to say in 1 Corinthians that if Jesus Christ was not raised from the dead then He, and all those who have preached and taught Jesus to be the Messiah and the Savior of mankind, are liars and not worth being followed. Paul even goes farther than that. He declares that those who have already died but did not believe in God's promise of the coming Messiah as their hope for eternal salvation, are condemned to eternal separation from God and will eventually be caste into the Lake of Fire. However, Paul reassures us that all is not lost because Christ has been raised.

1 Corinthians 15:20
"But in fact, Christ has been raised from the dead, the first fruits of those who have fallen asleep."

Paul assures all of mankind that the truth is that Jesus Christ was raised from the dead. God promised His resurrection and God delivered. Many hundreds of people, living in the day of His resurrection, testify as to having seen the resurrected Lord. God's Word tells us that to be saved, man must believe Jesus Christ died for us on Calvary, that he rose again and conquered death so that we might be saved. We must believe Jesus rose again and has paid for our personal sins. We must put our total trust in Him.

During his ministry on earth, Jesus brought a number of people back to life after they had died. Martha's brother Lazarus had been dead for four days when Jesus brought him back to life. But the resurrection of Jesus Christ was different. Jesus would never have to die again. Jesus did not die for His sins but for our sins. It was not just a postponement of physical death, as was the case with Lazarus, who later died again. On the third day Jesus was raised from the dead with a transformed body that was clothed with immortality and glory. His resurrection body could appear and disappear, go through material objects, and ascend to and descend from heaven.

Significance of the Resurrection

God's Word teaches a literal bodily resurrection of Jesus. Believers in Christ accept the New Testament scriptures as historical accounts of an actual event central to their faith. The resurrection is a fundamental tenet of our belief. Humanity sinned and God, as a Holy God, was therefore required to separate Himself from sin and therefore from sinners. However, God sent His Son, who was sinless, to take the sin of the world on His shoulders. Therefore anyone who believes upon His name, accepts the gift of Jesus's death, burial, and resurrection, and commits in their heart to become what Jesus wants them to become; will be freed from the consequences of their sin, without violating God's judgment. The resurrection of Christ validates the power of God. It proves that God can conquer sin and validates the claim of Jesus to be God.

Romans 1:4
"And was declared to be the Son of God in power according to the Spirit of holiness, by the resurrection from the dead."

It is impossible to explain the origin and existence of the Church without resting on the foundation of Christ's death, burial and resurrection. It is not unusual to describe the death and burial of Christ because crucifixion was a common method of Romans to execute criminals. We know from history even Philip the Great at one time used crucifixion to kill two thousand of his enemies. The crucifixion of Christ and His burial within themselves do not fulfill the promise of God. But the resurrection of Christ combined with the Crucifixion of Christ and His burial is the miracle from God the Father that is the cornerstone of the Church. The resurrection of Christ is the cornerstone of Christians worldwide because without the resurrection they would have no promise from God. Without the resurrection Jesus would be a liar because He promised often He would be raised the third day and would conquer death. God Himself said at the Baptism of Christ, *"This is my Son in whom I am well pleased."* If Jesus had not been raised from the dead then God's promise of a coming messiah would have been false and God would have sinned.

The resurrection of Jesus Christ was also necessary to fulfill biblical prophecy. In Psalm, David prophesied God would not abandon His soul to Hades but would come to take it home with Him. That could only be done if Christ were alive and Christ could only be alive if He was raised from the dead. The resurrection of Jesus Christ was and is absolutely essential to the completion of the Plan of Salvation of God for mankind. When people accept Christ and God changes their heart to one of obedience they are spiritually following the pattern of Christ in the resurrection. This is shown in physical baptism that is a symbol of the death, burial, and resurrection of Jesus Christ. When one goes down into the water they symbolize the death of Jesus for their sins. When they are at the bottom of the water they symbolize the burial of their sinful body. Then when they are raised up out of the burial waters they symbolize their commitment to a new life of following God's will. Let us forever praise God for His Son whom He sent to earth to die on Calvary, to be buried and then rise again the third day.

CHAPTER SEVEN

The Doctrine of God the Holy Spirit
God's Communication with Man

Who Is the Holy Spirit

Slightly more than two thousand years ago, a miraculous, incredible event occurred. The New Testament Church was initiated into the Hearts of believers at the Feast of Pentecost. What made this occurrence so astounding? John 14:16-17 records that the circumstances of that day were truly dramatic because God sent His Spirit to the followers of Jesus Christ, as He promised.

John 14:16–17
"And I will ask the Father, and He will give you another Helper, to be with you forever—even the Spirit of truth, whom the world cannot receive, because it neither sees Him nor knows Him; you know Him, for He dwells with you and will be in you."

To understand what God has done for us, we must first understand who the Holy Spirit is and who He is not. Yes, the proper question is who is the Holy Spirit? Not what is the Holy Spirit. The Holy Spirit is a person. The Holy Spirit is a person of the Godhead. To grasp that, we must try to understand the roll of the Holy Spirit in the Godhead.

Two Hebrew words and two Greek words are translated "spirit" in the Bible. Of these four, two are used only twice: the Hebrew word *neshamah,* which means "breath," and the Greek word *phantasma,* which means "phantom" or "apparition." The other two words are the Hebrew *ruach* and the Greek *pneuma,* each used several hundred times.

Ruach means "breath, air; strength; wind; breeze; spirit; courage; temper." Of the 378 times it is used in the King James Version, it is translated "Spirit" 272 times, "wind" ninety-two times, "breath" twenty-seven times and in other ways twenty-seven times. The concepts of "wind," "breath" and "spirit" were all related in biblical thought and language. We see these intertwined in the use of *ruach* in Ezekiel 37, which describes a great multitude of people being resurrected and restored to physical life to understand God's truth.

What is the meaning of *pneuma?* This word "primarily denotes 'the wind' (akin to *pneo,* 'to breathe, blow'); also 'breath'; then, especially 'the spirit,' which, like the wind, is invisible, immaterial and powerful." It is used 385 times in the King James Version and is usually translated "Spirit."

Jesus Christ made this connection Himself. After Jesus showed them the wounds in His hands and side, verifying that He had indeed been raised from the dead, John records that Jesus said: *"Peace to you! As the Father has sent Me, I also send you."* And when He had said this, He breathed on them, and said to them, *"Receive the Holy Spirit."*

John 20:21–22
"Jesus said to them again, "Peace be with you. As the Father has sent me even so I am sending you. And when He had said this He "breathed" on then and said to them, "Receive the Holy Spirit."

In John the fourteenth chapter Jesus told the Hebrew people He would send them a "Helper" also referred to as a "Comforter" because He, Jesus could not always be with them. Jesus described the coming "Helper" to be like a breath of air, or like the wind because they would not be able to see or touch the "Holy Spirit." They would, however, see the results of His actions. Actually we, as God's people should have a better understanding of the Holy Spirit because in Genesis 2:7 God told us that when He formed mankind out of the dust of the ground He breathed into man's nostrils the breath of life. Or another way of saying it He breathed into man His Spirit that He intended man to use to communicate daily with God. The parallel of breathing life into mankind and breathing life into a redeemed sinner is glorious. In Genesis God inserts His Spirit into man to establish physical life. Now in John Christ inserts Spiritual life into all men who will believe on Him so they can have eternal life as a Child of God.

The Holy Spirit is part of the Trinity

The Holy Spirit is one third of the Trinity. The Holy Spirit is a being and has a significant role in everything that happens. Jesus relies on the Holy Spirit to be our comforter and our communicator regarding God's will for our life.

John 15:26
"But when the Helper comes, whom I shall send to you from the Father, the Spirit of truth who proceeds from the Father, He will bear witness about me."

This verse from God's Word is fascinating. Jesus is speaking. He clearly outlines the trinity as part of our salvation. "When the Helper" (Holy Spirit) comes (at the day of Pentecost) *"whom I shall send to you from the Father,"* Jesus the Son asks God the Father to send the Holy Spirit, *"He will testify of me."* (Means the role of the Holy Spirit after the birth of Christ is to testify who Christ is to mankind.

Jesus tells us the Holy Spirit is clearly a part of the Trinity. Jesus tells us the Holy Spirit is a person *(He will testify of me)* and Jesus tells us the role of the Holy Spirit in the Trinity is to testify of the saving grace of Christ.

Led by the Holy Spirit

Perhaps you have heard much about being "Led by the Holy Spirit." Christians talk about this phenomenon without being conscious of the reality that we do not know a lot about what we are talking about and non-Christians know nothing about what we are talking about. Simply put, to be led by the Holy Spirit means to be ready and willing to do what the voice on God in our heart tells us to do. We have been told that the Holy Spirit dwells in our heart (better said to be our soul) if we have placed our trust in salvation to be in Jesus Christ the Lord. Since the Holy Spirit dwells in our soul He, not it, speaks to us continuously. The Holy Spirit encourages us to worship Jesus. The Holy Spirit discourages us in thinking thoughts that are not righteous. The Holy Spirit will chastise us for doing things that are disappointing to God. But the primary work of the

Holy Spirit in our soul is to instruct us in how to be a servant of God and to please Him.

There is much we do not know about the roles of God the Father, God the Son, and the Holy Spirit. We know God is Spirit. The role of the Holy Spirit changed to some extent when the Son of God came to earth and became man. Jesus told us the role of the Holy Spirit was to become the "breathed" voice of Christ. Another way to say it is the Holy Spirit projects the spirit of Jesus. We also know that Jesus is God and when we refer to God the Son, we are also referring to God the Father because they are one. So when we speak of the Holy Spirit we are speaking of the Spirit of God the Father and the Spirit of Christ. This thrusts us into the definition of the Trinity which man cannot totally grasp

As we try to think about the Trinity let's consider three brothers. If it could be that three male triplets could ever be created exactly alike, they would have the same personality, the same desires, the same abilities, the same power, the same character and the same nature. We understand this cannot be in our physical bodies. But that is what God the Father, God the Son and God the Holy Spirit are. They are one in personality, desire, ability, power, character and nature. Yet they are three in roles they play in accomplishing the will of all three. And we see that God the Father and God the Son have a relationship of Father and Son. The Holy Spirit was identified, primarily, as the spirit of God the Father, as outlined in the Old Testament before the birth of Jesus. The Holy Spirit emphasizes the role of the Spirit of Christ after the coming of Jesus to earth.

The Role of the Holy Spirit in Creation

God the Father, the author and designer of all that is or ever has been created, designed and conceived. He conceived the desire to create the world and set in motion the acts of creation. The Bible says He "spoke the world" into existence. This means He authorized God the Son to carry out His plan of creation.

Hebrews 11:3
"By faith we understand that the universe was created by the Word of God, so that what is seen was not made out of things that are visible."

God the Son, not yet named Jesus Christ, followed the desire of God the Father to create from nothing the universe. Jesus, being totally in harmony with His Father, knew what God the Father wanted, and acted to meet His expectations.

John 1:3
"All things were made through Him, and without Him was not anything made that was made."

John 1:3 tells us all things were made through the Son of God, who would become Jesus Christ after the virgin birth. The key word to understand the role of God the Father and God the Son in Creation is perhaps the word through. God spoke the world into existence. This authorized the God the Son to do it. It is conceivable that every day God the Father relayed to God the Son what would be done that day. We see that in creation God the Son was busy doing the will of the Father and likewise God the Holy Spirit was doing the will of God the Son.

Genesis 1:1–2
"In the beginning, God created the heavens and the earth. The earth was without form and void, and darkness was over the face of the deep. And the Spirit of God was hovering over the face of the waters."

What does this Scripture mean when it says the Spirit of God was "hovering" over the face of the waters? We already know the responsibility of implementing God's act of creation belonged to God the Son. This means the Holy Spirit maintained a support role for God the Son in creation. The Spirit of God hovered over the face of the waters means the Spirit of God stood ready to assist God the

Son as needed in creation. In Psalm 33:6 we have confirmed both the Son of God and the Holy Spirit were involved in creation. God's Word often refers to the Holy Spirit as breath, or God breathing. Look what Psalm 33:6 tells us.

Psalm 33:6
"By the Word of the Lord the heavens were made, and by the breath of His mouth (the Holy Spirit) all their hosts."

The Role of the Holy Spirit in Redemption

God the Father designed and organized every detail of His plan of redemption of mankind. Even before God created man He knew man would sin. So the plan of Redemption was created even as the plan of creation was created. Likewise the plan of redemption was implemented as was the plan of creation.

Galatians 4:4–5
"But when the fullness of time had come, God sent forth His Son, born of woman, under the law, to redeem those who were under the law, so that we might receive adoption as sons."

Look at the words "when the fullness of time had come." That does not just refer to when Mary was ready to have child. It also means that when the plan of salvation, created by God at the time of creation of the universe was ready, God implemented His plan to redeem lost mankind unto Him. God the Father conceived of and created the Plan of Salvation for lost mankind. But as in creation, who implemented God the Father's plan? It was God the Son. So in the Plan of Salvation, who implemented God the Father's plan? It was God the Son.

John 6:37–38
"All that the Father will gives to me, and whoever comes to me I will never cast out, For I have come down from heaven not to do my own will but the will of Him who sent me."

What a powerful scripture. This confirms that God the Son implements the will of God the Father's original Plan of Salvation. "All (whoever) that the Father gives to me (the children of God) and whoever comes to me (The Church) I will keep forever and their salvation eternally guaranteed. Jesus implemented the will of God the Father to come down from Heaven to earth even though He would be crucified, tortured, and killed. What then is the role of the Holy Spirit in Redemption? As in creation, God the Father was assisted by God the Son and God the Son was assisted by the Holy Spirit. Likewise in redemption God the Father is assisted by God the Son, and God the Son is assisted by the Holy Spirit. It is the role of the Holy Spirit to teach mankind what God the Son did under the direction of God the Father.

John 14:26
"But the helper, the Holy Spirit, whom the Father will send in my name, He will teach you all things and bring to your remembrance all that I have said to you."

It is the Holy Spirit that makes sure every person in the world feels a call from God's (God the Fathers) amazing grace, and feels a call from God the Son's amazing price paid for our salvation. It is the role of the Holy Spirit to take on the spirit of Christ to win hearts from the clutches of Satan. Furthermore, it is the Holy Spirit that transfers the sinful heart of mankind from lost to saved and gives to that one a new heart that will never cease to want to please God even though from time to time that one will commit acts that will disappoint them and God the Father.

It takes the full complement of the Trinity, God the Father, God the Son, and the Holy Spirit to save us. They are equal in their divine roles even through God the Son and the Holy Spirit recognize God the Father to be number 1 in the roles of the Trinity. This is because all of creation, all of redemption, and all of the End Times start with God the Father.

The Role of the Holy Spirit in the Resurrection

Romans 8:11

"If the Spirit of Him who raised Jesus from the dead dwells in you, He who raised Christ Jesus from the dead will also give life to your mortal bodies through His Spirit who dwells in you."

The power God the Father used to raise Jesus Christ from the grave was the Holy Spirit. That same Spirit dwells in the heart of those Christ has redeemed. The power God the Father will use to raise us from the dead will be the Holy Spirit. We need not think of who is in charge because all three members of the Godhead think alike, all three have the same objectives and all are supportive of each other. Thus we see the role of the trinity in the death, burial, and resurrection of Jesus Christ.

Each member of the Trinity are spiritual beings. After Jesus ascended back into the heavens to be with His Father He took with Him a glorified physical body as well as a spiritual body. Christ will come back in His second coming in that glorified body. God the Father and the Holy Spirit have not taken on a physical glorified body but will in some form take on such a body when they walk and talk and live with mankind after the Millennial reign, and in the new heaven and new earth.

1 Corinthians 8:6

"Yet, for us there is one God, the Father, from whom all things are, and for whom we exist; and one Lord, Jesus Christ, through whom are all things are, and through whom we exist."

The Works of the Holy Spirit

A largely unknown fact is the Holy Spirit maintains the order of the Universe and all that is in it. In addition, the Holy Spirit, in the role of the Spirit of Jesus Christ, is God's communicator with us as well. Each of the Trinity, God the Father, God the Son, and The

Holy Spirit, have unique roles to play. Look at what God's Word tells us the role in the Trinity God has outlined for the Holy Spirit.

Ephesians 2:1, 2
"And you were dead in trespasses and sin in which you once walked, following the prince of the power of the air, the spirit that is now at work in the sons of disobedience."

Ephesians 2:1 tells us the Holy Spirit has now broken our old union with Satan and has reunited us with God. God gives us His promise of eternity, and forgives us of our sin. After this life is over He will reunite us with Jesus Christ and God the Father in eternity. Christ paid the price of our reunion with God, but the Holy Spirit actually gives us the new spiritual body and through Him we are born again.

Ephesians 2:18
"For through Him we both have access in one Spirit to the Father."

The Holy Spirit gives us access to God the Father. We cannot come into the presence of God the Father while we live this life because we have a sin nature. But because Jesus Christ gave His blood on Calvary to pay the price of our sins, the power of God gives us access to God the Father. The Holy Spirit appoints us and selects us for specific jobs to do in the Kingdom of God. Doctor Luke said the Holy Spirit appointed Him to preach. The Holy Spirit touches our hearts and gives us instruction of what we are to do for the Kingdom of God. Through the Holy Spirit we feel a tugging to be righteous in all aspects of our life. And that feeling is more than avoiding evil. It includes the desire to be good. It includes the desire to demonstrate the love of God toward all mankind.

Luke 4:18
"The Spirit of the Lord is upon me, because He has anointed me to proclaim good news to the poor; He has sent me to proclaim liberty to the captives and recovery of sight to the blind, to set at liberty those who are oppressed."

The power of God, the Holy Spirit, brings about the change in our heart after we accept Jesus Christ as our Savior. The Holy Spirit makes us a new creature and reunites us with God. The Holy Spirit baptizes, what means immerses, us spiritually into the new life with Christ. What then, is the role of the Holy Spirit in our life after we have been reunited with Christ? God told John to record that when the Holy Spirit descended into the hearts of man He would convict us of our sin. He would serve the role the law did not accomplish. The Holy Spirit teaches us to pray to God and helps us voice the utterings of our heart. In Romans chapter 8, Paul, recording for God, says we do not know what to pray for but the Holy Spirit makes intercession for us with Christ and explains the feelings we do not understand. The desire we have to communicate with God comes from the Holy Spirit who makes intercession between us and God the Father. We do not understand Scripture unless the Holy Spirit interprets is for us. This is because we think in a carnal nature not a spiritual realm and we do not have the knowledge of our God.

John 3:3–6
Jesus answered him, "Truly, Truly I say to you, unless one is born again, he cannot see the kingdom of God." Nicodemus said to Him, "How can a man be born when he is old? Can he enter a second time into his mother's womb and be born?" Jesus answered, "Truly, Truly I say to you, unless one is born of water and the Spirit, he cannot enter the kingdom of God. That which is born of the flesh is flesh, and that which is born of the Spirit is spirit."

1 Corinthians 2:1, 14
"And I, when I came to you brothers, did not come proclaiming to you the testimony of God with lofty speech or wisdom. The natural person does not accept the things of the Spirit of God, for they are folly to him; and he is not able to understand them because they are spiritually discerned."

In the above scripture Paul explains the Holy Spirit makes us a new creature, gives us a new heart, and spiritually release's us from our sinful nature. The "natural person" cannot understand the voice of the Spirit of God but the redeemed can through the Holy Spirit. We are reminded of the young boy flying his kite on a very low hung, cloudy day. His kite was lost to sight in the clouds as he used the strings of the kite to maneuver it. A stranger asked how do you know what the kite is doing and where it is. The boy said, "No I can't see it but I can feel its tug through the strings." That is a simplified answer about the Holy Spirit. We cannot see the Holy Spirit but we do feel the Spirit's tugs on our heart. When we speak of the Spirit speaking to us it means the tugs of the Holy Spirit on our soul, which is our inner direction of our life, is directing us.

Ephesians 1:13–14
"In Him you also, when you heard the word of truth, the gospel of your salvation; and believed in Him, were sealed with the promised Holy Spirit, who is the guarantee of our inheritance until we acquire possession of it, to the praise of His glory."

How can we be assured of our Salvation? How can we be certain we will not become unsaved? Because the Holy Spirit sealed us with the power of God's promise of eternal life, we can be certain of once saved always saved. The Holy Spirit, the power of God, is the guarantee of our inheritance until He (Jesus Christ) comes again to take us home.

Evidence of the Holy Spirit's Presence

In the second chapter of Acts we read of the fulfillment of the promise that the Holy Spirit would come to the followers of Jesus.

Acts 2:1–4
"When the Day of Pentecost had fully come, they were all together in one place. And suddenly there came from heaven a sound like a rushing mighty wind, and it filled the entire

house where they were sitting. And divided tongues, as of fire, appeared to them, and rested on each one of them. And they were all filled with the Holy Spirit and began to speak with other tongues, as the Spirit gave them utterance."

This was a supernatural event. Nothing like this had ever happened before and will not happen again. The sound that accompanied the sending of the Holy Spirit was that of a rushing, mighty wind. The sound was of **wind**, again demonstrating the connection between wind and spirit. The sound was of a mighty wind because of the nature of the Holy Spirit.

Jesus Christ promised He would not leave the world without communication between God and believers. He promised He would send the Holy Spirit as a comforter and counselor to man. Jesus was quite clear that the Holy Spirit would be known to believers but a mystery to nonbelievers. There is no question God told the Holy Spirit to make this such a significant event to believers that it would be remembered and recorded for the remaining existence of His children. Yet God did not make the same effort to make this event aware to the lost majority. This was God speaking to His people. He was speaking to His people in the past, present and future of this event. This ushered in the new covenant God would make with mankind. This ushered in the age of Grace and fulfilled the Law.

John 14:15–18
"If you love Me, you will keep My commandments. And I will ask the Father, and He will give you another Helper, to be with you forever, even the Spirit of truth, whom the world cannot receive, because it neither sees Him nor knows Him. You know Him, for He dwells with you and will be in you. I will not leave you orphans; I will come to you."

In his book Systematic Theology, Wayne Grudem says the work of the Holy Spirit is "to manifest the active presence of God in the world, and especially in the Church." He is telling us the role of the Holy Spirit in the Trinity includes being a communicator and interpreter of God's will to man. In addition, the Holy Spirit is, to us humans, the active presence of God that makes things happen. And the Holy Spirit is a comforter to believers.

In the first chapter of Acts we read of another of Christ's appearances to His followers after His resurrection. A vital question burned in their minds: "Lord, will you at this time restore the kingdom to Israel?" Jesus then refocused their thinking regarding when He would return to the mission He had in store for them.

Acts 1:7–8
"He said to them, "It is not for you to know times or seasons which the Father has fixed by His own authority. But you will receive power when the Holy Spirit has come upon you; and you shall be my witnesses to in Jerusalem, and in all Judea and Samaria, and to the end of the earth."

Jesus told his disciples they would receive the power of the Holy Spirit. They did not know what this meant. The disciples wanted the power to enable them to set up a kingdom that would rid the people of the oppression of Rome. They wanted a physical kingdom on earth but Christ had much more in mind that than. He said the power of the Holy Spirit would be directly connected with their work of being witnesses of Him, starting in Jerusalem, then spreading throughout Judea and Samaria and ultimately to the end of the earth. The book of Acts records the beginning of this mighty work with Christ's followers. It began with believers receiving the Holy Spirit in the Feast of Pentecost. Then, empowered by that Spirit, they went out proclaiming the gospel of the Kingdom.

Christ made it clear that the Holy Spirit is connected with power. The Greek word translated "power" is **dunamis.** It is translated "power," "mighty work," "strength," "miracle," "might," "virtue" and "mighty." It is the same Greek root from which we get modern English words like **dynamic,** which means active, forceful and energetic; **dynamo,** which is a device for generating electric power; and **dynamite,** which is an explosion of great power, energy and force.

These give us a sense of the power that would result from the Holy Spirit being given to the early Church.

The Holy Spirit gives us power

Man cannot live the righteous life God wants us to live in his own power. We are assured, however, that righteousness is attainable through the Holy Spirit which continues to intercede with our Spirit and convict us of sin. This is true because the Holy Spirit not only convicts us when we sin but also empowers us to not sin. We are also assured that everyone who believes in Jesus Christ and commits their life to being His disciple is given the gift of the Holy Spirit to live in their heart. While no one is without sin, before or after they are saved, the work of the Holy Spirit is a continuing work of helping us grow toward the state of being more and more like God. When we are saved, the Holy Spirit gives us a new heart that always desires to please God. This heart, described is being, "Born Again," means we live and walk in the Spirit of God with our sins blotted out because of the price Jesus paid for our sin.

Romans 8:9–11
"You, however, are not in the flesh but in the Spirit, if in fact the Spirit of God dwells in you. Anyone does not have the Spirit of Christ does not belong to Him. But if Christ is in you, although the body is dead because of sin, the Spirit is life because of righteousness. If the Spirit of Him who raised Jesus from the dead dwells in you, He who raised Christ Jesus from the dead will also give life to your mortal bodies through His Spirit who dwells in you."

The Holy Spirit also gives us the power to live for righteousness and to serve God the Father and God the Son. God tells us the Holy Spirit, which has the power to raise Jesus Christ from the dead, also has the power to enable us to resist the temptations of sin. Fortunately for us, the Holy Spirit understands our weakness and our lack of understanding of God. He intercedes for us making it possible for us to do God's will.

Romans 8:26–27
"Likewise the Spirit also helps us in our weakness, for we do not know what to pray for as we ought, but the Spirit Himself intercedes for us with groaning too deep for words. And, He who searches hearts knows what is the mind of the Spirit is, because the Spirit intercedes for the saints according to the will of God."

Jesus Christ, the risen Savior, knows our mind and heart. In addition the Scripture says the Son and the Spirit are the same even as the Son and the Father are one. The Holy Spirit intercedes between us and Christ, and in so doing, provides a medium of communication enabling us to know God's will and to do it.

The Holy Spirit provides spiritual insight

As believers in Jesus, our knowledge of God comes to us through the Holy Spirit. Man cannot know God unless the Spirit teaches him. In addition our knowledge of ourselves, our sinful state, our need for God, and our hope for the future comes to us through the Spirit.

1 Corinthians 2:9–14
"But as it is written: what no eye has seen, nor ear heard, nor the heart of man imagined, what God has prepared for those who love Him, these things God has revealed to us through the Spirit. For the Spirit searches everything, even the depths of God. For who knows a person's thoughts except the spirit of that person, which is in him? So also, no one comprehends the thoughts of God except the Spirit of God. Now we have received not the spirit of the world, but the Spirit who is from God, that we might understand the things freely given us by God. And we impart this in words not taught by human wisdom but taught by the Spirit, interpreting spiritual truths to those who are spiritual. The natural person does not accept the things of

*the Spirit of God, for they are folly to him, and he is not able
to understand them because they are spiritually discerned."*

God tells us that we, as humans, have no concept, and no capacity to even dream of the marvelous things God has prepared for us in His eternal kingdom. It also tells us that we have no concept of what good and wonderful things God has for us here on earth. Yes, horrible things happen to believers and unbelievers alike here on earth. But God can fill our hearts with such peace, such joy, and such faith that anything here on earth is just an inconvenience compared to the joy of having Him our Lord and Savior here, as well as eternally. We think we are smart but we are not. We think we have things figured out but our knowledge is not a drop of sand in the vastness of desert compared to God's knowledge.

When the Holy Spirit comes into our heart we take on the nature and desire to become like Jesus Christ. We do not become perfect creatures but we do take on a heart for perfection and eternal pleasing of our Lord and Savior. Our base nature ceases to become consumed by lust and sin. It becomes a nature of love, compassion, peace, and goodness.

Ephesians 4:29–32
*"Let no corrupting talk come out of your mouths, but only
such as is good in building up, as fits the occasion that it
may give grace to those who hear. And do not grieve the
Holy Spirit of God, by whom you were sealed for the day
of redemption. Let all bitterness, and wrath, and anger,
and clamor, and slander be put away from you, along with
all malice. And be kind to one another, tenderhearted,
forgiving one another, as God in Christ forgave you."*

As the Holy Spirit comes into our heart we do not lose our carnal nature. We do gain a new nature of desire to honor and glorify God. This new nature enters into war with the old nature and, yes, we often grieve God by yielding to the old nature. But in our heart we have a continuous desire to honor and glorify God.

"Filled with the Spirit"

The apostle Paul commands in Ephesians 5:18 that we be filled with the Spirit. That raises three questions that must be answered. What does it mean to be filled with the Spirit? How can we be filled with the Spirit? And when are we filled with the Spirit?

To be "filled with the Spirit" is to be completely controlled by the Spirit of God. It means earthly desires that are selfish and prideful are put aside. It means our total motivation is to serve God and to please God. This means pride, anger, greed, lust, impatience, and other manifestations of the flesh no longer reign in our life. It means the urging of the Holy Spirit and the teachings of God's Word directs our every path and thought. Many people think, and many scholars teach, that to be filled with the Holy Spirit is to have overwhelming joy. They get the cart before the horse in such theology. Overwhelming joy is the result of being filled with the spirit, not its definition. When we totally submit ourselves to the control and direction of God we will as a result, be filled with total satisfaction. This is not a shallow emotion of happiness but deep seated satisfaction that we are pleasing God. As we consider the instruction of God to be filled with the Spirit, we should consider other terminology used by Christians that can be confused as being "Filled with the Spirit." These concepts are:

Baptism by the Holy Spirit: "Baptism by the Holy Spirit occurs when the Holy Spirit places us into the body of Christ (The Church) and anoints us as part of the family of God. Man does baptize us into a permanent relationship with God. Only God can do this. We understand the Scripture to say we are "saved by faith through grace." This is true. Through faith we believe Jesus died on Calvary for our sins and that Jesus died to pay the price of our sins. However our faith does not save us. Our faith presents us to God for salvation and God's Grace saves us. God's Grace changes our heart from being self-possessed to being a heart that has a deep abiding love for Christ and a desire to please Him. Only the Grace of God can make this change. The act of changing our heart, joining us with the family of God is said in God's Word to be "Baptism of the Holy Spirit." This is not a physical immersion of man down into water. It is a spiritual immersion of our hearts, soul, and being into the family of God.

Romans 6:3–4
"Do you not know that all of us who have been baptized into Christ Jesus were baptized into His death? We were buried therefore with Him by Baptism into death, in order that, just as Christ was raised from the dead by the glory of the Father, we too might walk in newness of life."

The indwelling of the Holy Spirit refers to the place, in humans, where the Holy Spirit dwells. It is the ongoing residence of the Holy Spirit in our souls after we have been "Baptized by the Holy Spirit" (a spiritual baptism). When we are saved from the price of our sins the Holy Spirit comes to reside within our hearts. He gives us the power for holiness, worship and righteousness. Without the guiding and urging of the Holy Spirit we could not maintain the desire we have to please God and be His servant. Indwelling of the Holy Spirit, means the Holy Spirit resides in our soul. In the Old Testament, the Holy Spirit accepted those who believed in God and desired to be His followers, just as in the New Testament. But the Holy Spirit did not necessarily remain in those who were converted. In the New Testament, Jesus revealed to His disciples the new role the Holy Spirit would hold in our lives.

Romans 14:17
"Even the Spirit of truth, whom the world cannot receive; because it neither sees Him nor knows Him. You know Him for He dwells with you and will be in you."

The truth of the Holy Spirit is different than being "Filled with the Holy Spirit" in that it is an understanding of our inheritance laid up for us in heaven. This partial understanding is given to us by the Holy Spirit and is for the purpose of encouragement and strengthening our walk with the Lord. This truth gives us the assurance of our salvation. Ephesians 1:13-14 in the New Testament God tells us He guarantees our salvation.

Ephesians 1:13–14
"In Him you also, when you heard the Word of truth, the gospel of your salvation, and believed in Him, were sealed with the promised Holy Spirit, who is the guarantee of our inheritance until we acquire possession of it to the praise of His glory."

The Sealing of the Holy Spirit: "The Sealing of the Holy Spirit" is different than being "Filled with the Holy Spirit" in that it is given to believers as absolute certainty that they belong to the family of God and are saved. This certification that the Holy Spirit gives our heart reassures us of the ownership of eternal salvation we have of with the Lord.

Those who believe Jesus died on Calvary and conquered death for them are assured by the Holy Spirit that their salvation will never be taken away. Some, however, ask can one who is saved reach the point they want to give their saved relationship with Jesus back and cease to be a follower of Christ. Is there anything we can do to lose our salvation? The answer is a strong NO! Our faith in God as the promised redeemer brings us into a grace relationship with God. If we could be saved by our faith we certainly could lose our salvation because of our lack of faith. But the Bible tells us that we are saved by the Grace of God. When we are saved we are made a new creature. We call this being "Born Again." This new creature is given a desire in our sole to want to please God. This is a desire lost people do not have. This nature is permanent and will not go away. John 10:29 affirms that we are protected by the power of God and no power on earth or heaven can break the power of God.

John 10:28
"And I give them eternal life and they will never perish; and no one will snatch them out of My hand."

We are not filled with the Holy Spirit *if* we have the joy of the Lord. We have the joy of the Lord *if* we are filled with the Holy Spirit. We get that joy when we begin to fully put every situation that comes up in life in the hands of God. Every event that looks tragic we ask God to handle and do the best we know how to do and leave the outcome in God's hands. God is interested and involved in every aspect of our life. God does not stand aside as one who observes but does not become involved. Could the God that is interested in every sparrow that falls to the ground be less interested in those He sent His Son to die on the Cross of Calvary to save?

Matthew 10:29
"Are not two sparrows sold for a copper coin? And not one of them falls to the ground apart from your Father's will."

Baptism of the Holy Spirit

All four of our gospels record that John the Baptist said, "I have baptized you with water, but He (Jesus) will baptize you with the Holy Spirit." Clearly the reference to Baptism with water is different than the Baptism of the Holy Spirit and God is describing two different spiritual events. The Gospels of Matthew and John compare the water Baptism of John the Baptist to a more complete, more perfect Baptism of the Spirit with Jesus Christ. Matthew reports John the Baptist stated; "He that cometh after me is mightier than I…and shall baptize you with the Holy Ghost, and with fire."

Matthew 3:11
"I indeed baptize you with water unto repentance, but He who is coming after me is mightier than I, whose sandals I am not worthy to carry. He will baptize you with the Holy Spirit and fire."

The only other two writers in the New Testament who refer to the phrase, "Baptize with the Spirit," are Luke in the book of Acts and Paul in 1 Corinthians. Paul's reference to "Baptize with the Spirit" is identical to salvation. To be baptized with the Holy Spirit, then, is when the Holy Spirit transforms a believer into a saved child of God. The word Baptize means to immerse and *"to be Baptized with the Holy Spirit"* means to be totally immersed in the Holy Spirit. In other words it means to ask God to take control of our lives.

Luke, like John the Baptist, refers to *"Baptized with the Spirit"* as a reference to the coming of the Spirit at Pentecost. This is when God sent the Holy Spirit to dwell in the hearts of believers. This is a different reference of the work of the Holy Spirit than regeneration or salvation. The two writers are referring to different spiritual events when they refer to *"Baptize with the Holy Spirit."*

Acts 1:5
"For John truly baptized with water, but you shall be baptized with the Holy Spirit not many days from now."

Luke, the chosen one God used to record the book of Acts, tells the people they are to wait a few days when the Holy Spirit will descend on man and a new era of Christianity will be ushered into existence. The new era of Christianity meant the change from the Dispensation of Law to the Dispensation of Grace. It meant the massive difference of the Holy Spirit coming to live in the hearts of believers. That event is known as the day of Pentecost. It was a onetime event that will never happen again. Luke clarifies that at the time of the statement of John the Baptist the event of the descending of the Holy Spirit had not yet happened.

Paul however in Corinthians, makes reference not to the descending of the Holy Spirit at Pentecost, but to the transformation the Holy Spirit brings to the hearts of man when man accepts Jesus Christ as Savior.

1 Corinthians 12:13
"For by one Spirit we were all baptized into one body—whether Jews or Greeks, whether slaves or free—and have all been made to drink into one Spirit."

Baptism of the Holy Spirit at Pentecost

Pentecost is universally recognized as the great feast of the Jews in which they remember and honor as a great happening for Jewish people. In Acts the second chapter, Luke records that the Feast of Pentecost occurred ten days after Jesus Christ ascended into the heavens, as witnessed by the Apostles. The apostles, and certain other followers of Christ, were all together in a room in Jerusalem.

Acts 2:2–4
"And suddenly there came a sound from heaven, as of a rushing mighty wind, and it filled the whole house where they were sitting. Then there appeared to them divided tongues, as of fire, and one sat upon each of them. And they were all filled with the Holy Spirit and began to speak with other tongues, as the Spirit gave them utterance."

Thus the Holy Spirit, according to the promise of the Savior, descended on the apostles in the form of ***tongues of fire*** as a sign that He gave the apostles the ability and zeal to preach the teachings of Christ to all peoples. He descended in the form of fire as a sign of the power to cleanse sins and to sanctify and warm souls.

John the Baptist, in his preaching, spoke of this coming event God revealed unto him. John the Baptist baptized people who believed in the forthcoming of the Lord as their Savior. To John the Baptist, Baptism was a sign of their conversion and their decision to follow Jesus. It was a symbol of death of the old self-serving, God denying soul and the burial of that soul forever. And it was a symbol of the resurrection of that soul as a new soul empowered by God through the blood of Jesus Christ. John the Baptist continuously tried to differentiate that his baptism was symbolic of the real coming of the Holy Spirit that would soon fall on believers. John the Baptist referred to the forthcoming day of Pentecost when God would honor His promise and send the Holy Spirit to be a comforter to man. The day of Pentecost was a onetime event that included miracles of speaking in unknown tongues to establish the magnitude of the event of the sending of the Holy Spirit to dwell in man.

Prior to this, the Holy Spirit had dwelt among man and worked with man but did not live and dwell as a constant companion inside the heart of man. The day this monumental event occurred is called the "Day of Pentecost" to indicate its significance. The Bible tells us about three thousand people believed the Word of God that day and were baptized. Most Bible scholars refer to this event as the day that God established His Church. In so saying, scholars are not referring to a local body of believers, nor to a denomination, but to the universal Church made up of all who believe in Jesus Christ as their personal Savior. Other scholars contend the God's Church was established when Christ was resurrected from the grave because that event ushered in the dispensation of Grace. These scholars count the "Day of Pentecost" as the original population of "The Church."

It will never be necessary to send the Holy Spirit to dwell with man again nor to reestablish the Church. From the day of the descent of the Holy Spirit the Christian faith quickly began to spread with the help of God. The number of believers in the Lord Jesus Christ multiplied. Instructed by the Holy Spirit, the apostles boldly preached about Jesus Christ. They preached about the Son of God. They preached about His suffering and His resurrection from the dead. The Lord empowered them with many great miracles that were performed by the apostles in the name of the Lord Jesus Christ. At first, the apostles preached to the Jews and then dispersed to various countries to preach to all people.

Baptism of the Soul at time of Conversion

When Paul speaks of Baptism of the Holy Spirit in 1 Corinthians, he is clearly not talking about Pentecost. Paul is referring to that point it which a person repents of his sins and decides to turn over to Jesus Christ his whole being while trusting Jesus for salvation. Paul tells us that it takes an act of the Holy Spirit to change our heart and make us acceptable in the sight of God to become part of the family of God. Paul refers to this act of the Holy Spirit as the "Baptism of the Holy Spirit." This is clearly a different, distinctly different spiritual event than Pentecost. Once we were alienated from God, cut off from Christ (Ephesians 2:12), but then the Holy Spirit swept over us and brought us to life by uniting us to the living Christ and thus to His people in one body. This is a once-for-all event. It is never repeated. Paul teaches being filled with the Spirit is to be born again, or to have a new spirit in which Jesus saves us.

Two events Pentecost and Conversion

When a non-believer receives Jesus Christ as Lord and Savior they receive the Holy Spirit to come live in their heart. They will not have a second filling of the Holy Spirit. For a Christian to receive a second filling of the Holy Spirit they would have had to only partially had the Holy Spirit come to live in their heart when they were saved. This is contrary to scripture.

Those who believe in a second filling of the Holy Spirit read scripture like Matthew 3:11, Acts 1:5, and Acts 11:16, and read how the Holy Spirit came to believers and filled them with great power. We want that kind of power and tend to desire something from God without having to do a thing. Prior to Pentecost, people believed in Jesus also but the Holy Spirit had not yet come to live in the hearts of man. Now the Holy Spirit lives in the heart of believers forever and is available for us to have the power of God if we will claim it in the name of God

Progressive Grasping of the Holy Spirit

Many believers who refer to the "Second filling of the Holy Spirit" are referring to a time in their lives when they feel the Holy Spirit takes control of their lives and they enjoy the warmth and joy of being really close, spiritually, to God. The interesting fact here is to go back and remember a characteristic of God. He is immovable and unchangeable. God saved us and made us His child and gave us the Holy Spirit as our companion. The Holy Spirit does not change. The Holy Spirit does not draw close to us and then back away and come close to us again. We are the ones who open our hearts to God and then drift away. We then continue our part of life of moving to and from the closeness to the Holy Spirit that God desires for us. We should call this our progressive grasping of the Holy Spirit not the second filling of the Holy Spirit. Ephesians 1:13–14 states He, The Holy Spirit, dwells in every believer.

Ephesians 1:13–14
"In Him you also trusted, after you heard the word of truth, the gospel of your salvation; in whom also, having believed, you were sealed with the Holy Spirit of promise, who is the guarantee of our inheritance until the redemption of the purchased possession, to the praise of His glory."

Look at what God told us in Ephesians. He told us that when we were saved our salvation is sealed in and by the Holy Spirit. The Holy Spirit guarantees the security of our salvation and there is nothing we or anyone else can do to change this. It also states every believer receives the same filling of the Holy Spirit. It does not leave room for later completion of our soul being united with God. The eighth chapter of Romans completely rules out a second filling of the Holy Spirit.

Romans 8:9
"But you are not in the flesh but in the Spirit, if indeed the Spirit of God dwells in you. Now if anyone does not have the Spirit of Christ, he is not His."

This verse tells us that, after salvation, we are no longer in the flesh. We are in the Spirit. It leaves no room for us to be partially in the spirit and partially in the flesh awaiting a second filling of the Holy Spirit. In fact it tells us that if any believer is not in the Spirit of Christ he/she is simply not saved.

CHAPTER EIGHT

The Doctrine of Salvation
God's Redemption of Man

What is Salvation?

The central theme of God's Word is God's love for all people. This love was revealed when Jesus Christ, the Son of God, came into the world as a human being, lived a sinless life, died on the Cross of Calvary, and rose from the dead. Because Jesus died, our sins can be forgiven, and because He conquered death we can have eternal life. When Jesus Christ died for our sins, arose from the dead and conquered death, He made it possible for us to have His righteousness "imputed" or transferred to us. Adam "imputed" sin to mankind, but Jesus Christ's sacrifice and victory over death "imputed" salvation to mankind.

What is Sin?

If almost any group of people are asked, "Are you perfect?" they will answer "No." We understand that we are not totally righteous. We know we are not eternally consumed with moral, just, fair, compassionate, thoughts that are pleasing unto God. We know we fall short of the example God set for us in the life of Jesus Christ. It is interesting to understand that God told us exactly the same thing. He said that all, everyone ever born by man into this world, falls short of the glory or the righteousness of God.

Romans 3:23
"For all have sinned and come short of the Glory of God."

Sin, put as simply as possible, is any deed, any thought, any intention, and any action that displeases God. God created us in His own image. God desired mankind to be totally righteous. Only through the ultimate righteousness of mankind could God fellowship with man, whom He created for fellowship. God is righteous and man must also be righteous for that Holy fellowship to be born, to flourish and to blossom. When mankind disappointed God or made God angry at our disobedience, God did separate himself from us. Therefore sin is what separates man from God, and from the reality of ultimate happiness. The Greek word translated "sin" in the Bible (hamartano), literally means, "to miss the mark." God has a plan for each person ever born. God has an image He wants that person to live up to and things He wants that person to accomplish. He has, more than anything else, a nature He wants that person to be. If our lives fall short of the will of God by not doing things commanded by God; if by being less that God wants us to be; if we veer away from God's will, doing things for which we have no authority; we "miss the mark." This means we sin. The Scripture is clear that mankind is a sinner because we miss the mark of what God wants us to be and we missed the mark from our very beginning. We missed the mark when Adam sinned. That point of time in which Adam disobeyed God and ate from the tree of knowledge of good and evil disappointed God in His creation of man. At that early date all of mankind, starting with Adam but succeeding Adam throughout the birth of all other humans, sinned and became sinners.

"Imputed" Sin

When God created Adam He also created mankind. God did more than create a man. He created people and Adam was the first of the species. Because of Adam's sin mankind disappointed God and disappointment of God is sin. Cain and Abel were born unto Adam and Eve and they were created "in the image" of Adam which means they inherited the sin nature of Adam. We know that when Adam was 130 years old God gave him a son named Seth. In addition to Seth Genesis 5:3–4 tells us Adam begat sons and daughters. We do not know how many. When a baby is born into this world that infant is born with a nature to sin. That nature to be selfish, to be rebellious of authority, to want to do things the way he or she wants to do them and ignore others is part of the sin nature we inherit from Adam.

This nature is called original sin. Original sin consists of those tendencies, desires and natural instincts that lie in our soul and are disappointment to God. The source of original sin is Satan. Satan places in the heart of every newborn baby the desire to be selfish, to instinctively live to satisfy self. Original sin comes natural to us.

We do not even have to think to follow the instincts of original sin. The Bible describes original sin as a morally ruined character. This natural tendency of our actions thoughts, and feelings, violate God's moral commands. So our sinful hearts (original sin) cause us to make sinful choices, think sinful thoughts, and feel sinful feelings (actual sins). We are not sinners because we sin; rather, we sin because we are sinners. We are all born totally imprisoned in original sin. There is no island of goodness left in us.

When God created the original man, Adam was just the first of a parade of millions of people called mankind. What Adam was or decided to be was what man was and would decide to be. But Adam was the one who elected to disobey God thus the cloak of Adam's original sin is imputed to us and we begin life with a sinful nature and the responsibility of a destroyed relationship with God. This is because when Adam sinned, mankind for all eternity sinned.

1 Corinthians 5:22
"For as in Adam all die, even so in Christ
all shall be made alive."

Romans 5:14
"Nevertheless death reigned from Adam to Moses, even over
those who had not sinned according to the likeness of the
transgression of Adam, who is a type of Him who was to come."

Psalm 51:5
"Behold, I was brought forth in iniquity,
And in sin my mother conceived me."

"Willful" Sin

Although all of mankind was lost to sin because of the failure of Adam in the Garden of Eden we cannot blame our lost condition on Adam alone. Because of our sinful nature inherited from Adam we each individually commit transgressions against God. This means we fall short of the pedestal God expects us to maintain of righteousness every day. It is our natural instinct to disobey authority. The greatest authority is God and it is our natural instinct to disobey God. It is also our natural instinct to seek immorality. Satan taunts immorality at us continually, and it looks exciting. It looks self-fulfilling. It is made to look wonderful by Satan. Such thinking and such actions are displeasing to God. They are transgressions against God and when we partake of Satan's temptation we sin against God. This sin is because Adam sinned. Willful sin is our decisions that we have the freedom to think and do or not think and do. We are responsible for willful sin.

Isaiah 64:6
"But we are all like an unclean thing, and all our righteousness are like filthy rags; We all fade as a leaf, and our iniquities, like the wind, Have taken us away."

Isaiah 53:6
"All we like sheep have gone astray; We have turned, every one, to his own way; And the LORD has laid on Him the iniquity of us all."

1 John 1:8
"If we say that we have no sin, we deceive ourselves, and the truth is not in us."

But God...

Perhaps to mankind two of the most precious words in existence are "But God." God knew, before we were born that we would sin. God knew before He made Adam, and Eve, and Cain, and Able, and Seth, and all the sons and daughters that Satan would temp Adam and Eve and they would give into their weakness and disappoint Him. They did not have to sin but they did. How could God know what mankind would do before mankind did it? This is possible because God is not limited to time as we are. God was present before time began. God is present now and God is, not will be, but is present at the end of time. God does not look back on what man does, nor does God look forward to what man will do, God sees what man does as we are doing it and yet know what we will do before we do it. Look at what the Bible tells us.

Ephesians 1:4
"Even as he chose us in him before the foundation of the world, that we should be holy and blameless before him, In love."

Paul teaches us that God chose us to be blameless before Him and He chose us before the foundation of the world. Then He goes on to say He choose us in love. Who are us? We know in other scripture that us, to whom Paul speaks, are those who chose to believe in Jesus Christ as their Savior. Us refers to those people of all ages who decide to turn from the original sin and willful sin Satan laid on us and believe God would (in the Old Testament) and had (in the New Testament) provided a divine payment for our sins so we could be viewed as holy and blameless in the sight of God. We know that this payment would be in the Old Testament the promised Messiah (who unknown to Old Testament Saints) would be Jesus Christ the Son of God. Because God is timeless God has the foreknowledge to know what will happen before it happens as we understand time.

1 Peter 1:2
"According to the foreknowledge of God the Father, in the sanctification of the Spirit, for obedience to Jesus Christ and for sprinkling with his blood: May grace and peace be multiplied to you."

What is this grace and peace that is to be multiplied to us? It is the sanctification of the Holy Spirit, or the changing of us from a sin infested creature to a creature no longer accountable for sin. This all happens because of the blood of Jesus that was shed on Calvary. The price of our sin had to be paid for. God is a just God and the wages of sin is death. The only price that could pay for our sins is death.

But Jesus Christ who came to earth died for our sin and through His death and the grace of God amazing peace and love will be multiplied to us throughout eternity. We call this the Doctrine of Regeneration.

The Doctrine of Regeneration

When we as sinners, who are eternally separated from God because of sin, reach the point of believing that Jesus Christ died to pay the cost of our sins we are approaching the throne of God and becoming justified in asking God to save us. When we reach the point of deeply regretting we have disappointed God, and desire to change the way we live; we are approaching the throne of God. The process of reaching this point results in our asking Him to save us. At this point we have a shallow faith, not fully grown, that believes Jesus died for our sins and can save us. God looks upon us and determines if we are sincere in our desire to trust Jesus. If we are sincere God gives us the faith to put our full trust in Jesus Christ. Then, through His amazing grace, the Holy Spirit changes us into a new person. We refer to the process of God creating a new person the Doctrine of Regeneration.

Regeneration is the exclusive work of God. Man has no part in regeneration. God gives new life to an individual. It is what the scripture calls the new creation or being spiritually "Born Again."

God's Word is very clear that we must be spiritually "Born Again" to be saved. Without our faith we cannot be spiritually "Born Again." However, our faith does not make us spiritually "Born Again." Because of our faith, through the grace of Christ, God creates the new person. In the book of John Jesus tells Nicodemus something he had never heard before. The focus of Jesus here is on the need Nicodemus had for a total transformation from the old sin driven, selfish person; to a new righteous driven, God loving person. Regeneration is part of the overall work of salvation. It is a transformation and renewal of the inner being where love for self is replaced by love for God. Regeneration is the sovereign work of God in that no one else can do it but God. God does not leave those He saves in sin and bondage.

God does not take away the old sin nature we were born with but He gives us a new nature that combats the old sin nature.

The Doctrine of Justification

What makes it possible for God to listen to the prayer of saved people, although God will have nothing to do with us when we were lost in sin? If God will not co-exist with our sin, and after regeneration we still have a nature of sin and a nature of grace, how is God able to look upon man? Just like the Doctrine of Regeneration is part of Salvation, the Doctrine of Justification is the final act of Salvation. God, in the act of Regeneration, allows the blood of Christ at Calvary to cover up mankind's sin, therefore creating the reality that we become just as if we had never sinned. The only way that is possible is that the price of our sin was paid for by Jesus Christ on Calvary's hill.

Our righteousness cannot stand before God. This means that if we are to be able to ever come into the presence of God we must have another path toward righteousness. Our own righteousness is not sufficient. The only righteousness that will stand is that of Jesus Christ. He became our substitute and suffered the penalty of death for our sins. We call His substitute for us *"Substitutionary Atonement"* because God allows the price Jesus paid for our sin to be substituted for the price we had to pay for our sin. The Apostle Paul describes justification as the judicial act of God supernaturally pardoning all the sins of those who believe on Jesus Christ and henceforth treating them just as if they had never sinned. The Doctrine of Justification does not ignore our sin. It very definitely recognizes our sin but places it on Jesus Christ who died on Calvary to pay the cost of our sin. We are pardoned because Jesus paid for our sin. Those who trust in what Jesus Christ did in His death, burial and resurrection; are declared as "righteous" by God. They are then given access to His presence. Faith in Jesus is the means by which God accepts us as candidates for this transformation.

The Doctrine of Justification is the completed act of salvation that starts with man's faith, is made possible because of the grace of our Lord and Savior Jesus Christ. It is consummated by the act of Regeneration by God in which we become a new creation with a desire to love and serve God. It is completed by the Act of Justification in which God transfers our sin to Jesus and lets us come into the presence of God just as if we had never sinned.

The decisions to believe, repent, confess, and accept Jesus into our heart, are not three separate decisions. They are all part of our request of Christ for salvation. If we truly believe in Jesus Christ, not just about Jesus, we will repent and receive Him into our heart. Our faith in Jesus makes us eligible for salvation. God's act of changing our heart into a new person completes the act of regeneration and enables us to be born again. The total encompassing process of faith, grace, and regeneration completes the act of justification. With justification we start the road toward sanctification.

Salvation by God Alone

The great Martin Luther should be listed as one of our "heroes of the faith." Martin Luther lived in an age in which the Catholic Church was supreme. Church sovereignty was unquestioned and the Catholic Church had instituted several practices that guaranteed the continuation of that culture. One was that the members or rank and file of the church did not know the Latin language. But the services of the Church were in Latin. This was done at least in part to keep the membership dependent upon the Priest and Bishops so far as interpretation of religion was concerned. A false teaching of the Catholic Church was that Salvation required not only belief on Jesus Christ as Lord and Savior but also demanded membership and faithful following of the Catholic Church. Luther, a priest of high standing, was troubled by the teaching of the Church because he could not find authentication in the Bible of these practices of the Church. His teachings led to the protestant revolution against the Catholic Church and a massive searching of people for truth in Salvation. Luther's teachings, which were in massive opposition to the Catholic governing body, taught these basic truths.

- **_Grace Alone_**: To Martin Luther the Bible taught that the power of salvation was solely by the Grace of God. He believed God's Word taught that there was nothing man could do to earn Salvation. The only hope of man for Salvation was dependent on the Grace of God. He also was outspoken that the practice of the Catholic Church of demanding, in addition to Grace of God, membership and good standing with the Catholic Church was in error. Luther introduced to a hostile religious culture the fact that Church membership, affiliation, or standing is not a prerequisite for Salvation.

- **_Faith Alone_**: Luther also taught that Scripture revealed truth to be that man could not ever earn salvation by works. The Catholic Church taught that Catholics must do good works and earn a good standing with the Church to, in part, earn salvation. Catholic doctrine taught not only that people had to be part of the Catholic Church to be saved but they had to have good enough works to earn good standing in the church and that meant good enough works to earn salvation. The Church exercised that practice through the requirement of members to faithfully practice the sacraments of the church. And sacraments of the church were taught to facilitate salvation.

- **_God's Word Alone_**: Luther, in reading God's Word, had revealed to him by the Holy Spirit that the only authority of truth rested in God's Word. In so teaching; Luther confronted Catholic doctrine that taught Church tradition and Church ritual were part of Salvation. Luther taught that Church tradition was man-made and therefore included mistakes of thought and interpretation. However he taught that the Bible was without error and was the only source of eternal accurate and timely truth.

- **_Christ Alone_**: Martin Luther's study of Scripture gave him revelation that only Jesus Christ is the mediator between God and man. This violated the idea of having priests who prayed to God the Father in intercession for people. Thus,

Martin Luther largely invalidated the need for Priests in the role of being a mediator between God the Son and themselves.

- **_Glory to God Alone_**: Martin Luther finally taught that the Church deserved no credit and no glory for the salvation and guidance of man.

Martin Luther simply retaught a truth taught to us by Jesus Christ and continued to be taught by Paul and the Apostles. This truth is that Salvation comes to us by the blood shed by Christ on Calvary and there is nothing man can do to earn Salvation.

Ephesians 2:8–9
"For by grace you have been saved through faith. And this is not your own doing; it is the gift of God, not a result of works, so that no one may boast."

This means we cannot be righteous enough to earn Salvation.

We cannot do enough good deeds to earn Salvation. We must not rely in part on anything but the Grace of God to save us because in so doing we are not fully trusting God for Salvation. One who relies on God's Grace but also relies on good works, church membership, on family affiliations, or anything other than God's Grace does not fully trust Jesus Christ as being sufficient for Salvation. One who does not fully trust Jesus Christ as being capable and willing to save us from our sins; but who partially relies on something else, is lost.

Salvation because of our Faith but not by our Faith

The fact that our salvation is of God and God alone, does not diminish the importance of faith in salvation. God's Word tells us that faith through grace is how we are saved. That means we cannot be saved without faith. We can better understand this when we correlate the word faith to a much stronger belief than we give the word in today's world. The Scripture is full of truths telling us all we have to do to be saved is believe on the name of Jesus Christ.

John 11:26
*"And everyone who lives and believes in me
shall never die. Do you believe this?"*

Romans 1:16–17
*"For I am not ashamed of the gospel of Christ, for it is
the power of God to salvation for everyone who believes,
for the Jew first and also for the Greek. For in it the
righteousness of God is revealed from faith to faith; as
it is written, "The righteous shall live by faith."*

Belief (faith) comes first then salvation. We are saved by God's grace. However, God selects us for salvation because of our faith. The act of employment in the secular world gives us some secular parallel of this truth. When a candidate recognizes they are unemployed and desperately needs a job, they begin to seek employment. When a candidate believes a company has a job opening and believes the company can hire them if the company wants to, the candidate applies for the job. They have faith to believe that if the company chooses they can be hired. If that candidate never applies for the job they will never get hired. But the total decision to hire or not hire is the company's decision. The applicant is hired because they put in an application and asked for the job, but they are not hired by the application.

In salvation we come to the point of believing we are sinners and as such we are separated from God. We recognize we need God to take over our life and we regret or repent that we have been so unfaithful to God. Then we recognize that God provided a plan for our salvation and we have enough faith to come to God and ask for salvation. This is faith to be saved. God gives it to us. It does not save us but we cannot be saved without this faith. To say we are saved by our faith implies we can save ourselves. This is not true. We apply for salvation because of our faith. And because of our faith, we are saved solely by the Grace of Jesus Christ.

Instant Salvation

Throughout the New Testament we find people were saved instantaneously without any process and without any period of preparation. In the first chapter of John, verses 35 to 49, we see where Andrew, Simon Peter, and Philip were all converted, one by one, immediately by faith in Christ. There is no record in the Bible of any person ever being told to wait, to do penitence, or to do any kind of good work to earn salvation. When we trust Jesus and place our faith in Him, salvation is instantaneous. God gives us numerous examples of saints who died and were immediately taken by God to be with Him.

Luke tells us there is joy in the presence of the angels over one sinner that repents and is saved. While this teaching does not rule out joy of the angels, the joy spoken of is not recorded as being just from the angels but from someone in the presence of the angels. The joy is of other saints who have gone on before. God's Word tells us that Enoch walked with God and was taken by God. He was not left behind until a day to be arranged. The scripture says Elijah was caught up in a whirlwind by God and taken to be with God. In the transfiguration of Jesus the disciples saw Moses and Elias talking with Jesus. There is clear evidence that saints of old went to a place prepared by Jesus when they died. Paul is quite clear 2 Corinthians 5:8 that people saved after the resurrection of Christ spiritually go to be with Jesus. For us to be absent from the body is to be present with the spirit. Paul also corresponded with the Philippians regarding this same subject.

Philippians 3:20
"For our citizenship is in heaven, from it we await a Savior, the Lord Jesus Christ."

Not Saved by Good Works

We do not deserve salvation. There is nothing we can do that will make us worthy of it. Salvation comes because of our faith in

Jesus Christ through the grace of Jesus. Jesus did not have to die for our sins but in love He elected to do so. We believe and trust and after we believe and trust God saves us. Our salvation is not because of good works on our part. It is not because of our connection with any Church or because we have Christian parents or any other reason except that we decided to follow Jesus and ask Him to save us.

Ephesians 2:8–9
"For by grace you have been saved through faith, and this is not your own doing; it is the gift of God, not the result of works, so that no one may boast."

Neither, Baptism, Church membership, good works, tithing, or anything we can do; other than believe on Jesus Christ as the one who paid the price for our salvation, will save us. Our faith in Christ as our Savior and Lord is the only condition we have to meet to be cleansed of our sin.

Nothing Needs to Be Added to Be Saved

The Word of God does not state Baptism is required for Salvation. We will have a total chapter on Baptism that will detail why it is a command immediately after salvation but not required for salvation.

Likewise the scriptures do not require us to join a Church to be saved. When we are saved we become part of the universal Church of God. The Scripture encourages us to join and be active in a local body of believers called the local Church. But membership in a denomination is not part of salvation.

Our Salvation is paid for by the Blood of Jesus

No other price can be paid for our sins but the blood of Jesus. In the Old Testament every lamb, bullock, heifer, goat, turtle dove and pigeon offered on the altar demonstrated that man, a guilty sinner, must have some innocent one to shed his blood to pay for man's sins.

Jesus died for our sins, and, thank God, salvation is bought for every person in the world, if we will have it, as the free gift of God. Peter emphasized that all the redeemed are bought by the blood of Christ:

How will we feel when we are saved?

Some people have an idea that the change of heart is a matter of feeling. Some do not want to claim Christ as savior until they have the mysterious feeling that they want. Do not let the Devil deceive you. God wants us to have a heartfelt religion. We thank God for the joy which He gives to us day by day. But the Bible simply does not tell how one must feel before he is saved, nor does it tell us how you feel after you are saved. All people do not feel the same immediately after Christ saves them.

No one is more saved than another but some may feel the primary emotion of relief. Others may feel jubilation while others feel immense gratefulness. We cannot feel right until we get right. Rejoicing does not come before we trust the Lord. We do not feel the result of medicine before we take it. The Children of Israel in the wilderness, bitten by fiery serpents and at the point of death, were not healed and did not feel healed until they looked to the brass serpent on the pole (Num. 21:6–9). People are not saved by feeling; they are saved by trusting in Christ.

The prodigal son, away from home in the hog pen, decided to arise and go to his father, but he did not feel good. He was without shoes, clothed in rags, without the ring of son-ship, without any evidence of his father's forgiveness, perishing with hunger. Yet he arose and came to his father, not by feeling, but by faith in his father. And his father received him, like God receives every sinner who will come. And when the prodigal son sat down at his father's table, with shoes of the gospel of peace, clothed in the garments of righteousness of Christ, with the ring of son-ship on his finger, eating the fatted calf at the right hand of the father, happy in his love, then he has plenty of feeling.

What about Public Confession?

God tells us to not make salvation an act that man can do. It is true that God told us to publicly confess our faith in Jesus. To publically claim Christ as your Savior simply tells others that you trust Him in the heart. But we cannot come to Christ without trusting Him, and John 1:12 shows that receiving Jesus is the same as believing on His name. Public confession is a result of salvation not part of salvation.

Can you lose your salvation?

Many people who outwardly profess to be Christians believe that if they do not live a good Christian life, God will take away their Eternal Security (Salvation). This belief brings into question the reality of their salvation. Earlier in this chapter we stressed the point God makes in Scripture when he very bluntly tells us that man is not saved because of anything he does. Salvation happens because of the Grace of God that is granted to man if man will decide to put his faith in Jesus Christ to save us from our sin. No actions of man can justify our salvation and no action of man can take away our salvation.

Chapter 10 is devoted to the Doctrine of Security of the Believer. We will deal in depth with this vital teaching of scripture in that section.

Four Spiritual Laws

Bill Bright, founder of Campus Crusade for Christ, a fantastic Christian evangelistic ministry, is credited as having conceptualized and implemented "The Four Spiritual Laws" as a way to clearly explain God's plan for Salvation of the lost. He breaks it down in simplistic terms. This listing of four basic rules of nature and God's will simplifies explaining the Plan of Salvation to the lost. The four Spiritual Laws are as follows:

Spiritual Law Number 1
"God loves you and has a wonderful plan for your life"

This spiritual law is based on the biblical truth that God loves every person He has ever created regardless of what sin they have committed. This does not mean they do not have to pay the penalty for their sin but it does mean God loves them so much He provided His own begotten son, Jesus Christ, to die on Calvary to pay for our sins conditional upon us trusting Jesus, asking Jesus to save us and wanting to be more like Jesus. John 3:16: *"For God so loved the world that He gave His only Son that whoever believes in Him shall not perish but have eternal life."*

The reality of truth is that God loves you and has a wonderful plan for your life. Before you were born God knew you would be born and He provided a way that your life can be wonderful, have purpose and be forever in harmony with our creator. Isn't it amazing that God would love us so much He would send His only beloved Son to die for us and thereby create a plan for our salvation? God wants every person ever born to enjoy a peaceful relationship with Him through the blood Jesus shed on Calvary to save us. But sin has to be paid for and the wages of sin is death. That means someone must die for our sins. God loves us so much He sent His Son Jesus to die for our sins. God still wants us to have a wonderful life even though we have disobeyed Him.

Spiritual Law Number 2
"Humanity is tainted by sin and is therefore separated from God. As a result we cannot know God's wonderful plan for our lives."

God is Holy. God is Just. God is Righteous. Man is, by nature, none of these. God cannot coexist with the sin of mankind because God is exactly opposite of sin and yet God loves us and wants a relationship with us. John 3:23: *"For all have sinned and come short of the glory of God."*

When Adam sinned against God by disobeying God's will, a barrier of sin was created that separates God and man. That barrier is man's sin. All human beings are cursed with that sin and it is referred to as a sin nature. It is a natural impulse of mankind to always act, and think trying to advance ourselves rather than trying to please God. That is not how we were created. Because of this sin barrier that keeps us from have a relationship of love for God we cannot know of God's wonderful plan for our lives.

Spiritual Law Number 3
"Jesus Christ is God's only provision for our sins."

The truth in God's Word tells us that even though we are sinners, God still loves us. In fact He loves us so much He sent His Son, Jesus Christ, to die for our sins and therefore we can be cleansed of our sins and our relationship with God restored. Romans 5:8: *"But God shows his love for us in that while we were still sinners, Christ died for us."* The death of Jesus to pay for our sins is essential because without His death we would have to pay for our sins with our own death. Romans 6:23 *"For the wages of sin is death, but the free gift of God is eternal life in Christ Jesus our Lord."* Death does mean the end of our physical live here on earth but it also means total separation from God throughout eternity and eternal punishment in Hell for our sins.

Spiritual Law Number 4
"We must place our faith in Jesus Christ as Savior in order to receive the gift of salvation and know God's wonderful plan for our lives."

The only way we can avoid Hell and eternal torment and the only way we can avoid total separation from God and the wonderful plan He has for our life is to believe Jesus Christ died for our sins. Then we have to want Jesus to save us from our sins and in our heart ask Jesus to save us. John 1:12: *"But to all who did receive him, who believed in his name, he gave the right to become children of God"*

By faith we are saved through the grace of our Lord and Savior Jesus Christ. But it is not faith that saves us. We have to approach God for salvation through faith to believe on Jesus but it is God's Grace that allows us to be saved. Our faith gives us the right to become the children of God but then God has to receive us. He has promised that if we believe on Jesus we will be saved. Acts 16:31 *"And they said, "Believe in the Lord Jesus, and you will be saved, you and your household."*

Salvation is a free Gift

We can never earn Salvation because we are by nature sinners. Spiritually we have a huge debt and no collateral. We owe the price of death to pay for our own sins. But God loved us so much He gave His only begotten Son, who lived a sinless life, and could therefore use His death to pay for our sins. This price of our salvation is not earned by our works. It is paid only by the grace of God through our faith in Jesus Christ.

The word grace means unmerited favor. It means God is offering us something we do not deserve. We do not have to work for it and we cannot earn it. But we have to be willing to receive it and desire to become a follower of Jesus Christ. Jesus Christ wants to have a personal relationship with each of us. We do not have an automatic right to become a child of God. We are sinners and God is holy. Yet God grants us that right or privilege on the condition that we repent of our sins and place our faith in Christ Jesus. This privilege is granted only to those who believe Jesus is the Son of God. It is given only to those who believe He came to die for their sins, and who believe He rose from the grave and conquered death. And then they must decide in their hearts they want to please God and honor Him for the rest of their life.

Ephesians 2:8–9
"For by grace You have been saved through faith, and this (faith) is not your own doing it is the gift of God, not of works so that no one may boast."

Paul wanted to teach the churches and therefore teach us, that while we have to have faith to believe in Christ to be saved our salvation does not happen because of our faith. It is essential that we have enough faith in Christ to believe in Him but God even gives us that faith if we will accept it. That much faith is available to everyone if they will accept it. Our salvation is an act of the Holy Spirit empowered by the Son of God. At no point does our salvation come about because of what we do. In part, our salvation comes about because of what we believe. But belief alone does not save us.

CHAPTER NINE

The Doctrine of Progressive Revelation

God's Progressive Revelation of His Plan for Man

What is a Dispensationalist?

N o one knows how long people have been on the earth. The Bible does not give us a definitive number of years since the creation of Adam. However, by a close review of the lineage of people in both the New and Old Testament we can come to a reasonable estimate that people have been on this earth approximately six thousand to seven thousand years. Yes those who want to believe in evolution claim we are millions of years old. The problem of evolution as the basis of creation, discounts what God clearly states in Genesis and much of the first five books of the Old Testament. We do know that from the days of Adam and Eve to now, the Bible gives us a clear documentary of God's creation and changes that have occurred. In the Doctrine of Progressive Revelation God's Word gives us a clear picture of God working with His creation and desiring to have a better relationship with mankind. God is almost always disappointed with man's unwillingness to allow Him to direct our lives. God has always wanted mankind to put Him number 1 in our life priorities. God has always wanted mankind to love Him even as God has loved His creation. Man has failed and God has, with each failure, changed His method of communicating with mankind. As these changes are recorded in the Bible the changes have evolved to be called Dispensationalism.

A Biblical Dispensationalist is one who looks upon the history of God's relationship to mankind and measures the changes God has made over time trying to convince man to love Him and be faithful to Him. A Dispensationalist interprets the Word of God literally. If the Bible says the Millennial Kingdom will be one thousand years the Dispensationalist believes it will last one thousand years. The Dispensationalist believes the Seven-Year Tribulation prophesied in the Book of Daniel and the book of Revelation will be exactly seven years. Likewise the Dispensationalist believes that when God gave Daniel a seventy-week prophecy until the end of time God takes the Bible as truth without man's interpretation. It is true the Dispensationalist allows for symbols, figures of speech and parables to influence what is recorded by God. For instance Daniel's seventy-week prophecy was done using the Hebrew idiom of one week equaling one year. This was a common understanding in the Hebrew language and was therefore recorded in God's Word. But there is no room for mankind to read where God spoke the world into existence and then rationalize that God really meant it took millions of years for the world to evolve into the shape it is today.

A true Dispensationalist believes God's Word teaches two foundational beliefs on Scripture interpretation. One is that what God says must be accepted as literal. The second is that God has identified three distinct divisions of people so far as dealing with them. These are the following: (1) the nation of Israel prior to the death, burial and resurrection of Jesus, (2) the Church, as created by Christ after His resurrection, and (3) the Seven-Year Tribulation period that began after the Rapture of the Church and ends with the Second Coming of Christ.

The Dispensationalist recognizes that people of all ages have available to them God's Plan of Salvation from their sins. And it is the same plan for all three groups. People of all ages must believe in God the Father and the promises of God the Father. More specifically they must believe in the Messiah God promised to send to save His believers of their sin. The only difference is related to the revelation of detail God delivered to His people.

Old Testament Saints believed God promised the Messiah to save them and they looked forward to the coming of the Messiah. They knew the Messiah would suffer and they had limited understanding of the price He would pay for their sins. They had a very limited understanding that the Messiah would be the Son of God and had no understanding He would be named Jesus Christ. Likewise they did not know Christ would come from Heaven to become both man and God. Old Testament Saints had the teachings of their fathers and God gave them "The Law" as a measuring device to help them understand when they were committing acts that were displeasing to God. They also had the Holy Spirit to teach and talk to selected people and anoint these people to be prophets. The prophets instructed the people concerning God's will for them.

New Testament Saints believe in God the Son as the promised Messiah. So New Testament Saints believe Jesus Christ the Son of

God is that promised Messiah and they look back in faith to Jesus and the price He paid for them on Calvary. For New Testament Saints their measuring device to teach them when they were committing acts displeasing to God was the life of Jesus Christ. New Testament Saints have the Holy Spirit living in their hearts to instruct, counsel, and chastise them, helping them to stay within the will of God.

The Tribulation Saints will believe in Jesus Christ as the Son of God in spite of the most incredible physical price anyone could every face paying for their faith. They will face torture and death if they confess Jesus Christ as their Savior. And they will be required to wear the "Mark of the Beast" to certify they worship the Antichrist. They will be required to publically confess to be believers in the Antichrist thus not believers in Jesus Christ. However, in their presence will be selected men, chosen by God to be evangelists preaching faith in Jesus Christ. These men, protected by the Holy Spirit, will preach and teach salvation by believing in the price Jesus Christ paid for their sins.

The Doctrine of Dispensation is often said to be an interpretation of biblical history in different time sequences recording the way God related to mankind. That is almost correct. The Doctrine of Dispensation is an interpretation of biblical history recording the way God chose and will choose to communicate His love and expectation for mankind. God did not change His plan of communication to man based on time. He changed based on mankind's reaction to His message. God's expectation of mankind has always been the same and has never varied. God wants mankind to love Him, to express love back to God, to desire to always please God and to do this mankind has to be a righteous, just, holy, and truthful believer in God.

God's Word does not tell us exactly why He has revealed His plan for mankind in a progressive pattern. Yet there is a clear and undeniable progressive pattern to the amount of Himself God revealed to man with each new Dispensation. With each new Dispensation God revealed more of Himself trying to help man make the life changing decision to trust God in all things. We know God wants a free love coming to Him from His creation without the need of coaxing it from us. God wants us to love Him without the need for revelation of who He is or what He wants from His creation. The Bible is very clear that we have in every stage of revelation substantially disappointed Him and yet His love for us does not dim. He remains faithful to us and continually reveals more and more of whom He is and what He wants us to be. God is trying to convince us to be faithful to Him and trust and love Him. And He wants us to love Him and be faithful to Him with as little as possible reaching out to us to obtain that relationship.

What do all Dispensations have in common?

God's Word tells us that all Dispensations have sinned and come short of the will of God. All are separated from God because of their sin and have no hope of restoration based on their actions. Jesus Christ dying on Calvary for their sins and conquering death by rising from the dead the third day is the only hope any of these Dispensations have to ever be reconciled to God. God's plan of salvation for all five groups is exactly the same. That plan for all of them is that they must believe on the Messiah God the Father promised all mankind. He (Jesus) is our hope for salvation. Without their faith in Jesus they are hopelessly lost.

Galatians 3:22
"But the Scripture imprisoned everything under sin, so that the promise by faith in Jesus Christ might be given to those who believe."

There is one plan of salvation and only one path of meeting the requirements of that plan for all of mankind regardless of when we were born or what God's revelation to us has been. However, God has revealed more and more of His plan of salvation too successive generations of people. His plan for salvation has never changed. God Himself has never changed and His expectations of His people have never changed. In the first dispensation of revelation, given to Adam and Eve in the Garden of Eden, we can assume mankind had broad revelation of what God wanted them to be. Adam and Eve had God

Himself who walked and talked with them in a glorified way and personally communicated with them and everything was perfect. We do not know how many years this experience lasted.

The Dispensation of Innocence

The word dispensation simply means a period of mankind's existence in which God relates to His people in certain distinct ways. The first age or dispensation is that of innocence. This age occurred for an unknown number of years in which Adam, and later Eve, walked and talked with God in the Garden of Eden. They shared absolute, total trust with God. Adam and Eve were innocence, happy, fulfilled and God was happy with them. Sin was not part of mankind's world.

During the Dispensation of Innocence, from the time Adam was created to the time Eve was created God often visited directly with Adam. They walked and talked together. This was the relationship God wanted with His creation man. We do not know if God came to Adam in a bodily form or if He came in spirit. But we know God had a close, personnel fellowship with Him. At some time God decided it would be good for Adam to have an earthly companion and He created Eve to be Adam's companion. There was a period of time in which God visited and had fellowship with both Adam and Eve. Adam had work to do in caring for the world around him but he enjoyed it. Adam had certain responsibilities assigned by God for Adam's benefit. There was no death. Animals, birds, and reptiles were not afraid of Adam or each other. They did not eat meat and did not destroy each other. Adam's dominion was very pleasant.

Genesis 1:28
Then God blessed them, and God said to them, "Be fruitful and multiply; fill the earth and subdue it; have dominion over the fish of the sea, over the birds of the heavens, and over every living thing that moves on the earth."

Genesis 2:15–17
Then the LORD God took the man and put him in the
Garden of Eden to work it and keep it. And the LORD
God commanded the man, saying, "You may surely
eat of every tree of the garden; but of the tree of the
knowledge of good and evil you shall not eat, for in
the day that you eat of it you shall surely die."

This beautiful relationship, called the Dispensation of Innocence ended when Adam and Eve elected to disobey God and eat of the Tree of knowledge of good and evil. Because of this act of sin they were forced out of the Garden of Eden.

God's Expectations of Man

During the Dispensation of Innocence, God expected to have a relationship of love with mankind. This is the expectation God had for man when He created us. God wanted mankind to be like Him in every sense. God wanted mankind to choose to be like him by our own free choice. Only then could man return a free love back to God. Only then could man share the love God had for man. God wanted man to be pure, to be Holy, to be just, and to love Him. During the Dispensation of Innocence, man fulfilled this expectation for an unknown period of time.

God's Freedom given to Man

During the Dispensation of Innocence God gave man the freedom to do anything he desired except one restriction. Mankind had no concept of evil. Mankind had not disobeyed God by eating of the Tree of Knowledge of Good and Evil. Mankind only knew holiness and righteousness and was fulfilled and happy. God's only restriction on man was to not eat of the Tree of Knowledge of Good and Evil.

God's Test of Man

God's purpose in creation of man was to create a being that had the capacity to return a free love back to God. God is love and love must be returned or it is empty. At creation God gave man the freedom to disobey Him. Without that freedom, man would have made been unable to return a pure love back to God. Therefore, God created a simple test of man in the Dispensation of Innocence to give man the choice of obeying God or not obeying God. That test was to not eat of the tree God placed in the middle of the Garden of Eden. It was the Tree of Knowledge of Good and Evil. Man could eat of all other trees in the Garden. Man was not informed much about the tree except that if he ate of it man would surely die. God gave some revelation to mankind concerning death. Death meant God would separate Himself from man if man disobeyed God.

But Adam was disobedient to God. Adam listened to Eve and ate of the Tree of Knowledge of Good and Evil and the dispensation of innocence was gone. God's relationship with his creation, man, was changed.

God's Revelation to Man

During the Dispensation Innocence God gave full revelation to man relating to the identity of God. God and mankind walked and talked and maintained a relationship of deep love. During this dispensation man knew God better than at any other time outside of the seventh Dispensation. That seventh dispensation will be the last dispensation or the Dispensation of the Millennium reign of Christ. God chose to not inform man what evil was because evil is not the nature of God. God gave man no knowledge of evil. God only told man he was not to eat of the Tree of Knowledge of Good and Evil for if he did on that day man would surely be totally and permanently separated from God. God's promise to Adam was that if he ate of the Tree of Knowledge of Good and Evil then all of mankind would be separated from God. And if Adam ate of that tree then death would enter the world.

God's Punishment of Man

In the Dispensation of Innocence there was no punishment of man because man had not sinned. Man was still in a loving, close, and mutual relationship with God.

Man's Response to God

For an undetermined period of time the relationship of man to God was wonderful. Man walked and talked with God. Man enjoyed God the Fathers presence. It may be that man understood the Trinity of God the Father, God the Son and God the Holy Spirit. The Bible tells us God came down to visit with man. Man was eager to see God and the relationship was what God intended. But Satan tempted Eve and Adam followed Eve's lead. Both Adam and Eve disobeyed God and the perfect relationship was broken. Man sinned and fell from the Grace of God into eternal damnation. Death, meaning physical and spiritual separation from God, entered the world. In addition, as a punishment to man, physical death was pronounced upon mankind. And man was given a new nature and that new nature was a sin nature. This means that for the first time, man's natural desire was to be independent and to be disobedient to God. This sin nature was imputed to all mankind including all the descendants of Adam. Thus the Scripture tells us that from Adam sin came into the world.

Romans 5:12
"Therefore, just as sin came into the world through one man, and death through sin, and so death spread to all men because all sinned."

What was required of man to be saved?

Every day, every moment, every second of Adam's life he had to have faith in God the Father. Through Adam's faith God would keep him righteous and holy and to maintain the relationship of love they enjoyed. Adam knew he had a choice. God Himself informed Adam that if he ate of the Tree of Knowledge of Good and Evil he would surely die. Adam's only hope of maintaining the relationship of love with God was to be faithful to the desires and expectations of God. Adam lived by faith. His faith was not in the resurrection of Jesus Christ because Adam did not have revealed to him the name of Jesus Christ. But God revealed to Adam and Eve, the first of God's creation, that He, God, would send a promised one who would some-day deal justly with Satan.

Genesis 3:15
"I will put enmity between you and the woman, and between your offspring and her offspring, He shall bruise your head and you shall bruise you're his heal."

In this verse God outlined the plan of Salvation for Old Testament people. They were informed by God that God would send one, sometime in the future, to deal justly with Satan for what he had done and to deal with Adam and all mankind based on their faith in God. In the Dispensation of Innocence mankind was saved because of his unwavering faith and trust in God the Father. Salvation was not applicable to this dispensation because man had not sinned and therefore was not lost. But the plan of God's Salvation for mankind was revealed although vaguely, and Adam was, after He sinned against God given the promise He could be saved if He would remain faithful to God.

Thread of Grace

In the Dispensation of Innocence the grace of God was demonstrated through His creation of Adam and His creation of Eve for Adam's good. God loved and still loves His creation. His grace prepared a wonderful world of beauty beyond man's descriptive power for man's enjoyment. Yet the Bible tells us that God knew, even before He created man, that man would eventually disobey Him and sin. The love and grace of God to create man even though He knew man would fail in his faith is beyond our ability to comprehend.

Let's look at each of the Dispensation periods to compare them regarding God's expectations of man, God's test of man, God's revelation to man, and man's response to God. Then we want to know what was required of mankind to be saved, and to follow the thread of God's grace through each of the dispensations.

The Dispensation of Conscience

The second dispensation is called the Dispensation of Conscience. Conscience refers to that part of mankind that houses our innermost being. That part of man is the soul. The soul determines what our values will be. The soul determines the direction we will go with our life. The soul receives the knowledge gained in the brain, and the information obtained through our senses of touch, smell, hearing, sight and taste; and filters this into actions and decisions. Man's conscience, the soul of mankind, is that part of mankind into which God stored an understanding of right and wrong.

When Adam disobeyed God and was separated from God, mankind did not lose his understanding of what was right and wrong. They just gained, through the eating of the Tree of Knowledge of Good and Evil, a desire to experience wrong for his own self-indulgence. Mankind had added a desire to follow his own will even through it was disobedience of God. Mankind, all of mankind including us did, however, lose an instinctive love for God and things that were righteous. We gained an instinctive love for independence, for unrighteousness, and for disobedience of God.

The Dispensation of Conscience was a time period lasting from the fall of Adam to the days of Noah. During this time period each person was held responsible for remaining faithful to God based on what he/she knew to be right, without any further revelation from God. Conscience was the accountability God placed on mankind to remain faithful to God.

Romans 2:15
"They show that the work of the law written in their
hearts, their conscience also bearing witness, and their
conflicting thoughts accuse or even excuse them."

Romans 2:15 reveals to us that in the Dispensation of conscience God relied on mankind to be faithful to Him on the basis what they believed to be right. This may sound shallow for God to rely on man's conscience for faithfulness. But Adam and Eve and their children had the testimony of Adam and Eve and their memory of how it was walking and talking with God. Why should greater revelation be needed? Adam and Eve knew what they had done wrong. They knew and remembered the price they paid for their disobedience of God. Surely they taught their children. It would appear from the life of Abel they did and Abel listened. But Cain yielded to his selfish desires. As they grew to adulthood Cain made his living working the soil and growing crops. Abel was a shepherd and apparently raised sheep. They traded product with each other and used their product to make sacrifices to God. The fact they made sacrifices to God speaks to the reality that Adam and Eve taught their children the expectations of God. God viewed the sacrifice of Abel to be given with the right attitude while Cain's was unsatisfactory. Cain became jealous of Abel and murdered him. The Bible says Cain wandered, built a gathering of people and fathered the line of descendants of Enoch.

During the Dispensation of Conscience God wanted man to come back to Him and gave all of Adam's descendants the freedom to worship. God waited on His creation to turn back to Him and choose the path of righteousness. But mankind kept getting more sinful, selfish, and defiant. The Dispensation of Conscience lasted from the fall of Adam to the flooding of the world in the days of Noah. It was brought to an end by the almost universal sinful domination of mankind and God's disgust with man's actions.

In the Dispensation of Conscience Adam, and His family, had a different relationship with God. They had a steep price to pay for their disobedience of God. That price now meant they did not have

God to talk with and to listen to them on a constant basis. And ultimately, man must now constantly demonstrate to God his love for God through offering of sacrifices to God. Because of His sin man would die separated from God throughout eternity. Today, as a descendant of Adam we also have that same relationship. We must demonstrate to God our love for Him or be separated from Him.

God's creation of people from Adam to Abram, were not part of a chosen people because God had not yet chosen Israel as His "Chosen People." The descendants of Adam include the Israelites but also all other people to be born in the world. This is different than the Bible reference to the Hebrew people being the descendants of Abraham. God did not create a special plan for these people to demonstrate their love for Him as He does in forth-coming dispensations.

God's Expectations of Man

During the Dispensation of Conscience God expected mankind to love Him, to do, to think, to act and to reason just as God thought acted and reasoned. God wanted mankind to be like Him. God is and was and will be Holy. God is love. God is just. God will not and cannot tolerate evil because to do so totally changes whom God is; and God does not change. God's expectations of mankind did not change from the Dispensation of Innocence.

God's Freedom given to Man

God gave mankind the freedom to choose to obey God or to obey Satan. God did not take away from mankind the sense of right he had been given in the Dispensation of Innocence but because of the sin of Adam, man was given another additional nature. That nature was a nature of sin. God wanted mankind to decide, based on his understanding of what was right, to follow God's will and God's teachings. God wanted man to reject his own nature of sin. Man was given total freedom to choose to follow God, his own desires, or the influence of Satan every day of his life.

God's Test of Man

God knew before the beginning of time that man would fail in the Dispensation of Innocence and in the Dispensation of Conscience. Yet God also knew it would be much more difficult for man to be faithful to Him in this age where the nature of sin permeated his soul and thinking. Man needed help to identify when he failed to measure up to the righteousness of God. At the creation of man, God imbedded His Spirit into the very soul of man. That spirit of man enabled Adam and Eve to communicate with God until they disobeyed God. So God relied on mankind's conscience, his knowledge of right and wrong, his very soul as his tool to fight the will of Satan. Would man resist the lure of Satan or would man give in to selfishness and wickedness? This test gave mankind a choice of serving God or rebelling against God. This is the ultimate test man will face in every dispensation of time. Will man serve God and be faithful in heart, mind and action to God's will or will man choose to do what he wants at the displeasure of God? During the Dispensation of conscience, man was held responsible for rejecting the influence of his sin nature while being obedient to his Spiritual nature. In so doing mankind would be pleasing in the sight of God.

God's Revelation to Man

Man needed help. Previously, in the Dispensation of Innocence Man had no sin and therefore had no need to ever be forgiven for anything. Now man did sin daily and yet, God did not turn His back on mankind. God gave to man a new revelation never previously given to man. God gave mankind a method of demonstrating his sorrow for having disappointed God and to ask God for forgiveness. We must realize that man was now separated from God. Man had no avenue to communicate with God although The Holy Spirit communicated with Adam and other select individuals as God so ordained. The Holy Spirit told Adam that God required a blood sacrifice to atone for their sins. God demanded they offer a burnt offering of flesh signifying their repentance of sin and their desire for

God to forgive their sins. However the sacrifice did not cause God to forgive their sins. It was the mindset of the heart that caused God to forgive their sins. The burnt offering was merely a way man could communicate to God that mind-set. Man obtained God's forgiveness by having a heart that was sorry he had disobeyed God. Man obtained God's forgiveness by having a heart that desired to renew a close relationship with God. Man obtained God's forgiveness by having faith to believe God loved him and would forgive him if his heart was right. Man did not gain God's forgiveness by works but by faith. In the Dispensation of Conscience man had no knowledge of Jesus Christ and certainly had no understanding that Jesus would someday be the promised Messiah. Therefore mankind, during this dispensation, had revealed to them that God had promised a coming Messiah. But they had no basis to place their faith in Jesus Christ. Their faith rested on God the Father's deliverance of His promise of one who would somehow handle the sin of mankind. God's plan of salvation for man was not different than today, but to that dispensation the definition of faith was different. Mankind is not saved by good works but by having a repentant heart, by asking God to forgive us of our sins, and by faith to believe He will do so.

Many scholars feel Old Testament Saints were saved quiet differently than are saints in the Dispensation of Grace. They feel the act of regeneration or being "Born Again" only applies to the Dispensation of Grace or to the Church. Much of their justification for such a position is that the Holy Spirit did not live in the hearts of man and therefore was not a constant urging of man to trust God and repent of sin. They are correct that the Holy Spirit only spoke to man on an individual basis and was quiet selective regarding to whom He spoke. But they miss the point of the sacrifice required of God. The sacrifice was the act of man that invited the Holy Spirit to touch the heart of an Old Testament Saint, change that heart into a new creature and save that soul. The burnt offering said to the Holy Spirit this is my heart, I am sorry about my sins and I ask God to forgive me.

The undeniable truth is that God reveals to us that many great saints of the Old Testament had a heart that loved God. Abraham,

Noah, Enoch, David, Joseph, Elijah, and many of the great females of faith in the Old Testament, had a heart of love for God. Based on their faith they were given a new nature. The old nature of sin was present in them just as it is in us. Yet they were given a new nature. But this new nature was not completed. It could not be completed until Jesus Christ would, in the future, die on Calvary, be buried and rise again in victory over their sins. That is the act of being "born again." That is the act of regeneration just as believers today are "Born Again" when they are saved. The Old Testament tells us that the Old Testament saints were preserved forever because of their faith.

Psalm 37:28
"For the LORD loves justice, He will not forsake His saints;
They are preserved forever, but the children
of the wicked shall be cut off."

Old Testament Saints had no knowledge of Jesus Christ and certainly did not know He would be the Messiah. Therefore they could not have faith in Jesus Christ but could have faith in God the Father, the one who promised the coming Messiah. They had some degree of understanding that God the Father would provide a plan whereby their sins could be forgiven. Such scholars ask, "How can Old Testament Saints be regenerated when they did not believe in Jesus Christ?" They did believe in Jesus Christ as the Messiah and Savior of their sins to the extent God revealed such truth to them. Their belief, limited in scope as it was, was counted unto them as righteousness.

Genesis 15:6
"And he believed in the LORD, and He
accounted it to him as righteousness."

God's Word is clear in explaining that the sacrifices themselves were not the objective of God. God's objective for Old Testament Saints was the same as is His objective for us in the Dispensation of Grace. He desired a pure heart of love toward God.

Psalms 51:16–17
*"For You will not delight in sacrifice, or I would give
it; You will not be pleased with a burnt offering.
The sacrifices of God are a broken spirit,
A broken and a contrite heart—O God, You will not despise."*

Man's Punishment from God

In the Dispensation of Conscience God gave Adam and all his seed the reminder of pain. Adam and his seed now had to work for a living. Childbearing to Eve and all women was with great pain. There were weeds, thorns and corruption to the land that caused making a living hard. These were punishment to Adam and his seed and also reminders that their disobedience of God caused the pain. The pain was intended to tell mankind that he needed to be faithful to God.

However, the greatest punishment is that death entered the world. The days man would live on earth became numbered. Yes, man lived much longer in the days of Adam to Noah but still God imposed physical death to all mankind as part of the punishment of having disobeyed God.

Man's Response to God

Mankind failed totally to be faithful to God based on his conscience of what was right and wrong. Man's basic sin nature that was imputed to mankind when mankind fell from the Garden of Eden proved too great for man to respond favorable to God. God gave mankind five different types of offerings that man could use to communicate to God his repentant heart. All offerings were voluntary offerings that required sacrifice on the part of the participant. They were made to demonstrate to God a voluntary act of worship toward God, an atonement sin, a commitment to God Jehovah as the Lord and Master of the participant's life, and complete surrender to God Jehovah.

- The burnt offering was a ram, bull or bird, bought or brought by the one making the sacrifice and offered to God.
- The grain offering was an offering of Grain, Fine Flour, Olive Oil, Incense, or baked bread. This offering was made in combination with burnt offerings.
- The peace offering was any animal offered as a burnt offerings combined with a communal meal with other believers.
- The sin offering was a young bull and this was offered in atonement for specific unintentional sin.
- The Trespass Offering was always a ram offered for unintentional specific sin.

Genesis 6:5
"The LORD saw that the wickedness of man was great in the earth, and that every intention of the thoughts of his heart was only evil continually."

What was required of man to be saved?

Through the Dispensation of Conscience God expected man to trust Him to take care of every need man would have. God wanted man to be totally dependent on God and to obey Him with a loving, willing heart. To do so required faith by man in Jehovah. When the Dispensation of Conscience began every human on earth was doomed to eternal damnation. God however gave man, in spite of his sin, a way to ask God for forgiveness and to demonstrate his faith and trust in God through burnt offerings.

The burnt offering sacrifices man made in Old Testament times, were merely the means by which mankind communicated to God. God gave them this avenue to communicate with Him and express their sorry for having disappointed God and to tell God they had a repentant heart. The burnt sacrifice was man's way of asking God for forgiveness. The burnt sacrifice in many ways took the place of our prayer to God, which is possible because we have the Holy Spirit living in our heart as a believer.

To be saved, mankind, in the Old Testament, had to believe in God Jehovah to the point they were ready to sacrifice of their worldly possessions to appease God. They had to believe to the point they were ready to commit their lives and heart to God and were ready to ask God to change their heart and forgive them for their sins. That is not unlike our salvation today except we have an understanding of Jesus Christ as the Messiah who died for our sins. We must have faith in Jesus to the extent of God's revelation to us. The Old Testament Saint did not have that revelation but they had to have faith in God Jehovah and had to ask God to forgive their sins. They did this through the burnt offering. If their heart was not right before God their burnt offering was rejected by God.

The Thread of Grace

Even though mankind failed in the age of conscience, God did not destroy the human race. In His total disgust, when He saw mankind so consumed with evil, God considered destroying the world. But in His Grace God gave mankind another chance. Therefore God gave to man, first, the opportunity to ask for God's forgiveness. Man had no assurance that his sins were forgiven because God did not communicate to every individual believer. But God gave man, through His grace, the burnt sacrifice to ask for forgiveness. The Bible tells us of a few who were redeemed because of their desire to follow God and be forgiven for their sins.

Why was God pleased with the offering of Abel but displeased with the offering of Cain? This is a foundational fact that establishes the trend throughout all dispensations. God was pleased with Abel's offering because Abel's heart was right and his offering was given with a repentant attitude. Abel had a desire to seek the forgiveness of God. Cain, on the other hand, was told by God that if his offering, intended to gain God's forgiveness for his sin, was not given with the right mindset and heart it would be unacceptable to God. This foundational fact establishes that in the Dispensation of Conscience forgiveness by God came by a repentant heart not from works. The failure of Cain and the success of Abel in gaining the forgiveness of God is revealed in Genesis 4:8, with the murder of Abel.

Genesis 4:8
"Cain spoke to Abel his brother an, when they were in the field, that Cain rose up against his brother Abel and killed him."

Mankind continued to not listen to his conscience. Mankind continued to not listen to the Spirit of God imbedded in his soul. Mankind continued to not pay attention to the reminder of pain God sent to remind him of his obligation to be faithful to God. In Genesis 6:1–5 more violence and corruption evolved and mankind became increasingly sinful. The Dispensation of Conscience lasted from Adam to Noah when God, seeing that mankind was totally corrupt again increased his revelation to mankind and his method of influencing mankind to be faithful to Him. The Dispensation of Conscience ended in the worldwide flood in which only Noah and his household were saved. They were saved because of Noah's faith. Faith continues to be the evolving truth as the constant requirement of God of mankind. Likewise the Grace of God is evident in God instructing Noah to build an ark and to spare the family of Noah because of Noah's faithfulness.

The Dispensation of Human Government

We know the Dispensation of Conscience ended with the worldwide flood from which God saved only eight people. These were not all believers but were of the family of Noah and were saved because of the faith of Noah. Because of the flood and the warning Noah gave to all who would listen, any thinking man would have been so grateful to have survived they would praise God forever. God gave man a period of time to test how he would respond. This period is known as the dispensation of Human Government. It began when Noah's Arc rested on dry ground and closed in the confusion of tongues.

Genesis 9:1, 2
And God blessed Noah and his sons and said to them,
"Be fruitful and multiply and fill the earth. The fear
of you and the dread of you shall be upon every beast
of the earth and upon every bird of the heavens, upon
everything that creeps on the ground and all the fish
of the sea. Into your hand they are delivered."

During both the dispensation of Innocence and the dispensation of Conscience, God took on the role of directly judging the earth. This was not effective because man revolted against God. Therefore, in the dispensation of Human Government God ushered in an age in which man would be given certain penalties God would impose on man for not obeying Him. God let man form governing bodies to self-discipline their selves. Noah and his wife and his three sons and their wives began to repopulate the earth. Noah spoke to God and asked for authority to form a governing body to enforce righteousness and to apply discipline over those who would lead the body of people away from God. God granted this request. Shem became the father of the Mediterranean region dwellers and eventually the Jews. Ham's descendants spread into Africa, and Japheth's into Eurasia. The one law God demanded Noah enforce was no killing of human flesh.

Genesis 9:3–6
"Every moving thing that lives shall be food for you. And
as I gave you the green plants, I give you everything. But
you shall not eat flesh with its life, that is, its blood. And
for your lifeblood I will require a reckoning: from every
beast I will require it and from man. From his fellow man
I will require a reckoning for the life of man. Whoever
sheds the blood by man shall his blood be shed.
for God made man in his own image."

God gave to mankind the responsibility of governing themselves and the authority of taking human life if one murders another.

And with the ushering in of the dispensation of man's rule God give mankind a promise.

Genesis 8:21–22

"And when the LORD smelled a soothing aroma the LORD said in His heart, "I will never again curse the ground because of man, for the intention of man's heart is evil from his youth; Neither will I ever again strike down every living creature as I have done. "While the earth remains, seedtime and harvest, cold and heat, winter and summer, and day and night shall not cease. "

In the Dispensation of Human Government, God changed the way He governs mankind. He took on a more hands off approach relying on eternal judgment. The content of the new contract with mankind was as follows:

- God will not destroy mankind with a flood of waters every again.
- Man may now eat animal flesh but may not drink blood.
- There will be fear between man and beast.
- People will be responsible for creating human governing bodies to impose punishment up to and including capital punishment.

God's Expectations of Mankind

God's expectation for man does not change. God still wants man to be righteous. God still wants man to be like God Himself. God wants man to resist Satan and to be faithful to God. God wants man to listen to God. God wants man to continue to use burnt offerings of animal flesh and of valuables to God to show God their trust in Him and their repentant heart.

God's Freedom of Mankind

God now gives man more authority toward self-government and gives man responsibility to help others be faithful to God. Man still has the right to choose righteous living or evil living. Man still has the power to choose right or wrong. But man is now granted the authority to identify those of their group who are falling away from God's expectations and to discipline them. Man is even given the authority to kill a person who takes another person's life.

God's Test of Mankind

God's test of mankind was to rule over men in such a way that the righteousness of God would be revealed. Man was not to rule for the power and glory of that rule. Man was not to abuse the power God gave them. Man was to rule with compassion but with justice. Man was to forever reveal to others the will of God in the laws they created. And God specifically told mankind they were not to unite under one government but were to disperse and in so doing populate the earth while stressing the righteousness of God.

God's Revelation to Mankind

God's revelation to mankind was the authority of human government. God continued to require burnt offerings as a symbol of man's repentant heart. God continued to require mankind to ask for forgiveness for sin and was willing to grant forgiveness from sin if the request was sincere.

God's Punishment of Mankind

God's punishment of mankind was the same as in the Dispensation of Conscience. The people violated God's orders in several specific ways other than just not loving Him. First they had no desire in their heart to focus their culture on God. They fell to the prey of Satan's temptations to seek their own authority and power, even to the point of separating from God. They were not unlike Adam. This age ended in a place called Babel where they united their efforts in an attempt to build a tower that would allow them to reach the heights of God. God, therefore, gave them different languages so they could not understand each other and could not complete their effort to become equal with God. The confusion of different languages forced them to scatter across the earth and to finally begin populating the earth.

Man's Response to God

Man's response to God's Dispensation of man's rule was immediately a failure. Noah got drunk and failed to rule as God had ordained. The people failed to dispense but gathered together specifically for the power of numbers and they decided they would build a tower to reach the heavens. They literally built a tremendous tower that, of course, did not begin to reach even the lower heavens, but their will was in direct violation of God's command. These people did not continue to believe in one God but invented Gods to worship. They became obsessed with the worship of idols. This age failed with the Tower of Babel.

What was required of man to be saved?

The responsibility of mankind to God remained the same as in the previous two dispensations. Man was responsible to have faith in the commands of God and to obey God. Man was not responsible to always understand what God commanded but was responsible to obey. Man was also expected and commanded to trust God to see them through trials. Man was to trust God for their daily needs but man failed and began trusting his own ability to provide.

Thread of Grace

God dispersed the people to protect them from themselves. Had God not dispersed them they would have continued to grow more evil. Chapter 11 of Genesis traces the genealogy of Noah and Shem all the way to Abraham who becomes the focal point of God's next dispensation. So God does preserve the seed line of faith promised in the fall of Adam. This seed line was that God would protect the seed line started and promised with the fall of Adam so that all men might someday be provided a Savior who would pay the price of their sins.

The Dispensation of Promise

With the failure of the people on earth to turn to God during the Dispensation of Human Government, God implements a plan to reveal more of who He is to His creation. God looks down on earth and sees one man who worships Him and is pleased by the heart of Abraham. Therefore, God ushers into His relationship with man a new unique effort to draw man to Him. This period of time is known as the Dispensation of Promise because of a covenant God made with Abraham.

Genesis 12:1–3
Now the LORD *said to Abram, "Go from your country and your*
kindred and your father's house to the land that I will show
you; and I will make of you a great nation, and I will bless you
and make your name great, so that you will be a **blessing. I will**
bless those who bless you, and him who dishonors you I will
curse, and in you all the families of the earth shall be blessed."

The unconditional promise in Genesis 12:1–3 was made to Abraham, his descendants Isaac and Jacob and all people of the soon to be nation of Israel. In making this promise or covenant, God wanted Abraham's descendants to be faithful to Him but did not make the promise conditional. With this promise, a new age or dispensation called the Dispensation of Promise was created by God. It is called the Dispensation of Promise because for the first time ever, God chooses one group, the descendants of Abraham, to be His choice to worship Him and to evangelize the world. This does not mean so much that the Israelites would get special privileges. Although they did get special gifts from God, as His chosen people they were given special responsibilities. God's communications and directions from this time forth are through the descendants of

Abraham. This nation of people would become the house of Israel and the promises of God to these people will be fulfilled.

In recognition that the Dispensation of Human Government failed, God selects Abraham because He knew Abraham would be faithful to the revelations of God. Therefore God created a covenant with Abraham. The Abrahamic Covenant included these promises:

- God would make Abraham a great Nation.
- God would make his name great.
- Abraham would be a great blessing to the world.
- God will bless those who bless Abraham.
- God will curse those who curse Abraham.
- All the families of the earth will be blessed through the house of Abraham.

God's Expectations of Mankind

God's expectation of His people never changes. God demands righteousness. God demands mankind wants to be like Him. God hates evil and God will not tolerate sin. God demands that man trust Him and believe on Him.

God's Freedom given to Mankind

God radically changes how he deals with mankind. In the first dispensation (The Dispensation of Innocence) God dealt with all people individually and personally. In the Dispensation of Conscience God relied on the teachings of Adam and Eve to their children. After all Adam and Eve knew how it was to walk and talk with God. They knew what was lost because of disobedience of God. They should have been the best teachers in creation to keep their children on the path of worship of God. In the Dispensation of Human Government God delegated to people the right to govern their selves. God now changes again and selects a people, a nation; that will set the example of how people are to live and act. This nation will be Israel or the descendants of Abraham. God ordains that the only way someone outside of the House of Israel could partake of God's promises was to become part of the House of Israel. They had to be adopted into the Jewish heritage.

God's Test of Man

God's test of mankind was to be circumcised for the right reason. Circumcision signified acceptance of God Jehovah. The test of burnt offerings continues as in past dispensations. The conscience given to man continued to be a gift from God. During the Dispensation of Promise God demanded His "chosen people" would be led by men of faith as evidenced by their having been circumcised. But mankind still had to make daily decisions of choosing God or Evil.

God's Revelation to Man

The people were given a sign of circumcision that signified their acceptance and adoption into the House of Israel. This sign also indicated their willing acceptance of God Jehovah as their God. Mankind's freedom outside of the House of Israel ceased to exist. The freedom of people inside the House of Israel was vast. God gave to His people the promise of becoming a great nation. This was a great revelation. Abraham was chosen to be the father of this great nation because of his faith.

God's Punishment of Mankind

The nation of Israel suffered severe famine that made them elect to go to Egypt even thought it was not the will of God for them to ever leave the land God had provided. In Egypt they eventually fell into bondage and persecution. They suffered 430 years from the call of Abraham and the establishment of the Abrahamic Covenant to the exodus from Egypt. The exodus from Egypt was the close of the Dispensation of Promise.

Man's Response to God

Abraham was a man of faith. He led His people in a marvelous way and was honored by God for His faith. But Abraham was also a human whose faith failed him in many instances. One of those instances was when the people of Abraham suffered severe famine in Canaan, He disobeyed God's commandment to stay in the Canaan, and led his people to Egypt. Abraham's descendants were also of inconsistent faith. Isaac was not faithful to God in Genesis 26:7. Jacob's very name meant deceiver. Jacob's sons, other than Joseph, were corrupt and not faithful followers of God. It was this continual pattern of corrupt, evil leadership of the people that caused God to put the people into bondage. The Dispensation of Promise failed.

What was required of man to be saved?

Again, we see the only path toward a relationship with God was for the people to believe and trust in God. Their trust was focused on God the Father. They had little understanding of the coming Messiah. They knew God had promised to send "An anointed one" to defeat Satan and rescue the children of God. However they did not know that anointed one would be Jesus Christ the Son of God. They did not know Jesus would be the promised Messiah. They continued to be required by God to be active in burnt offerings as their way of communicating to God their repentant heart. The ultimate price that would have to be paid for their sins was Jesus Christ's death and resurrection. They did not understand that. God expected his chosen nation to believe in Him to the extent of the revelation God provided. God's plan for the people of the Dispensation of Promise, as it was in the Dispensation of Human Government and the Dispensation of Conscience and the Dispensation of Innocence, was to demonstrate their faith in Jehovah.

Thread of Grace

God still loved His people. In spite of the fact they deserved to be destroyed God provided for them. The Dispensation of Promise is the first of the Dispensations that does not end. God's promise to the descendants of Abraham has come to pass, is coming to pass, and will be completed in dispensations to come. God's revelation to His people will continue to evolve as He reveals more and more of Himself to them but the promise of God in the Dispensation of Promise will still be fulfilled.

Dispensation of Law

In the Dispensation of Innocence God depended on His personal relationship with mankind to keep mankind close to Him and righteous. In the Dispensation of Conscience God depended on the internal conscience of man to know what was wrong and right and He depended on the teaching of Adam and Eve. They were to be aware of their need for God. In the Dispensation of Human Government, God entrusted that responsibility with the people themselves at the request of Noah. In the Dispensation of Promise God changed the way people would be governed. He developed a nation of people that He intended to lead the world toward Christ. These chosen people were to make them aware of their sin and their need for God. In each dispensation God laid out laws the people were to follow. In the Dispensation of Conscience they were not allowed to murder and that law still exists. In the Dispensation of Human Government the people were to disperse and populate the world. God commanded them to do so but they did not. In the Dispensation of Promise God told the people to stay in the Land of Canaan and they did not. In all ages God told the people to be righteous and they failed each time. God has from the beginning laid out laws for the people to follow and they failed.

Now in the new dispensation of "The Law" God provides a list of do's and don'ts for His chosen people to obey. These are not the first rules God has given to His creation. It is the first set of very specific, very detailed rules given only to the Children of Israel. These rules become known as "The Law." They are given to God's Chosen people only and not to Gentiles. God is dealing only with His people. They are the nation of Israel. Now God is not relying of Conscience, Human Government, or His Promise although His promise still applies. If they try to keep these laws, with a desire in their heart to please God, God will forgive their trespasses. In those instances where the people sin against God but genuinely regret having sinned, God maintains burnt offerings as a way of communicating to God their repentance of sin and their asking for God's forgiveness.

In the Dispensation of "The Law," God sends Moses back to Egypt to lead His people from their bondage. As Moses takes them out of bondage through a series of amazing miracles, God takes Moses up on Mt. Sinai and gives him "The Law." "The Law" is not an unconditional promise as was the Abrahamic Covenant. "The Law" is a conditional promise of God that He will protect His people and forgive their sins if His people will remain faithful to Him. "The Law" is added to the Abrahamic Covenant in which God promised certain things to the Hebrew people. Why did God only give "The Law" only to His chosen people? The answer is that God intended for "His people" to become the evangelists whereby the rest of the world was to find Jesus Christ as Savior. God takes this extraordinary effort of revelation to the Hebrews so they might be equipped to do God's work as evangelists, worldwide.

"The Law" is made up of three divisions. Division one is the Moral Law, which is the most famous, because it includes the Ten Commandments. Then God gives to Moses the Civil Law followed by the Ceremonial Law. These laws were all designed and intended to lay out in great detail exactly what the people were to do and how they were to live to be pleasing unto God.

God's Expectations of Man

God's expectations of mankind never change. God wants man to become a righteous person, consumed by righteousness and love. God wants man to become like Him so they can have a relationship of love.

God's Freedom for Mankind

God commands His people to be righteous and to love Him. Yet He does not demand it. God gives His people the choice to follow Him, to love Him, to become like Him. This choice continues in the Dispensation of "The Law." Yet God increases His effort to persuade man to willingly become the person God wants us to be. God wants man to love Him and to seek righteousness without this degree of revelation from God. God wants a loving relationship with mankind. However, the Dispensation of "The Law" proves to be unable to penetrate a rebellious heart. Mankind is, and has always been from the fall of Adam corrupt and evil. Virtually no one remains faithful to God. How can God still love these people? Yet He does continue to love them.

God's Test of Mankind

During the Dispensation of "The Law" all the Hebrew people have to do to be acceptable in the sight of God is to keep "The Law." Yet they cannot keep "The Law." God knows, and knew, it was impossible for the Hebrew people to keep "The Law." But God wanted to communicate to His people when they were falling short of the expectations of God and so He gave them "The Law." The conscience of man was still available. The guidance of Human Government still existed. But God, knowing none of these efforts had brought man to God took another step. He gave them the test of keeping "The Law."

God's Revelation to Mankind

Never before had there every existed such an extensive set of detailed instructions of how to live than were revealed in "The Law." Man just did not get it. As Old Testament years rolled on, God gave the Hebrew Children a great revelation in the form of His written Word. They were given the Old Testament. They were also given one great prophet after another who tried to lead them back to God and they rebelled. They were given the great King David who tried in his un-perfect way to bring the people of Israel back to God. They had miracle after miracle that demonstrated God's power, His love, and

His faithfulness but yet they always reverted back to their basic sin nature.

God's Punishment of Mankind

The Dispensation of "The Law" lasted from the exodus out of Egypt of the Israelites until Jesus Christ died on the Cross of Calvary. This was a period of about 1,500 years. During this time the Hebrew people continually rebelled against God. They suffered hard times and often bondage of slavery. They would be led by a prophet of God back to faithfulness and then would stray again. Their suffering was severe but they never learned. God led them in the wilderness for forty years because of their lack of faith but He stayed with them and kept His promise to Abraham. He gave them the promised land of Canaan and they failed to keep His command of destroying the inhabitants of that land. God led the Hebrew Children in conquering the land God gave them. He gave them Kings when they asked for them even though that was not God's desire. In every time the Hebrew Children rebelled against God they suffered and yet in every time, God, through His love, brought them back.

Even so, God's punishment of Israel for their great unfaithfulness is not complete even at the end of the Dispensation of Grace. The Dispensation of Grace, when concluded, ushers in the Great Tribulation. In that period of seven years, the last three and one half include incredible torture primarily for the Hebrew people. Then God will complete His punishment for nonbelievers and His rewards for His chosen few.

Man's Response to God

Much of the Old Testament is consumed by the unfaithfulness of the Hebrew Children. During these long years God did not work with other people. God intended for the Hebrew Children to be the evangelists who would lead the world to Christ. The Old Testament is a testimony of man's unfaithfulness and God's trustworthiness.

What was required of man to be saved?

Perhaps nowhere in Scripture do we see the thread of grace greater and more emphasized than in the plight of the Hebrew children. Why they could not see the amazing work of God is a mystery. They had the written word of God, in the form of the Old Testament for many of these years. They had every reason to trust God but did not. Paul, speaking to us through the church at Corinth, clearly stated the path of Old Testament Saints to salvation was the same path we must thread.

1 Corinthians 10:1–4

"For I do not want you to be unaware, brothers that our fathers were all under the cloud, and all passed through the sea, and all were baptized into Moses in the cloud and in the sea, and all ate the same spiritual food, and all drank the same spiritual drink. For they drank from the spiritual Rock that followed them, and the Rock was Christ."

Old Testament and New Testament Saints have all been saved by their faith in the promise of God and the Grace of God to forgive their sins.

Thread of Grace

Of course, the greatest demonstration of God's love and Grace in the history of the world takes place at the end of this dispensation. This is the virgin birth of Jesus Christ, followed by His perfect life without sin, followed by His death, burial and resurrection from the grave to pay the price of the sins of all mankind both Jew and Gentile.

The Dispensation of Grace

Many Scholars call the Dispensation of Grace the Dispensation of the Church. Both titles are correct because both "The Church" and God's Grace are the focus of this period of God's dealing with His people. God has continued to love His people when they did not deserve it and has poured out His grace upon them throughout the ages. Yet now His Grace is about to be revealed in abundance and in a new revelation of majestic miracle.

In the Dispensation of Grace God ceases to deal with nations, as He has for centuries, and returns to dealing with individuals. This dispensation begins with the death, burial and resurrection of Jesus Christ. It is set up with His virgin birth and His coming down from glory to live among men. It ends after an undetermined period of time, with the rapture of the church, when all believers will be taken up to Heaven to be with Jesus. They will first go through the Judgment seat of Christ and then follow Jesus into Heaven with God the Father. This dispensation is placed by God between the Dispensation of "The Law" and the Dispensation of "The millennial." During the Dispensation of "The Law" it was the responsibility of the Hebrew nation to evangelize the world. During the Dispensation of Grace it becomes the responsibility of the Church to evangelize the world. In this statement the Church is defined as all people who accept Jesus Christ as their Savior after His birth, life, death, burial and resurrection. The Dispensation of Grace will be followed by the Dispensation of "The Millennial." In that dispensation the responsibility of evangelizing the world will again rest with a newly redeemed and empowered Hebrew nation. God is not through working with His chosen people, the Nation of Israel. The Dispensation of the Millennial is initiated by the completion of the Dispensation of The Church. That completion is called "The Rapture" as outlined in 1 Thessalonians 4:13–18.

1 Thessalonians 4:13–18

"But we do not want you to be uninformed, brothers, about those who are asleep, that you may not grieve as others do who have no hope. For since we believe that Jesus died and rose again, even so, through Jesus, God will bring with him those who have fallen asleep. For this we declare to you by a word from the Lord that we who are alive, who are left

until the coming of the Lord, will not precede those who have fallen asleep. For the Lord himself will descend from heaven with a cry of command, with the voice of an archangel, and with the sound of the trumpet of God. And the dead in Christ will rise first. Then we who are alive, who are left, will be caught up together with them in the clouds to meet the Lord in the air, and so we will always be with the Lord. Therefore encourage one another with these words."

The Dispensation of "The Church" is a unique period in which God grants the believers many amazing gifts not granted to other Dispensations. These are granted because God gives "The Church" to His Son Jesus Christ as a reward for His faithfulness in keeping the plan of Salvation that was created before the beginning of mankind. Some of these unique gifts are:

- Believers in the Dispensation of "The Church" are given completed atonement for their sins. Previous dispensations were saved and given a new nature based on "the promise" that Jesus Christ would come and die on Calvary and be resurrected from the dead for their sins. Previous dispensations were saved without knowledge of Jesus Christ. They had only a vague understanding of God's plan, thus trusting in God Jehovah was difficult.

Hebrews 9:12
"He entered once for all into the holy places, not by means of the blood of goats and calves but by means of his own blood, thus securing an eternal redemption."

- Believers in the Dispensation of "The Church" are given everlasting life. This means they have security of believing they are saved forever and that security comes the second they accept Jesus Christ as Savior.

John 5:24
"Truly, truly, I say to you, whoever hears my word and believes him who sent me has eternal life. He does not come into judgment, but has passed from death to life."

- Believers in the Dispensation of "The Church" are given a much greater revelation from God of who the Messiah is and what Jesus Christ the Son of God has done for us. There is no excuse for any generation not trusting in and adoring God but there is even less excuse for people in the Dispensation of The Church. They have great understanding and much is expected of them.

Ephesians 2:8–9
"For by grace you have been saved through faith, and this is not of your own doing; it is the gift of God, not a result works, so that no one can boast."

- Believers in the Dispensation of "The Church" are given the indwelling of the Holy Spirit to help communicate with God, to help understand God's written Word, to chastise when sin occurs and to comfort in times of trial. The Holy Spirit also gives assurance of eternal salvation and security of the believer.

Ephesians 4:30
"And do not grieve the Holy Spirit of God, by whom you were sealed for the day of redemption."

- Believers in the Dispensation of "The Church" are adopted into the family of Christ and made as children of God. They are called the "Body of Christ."

Ephesians 5:30–32
"For we are members of His body, therefore a man shall leave his father and mother and hold fast to his wife, and

the two shall become one flesh." This mystery is profound, and I am saying it refers to Christ and the church."

- Believers in the Dispensation of "The Church" are guaranteed a supernatural body like unto that of Christ's resurrection body.

Philippians 3:21
"Who will transform our lowly body to be like his glorious body, by the power that enables him even to subject all things to himself."

- Believers in the Dispensation of "The Church" are guaranteed a future home in New Jerusalem or Heaven.

John 14:1–3
"Let not your heart be troubled: ye believe in God, believe also in me. In my Father's house are many mansions: if it were not so, I would have told you. I go to prepare a place for you. And if I go and prepare a place for you, I will come again, and receive you unto myself; that where I am, there ye may be also."

- Believers in the Dispensation of "The Church" are granted the privilege of praying directly to God through our Lord and Savior. No other dispensation has had individual access to God by simply talking with Him.

God's Expectations of Man

God still expects mankind to love Him, to be righteous, to be like God. But God also adds expectations to this dispensation. Mankind is expected to:

- Evangelize the world. When the Hebrew people failed to fulfill God's plan for them to evangelize the world that task fell to the Church. The Church is the second group of people challenged with this task.

- Be filled with the Holy Spirit. This means we are to be consumed with our desire to serve God, to exalt God, to evangelize others to Christ, to encourage other believers, and to be God's representative on the face of the earth. No other group received this challenge. No other group has had the Holy Spirit come and live in their hearts as a companion and helpmate.

- Present their selves as a living sacrifice to the work of God. This means God expects believers in the Dispensation of The Church to live every day toward the purpose of pleasing God. We are to seek to do God's Will above our own will. The people of this dispensation, more than any other group, have been challenged to totally put themselves and their own desires out of the question and focus on glorifying God.

We now see people who are believers in Jesus during the Dispensation of the Church try to please God not to be saved but because they are saved. They experience salvation by Grace not salvation by works. This experience is not different that the salvation experience of past generations. This is different than that of other generations because the Dispensation of Innocence, Dispensation of conscience, Dispensation of Government, Dispensation of Promise and Dispensation of "The Law" each had requirements of God of things they had to do to communicate their faith in Jehovah. But in the Dispensation of "The Church" the eternal relationship with God is guaranteed. Believers are not asked to do anything but are required to have a repentant heart and ask God for forgiveness of sin. They are required to trust Jesus Christ as their Savior. We are made Children of God when we are saved and it cannot be taken away.

God's Freedom for Mankind

God gives man freedom to think what he wants, to do what he wants, to be what he wants to be. However God has placed into man a new nature that is eternally at war with Satan regarding what we think, what we say, and what we do. Mankind has a new nature when he is "Born Again" and that new nature will not let him separate himself from God. That new nature will not let any other power separate him from God. In other words a new permanent spiritual relationship with God is established and in the future that relationship will also include a physical relationship of our glorified bodies and God the Father, God the Son and the Holy Spirit.

God's Test for Mankind

God's test for mankind is not an on-going, lifetime test as was in previous dispensations. This is a one-time test at the point of salvation. Does man have enough faith in Jesus Christ to believe Jesus Christ can and will save him from sin? And does the individual want Jesus Christ to come into his heart and take over his life? If the answer is yes at the point of salvation the individual is saved forever.

God's Revelation to Mankind

God's revelation to mankind is an abundance of Grace never experienced before in any dispensation. First and foremost is Jesus Christ's being sent, as God, to come live with mankind and to witness to mankind. Jesus paid the debt of our Salvation on the Cross. Second is Jesus's requesting of the Holy Spirit to be sent to live among men. Third is the total, absolute knowledge mankind can have that he has been saved and has eternal life with God. This security of the believer has not been available in any other dispensation. It is granted to the believers in the Dispensation of The Church as a gift from Jesus Christ to His body and is granted by God the Father as a reward to His only begotten Son. And as part of the Dispensation of The Church, mankind is given the New Testament as added revelation of His relationship with God. No grouping of believers has ever had more revelation from God than the Dispensation of The Church.

Man's Response to God

Amazingly, man does not respond to God as God desires and this dispensation also fails. This is already apparent in our Churches turning away from teaching the strict interpretation of God's Word. And it is seen in our people having less and less interest in God and the teachings of God. Man will fail and the world will have to go into the seventh and final Dispensation.

What was required of man to be saved?

Through the Dispensation of "The Church," man's faith is the sole and only factor, *on man's part,* necessary for salvation. However, man's faith has to be coupled with God's Grace. This means God takes us, unworthy people, and because of our faith, He changes our heart and redeems us because of His grace. Salvation comes about because of an act of God not man. But God will not bring about salvation without man's faith.

Thread of Grace

Mankind does not have to wait for the manifestation of God's Grace. Mankind experiences it immediately upon accepting Christ as Savior. It is the Grace of God that gives us a completely new nature. It is the Grace of God that changes us from what we used to be into a new person with a new desire to follow Christ. It is the Grace of God that gives us a desire to please God and that desire will last forever. Yes, we still have the old nature that battles in our physical body for supremacy. But God will win.

The Seven-Year Tribulation Period

The word *rapture* does not occur in the Bible. The term comes from a Latin word meaning "a carrying off, a transport, or a snatching away." Although the word *rapture* does not appear in Scripture, the concept of carrying off, or snatching away is a major theme in the New Testament. The rapture of the church is the event in which God "snatches away" all who believe in Jesus, from the earth in order to make way for His righteous judgment to be poured out on the earth during the tribulation period. The rapture is described in *1 Thessalonians 4:13–18*.

I Thessalonians 4:13–18

"But we do not want you to be uninformed, brothers, about those who are asleep, that you may not grieve as others do who have no hope. For since we believe that Jesus died and rose again, even so, through Jesus, God will bring with him those who have fallen asleep. For this we declare to you by a word from the Lord, that we who are alive, who are left until the coming of the Lord, will not precede those who have fallen asleep. For the Lord Himself will descend from heaven with a cry of command, with the voice of an archangel, and with the sound of the trumpet of God. And the dead in Christ will rise first. Then we who are alive, who are left, will be caught up together with them in the clouds to meet the Lord in the air, and so we will always be with the Lord. Therefore encourage one another with these words."

The Rapture The Church brings to a close of the Dispensation of The Church. All believers all over the world are taken out of the world in one supernatural event and swept up into heaven to go through the Judgment Seat of Christ. There they will be judged based on the good deeds and good intentions they have had on earth. This judgment has no bearing on their salvation but does have a bearing on their rewards to be granted in eternity.

With the close of the Dispensation of the Church it is important for us to consider the state the world will be in. First of all every believer in Jesus Christ will be taken and no one in the entire world will believe in Jesus Christ. Yet many Church buildings will continue to hold services as people worship their own pleasures and entertainment. Great confusion will exist, as perhaps one out of every ten (actual number unknown) people in the world will just vanish with no explanation.

Government leaders will begin to fabricate reasons that these people are missing but they will not admit it is because Jesus Christ has come and taken them as those believers said would happen when they lived on earth.

The Dispensation of Grace will close and God will reestablish both the Dispensation of "The Law" and the Dispensation of Promise both of which deal with the Hebrew Nation who are the chosen people of God. Therefore the Seven-Year Tribulation Period is where God completes His promise to Abraham about creating a great nation that would follow God.

The Great Tribulation period, following the Dispensation of "The Church," recognizes the failure of the Jews to accept Jesus Christ as the Messiah and yet recognizes the unfinished promise of God to Abraham that the Jewish nation would be the ones to lead the world back to God. God is not ready to implement amazing changes that will cause the Jews to recognize and accept Jesus Christ as the Messiah. But the Great Tribulation period places on God's Chosen People the incredible price the Hebrew nation has to pay for their lack of faith in Jesus. This price will be paid in the Great Tribulation. In the Great Tribulation Satan and "The Beast" will kill millions of Hebrew people, and Gentiles who believe in Christ. Yet at the end of this horrible period of suffering the Hebrew nation will emerge as confident in Christ and as faithful to Him. Through this period God will restore His promise to make the Hebrew nation a great nation who represents Him.

Chapter 23 of this book speaks specifically to what events will happen during the Tribulation.

The Dispensation of the One-Thousand Year Millennium Kingdom

At the close of the Great Tribulation period the Hebrew nation will have professed Jesus Christ as the Messiah, will have recognized God's plan for man's redemption comes through Jesus Christ and will be united in faith in Jesus Christ the Son of God. At this time God agrees to a new covenant with His children. Notice we say with God's children. God's children are a larger group than the "Body of Christ." The "Body of Christ" is the Church. God's Children include all who have ever been redeemed or forgiven of their sins.

This Dispensation will be for an exact one thousand years of time. It will include all of God's redeemed and will initially, not include anyone who refused to believe on Jesus Christ. The trigger to usher in the Dispensation of The Millennium is the Hebrew nation's repentance and turning to God. Their repentance shall be coupled with a belief that Jesus Christ, God's only Son, will return to receive and save them. They finally believe Jesus is the Messiah. Thus the chosen people of God must believe on Jesus Christ before God is ready to conclude the Dispensation of The Millennium. When they do so, God will forgive the Hebrew nation and restore unto them the promises He made. God will then judge all enemies of Israel and all who are unbelievers in Jesus Christ as the Messiah at the Great White Throne Judgment. There He will cast all nonbelievers into Hell.

The Dispensation of The Millennium is a covenant between God and the Hebrew nation. Because those who are saved in the Dispensation of "The Church," are adopted into the chosen family of God, we, The Church, will enjoy the one thousand millennium reign of Christ. But we will not be in charge of it. The leaders of the Nation of Israel, King David and the Apostles are the ones who will be Gods leaders in this period and the King in charge will be none other than Jesus Christ Himself.

God's Expectations of Man

God still expects mankind to love Him, to be righteous, to be like God. But everyone in the New Millennium reign will have a new nature. Satan will be cast into the "Pit" and will have no influence during this one-thousand-year period. Man will therefore have in his heart the desire to honor God and to Glorify Christ and will be consumed by it without the conflicting desire to be disobedient and selfish.

God's Freedom for Man

The freedom granted to mankind will be similar to that granted to Adam and Eve in the Dispensation of Innocence. The participants of The one-thousand-year reign of Christ will be allowed to do anything they wish. All believers who died before the Second Coming of Christ will have a glorified Body and will not commit sin. Those who are alive at the beginning of the one-thousand-Year Millennial must pass the test of God's judgment of nations to be qualified to enter the one-thousand-year Millennial Reign. They will not pass unless they also have given their heart to Jesus. Therefore ever person who enters the one-thousand-year Millennial Kingdom will be a believer in Jesus Christ. In addition the Hebrew Nation will have many people alive at the end of the Tribulation and they will enter the one-thousand-year millennial Kingdom. Therefore we will have many people enter the one-thousand-year kingdom as believers in Christ but without a glorified body. These people will be able to marry and reproduce during this one-thousand-year reign. Some of these saved peoples children will in the final days at the end of the one-thousand-year reign revolt with Satan against God. In the Dispensation of Innocence Satan was allowed to tempt man. In the one-thousand-year millennial reign Satan is bound and there is no possibility of evil having an influence on man. After the one-thousand-year reign Satan will be loosed for a short time and will be defeated by God and cast into the Lake of Fire.

God's Test of Man

There will be no test for believers with the glorified body in the one-thousand-year millennial reign because sin will not exist for them. Just as it was in the Garden of Eden for Adam, man will be given freedom to do anything he wishes but the Tree of Knowledge of Good and Evil will be Jesus Christ our Savior who will walk and talk with us, encourage us, love us, and enable us to be the Children of God we were intended to be. Children of those who enter the one-thousand-year Millennial Kingdom alive will be tested as are all people and will be given every opportunity to trust Jesus.

God's Revelation to Man

Man will have full revelation of whom and what God is. Man will have total understanding of God's nature just as did Adam in the Garden of Eden. The love and happiness will be full because to know Jesus is to know God.

Man's Response to God

Most people will faithfully be what God wants them to be. Without the temptation of Satan and with the ever presence of Jesus Christ, with our new changed nature, we will take our glorified bodies and worship Jesus Christ every hour of the one-thousand-year period.

What will be required of man to be saved?

Everyone with a glorified body will be present in the one-thousand-year millennial reign because of their faith in Jesus Christ and because of the Grace of God. Saints of the Old Testament did not have the same revelation of Christ that Saints from the Dispensation of The Church but they believed on God Jehovah and the plan God Jehovah had designed for their redemption. Saints from the Dispensation of "The Church" will be in the one-thousand-year millennial reign because of their faith in Jesus Christ as the resurrected Lord. Saints from the period of the Tribulation will be there because of their faith that Jesus Christ died for their sins and rose from the dead to pay for their sins with His blood. They will believe in spite of the fear, terror, and torture they faced for believing. No one enter the millennial reign without having practiced faith in Jesus Christ to the extent of their revelation from God. Children of parents who were alive at the close of the Seven Year Tribulation but whom believed on Jesus Christ, will not be saved because of their parents faith. They will not be tempted by Satan. However they will still have a basic nature of wanting self-satisfaction over God. They will have to turn their hearts to Jesus just as all the redeemed have done over the centuries.

Thread of Grace

Everything about the Dispensation of the Millennium is about Grace of God. No one throughout the ages will be saved except by the Grace of God. Yes, they will have had to demonstrate faith but that faith is only their qualifying for the request of God to save them. It is the act of God that saves anyone and that happens through the Grace of God.

What is the relationship of Gentiles in the Old Testament?

The dispensation periods of all dispensations seem to focus on either the Chosen People (Hebrew) or the Church. Did not non-Hebrews and non-church people exist? The answer is yes. What about the Gentiles who lived on earth during the days of Abraham, Isaac and Jacob. What about those who lived all the way up to the Dispensation of Grace also known as the Dispensation of the Church. This period covers some 1,500 years and millions of people.

The answer is that God continued to deal with these people but did not give special revelations of Him to them, as He did for the Hebrews. They continued to have the imputed sense of right and wrong in their soles. They continued to have the teachings of those who had experience faith in Jehovah to influence their thoughts. They also had the constant temptations of Satan to influence them to disobey God. And they did not have "The Law" as a measuring stick to tell them when they were displeasing God. Therefore their road to salvation was more difficult and perhaps this is the reason the vast majority of Gentiles in the Old Testament were not believers in God.

God's intention of giving special attention to the Jews was not just to favor that nation, although He certainly did reward the faith of Abraham in a favored role. His intention globally was for good for all mankind. God's intent of the Israelites was for them to be evangelists who would present the Word of God to all men regardless of whether they were Jews or Gentiles. God intended the Israelites to not only be evangelists to all lost people but to be examples of faithfulness to God. God intended that the whole world would see the faith of the Israelites and be influenced to trust Him.

Exodus 9:16
"But for this purpose I have raised you up, to show you my power, so that my name may be proclaimed in all the earth."

A great Scripture of God in Joshua 2:8–11 gives us a picture of how the faith of Israel, when it was properly done by believers, had influence on Gentiles everywhere.

Joshua 2:8–11
Before the men lay down, she came up to them on the roof and said to the men, "I know that the LORD has given you the land, and that the fear of you has fallen upon us, and that all the inhabitants of the land melt away before you. For we have heard how the LORD dried up the water of the Red Sea before you when you came out of Egypt, and what you did to the two kings of the Amorites who were beyond the Jordan, to Sihon and Og, whom you devoted to destruction. And as soon as we heard it, our hearts melted, and there was no spirit left in any man because of you, for the LORD your God, he is God in the heavens above and on the earth beneath."

There can be no question but that God had a vision of all creation on earth, whether Jew or Gentile and God desired everyone to be faithful to Him. This is pictures in Psalms 47:8–9. *"God reigns over the nations; God sits on his holy throne. The princes of the peoples gather as the people of the God of Abraham.*
For the shields of the earth belong to God; he is highly exalted!" The intent of God is clearly identified in Isaiah 49:6, *"He says,"* 'It *is too light a thing that you should be m y servant to raise up the tries of Jacob and to bring back the preserved of Israel. I will make you as a light for the nations that my salvation may each to the end of the earth."*

The failure of the Israelites and of "The Church" to trust God deemed millions to eternal punishment in Hell. These condemned millions are of both Jew and Gentile, male and female, children and adults, of all races, backgrounds, and religions. But Praise God, the love of God will complete the plan of Salvation and soon, perhaps very soon we will meet Him in the sky.

CHAPTER TEN

The Doctrine of Security of the Believer

God's Assurance to the Redeemed

One of the more controversial subjects in Christianity today is whether or not a person who has accepted Jesus Christ as Savior can lose their Salvation. Can a saved person ever be lost? Most of us answer from the wrong source. Either we rely on the teaching of our Church or we rely on human logic and reasoning. These sources of knowledge are unreliable in that both are teachings of man. Our correct source is God's Word. God's Word tells us a person who has truly accepted Jesus Christ as Savior has a change that happens in his/her heart and that change is of God. That person is "Born Again" or takes on a new nature. It is not that we can never commit sin again once we are saved. No, our base nature does not go away but we are given a new nature that co-exists with our base sin nature. Our new nature desires to serve and please Jesus Christ. Man cannot change his old nature. But God can give us a new nature that makes it possible for us to say no to sin. God's Word tells us that new nature, which God brings about in the Christian, is eternal and can never be taken away by anything.

What takes place when we are saved?

Many so-called scholars tell us it does not matter what you believe as long as you are committed to something. God's Word tells us that thought is foolish. It is dangerous. It is disastrous. That thought will send us to hell and eternal fire and brimstone outside of the comfort of God.

Only people who believe Jesus Christ died to pay the cost of redemption of our sins and that he was buried and rose again from the tomb for the sole purpose of paying the price of our sins, will be saved. And we have to believe this so strongly that it becomes a personal commitment of our life to change who we are and we must begin to become what God wants us to be. We must recognize Jesus Christ as the Messiah, the one God sent to pay for our sins and then we have to accept His gift of eternal life.

When we reach that point of belief in Jesus Christ, the Holy Spirit touches our life and changes us. The Holy Spirit gives us a new nature and that nature is one that loves God without condition, wants to serve and please God without reservation, and repents of our sins with deep remorse.

To be "Saved" means the same thing as some other words used in Scripture. To be "Saved" is to be "Redeemed" and is the same as being "Justified." Another term that means to be saved is "Born Again." To be "Saved" is synonymous with being "Born Again" and it means to be "Forgiven" of our sins and brought into the family of God. Each of these terms means Past, Present and Future. If we are saved from our sins, if we are justified from our sins, if we are redeemed from our sins and if we are forgiven of our sins we are saved for all past sins we have committed, all present sins as we are committing and all future sins we will commit.

Saved people are also often called "God's Elect." This term is controversial because there are two views regarding "The Elect of God." Chapter 16 of this book focuses on "The Elect." There are four groups in the Bible that are called God's elect. They are Old Testament believers, the Church, Tribulation believers, and one-thousand-year Millennial Kingdom believers. The definition of God's Elect involves those people that God, in His foreknowledge, knew would make the decisions to follow Him. When Christ died, God placed all the sins of all people on Jesus Christ. That means all past, present and future sins. Jesus Christ was and is God's plan of redeeming mankind to Him. Had Jesus failed, we and all believers of all generations would be eternally lost. But that gift of God was and is conditional on our belief. All we have to do is believe Jesus Christ paid the price of our sins and want with all our heart to be saved. If we believe in Jesus and trust Him for salvation God brings about the change in us that enables us to be forgiven of our sins and to become part of the family of God.

2 Corinthians 5:21
"For our sake He made Him to be sin who knew no sin, so that, in Him, we might become the righteousness of God."

When God saves us, through the sacrifice of Jesus, many things take place. None of these changes in us, are brought about by us. They are all changes brought about by the Holy Spirit. These changes include:

- **We are given a new nature that battles the sin nature we were imputed with when Adam fell from grace.**

2 Corinthians 5:17
"Therefore, if anyone is in Christ, he is a new creation; old things have passed away; behold, the new has come."

This point is crucial to understanding the doctrine of Security of the Believer. No one could ever be saved and certainly could not retain their salvation if it were not that God gives us a new nature. But God told us that if we are "in Christ" or redeemed we are a new creation. Old things have gone away. That means we have a constant urging from the Holy Spirit to do what is righteous. We have a new nature that welcomes that urging and does not resent it. Yes, we still have the old nature that tells us sin is wonderful. But God imputes a love for Him into us. God imputes into our soul a desire to be righteous. God does this. Man cannot make this change. Because God does it, God can keep it.

- **The Holy Spirit comes into our heart and soul and dwells with us. The Holy Spirit becomes our comforter as promised by Jesus Christ.**

Romans 8:9
"You, however, are not in the flesh but in the Spirit, if in fact the Spirit of God dwells in you. Anyone does not have the Spirit of Christ, does not belong to Him."

Another massive change that takes place when we accept Christ as our Savior is the Holy Spirit comes into our heart to dwell with us. The Holy Spirit is our comforter, is our interpreter of God's will, is our encourager, and is also the one who seals our salvation. If we could be lost after the Holy Spirit comes into our heart it means the Holy Spirit failed. It means the Holy Spirit could not keep what God the Father sent Him to keep. There is nothing we can do to defeat God and therefore there is nothing we can do to be lost once we are saved.

- **We become Children of God**

John 1:12
"But to all who did receive him, who believed in his name, he gave the right to become children of God."

This is the third, huge change that happens when we are saved. We are adopted into the family of God. The Bible tells us that when we are saved we are given the right to become children of God. We are given the power to join God's elect family. We become the elect of God. And who is given this right? Those who believe on the name of Jesus have that right. That means that when we believe Jesus Christ died for our sins and rose from death for us then God does three amazing things.

(1.) He gives us a new nature. After all, God would not allow us to even be in His presence, much less be His children, if we did not reject our old sin nature. And spiritually we do get rid of the old sin nature. This comes about because Jesus shed His blood to pay the price of our sin. Now God the Father no longer sees our sin when we come into His presence but sees the love of Christ who died for us. Physically we still have the old sin nature, but now we are given a new nature to battle the old sin nature, to guide us, to protect us, to inform us, and to empower us to be what we are "Born Again" to become.

Romans 8:17
"And if children, then heirs—heirs of God and fellow heirs with Christ, provided we suffer with Him, that we may also be glorified with Him."

God's Word tells us we inherit the kingdom of God. That begins when the Holy Spirit to come live in our souls. We inherit the promise of God to be with us in times of trial, times of trouble, and in times of confusion. We inherit God's love. God loved us before we were saved, but we could not experience His love. As part of His family we begin a road of learning to understand and relish His love for us. We also inherit God's promise of eternal security from hellfire and brimstone that awaits those who are not part of His family. We inherit the privilege of living every day through eternity with Jesus Christ, our Lord and Savior. We inherit Heaven and the glorified body God has promised us. In gaining the glorified body we inherit security from death, disease, sickness, aging, fear, despair and loneliness. But the greatest gift or inheritance we gain is the promise of eternity being loved and loving Jesus Christ our Lord and Savior.

Psalms 103:12
"As far as the east is from the west, So far does He remove our transgressions from us."

This verse in Psalms says that when we are saved our sins are forgiven. They are not only forgiven for the present and the past but also for all future sins. The verse tells us Jesus removed our transgressions from us. We no longer have them. We are not burdened with sin anymore.

- **We are set aside, or sanctified through the offering of the body of Jesus. We become a different person as viewed by God.**

Hebrews 10:10
"By that will we have been sanctified through the offering of the body of Jesus Christ once for all."

In the Old Testament the Bible tells us that Abraham's faith was counted unto him as righteousness. That is what happens with us when we are saved. We never, in this life, become as righteous as God. The very thought of that is beyond comprehension. But because of the sacrifice of Jesus Christ who died to pay for our sins, our faith in Jesus is counted as righteousness with God and forever more God no longer sees our sins but He sees Christ's sacrifice for us. God counts our faith and Jesus's sacrifice as righteousness for us.

- **Christ's Death makes those who are saved sinless in God's sight**

Hebrews 10:11–12
"And every priest stands daily at his service, offering repeatedly the same sacrifices, which can never take away sins. But when Christ had offered for all time a single sacrifice for sins, he sat down at the right hand of God."

Hebrews 10:11–12 promises us that the price Jesus paid for our sins will never need to be redone. The significance of that to us is we cannot lose our salvation. If the price Jesus paid for our sins was a single sacrifice for sins, and God Word tells us it was, then there is nothing we can ever do that will cause us to lose our salvation. Christ sits at the right hand of God. He is constantly representing us to God the Father and presenting the price He paid as the price that needs to be paid for our sins.

What role does Faith and Grace have in Salvation?

Ephesians 2:8–9
"For by grace you have been saved through faith. And this is not your own doing; it is the gift of God, not a result of works, so that no one may boast."

God tells us in Ephesians that it is by the grace of God that we are saved. This means our faith does not save us, the grace of God saves us. It also means that the reason God elects to give us a new nature and save our soul is because we have recognized we are a sinner, recognized we cannot correct our condition, and we have accepted that Jesus Christ died on Calvary for our sins and we ask Him to save us. This means that when we ask, spiritually not necessarily physically, we are placing our faith in Christ to save us. Without faith we cannot be saved. Our faith is a fervent request of God to accept us into His family and change us into a new creature. But faith is not what saves us. God's Grace saves us. Salvation is an act of God not man. Man just welcomes God's intervention into his life by our faith. God in His foreknowledge understood man would have a tendency to want to take credit for his own salvation. Therefore God specifically added the words that *It is the gift of God, not of works, so that no one may boast.*

God articulately tells us that being a good person will not earn us salvation. It means that giving to the poor, helping the needy, aiding the sick and a host of other wonderful things will not earn us salvation because man is a sinner in spite of the good deeds he might do. All the good deeds a man can do will never overcome his sin nature. This also means that our faith presents us as a candidate for salvation but does not save us. God will not save a person who does not believe in Jesus Christ. Mankind is certainly not good enough to earn salvation. We cannot do enough good works to ever overcome our sin, because if we commit even one sin, just one, we are sinners and face the penalty of sin.

This reality is important in considering whether or not we can be certain of our salvation. If mankind were saved by his actions or works then perhaps he could lose that salvation. But man is not saved by works. Man is saved by God. The reality that God makes us a new creature in God's sight when we are saved is monumental. When God forgives us for our sin he is forgiving us for having a sin nature. Then when The Holy Spirit comes to live in our heart and soul, our salvation is complete. The reality that God makes us part of His family and adopts us unto His own cannot be changed.

Paul, in Galatians, tells the New Testament Church that the Old Testament Saints were under the law. Paul told us "The Law" identified for the Old Testament Saints, how much they missed the mark of righteousness set by God. The Law showed them how much they needed God's forgiveness. Old Testament Saints were not saved by works but saved by their desire to be faithful to God and their faith that God would save them if they ask. New Testament Christians have the life of Jesus Christ that shows us where we fall short of God's expectations. The life of Jesus is more perfect than "The Law." God's Word teaches us that works cannot save and no one can ever be justified by works but only by faith through the Grace of God. During the Dispensation of Grace "The Law" is not needed because the Holy Spirit resides in our soul guiding us to be faithful to God the Father.

Galatians 3:24
"So then, the law was our guardian until Christ came,
in order that we might be justified by faith."

Bible-Based Reasons Why We Cannot Lose Our Salvation

Reason No. 1 God promised us Eternal Salvation

The first reason to believe in security of the believer is because God promised it to us. God keeps His promises. Just because a promise of God does not seem logical to man does not mean God cannot and will not keep it. It did not seem logical that Jonah would be swallowed by a whale and be coughed up on shore alive but it happened. It does not seem logical that Mary could have born a child when she had never known a man. Yet it happened. God is not limited by man's inability to understand. In the book of John God makes an eternal promise that if man will believe on Jesus Christ, God will give man everlasting life.

John 3:16
"For God so loved the world that He gave His only Son, that
whoever believes in Him should not perish but have eternal life."

Eternal life means more no ending. If man could be saved and then lose his salvation the scripture in John 3:16 is not true. God is truth. God does not lie. The scripture tells us that if man believes on Jesus Christ *"He will not perish."* This is the promise of God that if a person believes on Jesus Christ that person will never go to Hell and be punished throughout eternity for his sins. If one could be saved and then lose their salvation this scripture would be untrue because it tells us that if we believe we will not go to Hell. God deeply desires that man understand this illogical truth. It seems so simple. All man has to do is believe on Jesus Christ and God promises eternal life with God and a total escape from Hell. God further explains what it means to believe on Jesus Christ in the fifth chapter.

John 5:24
"Truly, truly, I say to you, whoever hears My word and believes in Him who sent Me has everlasting life. He does not come into judgment, but has passed from death into life."

At the moment of belief, eternal life is granted. It is a present possession, not something granted at a future judgment. There is a promise inherent in this verse— *"He that believes has everlasting life."* God's Word does not say that he that believes and continues to believe will receive eternal life. John 5:24 tells us that the moment we believe we are given eternal life that shall never be taken away. Then to emphasize that truth more God tell us that believer *"shall not come into condemnation."* How can this promise of God be misunderstood? God clearly says in absolute certainty that if we believe on Jesus Christ we will never, ever come into judgment. The phrase *"is passed from death to life"* is written in the perfect tense, meaning that the believer has passed and will always be passed from a state of spiritual death to a state of spiritual life. Satan would like for us to doubt our salvation because we are weak and ineffective as a witness when we doubt.

God wants us to be confident in our salvation. We need confidence in God's Word. We must trust in God to save us. But we also need trust in God to keep us. Jesus says in the Bible that no one can pluck us out of God's hand.

John 10:27–29
"My sheep hear My voice, and I know them, and they follow Me. I give them eternal life, and they shall never perish; and no one will snatch them out of My hand. My Father, who has given them to Me, is greater than all; and no one is able to snatch them out of My Father's hand."

God's people often miss a very important promise when they read this incredible scripture. God tells us that God the Father promised all believers would become the family of Jesus Christ. The verse that says, *"My Father who has given them to Me,"* means God the Father gave "The Church" to God the Son as a reward for His faithfulness in fulfilling God the Father's promise of salvation. When we were given to Jesus Christ we became His Family. Jesus Christ reassures us of His joy in being given these as faithful followers. He assures us of His joy of the gift God the Father gave to Him when the Church was placed into His care and love. If a believer, after being saved could become lost it not only becomes a broken promise between Jesus Christ and the believer but a broken promise between God the Father and God the Son.

Is this to say that every person who says publicly they are now a Christian and perhaps even joins a Church will not sin again? First of all every person who publicly says they are now a Christian is not necessarily saved. Salvation does not come because we say we are Christians. Salvation comes because we believe we are sinners, we believe Jesus can save us and we ask Him to save us and make us like Him. No, believers are saved because God forgives our sins of yesterday, today and tomorrow not because we will never sin again. We will continue to do things and think thoughts that are contrary to the will of God, thus we sin. But because of the new nature God gives us when we are saved we will never again want to displease God. We will never cease to have a desire in our heart to please Christ. God knows our heart while others see the surface of our lives. If a believer is truly a Christian and they appear to fall away, God will always draw them back to Himself in the end. If someone appears to fall away and they never come back to Christ, they did not have a change within their heart and God did not make them a new creature. They were not "Born Again."

The Bible speaks about God's promise telling us that God cannot lie and that God promised the believer in Christ eternal life even before the World began. This tells us that even before man sinned, God in His foreknowledge knew man would sin and provided a plan for the redemption of mankind. God's plan of salvation is not just for the sins we committed prior to our acceptance of Christ. The plan of salvation is for all past, present and future sins. The Bible, God's Word, says that redemption is permanent.

The great theologian W. A. Criswell sums up our faith as he speaks of our relationship to God when he stated:

"Our security lies not in the boldness or the courage of our faith; it lies in the faithfulness of God. Whether my faith is weak, trembling and hesitant, or whether my faith is bold and courageous, I am still saved by the faithfulness of God."

Reason No. 2: The Saved are the elect of God

God's Word tells us that once we accept Jesus Christ as our Savior we become predestined to eternal life with Jesus Christ. That predestination has no application of time as man knows it because time is not applicable to God. God is ALPHA, and the OMEGA, The Beginning and the End. God is already at the end of time as we understand it. God is still at the beginning of time as we understand it. The Scripture tells us that because of the foreknowledge of God, He knows what we will do because He is the past, present, and future. God already knows if we will decide to accept Jesus Christ as our Savior. And yet that does not take away the decision man has to make to accept Jesus Christ.

Ephesians 1:3–4
"Blessed be the God and Father of our Lord Jesus Christ, who has blessed us in Christ with every spiritual blessing in the heavenly places, even as he chose us in him before the foundation of the world, that we should be holy and blameless before him, in love."

Paul the apostle is speaking in this passage about the elect of God. The elect are those who choose to accept Jesus Christ as Savior. Look at the Scripture, "Just as He chose us (us being all that accept Jesus Christ as Savior) before the foundation of the world, that we should be holy and without blame before Him in love." This is amazing Scripture. Paul, under the divine inspiration of God the Father relayed through the Holy Spirit, tells us that all of humanity who elects to accept Jesus Christ as Savior become the elect of God and are predestined to become blameless, holy, and justified through Christ's blood. This means there is nothing that can change the election because we are predestined to be cleansed of our sin immediately with our Salvation. The cleansing and predestination of our souls takes place because the Holy Spirit does it. Man's decision to accept Christ opens the door and meets man's obligation to the contract of Salvation. But man is not saved until the Holy Spirit gives us a new nature and we are "Born Again."

The confusion in Christians about "The Elect" of God justifies chapter 16 of this book that studies this important truth in depth.

Reason No. 3: Believers are sealed in their faith, by the Holy Spirit.

God explains to us that if we trusted Jesus Christ to be the one who would save us from your sins, then the Holy Spirit seals us with the spirit of promise. This promise is that some-day we will be with Him not only in spirit but in a glorified body as well. This is a promise that means God's Word is true. Mankind who has been changed by God and predestined by God to eternal life cannot be lost.

Ephesians 1:13–14
"In Him you also trusted, after you heard the word of truth,
the gospel of your salvation; in whom also, having believed,
you were sealed with the Holy Spirit of promise, who is
the guarantee of our inheritance until the redemption of
the purchased possession, to the praise of His glory."

What a powerful promise. Let's break down Ephesians 1:13–14 to see what God told us. Verse 13 says that it is in Jesus Christ whom we trusted after we heard the word of truth (Gospel News) in whom (Jesus) we believed. And then we were sealed with the Holy Spirit of promise. Then to firmly anchor what God is telling us He goes on to say the Holy Spirit of promise is our guarantee of inheritance (eternal salvation). And God's promise lasts until the redemption of the purchased possession (our rapture to go to be with Jesus Christ in the air). Paul then expresses His inner feeling praise for the glory of Jesus Christ. There can be no doubt left. We are guaranteed salvation forever. We cannot be saved and later reject it because we are not the same person who was lost. We are different. God has changed us.

Reason No. 4: God forgives us of not only our "sins" but of our sinful nature.

Our understanding of time is so different from that of God. For God time does not exist. When God says He forgives us for our sin He is saying something far bigger than forgiving us of the times we failed God. He forgives us for even having a spirit of desiring to be disobedient to God. He forgives us of past, present and future sins. That is contrary to man's logic. We cannot conceive of being forgiven for something we have not yet done. However, to God there is no such thing as something we have not done. God is already at the end of time. Because God is yesterday, today, and tomorrow, He is not forgiving us for something we have not yet done. He is tomorrow just like today and when He forgives us, He forgives for all sins. He forgives us of the sins we have committed, the sins we are committing and those we will commit.

In Ephesians God tells us that *before the foundations of the world God chose us in Him.* Who was Paul, the writer of Ephesians speaking of when he says us? I emphasize again He was speaking of believers. Paul, under the direction of God, tells us that before the foundations of the world God knew who would be saved because he was already at the end of time as man understands time. So God, understanding who would be saved, predestined those who would believe to have everlasting life.

Reason No. 5: When we are saved we take on the righteousness of God

2 Corinthians 5:21
"For He made Him who knew no sin to be sin for us, that we might become the righteousness of God in Him."

This verse is staggering in its message of grace from God. God the Father placed our sin on Jesus Christ, who knew no sin, so we might be viewed by God as having the same righteousness of God through Christ Jesus. Who, therefore, paid for our sins? The answer is Jesus Christ. Who paid for our sins committed before we accepted Jesus Christ as our Savior? The answer is Jesus Christ. Likewise, the answer to who paid for our sins we would commit after we accept Jesus Christ as our savior is Jesus Christ. The answer is Jesus Christ. In the Old Testament the prophet Isaiah, though the vision God provided, saw the truth for his day just as it is the truth for our day.

Isaiah 53:6
"All we like sheep have gone astray; We have turned, every one, to his own way; And the LORD has laid on Him the iniquity of us all."

God's plan of salvation is timeless. The forgiveness of our sins is timeless. The security of our salvation is timeless because Jesus paid it all. According to human logic, Jesus died for all of our sins before the time we were saved in fact before the time we were born. The price for sin, however, was not paid just in our lifetime, but was paid when Jesus died on the cross for the sins of all those who believed from the beginning of time through the end of time. Therefore, if my sins are forgiven, then all of my sins were forgiven on the cross; past, present, and future. If Jesus died for Abraham's sins when He died for mine, surely He could die for the sins I will commit just as He died for the sins I have committed.

We can trust the word of God to be true. That means we can also trust the promises of God to come true. It may not be something we can logic out in our earthly intellectual limitations but we can trust God because He said it and that settles it.

When he wrote to the young pastor Timothy, Paul speaks with emphatic authority, "I know, I believe, I am confident, without a doubt..." We too can speak with this kind of confidence, so long as our faith is in His power and faithfulness and not our own. Let's give ownership of our salvation solely to the Lord and never to ourselves. We can be confident in the promises of God. Paul emphasizes His confidence in God and His confidence in the permanence of his salvation in Romans as he points out that nothing can ever separate us from the love of God.

Reason No. 6: No power exists that can take our salvation out of the care of God.

Romans 8:38–39
"For I am sure that neither death nor life, nor angels nor rulers nor things present nor things to come, nor powers, nor height nor depth, nor anything else in all creation, will be able to separate us from the love of God which is in Christ Jesus our Lord."

I have a precious relative who believes no power on earth can take away His salvation. However, he says what if, somewhere down the road of life, he decided he did not want to be saved, could he reject his salvation. Look at what the Scripture says. "Nor things present nor things to come" can take us out of God's hand. This means we cannot bring about that change. And remember we have in our heart the Spirit of God that is urging us to be faithful to God and will not let us ever decide we do not want to be a Child of God. Even if we could do so we could not request permission to lose our salvation and if we did so it would not be approved.

If we felt temptation to ask for our Salvation to be discontinued it would be the power of Satan causing us to ask. Romans chapter 8 tells us Satan is not powerful enough to separate us from God under any disguise of the truth.

Reason No. 7: We are part of the family of God

When we are saved we become part of two very important groups that we were not part of before. We become part of the family of God and part of the Body of Christ. The family of God is broad and inclusive of all people who have been saved by faith through the Grace of God because of the price Jesus Christ paid on Calvary for our sins.

The Body of Christ is the Church. Why should this group be called the Body of Christ? Why is it that although others in history have found salvation in the Lord they are not called the "Body of Christ"? The answer is that "The Church." "The Church" mean everyone who trusts Jesus during the Dispensation of the Church, also called the Dispensation of Grace. They become part of the "Body of Christ" because God the Father gave this body of believers to Jesus.

John 10:29
"My Father, which gave them me, is greater than all; and no man is able to snatch them out of my Father's hand."

When God put the Dispensation of Law on hold; He has not stopped the Dispensation of the Law but has it on hold because He has made promises that have not yet been fulfilled: He implemented the "Church" meaning people who find Jesus as their Savior in the Dispensation of Grace. The Church is unique and special. They are the people saved after Jesus died on Calvary and was raised again. They are the people to whom the Holy Spirit was sent to dwell in them and reside in them. They are the people to whom God the Father gave to Jesus and put The Church in His care and safekeeping. As part of the family of God and even more so the Body of Christ we are kept by God the Father whom the Scripture says no power can pluck us out of His care. Jesus Christ, to whom God endowed "The Church" for protective care, also protects us. No one who is saved can ever be lost without having broken the promise of God the Father and of God the Son.

Scriptures that state we cannot lose our Salvation

God wants us, the redeemed, to have total assurance that our salvation is permanent and irreversible. The Scripture gives us five things that must happen for one who has been saved to ever become lost again. They are as follows:

Someone has to pluck us out of the hand of
God Himself and that is impossible.

John 10:29
"My Father, which gave them me, is greater than all; and no man is able to snatch them out of my Father's hand."
Someone has to break the seal of ownership which make us God's purchased possession. This cannot be done.

Ephesians 1:13–14
"In Him you also, when you heard the word of truth, the gospel of your salvation and believed in Him, were sealed with the promised Holy Spirit, who is the guarantee of our inheritance until we require possession of it, to the praise of His glory."

Someone has to cast out the indwelling Spirit of God.

1 Corinthians 3:16
"Do you not know that you are God's temple and that the Spirit of God dwells in you?"

Someone has to separate us from the love of Christ.

Romans 8:33–34
*"Who shall bring any charge against God's elect? It is God
who justifies. Who is to condemn? Jesus Christ is the one
who died, more than that, who is raised, who is at the
right hand of God, who indeed is interceding for us."*

Once again, Paul clearly outlines God's elect by asking who has the power and authority to challenge Jesus Christ. He points out it is Christ who has adopted us unto salvation forever. He answers his question by saying it is Jesus Christ who died for our sins. Christ who is omnipresent, Christ who is omniscient, Christ who is immutable, Christ who loves us has saved us and the Holy Spirit has sealed us. To challenge this security one has to be more powerful than God the Father, God the Son, and the Holy Spirit. None such exist.

Romans 8:35–39
*"Who shall separate us from the love of Christ? Shall
Tribulation, or distress, or persecution, or famine, or
nakedness, or danger, or sword? As it is written:
"For Your sake we are killed all day long;
We are accounted as sheep for the slaughter."
"No in all these things we are more than conquerors
through Him who loved us. For I am sure that neither
death nor life, nor angels nor principalities nor powers,
nor things present nor things to come, nor height nor depth,
nor anything else in all creation, shall be able to separate
us from the love of God in Christ Jesus our Lord."*

*Someone has to erase the believer's name
from the Lamb's Book of Life.*

Revelation 20:15
*"And if anyone's name was not found written in the
book of life he was thrown into the "Lake of Fire."*

We are told by God that the elect have been written into the book of life and are predestined to be saved and not be cast into the "Lake of Fire." Who are the elect in Christ? In fact the elect or those who decide to trust Jesus Christ for salvation. The elect are those will go with Jesus first to live in the one thousand year millennial reign and then for eternity in the new heaven being prepared for God's children. When we are saved we are given a new nature, become a new creature and our name is forever written into the book of life. If we could lose our salvation someone would have to erase our name from the Lamb's book of life.

Why People Doubt Their Salvation

There are four significant reasons that people doubt the principle of "once saved, always saved":

1   They are not saved and have never been saved. People often want to be saved but have not reached the point of giving up self and trusting Jesus Christ to save them. In such cases the Holy Spirit continues to convict these of their sins. Of course they doubt their Salvation. It is not uncommon to have people confess their sins but not be willing to say to God, take me, us me, make me what you want me to be. A shallow confession of sins without a genuine desire to follow God is an act of man not an act of God.

2   They are trusting in their good deeds to be saved or to keep them saved. These people are not saved because they have not reached the point of trusting Jesus Christ and Christ alone for salvation. Again the Holy Spirit continues to strive with these as they doubt their salvation. Those who are trusting in good works for salvation are doomed to doubt because we can never be good enough or do good enough to earn salvation.

3   They have accepted Jesus Christ as Savior but have fallen away from Christ and His desire for their life to the extent they do not feel saved. Satan can put into our minds doubt

of our salvation simply to keep us from serving God. It is natural for all redeemed to at time feel we have not earned salvation. This is because we have not and cannot earn salvation. Many, trust Christ in truth and spirit, but later in life pull away from God and let Satan temp them to begin to trust their works. These are still saved but will not have the joy of their salvation until they return to Christ.

4   They simply have not understood the Bible's teaching on the subject of Security of the Believer.

Scriptures That Speak of Working out Our Faith

Human logic struggles with how man could be saved forever when we continue to sin after we are saved. If mankind can go to heaven then who pays for our sins? This is answered by God. Jesus Christ paid for our sins after we become believers just as He did prior to our salvation. However there are two main subjects of Scripture that God often addresses that do involve works. In neither case is salvation the object of the discussion but in both cases our interpretation of scripture could tie the two together if we do not research the base of the subjects and keep the scriptures in context.

Subject no. 1 is the Judgment seat of Christ. This is applicable only to Christians. The decisions made at the Judgment seat of Christ will be made based on the good works of Christians in this life. Yes, God tells us to persevere, to continue to do good righteous deeds that we may be found approved in the sight of God. But in these verses He is talking to those already saved and is discussing the subject of degrees of reward in heaven the saved shall enjoy. The Apostle Paul spoke often about fighting the good fight and persevering to the end. In such statements he was always discussing the subject to those already saved. And the subject was always his obtaining full rewards at the Judgment seat of Christ. This has nothing to do with obtaining salvation but has everything to do with obtaining full rewards of being a good servant of Christ.

Subject no. 2 is even more difficult. These are the Old Testament Saints who were required by God to perform acts of faith to communicate to God their request for forgiveness of sins. The Old Testament Saints never reached the point in their life they ever were released of the requirement of performing burnt offerings to ask God to forgive their sins. When God gave them "The Law" they were given rules they were expected to keep. God said if you keep these rules you will be saved. God was teaching the Old Testament people they could not save themselves unless they kept every point of "The Law." God also taught that because of the sinful nature of man, no man was capable of keeping "The Law." In fact God goes on in the Old Testament and New Testament to say over and over again that no man ever kept the "The Law," except Jesus Christ Himself. Our Lord was very clear that no man could be saved by "The Law." That is equivalent to saying no man can be saved by works. Scripture that speaks about God's requirement to keep the rules as acts of faith often are misinterpreted as saying salvation must have both faith and works. Let's look at several verses of Scripture many interpret to say one must "work out" their salvation. These scriptures are often misunderstood to mean we must combine faith and works to please God.

Luke 9:23
"And He said to all, "If anyone would come after Me, let him deny himself, and take up his cross daily, and follow Me."

Some say this scripture says that if anyone desires to accept Jesus Christ as Savior they must deny their earthly desires, become righteous and become followers of Christ. No, what Dr. Luke is saying is that if anyone desires to become a follower of Christ be warned what the result will be. After Salvation the Holy Spirit will enter your heart and you will become the recipient of a lifelong urging and powerful tugging to be righteous. This does not mean we must be righteous to be saved. It means that after you are saved you will be chastised if you are not righteous, you will feel the tugging of the Holy Spirit to be righteous, and you will change to the point you may face persecution from former friends. They may not like the change in whom you become. This is not salvation by works. This scripture identifies the results of Salvation.

1 Peter 4:18
"And If the righteous is scarcely saved,
What will become of the ungodly and the sinner?"

In 1 Peter 4:18 we are being taught that the righteous (people whose faith has been counted as righteousness), actually do little in works compared to what keeping "The Law" would require. They will suffer and find service for our Lord requires pain and effort. He then points out that if the saved suffer, how much more will the unsaved suffer and their suffering will be throughout eternity.

1 Corinthians 9:27
"But I discipline my body and keep it under control, lest after
preaching to others, I myself should become disqualified."

This is an excellent example of Scripture meant to refer to Christians who would receive a reward in heaven based on works. It does not refer to salvation. Some read this scripture to mean Paul is saying if he does not do what God wants him to do, he could end up going to hell. In 1 Corinthians 9 Paul begins talking about an Apostle and the rights of an Apostle of Christ. He says in verse 18 his concern is not this world but the life after and he wants full rewards in heaven. That is why he feels the tremendous pull to discipline his body and bring it into subjection so he, Paul, might have full reward at the Judgment seat of Christ that happens after the rapture of the Church. In verse 24 Paul begins discussing the prize associated with the work he was doing for God. Paul never talked about salvation as a prize. Salvation was and is a gift of God and man has no authorship of that gift. Paul in this passage of Scripture is clearly discussing his earthly goal was to do works that would earn him the full prize at the Judgment seat of Christ. It is understandable that some might misread this as applying to salvation but it is talking to one already saved who is seeking God's prize in the hereafter.

John 5:28–29

"Do not marvel at this; for the hour is coming in which all who are in the graves will hear His voice and come out— those who have done good, to the resurrection of life, and those who have done evil, to the resurrection judgment."

Does this verse refer to salvation or rewards after salvation? This verse clearly refers to resurrection of the dead or the results of mankind's decision to trust Christ or reject Christ while alive. The key here is what John means when he talks about "doing good"? A host of scripture tells us we have no hope to be 100 percent righteous in this life. So if this verse means we have to be righteous to be saved no one will be saved. That would be salvation by works. What is John talking about? In verse 24 just before verse 28 and 29, John described what he referred to as "doing good." That was the reference of hearing and believing on Jesus Christ. He went on to say those who believed on Jesus would not be condemned. Yes, this verse definitely refers to salvation and to the destiny of all people after death. But the reference, meaning of good works in this scripture; is our belief in Jesus Christ. Unto us, that faith is counted as righteousness.

Hebrews 6:4–6

"For it is impossible, in the case of those who have once been enlightened, who have tasted the heavenly gift, and have shared in the Holy Spirit, and have tasted in the goodness of the Word of God and the powers of the age to come, and then have fallen away, to restore them again to repentance, since they crucifying again the Son of God, to their own harm and holding Him up to contempt."

So many people are led astray on this verse. In being led astray they are ignoring a multitude of messages from God in which He clearly, without any hint of doubt, states the saved in Christ, those who believe in Jesus Christ, have been, are being and will be saved from their sins without exception. Then they take a vague verse such as this one and allow Satan to interpret it into confusion and doubt.

What did the author of Hebrews mean when he spoke of those who were once enlightened and have tasted the heavenly gift cannot come back to Christ if they fall away? Does this mean a saved person can fall away and never get back to Christ?

Most of the New Testament is written to Christians because the giving of God's Word is for the purpose of guiding Christians. Yes a significant part of the Scripture is also for the purpose of revealing to the lost how they can be saved. But to understand this scripture we must recognize why the author wrote the book of Hebrews. The letter was addressed primarily to Jewish converts to Christianity who were familiar with the Old Testament and who were feeling great pressure to revert to Judaism or to Judaize the New Testament Church. Acts chapter 6 verse 7 suggests there may have been a large number of Jewish Priests who became obedient to the Christian faith.

From initial review we know this verse was written to people who were saved and were part of the "Body of Christ" or "The Church." This understanding is important because it rules out the subject of this teaching being salvation. With that simple fact we now know this verse is about growth in the Christian faith. That is compliant with verses 1–4 in which the Author has told them they need to get past the basic understanding about Salvation.

Hebrews 4:1–2
"Therefore, since a promise remains of entering His rest, let us fear lest any of you seem to have come short of it. For indeed the gospel was preached to us as well as to them; but the word which they heard did not profit them, not being mixed with faith in those who heard it."

The author of Hebrews is comparing the Jewish converts, who are the recipients of this letter, to those ancient Jews who were promised the Land of Canaan. Almost all of those promised the Land of Canaan died before going into the Land of promise but their descendants entered into the Promised Land and in doing so felt the touch of the promise of God. This clearly does not say they were saved and then gave up their Salvation because the author says, ***"The word*** *which they heard did not profit them because it was not mixed with faith in those who heard it."*

God counted the people who went into the Promised Land and were faithful followers of Joshua as righteous. They were counted as righteous because of their faith in God Jehovah. The people who went into the Promised Land and experienced the blessing of God's promise but did so not because of faith but because they were followers of people only, were not counted as righteous and therefore were not saved.

The frustration of the author of Hebrews is that recipients of this letter, people already saved by faith not of works, now were being led to believe they had to have works mixed into their faith to remain saved. The author is saying to them you are already saved. You cannot become unsaved. It is impossible for you to be resaved.

As a father I have two daughters. If I decide to give them a gift of something they want very bad and something that is very expensive, and they accept that gift it belongs to them. If they then decide to pay for that gift again they cannot do so because it is already paid for. These Jewish converts to whom Hebrews 6 is written are told it is impossible to bring back to repentance those who have already repented of their sins (been enlightened). He could also say it is impossible for those who have been "Born Again" to be resaved because they have never become unsaved.

People today get confused that some degree of works must be necessary for salvation or at least necessary to remain saved. Shallow interpretation of the Old Testament requirements of God for His people can lead to this understanding. The people in the Old Testament had to keep certain requirements of "The Law" and they had to demonstrate faith in God Jehovah. But they were not saved because they kept the law, they were saved because, in their hearts they desired to keep the law. Their keeping the requirements of "The Law" was their demonstrating faith in God Jehovah.

During the Dispensation of Grace, however, Jesus Christ has completed the requirements of "The Law." Jesus Christ has completed everything we must do to be saved and all He asks of us is to believe He has done this for us.

Instead of this verse being proof that Christians must combine works with faith to remain saved, it does the opposite. It tells the Jewish converts and it tells us today, that even back in the day of the Jews going into the Promised Land, those who did so without faith were given entrance into the Promised Land but not entrance into the Kingdom of God. And it tells us that once we have been saved it is impossible for us to be saved again. Not because Jesus Christ will not take us but because we never became lost. You cannot resave someone who is not lost.

Salvation Is Not by "Faith Alone"

Many teach works plays some part in our salvation therefore when we cease to have interest in serving God we can lose our salvation. They go to the teaching of Paul who everyone would agree was saved. They say Paul taught no one can be saved by faith alone. They are correct.

However their human logic tells them (actually Satan temps them with this false idea), that surely we must demonstrate our love of God, and such demonstration, along with the grace of God will meet God's requirements of salvation. In this they are wrong. They should link grace with faith as the requirements for salvation. Paul does speak of life as a road or journey. He makes many comments showing that believers must grow in faith and it is never acceptable in the sight of God to remain stagnant in our growth.

Philippians 2:12
"Therefore, my beloved, as you have always obeyed, so now, not only as in my presence but much more in my absence, work out your own salvation with fear and trembling."

The Church Paul is writing to in Philippi, was once in good accord with each other but have had a falling away. In the above Scripture Paul tells the Church members in Philippi they are to "work out your own salvation with fear and trembling" Paul tells them to have bad feelings for another child of God should cause "fear and trembling." So many interpret that statement to say the people must earn their salvation through their work. But we have a host of scripture telling us we can never earn salvation through works. Paul is saying the Church members, meaning all converts to Christianity, must complete their part of their commitment to Christ. When we accept Jesus as our Savior, Christ forgives all past, present and future sins. We commit to love Him, to serve Him and to desire to never disappoint Jesus. We will have fear to the point of trembling as we learn how short we fall in keeping our promise to Christ. The greatest of these commitments are how we will treat others. Paul goes on to clarify what God expects of His Children and their relationship to each other.

Philippians 2:1–4

"So if there is any encouragement in Christ, any comfort from love, any participation in the Spirit, any affection and sympathy, complete my joy by being of the same mind, having the same love, being in full accord and of one mind. Do nothing from selfish ambition or conceit, but in humility count others more significant than yourselves. Let each of you look not only to his own interests, but also to the interests of others."

In the above verses Paul's subject was not salvation. He says "complete my joy by being of the same mind, having the same love and being in full accord with Him." His subject was harmony in the church. Paul is stating that "in the past, while I was with you and while I was absent from you, you have evidenced love for each other, respect to each other, affection and mercy because you had your eyes on Jesus Christ and were not pointing fingers at each other. You were of one accord and one mind and that was to be faithful servants of Jesus Christ." Paul tells them they need to return to that mindset. Note Paul is not telling them they need to be saved again. They had not lost their salvation. They simply were not acting like Children of God even though they were still children of God. Paul then reminds them of the beautiful example Jesus Christ set for all Christians. He was humble, He was self-sacrificing, He was full of love, and He was ever forgiving.

Paul then tells them they need to work out the problems they have with each other. "Work out your own salvation" recognizes that part of salvation that is the follow through of salvation which is sanctification. The members of the church at Philippi understood Paul to be saying.

1. "You need to grow in Christ because you are showing great spiritual immaturity" Work out your sanctification for your own sake, for the Lord's sake and for my (Paul) sake.
2. Your salvation is through Christ. This means you did not save yourselves. Your salvation was also your commitment to obedience of the Lord.
3. "Work out your own salvation" refers to the reality that Christ's atonement for our sins is complete after we accept Jesus Christ as our Savior. But our work of sanctification is only begun. "Work out your own Salvation" informs us that after we are saved we enter into a life-long process of growing spiritually with the Lord. That is called sanctification. It is similar to the laborer who is paid at the beginning of the day. That laborer now has an obligation to "work out your day's pay." This is not earning our salvation but it is completing our part of our covenant with God.
4. Our salvation is not contingent upon our growing in spirit and truth in Christ. However, our rewards at the Judgment seat of Christ are contingent on our good works desiring to please Him. Our example to the lost and dying world is contingent on our growth in spirit and truth.

Matthew 25:41
"Then he will say to those on his left, 'Depart
from me, you cursed, into the eternal fire
prepared for the devil and his angels."

The second coming of Christ will be to separate the righteous from the unrighteousness.

Matthew 25:31–34
"When the Son of Man comes in His glory, and all the angels
with Him, then He will sit on His glorious throne. Before
Him will be gathered all the nations, and He will separate
them one from another, as a shepherd divides his sheep from
the goats. And He will place the sheep on His right, but the
goats on the left. Then the King will say to those on His right
hand, 'Come, you blessed of My Father, inherit the kingdom
prepared for you from the foundation of the world."

The Catholic Church teaches works are required to keep Salvation

The Catholic Church does teach good works are a part of one's salvation. They also teach that after one accepts Christ as Savior, salvation is by inheritance because of faith. The Catholic Church also teaches that a saved person must have works to maintain salvation. They teach we can refuse to do the works required by God and thus lose our salvation which is another way of electing to give up salvation. A primary verse of Scripture they use to establish this doctrine is John the fifteenth chapter.

John 15:1–4
"I am the true vine, and my Father is the vinedresser. Every
branch in me that does not bear fruit he takes away, and
every branch that does bear fruit he prunes, that it may
bear more fruit. Already you are clean because of the word
that I have spoken to you. Abide in me, and I in you. As
the branch cannot bear fruit by itself, unless it abides in
the vine, neither can you, unless you abide in me."

In John 15 our Lord is teaching us that Jesus Christ is the source of who we are, what we become, and what fruit will emerge from our life. The teaching is clear that if we are children of God we will bear fruit of Christianity. We can do nothing else. An apple tree cannot bear forth oranges. Christians cannot bear forth a lifetime of hate, deceit, selfish behavior and hate toward God. This is because when we are saved we are changed into a different person than we were before we were saved. Yes, we can have periods in life in which we stray away from God. But even in such periods we never lose our desire to please God. It's just that our sinful nature has taken control of our life and temporarily drowned out the Holy Spirit.

In this verse, the Lord is comparing Himself with the Church. He points out that it is true sometimes Churches have people who proclaim to be Christians and for a time work feverishly toward that goal. But if the love of Christ is not in them they will not persevere. If they do not love God they cannot love His people.

The verse that says, "Every branch in me that does not bear fruit He takes away" is not saying we can lose our salvation. It is saying that if we are a Child of God we will bear fruit. If we are not a Child we will not bear fruit. Whether or not we bear fruit does not determine if we remain a Christian, it reveals that we never were a Christian.

When we consider the serious question about whether a saved person can lose salvation for any reason at all we must grasp the truth that God does not lie. Thus, God does not give us Scripture that contradicts other Scripture. God does always tell the truth and if two Scriptures appear to contradict each other we are misunderstanding one of those Scriptures and possibly both. That is a truth we can stand on and that we must stand on. Let's therefore, take another look at certain Scriptures that just give no other interpretation but that Salvation is everlasting and eternal.

John 6:37
"All that the Father gives Me will come to Me, and the one who comes to Me I will by never cast out."

This Scripture tells us that all that the Father gives to Me will come to Me. This embodies the two part sequence of Salvation. First God the Father gave to Jesus Christ "The Body of Christ" for Jesus to be our protector, our guide, our inspiration to righteousness living, and our eternal answer to our sin problem. However only those who, in God's foreknowledge would make the decision to come to Jesus, or believe on Jesus Christ will be sealed by the Holy Spirit and protected through eternity to glory with God. This verse tells us one who is saved, meaning he/she has believed on Jesus, will not be caste out or ever released from the protective care of Christ. Our Lord is even more specific in John 6:39.

John 6:39
"And this is the will of him who sent me, that I should lose nothing of all that he has given me, but raise it up on the last day."

What an amazing truth! What a secure promise of God! First this verse tells us it was the will of God the Father to give the Church to God the Son. Although not specifically stated this was because God rewarded Jesus Christ the Son for His fulfillment of the eternal plan of Salvation. Jesus Christ loved the Church and God gave Him the Church in total. Jesus tells us in verse 39 God gave to Jesus the Church ordained that no one, not one soul would ever be lost to Jesus Christ. If someone was saved and could and did decide later in life to renounce their Salvation, the promise of God to Jesus would be broke. This means God the Father was not truthful to Christ.

No, this amazing truth tells us that every person saved by believing on Jesus Christ is first of all saved, second of all guaranteed eternal salvation, and that that salvation will last not for just a time but until the last day of time and the beginning of the New Heaven and New Earth in which we will reign eternally with the Trinity of God the Father, God the Son and the Holy Spirit.

John 10:27–30
"My sheep hear my voice, and I know them, and they follow me. I give them eternal life, and they will never perish, and no one will snatch them out of my hand. My Father, who has given them to me is greater than all, and no one is able to snatch them out of the Father's hand. I and the Father are one."

Wow! This verse in John says Jesus knows everyone who is saved personally. He adopts us as His children. He gives us eternal life. Think what eternal life means. If one could be saved and given eternal life by Christ but later elect to renounce Jesus as Savior and in that action lose their salvation, then they were not given eternal life. Our salvation either lasts forever or it does not regardless of why it does not. God goes on to say they (the saved in Christ) shall never perish. Again if that one who was saved could become unsaved for any reason at all, then the promise God gave to Jesus; and Jesus gives to us; is false.

Now our Lord goes on to reassure us that there is no power on earth or heaven or any other realm that can make this promise void. The reason is that God the Father gave us this promise when He made the promise to Jesus. Jesus goes on to say He, Jesus, gives us this same promise and can be trusted to keep it because He, Jesus and God the Father are one. A promise from one is a promise from the other. Do you really think we as mere humans can break a promise of God the Father to Jesus and from Jesus Christ to us when even the power of Lucifer cannot break that promise? Of course not! Now let us cap off this incredible promise by another amazing Scripture. Look at John 5:24.

John 5:24
"Truly, truly, I say to you, whoever hears my word and believes him who sent me has eternal life. He does not come into judgment, but has passed from death to life."

God tells us in John chapter 5 that whoever, meaning anyone, who hears the good news which is the truth of Jesus Christ's death and resurrection and believes on Jesus not only has everlasting life but will not even come into judgment of their sins. This person, who is inclusive of believers in the "Body of Christ" will never have to account for the sins they commit. Why and how is this possible? Are not the wages of sin death? Yes, but that price was paid by Jesus Christ. We cannot pay a debt owed for our sins when that debt is already paid by Jesus.

Then Jesus explains how this not only is the case but has to be the case. That is because when we are saved we are "Passed from death to life." The very instant we ask Jesus Christ into our heart and ask Jesus to forgive us of our sins we are saved, past, present and future. We pass from this life that is consumed by death both physical and spiritual, and move into being a spiritual being. We still have our physical life and our spirit. But prior to salvation our life was dominated by the physical life that was separated from God the Father. After Salvation we are dominated by the Spiritual life that is united with God the Father not in separation but in eternal glory forever.

Did Old Testament Saints have Security of the Believer?

During the Dispensation of Innocence there was no issue about security of the believer on a day to day basis. Mankind walked and talked with God and they enjoyed a close, loving relationship. Yet the issue of security of the believer lay dormant waiting the time Adam and Eve would eat from the tree of knowledge, would be caste out of the Garden of Eden and would become physically and spiritually separated from God. God told them that if they ate of the tree of knowledge they would surely die. That meant spiritual separation from God immediately and physical death according to God's timetable.

During the Dispensation of Conscience, that followed Adam's being caste out of the Garden of Eden God did not walk and talk with mankind and did not have a personal relationship with man. God spoke with select individuals as He chose and had a teaching relationship. God expected those He spoke with to teach others to worship and praise Him. They failed God miserably. God knew mankind would sin and allowed man to ask for forgiveness of their sin by sacrificing burnt offerings to God. Did God speak to Noah? God's Word records God spoke directly with Cain (Gen. 4:6); Noah (Gen. 6:13–21, 7:1–4, 8:15–17), and Noah and his sons (Gen 9:1–17). However, they existed on a day to day relationship with God without certainty of eternal salvation. What we do know about this question is that the salvation plan for Old Testament Saints was the same as that for New Testament Saints. They were saved by faith in God through the grace of God. Likewise if the Grace of God saved the Old Testament Saints once they never had to be saved again. Remember when God was faced with the decision to grant anyone's request for salvation, God had in front of Him all sins this person ever had committed, all sins they were committing, and all sins they ever would commit. So with this knowledge if God granted that one salvation it was permanent.

During the following Dispensations of Human Government, Promise, and "The Law"; God had a close relationship with Elijah, Moses, Abraham, Joseph, David, Solomon and many others. God told Abraham his faith would count as righteousness with God. This meant that God will only associate with righteous people. But God would count the faith of Abraham and others as righteousness. This allowed a personal relationship with Abraham and others who continuously had faith in God. So people in these dispensations believed they were secure with God throughout eternity. They believed they could live with God eternally because they knew that God counted their faith as righteousness.

However, the Holy Spirit spoke to individuals according to the will of God the Father. Therefore man did not have the Holy Spirit dwelling in their heart even if they were believers in God Jehovah. We know Old Testament Saints were saved by faith through the Grace of God just as believers in the Dispensation of Grace are saved. However they had no understanding of Jesus Christ being the forthcoming Messiah. They could not therefore be saved based on faith in the death burial and resurrection of Jesus. They were instead saved on their faith that God Jehovah would provide a Messiah, at a time in the future, that would fulfill the plan whereby God would forgive them of their sins.

This indicates the Old Testament Saints were saved by their faith through the grace of God just as are New Testament Saints. It is also true they were given eternal salvation when God made the decision to accept their faith unto righteousness. But would they always know they had security in their salvation? The answer is no because the Holy Spirit did not speak to all people who were saved and assure them they were saved.

In addition, their faith in God was demonstrated to the outside world and to themselves as well, by following the commandments of God as given to them through whatever Dispensation of Revelation they resided. This included keeping the law of God, keeping "The Law" given unto Moses, and the burnt offerings to request forgiveness of God for their sins.

We can therefore see that those of us who live in the Dispensation of Grace are indeed blessed. We have clear definitive promise of eternal salvation whereas the Old Testament Saints had this promise but all who were saved did not understand they had security of the believer. The second we ask Jesus into our heart to save us we are eternally saved. Old Testament Saints did not have this promise unless the Holy Spirit spoke directly to a saved person and informed them of that fact. It seems to be scripturally accurate that certain of the Old Testament Saints who were very close to God such as Abraham, Isaac, and Jacob would have been given this promise. Yet all saved people are saved by their faith in God through the grace of God to, sometime in the future send an anointed one to pay the price of their sins and give them eternal salvation.

CHAPTER ELEVEN

The Doctrine of Grace
God's Mercy and Love of Man

A Definition of Grace

The grace of God has widely been described as God's unmerited mercy. This means that there is nothing man can ever do to deserve the mercy that God has elected to give us. Yet God's grace is conditional. Man has to believe on Jesus Christ. The last sentence is critical in that it says, "if man will believe." God's Grace is a free gift of salvation for those who believe.

God's Grace is given for the dual purpose of salvation, and for Godly or righteous living. God loves mankind so much He was willing to pay the price of our salvation. God is a just and Holy God and wants us to have a heart for the same. The Scripture tells us that His Grace and His plan of salvation are intertwined. They work together for His glory and honor. For those who elect to believe on Jesus Christ and to trust Him as their Savior and Lord, God offers his full, unlimited warehouse of Grace for every facet of our lives.

The Substance of Grace

The two critical concepts of Salvation are Grace and Faith. Grace is totally from God. Faith, also from God, is the decision of man in relation to God. The grace of God makes it possible for man to be redeemed. The principles of grace give believers the pathway to salvation and the sustaining power to live the Christian life. These principles include:

- Through Grace, God paid for our sins on Calvary and made it possible for us to be forgiven of our sins by God.
- Through Grace, God gives man enough faith to believe in Jesus and to place our trust in Him to deliver us from our sins.
- Through Grace, God places in the hearts of believers the desire to love God and to be righteous.
- Through Grace, God sends the Holy Spirit to commune with our Spirit so we might know the Will of God.
- Through Grace, God allows us to love one another and to love God.

- Through Grace, God allows us to understand that without God we are lost and doomed forever.
- Through Grace, God uses us to become conduits of His love to a lost and dying world.
- Through Grace, God sent His Church that we might belong to a Christian family and be part of a family with God and God's people.
- Through Grace, God has created Heaven for the permanent abode of His people.

The Source of Grace

God is the source of grace. God consists of the Godhead including God the Father, God the Son and the Holy Spirit. God the Father, God the Son and the Holy Spirit are one in that they think alike, have the same values, the same goals, the same desires and the same love. The grace of our Lord and Savior is the greatest treasure man can have. It is far better than all the gold at Fort Knox. The Grace of God is a spiritual fortune that time and man cannot corrupt. Grace is a showing of great mercy given to man with only the expectation of a returning love from man to God. Most of us have experienced grace from some kind person. We have also experienced the grace of God even though we may not know it. If you have ever been sick and got well that was because of the grace of God. If you have been unemployed and found a job it was because of the grace of God. If you have been in love with someone and they returned your love it was because of the grace of God. Human beings have a capacity for grace but it is almost always mixed in with an expectation of return. But the grace people show others is but a drop of water in the ocean in comparison to the amazing grace of God. Just consider that it was the grace of our Lord Jesus Christ, and the Love of God the Father, and the presence of the Holy Spirit that paid the price of our Salvation.

Acts 15:11
"But we believe that we will be saved through the grace of the Lord Jesus, just as they will."

The Grace of God is the result of God's Holiness, His Truth, His Righteousness, His Justice, His Love and His Mercy. Because we love our children we stand ever ready to forgive them for their mistakes and poor judgment. Likewise God loves us so much that He stands ready to forgive us of our sin. However, to have fellowship and a relationship with God a price had to be paid for our sin because God decreed that the wages of sin is death. However, because God is merciful and because God is love, His ever fiber called for forgiveness if a way could be found to forgive within the requirements of justice. Even when we were dead in transgressions, God's love combined with His mercy to provide a way we could live with Christ. We didn't do anything. We did not earn His forgiveness. We were dead in transgressions and sins. That means "separated from God" Even though we were not alive spiritually, even though we couldn't and wouldn't do anything spiritually to bring ourselves out of death, God loved us and showed us mercy. God demonstrates His grace through everything He does. He is holy, truthful, righteous, just, good, loving and merciful. God's grace proceeds from His nature. God the Father is our source of grace. Jesus Christ is our focus of grace. The Holy Spirit is our administrator of grace. God introduced grace into the human existence in creation. God granted Grace to Adam when he ate of the tree of Knowledge of Good and Evil. God granted grace to each of His prophets, to His apostles, and to each person who believes on His name.

2 Corinthians 8:9
"For you know the grace of our Lord Jesus Christ, that though He was rich, yet for your sake He became poor, so that you through His poverty might become rich."

A Saving Grace

In his second letter to the Church at Corinth, and therefore to all believers, Paul outlines to us that Salvation comes from the grace of Jesus Christ. He also points out that we can do nothing to earn such grace. If we could earn it, our treasure would no longer be grace. Grace is a gift we did nothing to deserve. The first and most obvious such gift, to a Christian, is that of Salvation. Paul the apostle taught that salvation is the gift of God. Paul was referring to man's need for salvation and his utter inability to save himself. Man has no hope for salvation unless God elects to grant forgiveness. And because man does not deserve forgiveness but deserves death and separation from God, then God's forgiveness is a gift that is not earned. It is granted without our merit. That truth is made stronger by contrast. It is "not of ourselves" and "not of works." Salvation is indeed the most extraordinary expression of God's grace.

God had no moral or legal obligation to provide man a way to not pay the price of his sins and yet be saved throughout eternity from Hellfire and damnation. God, however, is God, and as such He can do as he wishes. It is the result of His gracious will. Had it not been for His good pleasure, salvation would never have come. And yet, that unmerited gift of salvation is conditional. God states He will not give the gift of salvation to man without man's faith in Jesus Christ as his Lord and Savior. Is faith then, a gift of God? God's Word tells us our faith is made possible by the grace of God. God's Word tells us the decision of man to trust Jesus Christ for salvation is enabled by the Holy Spirit as a result of a demonstrated desire to follow Christ. That enabling process of God to trust Christ is God's granting us faith to believe. The enabling of us to believe comes from God's Grace. Paul explained where faith comes from in Romans 10:17.

Romans 10:17
"So faith comes by hearing, and hearing by the word of Christ."

God desires that mankind have a life of faith, righteousness, love, kindness, gentleness, and a servant's heart. These are attained through conscious effort of man combined with the Grace of God. Faith exists in the mind and has its birthplace in man's heart. Faith is offered by God in that God made man with the capacity to trust in Him. God then sent the Holy Spirit to encourage man and to witness to mankind for the purpose of convincing mankind to accept Christ. It is man's decision to request salvation. It is God's decision to grant salvation.

What is the faith man must have in God? Faith begins with an acceptance by man he is a sinner. Faith then proceeds to be an understanding of man that he cannot do anything to pay the price he owes God for his sin. Faith, then, consists of believing Jesus Christ can save us, and will save us if we ask with a sincere heart. Salvation is not something we decide to do on our own, whenever we decide to do it. Salvation requires a decision of man but it also requires an act of God. When we decide to put our trust in Jesus, and God accepts our request for salvation, the Holy Spirit cleanses us and joins us with Him. Then we become part of the family of God. Then we are saved by His grace.

Our decision to accept the salvation offered by Christ is not nearly sufficient to pay for our sins. So we cannot save ourselves. We have to depend on God to grant us forgiveness. It is through His Grace that God grants His conditional forgiveness and that condition is that we trust His only begotten Son Jesus Christ.

Ephesians 2:8
"For by grace you have been saved through faith, and that not your own doing; it is the gift of God."

God's sustaining Grace

As we considered the Doctrine of Salvation we agreed that we come to saving faith in Jesus Christ because of His Grace, through our faith, not of works, and no one has the right to become proud and boastful about what they have done. The above verse clearly says we are saved by the Grace of God, also known as the unmerited mercy of God to us. God goes on then to discuss our part of the step of salvation and that is faith. God tells us we have been saved by the Grace of God, through our faith and He goes on to point out that even the faith we use to request salvation is not something we do. It is the gift of God. We are not saved because we earned it. Why then does man tend to believe we retain our salvation because of our good works?

God's "sustaining grace" is just as amazing as his "saving grace." "Sustaining grace" is the undeserved kindness and mercy God gives to all believers so that we might remain in a state of being His redeemed and part of the family of God. After we are saved we retain our sin saturated earthly body, with its imbedded nature of sin. But God keeps us in His love by His grace. The grace of God allows us to accept the price Jesus paid on Calvary for our sins, and His grace makes it possible for the blood of Jesus to continue to pay for our sins. We are who we are because of God's grace. If we have talent to preach, to teach, to counsel others, to show mercy to the needy, to sing, or any of a thousand things, we cannot boast of our ability. We must praise God's grace for making us who we are. Arrogance is not part of the armor or God. Meekness is part of the armor of God. We have nothing to boast of when we consider what Jesus Christ has done for us. Paul has this attitude toward his work as he speaks to us and to the Church at Corinth.

Proverbs 16:5
"Everyone who is arrogant in heart is
an abomination to the Lord;
Be assured He will not go unpunished."

Paul tells us that God walks with and lives with us through the presence of the Holy Spirit who lives in our heart. His grace through the Holy Spirit:

1 Supplies spiritual strength when we would otherwise stumble
2 Enables us to maintain a positive, cheerful attitude in times of trouble
3 Enables us to resist temptation when presented to us on a daily basis
4 Allows us to face trials of health, finances, old age, family issues with comfort to know He will lead us through the dark days.
5 Gives us the courage to speak out against evil and unrighteousness.
6 Gives us the gift of friends and family as an encouragement and support.

7   Gives us the Word of God as a daily source of knowledge and strength.

8   Gives us assurance that we are saved and will be with Jesus Christ in eternity.

9   Enables us to resist the efforts of Satan to destroy our witness and our faith in Christ.

10 Gives us an understanding of God's character and a desire to be like God.

11 Keeps us from becoming bitter when faced with trials in this life.

12 Grants us the privilege of speaking with God directly through prayer.

Grace of God is now identified to be God giving us blessings we do not deserve. Is that the same thing as mercy? If not what is mercy?

The Mercy of God

We tend to blend in together God's grace and God's mercy. These are similar but different expressions.

God's Grace	God's Mercy
God's gift to us of blessings we do not deserve.	God's not turning upon us the punishment we deserve.
Romans 3:24 *"And are justified by His grace as a gift through the redemption that is in Christ Jesus,"*	*Romans 6:23* *"For the wages of sin is death, but the gift of God is eternal life in Christ Jesus our Lord."*
John 10:10 *"The thief comes only to steal, and kill, and to destroy. I came that they may have life, and that they may have it abundantly."*	*Psalms 51:1–2* *"Have mercy on me, O God, According to Your steadfast love; According to your abundant mercies, Blot out my transgressions. Wash me thoroughly from my iniquity, And cleanse me from my sin."*

Many places in Scripture God informs us, all have sinned and come short of the glory of God. This means we all have disappointed God severely and deserve punishment. In fact, we all deserve death, both physical death from this earthly life and spiritual death, which means eternal separation from God. The realization of this reality is clearly outlined throughout the book of Romans along with other places in scripture. Every day God gives us to live on earth without dying and going to the "Lake of Fire" is given because of His mercy. If God gave us justice we would all immediately go before the great White Throne of Judgment and be cast into the "Lake of Fire" known as Hell. Because of His love He grants us mercy and does not apply the justice we deserve. David voiced our condition when He cried out to God, *"Have mercy on me, O God, according to your steadfast love and according to your great compassion erase my sins as if they had not been committed by me."*

Because of the mercy and grace of God, our response should be to fall on our knees in worship and thanksgiving.

Hebrews 4:16
"Let us then with confidence draw near to the throne of grace, that we may receive mercy and find grace to help in time of need."

The Universal Grace of God

The universal grace of God refers to the unmerited mercy God has bestowed upon all mankind regardless of whether they have decided to accept Jesus Christ as their Savior or they have decided to continue in their sin.

Hebrews 4:16
"The LORD is good to all,
And His mercy is over all that He has made."

Jesus Christ told us in the book of Matthew (Matthew 5:45) that God causes His sun to rise on the evil and the good. He sends rain on the righteous and the unrighteous. He also told us in the book of Luke (Luke 6:35) that He is kind to the ungrateful and wicked. And perhaps, even more significant in the book of Acts; (Acts 14:17); He tells us He grants all mankind His compassion, goodness, and kindness while extending His patience upon the elect (saved) and non-elect (unsaved). It is the universal Grace of God that provides that patience upon the non-elect (unsaved) and thereby giving them more time to trust Jesus. It is also the universal grace of God upon the elect (saved) to give us more time to be His witnesses and to do the will of the Father who sent us to be His missionaries.

Nahum 1:3
"The LORD is slow to anger and great in power and the Lord will by no means clear the guilty. His way is in whirlwind and storm, and the clouds are the dust of His feet."

Another benefit of God's universal grace granted to both the elect and the non-elect is His restraint of sin in the life of individuals and society as a whole. God restrained the pagan nations from invading Israel time after time showing universal patience of a people who would not trust Him and would not do His precepts. God does not always restrain Satan from inflicting corruption and destruction, but He chooses the time and place to do so. God did not let Abimelech touch Sarah the wife of Abraham. God also, at times, chose to harden the hearts of certain people. One way God hardens the heart of an individual is by releasing His restraint on that person and let Satan take control of their lives to do evil.

Psalms 81:11–12
"But my people did not listen to my voice;
Israel would not submit to me.
So I gave them over to their stubborn hearts,
to follow their own counsels."

In Psalms 81 God is referring to His chosen people (the Jews). But they have rejected Him. Although they are His chosen people,

Jews who reject Christ are not saved. They are lost. God often dealt with the Jews by withholding His restraint and letting them become as bad as they wished. If God did not have restraint on the hearts of the saved and unsaved, our world would be lawless, corrupt, dangerous and very evil. We see some societies, in some countries, where witchcraft and Satanic demons rule. In such countries God has to some degree released His restraint of evil in the hearts of the saved and unsaved alike. Another product of God's universal grace is the implanting of knowledge of good and evil in all people even though those people do not believe on Jesus Christ and reject God. We know that many people who are not confessing Christians are very moral and decent people. The grace of God has universally placed into man something called a conscience that tells us of good and evil. Paul told a group of unbelieving Gentiles they had been imputed by God with a nature to do good. However that nature is also paralleled with a nature to do evil. It means all of mankind feels God's restraining hand and it means God is in control of Satan and limits the influence he can have on universal man.

Romans 2:14
"For when Gentiles, who do not have the law, by nature do what the law requires, they are a law to themselves, even though they do not have the law."

If God did not restrain Satan's influence on the hearts of believers and nonbelievers, all of society would fall into total depravity. Total depravity is the goal of Satan but God will not let that happen yet. But God tells us His patience is not eternal. We have in Scripture the foretelling of a time, after the Holy Spirit is withdrawn from earth that total depravity will reign. However, God is not yet ready for that to happen. He does not want man to totally destroy himself yet. Therefore the Sovereign God exercises His omnipotence to place restraint on the evil and to fulfill the promises of God."

CHAPTER TWELVE

The Doctrine of Sanctification
God's Plan for the Spiritual Growth of Mankind

The word *sanctify* has two meanings as used in God's Word and as the word applies to human life. The word Sanctification means to be set apart. In the Bible Sanctification literally means to be set aside for the exclusive use of God. It means to cease being focused on self and refocus on God. It means to be dedicated to please God. This requires a divine change in the life in an individual because we do not have the power or will to make such a change within our natural selves. Our nature is to serve self. Our instincts are to do what we want to do just because we want to do it. There are different terminologies used to describe the two meanings of spiritual sanctification. Let's begin with the concept of "Process Sanctification" and "The Act of Sanctification." These terms are also often called "Positional Sanctification" and "Growth Sanctification." The "Process of Sanctification" is not an immediate happening in this life but is a gradual process as we grow in the love and service of Christ. The "Act of Sanctification," however, is instantaneous and occurs when we accept Jesus Christ as our Savior. When we are saved we do not instantaneously become people who are sinless. No, we become people whose sins are forgiven and blotted out from the sight of God the Father because they are covered by the blood shed by Christ on Calvary. Immediately upon the act of sanctification (salvation) we begin the journey of the "Process of Sanctification."

In the seventeenth chapter of John, Jesus addresses the subject of sanctification, or being set aside, just for Christ.

John 17:16, 17
"They are not of the world, just as I am not of the world, sanctify them in the truth your word is truth."

The sanctification mentioned in this verse is a once-for-ever uniting of those who believe God. It is a work God performs in our salvation and it is an act mankind does not have the ability to accomplish. This is the sanctification theologians sometimes refer to as "Positional Sanctification"; it is the same as justification and regeneration. It is the result of God's regeneration of a lost soul. It means the Holy Spirit touches our heart and gives us a new nature. We are saved. The book of Hebrews verifies that those who are of the family of God are set apart from the world and made a new creature. This very process of giving us a new nature, or being "Born Again," brings about Positional Sanctification, as we understand the first meaning of sanctification. Some theologians call this "Granted Sanctification" because when we are saved we are granted the privilege of becoming a part of the family of God. First Corinthians 12:13 teaches us that the second we accept Jesus Christ as our Savior the Holy Spirit spiritually baptizes (spiritual not physical baptism) us into the body of Christ. Hebrews reinforces our understanding of **"Granted Sanctification"** by teaching we are all of one. This means we are part of the family of God after salvation.

"Born Again" means to be changed from a person whose life is focused on self and selfish desires, to a person who now, still has the old sin nature, but is also given a new nature. The new nature (Positional Sanctification also called Granted Sanctification) contains a desire to worship and praise God.

1 Corinthians 12:13
"For in one Spirit we were all baptized into one body—Jews or Greeks, slaves or free—and all were made to drink of one Spirit."

Hebrews 2:11
"For He who sanctifies and those who are being sanctified all have one source, that is why He is not ashamed to call them brothers."

The second meaning of Sanctify is the process of becoming Holy. Immediately after being saved we do not become Holy Creatures. We are people who still sin but we regret our sin. We must grow with the Holy Spirit toward the status of being Holy. When we are saved we are given a new nature and that is one of Holiness. Because this can only happen once and that must be at salvation we are authenticated forever into the family of God. This does not mean we are yet what God wants us to become. No, we are just forgiven of our sins and our sins are covered with the blood of Jesus. Therefore God sees us "as if" we had not sinned. Thus we hear this process called the act of justification meaning "Just as if we had never sinned." But God wants us to continue to grow in His likeness. This is a process that does not come about instantaneously or completely. We will call this "Growth Sanctification." As Christians, we will not be fully sanctified, in the sense of being a Holy creature made fully in the likeness of God, until after the rapture and the Judgment seat of Christ. There we will be finally cleansed of the impurity of the flesh that lives within us. This is an ever-increasing desire in our heart in which God, gradually, realigns us from a sin focus to a love of God focus. Regeneration, or Justification, or "Granted Sanctification" means we have been changed by the Holy Spirit and placed into the position of beginning "Growth Sanctification." "Growth Sanctification" is the decision man makes about what we are going to do with our new position of being part of the family of God. Will we gradually become more and more like Jesus Christ? That is God's plan. The Holy Spirit will work with us daily, for the rest of our life, to bring that about. We cannot become more like Jesus without the aid of the Holy Spirit. Yet The Holy Spirit will not change us to become more like Christ without our desire to change. Peter explained to the Churches the intent of God was that they be captivated by an overcoming desire to praise, honor and glorify God for the amazing work of Jesus Christ in their salvation, even though we have not personally seen Christ. This required continuous growth in the Spirit.

1 Peter 1:7–8
"So that the tested genuineness of your faith—more precious than gold that perishes though it is tested by fire—may be found to result in praise and glory and honor at the revelation of Jesus Christ. Though you have not seen him, you love him. Though you do not now see him, you believe in him and rejoice with joy that is inexpressible and filled with glory."

"Growth sanctification" is a wonderful adding to our personality and heart the desire to glorify God. But this thought pattern can miss a vital part of "Growth Sanctification." "Growth Sanctification" includes breaking down the old and cleaning up the flesh focused person to drop all selfish motives all deceit and all unrighteousness and replace those motives with God's righteousness. Dropping the old man is just as much a part of "Growth Sanctification" as is putting on the new creature in Christ.

1 Corinthians 1:2
"To the church of God that is in Corinth, to those sanctified in Christ Jesus, called to be saints together with all those who in every place call upon the name of our Lord Jesus Christ, both their Lord and ours."

1 Corinthians 6:10–11
"Nor thieves, nor the greedy, nor drunkards, nor revilers, nor swindlers will inherit the kingdom of God. And such were some of you. But you were washed, you were sanctified, you were justified in the name of the Lord Jesus Christ and by the Spirit of our God."

Growth Sanctification

When Paul used the terminology "sanctified" in 1 Corinthians 6:11, he was referring to "Justification" or "Granted Sanctification." But Paul was soon going to teach, both the Saints at Corinth, as well as you and I, that "Granted Sanctification" is not the end of God's expectations. It is, in fact, only the beginning. Paul's letters to Timothy gives us a revelation of God's expectations of our spiritual growth in the Lord. Paul's checklist of God's expectations for us is humbling.

1.   We are to be fearless in doing God's Work. When we were given "Granted Sanctification," God gave us, a spirit of confidence in God that overcomes our human fear. We were given the power of God and love of God as a resource to call upon so that we could represent Him without worry or

fear. We were assured that we could, of sound mind, believe that no man could do anything to harm us to the point of taking us out of the care of God. However, for most of us it takes time for us to grasp the full reality of claiming this promise. We grow to the point of gradually, increasingly accepting this truth and claiming it as our own. This is the process of "Growth Sanctification."

2 Timothy 1:7
"For God gave us a spirit not of fear, but of power and of love and self-control."

2. We are to be proud of our Lord and Savior and not ashamed of being His Child. Satan tries to tell us that our belief in Jesus Christ is something we should hide from the world because we will be rejected if they find out. Satan tries to tell us that we will suffer persecution and isolation from our family and friends if we publicly confess our love and adoration for Jesus. Paul tells us that "Growth Sanctification" is a process of overcoming the power of Satan. It is a process of becoming bolder in our witness about the Lord. We are to never be ashamed of whom we belong. We are, in fact, required to readily, without fear share to all we see what Christ has done for us.

2 Timothy 1:8
"Therefore do not be ashamed of the testimony about our Lord, nor of me His prisoner, but share in the suffering for the gospel by the power of God."

3. We are to be strong-minded about the Gospel. We are to turn our backs on any sense of evil, corruption, wickedness or unholy thing. The strong in Christ do not participate in lifestyles such as profanity. The strong in Christ do not participate in lifestyles including sexual misconduct. The strong in Christ do not allow their own desires for materi-

alism to overcome their desire to glorify God in all things. We are to resist Satan's attempt to ruin our witness. This is a twenty-four-hour-a-day battle, seven days a week. It requires mental strength beyond that which any of us have. This is why we must learn to rely on the Holy Spirit to be our strength. The process of "Growth Sanctification" teaches us to rely not on our own strength but on the Strength of the Spirit of God. In that manner we can reject the advances of Satan.

2 Timothy 2:1
"You then my child be strengthened by the grace that is in Christ Jesus."

4. We must be willing to endure hardship in our walk with the Lord. Christ tells us that Satan will pour his power upon us trying to nullify our witness. Just the normal trials of life can be discouraging. Add to that the attacks of Satan and we can be disheartened to the point of ceasing to be a witness for Christ. When we are given "Granted Sanctification" we are given the power, through Christ, to endure anything and everything Satan can throw at us. But we have to learn to use this power. We have to learn to ask for and seek the power of Christ to keep us on the right road.

2 Timothy 2:3
"Share in suffering as a good soldier of Jesus Christ."

5. We must call upon the faith that was given to us. When we were saved God gave us enough faith to accept Christ as our Savior. If we just ask, God will give us enough faith to overcome the trials of this life. We must, however, recognize when our faith is weak. The Scriptures tell us faith comes by the Word of God brought to us in preaching and in our reading of His Word. When our faith is weak we

are asked of God to study His word, pray, and step out on faith. God promises he will meet us at our point of need. However, accepting that without worry and trusting on the Holy Spirit is something that requires growth in the Spirit. We gradually gain the "Growth Sanctification" to claim His promises.

2 Timothy 1:5
"I am reminded of your sincere faith, a faith that dwelt first in your grandmother Lois and your mother Eunice, and I am sure dwells is in you as well."

6. We must be strict observers of God's Word just as Paul was a strict observer, first of God's righteousness and second of God's love. Paul stated he was imprisoned, was beaten, and was abused because He steadfastly preached and taught the Gospel of God without compromise. He did this so others might be become acquainted with the amazing grace available from God the Father, God the Son and the Holy Spirit. We gain this knowledge in "Growth Sanctification." When we are "Born Again" we are not complete with this maturity but God can and will empower us toward completeness in spiritual growth if we ask Him.

2 Timothy 2:9, 10
"For which I am suffering, bound with chains as a common criminal; but the word of God is not bound. Therefore I endure everything for the sake of the elect that they also may obtain the salvation which is in Christ Jesus with eternal glory."

7. "Growth Sanctification" is not accomplished by obeying a set of rules. God gave the Old Testament people the Law that was supposed to be a plumb line to help them understand when they were displeasing God. It was not enough because we must obey God out of love for Him not out of duty. We will not be successful in separating ourselves

from the world if we do not have a better place to be. But we have a better place to be. We have the state of "Granted Sanctification" that we can reside in and abide in the love of God. As we learn to abide or live daily in the place God has put us, that being "Granted Sanctification," we gradually do not care what the world thinks of us. Then we are growing spiritually in the Lord.

The more we grow in the Lord the more we hate sin. The more we understand what God wants from our life, the more we despise falling short of His satisfaction of our life. The Holy Spirit is working against our base nature. This is because when our base nature was changed from carnal to righteous, we retain our old carnal nature of sin. But the Holy Spirit can and will win the battle daily if we will trust Him. The Word of God says in Philippians:

Philippians 2:12–13
"Therefore, my beloved, as you have always obeyed, so now, not only as in my presence but much more in my absence, work out your own salvation with fear and trembling, for it is God who works in you, both to will and to work for his good pleasure."

God is not telling us that we are supposed to earn our salvation in Philippians 2:12–13. God is telling us that we are to continue the path we were sat upon when we were saved. At that time we were granted "Granted Sanctification." We were changed to become part of the family of God. We were granted entry into the Holy household of God the Father. We also were charged with the responsibility of being faithful to the commitment we made to God when we accepted Christ. We agreed to try with all our might, all of our mind, and all of our soul to please God. Paul now challenges us to work out the commitment we made to God at the time we were saved. That is the process of "Growth Sanctification."

We need to remember that when we accepted Christ as our Savior, we were given the name of Christians. We are to honor that name. We are to be proud of that name. We are to constantly study

God's Word, pray to our Father in heaven, walk and talk with His children of faith so that we might be humbled and yield not to our prideful temptation of Satan but yield to the amazing redemption of our Father.

The Spiritual Foundation of "Growth Sanctification"

We have seen a glimpse of what our goal or objective is in "Growth Sanctification." We tend to shutter when we think of the path we must tread to get there. We realize we can never get there on our own power. We would never arrive. We are too weak and too subject to the power of evil in our everyday life to steadily grow in Sanctification, much less approach the goal of being Holy. Even as we recognize we have to have God's help to grow in spirit we ask the question, "What can we do to position ourselves for Spiritual Growth?"

For an answer to this question we turn to the book of Romans. Romans chapter 6 puts the question of our spiritual growth in focus. Romans points out that when Christ died on the Cross of Calvary, God the Father gave Him the Church. We, The Elect of God, or the Church, belong to Christ for salvation, for regeneration, for protection, for justification, and yes for sanctification. The responsibility for our salvation, our regeneration, our justification, our protection and our sanctification was placed on the shoulders of our Lord Jesus Christ.

We the Elect of God, or the church, died spiritually when Adam disobeyed God and was caste out of the Garden of Eden. When Jesus Christ arose from the grave we spiritually arose with Him in the sight of God. When Jesus Christ ascended on High to be with His Father in the heavenly of Heavens we spiritually ascended with Him. We have a Spirit that is part of us here on earth but which also resides with Christ in Heaven. At the rapture of the Church our spiritual life will join our glorified physical body to be with God the Father. This is the reality of "Granted Sanctification" because of the drastic change in our position with Christ when we are saved.

Ephesians 2:5–6
"Even when we were dead in our trespasses, made
us alive together with Christ (by grace you have
been saved), and raised us up with Him, and seated
us in the heavenly places in Christ Jesus."

Know the Lord

Our life here on earth, is a spiritual internship teaching us to "Know the Lord." The Apostle Paul, through the Holy Spirit, teaches us that when the Holy Spirit changed our hearts and made us part of the Body of Christ (The Church), He changed us and gave us a new nature. Our new nature no longer is comfortable with the ways of the world. We were spiritually baptized, immersed, into the love of God the Father, God the Son and the Holy Spirit. Through the Grace of God we gave up the old self, put on a new self that is eternal and will never fail. Paul asks, "Did you not recognize this?" Now that you are a new person, entirely different than the old creature you used to be, don't you want to learn about who you are? This change is a spiritual baptism in which the old self is buried through death (The death of Jesus) and rises again with a new nature. Please understand, this is not water Baptism. Water Baptism is a symbol or remembrance of what happened when we were spiritually baptized into our new life. Spiritual Baptism is when we totally give ourselves to Jesus Christ and say do with me as you will Lord for I am yours. Paul says know and understand what happened to you at salvation. Know and understand what the marvelous gift of "Granted Sanctification" is. Recognize in your heart that Jesus died individually for you so you might be saved. The road to spiritual fulfillment or holiness begins with knowing our Lord and knowing what He did for us.

Romans 6:6
"We know that our old self was crucified with him in
order that the body of sin might be brought to nothing,
so that we would no longer be enslaved to sin."

Paul says, knowing what Jesus Christ did for us on Calvary and knowing how indebted we are to Him for eternal salvation, we come to the conclusion that; yes, the old man, the selfish man, the evil corrupt man, must cease to exist. The righteous man God wants us to be must emerge. As we recognize what Jesus did for us on Calvary, we then become aware of a growing need in our heart to do away with the body of sin that is still in us. We no longer want to be slaves to the urgings of Satan. We do not want to be slaves to sin. When we recognize this change in our soul, we must first accept this change came from the Holy Spirit not ourselves. Second, we accept that we have started the journey in our spiritual internship toward holiness.

Romans 6:9
"We know that Christ, being raised from the dead will never die again. Death no longer has dominion over Him."

Paul then emphatically points out that once we recognize that Jesus Christ was raised from the dead; once we realize Jesus conquered death, and we were raised from the dead with Christ; then we begin to learn we have already conquered death, We learn that we have absolutely nothing to fear. Mankind cannot defeat us because victory is already ours through Christ Jesus our Lord. Death has no dominion, or control, over Christ, and Death has no dominion over us as His children of faith. This is step one of the foundation of sanctification. It is not a step of action on our part that we earn something. It is a step of faith or a decision on our part that Christ has done something for us. Praise the Lord.

Evaluate your relationship to the Lord

Paul then tells us in Romans 6:11 that after we realize and grasp the reality of the gift of salvation Christ has given to us, we should use the intellect God gave us and reason about what we know about God wants from us.

Romans 6:11
"So you also must consider yourselves dead to sin and alive to God in Christ Jesus."

Therefore, let's consider the truth God told us and how it relates to our own lives. We know:

- Our sin driven life died with Christ Jesus on Calvary,
- Our sins, all of them, past present and future were buried with Jesus,
- We spiritually rose from the grave the third day with spiritual victory over death (separation from God), and
- Jesus conquered death when He arose from the dead, never to ever have to die again for our sins. His victory was our victory because we are why He died.

When Christians say they are dead to sin they first of all are referring to spiritual life not our bodily physical life. Spiritual death is permanent separation from God. So when Christians refer to being dead to sin they are pointing out they will spiritually live forever under the blessed protective care of God the Father, God the Son and the Holy Spirit. Christians are also referring to the reality they will not be held accountable for any sins we have committed or will commit. However, we cannot be dead to sin and not alive to something. We are alive to Christ Jesus, meaning the new focus of our life, the new purpose of our life and the new world we live in is totally consumed with the love of Jesus for us and our love for our Lord and Savior.

God does not want us to be people who just accept His promise blindly. He wants us to trust Him and trust His Word. Then based on our trust, make our decision based on the intellect God gave us to serve Him or to not serve Him. If we decide, as a rational Christian would, we are progressing well in spiritual internship toward holiness.

Part of our logic should be that we will not live this life without struggles, without disappointments, without tragedy. Jesus Christ experienced all these things and we are part of Him. We will experience all He experienced both good and bad. As we reckon or reason together, we gradually learn that we have victory in Christ Jesus not only of the life to come but of this world also. And our victory is not based on feelings that can vary from day to day but on Spiritual facts evidenced in the Word of God.

1 Corinthians 15:57
"But thanks be to God, who gives us the victory through our Lord Jesus Christ."

Yield to the Word of God

Romans 6:13
"Do not present your members to sin as instruments for unrighteousness, but present yourselves to God as those who have been brought from death to life, and your members to God as instruments for righteousness."

The Apostle Paul now reasons with all members of the Body of Christ to say recognize that you spiritually died with Jesus Christ, were buried with Him, and rose from the dead with Him. Paul tells us to also recognize we will someday ascend to the heavenly of heavens with Him to be with God the Father forever. It is therefore reasonable to decide we should live for Him and commit our heart, mind, soul, body, and spirit to please God. If we are a Child of God we will want to honor Him. Understanding this, and recognizing the amazing debt we have to our Lord and Savior, any reasonable believer would totally submit himself or herself to the will of Christ. Any reasonable believer would desire to be a servant of Christ and be consumed in His love and protection. Likewise, in our submission, any reasonable believer will dedicate their body, their mind, their heart and their very soul to please God and to honor His name. In so doing any reasonable believer will desire to do anything and everything He puts on our heart in service to Him. We will reject the urging of Satan to rebel against God and we will reject the will of Satan to do things to satisfy our carnal nature that stills exists. We will do this because our God makes us into a person who truly hates to disappoint Him. This is a significant step towards advancing in our internship toward spiritual Holiness.

Paul points out that we, as weak people will follow some superior force because we are too weak to not do so. Even those who take such pride in their own strength and independence are totally subject to either Satan or God. There are only three spirits in the world. These three include the Spirit of God, the Spirit of Satan and our human spirit. We are the weakest of the three and will be dominated by one or the other. Paul reminds us we were all, at one time, slaves to the dominance of Satan. This became true when Adam disobeyed God and was caste out of the Garden of Eden. At that point mankind was imputed with a sin nature. Satan rules the lives of everyone who does not have their faith in Christ. However, Praise the Lord, when we accepted Jesus Christ as our Savior that ended our slavery to Satan, so far as our eternal debt to God is concerned. But it did not end our weakness of falling into the prey of Satan on a daily basis so far as our works and thoughts are concerned. The only way Satan can bring damage and harm to God is through those whom God has elected to be His own. Thus, we must learn to obey the Lord God even when our logic says it does not make sense. We must learn to obey the Lord even when all those around us say we should do something else. We should obey the Lord our God when it makes us isolated from friends and family. We must obey the Lord our God based on our love for God and based on our reckoning that God is our world, God is our Savior, and God is our refuge in times of trouble. When we conquer this we are not ready to graduate from our spiritual internship but we are beginning to take the advanced courses.

No Condemnation for the Sanctified

Romans 8:1
"There is therefore now no condemnation to those who are in Christ Jesus."

In the eighth chapter of Romans, the Apostle Paul combines both concepts of "Granted Sanctification and Growth Sanctification" together so we can see the result. There is no condemnation to those who are in Christ Jesus because when we were saved we were granted full, complete "Granted Sanctification" in the Lord. This was not because of our actions but because of the actions of Jesus Christ. God offers us salvation, we decide to accept the offer through faith and we believe God can save us, and then God, through the Holy Spirit, changes us and gives us a new heart. When we are saved we instantly change from a state of spiritual filth to a state of spiritual holiness; *so far as God the Father is concerned.* This is possible because when God the Father sees us He sees Jesus Christ His Son. When we commit sin in this life God does not see that sin because the blood of Jesus shed on Calvary blots it out. We have been justified in the sight of God.

However, when we are saved we accept a commitment to serve God. We made a covenant with God when we accepted Jesus Christ as our Savior. He gives us a new nature that desires to please, honor and glorify God. We cannot be happy or complete unless we are pleasing God. Our new nature will overcome the old nature and we will try to walk according to the Spirit of God not the urgings of the flesh. Thus, we begin the journey of life trying to live a life acceptable to God. This is not out of duty but of love. As children we had a natural instinct to please our parents. As children of God we have a natural instinct to please our Savior. This is the path of "Growth Sanctification." We are on the road of our spiritual internship for Holiness all of our lives. We graduate at the Judgment Seat of Christ after the rapture of the Church and just before we are admitted to the heavenly of heavens to be with God the Father and the angels.

CHAPTER THIRTEEN

The Doctrine of Prayer
God's Communication with Man

What is Prayer?

Prayer is communication with God. God desires a relationship with us. Prayer is one of the greatest gifts God has given us because it opens the door to a dialogue with God. When we pray we communicate with God and the form it takes is not important. What is in the heart of man is what is important. The words we say are not important. What is in our heart is important. Do we want to communicate with our creator? To pray means we intentionally engage in a dialogue with God. To pray means we are establishing that connection within our mind, within our heart, and giving ourselves the opportunity to have a deeper experience with God. Prayer is our opportunity to transcend our world and connect with God's power, love and compassion. God cares deeply about our problems and our victories and is just waiting for us to come to Him and discuss our lives. The Bible tells us over and over to constantly bring our problems and victories to our heavenly Father. Prayer is not to inform God of something that He does not know. Prayer is not trying to convince God or change His mind. God already knows our needs. God also knows the future and wants what is best for us. Prayer's purpose is to build a relationship with God. God wants a relationship with us. He wants us to care about Him for He cares about us. That is the nature of love. Love seeks return of love. We should be able to pray to God in a state of mind of peace because we are speaking to the one who is all-powerful, all loving, all knowing and He cares for us.

Philippians 4:6
"Do not be anxious about anything, but in everything by prayer and supplication, with thanksgiving, let your requests be made known to God."

God tells us we should not worry and not be anxious about anything but take our troubles and trials to Him. He loves us and cares for us and will meet our needs.

Why should we pray?

The greatest reason to pray is that it pleases God when His children communicate with Him. We pray because we want things from God. We want relief from our perceived burdens. We want things for others. We pray to express our thanksgiving to God. We pray to express our despair and our depression.

Jesus thought it was worthwhile to pray, and we should also. If He needed to pray to remain in the Father's will, how much more do we need to pray? God wants to work with the will of man not in spite of it. God's seeks man's mind freely given with love and adoration. Therefore, prayer unleashes God's power inviting Him to work in our behalf. Prayer opens the channels of God's blessing. Prayer is a medium through which God accomplishes things He wants to see happen in our lives.

God has ordained that man would have freedom of choice and free will. When we pray to our Father through Jesus Christ the Son, as interpreted through the Holy Spirit, we ask God into our lives. God, in His sovereign will, has limited his powers in our lives to the extent necessary to give us free will. Prayer welcomes God into our lives to do what he has been longing to do all the time. God does not need our permission to intercede into our lives and at times does so. But God also wants to insure we have the free will to make our own decisions. Otherwise we become robots and cannot return to Him a free and heartfelt love. Even when we do not see anything significant occurring, God is still at work solving our problems. When we see no answers, God is still is waiting for the proper time to give us the solution.

How do we pray?

God is waiting for us to communicate with Him. He is waiting for those few brief moments when we acknowledge Him, think about Him, and show Him love, honor, and respect. God wants us to talk to Him and He sincerely wants to talk to us, not in words, but through our mind and our heart. God may speak vocally but seldom does. Instead our heart will feel that gentle tugging, an urging, and a pulling. That gentle tugging on our heart's door is the Holy Spirit speaking to us. The story goes that a little boy was flying his kite up in the air and the clouds descended to the point he could not see the kite. A man asked how can you fly the kite when you cannot see it? "Oh," the boy said, "I can still feel the tugging of the strings." Prayer is the tugging of our heart's strings. It is God, through the Holy Spirit, speaking to us. Our heart and mind will know what God is trying to tell us. Some basic considerations we should recognize in praying include the following:

1 Bring the issue to God immediately. Do not try to solve it on our own intellect and after failing, as a last resort, turn to God. Trust God to give you the answer to your problems.

2 We need to be honest with God when we pray. This often requires some meditation on our part concerning our attitude and our dependency on God. God wants to hear our confession of our failures and our need for Him.

3 Prayer must be God centered. We should not ask God to give us the power to solve problems in such a way that we receive glory, honor, or credit for the solution. We ask God to solve problems and give God the glory and honor that He is entitled to receive.

4 We should always give praise and honor to God giving thanks to Him for His great grace and mercy He has bestowed upon us.

5 We should not pray to gloat about what we did for God. Also we should not pray to gloat about what we did for ourselves or others. Our achievements are almost always made possible by God so it is foolish for us to gloat about what we did even if it is something of substance.

6 We should not pray to inform God of the latest news. God already knows.

Most people expect God to answer in a familiar way. We expect God to communicate as man communicates, perhaps by a discernable voice or in signs and demonstrations of His power. But that's seldom the way God operates. God speaks to a person's heart. God speaks to our mind, to our sense of moral righteousness and fairness, and to our understanding of what is right, holy and just. By speaking to our heart God instructs us, encourages us, warns us, and influences us but does so without taking away our free will. God wants us to listen to Him through faith. God wants us to ask of Him through faith. God wants us to understand Him because of our faith. We understand what God is telling us but often do not want to acknowledge it is God communicating with us. The person that has found Jesus and who has Jesus Christ dwelling within their heart listens to our Lord talk. If we are close to God and are seeking Him we can hear God. If we have faith to believe we will trust Him. However to have that type of communication with God we have to be receptive to God's Words. We have to begin to communicate with God and be mentally alert to discern God's communication. We have to get our heart in the right condition.

To become a positive, expectant, and vibrant communicator with God we must have a tremendous desire to understand God and to yield to His will. We also must have a desire to put in the time and effort to search for God's will. Many well-intentioned Christians see prayer as talking to God. Talking to God is one half of prayer. Listening to God is the other half. Unfortunately we talk more than we listen.

What God wants from His Children!

God wants people to recognize and honor His majesty, to trust Him and to love Him. Prayer is a step toward that purpose. Jesus prayed to God the Father because He needed the guidance, strength and holiness of His Father when He became man and walked among us. Jesus also prayed to His Father simply because He loved Him and enjoyed communing with God. Jesus also set an example to us of our need for prayer. He taught His disciples to pray. He brought His closest followers with Him to keep watch and to pray as He prepared for crucifixion. The apostles call on believers to be in "unceasing prayer"

God wants to have fellowship with us. We are his most precious creation and He loves us dearly. We are His creation, His children. He created us to return to Him a free love. God created man in His own image and God is spirit. God wants man to be consumed by spiritual values and be able to discuss spiritual values with Him.

God knows man is both physical and spirit and must discuss physical needs and desires. However, God wants man to reach above the physical and get in tune with his spiritual self and communicate that to God. Spiritual life is the highest form of life there is. Jesus did not give this life on Calvary for the animals that have no spiritual dimension. He gave it up for the benefit of man.

God wants man to share with Him righteousness and goodness. God is just, God is Holy, God is truth, and God wants man to desire those attributes and seek them. God wants man to seek God's help in making him as close to the image of God as he can be.

Everything that God originally made was very good. In the beginning man only knew good, not evil. There was no sickness, no depression, no discouragement, no pain, and no death. God knows that we constantly need direction in our life. The Bible talks about divine direction in the scriptures. God has a plan for each and every one of us. God does not want us to try to plan our lives. God wants us to seek out His plan for our lives. God goes step by step. He knows the end of this life and all steps in between but often elects to not tell us the final outcome. He wants us to trust Him one step at a time. God knows we are weak and must have help in forms of comfort and assurance to get through the trials of living in an evil corrupt world.

How does God answer Prayer?

God gave His Word to man as His primary tool of communication. The Bible is the Word of God. When we read the Bible we are hearing from God. If we get a letter from a trusted and loved relative we do not question that the words on the letter are the words of the loved one. God wants us to accept His Word as being directly from Him.

There was a time when God spoke to man directly from heaven and man heard the voice of God. God talked with Adam in the Garden of Eden. Later, God revealed His word to the Prophets and they spoke to the people. God told Moses that the time would come when He would no longer speak through the Prophets, but He, God, would raise up one Prophet, referring to His Son, Jesus. While we had Jesus with us on earth He was the spokesman for God. He taught directly from God using the Old Testament as the inspired Word of God.

God revealed His word unto the Prophets of old and the Apostles by the Holy Spirit. The Holy Spirit guided the writers of the Old Testament and the New Testament to record for all time to come God's message. God speaks to us today through His Holy Spirit speaking quietly to our heart. But God also speaks to us directly through His Word. We do not need Him to talk directly to us through a discernable voice. Paul declared God's Word was inspired and complete.

While Christ was on earth, He spoke the Word of God. But before Christ ascended to His Father in heaven, Jesus made all believers a promise. God promised He would send the Holy Spirit to speak to us. The Holy Spirit speaks directly to man through the heart of man. This is God speaking directly to man today although usually not in an audible voice.

Man's Responsibility in Prayer

Man has the responsibility to pray to God but not in a selfish, greedy way that would make God the provider of whatever we want. God is not at our beck and call. We are to be at God's beck and call. This means that when we come into the presence of God to pray we have the responsibility to be of certain frames of mind. These include:

1   We are to be mindful of the nature of God and our responsibility to come to God in His own image when we pray. We do not come to God as equals. We are not buddies with

God just because we are part of His family. We pray mindful of the great privilege we have to come into His presence not as a right but as a gift paid for by Christ.

2   We are to pray while submissive to God's will. God wants us to bring our petitions to Him. He wants us to share what we want but he also wants us to be willing to accept His decision about our requests. We are to have a spirit of ***"Not my will but Thine be done."***

3   We are to have a strong need to honor God in all things. If God answers our prayer as we ask, will that bring honor and glory to God? We are to not seek glory for ourselves but glory for God.

4   If God gives us the request we have of Him will that be a burden in someone else's life? Our concern for others should be greater than our concern for ourselves. That is love.

5   Will what we ask bring joy to God? We are created for the purpose of bringing joy to God. We forget that sometimes and believe God is to bring joy to us. Our number 1 goal is to bring joy, honor and glory to God.

6   Is my request in conflict with the Word of God and His will for my life? If I request freedom from an overbearing boss does that conflict with God's Word that tells us to be submissive to our supervisors even if they are less that godly?

7   Will my request hinder my ability to grow in the Spirit of my Savior? If I request riches, will God granting to me material wealth cause me to be less faithful to God?

Man has four things we are held responsible for when we pray. God wants these things to be present when we come into His presence. They are what follows:

1   We must believe in Jesus Christ as our Savior and have faith in who He says He is and what He says He will do. God will not interface with one who does not believe in Him.

2   We must be obedient to God. We must be people who desire in our heart to please God more than to please our own selfish wants. This means that even if God's answer is no we must be ready and willing to accept it because of our faith in God and our knowledge that He cares for us and seeks what is good for us.

3   We must have patience to wait upon the Lord. We are subservient to God not the other way around. God's timetable is different than ours. Our timetable is based on selfish, vaguely defined goals.

4   We must expect God to answer our prayer. This includes faith in God and it includes being positive regarding our request. However, we must recognize that God's answer to our prayer will also involve His will. God may desire that we go through a learning experience that is unpleasant. God may be trying to prepare us for an assignment He has in store for us later that will advance His kingdom. God's answer will not always be yes. Sometimes it will be no and sometimes it will be wait and have patience until He decides to respond to our request.

James recognizes the incorrect way mankind prays to God when he gave us the God inspired instruction that God wants us to focus on positive aspects and powers of God. God wants us to acknowledge that He is all-powerful and all-knowing. God wants us to also acknowledge that He is Holy, that He is Just, that He is love, and that He is Righteous. God wants us to remember His ability to raise the dead, heal the sick, make the lame walk, cause the blind to see, and forgive the sins of a multitude of believers.

No problem is beyond His ability to understand and solve. No problem is beyond His capacity to care and desire a wonderful result for His children. God also wants us to praise Him and exalt His name as we recognize His power, knowledge and love. We are to tell God how much we love Him and how much we trust Him even while we are telling Him about our needs and our concerns. When we pray God hears much more than our words. God hears our heart and understands our mind. God knows us because He created us.

Prayer changes us, it does not change God. God is immutable, unchanging. Man is fluid always in need of improvement. Prayer opens our hearts and minds to grow in His grace. Through prayer, God gives us strength to better reflect his character of love when we are tested. Through prayer God gives us courage and peace to trust Him in times that are beyond our control.

How to talk to God?

God is not seeking memorized prayer that is said with our mouth but not meant in our heart. God does not want repetitive words that become meaningless because our heart is not in them. God does not want us to read prayers recorded in books unless they are heartfelt and come from the depth of our soul. God wants to hear from our inner being. God desires our need to express to Him our praise and petitions. He wants us to need to communicate with Him so strong it feels like we will explode unless we talk with Him. In Matthew the sixth chapter Jesus gave us an example of how to pray to God. He told us to open our prayer with our utter amazement and incredible adoration for God. Even the name of God amazes and humbles us. *"Our Father in heaven, Hallowed be Thy name."*

Jesus told us next, after exclaiming our love and adoration for God, to express our ultimate desire that God's will be done over ours and over the entire universe. *"Your Kingdom come, Your will be done on earth as it is in heaven."*

At that point, Jesus taught us we are ready to express our desires and wants only after we have expressed our relationship to God in love and adoration. Our expression of our desires and wants should come after we have expressed our desire that His will be done over ours. Only then should we ask for the physical things we desire and need. *"Give us this day our daily bread."*

Jesus told us to purge ourselves of our requests, otherwise known as petitions of God. God wants to hear them, not because He does not know what we want, but because he wants to hear our faith in Him as the provider of what we want.

Then Jesus told us to not be negligent in expressing our sins. Forgive us our trespasses or sins as we forgive those who trespass against us. God makes it clear that one who requests forgiveness must be one who is ready to give forgiveness. *"And forgive us our debt (sins, trespasses) as we also have forgiven our debtors (those who sin or trespass against us)."*

Jesus tells us that the sequence of prayer should be that after asking for forgiveness of our sins we are ready to request God to protect us from Satan and Satan's lure of sin. *"And lead us not into temptation, but deliver us from evil."*

And Jesus tells us that the closure of prayer must also recognize the deity of God and His eternal reign as Lord of our life and master of our destiny. *"For Thine is the kingdom and the power and the glory forever. Amen."*

We were made in God's image and the Bible tells us repeatedly that He is very active in our lives. We are His children, and because of His love for us, He allows wonderful things to come into our lives each and every day. God loves to make his children happy. God told us He knows the hairs on our head and is aware of every sparrow that falls. He is telling us He is almighty and nothing in this world happens without his permission. We should then give God the glory for every good thing that happens to us. God wants us to acknowledge He provided us with a loving spouse. We should praise God for our children and for their love. We need to recognize God provides us a way to make a living. God keeps us safe on the roads.

We have a tendency to want to take credit for things for which God is responsible. We also have a tendency to blame God for things for which we bear blame. God does much more than save us as believers, he also sustains us and gives us life that we may have it more abundantly.

Can we change God's mind through prayer?

Can we change God's mind through prayer? This is a deep and controversial question that occurs to almost every Christian. We are so selfish in our prayer life that we have temptation to ask, "If we cannot change the mind of God what is the point of asking?" This answer implies that prayer must be one way, I ask and God delivers. No, much of prayer is simply communicating with God, thanking Him, praising Him, acknowledging His majesty and glory, and seeking His direction for our life. Yet we all reach that point in which we desire something greatly. We come to the Lord and ask. The correct response is to bring to God our petitions while ready to accept His answer whatever it is. Yet the question remains, can we change God's mind?

Perhaps James 5:16 gives us the clearest foundation to believe it is possible to change the mind of God.

James 5:16
"Therefore confess your sins to one another, and pray for one another, that you may be healed. The effective, fervent prayer of a righteous has great power."

The context of this verse in Scripture clearly has the intent of saying that if we pray fervently, believing and if our hearts are right with God our prayers are not without value. But how is it possible to influence God who has all knowledge and who surpasses the limits of time? Our first point of truth is that we cannot change God's mind. We must remember that to God time is meaningless because God created time for mankind. God is already at the end of our future. To God there is no past, present, and future because everything is present. Therefore to say we could change God's mind would mean we had the persuasive power to influence God to change what He has already approved.

We begin to grasp this truth when we remember that we are always to pray to God that all things we ask of Him be granted "within His will." If we have the attitude we need to go to God in prayer we will never endorse conflict with God's will. A prayer saying, *"God teach me to accept and rejoice in Your will"* is far better than *"God please give me the prayer I ask for today without consideration of the will of God."*

Ephesians 1:11
"In Him we have obtained an inheritance, having been predestined according to the purpose of Him who works all things according to the counsel of His will."

It is incorrect to think that finite man can change the mind of God. Yet James said prayer changes things. In Ephesians we are told all things will happen according to God's predestined purpose for us according to the counsel of His will. Are these statements in conflict? The answer is no. Let's think in terms of a child who loves his or her father and the father deeply loves the child. To have an accurate comparison we must assume the father and child love each other. This means both want the best for each other. If the child asks for something that can be granted ***"within the will of the father"*** it will be granted. But the child cannot ask for something outside of the will of the father and expect it to be granted. Suppose the child asks to stay home from school. If it can be granted, and not harm the overall purpose for the child to grow in maturity and knowledge, that request might be granted. But if in the opinion of the father granting the request harms the overall need for the child to grow in maturity and knowledge then all the pleading in the world from the child will not result in granting the request.

We likewise know that the child, because of his or her love for their father, would not ask anything that would knowingly be outside of the fathers will. But the child does not have anything close to the maturity and knowledge of the father. Therefore the child seeks guidance even as he or she seeks his or her own will. In other words they submit their will to the father while retaining the free counsel of their own will. So if the answer to their request is no, then they accept that answer because they know it is for their own good. If the answer is yes they accept it because they are still within the will of their father. Proverbs 21 tells us that we also allow God to shape and form our requests because of our love for Him.

Proverbs 21:1
"The king's heart is a stream of water in the hand of the Lord; He turns it wherever He will."

Likewise, if we have the right relationship with our Father, our heart's wishes are shaped and formed by our understanding of what God desires. We will not knowingly ask amiss from God's will. And if we unknowingly ask amiss we readily accept God's will as superior to ours. We accept His answers. Yet it is possible for our requests to influence God's guidance. We cannot influence God's overall will. Just like the child cannot change the father's overall will about what is right and good for the child and the child cannot change the over-all character and nature of the father, likewise we cannot change the overall character and nature of God. To believe we can change God's will conflicts with the sovereignty of God. God is all powerful, all knowing, all loving, and all holiness. He cannot and will not change. So if we are to influence God through prayer then our requests must be within the will and character and nature of God. And God will shape our requests to the point they are within His will if we have the right relationship with our Father.

Did Moses Change God's Mind?

Many people want to go to Exodus the thirty-second chapter to point out a time in which Moses did change God's mind. If Moses can do this then others could change God's mind. Let's look at this Scripture to give us insight of the answer.

Exodus 32:9–10
"And the LORD said to Moses, "I have seen this people, and behold it is a stiff-necked people! Now therefore, let Me alone, that My wrath may burn hot against them and I may consume them in order that I may make a great nation of you."

The background of this verse is that Moses had gone up into the mountain to receive the Ten Commandments from God. He was gone longer than the Hebrew children expected and they built a golden calf idol to worship. This infuriated God who wanted no graven images before them but to worship only God the Father. In anger God expressed his will to Moses and asked Moses to leave Him alone so He might destroy the idolatrous people. In this verse some question if God really intended to destroy the Jews who were worshiping a golden image. The answer is yes. We accept the Scripture as it is without putting our own concepts into it. God said He wanted to consume or destroy the people. But we also see that the will of God was not changed. "And I will make a great nation of you." His will was to rise up a nation of people who would be the evangelists for all of mankind to worship God. His will was not changed. Moses however pleaded with God to spare the people.

Exodus 32:11
"But Moses implored the LORD his God and said, "O LORD, why does your wrath burn hot against your people, whom you have brought out of the land of Egypt with great power and with a mighty hand?"

Note that everything Moses asked of God was within God's will. Moses did not ask God to forgive the people and leave them alone. To do so would be outside of the sovereign will of God. In fact, Moses asked God to give them another chance to be the people God chose to be His missionaries and to evangelize the world. That was the will of God. What Moses was really asking of God was to alter how He planned to accomplish His will. God consented with Moses. In this we see the fulfillment of our influence with God, yet our inability to change the mind of God if in so stating we mean the will of God.

Why should we pray?

Our first reason to pray is to ask God to forgive our sins, to imbed us with trust in Him, and to place us into the kingdom of God. We cannot accept Jesus whenever we wish. We must call on the name of the Lord and He will respond in His time to change our heart and bring us into His kingdom. We should consider how God came to Abraham and touched his heart resulting in Abraham's salvation.

Genesis 17:1
"When Abram was ninety-nine years old the Lord
appeared to Abram and said to him, "I am God
Almighty; walk before me, and be blameless."

The Holy Spirit is always reaching out to us to convict us we need Jesus Christ as Savior. Yet we must respond with a desire in our heart to follow God and trust Christ. When we answer the call of the Holy Spirit and demonstrate a desire to give our life to Christ He will change our heart and make us a new creature. He will adopt us into the family of God. This should be our first prayer request. Our Lord has told us that anyone who reaches out to Him with faith to believe on Christ will be saved.

Our second reason to pray to God is simply to worship Him. That means to tell Him of our Love, of our adoration, of our desire to please Him with our life.

Psalms 95:6
Oh come, let us worship and bow down;
let us kneel before the LORD, our Maker.

When we think of our Lord we should feel humble. We should want to bow down to show our appreciation of His greatness. Then we should just bubble up from our soul with praise and appreciation. God wants a relationship with us. There is nothing we can't pray about. God's Word tells us to *"pray without ceasing"* and *"in everything give thanks to the Lord."* We should go to Him in faith, knowing that He hears and answers all our prayers. We can also be confident that God knows and wants what is best for us. We should ask that His will be done in all we seek from Him. We should then thank Him for hearing us, thank Him for loving us, and we do this even though our request hasn't happened yet.

Our third reason to pray to our Lord is that we are sinners, we are steadily disappointing God and we should be sorry we sin. We should recognize that every time we disappoint God we choose the side of Satan against God the Father, God the Son and the Holy

Spirit. Therefore we should come to Him first in thanksgiving for His having already forgiven us of our sin and second to confess our sins to Him and seek His forgiveness even though it is already given.

Romans 3:23–26

"For all have sinned and fall short of the glory of God, and are justified by his grace as a gift, through the redemption that is in Christ Jesus, whom God put forward as a propitiation by his blood, to be received by faith. This was to show God's righteousness, because in his divine forbearance he had passed over former sins. It was to show his righteousness at the present time, so that he might be just and the justifier of the one who has faith in Jesus."

Our forth reason for praying to God is to seek the continual presence of the Holy Spirit as a witness to the lost. If we are grateful that we are going to Heaven then we should be greatly concerned about those about us who may be lost and doomed into Hell for eternity.

Luke 10:2

"And he said to them, "The harvest is plentiful, but the laborers are few. Therefore pray earnestly to the Lord of the harvest to send out laborers into his harvest."

We all know people who probably are not saved. This means they have never reached that point in which they came to God in prayer and asked Him to save their souls. In this prayer they would be professing a trust in God to save them and a request of God to save them. We are almost always uncertain if people we know or come across are saved. Certainly it is true some saved people have fallen away from God and are not showing Him in their life. Likewise sometimes people who appear to be serving God with a heart-felt trust are simply acting and do not really trust Him. God does not hold us accountable for knowledge of the lost but He does hold us accountable for concern about our fellow brothers and sisters here on earth. Luke 10:2 above tells us three requirements we must meet for the lost. No. 1 is to be concerned and ever alert to opportunities to witness. No. 2 is to pray for those whom God puts on our heart. No. 3 is to be laborers unto the harvest and go and witness.

Consider the compassion Paul felt for his lost Jewish brothers:

Romans 9:2, 3
"I have great sorrow and unceasing anguish in my heart. For I could wish that I myself were cursed and cut off from Christ for the sake of my people

Our fifth reason for praying to God is to seek God's care for us in trials we know will surely come in this life. Some, in fact many, of those trials are the result of imputed sin we inherit at birth because of the disobedience of Adam in the beginning. But some of our trials will be because of our own disobedience of God and His desire to help us sin our sin and come back to Him. These trials take many forms. They could be sickness, pain, fear, or depression. They could be mistreatment we receive from others. Some of our trials are the direct result of our standing up for our Lord.

James 5:14–16
"Is anyone among you sick? Let him call for the elders of the church, and let them pray over him, anointing him with oil in the name of the Lord. And the prayer of faith will save the one who is sick, and the Lord will raise him up. And if he has committed sins, he will be forgiven. Therefore, confess your sins to one another and pray for one another, that you may be healed. The prayer of a righteous person has great power as it is working."

God tells us in Hebrews the fourth chapter that we can pray boldly. "God tells us we have a great High Priest who has gone to heaven and that High Priest is none other than Jesus the Son of God. Let us spiritually hold on to Christ and never stop trusting him. Jesus Christ understands our weaknesses. He faced all of the same temptations we do, yet he did not sin. So let us come boldly to the throne of our gracious God. We are told by God that Jesus sits on the throne and is constantly interceding with God the Father on our behalf. There we receive his mercy. There we experience His grace and forgiveness." Our responsibility is to pray with sincerity, honor, and humbleness before the Almighty God. We are to pray with faith to receive, thankfulness to receive, and gratefulness for having receive even though in many cases we will not yet have received.

CHAPTER FOURTEEN

The Doctrine of Faith
Man's trust In God

What is faith?

God Word is very clear and definitive in defining faith. Faith is not tangible proof. Faith is belief in something to the point of acting upon it in spite of tangible proof. Faith is beyond hope. Faith is expectation because of a deep inner conviction. God explains the word faith in Hebrews.

Hebrews 11:1
"Now faith is the assurance of things hoped for, the conviction of things not seen."

The word "faith" in the Bible is used in two related but distinctly different meanings. What we believe concerning Christ and His plan of salvation is described as our faith. We say to others we are of the Christian faith as opposed to being of the Islam faith or of the Jewish faith. In so stating we are referring to a blanket of beliefs to which we intellectually and spiritually ascribe.

Jesus is the author and the finisher of what? He is the author and finisher of His plan of salvation for man. He is the author and the finisher of the reality that God the Father sent the Holy Spirit to be imputed into mankind. God did this to create a continuous relationship between with God and mankind. Jesus is the author and finisher of the blanket of beliefs in which we proclaim that Jesus Christ endured the cross of Calvary. He did this in spite of the pain both physically, spiritually and mentally so that we might enjoy salvation. Our joy of salvation is the joy Jesus Christ described as being worth the price of Calvary.

Yet that concept is connected to, but different than, the intent of saying, *"We have faith to believe in God's ability to save our sins."* The first is a blanket description of what we believe while the second is a specific description of the depth of our belief.

We have a strong faith when we believe in something in a very specifically experienced event in our life. That faith can come from our having actually, physically witnessed an event. If we see something happen we tend to believe it stronger than if we hear about it. If we have a faith that can easily be compromised, overturned, or caused to doubt we would be said to have a weak faith. The word "faith" in the Bible often refers to this inner feeling or inner conviction in a person. Jesus was talking about the strength of personal conviction when He said, *"O you of little faith, why did you doubt?"*

God tells us in His Word that every person is given enough faith to believe in God. We have built into us a basic desire to grasp the concept of God and to adopt that concept into our inner being. That faith is similar to a starter faith and requires man to act upon it. Having faith sufficient to be saved does not save us until we commit our heart to Jesus and ask Him to save us. To the extent we read the Word of God our starter faith becomes stronger. Many people accept the fact that Jesus Christ died for the sins of mankind and rose again the third day with victory over sin. But in spite of accepting this truth they have difficulty in deciding to trust their eternity in God's hands.

God holds each person responsible for his faith or lack of faith. Since the days of Adam God has placed in man enough understanding to put his faith in God. Mankind has to elect to trust that revelation from God. God is pleased when a person has faith to believe and displeased when he does not exercise the faith necessary to believe. God holds each of us responsible for our faith or our lack of faith. Hebrews 11:6 shows that each person is responsible for their own faith.

Hebrews 11:6
"And without faith it is impossible to please Him, for whoever would draw near to God must believe that He exists, and that He rewards those who seek Him."

The Scriptures clearly shows that faith comes from hearing and responding to the gospel. God uses people to present the gospel to others to help them, to encourage them and to enable them to commit their lives to Jesus Christ. God has endowed all human creation with enough faith to believe Jesus was born, lived a perfect life and died for our sins on Calvary. In talking to people all over the world people accept the concept of God. Even those who deny the Deity of

Jesus accept that a great God exists. Belief in God without believing in Jesus Christ and His death, burial and resurrection is not sufficient for salvation. The reason preaching is commanded in the Scripture is because hearing the Word of God enables the hearer to increasingly grasp the seed of faith God has placed in them. But preaching and teaching does not automatically increase our faith. We have to decide to believe.

When we hear the Word of God preached, or taught, or when we read the Bible ourselves and let the message of God penetrate our mind and touch our heart we place ourselves into a position to enable the Holy Spirit of God to plead with us to accept the message God sends. We call that saving faith.

Saving faith requires involvement of both God and man. Man cannot be saved unless God changes our heart and sends the Holy Spirit to dwell within our heart. That is a change Christian's call being *"born again."* Man cannot make that change happen. And God will not make that change happen unless man believes in Christ and commits our life to Him. Therefore saving faith requires three related but different parts of man.

People must believe in Jesus Christ. We do not have to be "in depth" theologians. We do not have to understand the mysteries of sanctification and justification, nor understand what the future holds. Mankind does not even have to understand creation. But man must believe

- that Jesus lived a perfect life and willingly gave up his life on the Cross of Calvary so that man might be saved, and
- that Jesus Christ overcame death when He was raised from the dead; and that, through His death, we too will be saved if we believe. Man must intellectually understand this doctrine and believe it.

Intellectual knowledge of God is not enough. Saving faith requires an inner conviction that the intellectual knowledge is true. We have to come to the point in which we believe in the death, burial and resurrection of Jesus even though we do not have physical, tangible proof of this teaching. God wants us to believe in Him because He said it; not because He gave us tangible proof. That is the faith God speaks of in His Word. We believe regardless of how we feel. We believe because we feel the Holy Spirit tugging at our heart to tell us the way of Jesus Christ is the only way to salvation.

The final step of faith man must make, is to take the seed of faith God has planted in us, and add our personal conviction of truth in God's Word concerning God's plan of salvation and ask God to change our heart to become part of His redeemed. We have to decide to ask God to save us. This is the outward component of saving faith. If God has changed our heart we have a new will to honor and please God. The saved man has a desire in his heart to honor and please God that was not there prior to being saved.

And yet, even these steps of faith by man alone are not enough for salvation. Salvation does not come because of man's faith alone. It comes because of God's Grace. That means God saves us, our faith is not what saves us. There is more than mere assent in the matter of believing in Christ. Saving faith involves the work of the Spirit as well as the whole person, meaning our intellect, sensibility, and will. Because a person is dead spiritually, it also requires the work of God to draw him to Christ.

God's Word Tells Us to Have Faith

Over and over again God tells us to have faith. It is clear that the faith He is speaking of is a saving faith and that is a decision man must make. God's Word tells us to have faith and makes it clear it is our personal responsibility for that faith. Jesus would not tell people to have faith in God if God were responsible for their faith. Doubt is the off spring of weak faith. Doubting is being uncertain about the truths of God. Doubting is fluctuating back and forth in placing our trust in God or placing our faith on man's logic. God always disapproves of doubting. Therefore doubting is sin. The Scriptures that warn us about doubting clearly show that faith, or the lack thereof, is our fault. Lack of faith is sin. God is not the author of sin.

The nature of man is to doubt and to not have faith. Satan encourages us to doubt. Our nature tells us to depend on our own logic. Testing the truths of God and leaning toward our own logic will result in doubt. Our greatest faith is minuscule in comparison to Christ's faith.

After we accept Jesus Christ as our Savior our journey of faith has just begun. Most Christians want more faith and seek it but they try to develop faith based on our own logic and information we hear from others. God wants us to develop faith based on listening to Him. He wants us to hear His Word and believe, not just for salvation, for to achieve a personal relationship with God. God wants us to hear His Word and believe on Him for the purpose of sustaining the Christian walk. Sustaining faith requires that we immerse ourselves in His Word. God wants to reveal Himself to man. As we get to know God we learn to trust Him. As we gain understanding of the works of Jesus Christ we will find it easier to rely on His understanding than our own logic. That is the beginning of true, deep faith. If we will seek Him, He will transform us into faith based people who seek and trust Him.

As we begin to allow God to transform us into a person more nearly like Him, as we learn to walk in the Spirit, not in the flesh, and as we learn to trust God our faith grows. To grow our faith we have to risk becoming His follower. If our trust in God is going to grow, we have to learn to step out in faith, moving out of our comfort zone and doing things our logic says are ill advised. As we experience God meeting us at our point of need, we learn to step out further always trusting in God. That is building faith. When we face temptations, God will meet us at our point of need if we will ask him and will deliver us from yielding to that temptation.

God knows that we grow in faith through testing and trials. As we learn to step out in faith we grow capacity to step out in faith. Therefore God's Word tells us we will have trials to test our faith and make us stronger Christians. When we fail and our faith is weak, God may chastise and rebuke us. God may bring hardships to teach us to trust Him. This growth in Christ is a process called sanctification. In an earlier chapter we called it "Growth Sanctification." As we grow in Christ we become more and more like Him. And as we grow more and more like Him the less and less the troubles of this world bother us. The perfect love of our Father will never change. His gospel plan gives life meaning and can assure our happiness.

Faith and Hope

Is there a difference between faith and hope? Much of the time, in our earthly life, we use the words interchangeably. Consider the definition of faith found in God's Word.

Hebrews 11:1
"Now faith is the assurance of things hoped for, the conviction of things not seen."

Let's look at Hebrews 11:1 and gain a deeper understanding of faith. Some translations use the word substance whereby the English Standard Version believes the best meaning to be assurance, certainty, or absolute confidence. Assurance means no doubt. Assurance means absolute certainty. "Hoped for" carries the thought of desire, want to, and maybe. And "things not seen" refers to the future beyond the realm of total certainty.

Faith is belief in something to the point of acting upon it in spite of the lack of tangible proof. Faith is beyond hope but is expectation because of a deep inner conviction. God explains the word faith in Hebrews. Hebrews the eleventh chapter verse 1, however, tells us that faith is assurance or absolute confidence in things we desire to happen, provided those things are within the will of God. It rests on evidence or proof of, God promised, events, things, activities that will come to pass in the future. How do these two statements correspond and merge?

The key is evidence. Faith requires evidence but the evidence we refer to is not physical but is the reality of God's Holy Word. So the evidence we can place our absolute confidence in, although we cannot see tangible proof, are the promises of God. We know God does not lie. God is truth. God is holiness. God deserves our trust.

When God speaks, that becomes proof to us because of who God is and what we are.

We can then say Faith is the proof (or evidence), based on promises of God in His Holy Word, of the reality that those things we hope will happen in the future. By Faith we are saved, not of our works, but by the grace of God. We can trust with confidence that when we die we will go to be with Jesus Christ in glory because God has promised it will happen. We do not have tangible proof because nothing like that has ever happened. But we have spiritual proof because God said it and that settles it.

John 3:16
"For God so loved the world that He gave His only Son, that whoever believes in Him should not perish but have eternal life."

God tells us that two things must be present for us to have faith as described in Hebrews 11:1. *First*, we must have total faith that Jesus Christ lived, was sent by God the Father to die for our sins. We must believe He lived among men and walked the face of the earth without sin. We must believe that He voluntarily gave His life on Calvary to pay the price of our sins. And we must believe that God raised Christ from the dead and fully paid the price of our sins. Without this belief we are not a child of God. Without this belief we cannot experience sustaining faith growing in our hearts. *Second*, we must believe that God desires to fulfill every desire of our heart and to reward us for every step we take of fulfilling His desire for our life.

Hebrews 11:6
"But without faith it is impossible to please Him, for whoever comes near to God must believe that He exists, and that He is a rewards those who seek Him."

This conviction causes us to accept His word without question and to trust His Word without hesitation. By faith we accept that the visible universe is created and controlled by God. Faith, by its very nature, begins and ends in the realm of the unseen. It is conviction supported by evidence concerning things we do not know by experience. By faith we accept that the invisible things of God are behind the visible universe (Heb. 11:3). By faith we hope for a home in heaven, though we have never seen that paradise (2 Cor. 4:18)

Faith as Compared to Belief

In American English, the word *belief* comes across weaker than the word faith. However in the day that the Scripture was recorded the intent of both the word belief and faith were the same.

Romans 1:17
"For in it the righteousness of God is revealed from faith to faith; as it is written, "The righteous shall live by faith."

The opposite of living by faith is to live by sight. Living by sight means the need for tangible proof of everything before placing trust. Paul said the saved or redeemed in Christ will be people who have so much faith or trust in Jesus Christ that they do not need tangible proof. That is how we as believers can trust the promises that are made by God that have so much importance in our lives. God wants a relationship with us as His children, that we will trust Him without need for tangible proof. God wants His people to believe on Him without much revelation from Him. In the Old Testament God's plan of salvation was the same as it is today but His revelation to His creation was much less. In the Dispensation of Conscience God wanted people to hear His Word and trust Him based on the seed of faith He has placed in all people. But Satan has such a mighty influence on our lives people in the Dispensation of Conscience failed to trust God by faith. They required sight. This same thing was true in the following Dispensations of Human Government, of Promise, and of "The Law." Even with the death, burial and resurrection of Jesus Christ and the ushering in of the Dispensation of Grace the Israelite nation still would not trust God.

Steps to Salvation in the Old Testament

In the New Testament book of Hebrews many beautiful revelations from God, often referred to as the "gallery of faith" and the "hall of fame of faith," reaffirm to us that the people of the Old Testament were saved by grace through their faith. They were saved by the Grace of God yet it was their faith that made the qualified to ask God to save them. So their faith, not works opened the door for their salvation. Yet we know the great names of faith such as Abel and Enoch, Joshua and Jeremiah, and Ruth and Rahab did not have a saving knowledge of Jesus Christ. We know, however, they had the promise of God that He would send a messiah to pay the price of their sins. And if they had faith to believe His promises they would be saved.

1 Peter 1:10–12
"Concerning this salvation, the prophets who prophesied about the grace that was to be yours searched and inquired carefully, inquiring what person or time the Spirit of Christ in them was indicating when he predicted the sufferings of Christ and the subsequent glories."

They had no ability to connect that messiah with the Son of God Jesus Christ. The prophets beginning with Moses told the people of a messiah who would come and pay the price of their sins if they were faithful to God. The miracle of the Virgin Birth of Jesus happened about four hundred years after the Old Testament was closed and many more years than that after the lives of Abraham, Isaac, Joseph and other great names of faith. Therefore we see the plan of salvation for Old Testament people was to believe in God with all their minds, all their hearts and all their soul to the extent God revealed Himself to them. The plan of salvation of New Testament Saints is the same but with the death, burial and resurrection of Christ the revelation of God was greatly intensified. God clarifies the plan of salvation for Old Testament Saints to be the same as that of New Testament Saints in Romans 4:1–5.

Romans 4:1–5
"What then shall we say was gained by Abraham, our forefather according to the flesh? For if Abraham was justified by works he has something to boast about; but not before God. For what does the Scripture say? "Abraham believed God, and it was counted to him as righteousness." Now to the one who works, his wages are not counted as a gift but as his due. And to the one who does not work but believes in him who justifies the ungodly, his faith is counted as righteousness.

In the above Scripture, Paul takes great effort to teach us Abraham, and all Old Testament Saints, were saved through their faith not because of good works. What then was Abraham's faith based on? He and all Old Testament heroes of faith had no knowledge of Jesus. They had no concept of Calvary. They had no revelation from God about the resurrection of Christ. Their faith could not have rested on events they could not conceive would happen. And yet, it did. God did reveal to the Prophets a coming Messiah would pay the price of their sins. However, even the Prophets did not understand the Messiah would be the only begotten Son of God. Yet Paul tells us Abraham was saved by faith. And Paul tells us Abraham's faith in God was counted as righteousness. What does it mean to be counted as righteousness? God is righteous. It means Abraham's faith in the revelation God gave him justified Abraham in the sight of God. Justified means *"Just as If"* Abraham had never sinned. It meant that after death, Abraham will be with us in Heaven around the throne of God. This is not because he was a fully righteous person but because he was faithful to God and God counted his faith as righteousness.

The Old Testament teaches us that people in the Old Testament were saved from sin by the grace of God through their faith in the Lord and His promises. In the book of Luke, Jesus teaches Old Testament Saints were saved by faith though grace. These same verses teach that the revelations of Old Testament Saints, of the coming Messiah, were revealed in the Law of Moses and the Prophets and Psalms.

Luke 24:44–47
"Then he said to them, "These are my words that I spoke to you while I was still with you, that everything written about me in the Law of Moses and the Prophets and the Psalms must be fulfilled."

The Definition of Faith

There is a simple story that is often used to describe faith. A man was hired to walk a tight rope across the Niagara Falls pushing a wheelbarrow. A large crowd was attracted to watch this act of courage. Hundreds of people watched as he successfully walked across the tight rope pushing a wheelbarrow. He then approached a person who had just seen this feat and asked him, "Do you believe I can walk across the Niagara Falls on a tight rope pushing a wheelbarrow?"

"Sure, was the answer, I just saw you do it."

"So you have faith I can perform this act?" asked the performer.

"Absolutely," said the observer."

"Then get into the wheelbarrow" was the reply of the performer.

This is the difference in today's understanding of the word belief and faith. To us, we may believe Jesus died for our sins, we may believe Jesus has the power to save us from our sins, but until we are ready to ask Jesus to forgive our sins and to change us into a person who desires to love and follow Him; we have not gotten into the wheelbarrow.

Where does faith come from?

As human beings we are given, at birth a basic concept of God's existence. It is interesting in witnessing that you can talk to lost people about God and they show little discomfort. But the discussion of Jesus makes them uncomfortable because the Holy Spirit is present on earth advancing the story of Jesus. As human beings, the creation of God, we have built into us enough faith to accept God's existence. But as human beings we do not have the capacity to have faith in

Christ as described in the wheelbarrow example. We cannot create that kind of faith because our basic nature is one of sin. Our basic nature is to not trust Christ but to trust ourselves. Our basic nature is to be independent of God. We are not born with faith or a nature of trusting God even though we have enough faith to acknowledge the existence of God. Yet God tells us we are saved by the Grace (undeserved mercy of God) but God will not give us Salvation unless we demonstrate belief that Jesus Christ died on Calvary for our sins and we want to belong to God. The book of Ephesians tells us we are saved by grace of God through the means of our faith in Jesus Christ the Son of God.

Ephesians 2:8–9
"For by grace you have been saved through faith,
and this is not your own doing; it is the gift of God,
not a result of works, so that no one can boast."

Ephesians the second chapter informs us we do not have the power or capacity to generate saving faith. The faith that qualifies us to be saved by God comes from God. Without the Grace of God reaching out for our souls we would have to pay the cost of our sin against God.

John 6:23
"For the wages of sin is death, but the free gift of
God is eternal life in Christ Jesus our Lord."

God has given us from birth enough faith to believe God exists. To be saved from our sins however, we must reach out to God and ask Him to save us. We must believe Jesus can save us and will save us if we will ask. Our salvation them comes through our faith and takes place because of the Grace of God. Our salvation is never because we have earned it or that we are in any way worthy of it. God gives us enough faith to believe in Jesus because of His mercy and His love for us. Therefore His grace provides an alternate way to pay for our sins. We do not have to go to hell and suffer through eternity. We do not have to be separated from God throughout eternity. We do not have to miss out on the amazing blessings God has in store for us in Heaven. But we have to decide to accept the offer of God. We have to make an active decision to follow Christ.

CHAPTER FIFTEEN

The Doctrine of Spiritual Gifts
God's Enabling of the Redeemed

W e are not saved from our sinful life just to sit and wait until the Lord raptures the church and we go to heaven with Jesus to enjoy eternity. That is a reward of salvation. But Christ has a plan for our life. Christ wants us to work and has enabled us with the power and ability to accomplish what He has assigned for us. God calls this enabling Spiritual Gifts.

Unfortunately Spiritual Gifts have become a division issue between Bible believing denominations and is often a dividing issue between churches. This is exactly the opposite of what God intended in giving us Spiritual Gifts.

What is a Spiritual Gift? A Spiritual Gift is an endowment from God to believers, according to God's Sovereignty, to build up the Church. The empowerment is in the form of ability and desire to do a particular work that edifies the Church. Some Spiritual Gifts, when granted in first century times, yielded supernatural powers. Some did not, but all Spiritual Gifts impute to the receiver interest, desire, and ability to perform specific work for the Lord's kingdom. A Spiritual Gift is not given to build up the recipient or to give fame, glory, or power to that one. It is not given as a reward for righteous living because none of us are righteous enough to earn even one gift for our righteousness. Those who receive Spiritual Gifts from God, and the Bible says every believer has at least one Spiritual Gift, are given that gift to enable them to accomplish something God has assigned them to accomplish.

God's Word gives us certain specific verses of Scripture that identify the Spiritual Gifts God gave to members of the New Testament Church. These are the following:

Ephesians 4:11–12
"And He gave the apostles, the prophets, the evangelists, the shepherds and teachers, to equip the saints for the work of ministry, for building up the body of Christ."

In Ephesians chapter 4 God identifies the gifts of Apostles, Prophets, Evangelists, Pastors and Teachers. All were given to build up the Church.

Romans 12:6–8

"Having gifts that differ according to the grace that is given to us, let us use them: if prophecy, in proportion to our faith; if service, in our serving; the one who teaches, in his teaching; the one who exhorts, in his exhortation; the one who contributes, in generosity; the one who leads, with zeal; the one who does acts of mercy with cheerfulness."

In Romans, God grants to Apostles, Prophets, Evangelists, Pastors, and Teachers the Spiritual Gifts of Exhortation, Giving, Leadership, and Mercy. God then proceeds to specifically point out the granting of gifts is not intended to give prestige, reward, or honor to individual Christians but is intended to assign work intended for the advancement of the entire Church body.

1 Corinthians 12:4–11

"Now there are varieties of gifts, but the same Spirit; and there are varieties of service, but the same Lord; and there are varieties of activities, but it is the same God who empowers them all in everyone. To each is given the manifestation of the Spirit for the common good. For to one is given through the Spirit the utterance of wisdom, and to another the utterance of knowledge according to the same Spirit, to another faith by the same Spirit, to another gifts of healing by the one Spirit, to another the working of miracles, to another prophecy, to another the ability to distinguish between spirits, to another various kinds of tongues, to another the interpretation of tongues. All these are empowered by one and the same Spirit, who apportions to each one individually as he wills."

In 1 Corinthians God informs us that although different Christians will have different gifts it does not make us different from each other. We all are of the same body and that is the Body of Christ. We all have the same motive and that is to build up the Body of Christ also known as the Church. This is because we all are Children of God, empowered by the Holy Spirit, directed by the Holy Spirit and led by the Holy Spirit.

1 Corinthians 12:28–31

"And God has appointed in the church: first apostles, second prophets, third teachers, then miracles, then gifts of healing, helping, administrating, varieties of tongues. Are all apostles? Are all prophets? Are all teachers? Do all work miracles? Do all process the gifts of healings? Do all speak with tongues? Do all interpret? But earnestly desire the best gifts. And I will show you a still more excellent way."

God specifically informs us the gifts of the Spirit are given within the Church, for the Church, and by the Holy Spirit Church members. But remember that in this statement, Church members are not just people who come and sign up to join a church. Church members by spiritual definition are people who have confessed their belief in Christ and to the extent of their knowledge have placed their trust in Him for forgiveness of their sins. They are people who have been accepted as part of the family of God. They are also people who have been truly granted membership by God to be part of the "Body of Christ."

Ephesians 4:7–13

"But grace was given to each one of us according to the measure of Christ's gift. Therefore it says, "When he ascended on high he led a host of captives, and he gave gifts to men." (In saying, "He ascended," what does it mean but that he had also descended into the lower regions, the earth? He who descended is the one who also ascended far above all the heavens, that he might fill all things.) And he gave the apostles, the prophets, the evangelists, the shepherds and teachers, to equip the saints for the work of ministry, for building up the body of Christ, until we all attain to the unity of the faith and of the knowledge of the Son of God, to mature manhood, to the measure of the stature of the fullness of Christ."

Spiritual Gifts are bestowed by God to selected Christians according to God's divine will. The reason God gives selected Christians certain Spiritual Gifts is to equip the Body of Christ in performing its mission. They are not given to enhance or empower individual Christians. They are not given to reward individual Christians. They are given to assist the Body of Christ in its mission. The mission of the Church, or the Body of Christ, is inclusive of the following:

- Exalt the Savior
- Equip the Saints
- Enlist the uncommitted
- Encourage the believer
- Evangelize the unbelievers
- Empower the laborers unto the task set before them

The work of the church will be done by believers in Christ who commit to accept the assignment of God in His service. God tells us that to accomplish the work of the Church each believer has been given at least one spiritual gift. We are challenged to accept that gift and step out in faith to use it.

1 Peter 4:10
"As each has received a gift, use it to serve one another, as good stewards of God's varied Grace."

Supernatural Gifts

Substantial differences of interpretation of the gifts God has bestowed to His children, according to His Sovereign will, exist. In general these differences become noticeable with regard to denominational lines. They often involve the concept of whether or not certain gifts were temporary at the time of Christ are whether they continue to exist today. The gifts that are cloaked with controversy are those that involve Supernatural powers. Supernatural gifts were designed to show the power of God not the power of the holder of this gift. They are called supernatural gifts because such gifts require

382

more talent than normal people possess. All Spiritual Gifts are supernatural in the sense they come from God. Supernatural Gifts put the spotlight on human attention of the bearer of the gifts. This attention often is a problem for the edification of the Body of Christ although Spiritual Gifts were all designed to edify the Body of Christ. They were not designed to replace the Word of God. The Bible is the single most powerful tool given to all believers to edify the Church, to exalt the Savior, to equip the Saints, to enlist the uncommitted, to encourage the believer, to evangelize the unbelievers, and to empower the laborers unto the harvest.

In areas of the world where Supernatural Gifts are not needed to affirm the legitimacy of the Word of God, they no longer are active as stated by none other than the Apostle Paul. In 1 Corinthians 13:8 Paul makes a very revealing statement regarding this controversial subject.

1 Corinthians 13:8
"Love never ends. As for prophecies, they will pass away; as for tongues, they will cease; as for knowledge, it will pass away."

In the above scripture Paul clearly tells us the Spiritual gift of tongues, of prophecy, and knowledge will cease to exist. When these will cease to exist is not clarified. We know from context of Scripture that supernatural gifts cease to exist wherever the Bible is available to teach people about Christ. Unfortunately, there continues to be substantial difference of opinion regarding the continued existence of Supernatural Gifts. Paul addressed it clearly. He told us the Spiritual Gift of love never ends. Paul puts love into such a dramatic different category he does not list it as part of the Spiritual Gift categories. He identifies love as part of the redeemer's Spiritual makeup. Paul states all redeemed will be imputed with love for God and for other people.

Paul then begins accountability of the lifespan of Spiritual Gifts recognized in the first century church. Paul tells us the gift of prophecy as given in the Old Testament will cease. He adds the Spiritual Gift of Tongues and interpretation will cease to exist. Then he concludes by telling us the Spiritual Gift of Knowledge will vanish.

Paul states the Spiritual Gifts of Prophecy and Knowledge will be done away with when the "perfect" comes. What does he mean when he says when the "perfect" will come? Paul is referring to the Word of God, which is the voice of God to all men. Supernatural Gifts were never intended to take the place of the Word of God but was intended to be a temporary revelation of God to establish the authenticity of the forth coming Word of God soon to be delivered to all mankind. The Supernatural Gifts were given to the Apostles to help them convince first Century people that the Messiah had come, that Jesus Christ was and is the Messiah. "Those who were imputed with Supernatural Spiritual Gifts were forerunners of the power of God's Word. This meant that when that which was "perfect," meaning the Word of God was available to men, the Supernatural Gifts would cease. What Spiritual Gifts are we speaking of?

1 Corinthians 13:9–10
"For we know in part and we prophesy in part. But when the perfect comes, the partial will pass away."

Let's break down the Spiritual Gifts as outlined in scripture to help us understand what each gift was intended to accomplish.

- ***The Gift of Faith:*** Every child of God has a certain amount of faith or they could not be saved. This amount of faith, called saving faith, is not what we speak of in the Spiritual Gift of Faith. No, the Spiritual Gift of faith is the ability to see what needs to be done and to trust God to make it happen even though all human logic says it cannot be done. It is the ability to see forthcoming trials and hardships but believe, without doubt, in God's ability to lead us through them. Noah had the Spiritual Gift of Faith to build the Ark even when the rest of the world said it was foolish. Moses had the Spiritual Gift of faith to believe God when God said He would deliver His people from bondage and slavery. The Supernatural Gift of Faith was granted to the Apostles and certain others for the specific purpose of demonstrating the power of God. This was a faith beyond the normal human capabilities of mankind. It was supernatural in source, in scope, and in results. This Supernatural Gift of Faith is no longer active today because the Word of God is the power of redemption and the power of introduction to all men of the power and will of God.

- *The Gift of Knowledge*: This was a Spiritual Gift that meant understanding the revelations of God beyond normal human ability to grasp. No person in scripture could be better understood as having the Gift of Knowledge than the Apostle Paul. But the other Apostles were also granted this gift. When mankind was given the New Testament, the Supernatural Gift of Knowledge no longer was needed and it ceased to exist. We site the New Testament because it reveals the coming Messiah. The New Testament finished the message of God to all mankind. The Gift of Knowledge was replaced by the Holy Spirit and the New Testament. Today the Holy Spirit interprets to all believers understanding of Scripture. The Holy Spirit puts into our heart a longing to understand His truth and then gives us understanding of His truth.

- *The Gift of "Word of Wisdom"*: The Word of Wisdom Spiritual Gift is the ability of a selected person to hear from God and apply a message that is intended to strengthen or reinforce the faith of others. This means this gifted person hears God give them messages that are to be relayed to others. In the first century Church people did not have the New Testament for the Holy Spirit to interpret. This Supernatural Gift was given to the Apostles to help edify the Church Body and teach them to rely on God for guidance. Today the Holy Spirit is quite capable of speaking directly to all believers and revealing to us the will of God. After all each believer has the Holy Spirit living in His own soul. God is quite sufficient to speak for himself. Second Timothy 3:17 states, His Word is sufficient to make us **"that the man of God may be complete, equipped for** *every good work.* " The presence of God's Holy Bible makes this Supernatural Spiritual Gift unnecessary today and it has ceased to exist.

- ***The Gift of Prophecy:*** The Supernatural Gift of Prophecy was in the Old Testament time a powerful leader of the Jewish people, anointed by God for the specific purpose of foretelling God's will for the people. This ability often came through direct revelation of God to the Prophet who then relayed the prophecy to the people. With the power and the complete revelation of God through the New Testament the Gift of Prophecy is no longer needed and if present would tend to detract from the intended purpose of God's Word.

  Many Christians today believe the Spiritual Gift of Prophecy still exists but in the reformed version of one who forth tells of God's will as proclaimed in the Scripture. Such gifts of the Holy Spirit do exist but they are imputed to Christians in the Spiritual Gifts of Teacher, Pastor, and Evangelist. Acts 16:16–18 specifically tells us that we are to beware of those who try to be fortune-tellers, or to predict the future because they are not of God.

Paul now comes to a grouping of Spiritual Gifts that are and were intended to edify God the Father but or frequently abused to personal edification of the one to whom the gift is given. He specifically mentions the Gift of Tongues because of the controversial burden it carried even in his day, but he also includes in this grouping the Gift of Healing, the Gift of Interpretation of Tongues and the Gift of Miracles. All four of these gifts were given to the Apostles for the specific purpose of affirming their appointment from God to be His messenger to the Church in its early days. The mission of the Apostles to the Church had some similarities of John the Baptist's mission as a forerunner for Christ. They were sent forth to prepare the way for the Church to flourish. The devotion, ability, conviction, and commitment of the Apostles were essential to the development of the first century Church. Although they had the Old Testament they did not have the New Testament in which the revelation of the Dispensation of Grace (or of the Church) was outlined. When the Word of God became alive in the minds of believers the need for the Supernatural Gifts of Healing, Tongues, Interpretation of Tongues and Miracles ceased to exist.

The Supernatural Gifts of Healing, Tongues, Interpretation of Tongues and the gift of Miracles were amazing revealing gifts that ended with the Apostles. The last recorded miracle in the New Testament occurred on the island of Malta when Paul healed Publius the chief of the Island. Miracles like tongues and healing are mentioned only in 1 Corinthians, which was an early epistle. Ephesians and Romans both address the subject of Spiritual Gifts but do not mention Supernatural gifts. The second chapter of Hebrews gives us a view that the age of miracles was already accepted as something of the past. This was because the Apostles needed no more confirmation through such gifts. By the end of the first century the New Testament was the accepted authority of God and had superseded that of God's appointed Apostles.

- ***The Gift of Healing:*** In the first century the Church did not have the New Testament to rely on or to serve as the undeniable source of truth from God. God gave the Church the Apostles to serve in that role. To further empower the Apostles and to strengthen the faith of first century believers, God gave to the Apostles the Spiritual Gift of Healing. This was the ability to heal people of their illnesses, of poor health, and of various infirmities, it was given to the Apostles to affirm that they were directly sent from God and to convince the first-century believers that the Apostles were to be followed. The Apostles always healed in the power of the name of Jesus Christ the Savior of mankind. They did not have in them the power to heal. Their power was from God and they faithfully gave full credit to God. Often they did not even understand the nature of illnesses they healed but they trusted God, having the Gift of Faith, and God worked through them. Today, God wants our attention to be totally directed toward the Word of God as His power and direction for His people. Supernatural Gifts of power that tend to take attention off His Word are set aside and cease to exist. Today the Spiritual Gift of Healing is not an active gift.

- **The Gift of Miracles:** We know that when Jesus Christ lived among human beings, during the first century church era, He performed all manner of miracles. He healed the sick, made the lame to walk, made the deft to hear, and made the blind to see. He even raised the dead. We also know the Jesus Christ had immense compassion for those he saw and those who called upon His name. Yet Jesus did not heal the sick, raise the dead, help the blind to see, or cause the lame to walk because of compassion. His primary purpose in performing amazing miracles was to affirm to the people that He was indeed, sent from God and that He was the Messiah, the Son of God. After all, it had been four hundred years since they had had a prophet preach to them the way of the Lord. For the same purpose, God gave to the Apostles the power of Miracles. They were empowered by God with the same powers of Christ. Their purpose was the same as was that of Jesus. They used their power of miracles to establish in the minds of man that the Messiah had come and that a new age of Spiritual revelation was at hand. This gift was a temporary gift just as the Spiritual Gift of Healing was temporary. The need for this gift to direct men toward God ceased to be the primary light of truth when God's Word was written and revealed to mankind. The Gift of Miracles does not exist today.

- **The Gift of Tongues:** The gift of tongues was another temporary Spiritual Gift of God to the Apostles so they might effectively preach and teach hosts of people that did not speak the same languages. The Gift of Tongues never was and has never been a secret spiritual language for God's select few. The gift of tongues enabled the Apostles to speak in languages they did not understand but always within the scope of languages that already existed. We need to remember that the Apostles scattered across the world preaching and teaching the Gospel of Christ. They effectively taught people whom they could not otherwise reach. Their effort was to build up the church, not to advance their own power and popularity. This gift was temporary and is not active today. The Spiritual Gift of Tongues and the relating Spiritual Gift of Interpretation of Tongues ended with the passing of the apostolic age. However the gift of tongues continues today to be the most divisive of all the Spiritual Gifts. It was not intended to be divisive but to be all encompassing of people of all languages into the body of Christ. Is the Spiritual Gift of Tongues active today? The answer is no. Paul clearly pointed out that with the passing of the Apostolic age the Spiritual Gift of Tongues ceased. First Corinthians 14:22 tells us that the gift of tongues was a sign for unbelievers. Today this gift is grossly misused when good intentioned Christians use it to build up their own spiritual growth as evidence to others of their relationship with Christ. Today our authority is the Word of God. We edify the Church whose purpose is to edify the Lord God Jehovah. The Spiritual Gift of Tongues no longer exists.

- *The Gift of Interpretation:* A person with the gift of interpretation of tongues could understand what a speaker was saying even though he or she could not speak in the language being used. The tongues interpreter could understand it by message from the Holy Spirit and would relay that message to the recipients. Both the Gift of Tongues and the Gift of Interpretation have passed away with the passing of the apostolic age and the imputation of the Word of God into our life.

Ministry Gifts

Ministry Gifts are not Supernatural Gifts. They are specific gifts of talent, desire and ability bestowed by God to selected Christians according to His divine will. Ministry Gifts are granted to those few who help all other Christians utilize the gifts God has given to them. These gifts include:

- **Apostle:** We should not allow ourselves to be confused with the position of Apostle as defined in the New Testament, first century Church. The first century Church did not have the New Testament available to be their primary guide for mankind in their daily walk with the Lord. The Apostles were a very select few who actually saw and heard the teachings of Jesus Christ. They were granted specific power to heal, to perform miracles, to teach supernaturally, and to start and build churches. By definition, and Apostle had to be one who had walked with Jesus. We no longer have people who meet this definition of Apostleship.

  Today the Spiritual Gift of Apostle means one who is empowered by God with the desire, the talent, the ability, and the power of God to start churches. This is not a Supernatural Gift. Today Christians with the Spiritual Gift of being an Apostle are often called church planters. An Apostle is a minister to ministers. Often offices such as Area Missionary are "called" leadership positions that utilize the scope of Apostleship. This is a position of leadership, a position of authority, but a position of high servant focus. It is usually a full time, paid professional person but certainly does not have to be such.

- **Pastor:** The Pastor is often one who utilizes much of the talents and abilities outlined in the Spiritual Gifts of Apostleship and Prophet but the Pastor also adds on the responsibility of guiding the Church. This does not mean directing the Church in the sense of a chief operating officer because Jesus Christ is the head of the Church in all ways. But the Pastor identifies thoughts, actions, concepts and doctrines the Church might develop that are displeasing to God. He then redirects that thinking into a healthy relationship with God. The Pastor has a responsibility to

God for his flock. Christ holds pastors accountable for the care they give their flock. Thus we often use the terminology Shepherd to define the Spiritual Gift of Pastor.

- *Evangelist:* The Evangelist is given the specific task by God to be a witness of what Jesus Christ did to provide a plan for the salvation of all mankind. The Evangelist works closely with the Church because he has responsibility to help the Church build but he is not responsible for the guidance, administration or spiritual direction of the Church. The Pastor often uses the Spiritual Gift of Evangelist in his administering the office of Pastor. The Evangelist does not use the Spiritual Gift of Pastor in performing the work God has given him.

- *Teacher:* All holders of the Spiritual Gifts of Ministry are related to each other in terms of gift content and gift usage. Yet they remain different. The teacher may or may not be connected to the work of Pastor or Deacon. The teacher is called by God to point out truth in Scripture as well as to point out canyons of false teachings we can fall into if we do not correctly interpret the Scripture according to the instruction of the Holy Spirit. The teacher often uses the Spiritual Gifts of knowledge and Wisdom as well as discernment in proclaiming the truth on a daily or on-going basis to his or her recipients. Teachers often have the gift of prophecy as well as Prophets often have the gift of teaching.

Service Gifts

When we get past the Ministry gifts, which are in general, position gifts to the ministry of the Church; and when we get past the Supernatural Gifts that are no longer active, we come to a large group of service gifts given to edify the Body of Christ. This means they are gifts given to select Christians according to the Sovereignty of God to help the Church grow, to help the Church reach its objectives, and to help the Church be pleasing unto our Lord and Savior. These are:

- **The Gift of Mercy:** Service in the Kingdom of God is the purpose and intent of these Spiritual Gifts of God. A key gift is that of mercy. Those who love the Lord and love the Children of God tend to be compassionate toward others. Most human beings have a certain amount of compassion for those in need but that compassion gets compromised with their own personal needs and desires. The believer who God gives the gift of mercy is sacrificial in caring for others. They are intuitive in understanding need when they see it and instinctive in reaching out with solutions, comfort, and peace of mind. This gift emphasizes giving people more than what they need. It helps grow the individual to be strong enough to cope with life's problems and to reach the point of learning to lean on Christ for life's solutions rather than on self and others.

- **The Gift of Discernment:** God gives certain believers the ability to determine the message source thereby defining whether messages received are from God or Satan. This is not a supernatural gift but a common sense gift. Satan is very deceitful and makes every effort to confuse believers. Satan practices the projection of false doctrine and can make it quite logical but not true. In Matthew 24:4–5 Jesus said many would come in His name and deceive many. The gift of discernment is needed by the Church to keep its witness and its effectiveness alive and well.

- **The Gift of Helps:** The Spiritual Gift of Helps is closely related to that of mercy. It involves compassion for others. However it is slightly broader than mercy. It features the desire to help others and often the recipient does not need to be in trouble to be offered such help. This gift is beautiful for building the Body of Christ because it teaches us love, it teaches us sacrifice, it teaches us respect of each other and it pleases God. The Gift of Helps is very helpful toward building a team and teaching trust. This is part of what God wants His people to exhibit.

- ***The Gift of Giving:*** Some people simple enjoy giving to others. They joyfully share what they have without regret or hesitation. This giving if often more than financial. The giving of time and energy is a prime example of this gift. It is very similar to the Spiritual Gift of Helps. The giver is concerned for the needs of others and actually looks for opportunities to help. This gift makes the Church more concerned for others and more responsive in times of trouble.
- ***The Gift of Leadership:*** The gifted leader is one who is strong in leading others in truth and righteousness. This believer often also has strong discernment, wisdom, grace and mercy. However this believer has to be equally concerned with accomplishing the mission of the Church as he or she is with meeting the needs of people. Again the mission of the Church is to exalt the Savior, equip the saints, evangelize the lost, encourage the believer, enlist the uncommitted and empower the laborers toward the harvest. The gift of leadership is often found in the position of Pastor, Teacher, Evangelist or Apostle.
- ***The Gift of Serving:*** This gift is a form of the combination of the Spiritual Gifts of Helps, Mercy, and Giving. This word "Serving" comes from the root word diakonian, which means serving. It is the basis of the office of Deacon as outlined to Timothy by Paul in the New Testament.

Fruit of the Spirit

Paul did not list love as a Spiritual Gift because love is the overwhelming fruit of being "Born Again" or of having been given a new nature when we accepted Jesus Christ as Savior. The basis of this new nature is that of love for Jesus Christ who died for our sins. The outgrowth of that new nature is love for people everywhere. A fig tree bears figs. An apple tree bears apples. An Orange tree cannot yield bananas. Likewise we who are part of the family of God as a result of God changing our heart will bear forth an image of God not selfishness. Love is not a Spiritual Gift it is better described as part of the DNA of the Christian. Love is who we are not what we do.

Romans 7:5–6
"For while we were living in the flesh, our sinful passions, aroused by the law, were at work in our members to bear fruit for death. But now we are released from the law, having died to that which held us captive, so that we serve in the new way of the Spirit and not in the old way of the written code."

In Matthew, we are informed that to be a Christian we must love God. If we are saved we are given a new nature that loves God. True love is eternal and faithful and our love for God does not diminish or fail. Our Lord pointed out that without love of God we cannot be saved.

Matthew 22:34–38
"But when the Pharisees heard that He had silenced the Sadducees, they gathered together. Then one of them, a lawyer, asked Him a question, to test Him, "Teacher, which is the great commandment in the law?" and He said to him, "'You shall love the LORD your God with all your heart, with all your soul, and with all your mind.' This is the first and great commandment."

Then God went the next step in pointing out what the fruit of loving God will be in our life. God is specific in outlining to us how important love is to our outside witness and to our pleasing of God.

Matthew 22:39
"And the second is like it: 'You shall love your neighbor as yourself.'"

God gives us a powerful challenge when He instructs His children to love others as we love ourselves. And He is talking about a sacrificial love that is not selfish but is giving. God knows all people are not lovable. He says to love them anyway because He loves them and we are to want to please God. How much are we to love them? We are to love them as much as we love ourselves. That is a challenge. It is a challenge we will constantly fall short on but it is a target of Christian living God has set for us. When we fail we get back up and ask God for help as we try again. Love is the foundation of all Christian living.

1 Corinthians 13:1–3
"If I speak with the tongues of men and of angels, but have not love, I have become noisy gong or a clanging cymbal. And if I have prophetic powers, and understand all mysteries and all knowledge, and if I have all faith, so as to remove mountains, but have not love, I am nothing. If I give away all I have, and if I deliver up my body to be burned, but have not love, I gain nothing."

Paul tells us the reality of Christian living. That is that people looking on our lives must see that we love them even as we love God. Otherwise, regardless of how deep our love is for God we appear to them to be empty vessels with nothing to offer. Regardless of how much faith we have in God and His ability and willingness to move mountains, if we do not show love in our relationships with others they will not see Jesus and will not see anything we have that they want. That means that to their view we are nothing. Love is the foundation of the Christian life. Paul then proceeds to explain in depth what kind of love Christ expects us to radiate to the outside world.

1 Corinthians 13:4–7
"Love is patient and kind; love does not envy or boast; it is not arrogant or rude. It does not insist on its own way; it is not irritable or resentful; it does not rejoice at wrongdoing, but rejoices with the truth. Love bears all things, believes all things, hopes all things, endures all things."

Paul then outlines to us that this love God speaks of is not conditional. It is not temporary and it is not selective. If we love God we will love His children. Paul clarifies that Christians will communicate to the outside world that they love Christ and have a changed, new nature, is the way they live. He starts with the most powerful of all. That is the fruit love. If we are Christians we will love others. In Galatians God gives us, in addition to love, eight outgrowths of salvation that will be evident in the Christians life.

Galatians 5:22–23
"But the fruit of the Spirit is love, joy, peace, longsuffering, kindness, goodness, faithfulness, gentleness, self-control. Against such there is no law."

The above verse does not say there are nine fruits of the Spirit. It tells us there is one fruit of the Spirit and it encompasses all of the following outgrowths of salvation. This is different than Spiritual Gifts. Spiritual Gifts are given by God according to His Sovereign will. To some, He gave certain Spiritual Gifts and to others He gave other Spiritual Gifts. But the Fruit of the Spirit, to all the redeemed, include love and these other eight outgrowths of Salvation. The fruit of the Spirit is a nature we are given upon salvation. Yes, we develop and increase of capacity for portraying the fruit of the Spirit as we grow in Christ. However we are granted the fruit of the Spirit when we are given the new changed heart for Christ. Some of us do not have the personality that is totally compliant or comfortable with the outgrowths of Fruit of the Spirit. There for some more cultivating of the new nature God has given us than others. But we are to recognize what God has made us and determine in our heart we will become what God has imputed into our heart to be.

The Personality of God

The Fruit of the Spirit is the personality of God. Forever God has been working with man trying to help man become by choice more like Him. God could force man to be just like Him but to do so eliminates man's choice and thus eliminates man's ability to return a free love back to God. When God instructs man that at Salvation, we are given a new nature that takes on the personality of God He is, in part, talking about the Fruit of the Spirit. These include the following:

Love: Love is a spiritual anchor of truth in relationship with God and neighbor. This love is a distinctly Christian love, which finds its source from God alone. Because He had and has this kind of love for us God sent his only Son to die for us. The Holy Spirit is battles continuously to reproduce this kind of love in us. We are to show this kind of selfless love to one another and to the world.

Joy: The word joy appears sixty times in the New Testament. It is not happiness. It is more substantial and deeper than the surface emotion of happiness. Joy comes from deep within the soul based on the relationship between Jesus Christ and the believer. Joy does not ebb and flow with surface happenings in our life. We have a bad day and our happiness vanishes until something good happens and it reappears. Joy is constant because it is the outgrowth of our present and future certainty of Christ's love for us. As Christians we are to radiate that joy in our life. Those around us should see our joy and seek it for themselves. God's Word says that the joy of the Lord is our strength and is the light to our path of Spiritual health.

Peace: God gives us peace of mind because we can be certain He loves us, He cares for us, and He is capable of conquering any problem we will face. God tells us the peace of mind He provides is not the same as the peace the world offers. Peace from God is based on our relationship with Christ. We know who we are and we know whose we are and that relationship will not change. Our peace is strongly reinforced with our certain knowledge of eternal salvation. God's peace is not temporary but permanent. Paul said the peace of God is a peace that passes all understanding. It is a peace that is illogical to the mind of a non-believer because it only comes when we have placed our total trust in the hands of our Lord and Savior.

Long-Suffering: This evidence of the fruit of the Spirit in our lives is called by some Bible translations patience. Certainly patience is part of this evidence of the change God has brought to pass in our lives but this evidence of the fruit of the Spirit goes deeper than patience. It recognizes that in our lives God did not promise a path of life without any trials and troubles. In fact, God told us that if we pick up the cross of Christ we shall suffer in various ways. However, He also assures us that His strength will give us what we need to bear the suffering and rejoice in the privilege of suffering for our Lord. And in our lives we will suffer often not because of our relationship with Christ but just because we live in a world that is corrupt, evil, selfish, and non-caring. We are not protected from the arrows of pain that all people suffer just because we are children of God. God said He may or may not protect us from certain things in life but He certainly will provide us the strength to get through the trials and rejoice in the Lord for the privilege of being His child.

Kindness: Many scholars call this sympathetic kindness but this is not what our Lord is speaking of. Rather than sympathetic kindness God wants us to have empathetic kindness. There is a lot of difference. Sympathetic kindness says "Oh my dear child, I feel so sorry for you that I will solve your problem for you." Empathetic kindness says, "I understand your problem, I am here to help you and walk with you. I am here to help you find the strength of our Lord and through His help solve your problem." Empathetic kindness grows the Christian in dependence on God and in self-confidence in God. When we are saved God gives us a love for people and that runs in tandem with our desire to help people. With God's help we can respond to the special needs of others who are hurting or in need. Those who have experienced the kindness of God's salvation in Christ are to exhibit that same kindness to the world. Empathetic kindness is a significant demonstration of the fruit of the Spirit God has endowed us with when we are saved.

Goodness: Goodness is generosity in our heart that urges us to share what we have with others for their good. Although goodness and kindness are similar, goodness is a more active term, which is often directed toward others in a benevolent way. This manifestation of the fruit of the Spirit would correspond well with the Spiritual Gifts of Helps and Giving. We, as saved believers, recognize the amazing gift of love God has given to us and we desire to pass it on. When we see a need we must meet it. When we see a hurt we must heal it. The virtue of goodness reminds us that we become the hands and feet of Jesus Christ.

Faithfulness: We are told in Scripture that faith is a gift of God and it comes from our reading God's Word, hearing God's Word preached and taught, and from our prayer life. We rely on God's faithfulness to us and He relies on our faithfulness to Him. This manifestation of the fruit of the Spirit is, in part, dependability. We should do what we say we will do. Our word must be true and accurate. We also are expected by God, and we owe it to God's children, to demonstrate to the outside world our total trust and dependence on God. Then we can demonstrate that we can do amazing things through Christ who strengthens us. When we are saved we have as part of our new nature the desire to be faithful to the promises and the expectations of God. Our walk toward sanctification involves growth of this manifestation of the fruit of the Spirit.

Gentleness: It means to be mild mannered and to have a calm personality. This does not mean to be weak or indecisive. It is closely associated to humility. It is the virtue that is needed when confronted by opposition. It is possible to be gentle with others even when they are in opposition to us because of the love for them God puts into our hearts. Peter tells us that gentleness is necessary to be a Christian witness. Without gentleness we give off an image of selfishness and anger that is not consistent with the personality of God.

Self-Control: The final manifestation of the fruit of the Spirit is to be able to control our desires and lusts. We are burdened with a nature of sin and we must recognize that urge lies within us. The desire to lash out in anger when things go wrong is ever present. The desire to seek materialism as part of our base nature is natural to us. The manifestation of Self-Control comes with growth in the maturity of Christ. We must control the flesh and let the Spiritual side of our "New Born" nature guide us rather than the carnal side of our physical nature. Self-control is closely associated to purity of mind, heart, and conduct. It is relying on the power of the Spirit to overcome the desires of the flesh.

Matthew 7:17–20
"So, every healthy tree bears good fruit, but the diseased
tree bears bad fruit. A healthy tree cannot bear bad fruit,
nor can a diseased tree bear good fruit. Every tree that
does not bear good fruit is cut down and thrown into the
fire. Thus you will recognize them by their fruits."

We cannot be something we are not. If we are followers of Satan we will demonstrate toward others selfishness, greed, thoughtlessness, and evil. If we are followers of Christ we will yield forth love, joy, peace, long-suffering, kindness, gentleness, gentleness and self-control. These manifestations of our "New Born" Christian nature are not Spiritual Gifts given to select believers. The Fruit of the Spirit is available to every believer to use. Manifestations of the Fruit of the Spirit lie in the arsenal of our heart and are ready for us to utilize them for our own growth in the Spirit of God and for the good and Spiritual health of others.

Growth Sanctification through Fruit of the Spirit

Earlier in this book we addressed the wonder of Growth Sanctification. In summery we outlined the reality that God expects us to grow continually toward the goal becoming like Him. He wants us to grow in mental thought, in spiritual desire, in actions of the body and above all in love from our soul, always advancing toward becoming like Him. When we pass on physically in this life and receive a glorified body, as all believers in Jesus Christ during this Church dispensation will receive, we shall be complete in that growth.

The fulfillment of the fruit of the spirit God has placed in us is that Growth Sanctification He expects of us. If you do not want to become like Jesus you should seriously examine your relationship with Christ so far as salvation is concerned. We should seek fulfillment of whatever fruits of the spirit God has given us. We need not seek more than God has given us but we should seek more ways to serve God. In such seeking God often grants us new tasks and responsibilities and in such we are given more fruit of the spirit. To better understand our nature and what God has done within us we should study Romans chapter 7.

Romans 7:5–6
"For while we were living in the flesh, our sinful passions, aroused by the law, were at work in our members to bear fruit for death. But now we are released from the law, having died to that which held us captive, so that we serve in the new way of the Spirit and not in the old way of the written code."

Before we were saved and became part of the Family of God we lived in the flesh meaning we were consumed to various degrees of always seeking what we believed to be good for us. Old Testament people were given the law to keep them aware of when they were thinking thoughts and doing deeds that were selfish and not pleasing to God. People convicted of their sins and saved in the New Testament have the life of Jesus and the Word of God to give them the same awareness. In addition we have the Holy Spirit to tell us when we are displeasing God. But God wants us to do more than not displease Him. He wants us to please Him with who we become in His Kingdom.

Now, however, being filled with the Holy Spirit we *"serve in the new way of the Spirit and not in the old way of the written code."* How do we accomplish this? We accomplish it through growth in our use of the Fruits of the Spirit God has endowed us with both at salvation and throughout our life on earth as His children.

CHAPTER SIXTEEN

The Doctrine of The Elect of God

God's Chosen Few

From the first Church in Jerusalem to today certain subjects have remained quite controversial. Undoubtedly in the first Church most of these subjects were not challenged. However as the years pass man cannot help but apply his logic to the interpretation of Scripture and thus we have mystery. In some of these subjects God did not give us much information, supposedly desiring that we not dig too deeply into these issues. In other subjects, however, man has applied his logic and twisted God's teachings to bring about the mystery.

An example of subjects that fit these categories is the question of whether Salvation is by works or by faith. This one is easy because God's Word is so clear that Salvation is through faith by the Grace of God lest anyone should boast of their good works. Yet mankind reexamines this concept and tries to put man's logic on it and too often twists this question to a different answer. Into this maze we can thrust Man's free will or God's Sovereignty and a host of other concepts. The doctrine of the elect of God involves some of these issues and has its own level of dispute.

Who are "The Elect"?

The word "elect" denotes the concept of choosing. We elect a President of the United States and in so doing Americans are privileged to choose who that will be. We elect Congress members and Senate members and that identifies who will serve in the role to which they have been elected.

All parties of the controversy seem to agree the "elect of God" are those whom God has predestined to salvation. They are called the "elect" because that word denotes the concept of choosing. God chooses those who will be saved. These are the elect of God. However the controversy gets involved with the process God uses for choosing. Does the faith of man and man's decision regarding who he will worship impact that choosing? Or does man become one who worships God after he has been chosen?

There are two dominant views today on the elect of God. One involves predestination that limits man's choice in salvation. The other involves God's foreknowledge. This means God knows who will decide to trust Him. After all, God is not limited by time. God is already at the beginning and end of what we call time. It is understandable that God knows who will decide to trust Him. God therefore commands that all humans who trust in the promise of Jesus Christ dyeing on Calvary and rising from the dead will be saved. These are called His Elect, because they meet His criteria for salvation. This criteria, is not a criteria of works, but of faith. As the Christian answers these choices we have to face the reality of some basic questions. They are:

1. Does God make the decision of who will be saved based solely on His right to make the choice?
2. Does man make the decision of who will be saved based on the simple question of who will believe on Jesus Christ to the extent of revelation they have been given by God?
3. Did God know, before the foundations of the world who would put their trust in God to redeem them and forgive their sins?
4. If God decided before the foundations of the world who will be saved what impact does that have on the free will of man in salvation?
5. If God decided before the foundation of the world who would be saved did He make that choice on an individual basis or a group basis?
6. If man has been given free will in the matter of salvation what does that do to the Sovereignty of God?
7. Is the doctrine of predestination and election the same thing?
8. Is there a doctrine of election that incorporates the free will of man, the sovereignty of God and predestination?

Faith + Grace = Election

The foreknowledge view of election, teaches that God, through His omniscience (meaning all knowledge), knows those who will, in the course of their life, choose of their own free will to place their faith and trust in Jesus Christ for their salvation. This teaching of scripture then tells us "The Elect" of God are those who will, by their own free will decide to trust God for Salvation. God, before the beginning of time declare these people, whoever they would turn out to be, to be predestined to be saved. It is hard for us to grasp the concept that God is past present and future. God was before the beginning of time. God is present and has been present from creation therefore God knows what every person ever born will decide. God recognizes the free will of man in decision-making that is taught in Scripture. This does not mean mankind has the ability to save himself. No, we are saved by faith through God's Grace. Every person who ever lived or will live is saved by having faith in Jesus Christ to the extent they have had revelation of God's truth. But even as we, in faith, ask God to save us, God makes the decision of whether our faith is real or fabricated. From the beginning of the world, God promised that the way to be saved is to believe in His only begotten Son. God created mankind to allow mankind to return a free will love back to God. If salvation comes only based on God's predetermined or predestined decision regarding who will be saved, the very purpose of man's creation is compromised.

John 3:16
"For God so loved the world that He gave His only begotten Son that whosoever believeth on Him shall not perish but have everlasting life."

God made the promise and asked the Apostle John, as well as countless others, to inform mankind that He will save all people who decide to accept Christ. Does this promise conflict with the Sovereignty of God? The answer is no. God, in His Sovereignty, elected to make Salvation a joint decision between God and man. Man must have faith in Jesus, as revealed to man by God, for God to accept him as saved. But God must, through His mercy, His grace, and His Sovereignty actually change the heart of man to be one who seeks God and trusts God.

A third factor must be considered. Yes Salvation requires the faith of man for salvation and the Grace of God for Salvation and yet, God, being not subject to time, knows in advance what mankind will decide. There is no controversy about the foreknowledge of God. God knows everything about the past, the present and the future. His knowledge is not dependent on anything. God does not have to wait on what Man is going to decide in order to know what man is going to think, say or do. The first reason this is true is because God is present from the beginning of time to eternity beyond the end of the world. The second reason is that God created us and knows what He created. It is like a parent turning a little two-year-old loose on land with mud holes. Sooner or later that child will get in the mud hole. That is who the child is. Therefore 1 Peter 1:2 tells us the people who will decide to trust in the promised Messiah (Jesus) for salvation are known by God from the beginning of time through eternity. Therefore, God in His Sovereignty declares these who will make that choice to be His elect. They are washed of their sins by the blood of Jesus and are, in the view of God, righteous. 1 Peter 1:2 then teaches us that those God declares to be His elect, or those destined to be saved, are so destined according to God's foreknowledge, not God's Sovereignty. And they are so chosen because God knows these believe Jesus (has, or will depending on when the decision is made) died for their sins and stands ready to use the blood He shed to cover their sins.

1 Peter 1:2
"Elect according to the foreknowledge of God the Father, in sanctification of the Spirit, for obedience and sprinkling of the blood of Jesus Christ."

We also know from Ephesians 1:4 that God created a plan for the salvation of His elect before the foundation of the world. That plan was that Jesus Christ would come to earth, live as a human man, remain sinless, and be crucified on a cruel cross for the sins of all mankind. Then God's plan for cleansing believers of their sins was and is that those who believe in Him and decide they want to be what Jesus wants them to become, will be made righteous (Holy) and sinless (blameless before God) because of the blood, shed in love, by Jesus. Ephesians 1:4 reveals that God chose His elect before the foundation of the world, as a family of God who would make the decision to seek God's salvation.

Ephesians 1:4
"Even as He chose us in Him before the foundation of the world, that we should be holy and blameless before Him in love."

God did not choose man individually with man having no part of that salvation decision. God declared, before the foundations of the world that those who believe in Jesus Christ as their Savior (even though the Old Testament Saints did not know who the Messiah would be) would be elected as His protected ones for salvation even to the point no power on earth or heaven could take them out of the hand of God.

Finally in Romans 8:28–30 God pointedly tells us those who work together for advancing the will of God the father and are called or selected to do His will, are those whom He foreknew would make the choice to be consumed with the will to please the Holy Spirit. Yes, these who are part of this elect group have to make a choice in their lives to be one who will work together to advance the will of God the Father. But because God foreknew all that would ever take place on earth He took those who would make that choice and pre-destined them to, through sanctification, conform to the image of Jesus, and after this life join Him in Heaven in a glorified body.

Romans 8:28–30
"And we know that all things work together for good to those who love God, to those who are the called according to His purpose. For whom He foreknew, He also predestined to be conformed to the image of His Son, that He might be the firstborn among many brethren. Moreover whom He predestined, these He also called; whom He called, these He also justified; and whom He justified, these He also glorified."

Salvation by God's choice therefore God's election

As a person who reads the Bible you will be familiar of the term predestination. And yes, the Bible does teach some things, some decisions of God, are predestined to happen. And many people who are strong Bible believing people believe God teaches us salvation is determined by predestination. This is to say they believe that before the foundations of the world God made the decision about who will be forgiven of their sins and will be saved. This belief of Salvation by Predestination totally eliminates any choice of man in whether or not he would be saved. Through the ages of time the doctrine of Predestination has been linked to the preaching of a great evangelist in the early 1500s named John Calvin.

Calvinism is a **very old doctrine that was first preached in 1519 by Huldrych Zwingli in Switzerland. However, the father of Calvinism was John Calvin, born in 1509 in France. John Calvin was active in the Catholic Church.** At the age of 21 he decided to change from Church-centered Catholicism to an evangelical faith in Christ. John Calvin chose trust what he believed to be the urgings of the Holy Spirit rather than the voice of the Catholic Church. The doctrine of Predestination became linked to Calvinism based on the preaching of John Calvin. Perhaps the most quoted Scripture to support predestination as the path toward Salvation is Romans 8:29–30.

Romans 8:29–30
"For those whom he foreknew he also predestined to be conformed to the image of his Son, in order that he might be the firstborn among many brothers. And those whom he predestined he also called, and those whom he called he also justified, and those whom he justified he also glorified."

Romans 8:29–30 is the basis of Calvinism concept of predestined salvation and God's intent in giving us this truth. Calvinism simply says man has no voice in being saved. This is totally out of context with the rest of God's teachings. God clearly teaches mankind must come to God in faith, believing on Jesus Christ for salvation and when man does this God will save him forever. Predestined simply means God in His foreknowledge knows who will elect to trust Jesus and God therefore guarantees eternal salvation for that person.

John 3:16
"For all have sinned and fall short of the glory of God."

John 10:27–29
"My sheep hear my voice, and I know them, and they follow me. I give them eternal life, and they will never perish, and no one will snatch them out of my hand. My Father, who has given them to me, is greater than all, and no one is able to snatch them out of the Father's hand."

Mankind is not on his own in deciding to believe in God. God has given to man enough faith to know God exists. God then gives man the Holy Spirit to interface with man's spirit to believe in Jesus Christ as our Savior. The concept that God elects people based on His will alone is just as inaccurate as the concept that God elects people based on their will alone. The concept that all who God has chosen will come to faith is reversed. Truth says all who come to faith in Christ, God has chosen. All those who are truly born-again will persevere in their faith is correct but not because of their strength. They will persevere because God counts their faith as righteousness as He did Abraham and the blood of Jesus Christ was shed at Calvary in payment for our sins. The belief that Jesus died for only the elect is misconstrued. Jesus died for the whole world but mankind has to accept the offering of salvation by expressing belief in Christ. Therefore Jesus died for the whole world but only the elect in Christ choose to accept the gift of love.

1 John 2:2
"And he is the propitiation for our sins: and not for ours only, but also for the sins of the whole world."

On what basis has God made this decision? Scriptures such as John 3:16 and Romans 10:13 are quite clear in which they say God made the decision on who would be saved based on who would believe in Jesus Christ as the resurrected Lord of Salvation. The tenth chapter of Romans, verse 13 tells us God wants every person ever born to be saved. If God wants every person ever born to be saved, and God in His Sovereignty has the power to make it happen, then God teaches **"The Elect of God" must decide to trust Jesus Christ as their Savior and yet must recognize their decision to accept Christ has done nothing unless the Holy Spirit changes us and gives us a new heart.**

John 6:44
"No one can come to Me unless the Father who sent Me draws him; and I will raise him up at the last day."

But wait, God also gives us unchallenged scriptures that says it is God's desire that every person who ever walked the face of the earth be saved.

John 3:16
"For God so loved the world, that he gave his only Son, that whoever believes in him should not perish but have eternal life."

Romans 10:13
"For everyone who calls on the name of the Lord will be saved."

God is in control of every aspect of our life. We know God chooses those whom He elects to receive certain revelations about Him. He chose Paul. He chose Moses. He chose David and we could go on and on. We can also equally be assured that if we have a gift to do something in the Kingdom of God it was God who chose for us to have it. Some people can sing and some cannot. Some can preach and some cannot. Some have the ability to preach but God did not choose them for that service. God chooses to whom he will give certain gifts. We do not make those choices. We also learn that we cannot come to Christ and accept Him as our Savior unless God draws us to Him. It is the Holy Spirit that urges us to be faithful to God. There is nothing in the Scripture that tells us God will save everyone. There is plenty of scripture that assures us God wants to save everyone but in His Sovereignty decided to give man a choice of who He would serve. He chooses who will be saved. But only those who chose to believe in Him will be saved.

Some say that there can be people who are morally very good people but just do not believe Jesus Christ is the redeemer of mankind. They would ask is it fair for these people to go to hell because they chose another thought pattern! This would encompass mases of people in the worship of Mohammed. So many good people who read the scriptures differently will go to hell because of their unbelief in Christ. This encompasses the Israelite people who are God's chosen people but have decided to refuse to accept Jesus as the risen Lord and Messiah. It is conceivable that some might feel God is not being fair. Paul knew some would feel this was unfair and clarified His will in His letter to the Church in Rhome.

Romans 9:15
"For He says to Moses, "I will have mercy on whom I have mercy, and I will have compassion on whom I have compassion."

God is sovereign over His creation. He is free to choose those whom He will choose, and He is free to pass by those whom He will pass by. In honor of His beloved Son who volunteered to come down from Heaven to be crucified for the sins of mankind, God elected to make the qualification for mankind's salvation, belief in Jesus Christ. That is the right of God. Mankind has no right to accuse God the creator of being unjust. So God issued His commandment that we should believe on the name of Jesus Christ.

1 John 3:23
"And this is His commandment: that we should believe on the name of His Son Jesus Christ and love one another, just as He has commanded us."

The Elect of God involve the total complete foreknowledge of God while yet yielding to the Sovereignty of God. The Elect of God also includes the Sovereignty of God without disregarding the free will of man. The desire of God that everyone be saved must not be overlooked. Yet the reality that all of God's creation may not be saved unless they meet the requirements of God toward salvation also must not be disregarded. The requirement that mankind believe in Jesus Christ is totally within the right of God to declare.

Matthew 7:21–23
"Not everyone who says to Me, 'Lord, Lord,' will enter the kingdom of heaven, but he who does the will of My Father who is in heaven. On that day many will say, 'Lord, Lord, did we not prophesy in Your name, and cast out demons in Your name, and do mighty works in Your name?' And then will I declare to them, 'I never knew you; depart from Me, you workers of lawlessness!'"

Conclusion Regarding Salvation

Neither the will of man, nor the goodness of man, determines salvation. Neither does the will of God alone. The combination of the will of man to trust and glorify God combined with the will of God to actually forgive man of His sins and adopt man into the family of God is both essential for salvation. Therefore, we establish several basic truths:

1. God is sovereign and in command of everything whether it is of man, of Satan, of angels, or creation of time.
2. God seeks a free love from man. He could have created Adam without a free will but to do so would mean Adam could not return a free love.
3. God knows everything. He is omniscient. He knows who will be saved because he is already at the end of our life. This does not mean God decides who will be saved without the faith of man. God has total foreknowledge but

has subjected himself to abide by the rules of salvation He imposed on Himself.

4. God has delegated to man the privilege of asking Jesus Christ to forgive man from sin and grant him membership in God's Kingdom. But with the privilege come the responsibility and the consequences.

5. The responsibility of becoming a member of the family of God is that you ask for God to change your heart and give you a new desire to serve Him forever. When you are saved that will be your heart's desire.

6. The consequence of accepting Christ and returning a free love to God is God's sealing our souls with eternal salvation. He guarantees that no power exists that can change God's decision to adopt us into His family.

7. However, our decision to accept Christ is not part of our basic nature. It is not possible for us to even desire to trust Christ without the Holy Spirit drawing us to Him. God explained that to us when He said man was imputed with a nature of sin.

8. The consequence of not accepting Christ is eternal separation from God and eternal persecution in the fires of the "Lake of Fire."

9. God did make the decision before the foundations of the world regarding who would be saved. God describes this as having predestined "The Elect" to salvation.

CHAPTER SEVENTEEN

The Doctrine of Priesthood of the Believer
God's view of Mankind

Definition of Priesthood

Many Christians do not understand the term "Priesthood of the Believer." Young Christians may not understand this term and many mature Christians have only a surface understanding. They practice "Priesthood of the Believer" without understanding its significance or appreciating the depth of God's grace in granting us this deep privilege. As we consider "Priesthood" we should look at several key characteristics. First, the Bible gave birth to this doctrine. In Exodus 19:6 God outlines His relationship with man as being a direct relationship, needing no one else to intercede.

1 Peter 2:5
"You, yourselves, like living stones, are being built up as a spiritual house, to be a spiritual priesthood, to offer spiritual sacrifices acceptable to God through Jesus Christ."

Peter, desiring to clarify to Christians their relationship with God, as opposed to their relationship with the world, stresses that the members of the "Body of Christ" (The Church) would have a close personal relationship that would be based on righteousness, love and service.

1 Peter 2:9
"But you are a chosen race, a royal priesthood, a holy nation, a people for His own possession, that you may proclaim the excellences of Him who called you out of darkness into His marvelous light."

An examination of scripture tells us Peter was speaking to believers when he recorded this message from God. Underlying his message is the believer's relationship with God that gives them the right and privilege to go directly to God with petitions, praise, concerns and desires. The price Jesus Christ paid on Calvary gave believers that right. It is not something we earn or deserve. In the Old Testament Jesus had not yet died for the salvation of believers in the coming

Messiah and God had not sent the Holy Spirit to dwell in man's heart. Therefore, except for selected people, Old Testament believers did not have "Priesthood of Believers" as a gift. "Priesthood of the Believer" is a gift of God. It is a right all believers have not had. Only believers in the age of Grace, or the Dispensation of the Church, have the right to go directly to God. This right and privilege is the right to go directly to Jesus Christ, the Son of God, who is part of the Godhead. Jesus then intercedes for us to God the Father, and living within us is the Holy Spirit. In this manner we are given the privilege of making contact with all three parts of the Godhead or Trinity.

1 Timothy 2:5
"For there is one God, and there is one mediator between God and men, the man Christ Jesus."

Religious bodies such as the Catholic Church teach people Jesus died for their sins, that is wonderful. But they then teach these people need the Church to be a mediator with God in their daily lives or to represent them to God. God tells us just drop on your knees and pray to me. My Holy Spirit dwells in your heart if you believe in Jesus. Confession needs be given to the Lord not to an earthly assigned "Priest." First Timothy 2:5 and many other scriptures give us three important foundations of faith.

- **The Priesthood of the Believer means each individual person has direct access to God.**

Because of Jesus Christ, who serves as propitiation for our sins with God, we have direct access to God through prayer because the Holy Spirit lives in our heart and directly mediates our prayers to God. Propitiation means to cover, or to justify, or to plead for one. We do not know how to pray but the Holy Spirit, sent by Christ to us, teaches us to pray. Our prayers, then, are received by Jesus and our cause is presented to God the Father. But our cause does not include sins we have committed because of the blood of Jesus shed on Calvary. We can receive a word, an interpretation, and a decision from the Lord directly from God. We require no pope, no confessor, no pastor, no saint of the Church, no Church Priest to guide us into God's presence. The only mediator between us is Jesus Christ the Son of God who is God Himself.

- **The Priesthood of the Believer means we have the responsibility for deciding to believe or deciding to reject our Savior. To that extent we are responsible for our salvation, and our walk with Jesus Christ.**

We cannot decide the salvation of our friends and family. No one else is responsible for our salvation. We alone must accept that responsibility. Church members can support, teach, and pray for each believer. Our Pastor and Church staff minister can pray for us and deacons and family can pray and minister to us. Ultimately, however, we are responsible for our own salvation, our own morality and even our own theology. God's Word teaches us that the Church has the responsibility to present to us the Word of God but the Church does not have the responsibility for our decision to accept or reject Jesus Christ.

- **The Priesthood of the Believer means each of us has the privilege and the responsibility of studying God's Word with the help of the Holy Spirit and making application of God's Word to our lives.**

Instead of relying upon one particular high priest who alone has the right to speak with God in our behalf, those who believe in Jesus Christ have the privilege and responsibility to go directly to God.

What is propitiation of our Sins?

We sometimes use words that sound good but most of us do not understand. This is true with the word propitiation when used with Jesus Christ. As we study the reality of Jesus giving to us the right to be our own priest, the concept of Jesus being the propitiation of our Sins is an important concept to grasp. God's Word clearly tells us Jesus Christ is the propitiation for our sins.

1 John 2:2
"He is the propitiation for our sins, and not for ours only but also for the sins of the whole world."

What does this mean? The Bible tells us Jesus is the propitiation of our sins because He became our substitute payment for our sins. So in the Bible Jesus as our propitiation means He takes on our obligations of guilt for our sins against God. The term substitution of payment requires that payment must be made to someone. In our state of sin, our payment for our sin has to be made to God the Father who created us to be sinless. So when 1 John 2:2 states "He is the propitiation for our sins," it means a number of different roles for Jesus.

First: When Jesus died on the cross at Calvary to pay the penalty for our sins He became the substitute for our sins. As the substitute for our sins He is something critical, something valuable beyond words. A vast number of verses in the Bible tell us Christ died for us and in so doing became the substitute for our sins. Romans 8:34 speaks to this fact. This verse emphasizes that Jesus died and even more than that rose from the grave. Jesus paid the price of our salvation. Therefore Romans 8:34 points out that Jesus intercedes with God the Father just on the basis of who He is, and that is the substitute payment of our sins.

Romans 8:34
"Who is to condemn? Christ Jesus is the one who died—more than that, who was raised—who is at the right hand of God, who, who is interceding for us from the love of Christ."

1. Jesus is not only the substitute for our sins, He is the voice of admittance into heaven for those seeking salvation. This is a powerful verse often overlooked. It says Jesus sits by the seat of God the Father, and as people continue to ask God

to save them He intercedes with God the Father for them. He tells God the Father, *"They are mine, You have given them to me."* In so doing Jesus is not convincing God these new believers are to be saved, no He is testifying to God the Father how much He loves them and how He paid the price of their sins on Calvary. Jesus testifies to His Father these new believers have met the test of belief in Christ for their salvation. He intercedes for believers as they join the family of God. Hebrews 7:25 reveals to us two important parts of Him being the propitiation for our sins. First is that through the price Jesus paid on Calvary our security as a believer has been placed, by God, into the hands of Christ. Hebrews 7:25 states He is able to save us to the uttermost. That means that when Jesus took on the role of being the substitute for our sins it was the substitute for all sins we would ever commit. No power can take us out of the hands of Christ.

Hebrews 7:25
"Consequently, He is able to save to the uttermost those who draw near to God through Him, since He always lives to make intercession for them."

2.   The same verse, Hebrews 7:25, tells us another great reward of Jesus being the propitiation for our sins. It says, *"He always lives to make intercession for us on a constant eternal way of life."* After Jesus died on Calvary, was buried and rose from the dead, we know He went down into Hades (inner part of the earth) and brought with Him all the souls of those Old Testament Saints who believed in God and God's promise of the coming Messiah. After that, we know Jesus ascended back into Heaven and sat at the right hand of God the Father. What role did Jesus accept sitting beside His Father? Jesus did not take time out to rest after He rejoined His Father. He began fulfilling the role of interceding with God the Father to bring in the host

of people who accepted Christ during the Dispensation of Grace. When someone asks Christ to save them, the Holy Spirit examines that person's intent and if they believe in Jesus Christ and want to be faithful to Him the Holy Spirit speaks to Jesus and Jesus tells God He has accepted that one as part of the family of God. Therefore, the third role of Jesus as our propitiation to God the Father is a intercessor to God for those who are turning their lives over to Him.

3. Hebrews 7:25 also tells us that Jesus saves us to the *"uttermost."* This is a reaffirmation of a host of scripture that tells us our salvation is protected by Jesus and can never be taken away from God. Some call this *"Once saved always saved."* Some call it *"The Security of the Believer."* Whatever we call it the forth role of our Savior as the propitiation of our sins is to secure our salvation throughout eternity.

But what about us, what about those millions who accept Jesus, pray to Him every day and ask for His help in living the Christian life. Romans 8:26 reveals to us the Holy Spirit, who dwells in our heart, intercedes with Jesus, and asks Him to help us with our Christian life.

Romans 8:26
"Likewise; the Spirit helps us in our weakness, for we do not know what to pray for as we ought, but the Spirit himself intercedes for us with groaning's too deep for words."

The Holy Spirit is the companion, the support, and the partner of Jesus Christ the Son of God in everything. We can say with accuracy that the Holy Spirit is to us as Christians the voice of Jesus. Jesus intercedes with God the Father to help us in our Christian life. What does this mean? Does this mean that God would not accept us every time we sinned but Jesus intercedes and changes God's mind? Absolutely not, the reality is the mind of Jesus and God the Father and the Holy Spirit are one. They think alike but have different roles. If then, Jesus as the propitiation of our sins is not interceding with God to change His mind, what is He doing? The answer is Jesus is helping us prepare our requests to Him so they correspond with the deep intent of our heart. The Holy Spirit brings to Christ requests we do not mentally think of but they are buried deep in our heart. Because of the Holy Spirit knowing us and knowing what our faith in Christ is, He helps us word our thoughts in prayer. God said, *"but the Spirit Himself intercedes for us with groaning's too deep for words."*

1 John 2:2
"He is the propitiation for our sins, and not for ours only but also for the sins of the whole world."

Isn't it interesting that almost all religions recognize the existence of God. God has installed in mankind enough faith to believe God exists. Mankind also intuitively understands God is vastly greater, smarter, and more intelligent than any man. But mankind does not gain forgiveness for our sins and membership in the close family of God because mankind believes God exists. Mankind has to trust God's promise of a coming Messiah as the answer to our need for salvation. Old Testament people were saved by looking forward toward the price Jesus would pay for their sins even though God had not given them understanding of who the promised Messiah would be. New Testament people and all to come after are saved by looking back at the death of Jesus on Calvary with trust His death and resurrection was enough to pay the price of our sins.

Jesus is the propitiation of the sins of the Old Testament believers, for New Testament believers, for Tribulation believers and for Millennial Reign believers. In other words no one can be admitted into the family of God without Jesus Christ cleansing that one by the blood He shed on Calvary.

There are two voices talking to God the Father regarding every deed we do and every thought we generate. One voice is that of Satan telling God we are hopeless, loveless people and He has won the battle of righteousness, while the other is Jesus Christ Son of God who is eternally telling God the Father that we, the ones who trusted Him for salvation, have in our heart a great love for God and desire to be the kind of children God wanted. God the Father listens only to His Son because Jesus, His Son paid God's price, paid God's penalty for our sin. Yes we are saved eternally but Jesus continues to interface with His Father for us.

Jesus is an advocate with God the Father

1 John 2:1
"My little children, I am writing these things to you so that you may not sin. But if anyone does sin, we have an advocate with the Father, Jesus Christ the righteous."

In 1 John 2:1 the Apostle John acknowledges that we as the redeemed will still sin. We do not want to disobey God and we are sorry we did it, usually immediately after doing it. However we are weak and will submit to Satan's urges occasionally. When we sin against God there is no need for Jesus to petition God to forgive us our sins. Jesus the Son of God and God the Father and the Holy Spirit are one and never disagree. They think alike. No, Jesus does not need to convince God to forgive our sins. God forgave all our sins, past present and future when we confessed being a sinner and ask Jesus to take over our heart. But we do not want to be out of favor with God. Jesus is our advocate that *(1)* **God the Father will not be angry with us because of our omission,** and *(2)* **We do not fall out of favor with God.** If either of the above happens we do not lose our salvation. But we can lose the joy of our salvation. We can lose the influence of our salvation and God can lose the worship of our obedience.

The battle between God and Satan is one of righteousness. God stands for righteousness while Satan stands for evil. God stands for love while Satan stands for greed and betrayal. God stands for adoration of His self while Satan stands for adoration of his self. Who will win the battle? There is no question who will win the ultimate battle between God and Satan in the world scene. It is recorded in the end of the book. God wins and Satan is locked up for eternity into the Lake of Fire. But the question is who will win the battle in your heart. Satan may win more hearts of mankind that God the Father because we have a selfish streak in us.

2 Corinthians 5:21
"For our sake he made him to be sin who knew no sin, so that in him we might become the righteousness of God."

God Established the Priesthood Relationship

Luke 23:44–45
"Now it was about the sixth hour, and there was darkness over all the earth until the ninth hour. Then the sun was darkened, and the veil of the temple was torn in two."

Prior to the death of Jesus Christ on Calvary and His resurrection from the dead, Hebrew people were separated from the Holy of Holies which was the inner sanctum of worship. God set aside the tribe of Levi, as people to serve as Priests for the people. Because of their sin, the Hebrew children were not allowed to look upon the face of God or to come into His presence. Yet God wanted to be in contact with His people because of His love. And God wanted to direct their path and keep them close to Him. In the Old Testament, a priest held a special place in the worship of God. Priests were responsible for certain aspects of worship, such as the sacrifice of animals. Priests reminded the people to worship God and led them in worship. They served as mediators between the people and God. The High Priest was the only one, however, allowed to enter the Holy of Holies in the Jewish temple. This especially sacred place was separated from the rest of the temple and from the other priests by a great curtain or veil.

The people outside the sanctum were divided according to their race and gender. The Gentiles were the greatest distance away from the Holy of Holies. The women were next, in the Court of Women.

The almost inner circle included the males of Israel and the final group was the priests. But even the priests couldn't go behind the veil. Only one person, the high priest, entered the Holy of Holies, and he went there only once each year, on the Day of Atonement. On that day he carried the sins of the people to the Lord and sacrificed for them so they could receive forgiveness. The curtain represented a stark reality. The people had to depend upon the high priest to convey their needs to God. They could not approach the Lord on their own. With the death, burial and resurrection of Jesus, the separation of people from God ended. Christ provided direct access to God for all believers. But God ripped that curtain, and with it the Jewish system of human mediation died. With its death mankind was given direct access, as believers, to God. That access is referred to as the Priesthood of the Believer.

The concept of the Priesthood of Believers comes from the New Testament. Every person who believes in the Lord Jesus Christ has access directly to God. Each is directly responsible to God. Each is to share the love of God with others. The priesthood of each believer is tied closely to another concept, that of soul competency. Each person has a God-given competence to know and follow God's will. A decision to follow Christ as Lord and Savior is an individual decision; no one can make it for another. Being a believer priest is a gift from God, not a human achievement; it is a gift of God given at the time of salvation.

Each believer becomes his/her own priest so far as having access to God. Each believer priest is responsible for his or her own actions. Individual believers can go directly to God without the aid of any human intermediary. Individuals can and should read and interpret the Bible for themselves without religious officials dictating to them what to believe. Each believer can and should pray directly to God without having to go through any human intermediary. This does not mean we as believer priests should not seek the counsel of more mature Christians for guidance. Certainly the Pastor of local Churches are ordained by God to aid members in discerning God's will for their lives and in interpretation of scripture. Nevertheless, mankind cannot relinquish his personal responsibility of being totally accountable to God for his/her relationship with God. We cannot say, "But the Pastor told me." We are given the gift of the Holy Spirit to interpret scripture and we are given direct access to God through the Holy Spirit. God will direct our paths.

Therefore, we must remember our Church leaders are people with a divine job. Pastors are not deity and are mortal as are members. Our Church leaders are not priests to represent us to God. They are helpmates to assist us in our relationships with God and others. God has granted spiritual gifts to assist us in worship. They however do not take the place of Christ in our lives. There is only one high priest for every believer. This means there is only one mediator for us to gain access to God and that is through Jesus Christ our Lord and Savior.

John 14:6
"Jesus said to him, "I am the way, the truth, and the life. No one comes to the Father except through Me."

1 Timothy 2:5
"For there is one God and one mediator between God and men, the Man Christ Jesus."

As believers, and therefore our own priests, we will seek knowledge of God. They will seek that knowledge through prayer, through reading God's Word, through conversing with other Christians, in Bible study and in evaluating life adventures. Much is to be gained from seeking the maturity and experiences of other Christians and of Pastors and teachers. But they are not the authorities of scripture. What we believe must come from our conviction based on interpretation of the Holy Spirit. This is the privilege and the responsibility of the priest believer.

CHAPTER EIGHTEEN

The Doctrine of the Church
The Body of Christ

Why did Jesus create the Church?

The Church has not always existed. When Adam was created there was no Church. In the days of Noah there was no Church. Abraham, Isaac, Joseph, and David were all believers, but they were not members of the Church. There was no Church in the days of the prophets. Isaiah was not a member of the Church. Even John the Baptist, the forerunner of Christ was not a member of the Church. In the days when Jesus walked on the earth there was no Church. Oh, when Jesus walked the earth the Jewish Synagogue existed for worship of Jehovah. But the Jews did not recognize Jesus as the Messiah. God did not create the Jewish Synagogue. The Church did not begin until after the death and resurrection of Jesus Christ.

Many people all over the world go to Church without conscious thought regarding what the Church is and why Christ created it. Jesus Christ built the Church to empower His believers and enable them to continue to do His work after He ascended back to heaven. Jesus loved the Church so much He gave His life for it. Jesus loved the Church so much that it is second only to God the Father in His love and adoration. Jesus knew that He was predestined to ascend to the Father in heaven a few days after His crucifixion and resurrection. He did not want to leave us here below without a direct connection with His Spirit. So Jesus said He would send us a comforter who would abide with us and live with us. The comforter is of course the Holy Spirit. However, Christ also created The Church as another comforter and builder whose mission is to protect those who come into faith believing in the death, burial, and resurrection of the Son of God.

In Matthew, we give a lot attention to Jesus's statement that ***"Thou art Peter and upon this rock I will build my Church."*** We ask was the Church built on the rock of Peter. The answer is no because we are not considering the context of the scripture. When Jesus said what is recorded in Matthew 16:18, He had not been crucified and therefore had not been resurrected but He knew what lay in His immediate future. He strongly desired a way to help believers in His death, burial, and resurrection stay strong together and to stay strong in faith in Him. The word *church*, as used by Jesus, is derived from the Greek *ekklasia*, which means the "called out" or "assembly."

Matthew 16:18
"And I tell you, you are Peter, and on this rock I will build my church, and the gates of hell shall not prevail against it."

In this creation Jesus is referencing as His church, the assembly of people who have been called out of the world by the gospel of Christ, and called out of the world for the purpose of evangelizing the unsaved multitudes. In this verse, Jesus is introducing us to the reality that His death, burial and resurrection will soon usher in a brand new dispensation. This dispensation was and is the Age of Grace, also known as the dispensation of the Church. This dispensation of Grace trusted believers on earth to spread the Word of God through preaching, personal witnessing, and reading God's ord. God established "The Church" to be a source of strength to believers. God ordained people would be saved during this age of the Grace of God by believing Jesus Christ died on Calvary for their sins and then conquered death by being raised from the dead. This dispensation featured the revelation of the death, burial and resurrected of the Messiah that God had promised for ages. Furthermore, God revealed to all mankind with the advent of this dispensation that the promised Messiah was the Son of God.

Jesus Verifies His Power

With the resurrection of Jesus from the grave, God the Father announces to all mankind that the focus of Salvation now rested on people believing Jesus Christ fulfilled God's plan of being the promised Messiah and everyone must now trust in Jesus Christ to be saved. In the book of Matthew Christ is very clear as to what incredible power God the Father is about to give Him.

Matthew 28:19–20
And Jesus came and said to them, "All authority in heaven and on earth has been given to me. Go therefore and make

disciples of all nations, baptizing them in the name of the Father and of the Son and of the Holy Spirit, teaching them to observe all that I have commanded you and behold I am with you always until the end of the world."

What a treasure of information. Look at the truths God reveals to us. The following truths are monumental.

1. Power has now passed from God the Father to God the Son. Revealed in the scripture *"All authority in heaven and on earth has been given to me."* We know that Jesus was before the creation of mankind equal in power with God the Father and the Holy Ghost. We know Jesus gave up His power when He came down to earth. Matthew 28:19–20 tells us that power has now been restored. Jesus is not superior to God the Father or the Holy Spirit but is equal to them.

2. Jesus adjusts the focus of faith mankind has to have to be saved. Now the lost must believe on Jesus Christ as the redeemer of mankind. The Old Testament Saints were allowed to be saved by believing simply in God and His promise of the coming Messiah. Now saving faith includes the new revelations God has given the world. God the Father has The Law and has ushered into time as man knows it, the Dispensation of Grace, also known as the Dispensation of the Church.

3. Jesus tells us the responsibility for evangelizing the entire world now lies with The Church and is now (for an unknown time) taken away from the Israelite nation. The advent of the Dispensation of The Church closed the practice of burnt offerings for an unknown time. And the advent of the Dispensation of the Church yields great privileges but also great responsibility to those who elect to believe Jesus died on Calvary for their sins and who ask Christ for Salvation. (*Go therefore and make disciples of all nations, baptizing them in the name of the Father*

and of the Son and of the Holy Spirit, teaching them to
observe all that I have commanded you.)

4. Jesus promises the Church He, Jesus, will be with us, in
    spirit not in flesh, always even until the end of the world.
    First, Jesus foretells that the world is going to go away.
    Second, Jesus tells us He will always be setting at the right
    hand of God the Father and standing up for us Christians
    even though we do not deserve it.

God Sends the Holy Spirit to the Church

John 14:16–17
"And I will ask the Father, and he will give you another Helper,
to be with you forever, even the Spirit of truth, whom the world
cannot receive, because it neither sees him nor knows him.
You know him, for he dwells with you and will be in you."

Jesus promises several amazing things in the above verse. He says
He, Jesus Christ, would ask God the Father to send the Holy Spirit
(a spiritual helper) and the Holy Spirit will reside in the Church.
Because the Church is the spiritual body of believers, this means
believers will live or abide with the Holy Spirit through the rest of
this life until the rapture. Throughout the millennial reign, and after-
wards throughout eternity in the new heaven, we as believers, will
walk and talk with the entire Godhead. Christ also announces that
the Holy Spirit would be only for those who believe on Him as their
Savior and Lord, meaning The Church. The rest of the world will be
unable to understand the Holy Spirit, abide with the Holy Spirit, or
communicate with the Holy Spirit because they were not born again
from death unto life.

Jesus goes on to say the work of the Holy Spirit abiding in The
Church would be to comfort believers (John 14:16), abide with
believers (John 14:16), live with believers (John 14:17) and teach
believers (John 14:26). The role of the Holy Spirit living in the hearts
of The Church, is to testify continually to us about Christ (John
15:26) and to guide us (John 16:13). Jesus promised His disciples

that the Holy Spirit would come on a special designated day and it would be a great day. Christ told the disciples that on that same day the Holy Spirit would descend, He would create the Church. Christ ushered in the Holy Spirit to live in the hearts of men.

Technically it is accurate to say the Holy Spirit came from heaven to live in the "Body of Christ." If we believe on Jesus Christ as our Savior then we are part of the Body of Christ and so the meanings are the same.

The Church Consists of Baptized Believers

Ephesians 2:22
"In Him you also are being built together for a dwelling place of God by the Spirit."

Ephesians 2:22 tells us it is by Jesus Christ (in whom) we (The Church) are built. We become the dwelling of the Holy Spirit because Jesus sent the Holy Spirit to be our helpers. Because the Church consists of baptized believers the primary difference between the Church and the Synagogue is where the Holy Spirit resides. The Holy Spirit came and descended to live in the Body of Christ (His believers). The Holy Spirit did not live in the Synagogue. The Worship of Christ is what Churches should thrive on. There are a lot of different verses in the Bible about worship, but one of my favorites is Psalm 29:2. It says, *"Ascribe to the Lord the glory due His name; worship the Lord in the splendor of holiness."*

When we arrive at Church meetings, our hearts should be prepared to worship. If there is anything that is not right in our hearts we should get it right before the Lord so that we can have a heart of worship. We should give glory where glory is due. *"For you were bought with a price: so glorify God in your body"* (1 Corinthians 6:20).

God's Word describes the Church in several terms to help us understand the depth of love Jesus has for her. None are more descriptive than when Jesus describes the Church as His "Bride." When we recognize the Church is not an organization, but a people, then we understand the imagery and symbolism. Christ uses this imagery to say we the people of God are like unto His Bride. In his letter to the saints at Ephesus, the apostle Paul describes how Christ has sacrificially and lovingly chosen the Church to be His bride.

The word Church refers to all those who have been redeemed of their sins because of their faith in Jesus. All these encompass the Body of Christ. The Church is, therefore, the spiritual extension of the Body of Christ in the world today for the purpose of exalting the Savior, evangelizing the lost, encouraging the Saints, equipping the believers, and empowering His elect to the work of Christ. God who dwells within the Church in the form of the Holy Spirit, rules over the Church through the Holy Spirit, and directs the Church toward the accomplishment of His ultimate plans.

1 Corinthians 12:13
"For in one Spirit we were all baptized into one body—Jews or Greeks, whether slaves or free—and have all been made to drink of one Spirit."

The Church is made up of all believers in Jesus Christ from the day of Pentecost (Acts chapter 2) until Christ comes back to take the Church out of this world. We should note this is a different point in the future than the second coming of Christ. The word "Church" comes from the Greek word *ekklesia* which is defined as "an assembly" or "called-out ones." The root meaning of "Church" is not that of a building, but of people. The Church is both of two definitions, each of which are related to each other but convey different revelations of the Body of Christ.

The Body of Christ

The root word of "Church" is not that of a building of wood, bricks, mortar and steel. It is of a spiritual body built on living blocks of redeemed believers. The Bible declares the Church is the Body of Christ.

Ephesians 1:22–23
"And He (God the Father) put all things under His
(God the Son) feet and gave Him as head over all
things over all things to the church, which is His
Body, the fullness of Him who fills all in all."

It is important to break down the above verse and consider exactly what God is saying to us. First of all this verse says God the Father moves all of creation under the authority of God the Son, Jesus Christ. We also know that neither God the Father, God the Son, or the Holy Spirit were created. And at the beginning of time, God's Word is clear to say each existed with equal power but different roles in the Godhead. Yet Ephesians 1 verses 22 and 23 clearly say the control over all things was not Jesus's until after His death, burial and resurrection. How can these diverging statements meet? They meet because when Jesus yielded up His glory in Heaven to come down to earth among men, He voluntarily gave up His supernatural powers. Jesus, on earth, clearly states He performed the miracles He performed, through the power of His Father. So Jesus was all powerful until He voluntarily gave up His glory in Heaven to come to earth. Then when He had completed His success in making possible the Plan of Salvation of God the Father, He was restored with the same powers He had when He created the world.

When God restored all power to Jesus, one very specific and important power God restored to Jesus, was total control of "The Church." "The Church" is not a kingdom but is a family. The Church is the family of God. We know the following differences exist between the Kingdom of God (a ruled body of people) and the Body of Christ (Meaning the spiritual gathering of Baptized believers.)

- The Bible does not present "The Church" as a kingdom and the Lord Jesus Christ as a King.
- The Bible presents "The Church" as a specific family of God with The Lord Jesus Christ as the head.
- God's Word consistently presents partakers of "The Church" to be members of the Body (family) of Christ. In a kingdom

workers are presented as slaves or workers in that Kingdom, without decision making authority. Jesus is not portrayed as the King with ruling authority. He is portrayed as Lord meaning one the members adore, praise, and serve willingly.

- It is accurate to define "The Kingdom of God" as the eternal rule of God over all of His creation. That includes mankind, earth, the atmosphere and all his creation. Psalm 103:19 tells us "The Lord has established His throne in heaven (King) and His Kingdom rules forever. Romans 13:1 tells us every authority that exists belongs to God. However, from the Spiritual viewpoint Daniel also stated in 2:44 that "The God of Heaven will set up a kingdom that will last forever without end. This is different from the physical earth which will someday be destroyed. And there is the Kingdom of God viewpoint from the future. Revelation tells us Christ has set up His spiritual reign with the Church on earth during the 1,000 year millennial reign. The Kingdom of God is broad in its application because everything belongs to God.

1 Peter 2:5
"You yourselves like living stones, are being built up a spiritual house, to be a holy priesthood, to offer spiritual sacrifices acceptable to God through Jesus Christ."

When can we as human beings become part of the spiritual house of God called the Body of Christ? The answer is when we accept Jesus Christ as our personal Savior and the Holy Spirit cleanses us of sin. When that happens, God gives us a new nature and makes us part of the family of God and the Body of Christ. The new nature still has the old body of flesh but has a new nature of redeemed spirit. It is this redeemed spirit that comprises the Church. No one can become a member of the Body of Christ (the Church) unless they go through the cross, meaning they have placed their faith in Jesus Christ as the propitiation of their sin. They believe in Jesus Christ as the Savior who will take them to heaven. When a person does this, God spiritually baptizes that one into His body

The Kingdom of God

The Kingdom of God, the Kingdom of Heaven, and the Church of our Lord Jesus Christ (also called the "Body of Christ"), are three significant but different terms we need to understand. Let's consider the difference in these three terms.

The Kingdom of God is the everlasting, universal, eternal, all-inclusive kingdom of God the Father. It goes from before the creation of the earth through eternity. It includes all of God's creation: it includes all time, and it includes all matter. It also includes all created people whether they ever believed in Jesus or not. It includes all the things in heaven including the host of angels. It includes all the things in earth, especially humanity. In Psalm 103:19 God tells us: ***"The Lord has established His throne in the heavens; and His kingdom rules over all."*** The author states everything ever created is subject to the deity and authority of God the Father. So the Kingdom of God includes the Body of Christ or "The Church." But the Body of Christ is less inclusive than The Kingdom of God. The Kingdom of God includes all who are faithful to God, who are willingly obedient to God, and are in fellowship with Him. Old Testament Saints, New Testament Saints, believers in the Seven-Year Tribulation period, and those who trust Christ in the thousand year millennial reign are all part of the Kingdom of God.

The Church, also known as "The Body of Christ," was built by Jesus Christ when He completed the plan of salvation ordained by God the Father before the beginning of time. The Church was conceived by God the Father as a new dispensation of time featuring Salvation coming to mankind through the Grace of God. It features the Holy Spirit coming to live in the heart of all who profess to believe in Jesus Christ as the resurrected Lord and ask Him for forgiveness of sin.

Ephesians 2:19–20
"So then you are no longer strangers and aliens, but you are fellow citizens with the saints and members of the household of God, built on the foundation of the apostles and prophets, Christ Jesus Himself being the cornerstone."

Because all translations of the Bible use "Kingdom of Heaven" and "Kingdom of God" interchangeably in places in the four Gospels, most Christians think they are one and the same. They will be one day, but not until the Second Coming of the Lord, Jesus Christ, when He rules the world for a thousand years on the throne of His Father. Jesus preached about four components of God's creation that is made up with people. These components were (1) All people who refused or will refuse to accept the forgiveness offered by God to them. These people will end up in the "Lake of Fire" for eternal damnation. (2) All saints in the ages prior to the age of The Church who maintained faith in God but did not have revealed to them that Jesus Christ was the promised Messiah. God counts their faith as righteousness and they joined Jesus Christ in Heaven when Jesus was raised from the dead. During that time He went down into the center of earth to redeem them. (3) All people, after the death burial and resurrection of Jesus who listen to the Word of God, and in faith believe Jesus Christ died on Calvary, was buried and rose again the third day for their sins. These people become part of "The Church" or "The Body of Christ" and will be raptured into Heaven with Christ. (4) All people who do not accept Jesus during the age of "The Church" but face death and accept death and tribulation from Satan during the seven-year tribulation in order to be followers and faithful to Jesus Christ will be taken with Christ after the battle of Armageddon.

The New Testament Church

The local Church created by Jesus is often referred to as the New Testament Church because it was not created until after the death, burial, resurrection and ascension of Jesus. "The Church" refers to all persons who believe Jesus Christ is the truth and the only way to salvation. "However, when using the "Local Church" Paul refers to the Greek word Ekklesia. *Ekklesia* is a Greek word defined as "a called-out assembly or congregation." *Ekklesia* refers to a local body of baptized believers is commonly translated as "church" in the New Testament. We should recognize the difference of "The universal body of baptized believers and the local body or congregation of believers. For example, Acts 11:26 says that "Barnabas and Saul met with the church [*ekklesia*]" in Antioch. And in 1 Corinthians 15:9 Paul says that he had persecuted the church [*ekklesia*] of God." "Ekklesia" then, is a congregation of believers whom God has called out of the world for the purpose of spreading His Gospel." The local church today needs to recognize and accept that they exist because God called each member to be part of that local body of baptized believers. God wants the local church to be different from the world. God wants the local church to always portray Jesus Christ and the teachings of Christ.

Galatians 1:1–2
"Paul, an apostle—not from men nor through man, but through Jesus Christ and God the Father, who raised him from the dead—and all the brothers who are with me."

When the Apostle Paul wrote to the "Churches at Galatia" he was not writing to all believers who had ever decided to put their trust in Jesus Christ. Paul was referring to a local body of believers in Galatia who had banded together, as instructed by God, to exalt the Savior, encourage the Believer, equip the Saints, and to evangelize the lost. In New Testament days the work of the Apostles was done to strengthen and guide the growth of the local Churches toward the goal of adding to the Kingdom of God. Yet his guidance to the local body believers at Galatia also applies to all bodies of baptized believers or local congregations. So when the Bible sends direction to one body of local believers it applies to all local believers.

What Jesus builds will be built on our faith in Jesus. Jesus said. "I will build my Church." When Jesus refers to "my Church," the Kingdom of God here on earth He is referring to the Universal Church. Yet the Universal Church is made up of a gathering of local bodies meeting and worshiping His name. Jesus did not want the work He had started to die. He wanted to energize and strengthen the work His Apostles with the help of the Holy Spirit would be successful. God's intent was to build the community of believers consisting of a multitude of local Churches of like mind and like faith. This body of baptized believers would be Jesus Christ's Church. It was to be built upon His life and His death and His sacrifice for man. In Acts 1:1–12, forty days after His resurrection, Jesus promises the Apostles that He would send the Holy Spirit to empower believers to do His work with power and authority in spite of the fact He would no longer be physically present with them.

In the New Testament Church denominations did not exist. Baptists, Methodists, Catholics, Presbyterians, and other denominations are not found in the scripture. The Churches were only distinguished by location. New Testament Churches were instructed by God to be of one mind, of one spirit, and of one baptism, and to stand for the same doctrine and same message.

Ephesians 4:4–6
"There is one body, and one Spirit, even as you are called to the one hope that belongs to your call; One Lord, one faith, one baptism, One God and Father of all, who is above all, and through all, and in all."

The fact that we have denominations today says someone has not interpreted the scripture, with relation to doctrine, correctly. God wants every local Church to be of exactly the same mind, same doctrine, same practices, and the same mission. Protestant Churches, in general, trend to believe in salvation by grace through faith, not of works. Nevertheless they differ in many aspects of biblical teaching. They do not cooperate with each other as Christ intended His Church to cooperate. Satan has led congregations to be independent, depending on their own interpretation of scripture rather than lean on the Holy Spirit.

Acts 1:4–8
And while staying with them he ordered them not to depart from Jerusalem, but to wait for the promise of the Father, which, he said, "you heard from me; for John baptized with water, but you will be baptized with the Holy Spirit not

many days from now. So when they had come together, they asked him, "Lord, will you at this time restore the kingdom to Israel?" He said to them, "It is not for you to know times or seasons that the Father has fixed by his own authority. But you will receive power when the Holy Spirit has come upon you, and you will be my witnesses in Jerusalem and in all Judea and Samaria, and to the end of the earth."

In verse 3 Jesus commands the Apostles to wait for the coming of the Holy Spirit and the ushering in of the Church age. In verse 8, Jesus told the disciples *"But you will receive power when the Holy Spirit has come upon you, and you will be my witnesses in Jerusalem and in all Judea and Samaria, and to the end of the earth."* Jesus told His disciples power that would enable them to evangelize the world would come to reign in their hearts. The power within the Church is the Holy Spirit. In the book of Mark we are told that, after Jesus ascended into heaven, His apostles "went out and preached everywhere," and the Church grew and prospered.

Jesus promised His disciples and all Christians that His Church would not perish. That is a comforting promise of our Savior as we look around at the division and lack of faithfulness within our denominations and the onslaught of opposition nonbelievers. Christ's promise that *"the gates of Hades shall not prevail"* against His Church is a divine guarantee that we can fight the good fight and be faithful to our Lord.

What is the purpose of the Church?

Jesus Christ created the Church to enable Christians to do His work after He ascended into heaven. Many Christians today believe the Church was created for their benefit so they would have a place to worship and witness. While not untrue this is a narrow view of the Church. A full answer to what is imbedded in the question; what was the purpose of Christ. Jesus Christ came to earth for the purpose of completing the plan of salvation that man might be saved. The Church is the spiritual extension of the body of Christ in the world today. The purpose of the Church is therefore to complete the work of Christ. The plan of salvation is already prepared, but the presentation of that plan to mankind is not complete. Therefore we find the true purpose of the Church is to glorify God and advance His kingdom. In business firms today we often find firms creating a mission statement so they will never get in front of themselves without a reminder of why they are created and how they are to conduct themselves. Ephesians 4:14 gives us a mission statement of the New Testament Church.

Ephesians 4:14
"So that we may no longer be children, tossed to and fro by the waves and carried about by every wind of doctrine, by human cunning, by craftiness in deceitful schemes."

The New Testament Church adopted the purpose of the Apostles. Their mission was to evangelize the world and spread the story of the resurrection of our Lord. In addition the Church was created to provide fellowship of Christians and to enable worship services in which God the Father, God the Holy Spirit, and God the Son would be exalted. The purpose of the Church is captured in the four steps of (1) exalt the Savior, (2) evangelize the lost, (3) encourage the believer, and (4) equip the saints to do the work of Christ. The Church is to teach biblical doctrine so we can be grounded in our faith.

Acts 2:42
"And they devoted themselves to the apostles' teaching and the fellowship, to the breaking of bread, and the prayers."

The Church is to be a place of fellowship, where Christians can enjoy the companionship of one another in brotherly love. Christians are supposed to prefer the company of each other to that of anyone else in the world because of our common bond in the love of Jesus Christ. The local Church, which is the assembling of our selves together, enables that fellowship to blossom.

Romans 12:10
"Love one another with brotherly affection,
outdo one another is showing honor."

Jesus understands man's propensity to sin and to be weak in the flesh. He understood we would need strength and encouragement as well as chastisement for our mistakes. Jesus sent the Holy Spirit to provide our needs but he also gave us the Church as a medium whereby Christians can and should encourage each other, chastise each other, and strengthen each other, always in the love of our Lord.

Romans 15:14
"I myself am satisfied about you, my brothers, that
you yourselves are full of goodness, filled with all
knowledge and able to instruct one another."

Ephesians 4:32
"Be kind to one another, tenderhearted, forgiving
one another, as God in Christ forgave you."

The Church is to be a place that promotes prayer, teaches prayer, and practices prayer. Prayer is a both a private communication with God and a public communication with God. God instructed us to pray and He uses His Church to encourage our prayer life. We are specifically instructed, as a member of the "Body of Christ" we will love one another. Therefore we are to be kind to each other, we are to treat each other in love, willing to be sacrificial in our loving. We must recognize that each person has different weaknesses and we are to be slow to chastise but quick to forgive. This is because God first, before we were a member of the Body of Christ, forgave our sins.

Philippians 4:6-7
"Do not be anxious about anything, but in everything by prayer
and supplication with thanksgiving let your requests be, And the
peace of God, which surpasses all understanding, will guard your
hearts and your minds in Christ Jesus" made known to God.

Jesus specifically empowered the Church to coat every day's activities with prayer. God wants every aspect of the Christian life to be communicated with God. God is interested in every aspect of what we do, what we think, and what we desire. God wants to hear our praise of Him and our thanks for His guidance of our life. He even wants to hear about our confusions regarding Him. The local church is intended to facilitate this lifestyle.

In 1 Corinthians God also outlines a specific remembrance, He wants the local Church to practice. This is the remembrance of the Lord's Prayer. This remembrance is more than a request. It is a command to the local body of Baptized Believers.

1 Corinthians 11:23–26

"For I received from the Lord what I also delivered to you, that the Lord Jesus on the night when He was betrayed took bread, and when He had given thanks, He broke it, and said, "This is my body, which is for you. Do this in remembrance of me. In the same way also He took the cup, after supper, saying, "This cup is the new covenant in my blood. Do this, as often as you drink it, in remembrance of me." For as often as you eat this bread and drink the cup, you proclaim the Lord's death until He comes."

The Roman Catholic Church, and other select religious groups, interprets the words of Christ in 1 Corinthians 11 to be a literal interpretation. They believe that in eating the bread, the apostles were actually, in essence, eating the body of Christ. Because of this practice and this belief; the pagan world claimed Christians were partaking in cannibalism through taking the Lord's Supper. They believed all Christians were actually eating of the body of Christ. The Roman Catholic Church, and all who do not understand the scripture, should be brought to recognize what Jesus meant when He said, "This is my body."

First we must understand the teaching practices of Christ. He often used symbolic references to help his listeners understand. For instance Christ said, "I am the Vine" and "I am the door" as well as saying "I am the bread."

John 15:1
"I am the true vine, and My Father is the vinedresser."

Jesus did not teach that He was a vine. He taught that the reality of His existence might be compared to that of the true vine and the vinedresser. This was an effort to help mankind understand His teachings. The same is true when He said "I am the bread." He meant I am represented in this event by the bread. And he did not teach that God the Father was a vine keeper. He taught that like the vine has many branches so does the kingdom of God and to understand the kingdom of God one might make the association to that of a vine with its many branches. In this teaching Christ's teaching of the vine was symbolic not literal.

John 10:9
"I am the door. If anyone enters by Me, he will be saved, and will go in and out and find pasture."

Likewise in the book of John Jesus taught us symbolically that we could visualize a door through which man must enter to get into a room. Likewise, Jesus taught He was not a literal door but was symbolically a door through which everyone must enter to experience salvation and eternal life. This is symbolic teaching. Christ did not intend for anyone to take this reference as literal and the listeners did not take it literal.

What is a Church Ordinance?

Our Lord and Savior Jesus Christ commanded his followers to continue two specific practices He initiated and ordained while on earth. These two commands were the Lord's Supper and Baptism. Jesus commanded believers to continue these two activities until He comes and takes the Church with Him to heaven. The word "ordinance" is derived from Latin. It means "that which is ordered or commanded." Jesus commanded His believers to continue these practices through the local church and they are therefore called Church ordinances. These two ordinances are always in remembrance of great truths God does not want His people to forget.

The ordinances of the Lord's Supper and Baptism have no saving power. They are not necessary for salvation and yet their importance cannot be overstated. They were direct commands from our Lord. Nonbelievers are not eligible to participate in these two ordinances because both are specifically directed at followers of Christ. How can nonbelievers do something in remembrance of something they do not believe and have never experienced? Nonbelievers are not eligible to be part of the "Body of Christ." They may very well be legal members of a local Church but nonbelievers are not spiritual members of the local church. This is because the first requirement of membership is asking Jesus to save our souls and forgive our sins. They are, therefore, not eligible to participate in the ordinance.

All Churches and all denominations do not agree that Church ordinances of Baptism and the Lord's Supper are symbolic and should be practiced in remembrance of what our Savior did. Some believe the ordinances themselves are used and are required by God to convey forgiveness of sin and saving power. Churches and denominations that believe Baptism and the Lord's Supper convey God's Grace toward forgiveness of sin recognize these two commands of God as Sacraments not as Ordinances.

What is a Sacrament?

Roman Catholics and other certain religious groups including members of several denominations believe certain rituals of worship they call sacraments, are more than just symbolic or reminders of the commands of our Lord. These Churches interpret the scripture as instructing that in partaking of these services, God actually conveys forgiveness of sin. They believe the sacraments, in and of themselves, are used by God as a means to communicate His grace to faithful recipients. The term sacrament is derived from the Latin word sacramentum, meaning "a consecrated thing or act." Catholics have seven Sacraments which are the following: (1) Baptism, (2) The Eucharist (Communion), (3) Matrimony, (4) Holy Orders, (5) Confirmation or Chrismation, (6) Penance and Reconciliation, and (7) Anointing of the sick. Protestant denominations almost universally recognize only two rituals of worship as being commanded by Jesus Christ for the Church to observe. They are Baptism and Communion which is more often simply called observance of the Lord's Supper.

What is Baptism?

Baptism is the immersion, by the proper authority, of a believer in Christ, in the name of the Father, and of the Son, and of the Holy Spirit. Immersion means to submerge a believer under water and therefore represent the burial of the old life of Godlessness and when brought up out of the water it represents resurrection to a new life of love for our Savior.

Acts 2:41–43
"So those who received his word were baptized, and there were added that day about three thousand souls. And they devoted themselves to the apostles' teaching and the fellowship, to the breaking of bread and the prayers. And awe came upon every soul, and many wonders and signs were being done through the apostles."

The Scripture gives us examples of people being saved, becoming believers in Jesus Christ and following the command of Jesus to be baptized. In every instance in the Scripture, baptism is by immersion. It always signifies the death of the old sinful self, the burial of that self to sin, and the resurrection of that new life to Jesus Christ.

Acts 10:47–48
"Can anyone withhold water for baptizing these people, who have received the Holy Spirit just as we have?" And he commanded them to be baptized in the name of Jesus Christ. Then they asked him to remain for some days."

When people are baptized it should always be because they are following the command of Christ after having accepted Jesus Christ. The Bible does not record any act of baptism in order to be saved. The author of Acts tells us these who are being considered for baptism have (already) received the Holy Spirit. Therefore, He commanded them to be baptized in the name of Jesus Christ. Baptism is and was an act of obedience to the Lord and Savior as part of our commitment to follow Jesus. It is the ongoing commitment we make to Jesus after we are saved. This is only the first of a lifetime of such commitments.

Three methods of baptism are used in Christian churches today. They are (1) Immersion, this method involves completely submerging the body in water. (2) Effusion, this method involves pouring of water on the body. And (3) Aspersion, this method involves sprinkling water on the body. Evangelical Christians are divided on the question of which method is the proper forms of baptism. However, the Bible teaches that Jesus outlined for us the only acceptable method of Baptism when He was baptized by immersion. The word baptizo in Greek, translated "baptize" in the New Testaments, meant to "dip" or "immerse." Romans 6:3, 4 outlines the correct method of Baptism is through Immersion.

Romans 6:3–4
"Do you not know that all of us who have been baptized into Christ Jesus were baptized into his death? We were buried therefore with him by baptism into death, in order that, just as Christ was raised from the dead by the glory of the Father, we too might walk in newness of life."

Baptism is specifically stated in the New Testament to represent the Christian's spiritual union with Christ in His death, burial and resurrection. The method used by the early Church in the first few centuries was immersion. Clearly immersion is the biblical method and preferred method of Baptism because it best portrayed the death burial and resurrection of Jesus.

Colossians 2:12–13
"Having been buried with him in baptism, in which you were also raised with him through faith in the powerful working of God, who raised him from the dead. And you, who were dead in your trespasses and the uncircumcision of your flesh, God made alive together with him, having forgiven us all our trespasses."

The Bible tells us baptism is an act Jesus Christ commands the saved to do as part of confessing their sins to the world. This is very different than an act we must do in order to be saved. We are saved by the grace of God through our faith in Christ Jesus. Then follow His command to use the ritual of baptism to confess to the world what has transacted in our life. The immersion into the water signifies the death of our old sin nature and the resurrection out of the water signifies that as Christ was resurrected from the dead so we also are resurrected spiritually to a new creation in our Lord. It signifies the new life, but it does not have any part of the act of salvation.

Jesus Elected to Be Baptized

Matthew 3:13–16
"Then Jesus came from Galilee to the Jordan to John, to be baptized by him. John would have prevented him, saying, "I need to be baptized by you, and do you come to me?" But Jesus answered him, "Let it be so now, for thus it is fitting for us to fulfill all righteousness." Then he consented. And when Jesus was baptized, immediately he went up from the water, and behold, the heavens were opened to him, and he saw the Spirit of God descending like a dove and coming to rest on him."

The purpose and importance of Baptism is evidenced in the baptism of Jesus by John the Baptist. The importance of baptism was emphasized by Jesus. Jesus demands believers confess publicly of their decision to follow the lifestyle of Jesus. Baptism is that first step. Jesus, who knew no sin, felt it necessary that He set an example toward that commitment. He was about to start His ministry that would end in His death on Calvary. Jesus certainly did not need to be baptized to evidence His commitment to God but He submitted himself as an example to those who would become believers.

Who May Be Baptized?

Many Churches, and many Christians, differ in Scripture interpretation over who can be baptized. The primary controversy lies in the baptism of infants. The issue has to do with the meaning of the act of baptism. If it is a Sacrament, that has something to do with the act of Salvation, then some credence to baptizing infants in hopes of getting them to heaven can be established. However God's Word establishes that we cannot perform any act that saves others. We can only give our heart to God and ask God for His forgiveness of our sin. Only those who have repented of their sins, turned their hearts to God and trusted in Jesus Christ as their only way to heaven can be baptized. For a person to be saved they must make an active decision to commit their lives to the Lord. They must be sorry they have sinned and deep in their heart desire to be righteous and pleasing to God. Infants do not have the capacity to be sorry they have sinned. Infants do not have the capacity to make an active decision of the heart to follow Jesus Christ. The very definition of what Baptism is excludes infant baptism.

Why Be Baptized?

Jesus commands us to be baptized after we are saved in order to make a public declaration of our faith in Him. It symbolizes the cleansing from sin which occurred when we were saved. We become a new member of the Body of Christ, the universal Church, when we have received scriptural baptism. Therefore, baptism is also recognized as the door to Church membership into a local body of baptized believers. The reason for baptism and what it signifies is also a primary reason that immersion rather than sprinkling or pouring on water is how baptism should be administered. When a new born child of God is immersed into the water it is a picture of the death of Jesus Christ who was buried in the grave for our sins. When that one is raised up out of the water it is a picture of Christ's victory over death and His having paid the price of our sins throughout eternity.

Romans 6:3–5
"Do you not know that all of us who have been baptized into Christ Jesus were baptized into his death? We were buried therefore with him by baptism into death, in order that, just as Christ was raised from the dead by the glory of the Father, we too might walk in newness of life. For if we have been united with Him in a death like His, we shall certainly be united with Him in a resurrection like His."

Baptism, according to God's Word, is not only a picture of the death, burial and resurrection of our Lord and Savior; it also symbolizes His coming again to take us to heaven that is promised in the Scripture. Therefore, when a person decides to accept Jesus Christ as Savior, they are commanded by God to confess their sins in public and be baptized. In this way they make a public statement that they have had a change come into their life. It says that God accomplished change.

Baptism was an existing practice long before John the Baptist baptized people as a forerunner to the coming of Jesus. However, it developed within the religion of Judaism, and was used by John the Baptist as a ritual to show repentance in which the water symbolized cleansing. Jesus continued this practice, and after his death and resurrection his disciples continued to use it.

Acts 10:47–48
"Can anyone withhold water for baptizing these people, who have received the Holy Spirit just as we have?" And he commanded them to be baptized in the name of Jesus Christ. Then they asked him to remain for some days.

Ordnance of the Lord's Supper

The second ordinance command of God to the Church is the observance of the Lord's Supper, also known as communion.

Believers in Jesus are commanded to periodically participate in the Lord's Supper in remembrance of the price Jesus paid for our sins.

1 Corinthians 11: 23–26

For I received from the Lord what I also delivered to you, that the Lord Jesus on the night when he was betrayed took bread, and when he had given thanks, he broke it, and said, "This is my body, which is for you. Do this in remembrance of me." In the same way also he took the cup, after supper, saying, "This cup is the new covenant in my blood. Do this, as often as you drink it, in remembrance of me." For as often as you eat this bread and drink the cup, you proclaim the Lord's death until he comes."

The Lord's Supper is a memorial service, instituted by Jesus before His death on the cross. He commanded His Church to observe this service in memory of His death until He comes back to earth again. It was practiced by the early Church. Acts records other instances of the early Church practicing the Lord's Supper. The Lord's Supper is an ordinance of the Church and is a remembrance of the death of our Lord Jesus Christ. Since the Lord's Supper is an ordinance of the Church it is important that we recognize some truths associated with its observation. It is intended only for believers.

How is the Lord's Supper to be administered?

This ordinance of the Church is to be administered as close to biblical instructions as possible. The night Jesus instituted the Lord's Supper He observed the Feast of the Passover. Jesus and His Disciples observed Old Testament practices, related to the Passover. These practices were changed to signify the approaching death, burial and resurrection of our Lord and Savior. We are commanded to eat unleavened bread to represent the broken body of Jesus on the Cross, and to drink fruit of the vine to represent His Blood shed for our sins. Jesus tells us the observance of this ordinance reminds of His sacrifice for our sins until He returns in glory.

1 Corinthians 10:16–17
"The cup of blessing that we bless; is it not a
participation in the blood of Christ? The bread that we
break, is it not a participation in the body of Christ?
Because there is one bread, we who are many are
one body, for we all partake of the one bread."

Who may partake of the Lord's Supper?

If a person is not part of the "The Church" also known as "The Body of Christ" they should not partake of the Lord's Supper. A person can't remember the Lord and what He has done through His death if they have never received His saving power. The Lord's Supper is also called the Eucharist which is from the Greek word eucharisteo which means to give thanks or to bless. Eucharist is a very beautiful and appropriate name for this ordinance since it is only for the individual who can genuinely give thanks for the sacrificial death of Jesus Christ. The Lord's Supper is for all believers if they are partaking of it for the purpose of remembering what Christ has done for us. Eucharist or Communion is closed to unbelievers. This ordinance was given to the "The Body of Christ," not to a particular local body of believers or denomination.

Matthew 26:26–29
Now, as they were eating, Jesus took bread, and after
blessing it broke it and gave it to the disciples, and said,
"Take, eat; this is my body." And he took a cup, and when
he had given thanks He gave it to them, saying, "Drink of
it, all of you, for this is my blood of the covenant, which is
poured out for many for the forgiveness of sins. I tell you I
will not drink again of this fruit of the vine until that day
when I drink it new with you in my Father's kingdom."

Literal or Symbolic

The wording of Jesus as He spoke to His disciples in reference to the bread and the cup has been a source of controversy and doctrinal difference between denominations for the last one thousand or more years. Was Jesus speaking literally when He said; "This is my body" and "This is my blood?" Two beliefs have emerged over the years regarding the words of Christ. One is that Jesus was speaking literally and meant the bread was actually His body and the wine was His blood. Others who contend Christ was speaking figuratively challenge this understanding. They contend that Jesus meant the bread was to be a reminder of His body and the wine was to be a reminder of His blood through the centuries to come. Let's first look at the two different views.

Transubstantiation

Roman Catholics believe the wine and bread used in communion actually change and become "in substance," part of the body of Christ. The term that describes this process is "transubstantiation." Catholic doctrine states that the bread appears to be bread and the wine appears to be wine, not the actual body of Jesus, but what appears to be bread and wine is not really bread and wine but has been substantively changed to be the body of Christ. They explain that although it still looks like bread and wine it has in substance or in reality been changed.

On November 28, 1518, Martin Luther appealed to the Pope, Head of the Catholic Church, for a general council to resolve differences in theology Protestants were raising regarding the interpretation of the Bible by the Catholic Church. This council was held at a city named Trent. The Catholic Church had demanded the council take place in Rome. However Martin Luther and his followers felt it should be held in Germany. The "Council of Trent" defined the Church interpretation of scripture regarding the bread and wine spoken of by Jesus Christ. Their statement that continues to this day as the official position of the Catholic Church is as follows: "Because Christ our Redeemer said that it was truly his body that he was offering under the species of bread, it has always been the conviction of the Church of God, and this holy Council now declares again, that by the consecration of the bread and wine there takes place a change of the whole substance of the bread into the substance of the body of Christ our Lord and of the whole substance of the wine into the substance of his blood. This change the holy Catholic Church has fittingly and properly called transubstantiation."

The Roman Catholic Church, therefore, teaches that once an ordained priest blesses the bread of the Lord's Supper, it is transformed into the actual flesh of Christ, although it retains the appearance, odor, and taste of bread; and when he blesses the wine, it is transformed into the actual blood of Christ, although it retains the appearance, odor, and taste of wine. The question that lingers over mankind for these centuries is whether this interpretation of the Catholic Church is scriptural. The Catholic Church refers to John 6:32–58, Matthew 26:26, Luke 22:17–23 and 1 Corinthians 11:24–25. The primary passage of scripture used to justify the belief of transubstantiation is John 6:53–57.

John 6:53–57
So Jesus said to them, "Truly, truly, I say to you, unless you eat the flesh of the Son of Man and drink his blood, you have no life in you. Whoever feeds on my flesh and drinks my blood has eternal life, and I will raise him up on the last day. For my flesh is true food, and my blood is true drink. Whoever feeds on my flesh and drinks my blood abides in me, and I in him. As the living Father sent me, and I live because of the Father, so whoever feeds on me, he also will live because of me."

Based on a surface interpretation of the above verse one would have to agree with Catholics that the bread does become part of the body of Christ and the wine becomes part of the blood of Christ. We must accept the Word of God as inerrant and true and accept it as it is. Yet we must also research to the point of understanding the meaning of the verse. Verses before and after a statement, give us a better intent of the verse and therefore a more thorough understanding.

Symbolic Interpretation

Jesus was well aware that even his disciples had substantial difficulty understanding what He had said as recorded for us in John

6. They reasoned together about how it could be that the bread would really become the body of Christ and the wine the blood. Jesus explained to His disciples, and thus to us, that when He spoke regarding the bread and the wine he was speaking about the spirit of man not the flesh. Jesus, seeing their consternation clarified the subject in John 6:63.

John 6:63
"It is the Spirit who gives life; the flesh is no help at all. The words that I speak to you are spirit, and life."

He told His disciples that the flesh was not lasting but the spirit would last. In telling His disciples that He also told us who would follow that what matters is who we believe in, not what we physically see or touch. Jesus wanted the disciples to remember His sacrifice in their heart and spiritually reunite with the Lord every time they partook of the Lord's Supper. He declared to them that the eating of the bread and drinking of the cup did not save them and had no part in the saving power. He proclaimed the entire salvation process is and was a spiritual rebirth, partaking of the Lords Supper is a physical event showing faith in the spiritual rebirth that took place between God and Man. God further enforces that by declaring the Lord's Supper to be a memorial in Luke 22:19 and 1 Corinthians 11:24–25.

Luke 22:19
"And He took bread, and when He had given thanks He broke it, and gave it to them, saying, 'This is My body which is given for you; do this in remembrance of Me."

1 Corinthians 11:24–25
"And when he had given thanks, he broke it, and said, "This is my body, which is for you. Do this in remembrance of me." In the same way also he took the cup, after supper, saying, "This cup is the new covenant in my blood. Do this, as often as you drink it, in remembrance of me."

Clearly Jesus is communicating to The Church, meaning all New Testament Saints, that the Lord's Supper is a spiritual remembrance of what He did for us on Calvary. When He says, this do in remembrance, that is totally opposite of the Catholic understanding of the bread and the wine being actually partaking of the body of Christ and it having some portion of saving power within itself. How can we equate the two views? To do so we have to go back to the words Jesus said "This is my body" and "This is my blood." Jesus did not mean the bread and the wine actually became his spiritual body.

Jesus liked to teach in parables. For example, Jesus referred to Himself as the Vine, and the Door, as well as the Bread.

John 15:1
"I am the true vine, and My Father is the vinedresser."

John 10:9
"I am the door. If anyone enters by Me, he will be saved, and will go in and out and find pasture."

In these verses, Jesus did not teach that He actually became a vine or that He actually became a door. He was comparing His ministry to be similar to some of the traits of a vine in that the vine has many branches all of which feed from the trunk. Christ was explaining His Kingdom has many branches that all feed from His strength and truth and grace. He explained He was not a door but that the door represented a narrow opening through which those who would enter must pass through. Christ was explaining that He, Jesus Christ was the one who every person must pass through to enter the Kingdom of God. He was teaching symbolic lessons so his hearers could understand the bigger truth. Likewise Jesus was teaching a symbolic lesson when He said "This bread is my body" and "This wine is my blood." In the same statement Jesus states the cup or the holder of the wine is a new covenant.

Luke 22:20
"Likewise the cup after they had eaten, saying, "This cup that is poured out for you, is the new covenant in My blood."

People who believe on the water being blood and the bread being Christ's body are so intent on a literal interpretation of scripture they miss the fact Jesus was teaching a symbolic lesson not a literal one. However the greatest reason transubstantiation stands in opposition to true understanding of scripture is that transubstantiation teaches the partaking of the bread and the wine has a saving aspect and actually becomes part of the believers continued salvation. That is in conflict with scripture that teaches the death, burial and resurrection of our Lord was done once and that once was sufficient for all time to come.

Hebrews 10:10
"And by that will we have been sanctified through the offering of the body of Jesus Christ once for all."

God's Word tells us Jesus, unlike the high priests who had to sacrifice first for their own sins and then for the sins of the people, only needed to sacrifice once for the sins of all mankind. These scriptures totally eliminate the possibility that transubstantiation can have any saving power. And the clarification of Jesus firmly establishes for all time to come that the Lord's Supper is done in remembrance of Him and only in remembrance of Him.

Should every member participate?

Every member of the Lord's Kingdom should keep themselves in such a frame of mind that they can worship God and remember the price Jesus paid for our sins as they observe the Lord's Supper. God tells us we are to examine ourselves before we partake of the supper because whosoever partakes unworthily eats and drinks to their own damnation. Does this mean that if we come to the Lord's Table with any sin we are unworthy to partake? No, man cannot come to the Lord's Table without sin. The key to this passage of Scripture is in verse 26 which outlines the reason we partake of the Lord's Supper. We do so to show, or demonstrate, and to remember the Lord's death until He comes again. The word wherefore clearly says that what follows relates to what was before. So whosoever shall eat of this bread and drink of this cup unworthily, relates to why they are partaking of the Lord's Supper. The scripture tells us to examine ourselves and determine if we are partaking of the Lord's Supper because we know Jesus Christ as our Savior and we wish to honor our Lord and praise Him for His sacrifice on Calvary. If we partake of the Lord's Supper just because others are doing it and we do not want to stand out we displease our Lord. If we partake without thinking, mindlessly we displease our Lord. If we partake because we are hungry we displease our Lord.

1 Corinthians 11:26–29
"For as often as you eat this bread and drink the cup, you proclaim the Lord's death until he comes. Whoever, therefore, eats the bread or drinks the cup of the Lord in an unworthy manner will be guilty concerning the body and blood of the Lord. Let a person examine himself, then, and so eat of the bread and drink of the cup. For anyone who eats and drinks without discerning the body eats and drinks judgment on Himself."

The Lord's Supper was instituted the day before the crucifixion, the night on which Jesus was betrayed. He was in the upper room with His disciples, and the Passover celebration had begun. The Lord's Supper was instituted in the midst of the celebration of the Passover. That is very appropriate because both of them are a memorial. Passover was a memorial of God's physical deliverance of His children from their bondage in Egypt through the blood of the lamb. The Lord's Supper is a memorial of the spiritual deliverance of God's people from their bondage to sin and death. That deliverance is through the blood of the Lamb, the Lord Jesus Christ.

Both the Passover and the Lord's Supper are in memory of an event that has happened. Both of them are in anticipation of an event that is yet to come. Passover anticipated the coming of the Lamb, the true Passover Lamb who would shed His blood in order to make atonement for God's chosen people. The New Testament tells us Jesus Christ is that sacrificial lamb.

1 Corinthians 5:7
"Cleanse out the old leaven, that you may be a new lump, as you really are unleavened. For Christ, our Passover lamb, has been sacrificed."

What the Passover lamb was to Israel, Jesus Christ is to Christians. The death of the Passover lamb and the application of its blood to the door posts of the home provided a covering whereby the inhabitants of that home were protected from the just judgment of God and entered into God's salvation. Just as the Passover Lamb died for Israel, Christ died for us and in so doing His death was a substitute for ours.

CHAPTER NINETEEN

The Doctrine of Life after Death
What happens to mankind after physical death?

Doctrine of Life after Death

Is death the end of man's existence, or will we be raised from the dead to face judgment? Will we be granted eternal rewards and privileges of heaven or endure the torments of the Lake of Fire also known as Hell? Some people deny life after death. Oriental religions teach reincarnation. Does man have a spirit that can achieve immortality? What awaits us? Is this life the end of everything or is resurrection the ultimate reward or eternal punishment of our fate? This is a question frequently asked in today's world. Throughout history people have asked this question. We can go back to what many consider the oldest book in the Bible and find Job asking the same question.

Job 14:14
"If a man dies, shall he live again? All the days of my service I will wait, till my renewal should come."

Job first asked the question of God *"Will I live again?"* God answered Job's question by assuring him that Job had an appointed time to live here on earth and an appointed time to die a physical death. God then told Job the answer he, as well as all mankind, seeks. God said that Job would be changed and have eternal life. We see this promise in Job's response, *"All the days of appointed time will I wait until my change comes."* This is the same consistent message God continues to give to people of all time including those who live today. However many refuse to believe God's Word or they twist God's Word to be a more comfortable understanding that does not cause them concern. In the New Testament, many scriptures assure us of life after death and after that we will experience judgment.

Hebrews 9:27
And just as it is appointed for man to die once, and after that comes judgment.

Some simply deny life after death.

First-century Sadducees claimed man is wholly material, having no immortal spirit, so at death he simply ceases to exist. Modern materialists and Humanists teach likewise. They say we evolved by natural forces from animals, so like the animals, we simply cease to exist at death. In our world a minority of people proclaim themselves to be atheists. They deny God exists, choose to believe creation is by evolution and therefore, of course, deny the existence of any form of afterlife.

Others believe in Reincarnation.

Hinduism, other Oriental religions, and the New Age Movement, teach that, after death, we simply are reborn in a different form, higher or lower, depending on how we lived. Reincarnation is a religious belief that people are given a soul soon after they are born and that soul is never destroyed. Followers of reincarnation believe that when our physical body dies our soul is reborn in a different physical body. This is sometimes called transmigration. It is the major religious doctrine in many of the world religions such as Jainism, Hinduism, Buddhism and Sikhism. Reincarnation was taught by historic Greek citizens such as Socrates and Plato. It is also prominent in Australia, East Asia, Siberia, and South America.

Still others say only the righteous will exist after Death.

Some claim the wicked simply perish, but the righteous go to heaven. What does God's Word say in reference to Life after Death? God's Word tells us everyone that ever lived or ever will live, will experience life after death. Therefore, our hope for life after death rests solely in the hands of our Savior and Lord.

Jesus's Resurrection Proves Life after Death Is Possible

1 Corinthians 15:12–13
"Now if Christ is proclaimed as raised from the dead,
how can some of you say that there is no resurrection
of the dead? But if there is no resurrection of the
dead, then not even Christ has been raised."

Every shred of Christian faith is based on the resurrection of Christ. The resurrection of Christ is true to the point that, if Christ's resurrection is false, the Christian faith is also false.

1 Corinthians 15:14
"And if Christ has not been raised, then our
preaching is in vain and your faith is in vain."

2 Corinthians 4:14
"Knowing that He who raised the Lord Jesus, will raise us
also with Jesus, and bring us with you into His presence."

Paul tells us the resurrection of Jesus is the prototype of the resurrection from death of all who believe in Jesus Christ. Jesus's resurrection and our resurrection are eternally connected. So that we might understand and believe, God recorded for us the experience of a Rich Man and Lazarus, both of whom died and what subsequently happened to them.

Luke 16:19–23
"There was a rich man who was clothed in purple and fine linen
and who feasted sumptuously every day. And at his gate was laid
a poor man named Lazarus, covered with sores, who desired to
be fed with what fell from the rich man's table. Moreover, even
the dogs came and licked his sores. The poor man died and was
carried by the angels to Abraham's side. The rich man also died
and was buried, and in Hades, being in torment, he lifted up
his eyes and saw Abraham far off and Lazarus at his side."

We have heard for most of our "Church" years the story of the rich man and Lazarus. Many Christians consider this story to be a parable or just a story to identify a spiritual truth. Did Christ intend for us to interpret the story as an event trying to teach a spiritual truth or does Christ intend for us to accept this happening as real and not just a teaching point used to address some other teaching? Those who teach the story of the rich man and Lazarus as a parable should perhaps review the following points:

- First and very significant, the story is never called a parable. In other stories that Christ used to teach a point He specifically called them parables. Consider the example Christ set in Luke 8:4: ***And when a great crowd was gathering and people from town after town came to him, he said in a parable.*** "Jesus often taught in parables because that is the way it would be most easy to believe. Christ does not tell us the story of the rich man and Lazarus is a parable. We must accept the Word of God as it reads without putting our own interpretation into it. We have to accept the story as truth and as being an actual occurrence.

- Second, the story of the rich man and Lazarus uses the actual name of a person. Other parables did not use real names.

- The third reason the story of the rich man and Lazarus is not a parable, but is true, is the story is not based on an earthly event. It is based on an event that happened outside of man's world of reality. Parables are based on earthly events people can understand to make the teaching point more clear.

- Jesus used this event to teach that after death the unrighteous are eternally separated from God. They know why they are separated from God and they remember their rejection of the Gospel. They are in torment, and their condition cannot be remedied. Most people think that in Luke 16:19–31; Jesus clearly taught the existence of heaven and Hell. Actually in this scripture Christ taught the existence of a holding place created by God for those who died prior to the resurrection of Christ. This place is named Hades. It has two different compartments. One is the upper department and it is called Abraham's Bosom. The other is the lower compartment and it is called "The Abyss" or Tartarus.

Luke 16:24–31

"And he called out, 'Father Abraham, have mercy on me, and send Lazarus to dip the end of his finger in water and cool my tongue, for I am in anguish in this flame. But Abraham said, 'Child, remember that you in your lifetime received your good things, and Lazarus in like manner bad things; but now he is comforted here, and you are in anguish. And besides all this, between us and you a great chasm has been fixed, in order that those who would pass from here to you may not be able, and none may cross from there to us.' And he said, 'Then I beg you, father, to send him to my father's house—for I have five brothers—so that he may warn them, lest they also come into this place of torment.' But Abraham said, 'They have Moses and the Prophets; let them hear them.' And he said, 'No, father Abraham, but if someone goes to them from the dead, they will repent.' He said to him, 'If they do not hear Moses and the Prophets, neither will they be convinced if someone should rise from the dead."

The Bible reveals to us several differing groups of people who have to be accounted for after physical death on earth. These groups exist because of their faith and because of the differing ways God related to people over the centuries of existence. Prior to the death, burial and resurrection of Jesus Christ God related His plan of salvation to people different than after Christ's resurrection. All human beings died and something happens to their souls after death. Let's consider these differences.

We know untold millions of people were born, lived and died from the original creation of Adam through the time that Jesus died on the Cross and was resurrected from the grave. The Bible tells us some small sampling of these people placed their trust of their afterlife in God's promise of a coming Messiah who would save them from their sins. We face the question of what happened to these people after they died. God's Word answers this question. Their bodies are buried somewhere and return to dust. Their souls or spirit went to a place God created called Abraham's Bosom. Abrahams Bosom is the upper part of a much larger place called Hades. Abraham's Bosom is where the spirit of this sampling of people rested awaiting the Messiah to come and take them to the Throne of God. These people trusted on God the Father to send a Messiah who would save them from their sins. God revealed to them that He would send a Messiah who would pay the price of their sins if they trusted God to redeem them. God did not reveal to them that the Messiah would be Jesus Christ the Son of God. Yet they were saved the same way all others are saved and that is through their faith in God's promise of the coming Messiah and God's Grace to accept them in His Kingdom of redeemed. Right after Jesus was resurrected from the dead He went down into Abraham's Bosom and took these people home with Him around the Throne of God.

1. Second, we must account for the massive millions of people who were born beginning with Adam through the resurrection of Jesus Christ from the dead. The vast majority of these people did not place trust in God for salvation from their sins. What happens to these millions? God's Word tells us the answer. At death, their bodies stay buried to return to dust. Their souls or spirit immediately went to a place called "The Abyss" or Tartarus, also known as "The lowest pit." This is the lower compartment of Hades and is recorded as a place of great torment. The spirit of these Old Testament people who did not believe in God, go, upon death, to "The lowest pit" and are stored there, in torment, until after the second coming of Jesus Christ, after the battle of Armageddon, and after the thousand year Millennial reign of Jesus.

465

2. What about the bodies and spirit of people born after the resurrection of Christ? Thousands of years have passed and millions of people have been born. Now we are in a different dispensation of time. Now God has sent the Holy Spirit to live in the hearts of believers. Now "The Church" is responsible for evangelizing the world. We know a minority of people, perhaps as small as 10 percent ever born, worldwide will believe in Jesus Christ as the resurrected God who died for their sins. What happens to these people who die? The Bible gives us the answer. Their bodies, as does all that die, return to dust. However, the Spirit of those that place their trust in Jesus Christ for salvation, do not go to Abraham's Bosom. Jesus Christ has already died and conquered death with His resurrection from the dead, these believers in faith through Grace of God go directly to the Thorne of God awaiting the one thousand year Millennial reign when they will live one thousand years and then go to heaven.

3. But what about the bodies and spirit of the millions, born after the resurrection of Jesus Christ through the second coming of Jesus Christ but who do not believe in Jesus Christ as the Savior of the world? Once again their bodies return to dust. But their spirits or souls go to the lower part of Hades, known as "The Lower Pit" and there they stay through the Second Coming of Jesus, through the battle of Armageddon, and through the one thousand year and then they will be thrown into an even more horrible place called in Scripture the "Lake of Fire."

4. Now, let's return in thought to Luke 16:24–31. Lazarus, who believed in Jesus Christ, died and the Scripture records that upon death He immediately went to be with the Lord in Abraham's bosom. The Rich Man, who was not a believer, also died and upon death he immediately went to Hades. God records for us this event so we might understand with certainty that life after death exists regardless whether we are saved or not. The difference is that the saved will go to heaven with Christ awaiting the New Heaven and the lost

go to "The Abyss," a place of torment to hold the lost until the "Lake of Fire" (Hell) is prepared. Death is the penalty for man's sin and his withdrawal from God.

The Resurrected Immortal Body

Paul explains that the body that dies is not the same one which rises up: What then will be the difference between the mortal body and the body of resurrection.

1 Corinthians 15:35–37
But someone will ask, "How are the dead raised? With what kind of body do they come?" You foolish person! What you sow does not come to life unless it dies. And what you sow is not the body that is to be, but a bare kernel, perhaps of wheat or of some other grain."

Paul compares the mortal body with that of the resurrection. He tells us the spirit and soul of man continues after death. The same person will rise, but not the same body. The "carnal body" which dies and the "spiritual body" which rises are the same person but not the same body. The Apostle Paul wrote to the Church at Corinth:

1 Corinthians 15:42–44
"So is it with the resurrection of the dead. What is sown is perishable; what is raised is imperishable. It is sown in dishonor; it is raised in glory. It is sown in weakness; it is raised in power. It is sown a natural body; it is raised a spiritual body. If there is a natural body, there is also a spiritual body."

In the resurrection of believers in Christ, the whole person is transformed and made into the likeness of Christ. The risen Christ is the prototype of the risen believer. Jesus Christ will transform our sinful body that it may be conformed to His glorious body. Jesus said, the resurrection is the work of the power of God in the person of the Holy Spirit. Many people who read this scripture fail to note the incredible truth when Paul tells us "There is a natural body, and there is a spiritual body." We have a tendency to believe the spirit is just a spooky, mysterious creation that we cannot identify with. God tells us everyone has a spiritual body. When we die as believers our spiritual body will be transformed into a glorified body.

Romans 8:11
"If the Spirit of him who raised Jesus from the dead dwells in you, He who raised Christ Jesus from the dead will also give life to your mortal bodies through his Spirit who dwells in you."

The Bible teaches us that Jesus was raised from the Dead and if we believe in Jesus Christ, so will we be raised. If we deny this how can we believe anything else written in God's Word? The total premise of Christianity is false if Jesus was not resurrected from the dead. The Bible tells us that there is not only life after death, but eternal life so glorious for believers that our minds cannot conceive it.

1 Corinthians 2:9
"But as it is written—what no eye has seen, nor ear heard, nor the heart of man imagined what God has prepared for those who love Him."

Where do we go after Death?

Because there is life after death for every one ever born God wants us to understand His provisions for all peoples. We understand that after death the spirit of believers immediately goes to be with Christ. It is also true that immediately after death nonbelievers go to Hades. As a way to examine the truth in Scripture regarding these complicated topics let's look at some biblical definition of terms:

- **Sheol:** Sheol is a word used in the Old Testament. Its roots are Hebrew, the language of the Old Testament. It is the temporary place where the souls of the unsaved dead are held until after the Great White Throne Judgment. We will discuss the Great White Throne Judgment in the chapter on End Times. The Great White Throne Judgment is where all nonbelievers will be judged according to their sins and will be cast into the "Lake of Fire." The "Lake of Fire" is Hell and Hell is the permanent place of torment and punishment for the lost. We must understand that Sheol is not the grave and is not Hell. It is not the place where the physical body is buried. However, in the King James translation of the Bible, Sheol is translated as grave thirty-one times, as Hell thirty-one times and as the pit three times. Thus we understand the confusion surrounding this term. These are translation problems.

- **Hades:** Hades is the equivalent of the word Sheol. Hades is a Greek word used in the New Testament that means the same as Sheol. It is a temporary place or a holding place for the non-believing dead. Again we stress Hades is not Hell. Hades is not the grave. Hades does not have the physical body of those who have died but holds the soul. Hades is translated "Hell" ten times and "Grave" one time in the King James translation of Scripture. Hades is a place holding the souls of those who have passed on. Hades is a place of torment and punishment.

- **Hades or Sheol** is constructed with two separate compartments. The upper level is used to contain the souls of those who believed in the coming Messiah and died prior to the resurrection of Jesus Christ. That compartment is called "Abraham's bosom." We get our best understanding of this in the revelation of God about the rich man and Lazarus in Luke the sixteenth chapter. We also know that when Christ was resurrected He led the righteous out of "Abraham's Bosom" to dwell with Him in heaven with God the Father. The second compartment is beneath Abraham's Bosom. It is called in Scripture the lower part of the earth or the lower compartment of Hades or Sheol. It is used to contain the souls of those who do not believe in the promise of God to send His Messiah or in Jesus Christ the Son of God. Occupants of this lower compartment did not and do not believe in Jesus Christ as the resurrected Lord after His resurrection. This compartment is called "The Abyss," "The Pit," and Tartarus. Death and Sheol/Hades are linked together thirty three times in Scripture. The grave always claims the part of the person called the physical body. Sheol/Hades claims the part of the person called the soul or the spirit of man.

- **Gehenna:** Gehenna is translated as "Hell" all twelve times in the King James translation. It is the permanent place of torment and the place of punishment for nonbelievers. Gehenna takes place after the Great White Throne Judgment, after the rapture and after the resurrection of the dead in Christ. Gehenna is created for Satan and his angels. However, people who reject Jesus Christ are followers of Satan and they also inherit the ultimate fate of Satan. They also go to the "Lake of Fire." We know that Gehenna, or Hell, or the "Lake of Fire" is a permanent place because Scriptures give testimony of this truth. Mark 9:45 is one of many Scriptures that state Gehenna is forever. It is clear that those who enter Gehenna or Hell do so in not only their spiritual body but also some form of physical body. We will see in the chapter on End Times that those who enter Gehenna must do so after the Great White Throne Judgment. It is therefore certainly separate from Hades. Gehenna is the "Lake of Fire" promised in Revelation chapters 19 and 20. The Beast and the False Prophet will be cast into the "Lake of Fire" after the one-thousand-year millennial reign of Christ with His Church.

Mark 9:45
"And if your foot causes you to sin, cut it off. It is better for you to enter life lame, rather than having two feet to be thrown into hell."

- **Limne pur which is Greek for "Lake of Fire"** is recorded four times in Revelation chapter 19. Limne means lake and pur means fire. Limne is translated "Lake" 10 times in the King James version while pur is translated seventy-three times as fire and one time as fiery. This term means Hell. It is also called the permanent Hell as opposed to "The Abyss" which is referred to as the Hades or Sheol.

- **Abraham's Bosom:** We understand the English word bosom to mean the chest area of the human body. Many people allow this understanding to create problems in grasping what God meant when He referred to Abraham's Bosom. Abraham's Bosom is first referred to as the place Lazarus was enjoying compared to the rich man who was in torment. Second, Abraham's Bosom is referred to as the place Christ went to following His resurrection, to retrieve the souls of the redeemed who had died prior to His resurrection. God was using the Hebrew expression called, an idiom, when He used the term Abraham's Bosom. In Hebrew this term refers to a comfortable place of rest and comfort where the redeemed in Christ are held awaiting His death, burial, and resurrection for their sins. It is often used parallel to the word Paradise.

- **Tartarus:** This word is used to describe a place of confinement for the nonbelievers who died prior to Christ's resurrection. It also is the place of confinement for all who die as nonbelievers after Christ's resurrection because they do not go with Christ to heaven. This place of confinement is also a place of torment and is also referred to as "The Abyss."

- **Paradise:** Paradise is either empty or has ceased to exist. It is not currently one of the two compartments of Sheol/Hades. This is because it has been vacated by the trip Christ made to Abraham's Bosom, when; following His resurrection; Jesus went down into Abraham's Bosom or Paradise and retrieved the redeemed in Christ who had died prior to His resurrection.

In 1 Corinthians the fifteenth chapter, Paul tells us the resurrection of mankind connects the dead physical body in the grave with the spiritual body known as the soul. Believers receive a new glorified body that is vastly changed from the physical body they had. We do not know everything about the glorified body but we know it will be like Jesus's glorified body. We know we can know others and be known. Attributes of the glorified body are covered previously in this book. The resurrection of the physical body and its reunion with the spirit is in preparation for the judgment. The just will be resurrected to eternal life with Christ in heaven. The condemned will be resurrected to eternal damnation, torment, torture, and separation from God in Gehenna, or the "Lake of Fire." In John the fifth chapter Jesus calls this the resurrection of life, and the resurrection of condemnation. Therefore we see that God's Word wants us to understand that in today's world the term Hades has little meaning to the redeemed in Christ. It is however the temporary home of those who do not believe in Christ. Clearly God communicates to us that Hades and Sheol are not Gehenna and are not the permanent place of residence of those condemned because of their unbelief.

The Resurrected Body of Believers

God wants us to have some degree of understanding of the glory and honor and power that awaits us in our glorified body. Paul, speaking directly to the church at Corinth but indirectly to all people all over the world wants to reveal more understanding of how wonderful our glorified body will be.

The first truth is that we will have a body like Jesus Christ. We know that when Jesus revealed Himself to His disciples after His Resurrection from the grave, He could be multiple places at the same time, He passed through walls and rooms without doors, yet he still had a physical body that could be touched, could eat and drink and be recognized as man.

1 Corinthians 15:42–45
So is it with the resurrection of the dead. What is sown
is perishable; what is raised is imperishable. It is sown in
dishonor; it is raised in glory. It is sown in weakness; it is raised
in power. It is sown a natural body; it is raised a spiritual
body. If there is a natural body, there is also a spiritual
body. Thus it is written, "The first man Adam became a
living being"; the last Adam became a life-giving spirit.

God reveals to us powerful facts about our resurrected bodies. These are as follows: (1) Our natural body is born to eventually cease to exist. We call that death but in God's word Death means separation from God. Physical death is for the shell that houses our spirit will decay. But the body we will be given at our resurrection will never grow older, never have sickness, no injuries and will never cease to exist. (2) Our natural body is born with a sin nature and a desire to do things, and think things that are displeasing to God. Because God will not coexist with sin our sin will bring dishonor to us. But our glorified body will have no temptation to displease God. (3) In this physical body we get tired at the end of the day but we project there will be no tiredness in heaven. We have things we cannot do because we are physically weak but in our resurrected body we will be very strong. We will have strong personalities all focused on worship of our Savior. In conclusion we are told we will have a spiritual body housed in a physical shell but in Heaven the Spiritual body will be predominant. Here on earth our physical body is predominant. What a glorious future our Lord has provided for us after physical death here on earth.

CHAPTER TWENTY

The Doctrine of Hell
Home of the Lost

The doctrine of eternal punishment is not widely preached or taught today. This is amazing because the doctrine or teachings of God are quite definite and clear that a true and literal hell exists. Perhaps pastors fear the congregation will be uncomfortable when Hell is taught and become discouraged with the Church. Perhaps many believe the lost may refuse to believe in Christ because of fear of Hell. What we do know is that natural men hate the idea of being held accountable for their lives to a Holy God. We love sin and do not wish to part with it. The carnal mind throws up objection after objection to the idea of Hell because it does not want to face the reality of it. Men live their lives thinking that maybe if they ignore a difficulty long enough, it will go away.

People do not enjoy hearing they are in danger of Hell and its fire and brimstone. In fact, many get insulted and defensive when informed of their fate. Most people think they have things figured out their own way and really think they are going to be welcomed into God's Kingdom. Satan has these people tricked into thinking they are safe. The Bible teaches us that there is a place for people who refuse to have a heart for God and decide in their heart to pursue their selfish desires. It is a place of eternal punishment and separation from God. God is quite clear the reason people go to Hell after death is because of their unbelief. However, we are given some indication of the kind of people we will find in Hell. The book of Hebrews connects death for the unbeliever with the consequences of judgment.

Hebrews 9:27
"And just as it is appointed for men to die once, but after that comes judgment."

In addition, the Bible tells us there is a no chance for the unbeliever after death. The Bible clearly states every man is born into sin and deserves death. By nature, man deserves separation from God and eternal torment. Our condemnation, however, comes because of our willful rejection of Jesus Christ. We are not condemned because of how we live our lives. Our redemption comes because of His willingness to pay the price of our sin on Calvary, combined with our desire to accept Him as our Savior and Lord. When we stand before God in judgment He will require justice for our sins that we have committed. For those saved because of God's grace through faith, their sins will be forgiven because of the blood of Jesus Christ. If people do not know Jesus as Lord and Savior, they are on their way to Hell. Hell may not be a politically correct topic these days, but many people enter Hell every day. Of the 7.6 billion people alive today many qualified statisticians estimate; 2.5 billion claim some connection with Christianity. In addition many qualified statisticians tell us there are about 745 million believers who believe Jesus Christ died on the Cross of Calvary for their sins and are saved; 745 million Christians, divided by a population of 7.6 billion people, estimates 10 percent of the world's population are saved. These statistics are not guaranteed in accuracy but they give us an estimate to work with. We should also consider that 120,000 people die every day, so an estimated 108,000 or better will end up in Hades awaiting their appointment in the "Lake of Fire." Hell is a real place but people simply do not understand how terrible Hell is. Just because you've never seen Hell doesn't mean it doesn't exist.

Hell was not prepared for man. It was prepared for Satan and his angels. Man was intended to live a sinless life and forever live with God the Father and the Son and the Holy Spirit in peace and happiness. In a 1991 study of Americans it was determined that 80 percent believe in life after death and 57 percent believe in the existence of Hell. But even within that 57 percent there was great debate of who would go to Hell. In his vision of the future, John in Revelation saw Hell and saw Satan and his angels cast into the "Lake of Fire."

Matthew 13:40–42
"Just as the weeds are gathered and burned with fire, so will it be at the end of the age. The Son of Man will send his angels, and they will gather out of his kingdom all causes of sin and all law-breakers, and throw them into the fiery furnace. In that place, there will be weeping and gnashing of teeth."

If Hell was prepared for Satan and his followers; then why should anyone, be forced to go to such a place? The answer is, of course, that if man does not choose to follow Jesus Christ then he has chosen to follow Satan and earns the just reward of Satan. If you do not belong to Jesus Christ you belong to Satan. As a follower of Satan you will go with him to the place prepared for him and his angels. It is right and just that the followers of Satan should follow him all the way. You do not have to be a drunkard, or drug addict, or rapist, or murderer to go to Hell. All you have to do to earn the reward of Satan and his angels is to ignore Jesus Christ and do what seems natural. And doing what seems natural is to be a person who seeks to satisfy self not to satisfy God and His righteousness.

How many times have we heard people say, "A loving God would not throw His creatures into "The Lake of Fire." Well, God does not throw us into Hell. A more responsible question would be, "Why did God not provide a way that His created people could avoid Hell." The answer if that He did provide a way for His people to avoid Hell. He sent His only begotten Son, to die on the Cross of Calvary, and to be raised on the third day so that if we believe on Him we will be saved. And if we do not believe on Him we are not His children. Hell is the natural place for all of mankind to go. This is because all of mankind is born into a sinful nature. We are born with a nature that does not, by instinct, want to be righteous.

The reality of Hell is why Jesus came to die

The Bible says that God loves us so much that the creator of this universe, Jesus Christ, came to be crucified for every human being ever born. He is God, come to earth in the flesh, to destroy the power of death and Hell. Jesus Christ holds the keys to Hell. If we say no to Jesus, Hell will be our eternal home. There will be no escape. There is no comfort. There is no end to Hell because it is everlasting. The reality of Hell is clearly outlined in the following scriptures.

Revelation 14:11
"And the smoke of their torment ascendeth up forever and ever;
and they have no rest day or night, who worship of The Beast
and his image, and whoever receives the mark of its name."

Revelation 20:12, 15
"And I saw the dead, small and great, standing before the
throne, and books were opened. Then another book was opened
which is the book of life. and the dead were judged by what
was written in the books according to what they had done."

From before the creation of mankind, Jesus Christ knew the price that must be paid for man's sin was the death of one who had never sinned. And from before the creation of man Christ volunteered to be the one who would pay that price. Jesus Christ paid that price because He knew intimately every soul that would ever live. He knew that everyone who did not or would not believe in Him were doomed to the horrible torment of Hell. Christ the creator, Christ the redeemer, Christ the Savior did not want man to die and was willing to pay the price to give man a choice. Let's look at what the Bible teaches us about the doctrine of Hell.

Doctrine of Hell Recorded in the New Testament

When Jesus Christ comes back to earth to take His believers up in the air with him, all non–believers, both alive and dead, including those in Hades, and those alive on earth, will immediately be cast into "The Abyss" or a holding place of temporary punishment. This is recorded in the book of Luke.

Luke 16:22–23
"The poor man died and was carried by the angels to
Abraham's side. The rich man also died and was buried,
and in Hades, being in torment, he lifted up his eyes
and saw Abraham far off and Lazarus at his side."

Revelation chapter 20:11–15 contains an amazing insight into what is to come. John the Apostle saw in a vision that was in the sky and was granted to him by God. He describes what he sees as a great white throne with Jesus sitting on the throne. John says that as he observes the vision, all of earth and the universe created by God just ceased to exist in His vision. Then John reveals the dead, meaning of all ages. Even the sea gave up their dead, and Hades gave up its dead and all nonbelievers were accountable to Jesus. Then John tells us he saw a vast number of books but one book in particular was the book of life. If a person's name was in the book of life they escaped the judgement that was to come. These people in the book of life were not present at this "Great White Throne" judgement. This incredible gathering was just for nonbelievers.

Then John had revealed to him, so he might reveal to us, that Jesus Christ on the Great White Throne judged every person who ever lived that did not in their life place their trust for salvation in God Jehovah (Old Testament) or Jesus Christ (New Testament). Then *"They were judged, each one of them, according to what they had done."* Then the three, Death and Hades and anyone's name not found in the book of life was thrown into the Lake of Fire."

Revelation 20:11–15

"Then I saw a great white throne and him who was seated on it. From his presence earth and sky fled away, and no place was found for them. And I saw the dead, great and small, standing before the throne, and books were opened. Then another book was opened, which is the book of life. And the dead were judged by what was written in the books, according to what they had done. And the sea gave up the dead who were in it, Death and Hades gave up the dead who were in them, and they were judged, each one of them, according to what they had done. Then Death and Hades were thrown into the lake of fire. This is the second death, the lake of fire. And if anyone's name was not found written in the book of life, he was thrown into the lake of fire."

Multiple judgments are spoken of in Scripture. The Great White Throne Judgment is for the dead in Christ. It is for all who lived and rejected Jesus Christ. At that Judgment, Christ will determine degrees of punishment the lost will suffer in the "Lake of Fire." The participants of that judgment will come out of Hades, meaning the compartment of Hades that holds the lost awaiting the Great White Throne Judgment. These will have suffered torment and separation from God without a physical body while in the "place for the dead." They will, however, know that their condition is about to get worse. It will move from temporary to final. They will move from torment of fire to fire and brimstone. It will move from just the spirit of the lost in torment to the physical body and the spirit being in torment. The lost ones will have been reunited with the physical body, but a changed body that is immortal and cannot die. After the Great White Throne Judgment the soul (spirit) of the lost and that one's changed physical body will be united and will be cast into the "Lake of Fire." They will be sentenced to an eternity of punishment based on their unbelief and on their actions in this physical life.

At the Great White Throne Judgment the scripture says "the books were opened." There may be millions of books. We do not know how many. They will be as numerous as the sand in the sea because every sinful deed, thought, intent, and every disappointment of God committed by every unsaved person every born will be recorded in the books. And the judge will be none other than Jesus Christ Himself.

The scripture does not say in words but tells us in implication that there will be degrees of punishment in Hell. God's Word does not reveal exactly what this means. We are told the degrees of punishment will be based on the intent of the heart of the one being judged. Then the scripture tell us that after the judgment, according to works of the unsaved, they will be cast into the Lake of Everlasting Fire also known as Hell. Just think about the eternal agony, the eternal depression, the eternal hopelessness for those in hell. Think about the eternal body that feels, suffers, grieves, and regrets. They will be cast into a punishment with multiple unspeakable torments. The word torments in scripture is plural.

The Bottomless Pit

Hell was not created by God for those who are unfit to dwell in His presence. In fact, Hell was not created for man but for Satan and his followers. The problem is that man elected to become a follower of Satan and therefore inherited his punishment. The lost will not go to hell because of what they did here on earth. They will be cast into Hell, also known as the "Lake of Fire" because of their decision to not trust and follow Jesus Christ the risen Messiah. Those who died before the Dispensation of the Church go to Hell because they did not have faith in God the Father. (They did not know of God the Son.) God also tells us that the angels who followed Satan and rebelled against God will be cast into hell also known as the Bottomless Pit. After the battle of Armageddon the Beast and the False Prophet will be cast into the Bottomless Pit. And after the one-thousand-year millennial reign of Christ and a brief war Satan tries to wage against God, Satan himself will be cast into the Bottomless Pit also known as the "Lake of Fire."

2 Peter 2:4
"For if God did not spare angels when they sinned, but cast them into hell and committed them to chains of gloomy darkness to be kept until the judgment."

Jude 6
"And the angels who did not stay within their own positions of authority, but left Their proper dwelling, He has kept in eternal chains under gloomy darkness until judgment of the great day."

These scriptures tell us that not only the unsaved people of earth will be cast into Hell but also the angels who joined Lucifer when he revolted against God will be cast into Hell on that great judgment day. We have already seen that both Hades and Death will be cast into Hell. The compartment that held the Old Testament saved in faith, called "Abraham's Bosom," will be empty. Abraham's bosom is empty because Christ took the saved Saints to heaven when He was resurrected from death and descended into the earth to get them. Hell is created to separate the wicked from God. Praise God, however, the scripture also tells us that "He who believes in the Son has everlasting life and he who does not believe the Son shall not see life but the wrath of God abides in him." What kind of prison is Hell? It is called the "Bottomless Pitt."

Revelation 9:2
"He opened the shaft of the bottomless pit, and from the shaft rose smoke like the smoke of a great furnace, and the sun and the air were darkened with the smoke from the shaft."

Hell is a pit of darkness. The term "Bottomless Pit" refers to more than its limitless size. It also refers to the hopelessness of those trapped inside. Imagine the despair of the sinner trapped in the bottomless pit forever and forever. Imagine the loneliness, the regret, the grieving, the horrible pain, and the separation from any kind of love especially the love of God forever and forever, with absolutely no hope.

The significance of where Hell will be is not important to the sinner or saint except to reemphasize the reality of Hell as a tangible place that God has prepared. God wants mankind to understand that Hell is real and therefore He gives us some understanding of its location. God gave us some insight into the location of Hades (The temporary home of the lost) when He told us where Jesus went while in the tomb. We must realize that all people who had believed on the coming Messiah prior to the advent of Jesus were saved as they looked forward, in faith, to the coming of our Lord and Savior.

We are saved looking back in faith to the death and burial of Jesus. Old Testament Saints believed in the future coming of the promised Messiah. We also know Jesus after His death but prior to His resurrection went somewhere to release Old Testament Saints from the confinement of Hades and into Heaven with Him. Where then did Jesus go to gather the Old Testament Saints and redeem them?

Psalms 49:15
"But God will ransom my soul from the power
of Sheol, for He will receive me. Selah."

In Ephesians, Paul is quiet explicit in stating Jesus descended into the "Pit," or the depths of the earth to bring back the saints who had gone on before He ascended into heaven.

Ephesians 4:9–10
In saying, "He ascended," what does it mean but that
He had also descended into the lower regions, the earth?
He who descended is the One who also ascended far
above all the heavens, that He might fill all things.

Based on these verses as well as much other Scripture we clearly know that Hades, or the "place of the dead" is located in the inner depths of the earth. There we have fire and smoke and torment of the occupants. The only occupants today of Hades are the lost who do not know Christ. There they await the coming of the Lord, the Great White Throne judgment and then the Lake of Fire.

Where is Hell or the "Lake of Fire" located?

Man does not know where Hell or the "Lake of Fire" is located. This is in contrast to our scriptural knowledge of where Hades or Sheol is located. We do however trend to speculate on the location of Hell. Some of the speculation versions are:

One popular version of that Hell is located is in the center of the earth. This understanding is based on a misunderstanding of Scriptures like Luke 10:15. However, upon examination we find this scripture speaks about Hades or Sheol not Hell or the "Lake of Fire."

Luke 10:15
"And you, Capernaum, will you be exalted to
heaven? You shall be brought down to Hades."

The interesting reality of Luke 10 verse 15 clearly says that the citizens of Capernaum would be thrust down into Hades not Hell. It first asks will the citizens be saved and join Christ in Heaven? No, the Bible says they are unbelievers and will be brought down (into the earth) to Hades. Other Scripture such as 1 Samuel 28:13–15 also refer to Sheol or the temporary place of the dead. From these scriptures we learn Hades and Sheol are located somewhere in the center of the earth but the location of Hell or the "Lake of Fire" is not revealed.

Matthew 25:30
"And cast the worthless servant into outer darkness. In that place where there will be weeping and gnashing of teeth."

One understanding or theory of where Hell is located is somewhere in outer space, possibly in a black hole. This theory is based on man's scientific knowledge that black holes are places of great heat and pressure from which nothing, not even light, can escape. Verse such as Matthew 25:30 might lead to this conclusion.

Another speculation is that the earth itself will be the "lake of fire." When the earth is destroyed by fire as recorded in 2 Peter 3:10 and Revelation 21:1 many decide two plus two equal what they want it to equal. To them that means Hell is located on earth after it is consumed by fire. This also may be true but we do not have Scripture to confirm or deny this thought pattern.

2 Peter 3:10
"But the day of the Lord will come as a thief in the night, in which the heavens will pass away with a roar, and the heavenly bodies will be burned up and dissolved, and the earth and the works that are done in it will be exposed."

The Bible does not tell us the physical location of Hell. We do know Hell is a literal place of real torment, but we do not know where it is. Hell may have a physical location in this universe, or it may be in an entirely different "dimension." Whatever the case, the location of Hell is far less important than the need to avoid Hell.

What will Hell be like?

Hell is a place of eternal fire that is never quenched. We know of people who burn to death and those who almost burn to death. We hear of the horrible pain they suffer. Yet the fire of Hell is much worse than the worst fiery death on earth. Earthly fire consumes the flesh of its victims. When the nerve endings are consumed the pain ceases. But for those in Hell, the pain will never cease because the fire does not consume. In Hell the nonbelievers will be given a physical body, but different than the physical body we have here on earth. This physical body cannot be destroyed, but it is built for the purpose of experiencing the horror of death by fire forever.

Revelation 14:10
"He also will drink of the wine of the wrath of God, poured out full into the cup of His anger. And He will be tormented with fire and sulfur in the presence of the holy angels and in the presence of the Lamb."

Revelation 14:10 tells us of the place where Satan will be cast forever and forever. It is a place of fire and brimstone. It is the same place where the unsaved people will go because they are followers of Satan. We are not given total insight to understand the flames of Hell. We do not understand completely the spiritual body that will have physical attributes. However, we do know Hades will a place of torment to the souls of men and women while their spirits are still in the grave before the resurrection. Their torment will continue throughout eternity when those souls are reunited with their bodies and both are caste into the "Lake of Fire."

Eternal Darkness

Hell is the place of outer darkness. Jesus Christ is said to be the light of the world. Those who are in Hell will have no contact and no support from Jesus Christ. They will therefore be in total absolute darkness. When you go down into Carlsbad Caverns there is a point in which they turn out the lights. You experience darkness of which you had no knowledge. At that point you cannot see even an outline of your hand when you hold it in front of you. Outer darkness is part of the punishment of those who refuse to trust Jesus Christ. This is part of their condemnation. John 3:19 says, *"That the light (Jesus Christ) has come into the world and men loved darkness rather than light."* Therefore God gives them what they elected to receive, absolute darkness. When you combine total sheer terror along with eternal multiple torments, combined with total absolute darkness we begin to get a glimpse of the horror of Hell. First Thessalonians tells us that those who continue in sin and do not commit to Christ are the children of darkness. The wicked will walk in darkness. Jude 13 tells us Hell is *"black darkness."* In the utter darkness the lost will have eternity to think about the multiple opportunities they had to accept Christ and avoid Hell. They will have eternity to dwell on a wasted life by serving their own selfish interests, lusts and vanities.

Matthew 25:30
"And cast the worthless servant into the outer darkness. In that place there will be weeping and gnashing of teeth."

Separation from God

One of the major torments will be total separation from God. God is love, holiness, trust, decency, hope, and the fountain of blessings. Without God there is no hope, no love, no holiness, no trust, no blessings and no decency. The lost do not love or delight in Jesus Christ therefore they may not fully comprehend what they are missing here on earth. But in Hell the nonbelievers will be able to look, pass the abyss and see into Heaven and behold the wonder and glory of those who trusted Jesus as their Savior. Those in Hell will have full understanding of the glory of Christ and their loss.

People in Hell will experience the loss of all the blessings they had on earth. Many of the lost in Hell will have been very blessed on earth. Remember the term lost does not relate to a scale of evil here on earth. Many people who were considered "great" people on earth will be in Hell. If they did not express their love for Jesus and ask Him for salvation they will go to Hell. Those who had a beautiful body will be corrupted and vile. Those who had power and glory on earth will be tormented by what they lost. Those who had possessions on earth will have nothing in Hell yet they will see those they scorned on earth as part of the blessed in heaven. Those in Hell will be totally separated from God and totally intermingled with the most evil of all creatures who ever existed. When the "Day of Judgment" comes the lost will hear Jesus say, *"I never knew you, depart from me, ye that work iniquity,"* they will hear our Lord say, *"Depart from me, ye cursed, into everlasting fire, prepared for the devil and his angels.'* And the lost will know that they have absolutely no one to blame but themselves. God is just, and His judgments are right.

Degrees of Punishment in Hell

A frequently asked question that is often avoided by theologians is whether there will be different degrees of punishment in Hell based on the heart or deeds of the lost. Many say we do not know but God wanted us to know the answer to this significant question. God answers the question clearly. In Revelation God simply stated that the dead in Christ will be judged according to their deeds. The subject of deeds includes both what one has done and why that one did it.

Revelation 20:13
"And the sea gave up the dead who were in it, Death and Hades gave up the dead who were in them, and they were judged, each one of them, according to what they had done."

Jesus taught different degrees of judgment and punishment in Hell. Those who do not obey God will receive "many stripes." Those people who are without God's Word and disobey ignorantly "shall be beaten with few."

Luke 12:47–48
"And that servant who knew his master's will but did not get ready or act according to his will, will receive a severe beating.

But the one who did not know, and did what deserved a beating, will receive a light beating. Everyone to whom much was given, of him much will be required, and from him to whom they entrusted much, they will demand the more."

Jesus clearly taught that those who lived in the cities where He preached and did many miracles would receive greater judgment that those living in cities where no mighty works were done. The Bible tells us that everyone will receive the punishment they deserve based on their works and the state of their disobedience to God. But it also teaches that regardless of how "good" they were on earth or how little exposure they had to Scripture, only those who know Jesus Christ as Savior and put their trust in Christ for redemption will go to Heaven and escape the torments of Hell.

Hebrews 10:29
"How much worse punishment, do you think, will be deserved by the one who has trampled underfoot the Son of God, and has profaned the blood of the covenant by which he was sanctified, and has outraged the Spirit of grace?"

In the Scripture quoted above we find confirmation that there will definitely be different degrees of punishment in Hell based on the heart of man or the intention of man. In the Gospel of Luke we find that the one who knows his master's will and does not do it will have greater punishment than one who does not know his masters will and does not do it. Then we find in Hebrews God clearly telling us there will be degrees of punishment in Hell. And finally in John we read where Jesus Himself confirmed there will be different degrees of punishment in Hell.

Hell is a place of Retribution

When God chastises a believer He does it for the benefit of the believer. Such chastisement is part of God's plan of sanctification. Sanctification means spiritual growth toward the example

God set in His Son Jesus Christ. Hell, however, is divine retribution. It is not a place of rehabilitation because the person in Hell can never get the debt paid. Hell is not Purgatory as taught by Catholics. Hell is permanent, eternal punishment. The retribution that the believer deserves was placed on the shoulders of Jesus Christ who paid the full penalty, retribution and wrath of God for that believer. Those in Hell pay their own price. They experience the full wrath of God in dolling out punishment for violation of God's will. If one dies without believing in Jesus Christ their fate is sealed because their decision to accept or reject Christ must be made while they live on earth. After this life on earth passes full retribution must be paid. Jesus had to pay that price on the cross, or the individual must pay his or her own cost in Hell.

Hell is a place of Justice

The eternal aspect of Hell reflects God's justice and majesty. Every sin man commits is a direct challenge of God's nature and authority. Every time we sin we are saying, "I am my own God and I will choose how I live and what my values will be." Every time we sin we say, "I will be my own God and I reject God my creator and my redeemer." We say, "I will glorify myself not God. Sinners cast contempt on God's honor and glory. They do not believe in a "Day of Judgment" and then eternity. God will glorify and exalt himself, in part, by the reigning down of eternal punishment on those who have demonized Him.

Hell is an expression of God's Wrath

Hell expresses God's wrath against Sin. God created us and gave us life. God created a magnificent world for us to live in and gave us dominion over the animals and all created beings on earth. Then, knowing in His foreknowledge that man would reject God, God sent His only begotten Son to die on Calvary so we might be redeemed. Mankind then took this Son God sent to earth to die for us, and treated Him with massive disrespect. Mankind humiliated, tortured and crucified Jesus who did all this to save us from our sins.

Romans 5:8–9
"But God shows His own love for us, in that while we were still sinners, Christ died for us. Since therefore we have now been justified by His blood, much more shall we be saved by Him from the wrath through of God."

God has every right to be angry with mankind. Praise the Lord, God's anger is answered by the blood of Jesus Christ who died for our sins, if we will simply believe on Him. Everyone who tramples on the Son of God shall receive the full wrath of God unless they have accepted the price Jesus paid for his sins. Eternal punishment will be ready to receive man when he dies. Unbelievers must consider the extreme danger they are in. God's great furnace of wrath is ready to devour them, not for a time, but throughout eternity without end. God's anger increases against the lost every day they live without Christ, not because of the passing of time, but because they are adding to the books of deeds they will be held accountable for in the great White Throne Judgment. God has nothing but contempt and anger for sinners who count the vanities and lusts of life more important than the life Jesus Christ gave to pay for our sins.

How long will Hell last?

Those who end up in Hell will be there eternally. People use different phrases and words used to describe the duration of Hell, but all of them indicate that it will never end. Jesus spoke of *"unquenchable fire...where the worm dieth not, and the fire is not quenched."* John wrote of people being in *"torment day and night forever and ever."* Again, Jesus said, *"These shall go away into eternal (or everlasting) punishment."* How long will Hell last, or how long will those confined there suffer? The answer is "eternally" or "for ever and ever." The word that is translated as "eternal" or "everlasting" in Matthew 25:46, is the same word that is used to describe the Holy

Spirit in Hebrews 9–14, It is the same word that describes God the Father in Romans 16:26. It is also used in Matthew 25:41 to describe the fire of punishment. Let me ask you, how long will God last? How long will the Holy Spirit last? That is, according to the scriptures, precisely how long the wicked shall be punished in Hell.

Matthew 25:46
"And these shall go away into eternal punishment: but the righteous into life eternal."

Is Hell fair?

Many people feel that the biblical concept of Hell is unfair. They challenge why someone should suffer forever for a short lifetime of sin. They feel the punishment outweighs the sin. It is God, however, who created us. God determines what is just and what is sin and God as our creator has the right to demand our obedience.

Deuteronomy 32:4
"He is the Rock, his work is perfect: for all his ways are judgment: a God of faithfulness and without iniquity, righteous and upright is He."

It's both foolish and dangerous for man to attempt to sit in judgment of God.

Isaiah 45:9
"Woe to him who strives with Him who formed him! A pot among earthen pots. Does the clay say to him who forms it, 'What are you making?' Or your work has no handles'?"

It is important that all understand that Hell is a place of punishment. A very popular view of Hell is that it is a place where the wicked will simply be burned up and cease to exist. That is a very comforting thought, just a brief period of pain and then it is over. But there is no scriptural support for that position. It isn't only that

Hell is eternal but the punishment to be endured there is eternal as well. Remember, *"These shall go away into everlasting punishment."* God has declared that eternal punishment is the just reward for sin. Man's recourse is not to question God but to repent of sin, believe on Jesus Christ and ask God for forgiveness. God in His love will forgive us and change our eternal destiny.

It is important and interesting for us to be aware of the fact that 'fire" is the most frequently used word to describe the nature of the punishment that awaits those who are lost. Jesus talked about the *"furnace of fire,"* the *"eternal (or everlasting) fire,"* where *"the fire is not quenched."* Paul spoke of the Lord returning *"in flaming fire"* taking vengeance on them that know not God, and that obey not the gospel our Lord Jesus Christ." John wrote of the *"lake that burns with fire and brimstone."*

Hell is not well received by the masses

In 2018 Pope Francis was reported widely to have supported the theory that Christians (members of the Catholic Church) would experience a wonderful life after death but those who did not believe according to Catholic doctrine would simply cease to exist. A vast majority of people in the world agree with the reported opinion of the Pope. Countries that do not tolerate or simply frown on any form of Christianity would agree that Hell as reported in God's Word does not exist. This is not because of intellectual study but because of human logic. Their theory is that hell is far too extreme a punishment for one's sin.

God does not work according to human logic. God makes decisions based on His Sovereignty and He had defined the penalty of sin. It is not death in the sense that people cease to exist. It is death in the sense of eternal separation from God and a penalty as defined by God that requires nor justifies any logic on human beings.

When we consider religious groups that deny the deity of Jesus Christ they are by far the majority of the world. That of course includes all Muslim religions. The traditional Muslim religion believes Jesus was born of a virgin, was a great Prophet and teacher but stop short of recognizing Jesus as part of the Trinity with God the Father and the Holy Spirit. People of Jewish faith believe Jesus was born of Mary but they reject the virgin birth. They believe Jesus claimed to have died on the cross and conquered death through resurrection. They believe Jesus claimed to be the Messiah but they still await the coming of the real Messiah.

Hindus recognize Jesus as having been a Holy man and a wise teacher and one of many Gods. Buddhists believe Jesus was a great leader and teacher but nothing more. Another religious group who worship themselves is those who simply deny there being a God. All of these groups deny Jesus and therefore deny hell. They will after this physical life go to Hades the temporary holding place awaiting judgment and sentence to eternity in Hell.

We either believe God's Word or we do not. We do not get to select that part of God's Word we want to believe. We do not get to believe in Heaven but reject Hell. We do not get to believe in the Christians judgment of good works (BEMA Seat) but reject the non-believers judgment of works (Great White Throne Judgment).

A Physical Body that Suffers

Some strenuously object to the idea of "Hell fire" because they contend the lost will not have physical bodies after death but will be spiritual beings. The Bible, however, tells us that the lost and the saved will be raised from the dead. The lost will stand before a judgment in which they will be condemned to Hell and will be given a physical body that is immortal to be cast into the "Lake of Fire." Revelation 20:11 says all the unsaved will "stand" before the Judgment of the Lord in the Great White Throne Judgment. This is giving evidence of a physical body. In addition the Scripture tells us the sea, death, the grave, and Hades delivered up the dead that were in them. We could understand that from Hades only the Spirit or soul of the dead in Christ would be given up. But from the grave and from Death we find the presence of the physical body. That delivered up from death and the grave has to be the body. So we learn that the soul (in Hades) will be joined with the body (death and the grave) to "stand" before the Great White Throne Judgment. The joined body and spirit of the lost will then receive sentence of their punishment throughout eternity in Hell and will be cast into the "Lake of Fire" with Satan and his angels.

John 5:29
"And come out—those who have done good, to the resurrection of life, and those who have done evil, to the resurrection of judgment."

We know that the lost in Christ will be resurrected in bodily form. We also know that that body will be different than on this earth. First of all it will be immortal. On earth if we suffer enough we will eventually die and that is the end of the physical body. In Hell the body will become immortal in that nothing can kill it. So the torment of eternal fire and brimstone will be incredible painful but will not kill us.

Hell is a place without Hope

Hell is the only alternative to heaven. Hell is a place of fire and brimstone, a place of torments, a place of pain, a place of thirst, and a place of separation from God. It is all that, but it's also even worse. Hell is also a lack of hope. Imagine being in a place of torments, knowing it will last forever, and on top of that, being completely hopeless. Imagine the deep depression, despair, and great sadness a total lack of hope will cause.

It is God's plan that we spend eternity with Him. God does not want us to go to Hell and be separated from Him. God loves us and He sent His son, Jesus, to pay the penalty for our sin. God's Son became our blood sacrifice for sin. God also made this plan a free gift. All we have to do is believe in Jesus Christ and accept God's gift of eternal life and it is ours.

Hell is a place with no rest

The Bible tells us the lost in Christ will go to eternal damnation in Hell and there they will have no rest day or night and the smoke of their torment will ascend forever and ever.

Revelation 14:11
"And the smoke of their torment goes up forever and ever; and they have no rest day or night, these worshipers of "The Beast" and its image, and whoever receives the mark of its name."

God's Word tells us that Hell is a place of total darkness with absolutely no light. In Revelation 14:11 the term "Day or Night" refers to our understanding of a twenty-four-hour day. In Hell twenty-four hours will have no meaning. We also know the body that goes to Hell will be changed and made immortal because this earthly body would eventually die without any rest. But the same earthly body, with its pain, and its suffering will be made immortal and changed to endure the eternal punishment of sin. The immortal body and soul will reside forever in Hell. Some people commit suicide because their problems on this earth are too many. If they died without professing Jesus Christ as their Savior and Lord they will take every trouble with them to Hell and wrestle with those troubles forever. Rest and peace can only be found in Jesus Christ as the resurrected Lord.

Fear of Hell

Many pastors do not preach the reality of Hell because their congregation is uncomfortable with such teaching. The Pastors want a church that is in harmony with each other and him and he justifies teaching other doctrine. This raises the question of whether it is fair to cause one to believe on Jesus for salvation because of their fear of hell. The answer to this question is found in God's Word. Did God use space in His Holy Word to tell us about Hell? Did God want us to be warned about Hell? Did God want us to trust Jesus Christ for salvation because we wanted to escape Hell? The answer to all is yes.

Revelation 21:8
"But as for the cowardly, the faithless, the detestable, as for murderers, the sexually immoral, sorcerers, idolaters, and all liars, their portion will be in the Lake that burns with fire and sulfur, which is the second death."

The glory of this horrible verse is that people can be forgiven of all these sins and because of the price Jesus paid for our sins on Calvary God the Father will view them as righteous. But those who do not believe will surely suffer Hellfire and Damnation.

CHAPTER TWENTY-ONE

The Doctrine of Heaven
Home of the Saved

Having established, based on Scripture, that life after death exists, and that nonbelievers will go to a place prepared for them called the "Lake of Fire" or Hell, the next logical question is of what happens to believers. God did not want this question to be a mystery to man. He gave us a lot of scripture in the New Testament to answer the question without any doubt. The basic answer is that those who believe in Jesus Christ will go to heaven and those who do not believe will go to Hell. Jesus Christ prepares heaven for those who believe in Him and put their trust in Him for salvation.

2 Corinthians 5:1
"For we know that if the tent that is our earthly home is destroyed, we have a building from God, a house not made with hands, eternal in the heavens."

As we study this Scripture from Paul we are reminded that our body is just a covering, a framework that houses the soul. Our body is not to be worshipped although we certainly can admire the work of God in the creation of our body. Paul then goes on to say that because our body is mortal it will decay and will not last. Therefore, as children of God we are promised a framework made by God Himself. And finally God tells us that framework that will house our souls will be in the heavens. It is also of value to note God uses the word heavens, plural. We should then start the study of heaven with an understanding of the plural usage God made of heavens.

The Hebrew word for "heavens" is shamayin. Shamayin means heights or elevations. This word is found in Genesis at the very creation of God.

Genesis 1:1
"In the beginning God created the Heavens and the earth."

Genesis 2:1
"Thus the Heavens and the earth, and all the host of them, were finished."

God created the heavens, plural, more than one heaven from the very beginning. He created the heavens as part of His act of creation. We also note that God created the heavens and the earth as part of His creation act but He created them separately in complement to but not equal with each other. The term heavens and earth encompass all of God's creation. The sea, the land, the sky, space, the animals, mankind and the abode of God Himself are all part of the creative act of God.

Three heavens are recorded in Scripture. All of these meet the definitions of "heights" or elevation because all are above us here on earth. The first heaven is earth's atmosphere, the second is outer space inclusive of the universe as we know it and the third is God's abode.

The First Heaven: God calls this the firmament. It is earth's atmosphere making it is possible for man to breathe and to live. It is the sky and is the home of birds that fly. This level of the heavens is the first or lower level and does not reach into space where we see the sun, stars and moon. This level of the heavens generate the rain that sustains earth, provides us air to breath, and is an integral part of the operation of God's life sustaining system He created for us. This creation is often called the atmospheric heaven. It includes the space that immediately surrounds the earth. The technical term for this is the "troposphere." It extends about twenty miles above the earth. The Scripture uses the term heaven to describe this area.

James 5:8
"And He prayed again and the heaven gave rain and the earth brought forth her fruit."

Second Heaven: The second heaven is the middle layer of the heavens that we call outer space. This creation begins beyond the twenty-mile barrier of the lower heaven. The second heaven is called the Celestial Heaven. It is also called the stratosphere. Mankind has not conquered space even though we have managed to travel in space. We are rapidly learning about space and as we learn we become more and more amazed at God's Creation.

Isaiah 13:10
"For the stars of the heavens and their constellations
will not give their light; the sun will be dark at its
rising and the moon will not shed its light."

Third Heaven: The third heaven is what we call heaven. But even the third heaven is not where we will spend eternity. This is because God promised He would create a New Heaven and a New Earth for eternity. The third heaven is also not where the thousand year millennial reign will take place. We will discuss this in the chapter entitled Eschatology. This third heaven is where God reigns and is where Christ ascended to after His resurrection from the grave. The third heaven is where the Church will go after the rapture. We will join with Jesus Christ waiting the Marriage Supper of the Lamb. The third heaven is called "The Heaven of Heavens."

1 Kings 8:27
"But will God indeed dwell on the earth? Behold,
heaven and the heaven of heavens cannot contain
You. How much less this house that I have built!"

Deuteronomy 10:14
"Behold, to the LORD your God belong heaven and the
heaven of heavens, the earth with all that is in it."

This creation of God is called the highest heaven thereby confirming that it is the highest of all three heavens created both in terms of physical creation and in terms of importance. It is the home of God the Father, God the Son and the Holy Spirit although Scripture tells us that God is not contained in any way by His creation of this third heaven. The Holy Spirit dwells today in the hearts of believers yet is not constrained to the hearts of believers but has residence in the third heaven as well.

This third heaven is beyond the space and stars. It is beyond anything man has seen by even his greatest and strongest telescopes.

We have the word of Paul who was called up into "the third heaven" by God.

2 Corinthians 12:2
"I know a man in Christ who fourteen years ago was caught up to the third heaven—whether in the body or out of the body I do not know, God knows."

This third heaven is not the same heaven that Jesus speaks of when He promises believers they will someday join with Him in eternity. That is the New Heaven the Lord promises. Therefore we need to take the time to briefly review the place the Church in Christ goes after the rapture and before they join with Christ when He comes back for His second coming and fights the war of Armageddon.

John 14:2
"In My Father's house are many mansions; if it were not so, I would have told you. I go to prepare a place for you."

The New Testament describes heaven as the place where God lives and rules. The angels who announced the birth of Jesus praise God in heaven. When Jesus was baptized, God's voice came from heaven and called Jesus "my own dear Son." Heaven is a real place. In the Scriptures it is called a place (John 14:2), a country (Hebrews 11:14–16), a city (Hebrews 11:10, 16, 12:22, 13:14; Rev. 21:10–27), and a house or mansion (John 14:23). The variety of expressions trying to explain heaven exists because of the human difficulty of understanding heaven. Heaven is all of these, a place, a country and a city. But God's Word specifically teaches us heaven is more than a condition of the soul, more than a state of mind, more than a spiritual dwelling without form or substance. It is a dwelling place consisting of material reality.

In addition to the biblical descriptions of heaven, there are two other biblical truths of the Christian faith that demands heaven be a real place. The first is the bodily resurrection and ascension of Christ. The other is the bodily resurrection of the believers. The nature of heaven must correspond to these two facts. It is inconsistent, on the one hand, to believe in the bodily resurrection of flesh and bones with the capacity to eat and drink (cf. Luke 24:39–43; Acts 10:41), and, on the other hand, to think of heaven as only symbolic and allegorical.

Matthew 5:34
"But I say unto you, do not take an oath at all; either by heaven; for it is the throne of God."

A good place to start in describing heaven is to acknowledge that heaven is the Throne of God. It is not adequate to say heaven contains the Throne of God. God is bigger than heaven. God swallows up heaven. It is more accurate to say the Throne of God is heaven. Everything about heaven is related to the Throne of God. The Bible is full of passages that establish heaven as the home of God. God's Word tells us the Jesus came from heaven when He came to earth and returned to heaven with His ascension. The Scripture also tells us He will come back from heaven at some time in the future to take the saved believers with Him for eternity.

God's Word tells us heaven is where Jesus dwells. We also rejoice because God's Word also tells us Jesus will take his believers with Him to heaven some day in the future.

Matthew 24:30–31
"Then will appear in heaven the sign of the Son of Man, and then all the tribes of the earth will mourn, and they will see the Son of Man coming on the clouds of heaven with power and great glory. And he will send out his angels with a loud trumpet call, and they will gather his elect from the four winds, from one end of heaven to the other."

When do we go to Heaven?

When a person believes on the Lord Jesus Christ, they receive eternal life. The Bible does not tell us they will receive eternal life when they die. The Scripture tells us they have it even as they continue to have their physical body reside on earth. The moment, the second, a lost person decides to put their trust in Jesus Christ for redemption, the Holy Spirit then changes that person into a new creature and they are "born again." They are immediately given eternal life not because of what they did but because of what the Holy Spirit does in the individual. When do we go to heaven? The answer for believers is you go to heaven when you die or whenever Jesus comes for The Church. We do not know when but we certainly know that day will come.

John 6:47
"Truly, truly, I say unto you, whoever believes has eternal life."

2 Corinthians 5:8
"Yes, we are of good courage, and we would rather be away from the body and at home with the Lord."

He that believeth on the Son hath eternal life;. This promise is in the present tense; it is ours now—if we believe. Salvation is the gift of God. We cannot earn it and we cannot buy it we simply accept it gratefully through our love, faith and trust in Jesus. We believe what Paul said: ***"To be absent from the body is to be present with the Lord."*** Upon salvation we are given a new spiritual body to be with the Lord. We shall experience no separation from God because Jesus conquered death in our place and gave us the gift of eternal life. We call that "Substitutionary Atonement." The spirit that was given to us when we were converted immediately created a new life and a new nature for us. We call that Regeneration. After physical death and the rapture we will be given a new, undefiled, perfect glorious body. That is when God comes back to take His Church home to heaven. It is a glorious thought to understand that death does not separate us from the Master. A great many people are living continually in the bondage of death, but if we have eternal life, we are freed from that bondage.

Hebrews 9:27
"And just as it is appointed for men to die
once, and after that comes judgment."

All unredeemed in Christ will face judgment before entering eternity. Revelation 20:11–12 tell us those who have to pay for their own sins in Hell will be judged in the Great White Throne Judgment where degrees of punishment will be passed out based on their works. This is a judgment of condemnation for the dead outside of Christ. The redeemed, however, will not go through the Great White Throne Judgment. They will face the BEMA seat of Christ that is a judgment of good works they have done on earth. The evil, corrupt, sinful things each redeemed has done will not be held against them, because Jesus Christ has paid for each of those sinful thoughts and acts. They are paid for by His blood spilt on Calvary. The judgment of works at the BEMA seat of Christ, however, will require that we account for the works we did and rewards for our Christian life will be passed out.

The first three chapters of Revelation gives us a partial understanding of what sort of good works the redeemed Saints could have done here on earth. Things done for our own self-gratification will not be counted as righteousness. However, works rendered out of total submission to our Lord and Savior will be counted as worthy for reward. It is critical to note the difference between the judgment of works for the redeemed and the judgment of faith. Many believers, unfortunately most believers will have no, or very little rewards built up for them in this judgment day. Yet they will be saved to live with Christ eternally. This is because salvation comes not of works but of faith through the grace of God. Rewards in heaven come by works coming out of a consecrated, dedicated, and committed heart to God.

Ephesians 2:8–9
"For by grace you have been saved through faith. And
this is not your own doing; it is the gift of God, not
a result of works, so that no one may boast."

Some Christians believe that when they are raptured they go straight to the place recorded in Scripture of golden streets, walls of precious stones and all of the glory of heaven. It is absolutely true that when raptured all Saints go to heaven but we are not ready to go to the New Heaven Christ promised us in John 14:2. This is because all Christians have some very important appointments with our Savior that must come to pass before we gain entrance into the New Heaven. After the rapture but before we pass into the New Heaven created for us by Christ we must encounter these events with Christ.

- The judgment of works also known as the BEMA seat of Christ (see 2 Corinthians 5:10).
- The "Marriage of the Lamb" when the redeemed of Jesus become the bride of Christ and are presented to God the Father—see Revelation 9:7–8
- The return to earth of the Church with Jesus Christ to fight the War of Armageddon—see Revelation 19:11–16
- We will observe the judgment of all Saints who survived and were faithful to Christ during the Great Tribulation and who refused the mark of the Beast—see Revelation 20:4–5
- We will observe the judgment of nations when the Lord will separate the sheep (believers) from the goats (nonbelievers) in getting prepared to enter the one-thousand-year Millennial Reign of Christ—see Matthew 25:31–34
- We will spend the next one thousand years with Jesus Christ as the King of Kings ruling from the throne in Jerusalem. Satan will be chained in the lower part of the earth. The Beast and the False Prophet will have been cast into the "Lake of Fire".

Then and only then, after the magnificent one-thousand-year millennial reign of Christ on earth will we as the bride of Christ enter into the New Heaven and the New Earth as foretold in Scripture.

A New Heaven and a New Earth

After the above five events are completed the redeemed in Christ will join Jesus in the New heaven and New earth prepared for the bride of Christ.

Revelation 4:1
"After this I looked, and behold, a door standing open in heaven. And the first voice I heard, speaking to me like a trumpet saying, "Come up here, and I will show you what must take place after this."

God is about to reveal to us a picture of the future. This revelation includes the New Heaven and New Earth He has prepared for us. God revealed this amazing truth through the eyes of the apostle John when He took John up into heaven to witness the final things that would happen just before eternity begins.

Revelation 4:2
"At once I was in the Spirit, and behold, a throne stood in heaven, with one seated on the throne."

The earthly body of John was corrupted with sin and could not go into the abode of God. This Scripture is interesting in that it is in confirmation of the separation of our Spirit and our physical body. It testifies of the reality that when we are saved we go to be with Christ spiritually and we are clean of sin in God's eyes because of the blood of Jesus spilt on Calvary. The Bible says John was "in the Spirit" which means his spirit entered into the New Heaven. This was possible because his spirit is and was sinless.

Revelation 4:3
"And he who sat there had the appearance of jasper and carnelian, and around the throne was a rainbow that had the appearance of an emerald."

Jesus Christ was sitting on the throne in all His beauty and glory. Around the throne were twenty-four elders. The majority of scholars believe the twenty-four elders are made up of the twelve tribes of Israel, and of the twelve apostles. Therefore the twenty-four elders represent The New Testament Saints (The Church), and The Old Testament Saints. What John saw was the Kingdom of God. The twenty-four elders were dressed in white to indicate total righteousness; they wore golden crowns to indicate the reward of their earthly deeds. The scene John saw was the gathering of the Kingdom of God as they were prepared for the second coming of Christ to defeat Satan.

God revealed to John the "Heaven of Heavens" that the Church will go to after they are raptured by Christ. This was the "Heaven of Heavens" but not the new Heaven. Then He revealed to John the New Heaven the Church as well as the Old Testament Saints and the Tribulation Saints will go to after the one-thousand-year millennial reign.

Many Christians would tell us that the New Heaven comes down out of the current heaven and resides somewhere above the earth or where the earth formerly was in existence. The Scripture says God sends down the Holy City or New Jerusalem. Yet we do not know exactly where this will be. First God revealed to us that this earth and the atmosphere (first heaven) created by God shall pass away. Other Scripture tells us the earth will be consumed by fire. The new earth will be startling different than the one we know. Let's take a look at the Holy City or New Jerusalem that John saw coming down out of heaven from God.

A Holy City

People make a lot of assumptions regarding what heaven is like. The world's understanding of heaven is a place where all good people go when they die. Many religious people think when they get to heaven they will see the Apostle Peter at the gate. But that is not scriptural. So let's look at New Jerusalem and what the Bible tells us of our eternal home if we know Jesus as our Savior.

Heaven is described as the place Jesus has prepared for those who love Him, trust Him, and believe Him. We know it is a real place because John was given the privilege of actually seeing it. The Scripture tells us that in heaven we will be interfacing with God on a personal and spiritual basis. God will actually dwell with us and we will be able to look upon God and know Him. We also have assurance that it is a physical place not just spirit. God's description of heaven is specific. We will know as we are known. Let's review some specific Scripture that gives us assurance we will know our loved ones in the New Heaven. Consider David and his sorrow that the son of Bathsheba was dead and yet assurance He, David, would see him again in Heaven.

2 Samuel 2:23
"But now he is dead, wherefore should I fast? Can I bring him back again? I shall go to him but he shall not return to me."

Moses and Elijah appeared with Christ on the Mount of Transfiguration. Even though it had been centuries since Moses died and Elijah was taken to heaven, Peter, James, and John were able to recognize them.

Matthew 7:3
"And behold, there appeared to them Moses and Elijah, talking with him."

We should also remember that in the book of John Jesus appeared to His disciples and was in His glorified body. Jesus recognized the doubt of Thomas and had him put his fingers into the places where the nails and spear had pierced His flesh. Jesus's body was a forerunner of our glorified bodies. If the Disciples could recognize Him it indicates we will know and be known in Heaven. We know our knowledge in Heaven will be vastly superior than it is on this earth therefore it is reasonable to assume we will know and be known.

God's Word gives us every reason to be confident that heaven is not a myth. When we come to the end of life the comfort of assurance about our eternal home makes physical death easier. There is comfort in following loved ones who have gone on before knowing they are with Jesus in heaven and we can join them. The apostle Paul said that those who are raised from death will have new bodies that are not stained with the corruption of this sin infested life.

The people around Paul did not understand the teachings of Jesus as well as we do because we have such better revelation from God. Yet they knew the contents of Corinthians 15:50–53

1 Corinthians 15:50–53

"I tell you this, brothers: flesh and blood cannot inherit the kingdom of God, nor does the perishable inherit the imperishable. Behold! I tell you a mystery. We shall not all sleep, but we shall all be changed, in a moment, in the twinkling of an eye, at the last trumpet. For the trumpet will sound, and the dead will be raised imperishable, and we shall be changed. For this perishable body must put on the imperishable, and this mortal body must put on immortality."

The Apostle Paul, inspired by God, tells us in Corinthians our new changed body will be like the glorious resurrected body of Jesus Christ.

Who will be in Heaven?

Earlier we established that Jesus Christ, God the Father, the Holy Spirit, and God's angels (the angels that did not rebel with Satan) resides in heaven. Those people on earth who choose to believe that Jesus Christ is the Son of God will also join with God the Father, God the Son, God the Holy Spirit, and the angels as residents of heaven. No human beings will be in heaven because they earned the right to go there. Every person in heaven will be there because of the Grace of our Lord and Savior and because of His blood shed on Calvary. Every person in heaven will be full of love and gratitude toward God for the gift of eternal life with God.

John 14:6
"Jesus said to him, "I am the way, the truth, and the life. No one comes to the Father except through Me."

The Saints of the Old Testament

We have previously seen those people who believed in the coming Messiah and devoted their lives to love of God the Father, and trusted God the Father and to the full extent of revelation given unto them, were saved from their sins. They were saved because of their faith in God the Father and the grace of God to redeem them subject to the forth coming death, burial, and resurrection of Christ. These will go to live throughout eternity with Christ just as the redeemed in the Church. However, when they died they could not join Christ around the throne of God. Christ had not conquered death through the Cross at the time of their death. Where then did the Old Testament persons of faith go awaiting their final entry into heaven? We know from previous scripture it is Abraham's Bosom. In fact, Jesus Christ told the thief on the Cross with Him that because of His faith he would go to Paradise, otherwise known as "Abraham's Bosom" or the holding place of the redeemed.

Luke 23:43
"And Jesus said to him, "Assuredly, I say to you, today you will be with Me in Paradise."

However, the Saints of Old Testament would not remain forever in Abraham's Bosom because their faith would be rewarded, even as would the Church's faith. That reward was to live eternally with God. After the resurrection of Christ from the grave we know He went down into Hades and gathered the Old Testament Saints and took them to the Throne of God in the Heaven of Heavens.

Hebrews 11:13–16
*"These all died in faith, not having received the things
promised, but having seen them and greeted them from afar,
and having acknowledged that they were strangers and exiles
on the earth. For people who speak thus make it clear that
they are seeking a homeland. If they had been thinking of
that land from which they had gone out, they would have
had opportunity to return. But as it is, they desire a better
country, that is, a heavenly one. Therefore God is not ashamed
to be called their God, for he has prepared for them a city."*

This "comfort" in Abraham's Bosom was not the ultimate salvation blessing anticipated by Old Testament believers. Hebrews
11:13–16 tells us that they were looking for a heavenly city.

Tribulation Saints

When the Church is raptured out of this world we do not know
what percentage of the living at that time will depart. We do know
that the Lord said the path is narrow and few there will be who
follow it to heaven. If we estimate or better stated, guess, that 10
percent of all living people on the earth are Raptured that leaves 90
percent of the words population on earth. We also know that the
Holy Spirit will be taken out of the world and its restraining power
on Satan will be gone. Demonic power will run rampant throughout
the world without the restraining force of the Church. The great
dictator called the Antichrist will emerge at the middle of the Great
Tribulation and declare he is God. He will then proceed to torture
and kill everyone who declares they are believers in God the Father
and Jesus Christ the son.

Yet a huge number of people will trust Christ in that time
period. That time period will be the greatest revival ever to happen
in creation. It will be the result of God's appointment of 144,000
Jewish evangelists who will be specially appointed by God, protected
by God from the wrath of Satan, and sent out by God to evangelize,
first the Jews and then the rest of the world left after the rapture.

Revelation 7:9–12
After this I looked, and behold, a great multitude that no one could number, from every nation, from all tribes and peoples and languages, standing before the throne and before the Lamb, clothed in white robes, with palm branches in their hands, and crying out with a loud voice, "Salvation belongs to our God who sits on the throne, and to the Lamb!" And all the angels were standing around the throne and around the elders and the four living creatures, and they fell on their faces before the throne and worshiped God, saying, "Amen! Blessing and glory and wisdom and thanksgiving and honor and power and might be to our God forever and ever! Amen."

Revelation 15:2–4
"And I saw what appeared to be a sea of glass mingled with fire—and also those who had conquered the beast and its image and the number of its name, standing beside the sea of glass with harps of God in their hands. And they sing the song of Moses, the servant of God, and the song of the Lamb, saying, "Great and amazing are your deeds, O Lord God the Almighty! Just and true are your ways, O King of the nations! Who will not fear, O Lord, and glorify your name? For you alone are holy All nations will come and worship you, for your righteous acts have been revealed."

So who will be in heaven? Three groups of believers will be with Christ in the New Heaven and New Earth for eternity. These groups are the Old Testament Saints who believed to the extent of revelation given them. They believed in the Messiah or the coming Savior sent from God to forgive men of their sins. The second group is the Body of Christ or the Church. They believe in Jesus Christ as the Messiah who died, was buried and resurrected for the sins of mankind. The third group will be the Tribulation Saints. They believe in Jesus Christ as Savior and trust in His second coming to take them home to glory. However, be not deceived. The 144,000

Jewish Evangelists will preach much more than the second coming of Christ to take the believers out of their pain and terror. The Jewish Evangelists will preach of the death, burial and resurrection of Jesus for the sins of all who would believe. After all, Tribulation Saints are looking back in faith to the price Jesus paid for their sins. Is that any different than "The Church" today looking back at the price Jesus paid for our sins? They also believe in spite of the pain and horror of the torment and terrorism placed upon them by the Antichrist. We see everyone in the heaven around the throne of God. They are saved by faith through the Grace of God not of works least any man could boast of their good deeds.

What will we be like in Heaven?

We will be changed into new, glorified bodies that are a combination of spirit (soul) and physical bodies. We know the new bodies will be beyond our ability to comprehend. We receive the glorified body at rapture with the Lord. The characteristics of the new bodies are the following:

- We will have new, perfect bodies. As Christians prior to the rapture we provide a dwelling place for the Holy Spirit but after the rapture when we join Christ in heaven we will become part of His Spirit.

1 Corinthians 15:42–44
"So is it with the resurrection of the dead. What is sown is perishable; what is raised is imperishable. It is sown in dishonor; it is raised in glory. It is sown in weakness; it is raised in power. It is sown a natural body; it is raised a spiritual body. If there is a natural body, there is also a spiritual body."

- Our minds will be made new with massive capacity and knowledge vastly beyond what we have now. This is not to say we will have equal knowledge with God, but the Bible tells us we will know so much more than we do now. This increased knowledge gives us increased capacity to rejoice in the presence and glory of God.

1 Corinthians 13:12
"For now we see in a mirror dimly; but then face to face. Now I know in part; then I shall know fully, even as I have been fully known."

- We will have moral perfection, for sin will be completely abolished from our nature and practice. Imperfection is such a part of our experience in this life that it is impossible for us to conceive what life in heaven will be like. We will have no temptation, no lust, no anger, no selfishness, no fear, no greed, no...we can go on and on.

Revelation 21:27
"But nothing unclean will ever enter it, nor anyone who does what is detestable or false, but only those who are written in the Lamb's book of life."

- Not only will we as individuals enter heaven as perfect people but we will enter as individual members of God's family. The church is "His bride." The Church is His beloved creation with glory and honor granted by Christ.

Ephesians 5:27
"So that He might present the Church to Himself in splendor, without spot or wrinkle or any such thing, but that she might be holy and without blemish."

- John's mind could not grasp the vastness of the revelation of God. He simply said we cannot comprehend in this life what we will be when be become like Jesus Christ.

1 John 3:2
"Beloved, we are God's children now; and what we will be has not yet appeared. but we know that when He appears, we shall be like Him, we shall see Him as He is."

- Paul wanted us to understand the vision given to him by God. He points out the difference between our earthly body and our new incorrupt spiritual body. Our new, spiritual body will be spirit and our glorified physical body. Paul then points out an interesting comparison of our spiritual body and Adam. He said Adam, as created a perfect creation, with a spiritual and physical body. But Adam sinned and was separated from God. We were born a sinful creation, but because of God's Grace He forgave our sin and we return to God as one who had no sin because of the blood of Jesus shed on Calvary.

1 Corinthians 15:44–49
"It is sown a natural body; it is raised a spiritual body. If there is a natural body, there is also a spiritual body. Thus it is written, "The first man Adam became a living being." The last Adam became a life-giving spirit. But it is not the spiritual that is first but the natural, and then the spiritual. The first man was from the earth, a man of dust; the second man is from heaven. As was the man of dust, so also are those who are of the dust, and as is the man of heaven, so also are those who are of heaven. Just as we have borne the image of the man of dust, we shall also bear the image of the man of heaven."

- The physical characteristics of our final heaven living place will be vastly different than we have here on earth. Scripture tells us John saw the Holy City, New Jerusalem come down to the New Earth. That Holy City is quoted as being 1,500 miles wide, 1,500 miles high, and 1,500 miles high. It has streets of gold and its gates are of precious stone. Evidently there is no gravity in heaven. Just as Christ was able to go through walls and not be encumbered with gravity so will we in the final heaven. There will be no sun, no moon, and no stars. God Himself will be the light in heaven. We will not need electric plugs to plug things in.

- We will not have any seas. This means we will not have a system in the final heaven of watering plants or of creating rain. We will have a brand new system mankind here does not comprehend.

Harmony in Heaven

Heaven will be a life of harmonious social relations. People from all walks of life and from all races and nations will be in heaven, and yet there will be no quarrels, disagreements, or crimes. There will be no wars to mar the fellowship. In heaven there will be no fear or mistrust of one another.

Revelation 21:24–27
"By its light will the nations walk, and the kings of the earth will bring their glory into it, and its gates will never be shut by day—and there will be no night there. They will bring into it the glory and the honor of the nations. But nothing unclean will ever enter it, nor anyone who does what is detestable or false, but only those who are written in the Lamb's book of life."

No sickness, No Pain, No Hunger, No Death

Life will be free from all the pain, sickness, hunger and death in Heaven. The body will no longer be subject to sickness, decay, hunger, pain, weariness, or death. It is impossible for us to grasp the joy of such an existence. We will have no fear, no stress, no anxiety regarding the health and welfare of ourselves or our loved ones and friends.

1 Corinthians 15:53
"For this perishable must put on imperishable, and this mortal must put on immortality."

We will not get tired in heaven. We will not need naps and will not have a shortage of energy. No medicine and no insurance companies will exist in heaven. The ravages of nature will no longer be a threat. There will be no car accidents. We will not need airplane tickets because we can just go wherever we want to go.

Revelation 7:16
"They shall hunger no more neither thirst anymore; the sun shall not strike them, nor any scorching heat."

Unbroken Fellowship with God

Heaven will be a life of unbroken fellowship with God. Our relations with God are so often hindered here. Satan often hides his face from us, and our limited understanding causes us to look through a glass darkly. But then we shall see Him face to face and behold Him in all His beauty. Who is the one here on earth you love the most and who loves you the most? Would you enjoy being with that one forever in total peace, joy, happiness and love? Multiply that joy and love by untold thousands and we begin to grasp our love for Jesus Christ. We will be with Christ walking and talking forever. This will undoubtedly be the greatest of joy in heaven, the bliss of all bliss. Oh, happy day!

Matthew 5:8
"Blessed are the pure in heart, for they shall see God."

We will know our loved Ones

Many want to know if they will recognize their friends in heaven. Matthew 8:11 tells us we will know not only our friends, but we'll know those who have gone on before us whom we never knew on this earth. Abraham, who lived so many hundreds of years before Christ, retains his identity. Christ tells us that the time is coming when the redeemed shall come from all over the world and shall sit down with Abraham and Isaac and Jacob in the kingdom of God.

Matthew 8:11

"I tell you, many will come from east and west and recline at table with Abraham, Isaac, and Jacob in the kingdom of heaven."

These great saints of the Old Testament did not lose their identity; they were known as Abraham, Isaac and Jacob. At the Transfiguration of Jesus, Moses who had been gone from the earth 1,500 years was there. Peter, James, and John recognized Moses on the Mount of Transfiguration.

We will have names in heaven. We will be known. Jesus told us that both Lazarus and the rich man knew each other after death here on earth. Our knowledge now is so small and insignificant compared to what it will be in heaven that God's Word tells us that here in this life we see through a mirror barely. However in eternity our understanding will be vastly expanded.

We look forward to seeing our families and friends in heaven. We also look forward to seeing and getting to know the saints of old who played a part in our heritage of God such as Abraham, Isaac, Jacob, and David. But the most wonderful experience will be to see our Savior and Lord Jesus Christ. And to God be the glory we will know Him and He will know us.

We will be like Jesus

We know that we will be like Jesus was in His resurrected body. This tells us a lot about our resurrected bodies. As saints in heaven we will see God in all His majesty. We will be amazed at His infinite glory. And the Bible tells us we will be "face to face" with God. The glory of God will swallow up the light of the sun as the brilliance of the sun now dispels the darkness of night.

Happiness in Heaven

All the joys we are to know in heaven will come from the presence of God. This is the leading thought in all that the Scripture has to say on the subject. It will be a sight like that far exceeds that of the prodigal son returning to his father. We cannot understand fully the rapture we will enjoy, but we know it will be centered on Jesus. Our perceptions of Christ will be clearer then, and that will make us love Him all the more.

The more we know God, the more we love Him. A great many of us would love God more if we only became better acquainted with Him. While on earth it gives Christians great pleasure to think of the perfection of Jesus Christ, but how will it be when we see Him as He is?

The Physical City

John the Apostle is given a glimpse of the City called, The Holy City or New Jerusalem. It is recorded in Revelation 21.

The City is 1,500 miles square. The city will be laid out like a cube. It is as long as it was wide as it is high. He measured the city with the rod and found it to be twelve thousand stadia (also referred to as a furlong) in length, and as wide and high as it is long.

- **Made of pure gold, like transparent glass:** The wall was made of jasper, and the city of pure gold (Revelation 21:18). The Holy city has an outside wall three hundred feet high made of jasper. There are twelve gates to the Holy City with three on each of the four sides. Each gate is made of one pearl and is guarded by an angel. Each gate has the name of one of the twelve tribes of Israel on it. The twelve gates were twelve pearls, each gate made of a single pearl. The great street of the city was of gold, as pure as transparent glass (Revelation 21:21).

Revelation 21:9–12
"Then came one of the seven angels who had the seven bowls full of the seven last plagues and spoke to me, saying, "Come, I will show you the Bride, the wife of the Lamb." And he carried me away in the Spirit to a great, high mountain, and showed me the holy city Jerusalem coming down out of heaven from God,

having the glory of God, its radiance like a most rare jewel, like a jasper, clear as crystal. It had a great, high wall, with twelve gates, and at the gates twelve angels, and on the gates the names of the twelve tribes of the sons of Israel were inscribed— mountain, and showed me the great city, the holy Jerusalem, descending out of heaven from God, having the glory of God. Her light was like a most precious stone, like a jasper stone, clear as crystal. Also she had a great and high wall with twelve gates, and twelve angels at the gates, and names written on them, which are the names of the twelve tribes of the children of Israel."

There will not be a Church or synagogue in heaven. There will not be a temple because Jesus Christ the Savior of the World will be the focus of worship. He will be imminently available for everyone at the same time to worship and adore and He will be the temple. There will not be a sun or moon in heaven because Jesus Christ will be the light. There will not be night. The City will never be closed and there will be no need of security for all evil and corruption will be gone and not be in heaven.

There will not be any clock in heaven for time will not exist. There will not be any alarms, no appointments for all the saints will be omnipresent or meaning able to be wherever they want to go instantly. The names of the twelve Apostles will be recorded on the twelve foundations. John said he saw the City descend out of heaven. This tells us John saw the third heaven descent out of the heavens or what we know as the new heaven. Our home, the New Heaven, will descend out of the third heaven and will be glorious beyond description.

CHAPTER TWENTY-TWO

The Doctrine of The Rapture of the Church
Jesus Christ comes Back for His Own

God's Word is very clear about the reality of Jesus Christ coming back to take the Church home with him. God promised this would happen and Paul speaks eloquently assuring Jews and Gentiles alike that they need not fear this life because eternity with Christ is our true reward. This event is not the second coming of Christ. It is, however, the prelude to the end times.

1 Thessalonians 4:13–14
"But we do not want you to be uninformed, brethren, concerning those who have fallen asleep, that you may not grieve as others do who have no hope. For since we believe that Jesus died and rose again, even so through Jesus; God will bring with Him those who have fallen asleep."

These are words the Holy Spirit told Paul to record in the book of Thessalonians so that the Jews and Gentiles of his day, and for all time to come, would have this message. God wanted the redeemed to be able to rejoice in comfort of knowing Christ would come again to take the Church home with Him. Paul is telling us God does not want us to be uninformed. He wants us to understand what will happen to those believers who have already died (sleep). And he gives assurance to us alive today that God will fulfill His promise to take us home to heaven with Him. His statement is so profound it sometimes gets missed. If you believe that Jesus died and rose again then you may also be certain that God will resurrect the dead in Christ and those still alive at God's rapture of His believers.

1 Thessalonians 4:15
"For this we declare to you by the word of the Lord, that we who are alive, who are left until the coming of the Lord will not precede those who have fallen asleep."

The Rapture, a promise to the Church

The promise of the rapture of the Church is a promise not given to all people. It is given to the Body of Christ, the Church. It is given to the Church alone. The reason only The Church will enjoy the rapture is because at Pentecost Jesus established the Church. The mission of the Church was to (1) glorify Jesus, and (2) evangelize the world. The Church has done an inadequate job of evangelizing the world but Jesus has perfectly performed His job of establishing The Church without error. The failure of the Church is man's fault. God is pleased with His Son and has rewarded the members of The Church, as an honor to Jesus.

Old Testament Saints were not promised the rapture. They did not know the Messiah would come in the form of Jesus Christ. Besides, Old Testament Saints who had died at the time of Christ's resurrection were taken to Heaven when Jesus left the grave and took them to Heaven to await the evolvement of The Church. They did not have the New Testament to record the coming of the Messiah. They were saved by having faith in God the Father to deliver for them a Messiah who would save them from their sins. They just did not know that Messiah would be Jesus Christ the Son of God. They were not part of The Church and therefore will not be resurrected from the dead at the rapture.

All New Testament Saints, meaning those who believe Jesus Christ died on Calvary to pay the price of their sins and who believe Jesus will save them from eternity in Hell, will be part of the great rapture.

1 Thessalonians 4:16–17
"For the Lord himself will descend from heaven with a cry of command, with the voice of an archangel, and with the sound of the trumpet of God. And the dead in Christ will rise first. Then we who are alive, who are left, will be caught up together with them in the clouds to meet the Lord in the air, and so we will always be with the Lord."

New Testament Scripture is even more precise as God tells His people of the approaching end of time to choose to follow Christ.

John 14:1–4
"Let not your hearts be troubled. Believe in God; believe also in me. In my Father's house are many rooms. If it were not so, would I have told you that I go to prepare a place for you? And if I go and prepare a place for you, I will come again and will take you to myself, that where I am you may be also. And you know the way to where I am going."

John, under the inspiration of God, wrote to us in chapter 14 many glorious points. First He points out that if we believe in God the Father we must also believe in God the Son because the two are as one. What God the Father wants, thinks, believes, desires and commands, God the Son also wants, thinks, believes, desires and commands. Second, because God the Father and God the Son are as one, we can believe Christ when He told us that just as surely as His ascension back into heaven was real we could also have faith that Christ was going to prepare a place in heaven for us as the redeemed believers to go with Him some day. Jesus promised His Word was true, and that He was going back to heaven to prepare a home for us in heaven. He also promised that He would return to earth and receive us, or take us into Glory to be with Him and God the Father. In writing this, Christ was not speaking of His second coming. The Bible is quiet clear that when He returns to earth the second time He will bring the Church with Him in our glorified bodies to wage war on Satan. That is called the second Coming of Christ. However in the rapture Jesus is talking about the time when He will come and take the Church out of the world, out of sin, out of pain, out of corruption. When Jesus comes to redeem "The Church," He does not touch the earth. When He comes back to defeat Satan in the battle of Armageddon, also called the Second Coming of our Lord, Jesus engages in battle while on the earth. Many people have mixed up the Second coming of Christ with the Rapture of the Church. Many of those who believe there will be a Rapture of the Church believe we have been promised a lot of signs announcing the coming rapture and because these signs are not completed they feel they have nothing to worry about. Beware, because they have mixed up the Second coming of Christ with the Rapture of the Church. God does not promise us signs announcing the rapture. God does give us signs that will announce the Second Coming of Christ. Nothing prevents the rapture to happen this very day. No man knows when this will happen but we do know it could happen this very day.

It is important as we study the End Times in the Doctrine of Eschatology, to pay attention to who is affected with the rapture. This is because all of the End Times events begin with the rapture and many of these events are happening at the same time.

The Bible gives us evidence that two resurrections of mankind will take place. Daniel 12:2, written way back into the Old Testament, reveals this occurrence.

Daniel 12:2
"And many of them that sleep in the dust of the earth shall awake, some to everlasting life, and some to shame and everlasting contempt."

This scripture, along with many more, tells us all of those who have died at the time of the resurrection of mankind, everyone who has ever lived and died up to that day will be raised from the dead. It is also very clear that there will be two resurrection categories, one for those who have shown faith and trust in God and one for those who choose to not believe. We will call these two separate resurrections from the grave to be the resurrection of the just (those who trusted God) and the resurrection of the unjust (those who rejected God).

John 5:28–29
"Do not marvel at this, for an hour is coming when all who are in the tombs will hear his voice and come out, those who have done good to the resurrection of life, and those who have done evil to the resurrection of judgment."

In John 5, verse 28 the resurrection of those who have done good to the resurrection of life mean those who have followed the commands of God and believed on Jesus Christ as their hope for salvation. Therefore those who have believed on Jesus and kept faith in God are the "Just." In verse 29 those who have done evil to the resurrection of judgement, are those who have rejected God's outreach to claim them unto His children. They have rejected God and are the "Unjust." The just will be raised to immortality and eternity. The unjust will be raised to condemnation, banishment from the presence of God, eternity, and torments.

Thessalonians 4:16
"For the Lord Himself will descend from heaven with a cry of command, with the voice of an archangel, and with the sound of the trumpet of God. And the dead in Christ will rise first."

Thessalonians 4:16 tells us the "Dead in Christ" will arise first. Who are the "Dead in Christ"? The "Dead in Christ" are those people who gave their heart to Jesus and asked Him for forgiveness of their sins, and did this in the time period between the Resurrection of Jesus and the rapture of the Church. The term, "Dead in Christ" then means the "Body of Christ" or the Church. When the "Body of Christ" dies their souls will immediately join with Jesus around the thrown of God but their bodies remain in the grave. Now with the Rapture, the souls are rejoined with the bodies but the bodies are now glorified bodies. The souls and now glorified bodies join with Jesus at the throne of God. That glorified physical body will be joined with their spirit and they will be caught up with Jesus in the air.

What do we mean when we say the "Dead in Christ" will be raised first? It means there is still work to be done. Christ will raise those who alive in Christ, or who have given their heart to Jesus and asked Him for forgiveness of their sins, directly from the life they are living to meet Him in the air. These people will also be transformed from the body they have had to a glorified. The promise of this activity is outlined in Matthew 27:51–53.

Matthew 27:51–53
"The tombs also were opened. And many bodies of
the saints who had fallen asleep were raised, 53 and
coming out of the tombs after his resurrection they
went into the holy city and appeared to many."

We know from 1 Kings 2:1–2 followed by 1 Kings 2:10 that the pattern of life is that when Old Testament people who believe and trusted in the promises of God died, they were put into a deep, unconscious sleep. In that sleep they had no knowledge are awareness of anything.

1 Kings 1:1–2, 10
When David's time to die drew near, he commanded Solomon
his son, saying, "I am about to go the way of all the earth.
Be strong, and show yourself a man, Then David slept
with his fathers and was buried in the city of David."

King David, like all other Old Testament Saints had to go to Abraham's Bosom, the upper part of Hades, to await Christ coming to Hades to redeem all believers. The sequence of resurrections is important in our understanding of how God will fulfill His Word to us. In Ecclesiastes 9:10 we are also assured there is nothing that happens that these Old Testament Saints were aware of while in Abraham's Bosom, which is the upper part of Sheol, also known as Hades.

Ecclesiastes 9:10
"Whatever your hand finds to do, do it with your
might, for there is no work or thought or knowledge
or wisdom in Sheol, to which you are going."

Sequence of Resurrections

Resurrection No. 1: The first resurrection was, of course, that of Jesus Christ. Jesus is the forerunner of all things. His resurrection gives us the assurance that we also, can conquer death because of the price Jesus paid for our sins. His resurrection is found in a host of scripture. God tells us the resurrection of Christ was the firstfruits of all "Dead in Christ" awaiting their resurrection. In this verse Paul is talking to and about the "Body of Christ" also known as "The Church."

1 Corinthians 15:20–23
"But in fact Christ has been raised from the dead, the firstfruits of those who have fallen asleep. For as by a man came death, by a man has come also the resurrection of the dead. For as in Adam all die, so also in Christ shall all be made alive. But each in his own order: Christ the firstfruits, then at his coming those who belong to Christ."

Before the resurrection of Jesus some small sampling of people who died were raised again through the miracles of Jesus. But no one had ever died, been raised from the dead and then did not have to die again. Therefore, no one had ever conquered death prior to the Resurrection of Christ. When 1 Corinthians chapter 15 records the resurrection of Jesus as the firstfruits of more resurrections, it is a guarantee or assurance of the possibility of all believers to come. Yet the resurrections of all who will follow the resurrection of Jesus could not be done without the death and resurrection of Jesus because He conquered death not only for Himself but for all believers who will follow.

Resurrection No. 2: This resurrection is often missed or overlooked by scholars. But the Word of God tells us that at the crucifixion of Jesus, when He cried out with a loud voice and yielded up His spirit, a great earthquake occurred. The Bible tells us the tombs were opened and many bodies of the saints who had fallen asleep (died) were raised and went to Heaven to be around the Throne of God.

Matthew 27:50–53
"And Jesus cried out again with a loud voice and yielded up His spirit. And behold the curtain of the temple was torn in two, from top to bottom. And the earth shook, and

*the rocks split. The tombs also were opened and many
bodies of the Saints who had fallen asleep were raised
and coming out of the tombs after His resurrection they
went into the Holy City and appeared to many."*

These were Old Testament Saints chosen by God to help celebrate the victory of Christ over death. We do not know who they were or how many were resurrected.

Resurrection No. 3: The third resurrection of the dead takes place at the rapture of the Church established by Christ. This is a time not announced in Scripture therefore it will be a surprise. God's Word is very clear that the "Body of Christ" also known as "The Church" members of the family of God who have had their physical body die will be resurrected. The spirit or souls of these people have been gathered in Heaven around the throne of God at the time of their physical death, but their earthly bodies have been asleep in the grave. At this Resurrection No. 3 they will have a glorified body unite with their spirit or soul and will go to heaven to rejoice with Jesus around the throne of God.

1 Corinthians 15:50–53
*"I tell you this brothers! flesh and blood cannot inherit
the Kingdom of God, nor does the perishable inherit the
imperishable. Behold! I tell you a mystery. We shall not
all sleep, but we shall all be changed, in a moment, in the
twinkling of an eye, at the last trumpet. For the trumpet
will sound, and the dead will be raised imperishable, and
we shall be changed. For this perishable body must put on
imperishable and this mortal body must put on immortality."*

Resurrection No. 4: Some will challenge whether this resurrection is separate or just the second part of resurrection no. 3. We see this as a separate resurrection that occurs seconds after the resurrection of the "Dead in Christ." This involves those who are believers in Jesus Christ as their Savior and are alive at the Resurrection of the "Dead in Christ." The Bible tells us in 1 Corinthians 15 that these people will also be changed and will put on imperishable and immortality. We do know that both the "Dead in Christ" and the "Alive in Christ" at the time of the rapture of the Church will be taken out of the world and join Jesus Christ in the air.

Resurrection No. 5: During the middle of the Seven-Year Tribulation, after the rapture of the Church but before the Battle of Armageddon, God will send two powerful witnesses to testify, along with the 144,000 evangelists, that Jesus Christ is the living Lord and belief in Him is the only way to salvation. These two witnesses will be publically killed in some way that the entire world will see. The two witnesses will lay where they are killed for three and a half days, before they are resurrected from the dead. These two powerful witnesses from God are a huge part of God's victory over Satan in this period.

Revelation 11:11–12
"But after the three and a half days a breath of life from God entered them, and they stood up on their feet, and great fear fell on those who saw them. Then they heard a loud voice from Heaven saying to them, "Come up here!" And they went up to heaven in a cloud, and their enemies watched them."

Resurrection No. 6: The Old Testament man of God Ezekiel tells us what God told him to write and informs us that the Old Testament people who believed in God the Father and of His promise of a coming Messiah will be raised from the dead and join God in Heaven. This could be millions of people but the amount is unknown. They will be raised from the dead, given a glorified body and that glorified body will unite with their spirit that has been in Hades awaiting this resurrection.

Ezekiel 37:13–14
"And you shall know that I am the Lord, when I open your graves, and raise you from your graves, O my people. And I will put my Spirit within you, and you shall live and I will place you in your own land. Then you shall know that I am Lord; I have spoken, and I will do it, declares the Lord."

Resurrection No. 7: At the end of the Seven-Year Tribulation in which those who believe Jesus Christ is the Savior of the world will be tortured and beheaded because of their refusal to wear the "Mark of the Beast" and their refusal to deny their faith in Jesus, the seventh Resurrection will occur.

Revelation 20:4
"Then I saw thrones, and seated on them were those to whom the authority to judge was committed. Also I saw the souls of those who had been beheaded for the testimony of Jesus and for the word of God, and those who had not worshiped the beast or its image and had not received its mark on their foreheads or their hands. They came to life and reigned with Christ for a thousand years."

Resurrection No. 8: The last resurrection will take place at the end of the one-thousand-year Millennial Kingdom rule of Christ. This resurrection is of the billions of people over the years of creation who are nonbelievers in Jesus Christ. They have rejected Him as the Messiah and only promise of victory over death. These people will go through the Great White Throne Judgment and will be found guilty and will be cast into the permanent Lake of Fire. God's Word assures us that these martyrs for Christ will be resurrected from the dead and will join Christ directly into the one-thousand-year Millennial Reign and after then Heaven itself.

Revelation 20:11–15
"Then I saw a great white throne and Him who was seated on it. From His presence earth and sky fled away, and no place was found for them. And I saw the dead, great and small, standing before the throne, and books were opened. Then another book was opened, which is the book of life. And the dead were judged by what was opened, which is the book of life. And the dead were judged by what was written in the books, according to what they had done. And the sea gave up the dead who were in it, Death and Hades gave up the dead

who were in them, and they were judged each one of them, according to what they had done. Then Death and Hades were thrown into the lake of fire. This is the second death, the lake of fire. And if anyone's name was not found written in the book of life, he was thrown into the lake of fire."

The Rapture

All believers are excited about the return of Jesus. God's Word tells us Christ will come and take The Church out of this world of pain, suffering, sin, and disappointment. He will take us home to live with Him throughout eternity. Although the English word rapture is not specifically used to refer to this event, the Bible does use the Greek word harpazo; which means "to snatch" or "caught up." God's Word says we will be caught up in the sky to be with Jesus. God specifically tells us that the Church, which means that body of believers who have placed their trust in Christ, will be caught up in the air with Jesus. God wants us to know this and to have unquestioned faith it will happen.

1 Thessalonians 4:16–17
"For the Lord Himself will descend from heaven with a cry of command, with the voice of an archangel, and with the sound of the trumpet of God. And the dead in Christ will rise first, Then we who are alive, who are left, will be caught up together with them in the clouds to meet the Lord in the air, and so we will always be with the Lord."

God does not give us a specific time that Christ will come "in the air" to redeem His Church. However in the first book of Corinthians God gives us new, dynamic revelations about that great event.

1 Corinthians 15:50
"Now this I say, brethren, that flesh and blood cannot inherit the kingdom of God; nor does corruption inherit incorruption."

Paul is establishing foundation for the great revelation He is about to give comfort to the Church at Corinth and to all believers throughout eternity. He tells us that this earthly body, corrupted in sin, cannot enter into eternity with Christ. He uses the wording "Kingdom of God" in this instance to refer to the glorified body of believers, after Rapture, who are reunited with Christ throughout eternity. We have too much sin, and our bodies are to corrupt to co-exist with Holy God.

1 Corinthians 15:51
"Behold, I tell you a mystery: We shall not all sleep, but we shall all be changed—"

Paul says, "Listen up Church," meaning all believers throughout eternity, because for the first time, ever, God is about to reveal, through Paul, the explanation of a mystery. How can we who have been promised eternity with Christ, but who know our earthly bodies cannot enter the Kingdom of heaven with God, have His promises of eternity with Him fulfilled? Paul tells us a marvelous promise. First, he tells us that everyone who believes in Christ will not die prior to the time Christ comes back for His Church. Then he explains a huge mystery. We shall be changed. Our earthly body will be changed into a glorified body that is not of flesh and bones but is still a tangible body not only of spirit but also of substance.

1 Corinthians 15:52–54
"In a moment, in the twinkling of an eye, at the last trumpet. For the trumpet will sound, and the dead will be raised incorruptible, and we shall be changed." For this corruptible must put on incorruption, and this mortal must put on immortality. So when this corruptible has put on incorruption, and this mortal has put on immortality, then shall be brought to pass the saying that is written: "Death is swallowed up in victory."

Paul now explains about the event in which we will be changed. He points out it will happen so sudden that no one will have any opportunity to prepare for it. Neither lost or saved will see it coming because it happens in the twinkling of an eye at the last of the seven trumpets recorded in the book of Revelation. When Paul tells us "the dead will be raised incorruptible it means we will not have the capacity to sin any more. We will no longer be conflicted by a desire to pursue earthly things while at the same time have a desire to please God and follow Christ. The incorruptible body will only have the nature of spiritual cleanliness granted by the blood of Christ. And in our resurrected, glorified body, we will be immortal while in this earthly body we are mortal. This means we will not be subjected to death. We will be immortal.

1 Corinthians 15:55–57
"O Death, where is your victory? O Death, where is your sting?"
The sting of death is sin, and the power of sin is
the law. But thanks be to God, who gives us the
victory through our Lord Jesus Christ.

Through the blood of Jesus Christ, shed for us on Calvary, and through the resurrection of Christ by God the Father; death will finally be conquered for us and the penalty of death will be paid. Paul's statement "O Death here is your sting, he is referring to the "place of the dead in Christ" awaiting the consummation of time that results in the dead in Christ going to the eternal "Lake of Fire."

We know that when we as believers in Christ die in this earthly world, we immediately go to be with Christ in heaven. How does this correspond with biblical teaching that tells us Hades is made up of two compartments? One compartment is for the unsaved and is a place of fire and torture, while the other is called "Paradise or "Abraham's bosom" and is a holding place for the completion of the Church age. This is because when believers in Christ die they pass from the realm of time into eternity. Time has no meaning because it is the opposite of eternity.

2 Corinthians 5:8
"Yes, we are of good courage, and we would rather be
away from the body and at home with the Lord."

Although God did not give us great depth of knowledge about our passage from time to eternity we do know certain things. Paul tells us to be absent from the body (speaking of the spirit of man) is to be home with the Lord. This scripture tells us that when we, as believers, die our spirit goes home to be with the Lord. We, as Christians, can rest in the comfort that as believers we will never experience separation from God.

Timing of the Rapture

The rapture will come as a thief in the night and will be a huge surprise to mankind. It is an event mankind is supposed to be expecting but does not expect. We do not know when the rapture will occur. God has specifically told us we have no need to know this information. God does not want us to waste time trying to determine this information but rather stand ready for that moment and expect it to happen imminently.

1 Thessalonians 5:1–6
"Now concerning the times and the seasons, brothers' you
have no need to have anything written to you. For you
yourselves, are fully aware that the day of the Lord will come
like a thief in the night. While people are saying, "There
is peace and security," then sudden destruction will come
upon them as labor pains come upon a pregnant woman,
and they will not escape. But you are not in darkness,
brothers, for that day to surprise you like a thief. For you
are all children of light. You are children of the day. We
are not of the night or of the darkness. So then let us not
sleep, as others do, but let us keep awake and be sober."

Luke 17:34–36
"I tell you, in that night there will be two in one bed. One will be taken and the other left. There will be two women grinding together. One will be taken and the other left."

God does not want us to know when He will come for His Church. He specifically tells us we are not to know that but we are to watch for His coming. Paul expected Christ to come for His Church during his lifetime. We too, are expected to watch with an anticipation of the Lord's return. The rapture is a rendezvous for dead and living Christians. The length of testing which the believer and the Church endure during the Church age is terminated with the timing of the rapture.

The Seven-Year Tribulation and the Rapture

The reality of the rapture is not questioned by the vast majority of Christians, but the timing of when that rapture shall occur is of vast debate. The issue has to do with whether the rapture will occur prior to, after, or simultaneous with the Seven-Year Tribulation that is revealed to us in Scripture. God's Word has a lot to tell us about the Seven-Year Tribulation because it is a very significant part of the end times.

The Tribulation period is a seven year period that occurs at the end of the Church age but prior to the millennium kingdom. Israel again becomes the focus of end times. In the book of Daniel, God outlines a seventy week period from the day he lived, until the first advent (or coming) of Jesus Christ. The period from Daniel to the resurrection of Jesus constituted sixty nine of those weeks. God installed a gap in time into Daniel's seventy weeks. We know this gap as the Age of the Church. This is a period granted to the Church to evangelize people and bring them to a saving knowledge of Christ. Once this age of the Church is exhausted the seventieth week begins. The seventieth week is also the "Seven years of Tribulation." We understand this period of time is a week on the seventy weeks of

Daniel's calendar. However we still do not know when the rapture will happen.

Daniel 9:27
"And he shall make a strong covenant with many for one week, and for half of the week he shall put an end to sacrifice and offering. And on the wing of abominations shall come one who makes desolate, until the decreed end is poured out on the desolator."

Daniel outlines the seven years of Tribulation into three distinct periods. The first half or three and one half years, the middle week of the seven year period, and the final three and one half years of the seven-year period. In Daniel, God tells us the Tribulation period begins with an agreement signed between Israel and "The Antichrist" that will bring about peace or the appearance of peace for the first three and one half years. We see in later Scripture that agreement angers God greatly because His chosen people trust in an agreement with Satan rather than God. But in the middle of the seven-year period Satan is banished from heaven and empowers the Antichrist who has stopped worship in the Jewish temple. The Antichrist now proclaims he is God.

Revelation 12:7–9
"Now war arose in heaven, Michael and his angels fighting against the dragon. And the dragon and his angels fought back, but he was defeated, and there was no longer any place for them in heaven. ⁹And the great dragon was thrown down, that ancient serpent, who is called the devil and Satan, the deceiver of the whole world—he was thrown down to the earth, and his angels were thrown down with him."

The Apostle John had revealed to him that when Satan is cast out of heaven he will know he has a very short time before he will be totally cut off from power by God. Satan knows he will lose the battle with God. But Satan is evil. That is who he is and he cannot change.

Therefore he elects to battle Christ for supremacy. Satan then selects a being called in Scripture "The Antichrist." This being is empowered by Satan and proceeds to set up relationships and world events that result in the world worshiping him and him alone. Yet through the God led 144,000 prophets of God a host of people will be saved and will refuse to worship "The Antichrist." These years will be the most horrific even known to mankind. They will be full of terror, fear, pain, grief, and amazing events.

Will the Church or the believers in Christ be left in the world to endure this horrible time? Believers in Christ have three distinct views of when the rapture will occur in comparison to the great Tribulation. Each of these views concerns timing. Let us consider the Pre-Tribulation rapture, the Mid-Tribulation rapture and the Post-Tribulation rapture.

Pre-Tribulation Rapture View

The Pre-Tribulation Rapture view simply means this view advances the understanding that the Church will be raptured or taken just before the beginning of the Great Tribulation seven-year period. God's Word provides ample reason to accept this view and believe it. Revelation 3:10 all promise the followers of Christ will escape the wrath of God. The great Tribulation is expressly a time of God's wrath.

1 Thessalonians 1:9–10
"For they themselves report concerning us the kind of reception we had among you, and how you turned to God from idols to serve the living and true God, and to wait for his Son from heaven, whom he raised from the dead, Jesus who delivers us from the wrath to come."

The key phrase in this verse is *"Jesus who delivers us from the wrath to come."* We have every reason to believe the reference of the wrath to come is the Tribulation period when Satan will be granted a period with power to rule on earth. But God specifically tells us He will deliver His Body of believers from that wrath.

In the fifth chapter of Thessalonians, Paul tells us again God did not appoint us unto the wrath of God. However, this verse specifically ties the fact God did not appoint us unto wrath but to avoid the Great Tribulation because of His rapture.

Revelation 3:10
"Because you have kept my word about patient endurance,
I will keep you from the hour of trial that is coming on
the whole world, to try those who dwell on the earth."

Now God speaks in Scripture more clearly. He tells us that because we believe on Jesus Christ (commanded to in Scripture) He will keep His commitment and in the hour or trial (Tribulation) that shall come on the earth, He will deliver His own from the earth. The Pre-Tribulation view of the rapture ties in closely with a view of how God has interfaced with man over the years. God has used different approaches to interface with man and convince man of his sin. This does not mean that there are different ways to be saved. In all ages, dispensationalists stress salvation comes by faith in the true God, and sins are forgiven only by Christ's payment of their penalty through His death on the cross. Yet depth of faith changes according to the revelation of Christ God has ordained. Each dispensation is a different covenant of faith man must enter into with God. The differences reflect the various amounts of revelation God has given to His people. Listed are the ages of Dispensation or ages of time:

- *Innocence (Genesis 1–3):*
- *God offers man eternal life for faith in Him demonstrated through man's obedience.*
  - *Man rebels, and is expelled from the Garden of Eden.*
  - *Man's knowledge of Jesus is unknown.*
- *Conscience (Genesis 4–6):*
- *God offers to govern man through his conscience, or the knowledge of right and wrong imputed into mankind.*

- ○ *Man sears his conscience, and God brings the universal flood.*
- ○ *Man has no knowledge of Jesus Christ as the promised Messiah*
- *Government (Genesis 7–11):*
- *God offers to govern man through civil government (Genesis 9:6).*
  - ○ *Man corrupts civil government, and God brings the confusion of tongues and scatters man.*
  - ○ *Man has no knowledge of Jesus Christ as the promised Messiah. Faith leading to salvation rests in believing the promises of God the Father, specifically the promised coming of the Messiah.*
- *Promise (Genesis 12):*
- *God promises to bless Abraham and his descendants, and all nations through them. This promise is fulfilled in part in the person and work of Christ, and fully realized and fulfilled in the Millennial Kingdom*
  - ○ *Jacob's sons fall into sin and God brings them into slavery in Egypt.*
  - ○ *Man has no knowledge of Jesus Christ as the promised Messiah Faith leading to salvation rests in believing the promises of God the Father, specifically the promised coming of the Messiah*
- *Law (Exodus 20):*
- *God promises to grant Israel the promises he made to Abraham conditional to their obedience to his Law. Like above, it is fulfilled in the Millennial Kingdom.*
  - ○ *Israel falls into sin, undergoes exile and dispersion, and is finally purified through the Great Tribulation in the form of the 144,000 who come to Christ during the Tribulation.*
  - ○ *Man has no knowledge of Jesus Christ as the promised Messiah Faith leading to salvation rests in believing the promises of God the Father, specifically the promised coming of the Messiah*

- *Grace or The Church Age (Pentecost—Rapture).*
- *The Birth of Jesus, the life of Jesus, the witness of Jesus and the Death, burial, and resurrection of Jesus reveals to man Jesus is the promised Messiah.*
  - *God temporarily suspends working through Israel as his chosen nation and offers to work through all believers in Jesus.*
  - *The Church apostatizes and is judged in the Great Tribulation after true believers are rescued through the Rapture.*
  - *Before the final Dispensation: The Seven-Year Tribulation*
  - *Jesus as the coming Messiah is history to these people. Their faith must rest in Jesus Christ coming again to conquer evil and deliver then into His eternal reign.*
  - *The Antichrist signs a covenant for seven years with the nation of Israel (Daniel 9:27).*
  - *Christ opens the first seal of a seven sealed scroll and a rider on a white horse who most probable is the Antichrist, appears on the world scene promising peace and established his one-world government (Revelation 6:2).*
  - *Christ opens the second seal of seven sealed scroll and it introduces a great world war. However this is not the battle of Armageddon. Not yet! (Revelation 6:3–4).*
  - *Christ opening of the third seal of seven sealed scroll brings famine and vast inflation (Revelation 6:5–6).*
  - *Christ opening of the forth seal of the seven sealed scroll brings death to 25 percent of the people and living creatures on earth (Revelation 6:7–8).*
  - *Christ opening of the fifth seal of the seven sealed scroll brings the beheading of a host but unknown number of people who refuse the Mark of the Beast.*

> *They are saved through the preaching of the 144,000 evangelists (Revelation 6:9–1).*
> - *Christ opening of the sixth seal of the seven sealed scroll unleashes the wrath of God in the form of a mighty earthquake. It is so severe people call for the rocks to fall on them. (Revelation 6:12–7)*
> - *Christ opening of the seventh seal of the seven sealed scroll opens an even worse period than ever seen before called the seven trumpets. (Revelation 8:1–6)*
> - *Millennial Kingdom (Revelation 20):*
> - *God fulfills all of his promises to the nation of Israel after the Second Coming of Jesus.*
>   - *Satan ignites a rebellion against Jesus, which God wins rather easily and then judges all men at the Great White Throne.*
>   - *All people in the Millennial period of one thousand years know Jesus because He comes down and lives with them very similar to the Garden of Eden before Adam fall from his relationship with God.*

Those who adhere to the Pre-Millennial view tend to have specific definitions of covenants God has had with his people. This view facilitates the clear definitions of time.

The following are some of the other arguments for a pre-Tribulation rapture:

- John was caught up to heaven in Revelation 4:1 as a picture of the Church being raptured prior to any of the other Tribulation events.
- Christ is coming "for" his saints (meaning the rapture) and then "with" the saints (meaning His second coming)—the interval allows for the judgment of believers and the marriage supper of the Lamb.
- The Tribulation Period is no. 1 to reclaim Israel to God and no. 2 to fulfill God's promise regarding His "Chosen

Nation" Israel—the Matthew 24 passage is for Israel, not for the Church.

- Believers (prior to the rapture) will escape The Tribulation and be delivered from wrath and judgment.
- The Church should have a constant expectation of Christ's (not antichrist's) coming.
- The "restrainer" of 2 Thessalonians 2:7 is the Church, or the Holy Spirit living in the body of believers, which must be removed before antichrist is allowed to appear.

Mid-Tribulation Rapture View

Mid-Tribulationists believe the same as Pre-Tribulationists except they believe the Church is raptured at the middle of the Seven-Year Tribulation Period not the beginning. However they still believe the Church will miss the great pain and torment of the last three and one half years called The Great Tribulation.

In substance the Mid-Tribulation Rapture view is not much different that Pre-Tribulation views. The Mid-Tribulation view simply believes the first three and a half years of Tribulation will be troubled and will have wars and rumors of war.

Mid-Tribulationists believe these first three and one half years will be difficult for Christians, but the effort of the government will not be totally focused on persecuting and elimination of all believers. They believe this happens at the middle of the Seven-Year Tribulation, after the Desolation of Abomination or the time the Antichrist takes the throne of Jerusalem.

A Millennial Tribulation Rapture View

A millennialists believe that many of God's promises regarding the end-times, are figurative and will not be literally fulfilled. They teach the boundaries of the figurative millennial reign, is between Christ's birth and His second coming. They do believe in the second coming of Christ but do not accept an earlier rapture of the Church. They believe that The Church will be taken up to meet Jesus in the sky with the second coming and that is the rapture. Amillennialists believe that when Christ comes for his own, in what they see as a combination of the rapture and the second coming of Christ, the judgment of the wicked and all end events outside of the millennial reign begin immediately. Amillennialists also believe that when Israel rejected Christ they sealed their fate and have no other part in end events. They believe the Church inherited the promises that were originally given to Israel. This means that Israel no longer has any special place in the plan of God. Amillennialists believe the Church has fulfilled the Old Testament millennial kingdom promises, in a spiritualized rather than literal way.

Post-Millennial Rapture View

Post-Millennial advocates believe the return of Christ is real and will take place at the end of the millennium. They teach the one thousand literal year reign of the millennial years are not a literal one thousand years but a long time. They teach that this unspecified period of time taught as the millennium corresponds to the "Church Age." They teach that during this long period of time called the "Church Age" or "Age of Grace" the world gets better and better socially, economically, politically and culturally. This belief teaches that the world will advance to a state of righteousness that exceeds anything experienced on earth before. They believe evil will be greatly curtailed and limited in power over the individual.

Post-Millennial teachings agree with Pre-Millennial, Mid-Millennial, and Amillennial teachings that the Church has been given the task of evangelizing the world from Israel. They teach that the Church is succeeding in this task. This view is not widely held today. It had its greatest followers in the eighteenth and nineteenth century.

Of all the four views Pre-Millennial advocators and Mid-Millennial advocators have the most scripture to support their views. Pre-Millennial teachings are most widely held.

Resurrected Bodies

At the time of the rapture the dead in Christ (believers who have died after the resurrection of Christ), will be resurrected from the dead and given a new glorified body. Immediately following those who are alive and are believers will be given a glorified body, will not require resurrection, but will be raptured.

1 Thessalonians 4:14
"For since we believe that Jesus died and rose again; even so, through Jesus, God will bring with him those who have fallen asleep."

God's Word tells us we will spend eternity in heaven with Jesus Christ. And this will be possible because God will give us a glorified, resurrected body that is physical, yet not corruptible or mortal. Certainly our current physical bodies we use here on earth will not meet the task for eternity. They must be glorified and substantially modified because

1. Our earthly bodies die and when we are raptured we will we will be given a glorified body that is immortal. In heaven there will be no death and no dying. However recognize there is a difference between the thousand year millennial reign and Heaven.
2. The bodies we have now are corruptible. First of all that means we have the results of sin and evil temptation that has ravaged us. We also have suffered from sickness, aging, accidents, stress, depression and evil of a corrupt people. In our glorified body all this will be taken away.
3. Our bodies have to eat, drink, rest, be clothed, and be shielded from the sun the weather and elements. We are weak and limited in where we can go and what we can do. We have to have the support of the universe that was created by God. We have to have rain, sun, the moon, the

stars, the sun, and oxygen to breath. In our glorified bodies whatever we need, will be supplied by Jesus.

4. We are also told in Scripture that our bodies are temporal which means we have a limited time to live. God has ordained we cannot live beyond a specific period of time. In fact everything we do and sense is related to time. We are not physically prepared for eternity. Our glorified bodies will have no awareness of need for time.

1 Corinthians 15:43–45

"It is sown in dishonor; it is raised in glory. It is sown in weakness; it is raised in power. It is sown a natural body; it is raised a spiritual body. If there is a natural body, there is also a spiritual body. Thus it is written, "The first man Adam became a living being" the last Adam became a life-giving spirit."

So it is obvious that we must have many physical changes if we are able to live through eternity and enjoy the rewards God has prepared for us in heaven. So what will our bodies be like? We will be:

- ○ *Immortal: 1 Corinthians 15:53. "This immortal must put on immortality. This means we will never die. So our new resurrected body will be perfectly fit for eternity.*
- ○ *Incorruptible: 1 Corinthians 15:42, 52–54. This means we can never take on a nature of evil. We will no longer have an evil nature within us and we cannot be converted to ways of Satan.*
- ○ *Glorious: 1 Corinthians 15:43. "It is sown in dishonor, it is raised in glory" Remember that our glorified body will be shaped like that of Christ. So we will in some way radiate light, we will be beautiful creatures but creatures that do not have the capacity to become enamored with our own beauty.*
- ○ *Powerful: 1 Corinthians 15:43. "It is sown in weakness, it is raised in power" - We are weak compared*

too much of the animal kingdom and compared to weather and nature. The body of Christ has amazing power. He is all-powerful because He is God. We will not be all-powerful. But we will have immense power to accomplish things.

○ *Spiritual: 1 Corinthians 15:44. "It is sown a natural body and it is raised a spiritual body" Paul tells us that somehow we will have real physical bodies that can be seen, can be known, can be touched because that is the kind of physical body Jesus Christ had after His resurrection. And in addition to our physical bodies we will be spiritual. In this life we are physical with a spirit. In our glorified bodies we will be spiritual with a physical body.*

○ *Holy: Ephesians 5:27. Paul told the Church at Ephesus that the entire Church would be presented to Christ without spot or blemish. This is not because we have never sinned but because the blood of Jesus has totally erased our sin. Not just forgiven our sin but erased it and our glorified bodies will be totally clean without blemish of sin and corruption. Just think this means we can trust everyone in heaven. We can and will love everyone in heaven. There will be no misunderstandings. There will be no hatred, no backbiting, no slander, and no grieving in heaven.*

1 John 3:1–3

"See what kind of love the Father has given to us, that we should be called children of God; and so we are. The reason why the world does not know us is that it did not know him. Beloved, we are God's children now, and what we will be has not yet appeared; but we know that when he appear we shall be like him, because we shall see him as he is. And everyone who thus hopes in him purifies himself as he is pure."

- ○ *We will be patterned after the body of Christ so we will be able to speak and hear—Christ in His glorified body spoke to Mary and the disciples. They heard Him and He heard them.*
- ○ *We will be able to be touched and to touch others— Christ's body was not a ghostly mysterious misunderstood body. It was real. It was tangible.*
- ○ *We will be seen and will see others -Christ was seen by over five hundred people.*
- ○ *We will be recognized for who we are Scripture tells us that we will be known and will know our loved ones.*
- ○ *We will have the marks of our physical journey on earth as a reward of our service -Christ showed his nail scarred hands and his side to the disciples.*
- ○ *We will have flesh and bones Christ was transformed and yet had flesh and bones. He had Thomas to touch his wounds.*
- ○ *We will not need the normal process of blood to live. Christ shed His blood for our sins. His glorified body did not need blood yet He was flesh and bones and had a glorified body.*
- ○ *We will be able to walk through walls and instantaneously go from one place to another in heaven.*
- ○ *We will eat real food in heaven.*
- ○ *And we will not be all knowing as is Christ, but we will have a much fuller knowledge than in this earthly body. We have all the knowledge we need for anything we endeavor.*

Purpose of the Rapture

We have discussed the reality of the Rapture. We have discussed the timing of the Rapture although we do not know the exact time and date. We have discussed the resurrected bodies we will be given when we as part of the Body of Christ will receive. Why, however, does God elect to Rapture us out of this world? The overall answer is we will be raptured to rescue the Church of Body of Christ from the Antichrist's persecution that occurs during the Great Tribulation.

Matthew 24:22
"And if those days had not been cut short, no human being would be saved. But for the sake of the elect those days will be cut short."

2 Thessalonians 1:7
"And to grant relief to you who are afflicted as well as to us, when the Lord Jesus is revealed from heaven with his mighty angels."

Following are five reasons for the Rapture of the Church out of this world. They are:

Reason number 1 for Christ's Rapture of His Church is to make sure His believers do not have to go through the Great Tribulation. In Matthew He tells us that the persecution will be so great and so totalitarian that if the days of the Church were not cut short all believers would be killed or murdered in the Great Tribulation. So God takes us home in such a way we do not face the persecution. Then, in Thessalonians, He tells us that the days of the persecution will bring great trouble and He wishes to simply take His Church home and to be with Him when He comes back to earth to conquer Satan.

Reason number 2 is to unite the glorified Church with Christ. We as the believers have been with Christ in Spirit but after the rapture we are given glorified bodies similar to that of Jesus Himself and we are reunited spiritually and physically with the glorified bodies to rejoice and honor and praise God.

1 Thessalonians 4:17
"Then we who are alive and remain shall be caught up together with them in the clouds to meet the Lord in the air. And thus we shall always be with the Lord."

John 14:3
"Then we who are alive, who are left, will be caught
up together with them in the clouds to meet the Lord in
the air, and so we will always be with the Lord."

Reason number 3 is to take all resurrected Christians, in their glorified bodies, to the BEMA or Judgment Seat of Christ for an evaluation where we will be given rewards for good works here on earth. These rewards will be place in our Crown of Life that we will wear in heaven.

Reason number 4 is to present the Church to God the Father as the bride of Christ. This will be done in the Marriage of the Lamb.

Reason number 5 is to end the age of the Church. God changes His revelation to this body of people to be the age of listening to the 144,000 evangelists and in so doing shifting the responsibility of evangelizing the world back to the Israelites.

Comparison of the Second Coming of Christ to the Rapture

The second coming of Jesus Christ is often spoken of by Christians when they in truth have in mind that time when Jesus Christ will come to receive the Church unto him and will take the Church out of the world. The second coming of Jesus is referred to as the second advent of Christ. The word advent means the coming of. Therefore Scripture actually refers to two advents or two comings of Jesus Christ. The first advent of Christ was His birth. The virgin birth of Jesus is when Jesus left His heavenly home to come to earth and dwell with man for the purpose of fulfilling the plan of salvation for all mankind that will believe on Him. The Second Advent will be when Jesus Christ comes, not as a humble servant but as a conquering king to establish His reign on earth. The Second Advent will display His royalty and His glory and He will fulfill all the covenants to Israel and to all believers on Him who are adopted unto His family. The Second Advent will also fulfill the promise of God to all nonbelievers as they are thrust into eternal punishment and separation from God because of their unbelief.

Many Christians speak of the rapture as the second coming of Jesus. The rapture is not the second coming of Christ. To be an advent Jesus must come to earth to dwell with man. At the rapture Christ will come to take the Church with him but does not actually set foot on the earth. The believers, both previously deceased and those still alive on earth will meet him in the air. Christ does not set foot on earth when He comes for His Church.

The Rapture of the Church and the Second Coming of Christ are separate events. If not then the Church will surely be present during the Great Tribulation and will suffer the horrible persecution of the Antichrist. But we have seen that they are separate events. They have separate and different purposes although they are connected.

The Rapture and the Second Coming of Christ are separate events because separated they allow the love and compassion Christ has for His Church to be manifested while yet rendering judgment and justice to the non-redeemed.

The Rapture and the Second Coming of Christ are separate events because they provide a pathway for other events promised in Scripture to take place in a sequence that compliments each other. During the time between the Rapture and the Second Coming of Christ God's Judgment of Good works takes place followed by the Marriage supper of the Lamb. This allows Christ to present the Church to God the Father and for the reunion of Christ and the Church to take place. This enables Christ to bring the Church with Him when He comes as a conquering King at the Second Coming of Christ.

The Rapture and the Second Coming of Christ are separate events because they allow the battle of Gog and Magog to take place. As separate events they provide the platform for the Abomination of Desolation to take place in which the Antichrist will seize the Throne of David in Jerusalem and declare himself God.

CHAPTER TWENTY-THREE

The Doctrine of the Seven-Year Tribulation
The Sequence of Events In The Final Days

Following the rapture of the Church it is hard for us to imagine the turmoil and fear our world society will experience. An estimated one million people will just be gone. There will be no explanation unless one wants to go back to the Bible and study what God said would happen. Many entire families will be taken. Babies that have not reached the age to know right from wrong will be gone. Airlines will have pilots who are flying and are suddenly gone. Insurance companies will be sued because of deaths that cannot be explained. It is hard to imagine the sorrow, fear and turmoil of that amazing moment when the saved on earth will be raptured. Because there are more Christians in America than anywhere else in the world, America will have the most turmoil following the rapture.

After the rapture "The Church" will leave this world. This does not mean all church members will be gone because many church members do not believe in Jesus. They may believe Jesus was born and even that He was crucified for their sins. But they have not reached the point of giving their life to Him and asking Him to change them, to redeem them and save them. The Bible tells us the world will be without anyone to speak for God. The Holy Spirit will no longer be present to hold back Satan. After the rapture we begin the Seven-Year Tribulation. This is a time plan that is voiced by God to Daniel thousands of years ago.

God's Vision to Daniel

In Daniel the ninth chapter, we find Daniel in deep prayer to God. Daniel acknowledges that the Hebrew people were not faithful to God and did not deserve His blessing. However, Daniel still pleaded with God to have mercy on his people. Daniel, who was in exile, specifically pleads for an understanding of when God will fulfill His promise of restoring the Temple in Jerusalem. God's answer, through Gabriel to Daniel, is recorded in Daniel 9. Gabriel said God's clock of prophecy would begin when a decree was issued to rebuild Jerusalem. Gabriel then revealed that the time from issuing the decree to the time "The Messiah would be cut off" would be 483 years.

God also revealed through Gabriel, to Daniel, for Daniel to reveal to the world that the future timeline for the Hebrew Nation from 445 BC (King Artaxerxes issued command to rebuild Jerusalem) to the end of time would consist of seventy weeks. These seventy weeks were identified based on the Hebrew practice of using idioms. One favorite idiom was the word week. So the Hebrew idiom of seventy weeks really meant 490 years. God gave the Hebrew nation the time line of seventy weeks until the end of sin and all unrighteousness (the end of the world), it meant 490 weeks in our measuring concept.

Daniel 9:25
"Know therefore and understand, that from the going forth of the word to restore and to build Jerusalem unto the Messiah the Prince shall be seven weeks, and threescore and two weeks: the street shall be built again, and the wall, even in troublous times."

The prophecy, as recorded in Daniel 9:25, says that "from the issuing of a decree to restore and rebuild Jerusalem until Messiah the Prince there will be seven weeks (49 years) to rebuild Jerusalem, and then sixty-two weeks (434 years) for the Israelites, God's Chosen People, to accomplish the tasks God chose them to do. Forty-nine weeks plus 434 weeks amounts to 483 weeks. This leaves one seven year week left. But God then said that after the sixty-two weeks (434 years) God gave His Chosen Nation to become what He wanted them to become; He would cut off the time prophecy because of Israel's failure to do as God commanded.

Daniel 9:24
"Seventy weeks are decreed about your people and your holy city, to finish the transgression, to put an end to sin, and to atone for iniquity, to bring in everlasting righteousness, to seal both vision and prophet, and to anoint a most holy place."

God identifies the things He demands the Hebrew people accomplish in the 434 weeks stated above. These are:

1. *To finish the transgression.* The revelation of this prophecy came after a prayer from Daniel to forgive the Israelite people for their transgression against God. Their transgression was to turn their backs on God and decide to do things their way not God's way. God told them this had to stop.

2. *To put an end to sin.* This means the Hebrew nation would become so close to God that they would be consumed with being like Him and in the Israelite nation sin would cease to exist.

3. *To atone for iniquity.* This means to make amends for something or to do what is necessary to correct something. And of course the Israelite nation had a lot to correct.

4. *To bring in everlasting righteousness.* This means God expected the Israelite nation to reach the point of not only being without sin but also returning to God a deep abiding love.

5. *To seal both vision and prophet.* This is hard to understand until we recognize the purpose of the seventy weeks (490 years) was to establish the time of the second coming of Jesus Christ. Understand the rapture of The Church is not part of the seventy weeks. The second coming of Jesus could not happen until the above commands of God were achieved. So God demanded the Israelite nation accomplish the above things and therefore "seal the vision of the seventy weeks. The Israelite nation by accomplishing the above commands were to make conditions right for the arrival of Jesus Christ. In that way there were to seal the arrival of the prophet Jesus Christ.

6. *To anoint a "Most Holy Place."* The "Most Holy Place" calls for a new, righteous, sinless temple built by God. In Ezekiel chapter 40–43 we learn of this temple. Ezekiel received the revelation that there would be after this

world ended, a new Temple to usher in the thousand-year millennial.

From the beginning of the seventy-week prophesy of God to Daniel through Gabriel, it was clear to God, after the seven weeks to rebuild Jerusalem, and the 62 weeks for Israel would fail to achieve the above commands, His "Chosen People" had failed the task. However, God knew from the beginning of time this would be the decision of His "Chosen People." However, God had a plan from the beginning of time. That plan was to *"cut off"* His dependence on the *"Chosen People"* to accomplish His plan, and to implement another. In the new plan God implemented a new dispensation of relationship to man. But it took a heavy price. **God sent His only begotten son Jesus Christ** to come to earth, to be tortured, humiliated, to suffer and to be crucified.

When God ceased to depend on the Israelites to reconcile man with God the new plan not only "cut off" His dependence on the Israelites to reconcile man to God, He "cut off" the prophesied seventy-week vision and implemented the Dispensation of The Church. This does not mean He stopped the seventy-week vision. No, God put the seventy-week vision in limbo while He implemented the age of The Church to accomplish the six points stated above and given to His "Chosen People." Now the Church has these responsibilities. After an unrevealed time period God will close the age of The Church with the rapture and will return to the Hebrew nation to fulfill His six demands. But when this happens God will take an active part in making His "Chosen People" fulfill His prophecy. The last week, number 70, after the seven weeks to rebuild Jerusalem, and the sixty-two weeks in which the "Chosen People" failed God is called the Seven-Year Tribulation.

The Seven-Year Tribulation is clearly presented by Christ in three distinct periods. These three periods are: **No. 1, *the first half of three and one half years*, No 2, *the middle week*, and no. 3 *the last half of three and one half years*.** The seven weeks or years are known as the Tribulation Period or the Seven-Period Tribulation. The first period is a cataclysmic, breath-taking, dynamic period such as the world has never seen before. The events that make this period so dynamic are the results of the rapture of the Church that introduces the Tribulation Period, worldwide war in which millions of people are killed, and horrifying treachery from government leaders. The Middle week is a terrifying, confusing, abysmal, betrayed week. There will be many, many people who have placed their trust in Jesus during the first half of the Tribulation Period. They will be beheaded in this week and the next year to come. In this week (remember the week is an idiom of Hebrew meaning a year) the expected outcome of world events is changed from hopeful to hopeless to people who have decided to follow Jesus. The middle week is so significant in the changes it brings to world order, that it overlays the first and third periods, and sets the scene for the excruciating last three and one half years.

In the last period of the Tribulation Period, the pain, fear, terror, death, disease, famine, and destruction of this period is greater than ever known on earth before. It is so great this period is known by its own special name; "The Great Tribulation."

The power behind the death, horror, and fear of the Tribulation Period is Satan. God allows Satan free reign to wage his war on everyone who shows any interest in trusting Jesus. The last three and one half years brings even greater death, fear, horror, and cataclysmic happenings to the earth. However, these events are brought on by God against those Jews and Gentiles who have chosen to follow the Antichrist and accept the Mark of the Beast. The wrath of God is amazingly greater than that of Satan.

When the rapture takes place (before the Seven-Year Tribulation), a host of believers will have already died. The souls of those believers will have joined Christ in heaven and their bodies will be buried. However at the rapture these believers, called "The Dead in Christ" will have their bodies resurrected from the dead and they will be given glorified bodies. All believers who are alive at the rapture will be transformed into their glorified bodies and will join the "Dead in Christ" with Jesus in heaven. God's Word says the Church will be removed from all tribulation because Jesus paid the price of our sins on Calvary.

And finally look at Mark 13:26. ***"Then everyone will see the Son of Man coming on the clouds with great power and glory."*** "Coming on the clouds" clearly refers to the rapture. This means all the redeemed will be raptured with Christ before the tribulation. This is also a preamble of how Christ will come to reclaim "The Church" at the time of the rapture. He will come in the clouds. When He comes for the rapture, Jesus does not set a foot on the earth. He calls the redeemed up to glory with Him. First the "dead in Christ" meaning those who believed in Him but have already died, will be resurrected from the grave. Then the "alive in Christ" meaning those believers who are alive at the rapture, will join Jesus in the air. Thus, the above verse speaks of meeting Him in the clouds.

Definition of Terms Used in Revelation

Revelation is in some ways, a simple book to understand. It rolls out in a natural sequence so that, if you understand certain terminology, it can be an exciting book to read and study. Unfortunately so many people get confused by certain terminology they give up and quit. To make it easier to understand "The Seven-Year Tribulation" we must have a general knowledge of the vision God gave to Gabriel to give in Daniel in the Old Testament. And we must grasp a general understanding of the vision God gave the Apostle John when John was taken by God up into Heaven, intending that John would report it back to the seven churches and ultimately to us.

We also need to have a basic understanding of certain symbols God uses to present the vision of Heaven to John. God gave to John an understanding of things no man had ever seen before when He raised John up to look over into Heaven. John was unable to describe much of what he saw and God enabled him to convey to us what God revealed to him and he did it mostly in symbols. Let's discuss some basic symbols used by God in Revelation and in the book of Daniel.

The Antichrist, the Beast, and the False Prophet

In discussion, the Seven-Year Tribulation Period we find Revelation often refers to "The Dragon," "The Beast," "The Antichrist," and "The False Prophet." Let's start by identifying these symbols. "The Dragon" is always referring to Satan himself. This does not vary. Reverence is made to the fiery, red, Dragon surrounded by fire. That is a symbolic way of referring to Satan and his destructive, frightening, deceitful fierceness.

Revelation 20:1–2
"Then I saw an angel coming down from heaven, holding in his hand the key to the bottomless pit and a great chain. And he seized the dragon, that ancient serpent, who is the devil and Satan, and bound him for a thousand years."

In the above verse, the angel is a messenger to John from God. The angel holds in his hand the key to eternal punishment prepared by God for Satan. Then the angel, a messenger from God seized the dragon, "who is the devil and Satan" and bound him for a thousand years. And the thousand years is the period of time the thousand year millennial kingdom of Christ will reign. So God tells us the dragon is Satan. Who is the Beast?

Revelation gives us the symbol of two beasts, not one. They are similar but not the same. They both report to Satan or the Dragon for direction, power, and purpose. Let's first look at Beast no. 1.

Revelation 13:1
And I saw a beast rising out of the sea, with ten horns and seven heads, with ten diadems on its horns and blasphemous names on its heads.

Beast no. 1 is the Antichrist. Rising out of the sea is a symbolic way of saying this servant of Satan begins to show himself in the first half of the Seven-Year Tribulation. As a servant of Satan, The Beast has always been with people but has not taken a previous visible role. He is rising out of billions of people from before the creation of Adam. So those who claim the Beast, or Antichrist, to be a Roman, or Muslim, or American, or some other nationality, are not visualizing this creature sufficiently. The Antichrist rises out of thousands of years of humanity of all races, nationalities, and practices. The Antichrist has always been with us in spirit but has been contained by God. Now God allows Satan to introduce the Antichrist, Beast no. 1, to the world. Satan, being a deceitful, devious being choses to introduce the Antichrist, not as a fierce satanic creature, pictured as "The Beast." No Satan elects to introduce the Antichrist as a brilliant businessman. He is introduced as an amazing peacemaker. He is introduced as a fantastic financier and human motivator. Beast no. 1, then, arises out of a vast sea of all humans ever born while Beast no. 2 arises, not out of the sea but out of land.

Revelations 13:11
"Then I saw another beast rising out of the earth. It had two horns like a lamb and it spoke like a dragon."

The beast in verse 11 is different from but complimentary to the Beast described in verse 1. This Beast rises up out of the earth which represents a more peaceful creature than the Beast that rises up out of the sea. This Beast looks much less fearsome than Beast no. 1. This Beast looks like a lamb and has horns like a lamb but speaks like a dragon. Why does this Beast speak like a dragon? It is because the old Dragon, or Satan, is the power behind both, Beast no. 1 and Beast no. 2. The purpose of Beast no. 2 is to implement the will of Beast no. 1 whose purpose is to implement the will of Satan. It is the second Beast that causes all the worshippers of the Antichrist to build an image of the Antichrist and to worship the Antichrist. The second Beast forces the whole world to cease all kinds of worship and to focus on worship of the Antichrist. The second Beast creates a worship religion that is worldwide and is the worship of the Antichrist. It is the second Beast that forces all people all over the world to wear on their right hand or forehead the image of the Beast. That image is a number and is 666. For these reasons the Second Beast is known as the "False Prophet."

The Ten Horns and Seven Heads

We understand the Antichrist is symbolized as a Beast in the vision God gave to the Apostle John. In fact both the Antichrist and the False Prophet are symbolized as Beasts. That is because God felt it best to give the Apostle John and you and I an understanding of how vicious, how evil, and how full of hatred the Antichrist and False Prophet could be. He felt the method used is to use a symbol of an animal that is consumed with the desire to kill, to torture, to hurt and to destroy. Now God gives us some insight into what means Satan (The Dragon) has used and will use through the Antichrist and the False Prophet to try to accomplish his desires. In Revelation 17 God reveals a glimpse of what is to come by telling us ten horns will receive power and authority for a short time in the horror that is to come. While various ideas have tried to emerge that differ; God is very clear in telling us who the ten horns are. They are as follows:

Revelation 17:12
And the ten horns that you saw are ten kings who have not yet received royal power, but they are to receive authority as kings for one hour, together with the beast.

The ten horns represent ten kings that will emerge on the scene of mankind as powerful rulers during the final battle of control between Jesus and Satan. The scripture says they are to receive authority as kings for one hour. This means their authority is permitted by God and is permitted for a short period of time. It ends because Jesus Christ comes back to earth and defeats Satan and all his followers. The verse also tells us that the reign of "The Beast" will also be terminated at that time. In this scripture "The Beast" refers to Beast no. 1 and Beast no. 2 because both are followers of Satan. To more clearly define for us what a horrible creature "The Beast" was, is, and will be, God gives us Revelation 13:2–7. Herein God reveals three horrible animals to the vision He gives John. The animals represent nations that have in the past fought God in His effort to communicate with us.

Revelation 13:2, 7

"Now the beast that I saw was like a leopard, its feet were like a bear's, and its mouth was like a lion's mouth. And to it the dragon gave his power and his throne and great authority. (7) Also It was permitted to wage war with the saints and to conquer them, and authority was given it over every tribe and people and language and nation."

It is significant that the first description of Beast no. 1 is like a leopard. This ties together the allusion given to Daniel 7:6.

Daniel 7:6

"And then I looked, and behold, another, like a leopard, with four wings of a bird on its back, and the Beast had four heads and dominion was given over it."

The tie in the above verse is the Kingdom of Greece that was the world power for a time, but was divided into four parts after the death of Alexander the Great in 323 BC. The bear gives reference to the Medo-Persia Empire while the Lion connects with the Babylon empire. These three great empires were anti-God in form and substance. But that brings us to the revelation of the fourth beast.

Daniel 7:19–20

"Then I desired to know the truth about the fourth beast which was different from all the rest, exceedingly terrifying, with its teeth of iron, claws of bronze, and which devoured and broke in pieces and stamped what was left with its feet."

This picture, given to John, parallels the vision given to Daniel so many years back. It also parallels with the Roman Empire of John's day because of the universal attempt Rome was making trying to eliminate any sign of Christian movement. For some three hundred years after the crucifixion of Christ, the Roman Empire planned implemented and sustained incredible persecution of any effort made by people in the provinces of Rome to worship Jesus Christ. However in 306 Constantine became emperor of Rome. His mother became a Christian and Constantine not only slowed down the persecution of the Church but declared Christianity to be the state religion of Rome. This created much dissension in the Church, primarily because of vast numbers of people who joined the Church but did not believe in Jesus. To settle the dissention, Constantine called a meeting in 325 AD to settle these issues. The result was the Nicene Creed. The greatest decision was that great power was given to the bishops of Antioch, Constantinople, Alexandria, Rome, and Jerusalem. These bishops would be Patriarchs and all authority would be given to them. This, in effect, established the Roman Catholic Church and linked the Catholic Church to the government of ancient Rome.

We have, now, identified three of the seven heads to be the ancient empires of Greece, Medo-Persia, and Babylon. The fourth is now established as the existing Roman Empire in the day of the Apostle John. Now God reveals an empire in the future as the future rebirth of the Roman Empire. Revelation 17 forecasts a future time when the Roman Empire will be reborn to wage war for the Antichrist against God and God's people. In the day the Apostle John saw this great vision Rome had just completed the torture, imprisonment, and murder of thousands of believers for the purpose of destroying any remembrance of Jesus Christ and His teachings. How do we know this is a forecast of a future army? We know it is because God's Word tells us.

Revelation 17:12–13
"And the ten horns you say are ten kings who have not yet received royal power, but they are to receive authority as kings for one hour (short time) together with the beast."

This is a power that will arise for a short time during the Seven-Year Tribulation. It shall be built along the lines of authority of the

Old Roman Empire. These ten kings represent a confederation of nations, past, present, and future that are dedicated to the destruction of Israel and the elimination of the worship of Jehovah. Their hatred for Israel, because Israel is witnessing for God, unites them with the Antichrist. However, at the close of the Seven-Year Tribulation, in the Battle of Armageddon, This force will be devastated in defeat by God. What do the seven heads represent?

Revelation 17:9
"This calls for a mind with wisdom: the seven heads are seven mountains on which the woman is seated."

We know Rome was built around seven mountains and we also know the ten kings represent a confederation of nations God allows Satan to use to fight God's efforts to worship with His creation. This connection is given in that the seven heads represent the seven mountains surrounding the Headquarters of the future confederation which will be Rome. Revelation 17:9 warns us the seven heads call for a mind of wisdom. Therefore we dig deeper and discover the seven heads are not only the seven mountains but represent seven kingdoms of Rome.

Revelation 17:10
"They are also seven kings, five of whom have fallen, one is, the other has not yet come, and when he does come he must remain only a little while."

God's revelation is exciting and amazing. It began with Daniel thousands of years ago, followed by God's revelation to the Apostle John and is being fulfilled even as we live today. The seven kings tell us who these kingdoms are. The above scripture tells us **"five of whom have fallen."** The five that have fallen must be great kingdoms that ruled the world in their time. In addition to meet the test each kingdom must have been devoted to the total destruction of the Hebrew people of their time. These five are: Egypt, Assyria, Babylon, Medo-Persia, and Greece. All were great but have fallen. The scripture then says **"one is."** In the day of John the Apostle going back to well before the virgin birth of Jesus the great worldwide powerful kingdom was Rome. So the **"one is"** has to be the world wide dominating power of John's day. That dominating power was the Roman Empire connected to the Catholic Church. Then Revelation 17:10 says **"the other is not yet come, and when he does come he must remain only a little while."** This message tells us a powerful view of the future for all of us. Now we read not only what was the history of the Jews we now see the future Seven-Year Tribulation and the force Satan will empower the Antichrist with to bring war on God and His followers. Yes, the sixth nation that will emerge will be the Roman Empire connected to the Catholic Church and the remaining four nations are confederation of nations that oppose God and the nation Israel.

"The Scarlet Woman" also known as "The Harlot" and "The Prostitute"

Revelation 17:1–4
"Then one of the seven angels, who had seven bowls came and said to me, "Come I will show you the judgment of the great prostitute who seated on many waters, with whom the kings of the earth have committed sexual immorality and with the wine of whose sexual immorality the dwellers on earth have become drunk. And He carried me away in the Spirit into a wilderness, and I saw a woman sitting on a scarlet beast that was full of blasphemous names, and it had seven heads and ten horns."

God refers to **"The Church"** as being the wife of Jesus. In so stating His reference to **"The Church"** is not inclusive of the Catholic Church. That is not to say there will not be millions of Catholics saved because if they believe in Jesus rather than the Catholic Church doctrine they will be saved. No, God's love for **"The Church,"** and the relationship of trust and faithfulness of the wife and Christ establish the faith God has in His believers. Revelation 17 refers to this relationship when God speaks of sexual immorality. The reference is to lack of faithfulness of **"The Church"** to Christ. Now we see the **"Great Prostitute"** known as the **"Great Harlot"** in many Bible translations representing a worldwide church body that has elected to be unfaithful to Christ. This unfaithful worldwide church body was in the day of John the papal Catholic Church. Papal meaning full authority given to the Pope and taking away direct access of man to God. Verse 4 states **"I saw a woman sitting on a scarlet beast that was full of blasphemous names and it had seven heads and ten horns."** We know from verses above the scarlet woman is **"The Beast"** also known as *"The Antichrist."* We also know this **"Beast"** is connected to the Roman Empire because of the seven heads and ten horns. Now we see the **"Great Prostitute"** known as the **"Great Harlot"** exercising control over the body of followers of **"The Antichrist"** also known as the **"Beast."** Wow this means that for a short time the future reinstallation of the Catholic Church will at lease influence **"The Beast."**

The overall lessen God desires to teach us is that in the Seven-Year Tribulation, we will see **"The Antichrist"** (The Beast), for a period of time, ruling the world through the use of the Old Roman Empire resurrected for his use but being controlled by the Papal Catholic Church. Note this does not say **"The Antichrist"** is controlled by the Papal Catholic Church. No, **"The Antichrist"** is solely controlled by Satan. This shows a conflict of authority within the enforcement body of **"The Antichrist."**

The Roman Catholic Church meets the test of who this scarlet woman is. First the Roman Catholic Church has ruled throughout the ages over kings of nations. Although Christian by name this church has tortured, killed, and devastated God's faithful people throughout the years. For the first three hundred years after the virgin birth of Jesus the Roman Church banned any form of Christianity and horribly persecuted and killed Christians. We can see therefore that the vision given to the Apostle John was of the Roman Catholic Church having successive control over continuous nations up to the end of the Seven-Year Tribulation. In the Seven-Year Tribulation the Roman Empire, that supports the evil of the Antichrist, will arise at the middle of the Tribulation Period and the ten kings will form a final but short-lived worldwide force dedicated to defeat God. The Roman Catholic Church will have amazing influence directing the war against those who elect to believe in Jesus during the Tribulation Period. But it will not last long.

The overwhelming control of Satan, combined with the powerful, worldwide influence of the Roman Catholic Church (the scarlet woman) **"will give their power and authority to the beast" (Revelation 17:13)** and will **"receive authority for one hour as kings with the beast" (verse 12)**. Empowered by the feeling of guaranteed success they **"will make war with the Lamb, and the Lamb will overcome them, for He is Lord of lords and King of kings"** (verse 14). When the Antichrist and the 10 kings realize they have been defeated by Christ and deceived by the Scarlet Woman (The Roman Catholic Church) they will turn on the Harlot. *"And the ten horns which you saw on the beast, these will hate the harlot, make her desolate and naked, eat her flesh and burn her with fire. For God has put it into their hearts to fulfill His purpose, to be of one mind, and to give their kingdom to the beast, until the words of God are fulfilled"* (verses 16–17).

"The Woman"

There is a massive difference between the definition of "The Scarlet Woman" and "The Woman." To best understand this symbolism we need to go back to Revelation chapter 12.

Revelation 12:1
"And a great sign appeared in heaven, a woman clothed with the sun, with the moon under her feet, and on her head a crown of twelve stars."

In the above verse God is referring to the nation Israel, His "Chosen People." God chose Israel because of the faith of Abraham. He promised the nation would spread to all parts of the world because of the faith of Abraham. In the verse above the woman is clothed by the sun in the day and the moon is at her feet. This represents the universal existence of Israel and God's universal love for her. On her head is a crown of twelve stars. The twelve stars are the twelve tribes God gave to Abraham. The twelve tribes represent the fulfillment of God's plan to have Abraham's people spread over the entire world. God's love for Israel is a theme throughout the Bible.

When Israel failed to fulfill God's six commands, one of which was to evangelize the world, God did not forget Israel. God set her aside for an unknown time period. In this time period God created **"The Church." "The Church"** is the body of believers who have put their trust in salvation in Christ Jesus. God's love for **"The Church"** is equal to His love for Israel. In Galatians 6:16 God refers to "The Church" as **"The Israel of God."** God has a specific role for the Church to execute. That does not mean God is through with Israel. In fact an overriding theme of the Seven-Year Tribulation is the restoration of Israel and the fulfillment of God's prophecy for Israel.

In the New Testament God uses the symbol of a woman to describe His Church just as He used the symbol of a woman to describe Israel in the Old Testament. This symbolism gives us a better understanding of God's love for "The Church" and Israel. The Church members are symbolized in 1 Peter 2:9 as a royal priesthood, a holy nation. It is not chance that God describes both Israel and "The Church" as His loving, devoted term "woman."

"The Child"

Revelation 12:1 speaks of **"the woman" clothed with the sun, with the moon under her feet, and on her head a crown of twelve stars"** it is followed up in verse 2 and three introducing *"The Child."*

Revelation 12:2–3
"She was pregnant and crying out in birth pains and the agony of giving birth. And another sign appeared in Heaven, 'behold, a great red dragon with seven heads and ten horns, and on his heads seven diadems."

The above verse maintains the imagery of Israel as "A Woman." Now she is giving birth to Jesus Christ who is the Messiah of the world. Do we find any connection of the birth of Christ and the nation Israel? The answer is absolutely yes. Jesus was born of an Israelite woman named Mary. He was of the lineage of David. God prophesied of the coming of The Messiah and Jesus Christ fulfilled that prophecy through the Israel nation. God tells us that at the end of the age Jesus will reign through the one-thousand-year millennial period and His throne will be in Jerusalem. God will rule the Gentile nations from Jerusalem. Jesus is **"The Child"** in this revelation however in other passages we see Jesus described as **"The Lamb."**

Micah 5:2
"But you, O Bethlehem Ephrathah, who are little among the clans of Judah, from you shall come forth for me one who is to be rule of Israel, whose coming forth is from of old, from ancient days."

Period one of the Seven-Year Tribulation, The First Three and One Half Years

We know the Church will not be part of the Tribulation. We know the Church will be raptured prior to the beginning of the Seven-Year Tribulation. In fact, the rapture is the measuring block to tell existing humanity when they are in the Seven-Year Tribulation. To understand what is happening in the first period of three periods of the Tribulation, we need to go to the vision God gave to John when He opened the doors of Heaven to let us have a glimpse of His revelation. In Revelation 1, John sees in a vision of elders and angels around the throne of God the Father. The One seated on the throne holds a mysterious scroll, written on both sides and sealed with seven wax seals, instead of the usual one. They search for one worthy to open the scroll and Jesus Christ is the only one found worthy. Jesus begins to open the scroll and as He opens the scroll the fate of all earthly inhabitants at the time of the Seven-Year Tribulation period is revealed.

The seals, the trumpets, and the bowls can be very confusing. They can be as confusing as The Dragon, The Beast, The Antichrist, and The False Prophet. But they need not be. The seals are a commitment made by God at the beginning of creation regarding events He knew would happen at the end of time. The seals of commitments are contained in a book God has created, in which He records every step He plans to take in the end of time. We can consider It part one of God's operational plan for all creation. God saw fit to outline seven seals or commitments. The seventh seal opens seven more commitments that are delivered to all mankind in the form of seven trumpets. Then the seventh trumpet open seven bowls of God's wrath. Human logic calls for the seals, trumpets, and bowls to happen in sequence but they basically happen in the same last three and one half years of the Great Tribulation.

The seals and trumpets reveal, mainly, the wrath of Satan poured out on people of the Tribulation Period who elect to believe in Christ. The seven bowls, however, record the wrath of God poured out on the unfaithful people of the Tribulation Period.

As we get ready to introduce the Seals, Trumpets, and Bowls discussed in Revelation we should consider the condition of the world right after the rapture. No one knows for sure but best estimates suggest as many as one billion people will just be taken out of the world because of the rapture. This means airplanes crash because of pilots who were Christians, taken from this world. Millions of people will be killed from car wrecks, airplane crashes and many other causes related to the rapture. There will be incredible confusion about what happened. The Holy Spirit will be taken out of the world to enable the entry of the Antichrist. Prior to the rapture the Holy Spirit is restraining the Antichrist from entry into the world. However, with the departure of the Holy Spirit, witchcraft, false religions, worship of idols and great crime and corruption will run rampant throughout the world. The country that will feel the greatest impact will be America. This is because the greatest number-of Christians reside in the USA. We could see almost 50 percent of some states simply disappear. The world will become ripe for the entry of the Antichrist because he will promise peace. He will promise what people want to hear but he will have no plan of delivering his promises.

God has a plan for every step of the Seven-Year Tribulation. It is a plan of what God intends to allow Satan to accomplish and how long Satan will have freedom to do what he wishes. It is also a plan in detail of what God will do and when He will do it. These instructions are located in a book of seven seals. After the rapture God opens the seven seals and His only begotten Son, Jesus Christ opens the seals. Let's look at the main events of Seal no. 1. These are events that begin right after the rapture of the Church.

The First Seal

Revelation 6:1–2
"Now I watched when the Lamb opened one of the seven
seals, and I heard one of the four living creatures say with
a voice like thunder, 'Come, and I looked and behold, a
white horse! And a rider had a bow, and a crown was given
to him, and he came out conquering, and to conquer."

The above scripture tells us that Jesus, The Lamb, opened the first seal. This means that God knows what is about to happen and He allows it to happen. Therefore He instructs Jesus to open Seal no. 1. The first seal is a revelation of the Antichrist. It is also known as the period of "The White Horse." White horse stands for peace and in the first period of the Seven-Year Tribulation the Antichrist appears to be anything but a warrior. The world is in total confusion. Wicked people are taking advantage of good people who did not trust Jesus for salvation. The nation of Israel, being hated by almost the total world, sees the Antichrist as one who can bring peace to the world and conquer the evil forces facing her. Therefore Israel will be ready and eager to turn their back on God and sign a peace treaty with the Antichrist for safety and protection. We know the Antichrist is also referred to as "The Beast." Prior to this revelation of God to the Apostle John, no knowledge of the Antichrist existed with mankind. Nevertheless, the Spirit of the Antichrist has always been with mankind. This is because the Spirit of the Antichrist is Satan. Satan is spirit and the Antichrist is a physical man consumed by Satan. However, Satan has been constrained in what he has been allowed to do to people because of the Holy Spirit. Satan does not blend the Spirit of the Antichrist into a human being until after the rapture of the Church and the departure of the Holy Spirit from the hearts of mankind. The rapture of the Church is when the Holy Spirit departs from mankind and is the beginning of the Seven-Year Tribulation. Now we see the Antichrist, a human, energized by Satan, who is beginning his campaign of world conquest. In the early months of the Tribulation He does not appear as a horrible or evil monster. In fact he appears to be a brilliant, benevolent business man who is capable of resolving almost any kind of problem. The multitudes see him as a messiah, who has come to solve the world's great problems. The Antichrist establishes his self as a great manager so he will be able to enlist the support of all world leaders and ultimately become the master of the world. He desires to feature himself as anti-war to accomplish what he will become.

This image the Antichrist builds is widely accepted in the world. He reshapes the world into four confederations of power. These federations of power are visualized in the ten horns of the Beast. (Remember, five done, one present, and four yet to come.) The Israelite people have much to fear and that is already obvious in our world today. The Israelites are weak and have little to no faith in God, when faced with the probability of the entire world going to war against them. They turn their back on God one more time. They decide to not trust God for peace but trust the Antichrist, a virtual unknown being but one who looks powerful.

The Second Seal

Revelation 6:4
"And out came another horse, bright red. Its rider was permitted to take peace from the earth, so that people should slay one another, and he was given a great sword."

God now instructs the Lamb Jesus to open seal no. 2. When God instructs Jesus to open the seal, He means God is giving Satan the authority to invoke havoc on the in habitants of the Tribulation Period. The Apostle John sees a rider of a bright red horse. The rider still represents the Antichrist but the color of the horse is bright red. The color red suggests blood-shed. It is also clear the second seal reveals a huge, massive war that affects much of the world. The primary participant countries engaged in this war will be nations having territorial connection to Israel. This war is not the battle of Armageddon. That comes at the end of the Seven-Year Tribulation. This battle is the Battle of Gog and Magog that was revealed to Ezekiel of the Old Testament. It is likely the Battle of Gog and Magog occurs in the first quartile of the Seven-Year Tribulation. God intervenes and swiftly defeats the enemies of Israel. Without God's intervention Israel will certainly be destroyed. It is most unlikely this Battle will be started by the Antichrist because he is still trying to establish himself as ruler of the world through manipulation. It is also probable that the Antichrist, who signed a peace treaty with Israel, does engage in military support of Israel. And although God Himself is the real defender of Israel, it is probable that the Antichrist claims victory over the opposing forces of Israel to better establish himself as the ruler of the world.

The Third Seal

Revelation 6:5
When He opened the third seal, I heard the third living creature say, "Come" and I looked and behold a black horse! And the rider had a pair of scales in his hand.

When Jesus opens the third seal, the symbolism of the punishment God allows Satan to utilize is that of great famine. The rider on the black horse is still the Antichrist. But now he holds a pair of scales in his hand. The scales symbolize measuring of food for purchase. This is likely happening in the middle of the Seven-Year Tribulation. The combination of plague, war, and disease contribute a horrible massive famine across the world. The price of food, for an example, will be prohibitive. The economic impact of this famine will undoubtedly prepare the people of the world to be willing to have a benevolent dictator. People will be required to have the **"Mark of the Beast"** in order to buy or trade food or any needed items. The Antichrist will declare he is God and the ruler of the world. God's Word speaks of food being weighed by scales. It speaks of food being in such short supply it has to be rationed, which creates black-markets, which creates corruption and greed. There will be only enough food for one person for a day. You would work all day long and all you would be able to earn, at best, only enough for your own physical needs. There would be nothing for your family or for anyone else.

Toward the end of the first half of the Tribulation four unfathomable events will occur on Earth. The first event is a firestorm that will burn a third of the Earth and then two huge asteroids will fall on the earth causing massive earthquakes. The impacts will be devastating to every human on earth. Finally, there will be many volcano eruptions and darkness will cover the Earth. This will cause global famine. The world's political leaders will not know what to do and will implement martial law taking away what rights are left. Every person on Earth will be dramatically affected. God's wrath will be so extensive, so pronounced, so overwhelming, and so far-reaching that many survivors will be afraid to even speak because they might further offend a very angry God. God will silence mankind's arrogance and impudence toward God and each other.

And yet, the most horrible of events has not yet come to pass. The fourth seal will be deadly and serious. Jesus will halt the ways and thoughts of mankind to inform us that the time has come for Him to judge and sentence the living.

The Fourth Seal

Revelation 6:7
"When He opened the fourth seal, I heard the voice of the fourth living creature say, "Come" and I looked and behold a pale horse and its riders name was Death, and Hades followed him. And

*they were given authority over a fourth of the earth, to kill with
sword and with famine and with pestilence and by wild beasts."*

The rider of the fourth seal is named "Death" and adds death by
plague to the horrors of the previous three seals. Following the fourth
seal named "Death," is another rider named "Hades." This implies
both the body and the soul will be affected in this horror. It gives
us a limited understanding of the forth seal. The fourth seal adds to
the horror inflected by the previous three seals with a vast number
of plagues racing across the world invoking death everywhere. The
destruction of human life in the days of the **"Fourth Seal"** is so
great that Isaiah 5:13–16 tells us **HADES** has to be enlarged signifi-
cantly. Ezekiel 14:21 reveals to us the four tools of the Fourth Seal
will be **Sword, Hunger, Death, and the Beasts of the Earth.** God
will accomplish two purposes: First, the death of an estimated two
billion people will almost end people depending on themselves. God
will put the entire world on notice that He, Jesus Christ, is Almighty
God, the Ruler of Earth, and the Judge of Mankind. Although a
massive revival is taken place with millions of people trusting Christ,
God's wrath will be a bitter surprise. While Earth's inhabitants are
reeling from the destruction of everything they once trusted Jesus
will issue demands through His evangelical servants, the 144,000. All
who put their faith in Jesus and obey His demands **"shall not perish,
but have everlasting life!"** This does not mean they will not die, for
they will surely die a physical death. But they will also inherit eternal
Spiritual life because of their faith in Jesus.

Understand, we are still in the first, three and one half years of
the Seven-Year Tribulation. In this time period the punishment, torture, murder, and destruction of religious, personal and government
ideals is growing to the point of hysteria. However the Bible teaches
us the first half of the Tribulation will be relatively mild compared
to the second half. Considering the reality of the horror of life in
the first half we cannot conceive of the living conditions in the second half. The Antichrist is becoming more and more impatient to
"take over" the earth and to destroy those who worship Jesus Christ.

However the Antichrist has not yet elected to reveal his true nature and discard his image of helping the people.

The combined efforts of the four horses usher in the horror, pain, death, and disease that affect everyone alive on earth after the rapture. The White Horse represents conquest. This refers to the conquest of the entire world that will be made by the Antichrist. The Red Horse represents blood-shed and terror as nations around Israel combine to attack her and millions are killed. The Black Horse represents famine. This refers to lack of food causes by plaques, war, earthquakes, meteorites and famine all over the world. Then the Pale Horse represents death. The four tools of the pale horse to bring death will be **Sword, Hunger, Death, and the Beasts of the Earth.**

The Middle Week of Tribulation

During the first half of the tribulation the whole earth has changed. An estimated 25 percent of the people on earth are now dead. This has happened in less than two years. That is approximately 2 billion people killed in a horrible way. This is because of the War of Gog and Magog, plagues, starvation, amazing storms, wild beasts, earthquakes, and unparalleled fear. Christians are being killed by Satan because of their faith in Christ. One hundred and forty-four thousand Jewish evangelists (see next article on the 144,000) spread the gospel, leading a vast untold number of people from all nations to faith in Jesus Christ. The message of the 144,000 evangelists will be, **"Yes, accept Jesus Christ as your Savior and experience physical death that is surely to come but also accept Spiritual Eternity with Jesus which is surely to come."**

Zechariah 14:1–2
"Behold the day of the Lord is coming, and your spoil will be divided in your midst, for I will gather all the nations to battle against Jerusalem, the city shall be taken. The houses rifled, and the women ravished. Half of the city shall go into captivity. But remnant of the people shall not be cut off from the city."

It is important to note that the horrors of the first half of the Seven-Year Tribulation have been allowed by God. In each of the above four horsemen we see Jesus opening the seals. This means God approves releasing Satan to do as he pleases for a period. In the second half of the Seven-Year Tribulation we see God releasing His wrath on the inhabitants of the world. These inhabitants will be nonbelievers. This is because the Church was raptured and taken out of the world before the Tribulation Period. It also means those who place their trust in Christ, even though they know it will result in death, have been transformed to Heaven with Christ. In the middle of the Tribulation Period, after God has released Satan to do as he pleases, Satan, through the Antichrist, decides it is time to declare he is God. This decision of Satan, against God, sets the stage for an incredible event called the Abomination of Desolation to take place.

The Abomination of Desolation

At the midway point of the seven-year tribulation, the Antichrist breaks his covenant with Israel. He commits an act in the new Temple the Jews built in Jerusalem. This act is called in scripture an abomination. The term "abomination" appears more than one hundred times in the Old Testament and just a few times in the New Testament. God's Word calls sexual sins like adultery, homosexuality and bestiality abominations. However, the Bible trends more often, in referring to abomination, to relate the word to major covenant violations of idolatry. Abomination also refers to idolatry in Daniel 9 and 11. We must remember Daniel was a vision of what would happen to the Jewish nation. In his vision he predicts a time when the Antichrist appears in the newly constructed Temple and commits some act that is repugnant, disgusting and terrifying. This act is not clearly outlined to us but it could be something like the slaughter of a hog or hogs and spreading hog-blood all over the temple. Anyone who had any leaning toward Jesus Christ would be appalled. Revelation 13:14 describes the Antichrist as making some kind of image which all people are forced to worship or face death by beheading. This act turns God's temple into a place of worship for the Antichrist. This is truly an "abomination." Desolation refers to those who are believers in Jesus who become desolate. They have no place to hide. They cannot get food or shelter. They face horrible death if they do not proclaim their worship of the Antichrist. This event is the beginning of three and a half years of the worst torture, harrow, and terror even known by mankind.

Matthew 24:15–16
"So when you see 'the abomination that causes desolation,'
spoken of through the prophet Daniel, standing in
the Holy Place, let the reader understand—then let
those who are in Judea flee to the mountains."

"Two Witnesses" Appear on the World Scene

"Two Witnesses" will appear in Jerusalem as promised by God. They are sent by God to preach Jesus Christ and His forth-coming Kingdom. They also represent the choice of God to go back to Israel and demand they witness for Christ as they failed to do prior to the establishment of the Church.

Revelation 11:3–12
"And I will grant authority to my two witnesses, and they
will prophesy for 1,260 days, clothed in sackcloth."

When will the two witnesses appear? The above scripture tells us they will prophesy, or preach and teach, for three and one half years. We know the last half of the Tribulation Period will be the outpouring of God's wrath on nonbelievers and the first half will begin with some degree of peace for most of the world, with that peace rapidly developing into horror and torture especially for believers. This leaves the three and one half years the "Two Witnesses" prophesy right in the middle of the Seven-Year Tribulation. **What will the mission of the two witnesses be?** Their responsibility will be to complement the work of the 144,000 and teach this lost world that this is their last chance to trust Jesus Christ. Nonbelievers in the Seven-Year

Tribulation have a last chance to trust Jesus if they believe He will take them to heaven after the absolutely sure death they will receive for having accepted Him. Who are the two witnesses? This is a most contested thought regarding the "Two Witnesses." It is also the most unimportant question about the "Two Witnesses." God does not tell us who they are and He did not think we needed to know who they were. The most popular guesses about their identity are "Moses and Elijah." Enoch and Elijah are considered possible candidates. It could be they are people not famous in God's Word. Regardless of their identity we know they are humans who come from Heaven at the command of God to witness to this lost world. It shows God's deep desire for all lost to trust Him and avoid the horrors of Hell.

The 144,000 Jewish Evangelists

God states in the book of Revelation that He sends exactly 144,000 Jewish evangelists, handpicked by Him, to present inhabitants on earth one last chance to be saved with Christ throughout eternity. People throughout the ages have enjoyed guessing who these select are. They guess at why God stated exactly 144,000 and are they really Jews." The selection of the 144,000 is made by God soon after the rapture of the Church. The exact number of 144,000 and the identity of this group are provided to us in Revelation 7:1–8. This is when God tells us twelve thousand were handpicked from the Jewish tribes of: Judah, Ruben, God, Asher, Nephthalim, Manasses, Simeon, Levi, Issachar, Zubulon, Joseph, and Benjamin. This scripture passage confirms the number of 144,000. It does not just symbolize a large number of people but teaches us the number will be exactly 144,000. It also confirms those selected will be Jews and will be people who make the decision to trust God regardless of the outcome.

When God selects these 144,000, Jewish people will be coming back to Israel as they are today. However Jewish people will still be spread all over the world. The selection of the 144,000 will put evangelists in every country in the world. What is the mission of the 144,000? Their mission is to provide one final opportunity for the Hebrew nation and Gentiles, who will decide to face the horrors of

"The False Prophet" and trust Jesus Christ. God tells us these are Jewish men who have never been with a woman. This significance is to indicate their commitment to God. It signifies they are pure, justifying them to be to be a witness for Christ. We also learn these selected witnesses will wear the name of God the Father on their foreheads.

Revelation 14:4
"It is these who have not defiled themselves with women, for they are virgins. It is these who follow the Lamb wherever he goes. These have been redeemed from mankind as firstfruits for God and the Lamb."

Revelation 14:1
"Then I looked, and behold, on Mount Zion stood the Lamb, and with him 144,000 who had his name and his Father's name written on their foreheads."

God so wanted to protect the 144,000 from the death and terror being dispensed by the Antichrist and the False Prophet that He held up or postponed the release of His wrath on the unbelievers until His name could be written on their foreheads. God so ordained that with His name on their foreheads they were immune to the death and devastation Satan would pour out on them.

Revelation 7:3
"Saying do not harm the earth or the sea or the trees until we have sealed the servants on God on their foreheads."

This passage of scripture reveals to us again how much God loves the people of this earth. God did not want anyone to have to go through the Seven Years of Tribulation. God's original plan of Salvation did not include a gap of seven years for the Seven Years of Tribulation. It was following the absolute failure of the nation Israel to witness to the rest of the world that God inserted the "gap" in His prophesied seventy weeks until the end of time. This week, based on the Hebrew idiom of a week equaling seven years, includes the Seven-Year Tribulation in the life of people. But God does not want the 144,000 to be killed or harmed by the Antichrist. So God held up releasing His wrath on mankind until the witness of the 144,000 could be made.

Revelation 7:1–4
"After this I saw four angels standing at the four corners of the earth, holding back the four winds of the earth that no wind might blow on earth or sea or against any tree. Then I saw another angel ascending from the rising of the sun, with the seal of the living God and he called with a loud voice to the four angels who had been given power to harm the land and the sea: 'Do not harm the land or the sea or the trees until we have sealed our servants of the Lord on the foreheads.' And I heard the number of those who were sealed: 144,000 from every tribe of the sons of Israel."

The above scripture tells us four angels were told by God to **"hold back the four winds of the earth so that no wind might blow on earth or sea or against any tree."** This scripture tells us several things. It tells us the sealing of the 144,000 happened in the first half of the Tribulation Period. By the middle of the Tribulation Period death and destruction was rampart and Satan had been released to do as He pleased. It also reconfirms that the number of the Jewish Evangelists will be 144,000. That is a real number not a symbolic number. It also tells us God is clearing the path for these evangelists to go all over the world preaching that the final day of redemption is at hand. It also tells us the four winds could very well be the four judgments Jesus reveals when He opens the fourth seal. The fourth seal is a release of the sword (war), famine (starvation), plague (illness), and wild beasts (starvation of animals). Jesus delays the opening of the fourth seal until the sealing of the 144,000 was completed.

The Fifth Seal

Revelation 6:9–10
"When I opened the fifth seal, I saw under the alter, the souls of those who had been slain for the word of God and for the witness they had borne. They cried out with a loud voice, "O Sovereign Lord, Holy and True, how long before you will judge and avenge our blood on those who dwell on the earth?"

With the opening of the fifth seal, Jesus waits until God the Father approves of the devastation that is to come on those who have believed on Him because of the witness of the 144,000 Jewish Evangelists and the Two Witnesses. This event ushers in the martyr-dom of those who give evidence of having trusted in Jesus Christ. And there can be no hiding of belief. Everyone on earth will be required to put on the "Mark of the Beast" and if they refuse they will be killed. However if they agree to put on the "Mark of the Beast" (that is the number 666) they will not be acceptable to Christ as a Tribulation Saint and go with Christ to Heaven. These believers will be told up front that to accept Jesus means immediate death and most of the deaths will be by beheading.

In the verse above the Apostle John **said, "*I saw under the alter the souls of those who had been slain for the word of God and for the witness they had borne.*"** Those who suffered so much under the Antichrist and the False Prophet want are eager for God to extract revenge. This shows the human nature of those redeemed in the tribulation. In the verse above, those who cried out in a loud voice, are those who choose death rather than to accept life under the Antichrist. These saints will trust Jesus because of their faith in God to bring Jesus back to conquer Satan and to redeem all of God's faithful.

Revelation 12:11
"And they conquered him (Satan) by the blood of the Lamb and by the word of their testimony, for they loved not their lives even unto death."

What a powerful testimony of truth regarding what faith was required by the Tribulation Saints to accept Jesus as their Savior. The above verse tells us they had to believe that Jesus Christ, the Son of God the Father, was crucified on the Cross of Calvary, was buried and rose again the third day to pay the price of their sins. That is exactly the same faith required by "The Church" to be saved. And Old Testament Saints had to believe on God's promise of a coming Messiah who would be crucified for their sins. The only difference in their faith and that of "The Church" and Tribulation Saints is that the Old Testament Saints had no revelation that the Son of God would be the messiah. In spite of the understanding that true, terrifying death would be dealt to those who refused the "Mark of the Beast" scripture tells us that the greatest worldwide revival in the history of mankind takes place somewhere in the middle of the Seven Years of Tribulation. God's Word gives us this information.

Revelation 7:9–10
"After this I looked and behold, a great multitude, that no man could number, from every nation, from every tribe, and peoples, and languages, standing before the throne, and before the Lamb, clothed in white robes, with palm branches in their hands; And crying out with a loud voice, "Salvation to our God who sits upon the throne, and to the Lamb."

Please note one of God's top objectives to come out of the Seven-Year Tribulation was for His "Chosen People" to step up to the faith He desired of them as far back as the days of Abraham. This has been accomplished by their faith even in the face of certain death. But the verse above tells us people from every tribe, all peoples and languages will be in that number of saved people. This means God has accomplished another objective and that is to give all mankind one more last chance to trust Jesus and avoid the Lake of Fire. Not only Jews but Gentiles will be saved in the Seven Years of Tribulation. And the verse tells us the number of believers will be so many no one can number them. Therefore it would be fruitless for us to guess how many. Will it be in the thousands? Certainly! Will it be in the

Millions? Probably! Will it be in the Billions? Possibly! All we know is that the number will be astounding.

We should note that in Heaven, around the throne will be a number that is too many to identify. They will be worshiping God the Father, God the Son and God the Holy Spirit. These will be the Old Testament Saints. And in another group will be another number that are too many to count and these will be **"The Church."** Separate from "The Church" will be a huge host of people whom we know will be the martyrs from the Seven-Year Tribulation?

Revelation 7:13–14
"Then one of the elders addressed me (John the Apostle) saying "Who are these, clothed in white robes, and from where have they come?" I said to him, "Sir, you know." And he said to me, "These are the ones coming out of the Great Tribulation. They have washed their robes and made them white in the blood of the Lamb. Therefore they are before the throne of God and serve Him day and night in His temple, and He who sits on the throne will shelter them with His presence."

We begin to see the vision God had and the reason He created and oversaw the Seven-Year Tribulation. Look at the joy of those in Heaven for they are with the Lord. But the suffering, now on those who choose to follow Satan, gets worse.

The Sixth Seal

Revelation 6:15–16
"And when I opened the sixth seal, I looked and behold, there was a great earthquake, and the sun became black as sackcloth, the full moon became like blood, and the stars of the sky fell to the earth as the fig tree sheds it winter fruit when shaken by a gale. Then the kings of the earth and the great ones and the generals and the rich and the powerful and everyone, slave and free, hid themselves in the caves and among the rocks of the mountains."

This verse tells us that Jesus opens the sixth seal and not only allows but causes the world wide devastation to take place. This is done in fulfillment of the promise of God in Romans 6:23 when God said, **"For the wages of sin is death, but the free gift of God is eternal life in Christ Jesus."** The host of believers in Heaven are about to enjoy the promise of eternal life with God. The Tribulation Saints are martyred because of their faith but they also will be rewarded with eternal love and care of our Savior. But the host of people, the billions of people left on the world now left alive are going to suffer all over the world as an announcement of their doom. To add to the horror of people who live in these times God outlines what physically happens on earth.

- There is a huge earthquake. It may not be worldwide but it is so huge it affects the entire earth.
- The sun becomes black meaning darkness prevails.
- The moon glows red like blood.
- The sky releases stars and clear distinction of earth and space ends.
- All powerful people on earth join billions of others asking God for death.

The Seventh Seal

Revelation 8:1–2
When the Lamb opened the seventh seal, there was silence in Heaven for about a half hour. Then I saw the seven angels who stand before God, and seven trumpets were given to them.

What was the half hour of silence for? It is in honor of the Tribulation Saints who are under God's altar. These have been taken from their place of physical death to Heaven, a place of spiritual eternity. They are pleading to God to throw His wrath against the evil forces who killed them. God responds and answers them to say "In just a little while." What we see is the wrath of God building against the Antichrist, the False Prophet and all their followers. God honors those who have died for Him. Therefore God uses the Seventh Seal to announce the seven trumpets. Remember that time is not an issue here on earth. The seven trumpets are revelation of God to the world of another round of punishment He is about to deliver, has delivered and will continue to deliver on earth.

The Seven Trumpets

To understand the Seven Trumpets we must remember this is a vision given to the Apostle John and it unfolds to give us an indication of God's wrath against the followers of Satan. This involves all the people who have had the Mark of the Beast placed on either their right hand or their forehead. Each Trumpet adds to the unbearable conditions for people on earth. We are coming to the close of the Seven-Year Tribulation. We are even coming to the close of the Great Tribulation, which covers the last three and one half years of this devastation. Many people think that because the Seven Trumpets are announced by the Seven Seals they have to come after the seals. This is not quite accurate. Yes, they come in the last quadrant of the Great Tribulation but there is plenty of room to overlap some of the Seven Seals. The Antichrist who was so confident at the Middle Week Abomination of Desolation and declared to be God now is beginning to understand he will lose the war with God. The False Prophet, who has totally destroyed all world religions including the Catholic Church as well, stops all worship practices of any kind that does not recognize the Antichrist as God. These events are called the Seven Trumpets because, before each is horrible event takes place, a trumpet in sounded in Heaven. Let's look at each trumpet.

Trumpet No. 1

Revelation 8:7
"The first angel blew his trumpet, and there followed hail and fire, mixed with blood, and these were thrown upon the earth. And a third of the earth was burned up. And a third of the trees were burned up, and all green grass was burned up."

The conditions in the world will be horrible. We know that war, and plaque, and wild animals as well as earthquakes, stars falling on earth have created a state of absolute fear in every living being. People who have accepted the Mark of the Beast still have trouble getting food to eat and now the angel throws fire upon the land and all green grass was burned up. In addition one third of the trees are burned. Our imaginations do not need to work overtime to realize the events that will happen on earth. With the difficulty of buying food, gangs will be created to take care of only gang members. Theft will put everyone on edge, scared, and quick to defend their meager possessions. It is probable the Antichrist government will have forbid any guns or weapons in homes to defend families. No one will trust anyone. Death will be a normal day's event. A vast number of people who, die will not even be buried but will just tossed into a pit. Any form of medical care will go to those with power and money. Group insurance to pay bills will become non-existent.

This event does not necessarily happen after the sixth seal. We just know it will be after God releases the angels at the four winds of the earth and begins to release His wrath upon the followers of the Antichrist and False Prophet. This places the Seven Trumpets in the latter part of the Great Tribulation. The wrath of the Seven Trumpets could be released concurrent with the Seven Seals.

Trumpets two, three, and four come very quickly after trumpet one. This is simply showing the wrath of God. God is not punishing the followers of Satan because He hates them. He is also fulfilling His plan of justice and what He has ordained for the end times from the beginning of time. The evidence of the book from which the seals are opened, inform us that God has not only planned every detail step of what will happen but has recorded it for us to study. It is recorded in the book of the Seven Seals, the Seven Trumpets and the Seven Bowls.

Trumpet No. 2

Revelation 8:9
"The second angel blew his trumpet, and something like a great mountain was thrown into the sea and

a third of the sea became blood. A third of the living creatures died and a third of ships were destroyed."

Very soon after trumpet number 1, God will release the angel to blow trumpet number 2. This attacks the ocean featuring the destruction of fish as a food supply and the destruction of shipping freight, in particular food. The verse above says one third of all living sea creatures will die. This tells us many million people will die. This affects not only food supply but jobs all over the world. Our imagination can run rapid on the adverse impact these events will have to living conditions on earth. Distrust of the government will exist in every heart but fear of voicing that discontent will be greater than ever. The voice of the 144,000 Jewish Evangelists will be active still but the forces of the Antichrist government will so fierce life will feel hopeless. A television show we used to see often used the phrase, gloom, despair, and agony on me. In this reality of life, not a reality television show, gloom despair, and agony on me will be real and hopeless outside of Christ. And even the decision to accept Jesus and place trust in His saving power brought absolute and certain immediate death through beheading.

Trumpet No. 3

Revelation 8:9
"The third angel blew his trumpet and a great star fell from Heaven, blazing like a torch, and it fell on a third of the rivers and on the springs of water. The name of the star is Wormwood. A third of the waters become wormwood and many people died from the water, because it had been made bitter.

How could it get worse? And then it does get worse. The great star likely is so massive it breaks into millions of small pieces before it hits earth and the impact on fresh water sources. Some scientists estimate that a relatively small asteroid falling on the Gulf of Mexico would cause massive flooding up into Kansas. Think what a star, perhaps half the size of earth that splits into millions of small pieces would do to our universe. In Trumpet number 2 we saw all one third of seawater contaminated resulting in one third of all seas and creatures of seas destroyed. Now in Trumpet number 3 we see one third of fresh water contaminated resulting in one third of all human usage of such water deadly.

Trumpet No. 4

Revelation 8:12
"The fourth angel blew his trumpet and a third of the sun was struck and a third of the moon and a third of the stars so that a third of their light might be darkened, and a third of the day might be kept from shining, and likewise a third of the night."

Trumpet 4 involves the Universe we take for granted. It causes one third of the sun, moon and stars to become dark. This is far more than comfort of having light. This severely affects the heat of the world. Bitter cold hits much of the earth and crops cannot grow in weather that is not at certain heat. Without the rays of the sun seeds will not sprout and life becomes that much more difficult. Trumpets one, two, three, and four sound and are implemented very close together. The net result of all these are to get the attention of everyone alive on earth and force them to realize God is real. They are also reminded by the world changing events that time is about to end. Everywhere they look they are seeing people accept Christ and then be beheaded because of it but they also see the wicked and unbelieving people also face horrible death. Who are they to believe? God is giving his people the last chance to avoid the Lake of Fire for eternity. The Two Witnesses and the 144,000 Jewish Evangelists are active preaching God's message. People all over the world are witnessing how the 144,000 and the Two Witnesses cannot be touched by the Antichrist or by any of his plaques.

The Three Woes

Revelation 8:13
"Then I looked, and I Heard a loud voice as it flew directly overhead, "Woe, woe, woe to those who

*dwell on the earth, at the blasts of the other trumpets
that the three angels are about to flow."*

A woe is considered to be something that causes grief, sorrow, pain, fear, of despair. A woe is also considered to be something that teaches a lesson and whatever caused it one would know to not do that again. In Revelation 8:13 God announces that the plaques He has caused to fall on earth have still not resulted in millions and perhaps billions of people to trust in Jesus as their Savior and Lord. We know this because Revelation 9:20 tells us exact that fact. **"The rest of mankind, who were not killed by these plagues, did not repent of the works of their hands nor give up worshiping demons and idols of gold and silver and bronze and stone and wood, which cannot see or hear or walk."** God therefore, not Satan, casts upon the people on earth three plaques more horrible that even the terror on ones before. The first four trumpets will have effectively destroyed houses, shelters, stores, towns, cities, roads, ships on the open sea, bridges across waterways and ability to communicate with each other. Food will be almost impossible to get at all and too expensive to buy when it is available. Millions of people will be dying from lack of medical care and from disease as well as injuries. People will see and understand God is delivering these plaques and will ask.

"Why is God doing this?" They will also be aware of many friends who decide to trust Jesus, perhaps through the preaching of the 144,000 and then be quickly and viciously beheaded. God is about to implement the last three trumpets that He calls woes because their devastation is so overwhelming.

Trumpet No. 5 and Woe No. 1

Revelation 9:1–4
*"And the fifth angel blew his trumpet, and I saw a star
fallen from heaven and he was given the key to the shaft of
the bottomless pit. He opened the shaft of the bottomless
pit, and from the shaft rose smoke like the smoke of a great
furnace, and the sun and the air were darkened with the*

*smoke from the shaft. Then from the smoke came locusts
on the earth, and they were given power like the power of
scorpions of the earth. They were told not to harm the grass
of the earth, or any green plant or any tree but only those
people who do not have the seal of God on their foreheads."*

We know from the above verse the 144,000 Jewish Evangelists are still at work on earth witnessing about Jesus because the locusts were informed to not attack those people who had the seal of God on their foreheads. Therefore we know God has not yet given up hope that some of His people will still in this late hour trust Jesus Christ as their Savior. The locusts are generally considered to be much more deadly, painful, and terrifying than normal locusts in the world today. Verse 5 tells us these locusts torment unbelievers for five months. Their stings are reported to be fierce, long-lasting torture to the victim. The pain is so much, those bitten are said to "Long for Death" but they are not granted death. Instead they are forced to endure the misery. The locusts were like, "locusts prepared for battle," their heads "were like crowns of gold," their hair "like women's hair," and their teeth "like lions teeth." They had "breastplates like breastplates of iron." The noise of their wings was like the noise of many chariots with horses rushing into battle. They have tails and stings like scorpions and their power to hurt people for five months is in their tails. They have as king over them the angel of the bottomless pit. His name is Abaddon and in Greek he is called Apollyon.

Trumpet No. 6 and Woe No. 2

Revelation 9:13–17
*"Then the sixth angel blew his trumpet and I heard a voice
from the four horns of the golden altar before God, "Release the
four angels who are bound at the great river Euphrates." So the
four angels, who had been prepared for the hour, the day, the
month, and the year, were released to kill a third of mankind.
The number of mounted troops was twice ten thousand times
ten thousand; I heard their number. And this is how I saw*

the horses in my vision and those who rode them; they wore breastplates the color of sulfur and the heads of the horses were like lion's heads. And fire and smoke came out of their mouths."

With the sixth trumpet, God declares that enough is enough. Amazingly the people of the Antichrists following go through the horrors of all that has gone before and they still refuse to follow Christ. Yes huge numbers of people do elect to face sure death from Satan's Lieutenants but the mass of people continue to ignore God. Therefore God implements a plan He knew would come to pass. He tells four angels to release an army of 2 million soldiers who will kill one third of mankind. All those who will be killed will have the "Mark of the Beast" on their foreheads to signify they are followers of Satan. The End of the World is now very close. This will happen close to the Battle of Armageddon and the return of Christ.

The purpose of God's Wrath

Revelation 9:20
"The rest of mankind, who were not killed by these plaques, did not repent of the works of their hands nor give up worshiping demons and idols of gold and silver and bronze and stone and wood, which cannot see or hear or walk, nor did they repent of their murders of their sorceries or their sexual immortality or their thefts."

What was the purpose of God's wrath falling upon mankind during the seven seals and the seven trumpets? It was to convince the rest of mankind that God is all powerful and God demands their trust and faith. God will destroy evil and reward people who put their trust in Him. This message was conveyed to the whole world by the 144,000 Jewish Evangelists. Satan, through his Lieutenants, the Antichrist and the False Prophet countered this message by telling the masses they were winning the war against God and to survive the masses must remain loyal to him. Besides they were forced to wear the "Mark of the Beast" which was number 666. If anyone was seen without that number they were immediately beheaded. Many millions of people were beheaded and taken to the altar of God in heaven where they awaited the close of Earth. The result of these two messages very clearly outlined to people was people still refused God and God had to keep His word and destroy unbelievers.

Trumpet No. 7 and Woe No. 3

Revelation 11:17
Then the seventh angel blew his trumpet, and there were loud voices in heaven, saying, "The kingdom of the world has become the kingdom of our Lord and of his Christ, and he shall reign forever and ever." And the twenty-four elders who sit on their thrones before God fell on their faces and worshiped God, saying, "We give thanks to you, Lord God Almighty, who is and who was, for you have taken your great power and begun to reign."

The seventh angel blew his trumpet and that announced to the world that the end was at hand for the earth. The twenty-four elders in heaven that sit on their thrones before God will fall on their faces and worship God saying **"We give thanks to You, Lord God Almighty who is and who was for You have taken your great power and begun to reign."** Most scholars believe the twenty-four elders will be leaders of "The Church." Some believe the elders will be twelve from the tribes of Israel and the twelve apostles. The Bible does not tell us this information. We do not need to know who they were. We do know they see, in their vision that the end of God's allotted time for people to choose Him over Satan was close at hand. The angel who blew the seventh trumpet brought down on earth the third woe. That woe will be the seven bowls of judgment. They also could see it was nearly time for the dead to be judged, referring to the coming judgment of nations to determine who could go into the one-thousand-year millennial reign, and for the saints to be rewarded with the one-thousand-year millennial reign was near.

Revelation 11:18
"The nations raged, but your wrath came, and the time for
the dead to be judged, and for rewarding your servants, the
prophets and saints and those who fear your name, both small
and great, and for destroying the destroyers of the earth."

The seventh trumpet does not announce another plaque that happens. However, it announces two significant and nonreversible events. Number 1 is the coming of divine wrath of the seven bowls. We can say the seventh trumpet's wrath is the seven bowls that follow. Number 2 is the reality that Jesus descends at the blowing of the seventh trumpet. This will be when the Tribulation saints left on earth will be caught up with Him and will be given a spiritual body. At the end of Revelation 11:18 the world is now ready for the Battle of Armageddon and the second coming of Christ.

The Mark of the Beast

Revelation 13:16–17
"Also it causes all, both small and great, both rich and poor,
both free and slave to be marked on the right hand or the
forehead, so that no one can buy or sell unless he has the mark,
that is, the name of the beast or the number of its name."

One of the most questioned parts of Revelation is the **"Mark of the Beast."**

This action taken by the False Prophet, who is the Beast that arises out of the Earth rather than the Sea, is taken to advance the power of the Antichrist. It is totally universal for every person alive that declares the Antichrist as God and who denies, publically, the reality of Jesus Christ. We can speculate that believers were hiding their belief in Christ even though, in their heart, they trusted in Jesus Christ as the Messiah of old and the Savior of their future. This was unacceptable to the Antichrist. No one was spared this action. Note that Revelation chapter 13 tells us that it, the declaration to be branded with the number 666, was applied to every human being, whether they were powerful or not powerful, whether they were rich or poor, and whether they were slaves or free. Yes, slavery will reinter humanity.

The impact of the **"Mark of the Beast"** is that without it on their right hand or their forehead no one will be allowed to buy or sell anything. In essence this means they will starve to death. Let us realize there will be no court system to appeal this legislation. There will be no Supreme Court. There will be no Congress. There will be no system law except for that of the Antichrist. Revelation chapter 13 verse 18 tells us the number 666 "calls for the number of a man." Biblical history does emphasize the number 6. Mankind was created on the sixth day. The Old Testament Law called for mankind to work six days of the week. Certain kinds of slavery, in ancient Rome became null and void after six years. The number use of the number 6, as will be used by the Antichrist is parallel with the Greek word *charagma.* In the Roman Empire the word was associated with the Roman government and was implemented under the power and authority of the Roman Emperor. In ancient Rome the passage of a mark was used with the word charagma and it involved authority to buy and sell needs of life. The parallel with the 666 number required of believers in the Antichrist reflect the power of the revived Roman Empire in the Great Tribulation.

Revelation 13:18
This calls for wisdom: let the one who has understanding
calculate the number of the beast, for it is the
number of a man, and his number is 666.

The **"Mark of the Beast"** will be, in the Great Tribulation, the output of the terrible battle going on between God and the Antichrist. The goal is the heart of mankind. The result for believers in Christ who reject the **"Mark of the Beast"** is death.

Revelation 14:9–10
"And another angel, a third, followed them, saying with a loud
voice, "If anyone worships the beast and its image and receives

a mark on his forehead or on his hand, he also will drink the wine of God's wrath, poured full strength into the cup of his anger, and he will be tormented with fire and sulfur in the presence of the holy angels and in the presence of the Lamb."

The horror of life is now evident. If one choses Jesus they will be tortured and beheaded by the Antichrist. If they chose the Antichrist they will suffer the full strength of God's anger and will be tormented with fire and sulfur. Death and terror surrounds all. The reality of life in those times to soon come on earth are that if one choses to be true to God, as the 144,000 evangelists are preaching and which you know to be the right thing to do you and your family will become unemployed, will have no money and even if you do get some you will be unable to buy food, clothing or maintain a place of residence. You will be totally isolated from all structures of government and will even be isolated from people formerly thought to be friends. They will shun you because to do otherwise could cause them to die as well.

However, if one choses to receive the **"Mark of the Beast"** they will be able to continue life in some shape for a short time until the wrath of God falls upon them. God has declared they will face cataclysmic earthquakes that affect the whole world, and will face the horrors of the seven seals and seven trumpets designed by God as punishment for sin. But the worst of all is they will be well informed by the 144,000 that they will not go with Jesus into eternity but will be caste into the "Lake of Fire" where they will be separated from God and will exist in fierce fire and brimstone forever and forever.

Those who choose to worship the Antichrist will not be the only ones with a sign of commitment and protection. The Bible tells us in Revelation 7:2–3 that those chosen by God to deliver His message of commitment to Jesus Christ will be given the **"Seal of God"** and no power of the Antichrist will be able to affect them.

Revelation 7:2–3
"Then I saw another angel ascending from the rising of the sun, with the seal of the living God, and he called with a loud voice

to the four angels who had been given power to harm earth and sea, saying, "Do not harm the earth or the sea or the trees, until we have sealed the servants of our God on their foreheads."

In these verses God tells us that the 144,000 evangelists and the two witnesses, who are challenged to present Jesus Christ as the Lord and Savior of mankind, will be given a seal placed on their foreheads in which they testify of the power of God. They are so important to the closing of the earth's rule that God holds back the fierce ravages of the seven seals, seven trumpets and even the seven bowls until the witnesses have been given the seal of protection so that the horrors of these events will not touch them.

The Seven Bowls

Revelation 15:1
"Then I saw another sign in heaven, great and amazing, seven angels with seven plaques, which are the last, for with them the wrath of God is finished."

Revelation 15:6
"And one of the four living creatures gave to the seven angels seven golden bowls full of the wrath of God who lives forever and ever."

The scripture relating to events God revealed to the Apostle John are recorded as past tense because John is reporting to us something he has just witnessed, not as an accomplished event but as a vision of a future event. We therefore write about the Seven Bowls as a future event because they are a future event to us but the vision John reports make that a past tense event for him.

The close of time will be very close at hand with the blowing of the seventh trumpet. But the Bible is not written chronologically. The seven bowls that will be delivered by the seven angels and will be delivered by the blowing of the seventh trumpet; not only will announce the end of time for the unsaved to choose Christ, they also will announce the seven bowls that are a final suffering of non-believers. God loves all of His creation. He even loves these stubborn people. Because of His love He will try to convince them to accept Christ as their Savior and to trust God for deliverance. The seven bowls indicate the end of time is soon approaching. These seven bowls of wrath, the seven seals, and the seven trumpets. Whereas the trumpets affect a large part of earth's population, the bowls, encompass every living person.

Bowl No. 1

Revelation 16:2
"So the first angel went and poured out his bowl on the earth, and harmful sores came upon the people who bore the "Mark of the Beast" and worshiped His image."

Concurrent with the horror of the seven trumpets the seven bowls intensify the devastation of God's Wrath. The seven trumpets happen quickly, too quickly for inhabitants to rationalize or understand what was happening. However, the 144,000 Jewish evangelists, who have God's "Seal" of protection against the Antichrist on their foreheads, will proclaim this horror comes from God onto the nonbelievers on earth. In the previous chapter of Revelation we have seen the angels accept from Jesus the seven bowls filled with seven plagues. Bowl No. 1 is the first of these seven plagues. Then a loud voice will tell the angels to pour out the seven bowls. The first angel will pour out the first plague which is **"harmful sores."**

Many Bible Scholars try to interpret the above verse that says, **"So the first angel went and poured out his bowl on the earth."** They simply do not want this horror on the entire world so they rationalize it really means Israel. When will we learn to accept the Bible to mean exactly what it records? God clearly says the bowls, full of His wrath, will be poured out on the earth. That means every bit of dirt in the whole world will have this bowl of sores poured out on it. To say they will be poured out on Israel only is to say that only Israel contains non-believing horrible people who deserve the horrors of punishment for their lack of belief. This is not true and God means exactly what His Word tells us.

The painful sores God tells us about will fall on the people who have the "Mark of the Beast and who worship Him Image." Only the people with the "Mark of the Beast on their forehead or right" hand suffer this horror. We also know that there will still be believers who have not yet been killed by the Antichrist. We know this because we know millions of people will survive the Great Tribulation and go through God's Judgment of Nations to determine who will go into the one-thousand-year millennial reign of Christ. Those who are believers and who go into the one-thousand-year Millennial Reign alive, and who do not experience physical death on earth, will be spared the suffering of these bowls.

Bowl No. 2

Revelation 16:3
"The second angel poured out his bowl into the sea, and it became like the blood of a corpse, and every living thing died that was in the sea."

In Revelation 16:3 Jesus authorizes the second angel to pour out his bowl on those who wear the "Mark of the Beast." But this verse, taken literally, is different because it says God kills every living creature in the sea as punishment to those who worship the Antichrist. By now there is no doubt but that God is pouring out His wrath on unbelievers but they are stubborn and will not repent. Understand when the Bible says the sea became like blood of a corpse God means all over the world. Every body of salt water in the world turns into something like the blood of a dead person. We know that 70 percent of the earth's surface is ocean. We know that 97 percent of earth's waters exist in the oceans. Now, after Bowl No. 2, this vast amount of contaminated water cannot support fish related food. Ocean fish make up 80 percent of the world's fish-food. Fish make up 17 percent of the world's protein. Now this critical food source is destroyed because it no longer exists in ocean waters that have been critical for survival. In addition the stench is horrible creating allergies beyond description and disease that rapidly covers the earth. The above verse tells us every living thing died that was in the sea. That includes death that occurs because great shipping freight that transfer food to needy places in the world can no longer travel in the sticky mass of this new liquid. And this change happens quickly, perhaps instantly. The fear and confusion cannot be described.

Bowl No. 3

Revelation 16:4–6
"The third angel poured out his bowl into the rivers and the springs of water, and they became blood. And I heard the angel in charge of the waters say, Just are You, o Holy One, who is and who was, for You brought these judgements. For they have shed the blood of saints and prophets, and You have given them blood to drink. It is what they deserve."

Every person who has accepted the Antichrist's **"Mark of the Beast"** will be held responsible for the murder of each and every saint they killed in the Great Tribulation. God is now giving them what they have earned and the Bible teaches the wages of sin is death. In addition to the horrors of the Seals and Trumpets now all fresh water will be changed into blood to drink. Note that in verse 4–6 the third angel pours out bowl number 3. In Bowl No. 2 the water was changed into something like blood. Now in Bowl No. 3 the scripture tells us the water becomes blood. The third angel, empowered by Christ, tells those who are dying the rivers and fresh waters are being changed into actual blood to represent the shed blood of saints and prophets. The angel tells these who have the **"Mark of the Beast"** on their foreheads or right hand, **"Just are You, O Holy One who is and who was, for You (God) brought these judgments. For they (nonbelievers) have shed the blood of saints and prophets and You (God) have given them blood to drink. It is what they (non-believers) deserve."**

Bowl No. 4

Revelation 16:8–9
"The fourth angel poured out his bowl on the sun, and it was allowed to scorch people with fire. They were scorched by the fierce heat and they cursed the name of God who had power over these plaques. They did not repent or give Him glory."

How can a people be so evil and so dumb? How can a people be so captivated by the promises of evil they cannot see and accept truth? The answer goes back to the days of Adam and Eve. Eve was tempted and she lured Adam who was tempted. They both knew better. God had warned them and taught them that eating of the tree of knowledge would bring death. The Garden of Eden was the beginning of this story and now we are almost at the end of this story. The fierce sun reaches not only Israel but everywhere in the world. This bowl of wrath is universal as will be all other plaques of wrath. It is significant to note that God will "scorch" severely all who have the "Mark of the Beast." And the fire that will scorch them will be so hot the nonbelievers will beg to die and be taken out of the torture. But the same people will have a hardened heart and will not repent. They will curse God and blame Him even though they understand God is sending the plague of fire. God loves these lost souls and is giving them this final chance to repent of their sins. But God's Word tells us the lost people will have a hard heart and will not repent.

Bowl No. 5

Revelation 16:11
"The fifth angel poured out his bowl on the throne of the beast, and its kingdom was plunged into darkness. People gnawed their tongues in anguish and cursed God of heaven for their pain and sores. They did not repent of their deeds."

Now God attacks the very throne of the Beast whom we know as the Antichrist and plunges the Antichrist's kingdom in total darkness.

What does that mean? The kingdom of the Antichrist will be those who have the **"Mark of the Beast"** on their body. These are the ones who will now be totally dark. This could be that the people with the **"Mark of the Beast"** lose sight. It could also mean darkness is only given to the home, businesses, and places where the **"Mark of the Beast"** people reside. This will be darkness to the point one cannot see images because of the lack of light. There will be no light for those who reject Jesus. Think about it. There will also be no light in the darkness of the Lake of Fire. This Bowl of darkness combined with Bowl No. Four render a glimpse of what Hell is going to be. Hell will be full of fear, horrible heat, incredible sulfur making breathing hard, and darkness. Yet the amazement is people do not draw to God. These seven plagues should draw many to God but they draw farther apart and their hatred of God grows.

Bowl No. 6

Revelation 16:12–13
"The sixth angel poured out his bowl on the great river Euphrates, and its water dried up to prepare the way for the kings from the east. And I saw coming out of the mouth of the dragon (Satan) and out of the mouth of the beast (The Antichrist) and out of the mouth of the False Prophet, three unclean spirits like frogs."

In the fifth bowl God attacked the throne of the Antichrist. Revelation 16:12–13 points out the sixth angel poured out his bowl on the great river Euphrates. What is so significant about Euphrates? The river Euphrates pictured life for the Holy Land that compromised this war. It is the largest river in the western Asia. The river Euphrates forms the eastern boundary of ancient Rome and countries they held under bondage. It formed the eastern boundary of land Abraham was promised. It has huge historical significance and is the major source of life for the people. More significant we see in these verses that God is arranging the movement of troupes of oriental kings to take position in the final Battle of Armageddon. God tells us the water of Euphrates is dried up to prepare the way for the kings from China, India, Persia, Japan and Afghanistan to attack Israel in the final war of Armageddon.

God arranges this to happen by gathering the Dragon (Satan) The Beast (overall commander of the rebellion against God) and the False Prophet (the organizer of universal worship of the Antichrist) together to form military force against Israel who has finally turned to God. The unclean spirits coming out of these three are demonic spirits and verse 14 tells us the thing they do. **"Who go abroad to the kings of the whole world (ten kings relating to the ten federations and the ten horns) to assemble them for battle on the great day of God the Almighty."** Verse 16 follows up and says **"The assembled them at the place that in Hebrew is called Armageddon."** Now we see the federations of force against God and His people unite. Bowl No. Six prepares the way for the final battle.

Bowl No. 7

Revelation 16:12–13
"The seventh angel poured out his bowl into the air, and a loud voice came out of the temple, from the throne, saying "It is done!" And there were flashes of lightning, rumblings, peals of thunder and a great earthquake such as there had never been since man was on earth, so great was the earthquake, the great city was split into three parts, and the cities of the nation's fell, and God remembered Babylon the great, to make her drain the cup of the wine of the fury of His wrath."

Clearly in Bowl no. 7 God is preparing for the great Battle of Armageddon. Although technically the Battle of Armageddon is not the last battle between God and Satan it is the most significant. The Bible tells us that at the end of the one-thousand-year millennial reign Satan will be loosed from the pit of hell below the earth and will gather an army and wage one more war against God. But that war and the forth coming war of Armageddon will not be a contest. God so dramatically defeats Satan that the war itself is no contest. The war at the end of the one-thousand-year millennial reign will be called a Battle of Gog and Magog but should not be confused with the Battle of Gog and Magog that occurred in the first quarter of the Tribulation Period.

The Battle of Armageddon

To understand the Battle of Armageddon we need to review the world situation at the close of the last bowl of plaques God sends down on lost mankind. The wild beast, the Antichrist, has successfully maneuvered the political kingdoms of the world into ten federations of power and each king of each federation has become fully under the physical, mental, and political control of the Antichrist.

Revelation 13:1–2
"And I saw a beast rising out of the sea, with ten horns and seven heads, with ten diadems on its horns and blasphemous names on its heads. And the beast that I saw was like a leopard, its feet were like a bear's, and its mouth was like a lion's mouth. And the dragon gave his power and his throne with great authority."

The rule of the Antichrist (beast) is like that of the Roman Empire at the time of Christ's crucifixion in that it applied to every person of every language, every tribe, and every domicile.

Revelation 13:7
"Also it was allowed to make war on the Saints and to conquer them. And authority was given it over tribe and people and language and nation."

The Roman Empire ruled with total control and any noticed restraint of or conflict with Roman rule was dealt with immediately with fierce and often deadly response. The Antichrist will deal the same way. It is therefore of no surprise that the kings of the ten most powerful nations and armies in the world will be in reality, puppets of the Antichrist. And because the Antichrist will be totally, 100 percent under the control of Satan, we understand that Satan has been given authority to control the entire world. That authority was given by God the Father. Satan is even given power to make war against those who trust Jesus and are willing to die to follow God's will.

Revelation 17:12–13
"And the ten horns you say are ten kings who have not yet received royal power, but they are to receive authority as kings for one hour (short time) together with the beast."

The ten horns then represent the ten-king federation that had, have, or will have total and complete control of the world in its day. Understanding that the ten horns represent ten kings ruling over a confederation of nations surrounding Israel what do the seven heads represent?

Revelation 17:9
"This calls for a mind with wisdom: the seven heads are seven mountains on which the woman is seated."

The seven heads are seven hills on which the woman is seated. The seven hills represent the seven hills upon which Rome was built. The Beast or Antichrist will at the middle of the Seven-Year Tribulation take over the Jerusalem temple and declare he is God. The woman, verse 9 refers reveals, is the Catholic Church. This woman (The Catholic Church) is referred to as **"The Harlot"** and **"The Prostitute,"** based on her claiming to be a Christian religion. In fact **"The Harlot"** is working continually to destroy Christianity. So the place the woman is seated is Rome and the kingdom she personally controls is the resurrected Roman Empire. In verse 10 God tells us **"They are seven kings, five of whom have fallen, one is, and one is yet to come."** This one "who is yet to come" will represent seven ruling powers that (1) are powerful enough to control the whole world, (2) have an overwhelming hatred for anything or anyone who support the work of God the Father or God the Son, and (3) have a connection to the Roman Empire either as ancestry of Rome, ruler of Rome or future ruler of Rome. The seven kings that have fallen are Egypt, Assyria, Babylon, Medo-Persia, and Greece. The kingdom *that is,* in the day of the Apostle John, was Rome. The one that is yet to come, will be the reinstallation of a Rome-like empire through which the Antichrist will implement so much of his conquest of the world. What does the Word of God mean when it says "on which the woman is seated?" This reference goes back to the verse in which we saw the "harlot" riding the "Beast" and having control of the "Beast" for a time. However, eventually the "Beast" (Antichrist) revolts and destroys the "harlot." In this scripture we know the "harlot" is the Roman Catholic Church. This Church, in the day of John the Apostle, was a false church in that they did not accept Christ. They not only did not accept Christ they fought every effort of Jesus and killed thousands of Christians. In the last days the False Prophet will likewise create a church, very similar to the Roman Catholic Church John saw in the vision and it will exist to support the work of the Antichrist.

The Battle of Armageddon that takes place at the end of the Seven-Year Tribulation is the result of Satan having gained total control of the world but not defeated God. In spite of amazing success in forming the political and military might to control the world and in being able to totally defeat any church effort that supports worship of anyone other than him, Satan has had many fierce road-blocks to winning the battle with God. These road-blocks include:

- The 144,000 Jewish Evangelists whom Satan has not been able to catch, to harm in any way, or to even be able to twist, or destroy the message of Jesus Christ as the savior of sins and eternal life with Christ. An untold number of people have decided to accept Satan's punishment of death and trust Christ.
- The "Two-Witnesses" likewise have witnessed to the lost and have had amazing success in converting the hearts of people from Satan to God.

- The plagues called the Seven Seals God has allowed Satan to impose on all people showing his power and forcing people to accept the "Mark of the Beast" have not worked but have actually driven a huge number of people to Christ.
- The Seven Trumpets of God in which horrible things have happened to the land have caused millions of people to see the power of God and turn to Christ rather than Satan.
- The final Seven Bowls have accentuated control God has over Satan and it is now a fear in the mind of even Satan's most loyal Lieutenants that they may not be able to defeat God.
- But Satan, through the Antichrist and the False Prophet, impose powerful demonic power on his Ten Kings of the Ten Federation of nations, thereby imposing total authority to force the Kings to build a great hatred of specifically God and secondarily Israel.

What Nations are engaged in the Battle?

God's Word tells us four powerful armies are involved in the Battle of Armageddon. One will be from the north, one from the east and one from the south. The ***northern political and military power*** is most like made up primarily of Russia with possible coalition with Germany, Turkey, and surrounding nations. Consider Jeremiah 50:41: **"Behold, a people comes from the north, a mighty nation and many kings are stirring from the farthest parts of the earth."**

The ***Southern political and military power*** will be a coalition of Iraq, Iran, Syria, Saudi Arabia and other Muslin nations. They will be limited in power because of the losses they sustained in the Battle of Gog and Magog. However, they may have the added support of India, one of the world's most populated countries.

The third political and military army will be located in the area close to Jerusalem and will be the resurrected Roman Empire headed up by the Antichrist. These people will include the Palestinians. The Antichrist himself will command the Roman Empire that includes followers all over the world. Because of the influence of the Catholic Church millions of people all over the world will side with the Antichrist. The False Prophet takes over the Catholic Church in the final days and creates a one world religion that worships the Antichrist. This puts these people on the Antichrist team.

The fourth political and military coalition comes from the Orient. Revelation 16:12 God tells us, **"The sixth angel poured out his bowl on the great river Euphrates and its water dried up to prepare the way for the kings from the east."** The Euphrates River is located as to be a natural divider of the East from the West. God dries up the river to symbolically enable the eastern powers to wage war on Israel. This coalition will probably consist of countries such as China, Japan, North Korea, and South Korea. God's Word tells us a massive oriental invasion against Israel will be implemented. This confrontation alone would be far beyond Israel's ability to survive without God.

The Union of these Great Armies

We know these great armies converge on Israel for the purpose of defeating and totally destroying Israel. They hate Israel largely because Israel has become a nation whose leaders promote and support the teachings of God. They hate the 144,000 Jewish Evangelists and the work they have done. They hate the fact that the Antichrist could not destroy the 144,000 or the "Two Witnesses" who helped convert millions of people from worship of the Beast to worship of the Messiah. But the most significant reason they hate Israel is that Satan is the power behind the Antichrist and the False Prophet. Satan is using demonic powers to twist the minds of the ten kings of the ten-king federation. And Israel is God's "Chosen" nation.

The four armies are directed by the ten kings of the ten-king federation. The ten federations will be molded into the four great armies mentioned previously. The ten kings rule the whole world but they are blinded to the truth by Satan and are little more than puppets of Satan. The minds of these ten kings know are twisted and deranged by Satan to think as he thinks. Satan, who knows the showdown between him and God is near, issues a worldwide order to nations under his command to attack Israel and representatives of God. He will point out the horrors God has created in the Seven Trumpets and Seven Bowls. These ten kings, representing the balance of the world do not know that Satan knows the battle will really be against God himself.

As the ten kings converge to defeat Israel they learn of the forth coming of Jesus Christ to earth with His army and they change tactics from fighting Israel to fighting God. Thus the Battle of Armageddon begins. Scripture implies to us that the king of the southern army will first attack Jesus and His followers.

Daniel 11:40
"At the time of the end, the king of the south shall attack him (Roman Empire), but the king of the north shall rush upon Him (king of the southern armies) like a whirlwind with chariots and horsemen and with many ships and he shall come into countries and shall overflow and pass through."

The kingdom of the south will probably be Iraq, Iran, Syria, Libya and other Muslin leaning nations. This king has great success and proceeds through the land of Israel devastating and destroying wherever he goes. The king of the southern army reaches as far south as Egypt and wages war. They are highly successful. Then things go wrong and they are attacked and decimated by the armies of the northern kingdom. The northern kingdom is almost certainly Russia although God's Word does not specify Russia. These armies are commanded by greedy, evil men who know no loyalty. They know force, and their commitment to the Antichrist is based on the apparent force of the Antichrist and his followers. However ancient hatreds come to play here as the south fights the north. This battle of the northern kingdom reaches out and conquers Egypt. However, news from the northern kingdom and the eastern kingdom cause this king of Russia, who wants to command the world, great anger.

Daniel 11:44
"But news from the east and the north shall alarm him and he shall go out with great fury to destroy many to destruction."

The king of the northern army learns two hundred million military men from the east are entering the battle. At that time the northern kingdom and the eastern kingdom join with the Antichrist in the Roman Empire to fight the armies of Jesus.

This is the last phase of the massive war that has touched the entire world. But the final battle between Jesus and Satan, who controls the Ten-King Federation and his two lieutenants the Antichrist and False Prophet, will take place in Jerusalem. God tells us in Zachariah 12:3, *"On that day I will make Jerusalem a heavy stone for all the peoples, all who lift it will seriously hurt themselves; and all the nations of the earth will gather against it."* Just before Jesus returns the battle of Jerusalem will be massive, violent and fierce. Large numbers of the northern and eastern armies are killed and injured. Much of Jerusalem is laid in ruins and a massive number of Israeli's are killed. But God steps in with miraculous intervention and prevents any force from totally capturing Jerusalem.

Zachariah 14:2, 3
"For I will gather all nations against Jerusalem to battle; and the city shall be taken, and the houses plundered, and the women raped; half of the city shall go out into exile, but the rest of the people shall not be cut off from the city. Then shall the Lord go out, and fight against those nations, as when he fights on a day of battle."

Jerusalem is in the process of being overtaken by Satan's forces. And we are now ready for the second advent of Christ.

CHAPTER TWENTY-FOUR

The Doctrine of God's Promise Fulfilled
Meanwhile in Heaven

In chapter 23, we picked up by stating "Following the rapture of the Church" and we proceeded to lay out what will take place in the Seven-Year Tribulation outlined by Scripture. In chapter 24, we pick up by stating, "Following the rapture of the Church" but we have a vastly different story to tell. Whereas the Seven-Year Tribulation is horror, fear, disease, and death, chapter 24 is jubilation, amazement, joy, peace, love, and eternal life with Jesus the Son of God.

But the agenda of what will happen in Heaven while the Seven-Year Tribulation takes place on earth is glorious. In this chapter, we want to take a look at what God does for His redeemed. We will also rejoice over God's fulfillment of His promise to all who believed. This rejoicing takes place for the Old Testament Saints, who have joined with Christ around the Throne of God, for "The Church," that has been raptured and taken out of the world just before the Seven-Year Tribulation, and the Tribulation Saints who have been redeemed because of their faith in Christ demonstrated by their willingness to accept certain death if they remained faithful to the Lord.

Several huge events take place in Heaven for "The Church" that reflects God's love for His redeemed and His love for His Son Jesus to whom He has given "The Church." The first great event is the Judgment of Good Works also known as "The Judgment Seat of Christ" or The "Bema" Seat. This takes place in Heaven even as the first quarter of the Seven-Year Tribulation is taking place on earth. The second great event is the Marriage Supper of the Lamb. This takes place in Heaven even as the second quarter of the Seven-Year Tribulation is taking place on earth. The third event is the second coming of Jesus Christ to end the Seven-Year Tribulation. Christ and His Church as well as angels and His armies come down from Heaven and completely thrash Satan and His followers. The fourth event is the Great White Throne Judgment in which God judges all lost mankind based on their performance on earth.

To understand the above judgement events that will happen we need to review judging events that have happened and shaped our world as God oversees the world and directs its path.

Confusion Regarding Judgments

Many Christians are confused regarding Judgments. We think, "If only the Church is judged at the Bema Seat Judgment then is there a judgment of works for Old Testament Saints? Is there a judgment for Tribulation Saints? What judgment will take place for non-believers? Many of us are unaware of judgments in the past by God the Father. Before we move on we should stop and consider the confusion regarding judgments.

Judgment of Satan and Fallen Angels

A huge, dynamic judgment of God against Satan and his fallen angels was made in Heaven before man was created. The most beautiful and magnificent of all angels was named Lucifer. The angel Lucifer and certain angels seduced and deceived by Lucifer, decided to contest God and rebel against God's authority. That Lucifer would decide to contest God seems so ridiculous to us because we know Lucifer could not win. Yet we make the same decisions daily. We challenge God and want to do things our way. Is it really any different?

Lucifer was so enchanted by His beauty and so caught up in his opinion of himself he elected to challenge God and take over from God the rule of the entire world. When Lucifer challenged God and waged war against God his name was changed to Satan. Later, in the book of revelation we see Satan called "The Dragon." Can any of us imagine what the world would be like had Satan won his war against God? Following this contest in which one third of the angels in Heaven were cast out of heaven along with Satan, God judged Satan and declared the penalty of Satan's sin. As we can see, those penalties have not been imposed yet, probably because Satan's challenge against God is still active. God has already determined that judgment. His judgment is that at the end, Satan will be cast into the Lake of Fire (Hell) for eternity. But Satan will continue to gather more damnation from God even through the last battle of Gog and Magog at the end of the one-thousand-year Millennial Kingdom. There is much we do not know about Satan, and yet the Bible constantly tells us more than we think we know. When will Satan fall from heaven or has that already happened? When will Satan be judged for his works or has that already been done? The Bible is our answer.

Revelation 20:10
"And the devil who deceived them was thrown into the lake of fire and sulfur, where the beast and the false prophet were, and they will be tormented there day and night forever and ever."

When will the Dragon, otherwise known as Satan, be sentenced for his sins? We know from the verse above that Satan will be sentenced for his sins after the beast and the false prophet. The Beast and False Prophet will be judged and sentenced at the end of the Battle of Armageddon. Satan has already been partially judged as evidenced in Scripture.

Genesis 3:14–15
"Because you have done this, cursed are you above all livestock and above all beasts of the field; on your belly you shall go, and dust you shall eat all the days of your life. I will put enmity between you and the woman, and between your offspring and her offspring; he shall bruise your head, and you shall bruise his heel."

The above verse is more an example of how Satan works with mankind than being an actual physical snake. Satan remains hidden from mankind doing his evil while poisoning us to the point of physical death and separation from God. Satan is cursed by God and by believers in Christ. He is considered to be the lowest of all creation. In verse 15 God proclaims there will be eternal war between the offspring of **"The woman."** This references **"The Church"** that is the **"Bride"** of Christ as **"The Woman."** And it forecasts unending conflict between God's people and the followers of Satan.

But Praise God! We know the answer. Satan loses, God wins and Satan will be sentenced at the end of the one-thousand-year Millennial Kingdom. He will, however, not be thrown into the Lake of Fire until after the one-thousand-year millennial reign of Christ and after his unsuccessful attempt to overthrow God at the last battle of Gog and Magog. Full judgment of Satan is delayed beyond that of the Antichrist and the False Prophet because Satan will be judged for the evil he commits once he is released for a short time after the one thousand Millennial Kingdom.

Judgment of Man's Sin

We do not know how many years Adam and Eve enjoyed walking and talking with God in the Garden of Eden. But we know both eventually disobeyed God. We also know that their disobedience judged mankind throughout eternity by inputting into our soul a sin nature. A sin nature is a natural desire to satisfy our own desires beyond those of God.

Genesis 2:17
"But of the tree of knowledge of good and evil you shall not eat for in the day that you eat of it you shall surely die."

This is a judgment of God and it has an overwhelming impact of every living creature, both man and animal, from Adam's fall forward. The curse of death was given to man. Mankind inherited the nature of pursuing his own plans, ideas, and desires rather than Gods. But praise the Lord! Mankind does not have to bear the burden of that judgment. Jesus Christ died for our sins and created a way for man to pass our sin burden to Jesus who is victorious over sin and death.

Judgment of Conscience

God wants mankind to worship Him and love Him just because of the understanding God has put into man's soul and into mankind's conscience. To give man freedom to choose God or to refuse God, man had to be given the right to make a choice. God will not plead with man to worship Him. But God will, has, and is, directing our part regarding what He wants us to do. After Adam and Eve were forced from the Garden of Eden because of their disobedience of God, they had knowledge of God and how wonderful their years with God had been. They had in their soul and conscience the call of God to remain faithful. Yet they also had the continual, call of Satan to be independent and to disobey God. Over the many years of God's relationship to man He has desired to keep the right to choose as pure as possible for man. Therefore, for all people born after the fall of Adam from the Garden of Eden, to Noah's flood, God simply asked mankind to return to Him based on man's conscience. Man's conscience is that understanding in his heart that worship of God is the right way. However, man continued to disobey God, ignore God, and in many instances be an enemy of God.

Genesis 3:87
"And they heard the sound of the Lord *God walking in the garden in the cool of the day, and the man and his wife hid themselves from the presence of the* Lord *God among the trees of the garden."*

Mankind failed miserably, however. Adam and Eve, who had to this point loved to have God come and walk and talk with them, now felt guilty and hid themselves from the presence of God. They hid themselves because they knew God loved them and was totally, thoroughly righteous. They knew God had taught them over and over again they must obey His commands. Yet they disobeyed the most important command ever given them. They had eaten of the tree of knowledge so they might become like God. They hid because they had a guilty conscience.

Thus the dispensation of conscience began. This dispensation is not a time period but is a manner in which God elected to reveal Himself to His people. This was the dispensation in which fallen angels (supporters of Satan) joined with human women and had yielded giants who opposed God. Mankind became so evil and far from God that **"every intention of the thoughts of man's heart**

was evil continually." The judgment rendered down to man for this dispensation was as follows:

- An eternal curse of death, sin, evil on the serpent and his followers
- Suffering to women in childbearing
- Women became subject to the rule of man
- All of nature was cursed in that animals became enemies of other animals
- Man had to henceforth work at providing food for his household
- God promised a messiah would be delivered to provide a way to escape the clutches of Satan.

God closed this dispensation or way of communicating to man with the flood that covered the world.

Judgment of Human Government

God then, after the failure of the Dispensation of Conscience promised Noah and his family He would never flood the world again. He commanded Noah to repopulate the world and scatter all over the earth. God allowed people to kill animals for food as He continues to make it easier for man to worship God. God instituted rules for man to live by such as capital punishment for certain crimes. But Noah's descendants became power hungry and refused to scatter all over the earth. They, instead, elected to build a tower trying to reach heaven. God decided to punish them by imposing different languages on mankind. This judgment forced man to create different nations and to scatter all over the world. The judgment rendered down to man for this dispensation was:

- God will not curse the earth again with a flood
- Noah and his family were commanded to replenish the earth with people

- Noah and his family are given control and right to rule over animals
- Noah and his family are allowed to kill animals to eat
- The Law of Capital Punishment was established by God

Judgment of the Son of God

John 3:16
"For God so loved the world that He gave His only Son, that whosoever believeth in Him should not perish but have eternal life."

Can you fathom the day, before the beginning of the world, that Jesus Christ came to God the Father to volunteer to sacrifice His seat around the Throne of God in heaven. Christ knew He would be coming down to earth to become a lowly man. Christ knew He would be denied by the masses, would be spat upon, would be ridiculed, would be heartbroken at the sinfulness of man and would be crucified. Even worse Christ knew He would have to take on Himself the sins of an entire lost, condemned world. He knew He would have to carry those sins to the grave for mankind. Then Jesus knew He would have His own loving Father, Yahweh, turn His back on Him because God could not look upon the ugliness of sin.

Oh, the pain of God the Father to say to His only begotten Son, Yes that will be our plan of salvation for mankind. Yes, that is how we will defeat death. Yes, that is how we will defeat Satan. And although God the Father had authority to make sure Christ would be successful in living the sinless life, and although God the Father had the authority to make sure Jesus would not have to be crucified; to do so would mean Christ could not be able to take on the sins of you and me. Jesus had to have the ability to fail to be able to succeed. But God believed in His Son. But God so loved you and I that He gave His Son.

So Jesus came to earth through the virgin birth. Jesus grew up as a sinless child, not once ever doing anything that was offensive to His Father in Heaven. Jesus became a man and began His ministry.

He spent the forty days and nights in the wilderness and did not eat or drink. He faced every temptation Satan could conceive of and He yielded not to temptation. Then Jesus faced Calvary. Then Jesus faced crucifixion. Jesus the man agonized over the pending cross but He remained faithful.

All this time, God looked down upon His Son. God knew what would happen because He is at the end of time and knows the future. Yet God allowed Jesus to have the opportunity to succeed or fail. God made the judgment of whether Jesus had met the task of becoming the price to pay for the sins of all mankind. He was able to say, "Yes, that is my beloved Son in whom I am well pleased."

Bema: The Judgment Seat of Christ

The Judgment Seat of Christ will take place in Heaven around the Throne of God during the first half of the Seven-Year Tribulation. The Judgment Seat of Christ will be taking place in Heaven while the Seven-Year Tribulation is taking place on earth. In the scripture below God reveals to us, "The Church," meaning all who were saved after the resurrection of Jesus and before the rapture, will be rewarded according to the good things they have done. Many question the fact that Christians will have rewards in Heaven. There can be no doubt, however, because God tells us it is true.

Romans 14:10–12
"Why do you pass judgment on your brother? Or you, why do you despise your brother? For we will all stand before the judgment seat of God; for it is written, "As I live says the Lord, every knee shall bow to me, and every tongue shall confess to God." So then each of us will give an account of himself to God."

Matthew 16:27
"For the Son of Man is going to come with His angels in the glory of the Father and then He will repay each person according to what He has done."

Will there be different levels of rewards for Christians in eternity? Will there be different levels of rewards for Old Testament Saints? What about Tribulation Saints? This is a contested doctrine that needs not be contested because Scripture clearly answers the question. The answer is yes; there will be different levels of rewards in heaven. Salvation comes to us all by grace through faith not of works lest anyone boast. But rewards to the Christian in heaven, comes through works and faith. Will there, therefore, be jealousy of each other in Heaven because that is exactly what different level of rewards on earth cause. The answer is no because on earth we build up our capacity to love and enjoy the good of others by our closeness to Christ. In Heaven everyone will have joy, peace, and happiness to the full extent of their capacity to love and enjoy good things. There will be no unhappiness in heaven because everyone will be happy, and rewarded to the full extent of their capacity and will not know or be concerned about others.

Another misconception is that the judgment seat in Heaven, known as the BEMA seat, will in truth be a salvation decision. Nothing could be farther from the truth. No one will be participating in the judgment seat unless they have already been forgiven of their sins and the blood of Jesus Christ on Calvary has covered their sins. Only the saved will participate in this evaluation and reward experience.

1 Thessalonians 2:19–20
"For what is our hope, or joy, or crown of boasting before our Lord Jesus at His coming? Is it not you for you are our glory and joy."

Paul, under the instruction of the Holy Spirit, further clarifies the works that will be judged. He classifies them as gold, silver, precious stones, wood, hay, and straw. Through this verse and others, we understand that some of the good works we think are so wonderful will not be accounted as such in God's sight. Some of the works we think very little of will be counted as precious in God's sight. Those works that are referred to as "gold, silver, or precious stones," will be those that we do in the name of the Lord and with a pure heart to help others with no interest is self-advancement. Works that are done with a secret desire to make us look good, or so we might obtain the good will of others, will be counted as wood, straw and hay. Paul then explains that the fire of God's judgment will burn up those works made of wood, hay and straw. In other words only the good works done to praise and glorify our Lord and Savior, or to help others with a pure heart, will be counted as righteousness. Only these will gain us rewards in heaven. Only these will be counted as jewels in our crown of life.

Paul then states that our rewards for the works that survive the fire of God's judgment will be granted to us for life through eternity with God.

1 Corinthians 3:14–15

"If the work which anyone has built on the foundation survives, he will receive a reward. If anyone's work is burned up, he will suffer loss; but he himself will be saved, but only as through fire."

The last magnificent promise is that even though we may have lots of deeds that were not done with the right motive and are not pleasing to God we retain our Salvation. This is a great promise of Security of the Believer. Verse 15 makes it clear that salvation is a permanent change made in the heart and soul of the believer. We did not save ourselves and we cannot do anything that will make us lose our salvation. The giving of salvation and keeping of salvation is an act of God.

The purpose of the judgment seat of Christ or BEMA, as it is known, is to prepare us to become the bride of Christ. The marriage of the Church and Jesus Christ is about to take place. To take place the members of the Church must be spotless. We are ready for the Marriage of the Lamb.

Judgment of Nations, Judgment of Sheep and Goats

The Judgment of Nations is often called the Judgment of Sheep and Goats. This is because soon after the Seven-Year Tribulation that ends in the Battle of Armageddon and the victorious second coming of Jesus Christ to bring to a close mankind's battle between good and evil, this judgment of God will take place.

Matthew 25:31–32
"When the Son of Man comes in His glory, and all the angels with Him, then He will sit on His glorious throne. Before Him will be gathered all the nations and He will separate the people one from another as a shepherd separates the sheep from the goats."

Jesus has just completed His famous Olivet Discourse in the book of Matthew when He announces a judgment that will take place. This will be a judgment of Gentile nations and the subject matter will be their treatment of Israel particularly during the just happened Seven-Year Tribulation. Most of the world joined forces with the Great Dragon (Satan) and his lieutenants The Antichrist and The False Prophet. The nation of Israel is still the "Chosen Nation" of God due to the faith of Abraham although Gentiles individually have been admitted to the family of God if they have faith in Jesus Christ as their redeemer of sin.

When does this judgment take place? The above scripture tells us **"When the Son of Man comes in His Glory."** The Son of Man clearly means Jesus and comes in His Glory clearly means just after His second coming in which He totally decimates the Armies of Satan and throws the Antichrist and False Prophet into the Lake of Fire. This will be just after Jesus has thrown the **"Great Dragon"** into the **"Pit"** to be sealed for one thousand years, but before He begins His reign in the one-thousand-year Millennial Kingdom. We know this because the purpose of the Judgment of Nations is to determine who will be allowed into the one-thousand-year Millennial Kingdom.

Scripture then tells us Jesus will separate the nations as a shepherd separates the sheep from the goats. **"As a shepherd separates the sheep from the goats. He will put the sheep on his right and the goats on his left."** Clearly, Jesus is separating those who have placed their trust in Him for salvation to go into the Millennial Kingdom.

They are identified as sheep because they have been followers of the great shepherd and the goats have been rebellious against the great shepherd. Jesus is the shepherd. Those who have shown faith in God and have had a will to follow Him are sheep because they have done His will. Those who have been against God and opposed His will toward Israel are goats because of their rebellious nature. Sheep will enter the Millennial Kingdom and Goats will be cast into the Lake of Fire alone with the Antichrist and the False Prophet. We in American often say those who support Israel will be supported by God and those who hate Israel will be despised by God. The fact this is a Judgment of Nations does not mean individual faith is not still required for salvation.

God's Word does not contradict itself so we must go deeper than surface understanding of what God means by the Sheep will be saved and the Goats will go to Hellfire and Brimstone. The overwhelming doctrine of the entire Bible is that salvation comes by faith through the grace of God. This means we apply to God for salvation through our faith in His ability and willingness to save us and that act of salvation is completed by a divine act by God individually to us. Our faith does not save us because God's Grace saves us. But our faith makes us eligible for God to save us. Nowhere is there any reference to or hint in works being part of our faith or God's Grace.

Romans 3:22–24
"The righteousness of God through faith in Jesus Christ for all who believe. For there is no distinction: for all have sinned and fall short of the glory of God, and are justified by his grace as a gift, through the redemption that is in Christ Jesus."

In this Judgment of Nations, we find those who treat Israel well do so because of their love of God and their total commitment to follow Christ regardless of the cost. And that cost was beheading, or certain, immediate death at the hand of the Antichrist. No one had the will to support Israel for any reason other than because they knew what God wanted them to do and they were willing to do so because they loved God. So the Judgment of Nations separates those who loved God through the Great Tribulation and survived. There will be a limited number of these. And the Judgment of Nations separates those who hated Israel because they were enemies of God, enemies of Christ and there will be mass numbers of these. In this judgment Jesus will be the Judge as so authorized by God the Father.

Judgment of Angels

When we get to the throne of God, whether as Old Testament Saints, or "The Church" or as Tribulation Saints, we will be changed. We will not look like we do here on earth and we will not think like we do here on earth. Our faith will not be mixed with a sin nature that strives for part of our attention. We will not be trying to do things our own way but will be totally dependent on the power and grace of Jesus Christ to guide us in all things. And that is the only way I can conceive of our capability to accomplish the Judgment of Angels outlines in 1 Corinthians chapter 6.

1 Corinthians 6:2–3
"Or do you not know that the Saints will judge the world?
And if the world is to be judged by you are you incompetent
to try trivial cases? Do you not know that we *are to judge*
angels? How much more then matters pertaining to this life?"

Which angels does this verse say will be judged by Saints in Heaven? Paul is referring to the angels that are cast out of Heaven because they chose to follow Satan rather than God the Father. He is giving us a revelation God gave to him that we as Saints, who have been adopted into the family of God and who have been made sinless; have openly accepted total dependency on our Lord and Master and will be delegated the judgment of Angels. And do not discount the job. There will be a massive number of angels who followed Satan. We do not know the number but we know one third of all angels serving God all over the world and the universe followed Satan. What a pity to have so many be caste into the Lake of Fire and to be done so by Saints through the delegated power of God.

The Marriage Supper of the Lamb

After the Judgment Seat of Christ, up in heaven we begin an event of great celebration for our Lord and Savior. He has accomplished an enormously difficult work for God the Father and He has experienced amazing success. Jesus met His own requirements and the requirements of God the Father in paying for the sins of all who will believe on Him. In celebration God has given the Church to Jesus and made Him the Head of the Church.

Ephesians 1:22
"And He put all things under His feet and gave
Him head over all things to the Church."

God has given **"The Church"** to Jesus and its victory is His victory. Jesus has referred to "The Church" in Ephesians 5:22–23 in the analogy of marriage. He says as the husband is head of the wife even as Christ is head of the Church. From that analogy we think of **"The Church"** as being the **"Bride"** of Christ.

Ephesians 5:22–23
"Wives, submit to your own husbands as to the Lord. For
the husband is the head of the wife even as Christ is the
head of the Church, His body, and is Himself its Savior."

The best way a marriage works well and can maintain a relationship as God outlines above, is if it is built on mutual love, always putting the other partner in marriage first. God tells us the same is true in our relationship with God. We are to lovingly, willingly, and happily recognize the superiority of God. We are to admire with awe, the price Jesus has paid for our sins and dedicate our lives to follow Him. This relationship between mankind and Christ has been a rocky one but now after the rapture of the church, and after the Judgment of Works by Christ, we have that kind of relationship between Jesus and His adoring followers. It is time for celebration. Jesus wants to show His new "bride" off to God the Father and officially bring each saved person into the family of God. I remember when as a very young man I took my newly engaged sweetheart out to my parents to tell them we were getting married. I was filled with love and pride and joy and admiration for her and I wanted to show her off to the people who raised me and loved me so much. That is what we see in the Marriage of the Lamb.

Revelation 19:8
"Let us rejoice and exult and give Him the glory, for the marriage of the Lamb has come, and His bride has made herself ready."

The Marriage of the Lamb is going to follow the Jewish custom of marriages. In considering this it helps to remember that Jesus was born into the nation of Israel and it was the nation of Israel God chose to be His **"Chosen People."** It is most natural that the marriage of the Lamb would follow the tradition of Hebrew marriages. Therefore we will see this event take place in three segments. We also can draw a beautiful parallel of the Marriage of the Lamb process and the salvation process as lost people accept Christ and are married into His family.

Segment No. 1 of the Jewish wedding custom is a marriage contract agreed to and signed by the parents of the bride and bridegroom. By Jewish tradition the parents of the bridegroom, or the bridegroom himself, brings a dowry to the bride or her parents. Once the dowry amount is agreed to by the bride to be; the bride and groom enter into the betrothal period. In our marriage we would call this the engagement period.

Segment No. 1 of our salvation relationship with Jesus is similar. A contract of love is offered by the bridegroom and agreed to by the bride and the bridegroom. The bridegroom has already paid for a dowry for the marriage. The dowry Christ offers to each of us is the death of Jesus on Calvary and His shed blood. The agreement is mutual. Jesus offers us salvation if we accept the dowry He provides. We agree to love God, and seek His forgiveness for sins and ask Him for salvation. The bride (The Church) then is converted from lost to saved but does not yet receive the reward of that marriage until segment two and three are completed. As in the Jewish wedding, we do not immediately enter into the union with our bridegroom but enter into an engagement period. The engagement period may take time to be fulfilled. In the Jewish wedding the waiting period is for the groom to go home and prepare a place, in his home, for his bride. In Salvation it still is true. The waiting period from the time we are saved until the Lord comes to collect His church is for the groom to complete all that must be completed to prepare the home for his bride, "The Church."

Segment No. 2 of the Jewish wedding is to come to the bride's home and take her to his home and present her to his parents at the feast prepared in her honor. This step demonstrates the bridegroom's love, approval, and pride for the bride, and his love, admiration, and pride in his parents.

Segment No. 2 of our salvation experience takes place at the end of the engagement period and that is when Jesus comes to take us home with Him. We call that the rapture of the Church. With the rapture of the Church Christ will come and take those who are alive in Christ and those who are dead in Christ, and will take us all home to Heaven. This is the home He has prepared for us. That is His contract with us. In our salvation experience we are betrothed to Christ until the rapture when He comes to take us home to the fabulous mansion He has prepared called Heaven. The bride of Christ should be always watching and waiting for the rapture to take us home as is the bride in a Jewish wedding always awaiting the coming of the groom to take her home.

Segment No. 3 of the Jewish wedding is a feast of celebration that can go on for days. God reveals to the Apostle John the third step of The Church's wedding feast. John's vision, given by God, begins with Segment No. 3. This is when the groom gathers the bride and celebrates with family and friends, the union between him and his bride. He then takes the bride in to the home provided and lives together forever in love and peace.

Segment No. 3 of our salvation is when Christ introduces the raptured church to His father and begins the celebration feast.

Revelation 19:6–7
Then I heard what seemed to be the voice of a great
multitude, like the roar of many waters and like the sound
of mighty peals of thunder, crying out, "Hallelujah! For
the Lord our God the Almighty reigns. "Let us rejoice and
exult and give him the glory, for the marriage of the Lamb
has come, and his Bride has made herself ready."

"The Church" (The bride of Jesus) will be the featured guest of Jesus at the Marriage of the Lamb. The "great multitude" includes the Old Testament saints who will be present in spirit but not in a glorified body. This is because they will not yet have been resurrected. The "great multitude" also includes angels that celebrate with Christ in His union with His bride. And "great multitude" will include an incomplete number of early Tribulation Saints who died in the first quarter of the Seven-Year Tribulation. This number will include all who have accepted Jesus as their Savior in the Seven Year Tribulation.

Revelation 19:6
"Then I heard what seemed to be the voice of a great
multitude, like the roar of many waters and like the
sound of mighty peals of thunder, crying out, Hallelujah!
For the Lord our God the Almighty reigns."

The above verse tells us the "great multitude" in attendance will be to many for man to count. Yes the saved for all eternity will be there. The peals of thunder may be hands clapping and feet stomping with delight and joy as they sing out "Hallelujah" which means Praise the Lord. It is worthy to note the great celebration of the Church to be in Heaven with Jesus. Yet the focus of joy and happiness is not of the church but is of the bridegroom. The focus of joy and happiness is on Jesus. The title of this great event is the "Marriage of the Lamb" not the "Marriage of the Church." Realize this is an event Jesus has been preparing from the beginning of time. This is the event Jesus came down from Heaven to be with the people He would save. This is the event for which Jesus willingly suffered humiliation, disobedience, being ignored, and great mental, emotional, and physical pain. Of course this is a great time of celebration for not only the Son of God but for God the Father and the Holy Spirit.

Ephesians 1:4
"Even as He chose us in Him, before the foundation of the world, and blameless before Him."

Can we grasp what an amazing accomplishment this is and will be for Jesus? Jesus took a people who had failed God in every trial they had been given. They failed Him in the dispensation of conscience. They failed Him in the dispensation of human government. They failed Him in the dispensation of promise. They failed Him in the dispensation of law and yes, they failed Him in the dispensation of grace. But because Jesus took up the price of salvation, not because the people were finally successful, the Marriage of the Lamb presents an unknown number of believers in Christ. These believers are qualified through the blood of Jesus to be part of the family of God. Yes it is true the most joyful one at the Marriage of the Lamb will be Jesus Christ.

An interesting note is that when Jesus walked on earth He was both God and Man. He was devoted to God the Father but subject to the evils of Satan. There is no reference to say that when Jesus ascended back to Heaven after His resurrection, that He gave up being God and Man. In fact we know Jesus will, in the one-thousand-year reign, actually live among us and rule over mankind as God. But all evidence leads us to believe He will still be both God and Man. So it was at the Marriage of the Lamb. Jesus the man was filled with love for His Father, love for His Church and joy of His achievement.

Likewise we should note that the joy of the multitudes is not for "The Church" although they rejoice greatly for the salvation of a multitude of saints. No the greatest joy and attention is not for the Church but for the Bridegroom. Jesus is loved on earth but He is adored in Heaven. And the greatest one to be proud of Jesus is none other than God the Father. Once again He can say, "This is my beloved Son in whom I am pleased."

The Second Coming of Christ

If the Rapture is not the Second Coming of Christ, then what is the Second Coming of Christ? It is the beginning of the "End Times" as outlined in Matthew the twenty-fourth chapter. A study of the words recorded in the book of Matthew give us much insight into the Second Coming of Christ. God tells us His Second Coming will be visible from every part of the world. Just as lighting can be seen from the east to the west it is also true that Jesus will come out of the clouds and the entire world will see His arrival. This differs from the Rapture which will be sudden, and not announced.

Matthew 24:27
"For as the lightning comes from the east and flashes to the west, so also will the coming of the Son of Man be."

We also know from the book of Matthew that at the end of the Tribulation period great unnatural cataclysmic events will take place announcing the coming of Christ.

Matthew 24:29
"Immediately after the Tribulation of those days the sun will be darkened, and the moon will not give its light; the stars will fall from heaven, and the powers of the heavens will be shaken."

The book of Matthew tells us that after the series of cataclysmic events take place that include the darkening of the moon, the falling of stars from heaven, and the disruption of the order of the earth as we know it the whole world shall see a sign that is the foretelling of the Coming of Christ again. It will be so clear that the whole world will see it and will understand it for what it is. And the entire world will grieve because the believers will have already been taken with Christ at the Rapture. Those left behind will understand their doom is at hand.

Matthew 24:30
"Then the sign of the Son of Man will appear in
heaven and then all the tribes of the earth will mourn,
and they will see the Son of Man coming on the
clouds of heaven with power and great glory."

God announces the Second Coming of Jesus Christ with the amazing earth changes mentioned in Matthew and in Revelation. The earthquake changes the entire world. Islands vanish and mountains crumble. Almost half of the people in the world die. The Son of God is about to come back to the earth as conquering King.

Revelation 16:17–21
"Then the seventh angel poured out his bowl into the air, and
a loud voice came out of the temple of heaven, from the throne,
saying, "It is done!" And there were noises and thundering and
lightning; and there was a great earthquake, such a mighty and
great earthquake as had not occurred since men were on the
earth. Now the great city was divided into three parts, and the
cities of the nations fell. And great Babylon was remembered
before God, to give her the cup of the wine of the fierceness of His
wrath. Then every island fled away, and the mountains were not
found. And great hail from heaven fell upon men, each hailstone
about the weight of a talent. Men blasphemed God because of
the plague of the hail, since that plague was exceedingly great."

All of the **"End Time"** events recorded in God's Word serve as signs that the Day of the Lord is at hand. When will Jesus Christ return? We do not know when Christ will return. We do not know when He will return for the rapture to retrieve the Church. And we do not know when He will return with His angels, His Church, and His followers; but, Praise the Lord, we are informed Christ will come the second time at the end of the Battle of Armageddon and soundly defeat Satan. We also know that when Christ returns to earth as a conquering King, it will be with His Church. He will wage war on Satan. He will defeat Satan and throw the Antichrist and False

Prophet in the Lake of Fire for eternity. God has revealed to us that at the end of the Battle of Armageddon He will throw Satan into **"The Pit"** and seal it for one thousand years. This will all happen about seven years after the Rapture of the Church. We do know the rapture will be total surprise to the saved and unsaved alike. But the Second coming of Christ will be announced with the greatest cataclysmic event ever recorded.

It is worthy to understand that when Jesus comes to rapture the Church He will not set foot on earth. However when He comes back to defeat Satan and to close the Church Age, He will come with a host of angels, with His Church and will defeat Satan here on earth.

Why does Jesus tarry in His second coming? No one knows. The Disciples expected Jesus to come back in their lifetimes. But God is very clear in His answer to this question.

Acts 1:7
"It is not for you to know times or seasons that the Father has fixed by His own authority."

CHAPTER TWENTY-FIVE

The Doctrine of The One-Thousand-Year Millennial Kingdom
Meanwhile in Heaven

THE DOCTRINE OF THE ONE-THOUSAND-YEAR
MILLENNIAL KINGDOM

After the rapture of the Church, after the Judgment Seat of Christ, after Israel signs a treaty of peace with the Antichrist, after the Battle of Gog and Magog, after the Abomination of Desolation, after the Battle of Armageddon, after the Antichrist and False Prophet are thrown into the **"Lake of Fire,"** and after Satan, **"The Dragon,"** is locked up in the **"Pit"** and after the Judgment of Nations, God the Father will establish a one-thousand-year reign for all believers in Christ and Jesus will rule on earth for one thousand years. Satan will be locked up in **"The Pit,"** an underground prison that becomes Satan's holding place, until after the one-thousand-year reign. The purpose of the Millennial Kingdom is to establish Jesus as King of Jerusalem sitting on the throne of David and to fulfill the promises made to Israel.

Luke 1:32–33
"He will be great, and will be called the Son of the Most High; and the Lord God will give to Him the throne of His father David. And He will reign over the house of Jacob forever, and of His kingdom there will be no end."

Israel will finally be the blessing to other nations God promised and God will fulfill the Abrahamic covenant. This covenant between God and Abraham promised that, some day, God would make Israel a great nation. Yes, Israel never deserved that promise but God still made it and God keeps His promises.

Genesis 12:2–3
"And I will make of you a great nation, and I will bless you and make your name great, so that you will be a blessing. I will bless those who bless you, and him who dishonors you I will curse, and in you all the families of the earth shell be blessed."

One of the reasons for the one-thousand-year millennial is for God to complete the promise He made to Abraham called the Abrahamic Covenant. God will make Abraham's name great and He has, through Abraham, created unknown masses of people. God will in the last half of the Seven-Year Tribulation punish many of those who dishonor Israel. He completes His promise in the one-thousand-year millennial reign. Likewise God has not yet completed His blessings for those who support the Israel nation. But He will in the one-thousand-year millennial reign.

A second reason for the one thousand Millennial Kingdom is to complete the promises made in the Palestinian covenant. This promise was that the borders of Israel would be precise and that day has not yet been fulfilled. It appears it will not yet be fulfilled in the Second Coming of Christ but it will be fulfilled in the one-thousand-year Millennial Kingdom.

Numbers 34:1–2
"The LORD spoke to Moses, saying, "Command the people of Israel, and say to them, When you enter the land of Canaan (this is the land that shall fall to you for an inheritance, the land of Canaan as defined by its borders)."

A third reason for the one thousand Millennial Kingdom is to finish the Davidic Covenant found in 2 Samuel. This is the promise that God made to David that David's heir would sit on the throne of Israel forever. They will live in an existence of peace and harmony. Jesus is that heir but He has yet to take the throne of the world.

2 Samuel 7
"And I will appoint a place for my people Israel and will plant them, so that they may dwell in their own place and be disturbed no more. And violent men shall afflict them no more, as formerly."

A fourth reason for the Millennial Kingdom is to fulfill the promise of the New Covenant. This promise from God states that Israel will return to God and worship their Messiah (Jesus Christ). To some degree this was fulfilled in the last half of the Seven-Year Tribulation. But it was fulfilled by individuals not as an existing nation.

THE DOCTRINE OF THE ONE-THOUSAND-YEAR
MILLENNIAL KINGDOM

Jeremiah 31:31–34
"Behold, the days are coming, declares the LORD, when I will make a new covenant with the house of Israel and the house of Judah, not like the covenant that I made with their fathers on the day when I took them by the hand to bring them out of the land of Egypt, my covenant that they broke, though I was their husband, declares the LORD. For this is the covenant that I will make with the house of Israel after those days, declares the LORD: I will put my law within them, and I will write it on their hearts. And I will be their God, and they shall be my people. And no longer shall each one teach his neighbor and each his brother, saying, 'Know the LORD,' for they shall all know me, from the least of them to the greatest, declares the LORD. For I will forgive their iniquity, and I will remember their sin no more."

A fifth reason for the one-thousand-year Millennial Kingdom is the promise made by God to Jesus. In the mind of God this promise was earned and God desired to give it to Jesus because of His love for His only begotten Son.

Psalms 110:1
"The LORD says to my Lord:
"Sit at my right hand, until I make your enemies your footstool."

Certainly the power given to Christ in the Seven-Year Tribulation fulfilled much of this promise. Yet in God's mind His love for Christ demanded more. The one-thousand-year Millennial Kingdom in which Jesus is on the throne, Jesus sets the tone of the entire world, without opposition, and revels in the joy of His victory over death and sin.

A sixth reason for the one-thousand-year Millennial Kingdom is the promise of God, to Jesus, through "The Church," meaning the believers who placed their trust in the Son of God for eternal salvation. This promise is not fulfilled by the Seven-Year Tribulation. The Seven-Year Tribulation is an event for the nation of Israel and for Gentiles who were not raptured. It was, however, not for "The

Church." The sixth reason for the one-thousand-year Millennial Kingdom is to fulfill God's promise to the Gentiles. That is that not only will we be saved from sin but we will be with Him in Heaven throughout eternity.

1 Corinthians 6:2
"Or do you not know that the saints will judge the world? And if the world is to be judged by you, are you incompetent to try trivial cases?"

A seventh reason for the one-thousand-year Millennial Kingdom is to restore nature and the original creation of God to the joy of God the Father. God's creation was wounded with the onslaught of sin into the world. Animals will live in peace again without fear of each other (Romans 8:18–23), fields will be productive and freed from the curse of weeds (Isaiah 11:6–9) and people who survive the Tribulation and populate the one-thousand-year reign will be free from disease (Isaiah 33:24).

The millennial reign of Christ will give us a taste of what it would have been like if Adam and Eve and everyone born after had not sinned against God. Jesus Christ will be judge and will dominate in love the world. There will be total peace in the Millennial Kingdom.

Who will be with Jesus in the one-thousand-year Millennial Kingdom?

Thessalonians 4:17 tells us believers who are raptured will be with Him forever. This, of course, includes those who had previously died. They are called the **"Dead in Christ,"** and will be resurrected first. It also includes those alive at the time Jesus raptures the Church. They are called the **"Alive in Christ."** These believers will be resurrected second. This means every soul that recognized they were sinners and desired Jesus to forgive their sins and save their souls will be with Jesus through the one-thousand-year Millennial Kingdom and through eternity thereafter.

THE DOCTRINE OF THE ONE-THOUSAND-YEAR MILLENNIAL KINGDOM

1 Thessalonians 4:16, 17
"For the Lord Himself will descend from heaven with a cry of command, with the voice of an archangel, and with the sound of the trumpet of God. And the dead in Christ will rise first. Then we who are alive, who are left, will be caught up together with them in the clouds to meet the Lord in the air, and so we will always be with the Lord."

God's Word also give every soul that refused to worship the beast and who finally saw and understood that Jesus Christ was giving them one more chance to be saved. These include all people who refused the "Mark of the Beast" in the Great Tribulation and were beheaded. These also include those who refused the "Mark of the Beast" and died of one of the outpouring of the seven seals, or the seven trumpets or the seven bowls.

Revelation 20:4
"Then I saw thrones, and seated on them were those to whom the authority to judge was committed. Also I saw the souls of those who had been beheaded for the testimony of Jesus and for the word of God, and those who had not worshiped the beast or its image and had not received its mark on their foreheads or their hands. They came to life and reigned with Christ for a thousand years."

Another group of people will be the Old Testament Saints who believed in God and the forth-coming Messiah but did not know the Messiah would be the Son of God, Jesus Christ. Yet God counted their faith as righteousness and gave them grace to become children of God. Ezekiel gives us confirmation they will be present in the one-thousand-year Millennial Kingdom.

Ezekiel 37:12
"Therefore prophesy, and say to them, Thus says the Lord GOD: Behold, I will open your graves and raise you from your graves, O my people. And I will bring you into the land of Israel."

The people who become believers during the seven-year tribulation, who do not die, will enter the millennial kingdom alive. These will have to go through the Judgment of Goats and Sheep but their faith will make them eligible for God's grace. They will not experience physical death in this life but in the one-thousand-year Millennial Kingdom they will live long lives but experience physical death.

Matthew 25:31–34
"When the Son of Man comes in his glory, and all the angels with him, then he will sit on his glorious throne. Before him will be gathered all the nations, and he will separate people one from another as a shepherd separates the sheep from the goats. And he will place the sheep on his right, but the goats on the left. Then the King will say to those on his right, 'Come, you who are blessed by my Father, inherit the kingdom prepared for you from the foundation of the world.'"

Where will the rest of humanity be?

Where will the rest of humanity be? God's Word reveals to us that every soul that ever places or placed their trust in Jesus to save them, even those who trusted "The Messiah" when they did not know who He was, will be in the one-thousand-year Millennial Kingdom. But that will represent, perhaps 10–15 percent of all mankind ever born. These numbers are estimates because we do not have these facts revealed to us. However based on the message of Matthew 7:13–14 God's Word says, **"Enter through the narrow gate. For wide is the gate and broad is the road that leads to destruction, and many enter through it. But small is the gate and narrow the road that leads to life and only a few find it."** We can estimate reasonably well. God gives us the answer.

Revelation 20:5
"The rest of the dead did not come to life until the thousand years were ended. This is the first resurrection."

This tells us that the millions of nonbelievers who died physically, whether they died before the Resurrection of Christ or after, or whether they died after the Resurrection of Christ or the Seven-Year Tribulation, their bodies stay in their grave through the one-thousand-year Millennial Kingdom. Their Spirit is in Hades and their body is in the grave. The resurrection of those who placed their trust in Christ is called in the Scripture as the first resurrection even though there were separate resurrections of those saints.

1 Thessalonians 4:17
"Then we who are alive, who are left, will be caught up together with them in the clouds to meet the Lord in the air, and so we will always be with the Lord."

What will the Millennial Reign be like? When will it happen? Why will it happen? Our foundation for discussion on this topic is Scripture. The foundation Scripture we will use for this discussion is Revelation 20:1–10. John the Apostle was given the vision from God of an angel coming down from heaven with the key to the bottomless pit and a great chain in his hand. God captured Satan, chained him, and cast him into the bottomless pit for one thousand years. Why was this done? Why was Satan not cast into the "Lake of Fire" as was The Beast and The False Prophet? We are not told. It may be God wanted to give Satan another chance. Perhaps the great love for Lucifer that God had at the beginning caused Him to want to give Lucifer one more chance. We do not know but we will very soon see the result of that trial.

The bottomless pit has been a subject of conjecture and disagreement among Bible scholars over the years. The King James Bible describes the Greek word abusso as **"The Bottomless Pit."** The Gospel of Luke, while talking about the swine being driven out of the man with demons, states the demons begged Jesus to not drive them out to **"The Deep."** In this instance **"The Deep"** was also used in replacement of abusso. We know that **"The Bottomless Pit"** was a hole so large and so deep that it seems to have no bottom. It is so dark that there is absolutely no light. It is not Hades and is not the place where the unsaved were temporarily held. And it is not the **"Lake of Fire"** where **"The Beast"** and **"The False Prophet"** will be caste.

Revelation 20:1–3
"Then I saw an angel coming down from heaven, holding in his hand the key to the bottomless pit and a great chain. And He seized the dragon, that ancient serpent, who is the Devil and Satan, and bound him for a thousand years; and he threw him into the bottomless pit, and shut it, and sealed it over him, so that he might not deceive the nations no longer until the thousand years were ended. But after that he must be released for a little while."

John the Apostle saw the Millennial Reign of Christ in the vision God provided. It is from this Scripture that we have the eternal promise of living with Jesus Christ, here on this earth for one thousand years. Satan will not have any influence.

Will there be unsaved people in the one-thousand-year millennial reign?

When Jesus comes to wage the war of Armageddon and defeat Satan, there will be people alive who trust Him for their salvation. There will also be people who hate Jesus, as well as people who do not hate Him but have not given their lives to Jesus to trust Him for salvation. We know the Judgement of Sheet and Goats, also known as the Judgement of Nations, will be conducted by Jesus to determine who goes into the one-thousand-year millennial reign. Those alive who have placed their trust in Him for salvation will enter the Millennial Reign in their natural state because they have never experienced physical death. They will not have a glorified body but are believers in Him. Those who have not trusted Jesus will be sent to Hades, a place of torment, and will not partake of the Millennial Kingdom.

Everyone on earth, during this period who will enter the one-thousand-year Reign in a glorified body will believe in Jesus Christ and will love Him with all their hearts. In addition to those with glorified bodies will be, perhaps millions of people who come into the Millennial Reign in their natural state without glorified bodies. These people will love Jesus but will continue life somewhat as they have in the past. They will partake in marriage, will have children and the children they yield will have to decide if they want to trust Jesus for salvation or not. These children have the advantage over this life in that Satan will not be there to tempt them. But they still have the imputed nature to sin from the days of Adam and they can eventually enter Heaven only if they trust Jesus Christ for Salvation. The one-thousand-year millennial reign will last one thousand years. People will have very long lifespans perhaps seven to eight hundred years. This means many generations of birth will occur in the one-thousand-year millennial reign. Amazing as it seems a massive amount of these people will elect to trust in themselves rather than Jesus and will be lost. Their future will be eternity in the **"Lake of Fire."**

Revelation 20:7–10 tells us that at the end of the one-thousand millennial reign Satan will be set free and will recruit from this host of nonbelievers a massive army to take one last try at defeating God. Perhaps this is why God only imprisoned Satan in the deep of the earth rather than throw him into the Lake of Fire after the Battle of Armageddon. God knew what Satan would do and will punish him for his deeds.

Revelation 20:7–10

"And when the thousand years are ended, Satan will be released from his prison and will come out to deceive the nations that are at the four corners of the earth, Gog and Magog, to gather them for battle; their number is like the sand of the sea. And they marched up over the broad plain of the earth and surrounded the camp of the saints and the beloved city, but fire came down from heaven and consumed them, and the devil who had deceived them was thrown into the lake of fire

and sulfur where the beast and the false prophet were, and they will be tormented day and night forever and ever."

From Revelation 20:4–6 we know there will be structure in the Millennial Kingdom. We have reason to believe people will continue to work at jobs, but they will love their work. It is reasonable to believe the Millennial Kingdom will be similar to that of the Garden of Eden before the fall of man. We know Christ will rule with a rod of iron. That means He will be totally in control. There will be no power struggles. Our Lord who is sovereign and knows everything, our Lord who is all-powerful, and our Lord who is all gracious is also totally holy. A sinless life, nothing less, will be required by Jesus in the Millennial Kingdom. Yet some will disappoint Jesus and in so doing will sin. They will be held accountable for their sin but can be saved if they confess their sins and ask Jesus to save them. It is understandable that many who are born in the Kingdom's lifespan, will resent this iron rule of righteousness and be ready for rebellion with Satan.

Who will be there? Certainly the Body of Christ, the Church, will be present in the millennial reign. In addition the Old Testament Saints who were saved because of their faith in the coming Messiah will be there. They were saved through faith just as was the Church although they did not know exactly what the coming Messiah meant. They will be saved through their faith in the revelations of God to the extent given and by the Grace of God. In addition we will have the Tribulation Saints with us. The Body of Christ arrives in Heaven through the rapture of Christ. But how do the Old Testament Saints and the Tribulation Saints arrive at the Millennial Reign? To better understand the subject of resurrections lets review the resurrections previously covered.

How Many Resurrections Will Take Place?

We know that, during the Dispensation of the Church; or perhaps known as the Dispensation of Grace, when believers die our souls go to heaven to be with the Lord. Our bodies go to the grave to await a resurrection in which our spirits in heaven are joined with glorified physical bodies. We also know that now, during the Dispensation of Grace, that when nonbelievers die their bodies go to the grave to await a resurrection. Their spirits however go to hades as a waiting place. Jesus tells us in Matthew 25:46 that spiritually everyone lives forever. There is no such a thing as ceasing to exist. And the vast majority of people will experience a resurrection. The question of massive importance is where will your spirits go at physical death and where will your resurrected bodies go at resurrection.

Matthew 25:46
"And these shall go away into eternal punishment but the righteous into eternal life."

When the Bible uses the term resurrections it refers to that point in which our bodies cease to function as a body here on earth and puts on immortality. Yes, both sinners who are saved by the blood of Christ and nonbelievers both put on immortality when they die. The question is what is the destination of the resurrection will they experience.

There are two kinds of resurrections. The first resurrection applies to people who die and during their life have asked Jesus to save them. They are the redeemed and we will call this resurrection the **"Resurrection of Life."** The second resurrection is for those who die and never asked Jesus to save them from their sins. They are lost and we will call this resurrection the **"Resurrection of Death."** People in the **"Resurrection of Life"** will be raised from death (physically) to life (spiritually) and will spend eternity with Jesus. People in the **"Resurrection of Death"** will be raised from death (physically) to death (spiritually) and will spend eternity separated from God in agony and punishment.

People in the **"Resurrection of Life"** will never face condemnation for things they did wrong on earth because their sins are covered by the Blood of Jesus who took their sins on Himself and paid for their sins by His death. People in the **"Resurrection of Death"** will be held accountable for every sin they ever committed.

People in the **"Resurrection of Life"** will enjoy eternity of rewards granted to them for good deeds they did while alive on earth. People in the **"Resurrection of Death"** will receive degrees of punishment throughout eternity in the Lake of Fire otherwise known as Hell.

John 5:29
"And come out, those who have done good to the resurrection of life, and those who have done evil to the resurrection of judgment."

When will these resurrections take place? The Bible does not give us exact dates but we can, in relation to other events that will take place, identify their place in the End Times.

There are a number of instances recorded in Scripture in which an individual, under the power of God, raised another person from death to life. We do not count these as resurrections in the **"Resurrection of Life"** or the resurrections in the **"Resurrection of Death."** While each resurrection was a magnificent example of God's power through His representatives on earth they did not bring the recipient back to everlasting status. Participants in the **"Resurrection of Life"** and **"Resurrection of Death"** have their future permanently determined either to be heaven or hell.

Resurrections of Life

1. The Resurrection of Jesus Christ

The **"Resurrection of Life"** for Jesus Christ, after He was crucified, is recorded by God, for our benefit, as the "first fruits" of forthcoming **"Resurrections of Life."** "First fruits" simply means Jesus was the first to be raised from the dead within the plan of salvation provided by God the Father. Yes, prior to the resurrection of Jesus, Jesus and a limited number of apostles raised certain individuals from the grave. They did this, in part, because of compassion for these raised, but primarily to demonstrate that Jesus had to power of God and was the expected "Messiah." They each did this through power given to them by God the Father.

The resurrection of Jesus is quite different. First it was done by God the Father Himself. But most important the resurrection of Jesus was a permanent, one time resurrection with victory over death. Other individual resurrections previously left the resurrected one to experience death again sometime in the future. Just think without the resurrection of Christ He would have the burden of sin on his back as we would have the burden of our sins on our back. Christ would have gone to Hell with us. Without the resurrection of Christ not one believer in Jesus Christ would ever be saved but would be accountable for our all our sins. Without the resurrection of Christ we all, including Jesus the Son of God, would be in Hell for eternity.

1 Corinthians 15:20–21
"But in fact Christ has been raised from the dead, the first fruits of those who have fallen asleep. For as by a man came death; by a man came also the resurrection of the dead."

Resurrections of Life
The Rapture of the Church

The next resurrection to be a **"Resurrection of Life"** is the rapture of the Church. This happens just before the beginning of the Seven-Year Tribulation and includes all people who confessed to believe Jesus Christ died for their sins, were buried for their sins, and were raised from the dead to pay the price of their sins. If you believe in Jesus Christ as your Savior this is your hope of eternal salvation. To be included in this resurrection we have to have been "born again" after the death, burial, and resurrection of Jesus. If so, we are part of **"The Church"** as ordained by God and given to Jesus. This means that all believers who died after the death, burial and resurrection of Christ up to the rapture of the Church were spiritually taken to heaven to be with Jesus but their bodies remained in the grave awaiting the rapture of the Church.

1 Corinthians 15:50–54
"I tell you this, brothers: flesh and blood cannot inherit the kingdom of God, nor does the perishable inherit the imperishable. Behold! I tell you a mystery. We shall not all sleep, but we shall all be changed, in a moment, in the twinkling of an eye, at the last trumpet. For the trumpet will sound, and the dead will be raised imperishable, and we shall be changed. For this perishable body must put on the imperishable, and this mortal body must put on immortality. When the perishable puts on the imperishable, and the mortal puts on immortality, then shall come to pass the saying that is written."

Resurrections of Life
The Resurrection of the "Two Witnesses"

The book of Daniel informs us that in the middle of the Seven-Year Tribulation Satan will forcibly take control of the worldwide worship system and will announce he is God. In so doing he demonstrates his hatred for Israel and especially his hatred for God or anyone worshiping God. When this happens the last three and one half years of the Great Tribulation will have great suffering poured out by God. At the same time we find two prophets from God receive power from God to begin witnessing Jesus Christ is the promised Messiah. The book of Revelation 11:3 announces all of this to the Apostle John in the vision God gave to him.

Revelation 11:3
And I will grant authority to my "Two Witnesses" and they will prophesy for three and 1,260 days, clothed in sackcloth.

What do the **"Two Witnesses"** prophesy about? They prophesy about the power of Jesus Christ, about the need of people alive to forsake "The Beast" and "The False Prophet" and be faithful to Jesus. They are extremely clear in their message and are amazingly well received by both Jews and Gentiles. Untold thousands, and perhaps millions, of people are saved to the point the **"Two Witnesses"** prove to be a successful deterrent to the success of The False Prophet. But God's Word says that **"When they have finished their testimony,"** meaning when they have accomplished the will of God the Father, He allows Satan to kill them only to be resurrected in three and one half days.

Revelation 11:7
"And when they have finished their testimony, the beast that rises from the bottomless pit will make war on them and conquer them and kill them."

Revelation 11:8–9 informs us that the **"Two Witnesses"** are publically killed in Jerusalem and their dead bodies are put on display to the public for three and one half days. This gross display of barbarism is done to demonstrate the power of The Antichrist and The False Prophet over God. We must remember this happens at the end of the Seven-Year Tribulation and most believers in Christ have now been beheaded and their souls resurrected to Heaven. So those left to view the bodies of the **"Two Witnesses"** are followers of Satan. The fact all believers have been removed is why the **"Two Witnesses"** are allowed to be killed. Their mission has been successfully accomplished and is finished.

Revelation 11:11
"But after the three and a half days a breath of life entered them, and they stood on their feet and great fear fell on those who saw them. Then they heard a loud voice from heaven saying, "Come up here!" And they went up to heaven in a cloud and their enemies watched them."

Resurrections of Life
Resurrection of Old Testament Saints

The Book of Daniel reveals to us that at the end of the Great Tribulation, right after Jesus Christ comes back to earth, right after He defeats Satan in the Battle of Armageddon, and right after He brings "The Church" with Him, Jesus will resurrect the bodies of all Old Testament Saints.

Daniel 12:1–2
"At that time shall arise Michael, the great prince who has charge of your people. And there shall be a time of trouble, such as never has been since there was a nation until that time. But at that time your people shall be delivered; everyone whose name shall be found written in the Book. And many of those who sleep in the dust of the earth shall awake, some to everlasting life, and some to shame and everlasting contempt."

Many quotes from Daniel's vision give us strong facts about Old Testament Resurrection of Saints and sinners. First we realize this resurrection will take place at the end of the Seven-Year Tribulation Period. This fulfills the seventy-week allowance God gave to Daniel regarding the future of Israelite people. It also is confirmed when the scripture tells us **everyone whose name shall be found written in the Book.** The Book of Life will not be opened until near the end of the Seven-Year Tribulation. We also know that reading from the Book of Life is the only way to know who will be saved and who will not be saved of the Old Testament people. So this resurrection will be separate from the resurrection of Tribulation Saints. In that resurrection only those **"Dead In Christ"** will be resurrected.

Could this resurrection be the same as the Judgment of Sheep and Goats commented on in other scripture? The Bible does not give us clear differentiation on this question. However, the purpose of both resurrections, are to determine who will go into the forthcoming one-thousand-year Millennial Kingdom. The purpose is to determine saved and unsaved.

Resurrections of Life
Resurrection of Tribulation Saints

The fifth resurrection of Life is for the group of people God gave a last chance to accept Jesus Christ as their Savior. God, in His love, gave this group of people one last chance to avoid eternity in Hell. This group is the Tribulation Saints. The vision given to John is quite clear.

Revelation 20:4

"Then I saw thrones, and seated on them were those who whom the authority to judge was committed. Also I saw the souls of those who had been beheaded for the testimony of Jesus and for the word of God and those who had not worshipped the Beast or its image and had not received its mark on their foreheads or their hands. They came to life and reigned with Christ for a thousand years."

It is fascinating to read the details of this information from God. First of all these people already have positions of command in the one-thousand-year Millennial Kingdom because John saw thrones upon which they were seated. He saw that these people had been granted authority to judge in the Kingdom. He also cannot be misunderstood about what group of people they were because they were the **"souls of the beheaded and they were beheaded because of their testimony of Jesus."** We see God told John and therefore us that the Tribulation Saints will be rewarded for their excellent faith to accept certain death by being beheaded in order to remain faithful to God. God tells us they take their position in the **"Resurrection of Life"** because it says **"they came to life and reigned with Christ for a thousand years."** This also confirms that the Tribulation Saints, along with "The Church" will be part of the one-thousand-year millennial kingdom.

Resurrections of Death
Resurrection of the Old Testament Nonbelievers

The book of Daniel informs us that believers in the Old Testament will be redeemed by the blood of Jesus shed on Calvary even though they did not know exactly who the Messiah would be. They knew and believed the Messiah would be promised by God and provided by God but could not place the Messiah with the "Son of God." Yet to the extent of their revelation, they trusted God and through God, trusted in Jesus to, some distant date in the future, pay the price of their sins.

Daniel chapter 12, however, also accounts for the vast host of people who did not believe in God as God gave them revelation. To these, millions of people over thousands of year's eternal damnation are foretold. Consider the words, **"And many of those who sleep in the dust of the earth shall awake, some to everlasting life, and some to shame and everlasting contempt."** God's Word tells us of a resurrection that takes place along with the resurrection of Old Testament Saints. These are the Old Testament nonbelievers in which the people therein face eternal shame, eternal contempt, and eternal punishment. This resurrection will occur at the end of the fierce Battle of Armageddon where Christ defeats Satan and seals the fate of all nonbelievers. These Old Testament Nonbelievers consist of those who reject God, purposefully fail to meet the Law as outlined by God from the fall of Adam and Eve up to the resurrection of Jesus Christ from Calvary. At Calvary Jesus was resurrected from the dead and the age of **"The Church"** begun. All others prior to that whose faith could not be counted as righteousness are condemned to eternal death.

Resurrections of Death
The Great White Throne Judgment

The Great White Throne Judgment is the final judgment and it takes place right after the end of the one-thousand-year Millennial Kingdom in which Jesus Christ personally served as King. It is just and fair that God would grant Jesus the right to be the final judge over all who appear before the Great White Throne. In a previous Judgment called the BEMA SEAT we saw that the saved were judged by the good deeds and thoughts they had done. In this judgment the lost are judged by the evil deeds they did while on earth. They stand in line waiting for their judgment into a future they dread. Revelation 20:7–15 tell us that this great judgment takes place after

Satan has suffered his last defeat and has been cast into the Lake of Fire forever. There is no better commentary than that given to the John in Revelation 20:11–15. The following is a break-down of these verses:

Verse 11 "There I saw a Great White Throne and Him who was seated on it."

The Great White Throne signifies the total, absolute power God has transferred to Jesus. Our Lord sits on the throne of judgment of all lost people to ever populate the world. God has passed the right and responsibility to judge to His Son Jesus Christ (John 5:22). His throne is great and majestic signifying His power and His rule over everything. His throne is also white. That tells us He is pure with His ruling, fair and just with His judgments.

Verse 11 continued: **"From His presence earth and sky fled away and no place was found for them."** God is telling us that this judgment takes place someplace other than earth or the sky. While the Scripture does not tell us where this takes place it does tell us the world as we knew it has ceased to exist. Believers are now in a "New Heaven and a New Earth." The lost can see into this new place but not enter it. This adds to their terror because they have a slight insight into their fate.

Verse 12: **"And I saw the dead, great and small, standing before the throne, and books were opened. Then another book was opened which is the book of life"** The Apostle John tells us he saw the vision of the future event in which the unsaved had no status of rich or poor, powerful or insignificant. No longer did politics count, wealth did not count, personality did not count, religion did not count and the only thing that had any value was their lack of belief in Christ and the deeds they had done. We also see that the answer is in detailed books recording every deed they had ever done. These had to be mountains of books but the one special book called the "Book of Life" contained the status for every person with relationship to being saved or lost for eternity.

Verse 13: **"And the sea gave up the dead who were in it. Death and Hades gave up the dead who were in them and they were judged, each one of them according to what they had done."** The picture here is one of millions of people standing, erect before Jesus Christ waiting on a sentence they know will be horrible but they do not know how horrible. No one alive can escape from this event. We should remember that the "Church-Age" Christians were raptured just before the Seven-Year Tribulation. They are not present. But there were, perhaps, 1 billion "Church-Age" believers so that left 7–8 billion people on earth. The number of people who came to trust Jesus as their Messiah in the Seven-Year Tribulation is unknown but said to be so many no man could count them. Although we do not know how many were converted to God we know it would have been difficult because to accept Christ and refuse to worship the Antichrist meant immediate death. Perhaps another billion were saved and resurrected from the Seven-Year Tribulation. That would leave 6–7 billion people still on earth. We know that of the 6–7 billion left on earth they all denied Jesus as Lord and Master and they came under the wrath of God in the seven Trumpets and seven Bowls. In Revelation 9:18 God tells John one third of all living on earth will be killed by fire, smoke, and sulfur. Perhaps that leaves about 4 billion people living at the beginning of the Battle of Armageddon. If another billion are killed then we still have 3–4 billion people alive on earth at the beginning of the Great White Throne Judgment. All of these will be lost and have no chance to escape their sentence in the Lake of Fire.

But wait, that only begins to be the picture of people waiting sentence from Christ. The scripture says that Hades and Death will release all their occupants to attend this great judgment day. No know knows how many but certainly as many as 3–4 billion because this number includes those who died from the beginning of time not trusting God. They have no escape.

Will there be degrees of punishment in the Lake of Fire? The answer is absolute yes. Look at what the Bible tells us: **"Each one of them according to what they had done."** Case closed! Those who were good people but just did not trust in Christ will have a lighter sentence that those who were bad, corrupt, Satan loving people. But all will be cast into the Lake of Fire.

Verse 14: **"Then Death and Hades were thrown into the Lake of Fire. This is the second death. The Lake of Fire!"** Now we see the books closed. The judgment is done and the satanic place of Death and Hades are also thrown into the Lake of Fire. Hades is the compartment created in the innermost part of earth where the souls of dead people, from the day of Adam to the last person on earth, were "stored" awaiting this very judgment. **"And many of those who sleep in the dust of the earth shall awake, some to everlasting life, and some to shame and everlasting contempt."** This verse refers to that resurrection of Old Testament Saints and all nonbelievers awaiting judgment in Hades. It takes place at the end of the Battle of Armageddon. After than battle Hades and Death give up their contents for judgment and Death and Hades have already been judged and they are thrown into the Lake of Fire forever.

Why the one-thousand-year Millennial Kingdom of Christ?

The Millennial Kingdom is a period of exactly one thousand literal years after the Seven-Year Tribulation, after the Battle of Armageddon, after the Second Coming of Jesus, and after Satan is locked up in **"The Pit"** for one thousand years. Jesus will reign as King over Israel and the rest of the world for these one thousand years. The reason God creates the one-thousand-year Kingdom is basically and primarily to fulfill promises God made to the nation of Israel, to His Son Jesus Christ, and to all mankind. These are promises that require faith and obedience of man to God and in the six dispensations previously, man has refused to follow the demands of God. Thus we move into the seventh and final Dispensation. The promises God has made are covenants between God and man that primarily involve the nation of Israel. However some promises were made to Jesus and some to creation as a whole. These promises are called Covenants in the Bible and are as follows:

When people talk about the Covenants of God, especially the Covenants with Israel, the first one we think about is the Covenant

God made with Abraham. Much of the Abrahamic Covenant has been accomplished before the Millennium. Abraham did go into the promised-land as promised. He did have a vast number of descendants. He is the forefather of the nation of Israel that is recognized as God's "Chosen People." However, there is one part of the Abrahamic Covenant that has not been fulfilled because of the hatred the world has had for Israel.

This part of the Abrahamic Covenant is often called the Palestinian Covenant because it involves not only the Jewish People but the Palestinian people as well. And as we know, there exists great hatred between these nations. Israel has never possessed the specific boundaries God promised in Genesis 15:18–20. God is faithful to keep His promises. He used the Millennium to complete The Abrahamic Covenant. Now Israel will control these promised lands forever and forever. He promised they would control that land forever in Genesis 13:15. This promise will be fulfilled in the one-thousand Millennial Kingdom that is under the total, absolute rule of Jesus Christ.

God promised David in 2 Samuel that the line of David would never die out and David's heir will sit on the throne of Israel forever (2 Samuel 7:16). **"And your house and your kingdom shall be made sure forever before me. Your throne shall be established forever."** Jesus Christ's earthly birth came through the lineage of David. Jacob the father of Joseph who was the husband of Mary who was the mother of Jesus set this lineage. And of course, Jesus the son of Mary satisfies the lineage of David. When Jesus sits on the throne of the one-thousand-year Millennial Reign He fulfills this promise of God. The one-thousand-year reign will be the start of Jesus's eternal reign over both, Israel and the rest of the world (Revelation 20:4, 6).

Jeremiah 31:33 outlines the third promise God made that has to be fulfilled in the one-thousand-year millennial reign. It states, **"For this is the covenant I will make with the house of Israel after those days, declares the Lord; I will put my law within them, and I will write it on their hearts. And I will be God and they shall be my people."** This has been called the New Covenant with Israel. It means every member of the Jewish Nation, alive on earth, will turn and worship Jehovah. As we have seen God accomplishes this by allowing His wrath to pour out on unbelieving Jews. He also institutes the greatest revival in the history of the world convicting both Jew and Gentile. However the Jews that return to faith in Him fulfill this Covenant. We know Israel will not turn, as a nation, to worship Jesus Christ until after the Seven-Year Tribulation. However, at that time God seats the surviving Jews, who believe in Him, to positions of authority in ruling the Millennium. This fulfills God's promise to the stubborn nation of Israel.

God made other promises that require unwavering support of mankind and Jesus Christ. He promised Jesus He would rule personally over His Church. Jesus rules over the Church spiritually now but in the Millennial Kingdom He will rule spiritually and physically over the Church. God promised all creation he would lift the curse of sin and this happens when Satan and his followers are cast into the Lake of Fire forever. God promised many things that can only happen with the creation and implementation of the one-thousand-year Millennial Kingdom.

Spiritual Life in the one-thousand-year Millennial Kingdom!

The one-thousand-year Millennial Kingdom will be a physical and spiritual union that enhances the relationship of man and Christ beyond our ability to comprehend. We have, here on earth, a spiritual kingdom with Christ now. This is true because we feel the Holy Spirit teaching us, correcting us, encouraging us, and guiding us in our daily life. But it is not a perfect union with Christ because of the presence of Satan who is always trying to temp us to forsake Christ and be carnal. In the Millennium, a term for the one-thousand-year Millennial Kingdom, Jesus will be both spiritual and visible. We shall see Jesus, touch Jesus, and talk with Jesus. How can we live all over the world and do these things. It is because Jesus takes on the physical body He exhibited while on earth as well as His Spiritual Body. We take on a glorified spiritual body that gives us amazing ability to conquer physical barriers that would otherwise make our close relationship with Jesus impossible. The prophet Isaiah was given a vision of this future relationship with Christ. He shares it with us in Isaiah 40:4.

Isaiah 40:4

"Every valley shall be lifted up, and every mountain and hill shall be made low, the uneven ground shall become level and the rough places a plain. And the glory of the Lord shall be revealed, and all flesh shall see it together, for the mouth of the Lord has spoken."

There can be no doubt but that Christ glorified is the center of worship and the center of life in the Millennium. The Bible is full of scriptures that support the future seventh Dispensation of God in His relationship with mankind. In much of the following comments we made regarding the Millennial Kingdom we will emphasize physical aspects of this great Dispensation of God that is yet to come. However we must always recognize the greatest give of God to mankind will be the Spiritual walk we will have with Jesus even as God is preparing us for eternity in Heaven that is to come.

Will the one thousand number be literal in the one-thousand-year Millennial Kingdom?

Revelation 20:2 tells us quite clearly that God took Satan and threw him in the "Pit" for a thousand years, shut it and sealed it so Satan could not deceive nations until the thousand years were ended.

Revelation 20:2–3

"And he seized the dragon, that ancient serpent, who is the devil and Satan, and bound him for a thousand years, and threw him into the pit, and shut it and sealed it over him, so that he might not deceive the nations any longer, until the thousand years were ended. After that he must be released for a little while."

The Millennium or Millennial Kingdom (meaning one thousand years) was created by God to fulfill His promises. These promises are primarily made to the Israelite nation, but also to His Son Jesus, to all of humanity, and to the laws of nature. God creates this time warp period and specifically confines Satan so Satan cannot influence the ideas of mankind. He does this by throwing Satan into a **"Pit"** or a prison for exactly one thousand years. This is the exact time God wants to create the time to fulfill His promises.

It is also of value to note that the one-thousand-year Millennium is not Heaven. It is heavenly reign that takes place on earth but an earth without Satan. It is quite different than Heaven. Verses in Scripture that refer to no sin at all and total perfect peace are referring to Heaven. The one-thousand-year Millennial Kingdom will begin with perfect peace and with no sin. However those who enter the Kingdom without glorified bodies still have the capacity to displease God. Each time they choose to satisfy self over God they sin. The inhabitants on the Kingdom with glorified bodies will not have the capacity to sin. They will not have any desire to satisfy self but just desire to please Jesus. As time passes toward the end of the one-thousand-year conflict will arise and this will lead to the brief war Satan chooses to wage against God after the one thousand years is complete.

Will we have a physical body in the one-thousand-year Millennial Kingdom?

Those with glorified bodies will be immortal, will live forever and not be subject to death. Those with glorified bodies will be imperishable. That means they will not be capable of sin. We will have a glorified body that is both physical and spiritual. So yes we will be able to recognize each other.

1 Corinthians 15:54
"For the perishable body must put on imperishable and this mortal body must put on immortality."

In the one-thousand-year Millennial Kingdom there will be people with glorified bodies and those with mortal bodies. Those with mortal bodies will be exactly the same as they are here on earth with the exception of the fact Satan and his followers will not be present to temp people to sin. Those without glorified bodies will be perishable, meaning capable of sin and will be mortal, meaning they can die. We know that in Romans 6:23 God told us **"The wages of sin is death."** And in 1 Corinthians 15:26 God told us **"The last enemy to be destroyed is death"** but that will not happen until the end of the Millennium. **"Then Death and Hades were thrown into the Lake of Fire."** The only reasonable understanding is that sin will be an existent and growing factor in the Millennium. That sin will not be from those with glorified bodies because they are imperishable and immortal. That leaves the fact that sin comes from the offspring of those who came to the Millennium alive. Over a one-thousand-year period of time, with no war, and little if any sickness or pain there will be many more people born than will die. It is not hard to understand where the followers of Satan will rise up from to fight the final Battle ever fought.

What will life be like in the one-thousand-year Millennial Kingdom?

About all we know regarding our glorified bodies is that we will be like Jesus.

1 John 3:2
"Beloved, we are God's children now, and what we will be has not yet appeared, but we know that when He appears we shall be like Him, because we shall see Him as He is."

We know, for instance that God is love. That means Jesus is full of love for all and we, who have a glorified body, will also be consumed with love for Him, and love for each other. Those who pass into the Millennium alive and are believers in Christ will initially be filled with love. However, they still have a human nature so that could fade with time. Believers who are alive when the Millennium begins will have their salvation secure as we do here on earth. But their children must find salvation the same way we have and that is by believing in Jesus Christ as the Savior of their sins.

Although we have said it before in this book lets reiterate that a huge reality in the Millennial Kingdom is that "**Satan will be bound.**" This means Satan will have no direct influence on those alive in the Millennial. But that does not mean Satan will have no influence. Those people who are believers in Christ and who come into the Millennial alive will not be given a glorified body. They will continue life much as here on earth because after all, they will still be here on earth. Their salvation is guaranteed but they will still have the human nature to be selfish and they can sin against what Christ teaches. There will be a strict ruling body made up of earth believers in Christ to oversee these possibilities. The influence Satan will have in the Millennial Kingdom is the nature the nature of sin God imputed into mankind at the fall of Adam and Eve.

God's Word also assures us somewhat of what the role of us as Christians will have in the Millennial Kingdom. Revelation 20:4 reveals that certain saints will be used in discipline, judgment, and order in the Millennial Kingdom.

Revelation 20:4
"Then I saw thrones, and seated on them were those to whom the authority to judge was committed. Also I saw the souls of those who had been beheaded for the testimony of Jesus and for the word of God, and those who had not worshiped the beast or its image and had not received its mark on their foreheads or their hands. They came to life and reigned with Christ for a thousand years."

The voice of God comes to us in the above verse to say clearly that certain Saints will be given responsibility of judging the citizens of the one-thousand-year millennial reign. This means the righteous believers in Christ will reign one thousand years and will be priests of Jesus Christ helping Him reign over the world in a physical reality. This is fulfillment of God's promise to both His Son and to Abraham. It is important to recognize and accept the role Israel will play in supervision of the Millennial Reign. Exodus 19:5–6 outlines this promise of God to Israel.

Exodus 19:5–6
"Now if you will indeed, obey my voice and keep my covenant you shall be my treasured possession among all peoples. For all the earth is mine, you will be to me a kingdom of priests and a holy nation, These are the words that you shall speak to the people of Israel."

The nation of Israel did not keep God's covenant, and did not obey His voice until the Seven-Year Tribulation. Certainly all Israelites did not turn to God even then. But the bulk of Israel citizens recognized God's plan for them and committed themselves in service to Him. The law, meaning the rules of Jesus regarding how we must live, will be taught and enforced by Saints who are appointed by Christ to make sure the Millennium does not become another earth. The Jewish nation will hold many of these positions. David will reign over the Jewish nation for the one thousand years of the Millennium. And Jesus, who lineage is Jewish, will rule the world for eternity.

Ezekiel 37:24
"My servant David will be king over them, and they will all have one shepherd. They will follow my laws and be careful to keep my decrees."

All over the earth there will be much admiration and love for Jesus. Believers will do as He wishes because they want to; not because we are forced to worship Him. Animals will not fight other animals. Yes we will have animals in the Millennium, because the one-thousand-year Millennial Kingdom will be the same earth that existed at the end of the Battle of Armageddon. The difference is that Jesus is in charge.

In Isaiah's vision God told him the way things would be in the Millennial. Mankind would still work. In fact it tells us clearly that we will build houses just as we do today and live in them. We have not yet reached heaven where God has prepared for us a mansion.

We have to prepare our own house. We will live in what we build. Some people will be farmers because we will grow fruit trees and care for them. We will eat the fruit we grow and maintain.

Isaiah 65:21
They shall build houses and inhabit them;
They shall plant vineyards and eat their fruit.

There will be no freeloaders in the millennial reign. Scripture is quite clear that we will build houses and live in what we build. It says we will not plant and sell our goods but will eat what we grow. Scripture goes on to say trees will live as long as the man. This means trees are cared for by God. We will work for a living but it will be pleasant as it was in the Garden of Eden. It also tells us that we will love our work and will find the work God has laid out for us to be fulfilling.

Isaiah 65:22
"They shall not build and another inhabit,"
They shall not plant and another eat;
For like the days of a tree, shall the days of My people be,
And My chosen shall long enjoy the work of their hands."

In the Millennial when we ask of the Lord we will get instantaneous answers. Scripture says that before we ask, Christ, who knows our heart will give us answers. We will have a comfort of total peace and still be totally dependent on Christ as our Lord and Savior.

Isaiah 65:24
"Before they call, I will answer;
While they are yet speaking, I will hear."

We know there will be peace in the millennial reign.

- *Animals that are presently carnivorous, will begin to eat vegetation only*
- *Humans will be vegetarians also and will not eat meat*

- *Animals that are now wild and unable to be controlled will be led by children and can play with children without fear.*
- *Snakes will cease to be objects of fear in fact fear will be removed.*
- *The entire earth will be consumed and maximally influenced by the Word of God.*
- *In the Garden of Eden man was given herbs and fruit to eat and man did not crave meat. After the fall of man this all changed with the new dispensation of God's governing. We will go back to the age of innocence, which is what we had in the Garden of Eden.*
- *Note that the Millennium becomes very similar to what the Garden of Eden was before the fall of man.*

Isaiah 65:25
"The wolf and the lamb shall graze together,
The lion shall eat straw like the ox,
And dust shall be the serpent's food.
They shall not hurt nor destroy in all My holy mountain,"
Says the Lord.

This will be a one-thousand-year period in which wars shall not be a fear on the coming horizon. Yes, at the very end of the Millennial Kingdom Satan will be set loose and will wage a brief war against God. But the bulk of the one-thousand-year Kingdom will be total peace. Not only will there be no war. Nations will not build up huge costly defenses. They will even destroy their weapons because of their comfort that they do not face a threat from other nations. All of this is because Jesus Christ is clearly in control and will not allow war.

Isaiah 2:4
"He shall judge between the nations,
And decide disputes for many peoples;
And they shall beat their swords into plowshares,
And their spears into pruning hooks;

Nation shall not lift up sword against nation,
Neither shall they learn war anymore."

The above verse, as well as Scripture in Jeremiah and Micah, states that Jesus will be a literal King ruling the world for one thousand years. The Gentile Nations will be imperfect and will make poor decisions and mistakes. They will not do so with a desire to oppose Jesus but they will require correction. Christ will simply not allow the society to degenerate as other lifestyles have over the years.

Jesus Will Rule and Reinstitute the Judge System for Israel

Why will it be different in terms of the ruling system for Israel and for the Gentile Nations? The answer is that Christ will institute the Judge System of ancient Israel as the governing system for Israel in the millennial years. The Israel Nation will be divided back into the twelve tribes and an Apostle of the twelve Apostles will rule the tribes. And of course all twelve tribes will be under the authority and spiritual guidance of Jesus Christ. Other scripture tells us that Christ will have a more direct role in the judgment of Gentile Nations. Martyred Saints will assist in the ruling over these nations. Therefore we see in the final reign of one thousand years the chosen nation of Israel takes its intended place in world leadership and in God's chosen plan.

Israel will become a Kingdom of Priests for the rest of the world. Scripture tells us that nations will come to Jerusalem to pray before the Lord. Prayer will still be a mainstay of society. People will trust Jesus and depend on Him and will view Israel as the seat of religious worship. This is because Israel is still vital in God's plan of rule over the one-thousand-year reign.

Exodus 19:5–6
"Now therefore, if you will indeed obey My voice and keep
My covenant, then you shall be my treasure possession among
all people; for all the earth is Mine. And you shall be to

Me a kingdom of priests and a holy nation.' These are the words which you shall speak to the children of Israel."

Now let us review some of the information God teaches us about the one-thousand-Year Millennial Kingdom that Jesus Christ will rule.

- *We know the Church will be in the one-thousand-year reign. They were raptured and will be with Jesus Christ forever more.*
- *We know the Old Testament Saints will be in the one-thousand-year reign because they are part of the "first resurrection" that takes place at the beginning of the one thousand years.*
- *We know the Tribulation Saints will be in the one-thousand-year reign because they also are part of the "first resurrection" that takes place at the beginning of the one thousand years.*
- *We know Jesus Christ will be the King and occupy the throne called in the Old Testament "David's Throne" and establish His Kingdom with the Jews.*

    In Isaiah the sixty-fifth chapter we find amazing revelations of God that so many people never take time to study. God tells us these things about the one-thousand-year millennial reign.

- *Verse 20 tells us life span will dramatically increase in the millennial reign similar to what it was in the Garden of Eden. In the garden life span of most people was over seven hundred years. Verse 20 tells us life spans will return to something like that.*
- *Verse 20 however also introduces to us the existence of death in the Millennial. Many of the inhabitants of the Millennial will be immortal but an ever growing number will not have been given a new spiritual body and will not be immortal.*

- *We know that many more people will be born than will die in the Millennium. At the end of the one-thousand-year reign a great uprising of those born in the Millennium but who do not place their trust in Jesus will be seduced by Satan who will be released out of the "Pit" for a short time. This will be the second battle of Gog and Magog.*

The Great White Throne Judgment

We have reviewed many judgments by God to direct the earth's people and to protect us against ourselves. One more great judgment is yet to be reviewed. It is possibly the most discussed, and most mis-understood judgment of all. Some Bible scholars try to rationalize that the judgment of believers and nonbelievers take place in the Great White Throne Judgment. This is incorrect. Revelation chapter 20 tells us this judgment will take place after the one-thousand-year millennial reign, after Satan has been loosed from "The Pit," and after he has waged war against God and been severely defeated. The Bema Seat Judgment will take place immediately after the rapture of the church. Therefore The Bema Seat Judgment cannot be the same judgment. The Bema Seat Judgment is for the saved to be given rewards for good works. The Scripture below tells us the Great White Throne Judgment is for those whose name is not in the Book of Life. Those whose name is in the Book of Life have already been judged at the Judgement Seat of Christ. Furthermore the Scripture tells us "The dead were judged by what was written in the Book of Life. The dead refers to those who are not believers and are separated from God. Death relates to separation from God. The Great White Judgment does not judge believers in Christ.

Revelation 20:11–15
"Then I saw a great white throne and Him who was seated on it, from His presence earth and sky fled away and no place was found for them. And I saw the dead, great and small, standing before the throne and books were opened. Then

another book was opened, which is the Book of Life. And the dead were judged by what was written in the books according to what they had done. And the sea gave up the dead who were in it. Death and Hades gave up the dead who were in them. And they were judged each one of them according to what they had done. Then Death and Hades were thrown into the lake of fire. This is the second death the lake of fire."

The Apostle John states he "saw the dead, great and small stand before God to be judged based on their works." This means the dead unbelievers all over the world, regardless of when they died or when they were buried. Over the years it has been a general understanding that if you died at sea the chance of every finding any part of a body was almost none. But God knows ever particle ever created because He created it. God who made mankind can sure recreate a glorified body for the saved and a transitional body for the lost. We also see that the Scripture tells us **"Death and Hades gave up the dead who were in them."** This means several things. First it means souls of lost people waiting in Hades for this Great White Throne Judgment are about to come forth out of the waiting place to face God. It also signals the end of time because Judgment follows life.

The Battle of Gog and Magog at the End of the Millennium

Revelation 20:7–10
"And when the thousand years are ended, Satan will be released from his prison and will come out to deceive the nations that are at the four corners of the earth. Gog and Magog, their number is like the sand of the sea. And they marched up over the broad plain of the earth and surrounded the camp of the Saints and the beloved City, but fire came down from Heaven and consumed them. And the devil who had deceived them was thrown into the lake of fire and sulfur where the beast and false prophet were, and they will be tormented day and night forever and ever."

THE DOCTRINE OF THE ONE-THOUSAND-YEAR
MILLENNIAL KINGDOM

There will be peace and happiness for God's elect during the one-thousand-year Millennial Reign of Christ. This is not because every person in the Millennium will be sinless. The people who do not have a glorified body in the Millennium will have the capacity to sin. Those who enter the one-thousand years alive without the glorified body will most likely pass away during the one thousand years. However, because for them, death is still alive and well. For us with glorified bodies we will be imperishable meaning we cannot sin, and immortal meaning we cannot die. But the offspring of those who are alive when they enter the Millennial Kingdom will have the capacity to sin and the weakness of death.

When we consider how long for us a thousand years is, we can grasp an understanding that there will be many people who have never experienced death at the end of the one thousand years. They will be restrained and unable to create any disturbance for the one thousand years but immediately after the one thousand years Satan will be loosed and will begin to plant deceit into the hearts of all who are not imperishable. Soon after the one thousand years Satan will gather a great army from all over the world. There will be groups of people extending even to whole nations that will rebel against the Lord's rule at the end of the Millennium. They will create a huge army that is as large as the sands of the sea.

We remember that at the beginning of the Seven-Year Tribulation a body of Anti-Israel forces attacked Israel trying to destroy her. This battle was called the Gog and Magog battle because of the groups of people fighting Israel. The reality of this battle now at the end of the one-thousand-year millennium is not the same battle as discussed in the early Tribulation period. But it is the same group of nations who evident arise one more time against God. Satan has been released from prison and of course who is he likely to approach to convert them into his army to fight God. He will approach the same group that hated Israel more than one thousand years ago. But in the first Battle of Gog and Magog Satan used the Antichrist and False Prophet to arm and motivate the battle against God. Now Satan himself leads the worldwide forces against God.

The reality of Satan being able to gather a worldwide army to fight God seems incredible. For one thousand years those participating in the Millennium have seen the power of God. They have seen the love of God. They will have experienced the love and teaching of immortal Saints for one thousand years. They will have mental knowledge of God but not heart conversion of God. They have seen the peace and happiness possible when God is worshiped and yet they rebel. The sin nature implanted in Adam in the Garden of Eden still exists in these people. Once again these who follow Satan are not Saints who have a glorified body but are people whose parents came into the Millennial alive but saved. A large number of the descendants will be saved during the one thousand years. But a number so large they are like the sands of the sea will rebel.

Isaiah 26:10
"If favor is show to the wicked, he does not learn righteousness, in the land of uprightness he deals corruptly and does not see the majesty of the Lord."

This battle will be the last conflict of faith God will allow to happen on earth. Just as Adam and Eve were seduced by Satan, just as hordes of people have been deceived by Satan over six past Dispensations of God reaching out to mankind these people who have capacity left to make their own decisions are deceived by Satan. But Satan led rebel armies will march on Jerusalem. ***"And they marched up over the broad plain of the earth and surrounded the camp of the Saints and the beloved City,"*** This is not the New Jerusalem God refers to in the New Heaven and the New Earth. Mankind is still in a test to determine who they will serve. But even greater Satan is still in a test to determine what his level of punishment will be. Satan has been bound for one thousand years waiting for the Millennium to be fulfilled and the promises of God completed. Now is the time to give Satan his last chance. If Satan would have repented of his sins and ask God for forgiveness would God have spared him eternity in torment? We do not know the answer but this is the nature of God. God does not want to punish but wants to love. God does not want to condemn but wants to forgive. But man and perhaps, Satan as well, must have a heart that asks forgiveness of sin.

This time, however, God is ready to end it all. So He sends down fire from Heaven to eliminate this enemy.

Revelation 20:9–10
"But fire came down from Heaven and consumed them. And the devil who had deceived them was thrown into the lake of fire and sulfur where the beast and false prophet were, and they will be tormented day and night forever and ever."

God annihilates Satan and every follower he has. They are thrown into the "Lake of Fire." Then God causes such a great fire to come down from Heaven that the entire surface of the earth is destroyed. The world is set now for the final scene because God now reveals the new heaven and new earth He has created not for nonbelievers but for the redeemed. God destroys the surface of the Earth. That is interesting because God is going to create a New Heaven and a New Earth.

The New Heaven and New Earth

As fantastic as the Millennial Kingdom will be, God is not through with us yet. Many, in fact most Christians get the Millennial Kingdom and the New Heaven and New Earth mixed up. They are very different. They are both marvelous. They are both literal and real. God promises them, and God does not fail to fulfill His promises. To describe the New Heaven and New Earth we can best compare the two. But first, where do we get the promise of a New Heaven and New Earth? The answer is Revelation the twenty-first chapter. Let's see what God has in store for us.

Revelation 21:1
"Then I saw a new heaven and a new earth, for the first heaven and the first earth had passed away. Also the sea was no more."

Wow, what a Scripture. These few words are full of massive changes in our lives and eternal future. First the Apostle John had revealed to him by God a New Heaven and a New Earth. Isn't it fascinating what John saw. He saw a New Heaven and a New Earth. This indicates tremendous changes in our atmosphere. We will see this is true because in eternity Scripture tells us that there will be no sun on the New Earth because Jesus Christ will be our light.

The second point of amazement is that the first heaven and first earth are passed away. This means the world we live in during the Millennial Kingdom has passed away. We get more clarification in Revelation 20:11.

Revelation 20:11
"Then I saw a great white throne and Him who was seated on it, from His presence the earth and sky fled away. And no place was found for them."

Earth and heaven fled away from the face of God. It is God the Father who is coming down on the great white throne in New Jerusalem to live with the redeemed forever. God will not tolerate sin. Earth is and was corrupted with sin. Even the one-thousand-year millennium was conflicted with sin of certain occupants. Earth had to go. And God even decided to create a New Heaven. Perhaps the fact that Lucifer had lived in heaven and left a residue of sin caused God to create a New Heaven. Perhaps God simply wanted a heaven that is more glorious and wonderful than even the heaven He had lived in was. We do not know but we know He created a New Heaven and the old earth passed away. What does that mean when God says it passed away? The Apostle Peter deals with this question in 2 Peter 3:10–13.

2 Peter 3:10–13
"But the day of the Lord will come as a thief and then the heavens will pass away with a roar, and the heavenly bodies will be burned up and dissolved; and the earth and the works that are done on it will be exposed. Since all

these things are thus to be dissolved, what sort of persons ought you to be in lives of holiness and godliness, waiting for and hastening the coming of the day of God, because of which the heavens will be set on fire and dissolved, and the heavenly bodies will melt as they burn. But according to His promise we, according to His promise we are waiting for new heavens and a new earth in which righteousness dwells."

We see that at the end of the Millennial Kingdom the destruction of the earth and heaven, as Christians have experienced it, will be sudden without warning. The elements, meaning both earth and everything on it and the atmosphere we have experience with, will melt with fervent heat. Many have tried to interpret this verse as proof that the end of the earth will be nuclear war. It is very unlikely this is the correct interpretation. Remember that at the end of the Millennial Reign, Satan will come out of prison and wage war against God. Satan and all of his followers will be devoured in fire. Could this be a nuclear war? Yes but we do not have enough revelation to make that statement. God does not need to use nuclear weapons to destroy the world. He has the power within Himself. Quite possibly this is the fire Satan is devoured up in and that melts the earth. Satan is cast into the "Lake of Fire." We do not know where the "Lake of Fire" will be located. Scripture does tell us the earth and all connected to it, will be consumed by the fire. Scripture tells us the earth and the atmosphere melts. Does it melt into a "Lake of Fire" a lake of fire and brimstone? It is possible and even probable this is true. But it is conjecture on our part.

To take the place of the current earth and heavens God will create a New Heaven and New Earth.

Isaiah 65:17
"For behold, I create new heavens and a new earth;
And the former shall not be remembered or come to mind."

In this new heaven, we will not have any memory of the world we lived in. We will not have memory of our people or things we did while on the first earth. We will not regret that we did not do this or that. There will be no sorrow or regret in heaven. Perhaps one of the reasons for the creation of the new heaven and new earth was so we could put everything connected to our sinful past behind us.

A comparison of our new heaven and new earth and the Millennium reign gives us these comparisons. They demonstrate the vast difference in our new home to our old home.

The Millennial years compared to the New Heaven and New Earth	
Jesus Christ the Son of God comes and physically reigns with us on earth.	God the Father comes down from Heaven to physically live among us. We have God the Father and God the Son as companions for eternity.
The Millennial years are spent on the same physical earth we currently live. Yes, the earth has been changed by earthquakes and fire but it is essentially the same earth.	The New Earth will be totally new. It will have no sea so it will be three times larger than what we live on now. All signs of corruption, decay, or sin are totally gone.
Jesus Christ is said to be the light of the Temple but the earth continues to have the Sun, Moon, Stars and the atmosphere.	God the Father is the light of the world. There is no more sun, no moon, no stars. There is no atmosphere just heaven and earth.
Jesus Christ will physically occupy the Throne of David in the Holy City of Jerusalem. He will rule from that literal throne. The throne will be in the temple in Jerusalem.	The New Earth will have no temple. God the Father does not need a temple. He will reign together with God the Son forever and forever.
In the Millennial reign Jerusalem will be the same Jerusalem city it was on earth. It will be without the presence of religions that are against Jesus and Satan will be removed.	In the New Heaven and the New Earth we will get a New Jerusalem. It will be a glorious marvelous place of worship and praise. There will be no sin, no sorrow no grief.
In the Millennial reign Tribulation Saints who transferred into the one thousand years without having died were mortals and died during the one thousand years. So death, although limited to those with mortal bodies, still existed.	At the end of the Millennial reign God defeated Satan, caste him into the "Lake of Fire" and cast Hades and Death into the "Lake of Fire" also. At that time death ended. There will be no death of any kind in the New Heaven and New Earth.

The Millennial years compared to the New Heaven and New Earth	
There is no Scripture that tells us there will not be pain in the one thousand year reign. We know those with mortal bodies will be able to bear children. Therefore we expect those with mortal bodies will experience pain, sickness and accidents even to the point of death.	Scripture specifically tells us there will be no pain in the New Heaven and the New Earth. All present in the New Heaven and New Earth will have glorified bodies and will have no pain, no sickness, and no death.

What Will the Holy City Look Like?

Most Christians think of "The New Jerusalem" or the "The Holy City" as all of heaven. They fail to understand that the total new earth will be part of heaven. The "Holy City" will be the central focus of everything because that is where God the Father and God the Son will reign. Therefore it is magnificent that God gave us some limited understanding of what that Holy City will look like.

Revelation 21:16
"The city lies foursquare; its length the same as its width. And he measured the city with his rod: twelve thousand stadia. Its length, breadth, and height are equal."

The New Jerusalem will be a laid out as a square but will actually be a cube. It will be 1,500 miles wide, 1,500 miles long, and 1,500 miles high. This is so huge it would occupy most of the United States. Where will the New Jerusalem be located on earth? That question is impossible to answer because earth as we knew it has passed away. The New Earth will be different and will not give us remembrance of the nations we have now.

Revelation 21:18–20
"The wall was built of jasper; while the city was pure gold, like clear glass. The foundations of the wall of the city were adorned with every kind of jewel: the first foundation was jasper, the second sapphire, the third agate, the fourth

emerald, the fifth onyx, the sixth carnelian, the seventh
chrysolite, the eighth beryl, the ninth topaz, the tenth
chrysoprase, the eleventh jacinth, and the twelfth amethyst."

The wall around the city is made of jasper and the foundation is pure gold like clear glass. The wall is imbedded with all kinds of precious stones. Can you imagine a foundation of 22 million square miles all of gold. And the city has a wall around it of unbelievable beautiful jasper and precious stones.

Revelation 21:21
"The twelve gates were twelve pearls: each of the
gates made of a single pearl. And the street of the
city was pure gold, like transparent glass."

The city will have twelve gates. The twelve gates are not so numerous when you consider the size of the city. Each gate will be made out of one pearl. What huge pearls. Consider the cost of building such a city in our world. It would be impossible to consider. It is a task only capable of God. He can speak it into existence. The streets of the city are pure gold that are so pure that they look like clear glass. We will see later each of the gates is in honor of one of the Apostles.

What will we do in Heaven?

Christians do not know the answer to the question, "What will we do in Heaven?" We do not worry about it because we will be with Jesus Christ, God the Father and the Holy Spirit. However, God gives us limited insight to this mystery.

Ephesians 2:6–7
"And raised us up with Him, and seated us with Him
in the heavenly places of Christ Jesus, so that in the
coming ages He might show the immeasurable riches of
His grace in kindness toward us in Christ Jesus."

THE DOCTRINE OF THE ONE-THOUSAND-YEAR MILLENNIAL KINGDOM

The Bible tells us God has raised us up to sit together in the heavenly places because we are His children and are heirs to Jesus Christ and His love. Therefore He answers part of the question about what we will do in the New Heaven. God wants to be able to reveal to us gradually throughout eternity the amazing riches of His grace. God wants to do this because He loves us but even more so He wants to do this because He loves His only begotten Son Jesus Christ and Jesus Christ loves us. God rewards Jesus for His faithfulness by His kindness, mercy, and love to us the Body of Christ. We will spend much of eternity simply being amazed at God's grace, love, power, mercy, and creation.

One thing we will not do that everyone seems to think they will do is to go around asking questions about this life. We hear all the time people say, "When I get to Heaven I am going to ask Jesus." No, we will not be asking why Hitler was allowed to slaughter so many Jews. We will not be asking questions about life on earth because Scripture tells us clearly that former things, things of the earth bound life, shall not be remembered or even come to mind. We will be totally focused on Jesus Christ the Son of God. We will know others in heaven and will be known in heaven. But we will not remember people we knew on earth who did not accept Christ. To remember such would cause pain. There will be no pain in heaven. Now that does not mean that in the Millennial Kingdom we will not remember anything. Scripture tells us there are substantial differences in the Millennial Kingdom and in the New Heaven and New Earth.

Isaiah 65:17
"For behold, I create new heavens and a new earth;
And the former things shall not be
remembered or come into mind."

In conclusion, I offer my thanks to a host of those
who have assisted me in writing this book.

This book is the result of years of hearing sound gospel
preached from a wide number of pulpits. I also am
grateful for the privilege of participating in a host of
Bible study sessions over a lot of years as a layman.

I am grateful to many books and articles written covering
the topics and the voices of opinions. Collectively they
challenge each other and drove me back to God's Word.
A host of them, however, have collectively enlightened
me and sharpened my receptivity of truth.

But the final authority and source of everything written
in this book comes from God's Holy Word.
It is my prayer that you will use my thoughts and research
the Scripture recorded to reach your own divine answers to

God's Doctrine for Dummies

God's Doctrine for Dummies

I visualize *God's Doctrine for Dummies* to be a broad,
Bible-based source of God's directions (doctrine) to His
children. Pastors, teachers, and especially individual
worshipers of our Lord will find this writing to be easy to
teach and a blessing of worship. To facilitate the usage of
the book I include this suggested lesson plan outline.

The book *God's Doctrine for Dummies* is taken from God's Word
and contains quotations from God's Word as the foundation
of the book. I encourage all users to let God speak to you
through prayer and through basic study of God's Holy Word.

1 Peter 3:15
*But in your hearts honor Christ the Lord as holy, always being
prepared to make a defense to anyone who asks you for a reason
for the hope that is in you; yet do it with gentleness and respect.*

I. Why and How God reveals Himself

- **2 Timothy 3:16:** "All Scripture is breathed out by God and profitable for teaching, reproof, for correction, and for training in righteousness."
- God Breathed
- Never out of date

II. Inerrant,

- **Hebrews 6:18:** "That by two unchangeable things, in which it was impossible for God to lie, we who have fled for refuge might have strong encouragement to hold fast to the hope set before us."
- Challenges of man
- Accuracy of God

III. Sufficient

- **2 Corinthians 3:5:** *"Not that we are sufficient in ourselves to claim anything as coming from us, but our sufficiency is from God."*
- *Sufficiency is of God not Man*
- *Word is living and active (Hebrews 4:12)*
- *Man needs, God provides (Psalms 19:7–9)*

IV. Taught by the Holy Spirit

- **1 Corinthians 2:13:** *"And we impart this in words not taught by Human wisdom, but by the Spirit, interpreting Spiritual truths to those who are Spiritual."*
- *Jesus is in charge (Ephesians 1:22)*
- *You have put on Christ (Galatians 3:26–27)*

V. Construction

- The Pentateuch
- The Historical Books
- The Books of Wisdom
- Canonization
- Translations

VI. Value of the Old Testament

- The Book of Creation
- The History of Sin
- The Coming Messiah

VII. Composition of the New Testament

- The letters of Paul
- The Books of Gospel
- The Book or Prophecy

I.   God's Word is truth

- ***God and God alone Created***
- Spoke the world into Existence
- Evolution is false

II.   Day One: Matter and Light (**Genesis 1:1–5**)

- ***Day One: Matter and Light (Genesis 1:1–5)***
- Created from nothing, Light, Time, Matter
- God spoke Matter (Water, Gaseous Liquids) into existence
- God created twenty-four-hour day (1 John 1:5)

III.   Day Two: Atmosphere, Space, and beyond

- **Creates expanse to divide the waters (Genesis 1:6–8)**
- *Troposphere*
- *Middle Heaven*
- *Throne of God*

IV.   Day Three: Land, Sea, Vegetation

- **God spoke into existence Land in the midst of the waters (Genesis 1:9–13)**
- *God prepares creation for Man's enjoyment*

V.   Day Four: Sun, Moon, Universe

- ***"Then God said, "Let there be lights in the expanse of the heavens to separate the day from the night (Genesis 1:14–19)***
- Separates day and night
- Sets Sun to give light in day, moon and stars at night

VI.   Day Five: Fish, Fowl

- ***"Then God said, "Let the waters swarm with swarms of living creatures, and let birds fly above the earth across the expanse of the heavens." (Genesis 1:20–23)***
- Every living thing, "According to its kind." (No Evolution)
- Getting ready for creation of man

VII.   Day Six: Creation of man and animals

- ***"Then God said, "Let the earth bring forth the living creature according to its kind: livestock and creeping things and beasts of the earth, each according to their kinds." (Genesis 24–26)***

VIII. Godhead involvement in Creation
IX.   Creation versus Evolution
X.   Creation accepted by Faith not Fact

- God creates our world in six twenty-four-hour days then rests on the Seventy

XI.   Day Seven: God Rests (Genesis 2)

I.   Sin originates with Lucifer

- *God loved Lucifer, most beautiful of all creation (Ezekiel 28:12–17)*
- Unknown years of peace, love, harmony passed
- Lucifer overcome with selfish pride, starts way against God
- Lucifer chooses man as His tool to defeat God

II. The Fall of Man: *"But of the tree of the knowledge of good and evil you shall not eat, for in the day that you eat of it you shall surely die." (Genesis 2:17)*

- The original Sin
- Why God created Satan—Need for man to have capacity to love
- What is Sin? Sin of Omission, Sin of Commission
- Lack of faith in Jesus is the state of Sin (Hebrews 11:6)

III. The Unpardonable Sin: *"Truly, I say to you, all sins will be forgiven the children of man,…but whoever blasphemes against the Holy Spirit never has forgiveness…" (Mark 3:28–30)*

- **Man's Sin Nature (Romans 3:23)**
- *All have sinned*
- *Sin vs. Temptation (James 1:15)*

IV. The Price of Sin. *"For the wages of Sin is death but the free gift of God is eternal life in Jesus Christ our Lord"* (Romans 6:23)

- Spiritual Death is separation from God
- Physical death applies to all

V.   Why does God hate Sin? (Psalms 5:4)

- Sin separates us from God
- Sin blinds us to truth
- Sin temps us to partake is ways of Satan

VI. Every activity, thought, desire of man comes from one of two sources

- Source one is of Satan because we have a sin nature
- Source two is of Christ because He paid for our sin

VII. Imputed Sin

- Adam's fall
- Passed to all born of man
- Jesus Christ was born of God and woman, no imputed sin

I.   The Trinity (Godhead)

- ***Three yet One***
- God the Father is God (Philippians 1:2)
- God the Son is God (Titus 2:11–13)
- Holy Spirit is God (Act 5:3)

II.   God is both Three and One
III.   Attributes of God the Father

- God the Father is Eternal
- God the Father is Holy
- God the Father is Truth
- God the Father is Righteous (Just)
- God the Father is Love
- God the Father is Omnipotent (All-Powerful)
- God the Father is Omniscient (All-Knowing)
- God the Father is Immutable (Unchanging)
- God the Father is Omnipresent (Everywhere)
- God the Father is Timeless
- God the Father is Sovereign

IV.   God's Grace (John 1:14)
V.   God's Wrath (Romans 1:1)
VI.   The Names of God
VII.   The Father of Israel (Jeremiah 31:9)
VIII.   Christian Relationships with God the Father

- No man can know the Father except through the Son (Matthew 11:27)
- We cannot go directly to the Father, we go through the Holy Spirit
- He is the Head of the Family of God to whom we belong (Galatians 3:26)

I.   Prophecy of the coming Messiah

- *__To who and when did God reveal a coming Messiah__*
- Salvation through Jesus applies to all generations
- Why did the Old Testament people reject the Messiah (Acts 7:51–53)
- Gap of the Old Testament and New Testament

II.   The Promised Messiah (Malachi 3:1)
III. The Role of John the Baptist (Matthew 11:13–14)

- New Testament: Introduction to the Church
- Persecution and Murder: Christianity spread
- Church then draws cold

IV.   The Fulfilment of Prophecy
V.   The Virgin Birth of Jesus

- Foretold in Old Testament
- Foretold by Man: John the Baptist

VI.   Doctrine of Incarnation (John 1:14)
VII. Christ's Sinless life (2 Corinthians 5:21)

- All have sinned
- But Christ was sinless
- "This is my Son in Whom I am well Pleases" (Matthew 3:16–17)

VIII. The Miracles of Jesus

- Reason for the Miracles
- The amazing response of the people to Christ
- Thirty-six miracles identified

IX.   Prophecy of His Death and Resurrection

- Prophecy made
- Fulfillment of prophecy
- Accuracy of each prophecy

I.   Why the Cross?

  - *The Price of our sins had to be death*
  - *Was there no alternative for God but Jesus crucified?*
  - *Was there not a way to die less painful?*
  - *The commitment of Jesus to the Cross*

II. Why the Jews hated Jesus

  - Pilate had Jesus scourged because of the Jews
  - The Trial
  - Carry the Patibulum
  - Jesus was sinless

III. Jesus faced temptation to resist the Cross

  - *"My God, My God, why hast Thou forsaken me?"*
  - *"It is finished; Father into Thy hands I commend my spirit"*

IV. Sequence of Events at Calvary

  - On the Cross for six hours
  - Crucified at 9:00 AM
  - First Words: *"Father forgive them for they (us) know not what they do"*
  - Thieves rail on Him (Luke 23:39–43)
  - Second Words: *"Truly I say to you, today you will be with me in paradise."*
  - Third Words: *"Woman this is Your Son, then to the disciples He said, This is Your mother"*
  - Fourth Words: *"Eloi, Eloi, lema sabackthani?"* which means *"My God, my God, why have you forsaken me?"*
  - Fifth Words: *"I Thirst"*
  - Sixth Words: *"It is finished"*
  - Seventh Words: *"Father into Your hands I commend my spirit"*

V.   Between the Crucifixion and Resurrection

  - Three days and three nights in the heart of the earth.
  - While in the tomb what did He do?
  - The rich man and Lazarus

VI. Resurrection from the Dead

  - First fruits of those who sleep (1 Corinthians 15:20)

VII. Significance of the Resurrection

  - Victory over death
  - Fulfillment of Biblical Prophecy

I. Who is the Holy Spirit?

- Two thousand years ago Jesus sent: *"And I will ask the Father, and He will give you another Helper, to be with you forever.* (John 14:16–17)
- A person, a Spirit, a Breath, the Wind
- A Helper: A Comforter
- Part of the Trinity: One-Third of the Godhead

II. To Be Led by the Holy Spirit

III. The Role of the Holy Spirit in Creation

- God the Father, author and designer of all that has been created. *"By faith we understand that the universe was created by the Word of God, so that what is seen was not made out of things that are visible."* (Hebrews 11:3)
- God the Son, the creator of all that has been created, the implementer of the Will of the Father *"All things were made through Him and without Him was not anything made that was made."* (John 1:3)
- God the Holy Spirit, the administrator or user of all conceived by the Father and created by the Son provides to us a "Support" Role, or Administrator Role, or Comforter Role in the Church Age. *"By the Word of the Lord the heavens were made, and by the breath of His mouth (The Holy Spirit) all their hosts."* (Psalms 33:6)

IV. The Role of the Holy Spirit in Redemption

- God the Father determine what, when, and how everything happens.
- God the Son was accepted as the primary implementer of the Plan of Redemption
- The Holy Spirit made it happen. (John 14:26)

V. The Role of the Holy Spirit in the Resurrection

- God the Father created the plan and concept of Christ's Resurrection
- God the Son volunteered to be the principle one involved in the Resurrection
- The Holy Spirit is the power God the Father used to raise Jesus from the grave.

VI. The Works of the Holy Spirit

- Provides evidence of His Presence
- The Holy Spirit gives us power to do God's Will
- The Holy Spirit gives us spiritual insight

VII. Filled with the Spirit

- Baptism of the Holy Spirit
- Sealed by the Holy Spirit

VIII. Baptism of the Holy Spirit at Pentecost

IX. Baptism of the Holy Spirit at Conversion

X. Progressive grasping of the Holy Spirit

I. What is Salvation?

- Definition of Sin
- All have sinned **(Romans 3:23)**
- Imputed Sin: Willful Sin
- But God!

II. The Doctrine of Regeneration
III. The Doctrine of Justification
IV. Salvation by God, and God alone

- Grace Alone
- Faith Alone
- Word Alone
- Christ Alone
- Glory to God Alone

V. Salvation because of Faith but not by Faith

- Instant Salvation
- Not Saved by Good Works

VI. Salvation paid for by the Blood of Jesus
VII. Salvation fact not feeling

- God's command to publically testify of our Salvation through Baptism
- Salvation is of God not Man

VIII. Four Spiritual Laws

- No. 1: **"For God so loved the world that He gave His only Son that whosoever believes in Him shall not perish but have eternal life."** (John 3:16)
- No. 2: **"All have sinned and come short of the Glory of God"** (John 3:23)
- No. 3: **"But God shows His love for us in that while we were still sinners, Christ died for us.** (Romans 5:8)
- No. 4: **"But to all who did receive Him, who believed in His name, He gave the right to become children of God."** (John 1:12)

IX. Salvation is a free Gift

- Grace = unmerited favor—something God has given not that we have earned
- Must reach a point in which we make a spiritual decision that we want to follow Jesus
- Must in our heart ask Jesus to forgive our sins
- Christ will save us

I.   What is Dispensationalist?

- God has always wanted the same thing from His children.
- The way back to God has always been the same—through belief in Jesus (Galatians 3:22) *"But the Scripture imprisoned everything under sin, so that the promise by faith in Jesus Christ might be given to those who believe."*

II.   The Dispensation of Innocence

- Began with the creation of Adam—ended with the disobedience of Adam
- Innocence means Adam had not sinned, had not displeased God
- God communicated with man personally, spiritually, and physically

III. The Dispensation of Conscience

- Began with the fall of Adam from the Garden of Eden—ended with the Noah's flood
- Mankind was given a nature of sin and imputed with the sins of Adam

IV.   The Dispensation of Human Government

- Began with the end of God's flooding the world during the days of Noah
- God directs man to form human governments and established rules to live by
- Closed in the attempt to build ladder to Heaven and God's confusion of tongues.

V.   The Dispensation of God's Promise

- Began with the Covenant God makes with Abraham (Genesis 12:1–3)
- God choses Israel as His "Chosen People"
- This Dispensation is current put "on hold" but has not ended

VI.   The Dispensation of "The Law"

- God provides list of "Do's" and "Don'ts" to help them know when they disobeyed
- God, through Moses leads His people out of bondage
- The Dispensation is currently put "on hold" but has not ended

VII. The Dispensation of Grace (also known as Dispensation of "The Church")

- Began with the Day of Pentecost when God created the Church
- Relies on Holy Spirit to witness to people about Christ
- Will end with the Rapture of the Church

VIII. The Dispensation of the One-Thousand-Year Millennial Reign

I. What happens when we are saved?

- To Be: Saved, Redeemed, Justified, Born Again, Forgiven of Our Sins
- We must take the faith God has given us and decide to trust Jesus to save us
- We become the "Righteousness of God."
- We become Children of God and part of God's Family
- We are "set aside" or "sanctified." We are viewed as a new person by God
- The Blood of Jesus makes us sinless in the sight of God the Father

II. What is the role of Faith and Grace in Salvation

- Ephesians 2:8–9: *"For by grace you have been saved through faith. And this is not of your own doing, it is the gift of God, not a result of works so that no one may boast."*
- Our faith is the path for us to ask for Salvation
- God's Grace is the unmerited mercy of God to grant us Salvation

III. Why the saved cannot lose their Salvation

- God promised us His Children will never perish. (*John 3:16*)
- Saved "Pass from death (Separation from God) to Life (present with God) (*John 5:24*)
- At Salvation, we become part of the family (inner circle) of God (*John 10:27–29*)
- Our Security of Salvation lies not in the power of man but the faithfulness of God
- The Saved are the Predestined Elect of God (*Ephesians 1:3–4*)
- Believers are sealed in their faith by the Holy Spirit (*Ephesians 1:13–14*)
- God forgives us of not only our past, present, future sin but also our sinful nature.
- When saved we take on the righteousness of God (*2 Corinthians 5:21*)
- No power exists that can take us out of the care of God (*Romans 8:38–39*)

IV. Why people doubt their Salvation

- They doubt because they have never given their heart to Jesus and trusted Him
- They doubt because they are trusting good deeds to earn salvation
- They doubt because they have allowed the world's draw pull them away from God
- They doubt because they do not understand what happened when they were saved

V. No amount of "works" can lead us to salvation

I.   What is the Grace of God?

- Something God does that man can never earn
- Unmerited mercy of God to mankind

II.   The Substance of Grace

- Through Grace, God paid for the sins of all mankind
- Through Grace, God gives man enough faith to believe in Jesus Christ
- Through Grace, God gives mankind a new inner nature dedicated to loving God
- Through Grace, God sent the Holy Spirit to be our "Comforter"
- Through Grace, God overcomes our basic nature and allows us to love

III.   The Grace of God is the result of His Holiness, His Righteousness, His Justice, His Love

- 2 Corinthians 8:9: *"For you know the grace of our Lord Jesus Christ, that though He was rich, yet for your sake He became poor so that you through His poverty y might become rich."*

IV.   A Saving Grace

- Man must demonstrate faith in Christ to be saved
- God's Word tells us our faith is possible because of the Grace of God
- Romans 10:17: *"So faith come by hearing and hearing by the Word of Christ"*
- Faith alone cannot save us. God's Grace converts us from sin

V.   A Sustaining Grace

- At Salvation, He gives us a new nature, a nature to seek and love God
- Our faith in God is counted as Righteousness by God
- We become in the sight of God sinless
- Twelve gifts of the Holy Spirit that enables us to have sustaining faith

VI.   God's Mercy
VII.   The Universal Grace of God

I.   What does Sanctification mean?

- To be set apart or designated for something
- Biblical sanctification means to be designated and set aside to serve God
- Sins not only forgiven but blotted out, eliminated by the blood of Jesus
- John 17:16–17: *"They are not of the world, just as I am not of the world, sanctify them in the truth your word is truth."*

II. The Act of Sanctification (Granted Sanctification)

- We are sanctified when we are saved.
- We are given a new nature, a new heart, want to please God
  - *We are expected to praise God and worship Him*
- An act of God, man cannot sanctify himself

III. The Process of Sanctification (Growth Sanctification)

- Sanctification granted at salvation is the beginning of growth sanctification
- Our new nature encourages us to become more like Christ

IV. The content of Growth Sanctification

- Know the Lord
- Death no longer has dominion over Christ therefore no longer over the saved (*Romans 6:9*)
- Evaluate Your Relationship with the Lord (*Romans 6:11*)
- Yield to the Word of the Lord (*Romans 6:13*)

V.   There is no condemnation for the sanctified (*Romans 8:1*)
VI. The combined Granted and Growth Sanctification yields a righteous being

- The result is a servant for the Lord
- The result is a passion for the Lord
- The result is an extension of our Lord

God's Doctrine for Dummies
Doctrine of Prayer—Lesson Plan No. 13—Page 345

I. What is Prayer?

- Communication with God
- Not to inform God of anything
- Two-way communication: Speak and Listen

II. Why should we pray?

- We love God and want to please Him
- We love our children, God loves His children

III. How should we pray?

- Bring every issue to God immediately. Do not try to solve issues by yourself
- Be honest with God. Do not try to hide our sin or weakness
- Express to God our praise, admiration, love, and amazement of Him
- Pray always for God's Will to be done

IV. What does God want from His Children?

- To hear from us about our love for Him
- To hear from us of our willing dependency on Him
- To simply have fellowship with God

V. How does God answer prayer?

- God talks to us through His Word
- God has sparingly spoken directly to select men
- God speaks to us primarily through the Holy Spirit

VI. Man's responsibility in Prayer

- We do not come to God as equals. We come in awe.
- Express our desires, requests, fears, hopes, but always be submissive to God's Will
- Don't request anything that would hinder the work of god or conflict with His Word.

VII. The Lord's Prayer is our example.

I.   What is Faith?

- Overall faith = the set of doctrine we believe about God's Word
- Specific Faith = Complete reliance on Jesus Christ to save our souls, save our spiritual bodies, save our future existence from the pit of Hell to the glory of Heaven
- Hebrews 11:1: *"Now faith is the assurance of things hoped for, the conviction of things not seen."*
  - *The belief that the promises of God that we cherish and believe will happen*
  - *The comfort that we do not need to see or touch, belief in God is sufficient*

II.   What "Specific Faith" is required of God

- Jesus lived a sinless life and willingly gave up His life for our sins
- Jesus overcame death when He arose from the grave and we will also conquer death
- Use this "Specific Faith" as the substance to support our asking Jesus to forgive our sins, past, present, and forever.

III. "Specific Faith" does not save us. It allows us to make application to God for Salvation

IV.   The "Grace of God" acts on our faith and completes the salvation experience

V.   "Growth Sanctification" includes "Growth Specific Faith"

- We learn to walk in Spirit not in Flesh

VI.   Faith vs. Hope

- Faith = belief in something sufficient to act without tangible proof
- The presence of proof hinders faith
- God's Word is our Spiritual proof of those things we hope for

VII. Where does Faith come from?

- The Grace of God: Ephesians 2:8–9—*"For by Grace you have been saved through faith, and this is not your own doing, it is the gift of God, not of works, so that no one can boast."*
- God tells us to pray for greater faith
- We cannot earn Salvation, we must ask and rejoice when given

I. What are Spiritual Gifts?

- An endowment from God to believers to edify the Church
- They are not given to edify the believer
- Ephesians 4:11–12: *"And He gave the apostles, the prophets, the evangelists, the shepherds and teachers, to equip the saints for the work of ministry for building up the body of Christ!"*

II. Different gifts, but all of the same Body, The Body of Christ, The Church

- God only give Spiritual Gifts to believers
- Gifts are to enable that one to do something specific for God
- Gifts may be permanent or temporary according to God's Will

III. Mission of the Church (Also known as the "Body of Christ"

- Exalt the Savior, Equip the Saints, Enlist the uncommitted
- Encourage the Believers, Evangelize the Unbelievers, Empower laborers to harvest

IV. Supernatural Gifts (no longer necessary with the advent of the Word of God

- Gift of Supernatural Faith; Gift of Knowledge, Gift of "Word of Wisdom," Gift of Prophecy, Gift of tongues, Gift of Interpretation, Gift of Miracles, Gift of Healing

V. Ministry Gifts

- Ministry of being an Apostle, Ministry of being a Prophet, Ministry of being a Pastor, Ministry of being an Evangelist, Ministry of being a Teacher

VI. Service Gifts

- The Gift of Mercy, The Gift of Discernment, The Gift of Helps, The Gift of Giving, The Gift of Leadership, The Gift of Serving

VII. The Greatest Gift of all—Love
VIII. The Fruit of the Spirit

- Galatians 5:22–23: *"But the fruit of the Spirit is love, joy, peace, longsuffering, Kindness. Goodness, faithfulness, gentleness, self-control. Against such there is no law."*

I.   What are the Elect of God?

- Denotes the concept of choosing and "Of God" choosing of God
- Focus is on those God has Predestined to be saved
- Does "The Elect of God" compromise the freedom of choice of man

II. Who are the Elect of God?

- Concept No. 1 = God's Sovereign nature demands man's choice of salvation is limited
- Concept No. 2=God's Foreknowledge acknowledged God's knowledge without action

III. Faith + Grace = God's Election

- God is not subject to time. Sees all things past, present, future as one event
- God through omniscience knows who has and will elect to trust Jesus for salvation
- Mankind has a decisive role in Salvation. John 3:16: *"For God so loved the world that He gave His only begotten Son that whosoever believeth on Him shall not perish but have everlasting life."*
- God in His Sovereignty, elected to require of mankind the decision to trust "The Son" in order to be saved.

IV. Election and Predestination are truth

- God in His foreknowledge knew who would be saved before the world was formed. Romans 8:29–30: *"For those whom He foreknew He also predestined to be conformed to the image of His Son, in order that He might be the firstborn among many brothers, and those whom He predestined He also called, and those whom He called He also justified, and those whom He justified He also glorified."*

V.   God requires man to choose Jesus in order to be saved

- If man has no ability to choose or reject Christ He has no ability to return a free love
- God created man to return a free love back to Him

VI. Conclusion on Predestination and the Elect of God

- God knew through foreknowledge yet requires man to choose
- God's predestination is assurance that once saved man cannot ever be lost

I.   What does Priesthood of the Believer mean?

- God's relationship with each believer is precise and direct
- God dictates we 1 Peter 2:5 *"You, yourselves, like living stones, are being built up as a spiritual house, to be a spiritual priesthood, to offer spiritual sacrifices acceptable to God through Jesus Christ."*
- Believers are chosen, righteous, owned by God, sanctified for the purpose of proclaiming the glory of God. 1 Peter 2:9: *"But you are a chosen race, a royal priesthood, a holy nation, a people for His own possession, that you may proclaim the excellencies of Him who called you out of darkness into His marvelous light."*

II.   Yet with one mediator between God and man

- We need Jesus Christ as our sole mediator with God. 1 Timothy 2:5: *"For there is one God, and there is one mediator between God and men, the man Christ Jesus."*
  - ○ *No human priest who is with sin can be our mediator*
  - ○ *The human side of Jesus, the one who knew no sin, is our mediator.*
- This means every believers has direct access to God the Son
- The man's every believer has access to God the Father through God the Son

III.   The responsibility for our salvation and sanctification rests solely on our shoulders.
IV.   What is the Propitiation for our sins?

- Jesus is our propitiation meaning He is our substitute payment for our sins
- He is the voice of admittance into Heaven of those seeking Salvation
- He intercedes with God the Father with assurance we belong to Jesus
- Hebrews 7:25 and other scripture says we are saved to the uttermost meaning the security of our salvation is not in our hands but in the hands of Jesus

V.   The Holy Spirit is the administrator of the Trinity.

- The Holy Spirit speaks to us as the voice of Jesus
- Jesus speaks to God as our mediator
- Our requests, desires, needs are granted by Christ, implemented by Holy Spirit

I.   Why did Jesus Create the Church?

- The Church did not exist before the Dispensation of Grace
- That mission was to evangelize the whole world.

II.   The Church was built upon the sinless righteousness of Jesus Christ's desire to please God

- Church was not built on the Apostle Peter Matthew 16:18: *"And I tell you, you are Peter, and on this rock I will build my church, and the gates of Hell shall not prevail against it."*

III.   The Power of Jesus Christ given to Him by God the Father

Power is passed from God the Father to God the Son. *"All authority in heaven and on earth has been given to me."*

- Jesus changes the focus of faith believers in the Dispensation of Grace must have to be saved.
  - *Old Testament focus was on the promise of God for a coming Messiah (who would be Jesus the Son of God but that was not revealed to them)*
  - *New Testament focus was on Jesus Christ the Son of God as the accomplished Messiah because He had fulfilled the promise of His Father*
- The responsibility for evangelizing the whole world passed (for unknown period of years) from the "Chosen Nation Israel to the body created by Christ, The Church.

IV.   God sends the Holy Spirit as a comforter, teacher, chastiser, and guide for "The Church"

V.   "The Church" consists of Baptized (spiritual baptism) Believers in Christ

VI.   The New Testament Church

- *Ekklesia* is a Greek word defined as "a called-out assembly or congregation."
- The "Body of Christ" includes all people saved during the Dispensation of Grace

VII.   The purpose of "The Church"

VIII.   What is a Church Ordinance vs. a Sacrament?

IX.   Spiritual Baptism and Physical Baptism

X.   Ordinance of the Lord's Supper

I. Is there life after death?

- Old Testament Job gives first assurance of life after death Job 14:14 *"If a man dies, shall he live again? All the days of my service I will wait, till my renewal should come."*
- Not only life but Judgment as well Hebrews 9:27: *"And just as it is appointed for man to die once and after that is judgment."*

II. The Resurrection of Jesus proves life after death is real

- Every shred of Christian faith rests on the resurrection of Jesus
- 1 Corinthians 15:4: *"And if Christ has not been raised, then our preaching is in vain and your faith is in vain."*
- Jesus Resurrection is prototype of the Resurrection of believers

III. Revelation of Lazarus and the rich man

- After death unsaved go to Hades, a place of darkness, and torments
- In Old Testament believers go to Abraham's Bosom
- In New Testament believers spirit goes to Heaven with the Lord

IV. Teaching points

- Jesus clearly teaches reality of a holding place for saved as they await judgment
- Unsaved are immediately sealed in temporary place of torment awaiting judgment
- Bodies are separated from Spirit of saved awaiting being reclaimed by Christ
- Bodies are separated from Spirit of unsaved in Hades awaiting judgment

V. The Resurrected Immortal body (1 Corinthians 15)

- Made into the likeness of Jesus Christ
- What is sown is perishable—raised imperishable
- "Sown in dishonor—raised in glory"
- "Sown in weakness—raised in power"
- Sown a natural body—raised a spiritual body

I.   Is Hell real?

  •   Billions of people worldwide elect to not believe in Hell
  •   The Bible is very clear in teaching Hell is real
  •   Hebrews 9:27: *"And just as it is appointed for men to die once, but after that comes the judgment"*
  •   Estimated 10 percent of world's population is saved. 90 percent are going to Hell
  •   Satan, His angels, "The Beast," "The Antichrist," and the false Prophet will be in Hell

II. The Reality of Hell is why Jesus came down from Heaven to be crucified.

  •   There will be no escape
  •   There will be total separation from God and all that is righteous
  •   There will be no such a thing as time because Hell will last through eternity
  •   There will be total darkness
  •   There will be fire, horror of burning but not dying
  •   There will be no friends, no one to confide in, no comfort at all

III. There will be degrees of punishment in Hell

  •   Revelation 20:12: *"And I saw the dead, great and small, standing before the throne, and books were opened. Then another book was opened, which is the book of life. And the dead were judged by what was written in the books, according to what they had done"*
  •   The Great White Throne Judgment will be the judgment of sinners based on the evil they practiced on earth

IV. The Bottomless Pit

  •   Hell was not created for man but for Lucifer and his followers
  •   However those people who choose to follow Satan will be with him in eternity
  •   Hell is the same as the "Lake of Fire" recorded in Revelation
  •   One-third of all angels, those who followed Satan and rebelled against God will be in Hell with all sinners

V.   Hell is a place of retribution, of God's Wrath, of justice,
VI. Hell is a place of no hope, no rest, and no ending

I.   Is Heaven real?

- Paul was inspired by God to tell us we (Believers) have a home built for us in Heaven
- 2 Corinthians 5:1: *"For we know that if the tent that is our earthly home is destroyed, we have a building from God, a house not made with hands, eternal in the heavens"*

II. Three Heavens created by God

- First Heaven is the firmament. Earth's atmosphere, the Troposphere,
- Second Heaven is outer space. Begins about twenty miles out from earth
- Third Heaven is what we call heaven. It is where the Church shall be raptured
- Fourth Heaven is created by God or is being created by God as the New Heaven and New Earth to be used after the one-thousand-year millennial reign

III. The Third Heaven is the Throne of God

- Where Jesus dwells now
- Where some Old Testament Saints who were rapture await
- Where All Old Testament Saints not raptured will be raised to join with God
- Where the Church will be raptured to join with God the Father

IV. When do we (The Church) go to Heaven?

- Spiritually we go to Heaven the instant God gives us a new heart and saves us
- Physically we go to Heaven at the rapture of the Church
- A Holy City
- Who will be in Heaven?

V.   After the rapture five events the redeemed Saints will experience

VI. The New Heaven and the New Earth

VII. What will it be like in Heaven (1 Corinthians 15:42–44)

- Harmony and love in Heaven
- No sickness, no pain, no hunger, no death
- Unbroken fellowship with God

I.   Is the Rapture Real?

- 1 Thessalonians 4:13–14: *"For we believe that Jesus died and rose again, even so through Jesus; God will bring with Him those who have fallen asleep."*
- If you believe Jesus died and rose again you must also believe in our resurrection

II.   The rapture, a promise to the Church

- Rapture applies to "The Church" because God gave believers to His Son
  - *Dead "In Christ" will rise first, then those alive, (1 Thessalonians 4:16–17)*
- Jesus promised He was gone to prepare Heaven for us (John 14:1–4)

III.   The rapture is different than the Second Coming of Jesus

- Just for believers in "The Church" or the "Body of Christ"
- Sets in motion Daniel's "Final Week" the Seven-Year Tribulation

IV.   The Sequence of Resurrections as outlined in Scripture

- No. 1: When Jesus arose from the Grave (1 Corinthians 15:20–23)
- No. 2: At the crucifixion many Old Testament Saints were raised (Matthew 27:50–53)
- No. 3: When the "Dead in Christ" (of the Church) are raised (1 Corinthians 15:50–53)
- No. 4: When the "Alive in Christ" (of the Church) are raised (1 Corinthians 15:50–53)
- No. 5: When the "Witnesses in Revelation are raised (Revelation 11:11–12)
- No. 6: All Old Testament Saints not raised at Crucifixion are raised (Ezekiel 37:13–14)
- No. 7: At the end of the Great Tribulation those saved will be raised (Revelation 20:4)
- No. 8: At the end of the one-thousand reign those saved will be raised (Revelation 20:11–15)

V.   Timing views of The Rapture

- Pre-Millennial; The Church will be raptured before the Seven-Year Tribulation
- Mid-Millennial: The Church will be raptured in middle of Seven-Year Tribulation
- Amillennials: Events prophesied are figurative not literal—Church will not be rapture
- Post-Millennial: One-thousand-year millennial is "long time" and is taking place with church age

I.   What is the Seven-Year Tribulation?

 • World turmoil following the Rapture of the Church
 • Prophecy of the world from Daniel to the Rapture

II.   God's Vision to Daniel

 • The Seventy Weeks (using the Idiom of the word week seventy weeks =490 years
 • God's command and timeline to Israel
 • God "cuts-off" the seventy-week vision by one week to implement the Church Age
 • Week No. 70 = the Seven-Year Tribulation reaching toward fulfilling God's promises

III. Definition of Terms

 • The Antichrist, The Beast, The False Prophet, The Ten Horns and the Seven Heads
 • The Scarlet Woman, The Harlot, The Prostitute, The Woman, and The Child

IV.   The First Three and One-Half Years

 • The First Seal (The White Horse)
 • The Second Seal (The Red Horse)
 • The Third Seal (The Black Horse)
 • The Forth Seal (The Pail Horse)

V.   The Middle Week of Tribulation

 • The Abomination of Desolation
 • The "Two Witnesses" appear
 • The 144,000 Jewish Evangelists
 • The Fifth and Sixth Seal
 • The Seventh Seal releases the Seven Trumpets

VI.   The Seven Trumpets concurrently The Seven Bowls upon inhabitants

 • God's Wrath as opposed to the Wrath of Satan
 • The Mark of the Beast
 • The Battle of Armageddon = God's Great Victory

I.   All believers events after the Rapture of the Church!

   • The "Bema" Seat
   • The "Marriage Supper of the Lamb"
   • The Second Coming of Jesus
   • The Judgment of Sheep and Goats
   • The One-Thousand-Year Millennial Reign
   • The Great White Throne Judgment

II.   The "Bema" Seat

   • Judgment of Believers in Jesus the Messiah only
   • Judgment of "Good Works" with relationship to rewards in Heaven

III.   The "Marriage Supper of the Lamb"

   • Jesus presents "The Church" as His bride to God the Father
   • All members of "The Church" are seen by God the Father as righteous
   • "Marriage Supper of the Lamb" process parallels the process of Salvation

IV.   Judgments

   • Judgment of Satan and fallen Angels before the fall of Adam
   • Judgment of man's sin at the time of Adam's fall from God's Grace
   • Judgment of man in the Dispensations of God's voice to His people
   • Judgment of The Son of God while on the Cross
   • Bema Seat of Judgment of Good works of believers
   • Judgment of nations (Sheep and Goats) to populate the One-Thousand-Year Millennial Reign
   • Great White Throne Judgment - Judgment of works of nonbelievers
   • Judgment of fallen Angels by redeemed believers

V.   The Second Coming of Christ

   • Will be visible from every part of the world
   • Great unnatural cataclysmic events will take changing the earth
   • Jesus brings His Angels and His followers back to earth with Him
   • Satan is defeated and locked in "The Pit" for one thousand years

God's Doctrine for Dummies
One-Thousand Millennial Reign—Lesson Plan No. 25—Chapter 25, Page 633

I.   The One-Thousand-Year Millennial Reign

- All nonbelievers are housed in Hades (place of torment) awaiting final judgment
- The False Prophet, The Beast, and The Antichrist are imprisoned in Hades
- Satan is cast into "The Pit" (bottom of earth) awaiting final judgment
- All believers who have physically died are in the One-Thousand-Year Millennial Reign
- All believers who pass from Battle of Armageddon alive go to Millennial Reign

* Believers who physically died come back with glorified bodies.

II.   Those who enter the One-Thousand Millennial Reign alive

- Will go in naturalized bodies
- Will go as husband and wife and will have children
- Children of these will have to decide to trust Jesus and be saved or Satan and perish
- Thus over a period of one thousand years an army of lost who support Satan arise

III.   Resurrections that will take place (means raised from death never to die again)

- Resurrection of life (meaning resurrected to join Christ in glory)

* The Resurrection of Jesus Christ from the Grave
* The Resurrection of believers in Jesus who had physically died at the Rapture
* The Resurrection of believers in Jesus who were alive at the Rapture
* The Resurrection of the "Two Witnesses" in Jerusalem
* The Resurrection of Old Testament Saints
* The Resurrection of Tribulation Saints

- Resurrection of Death (meaning resurrected to have physical body join with spiritual body in the Lake of Fire forever

* Resurrection of Old Testament Nonbelievers
* Resurrection to attend the Great White Throne Judgment

IV.   Why God has ordained a One-Thousand-Year Millennial Kingdom

- Fulfill His promises to first of All Jesus, second of all Israel
- Fulfill the promise of what the Garden of Eden was supposed to be

V.   A New Heaven and New Earth

About the Author

B. V. Lightsey is a professional human resources executive of over fifty years' experience. He is husband of one wife, two children, six grandchildren, and seven great-grandchildren. He has been an active member local evangelical churches since the age of nine. He has served as teacher, music director, and as an ordained deacon for over fifty-five years. Bill joined the Giddeons International in 1987 and has, for over thirty years, been involved in spreading God's Word to a lost and dying world. His greatest treasure was when he experienced the amazing grace of Our Lord and Savior, and was called by the Holy Spirit to accept Jesus as Savior at the early age of nine.

As the executive representative of oil and gas and manufacturing employment, Bill has negotiated labor disputes and contracts with some of American's leading labor unions. As his employer's expert at employment law he has often faced the challenge of blending corporate rules, government regulations, and the emotions and needs of involved human beings.

Yet Bill's greatest challenge has been to simplify the Word of God thus enabling God's people, who do not understand Greek, Hebrew, or Aramaic languages to gain a practical level of understanding of what God desires His people to grasp.

The Gospel product of our scholars who are graduates of our great colleges, universities and theological seminaries often leave us confused and at the point of feeling like we are gospel dummies. This book is for these children of God who seek His will. May your study of doctrines for dummies be blessed by your devotion and hunger for God's Word.

CPSIA information can be obtained
at www.ICGtesting.com
Printed in the USA
LVHW031933110720
660354LV00001B/5